Something about
the Author *was named
an "Outstanding
Reference Source,"
the highest honor given
by the American
Library Association
Reference and Adult
Services Division.*

ISSN 0276-816X

SOMETHING ABOUT THE AUTHOR®

**Facts and Pictures about Authors
and Illustrators of Books for Young People**

EDITED BY

ALAN HEDBLAD

VOLUME 96

GALE

DETROIT · NEW YORK · TORONTO · LONDON

STAFF

Editor: Alan Hedblad
Associate Editor: Sheryl Ciccarelli
Assistant Editor: Marilyn O'Connell Allen

Sketchwriters/Copyeditors: Marie Ellavich, Ronie Garcia-Johnson, Mary Gillis, Motoko Fujishiro Huthwaite, Arlene M. Johnson, J. Sydney Jones, Thomas F. McMahon, Susan Reicha, Gerard J. Senick, Pamela L. Shelton, Diane Telgen, Crystal Towns, Arlene True, and Kathleen Witman

Managing Editor: Joyce Nakamura
Publisher: Hal May

Research Manager: Victoria B. Cariappa
Project Coordinator: Cheryl L. Warnock
Research Specialists: Andrew Guy Malonis, Gary J. Oudersluys
Research Associates: Laura C. Bissey, Norma Sawaya
Research Assistants: Talitha A. Jean, Jeffrey D. Daniels

Permissions Manager: Susan M. Trosky
Permissions Specialist: Maria L. Franklin
Permissions Associates: Edna M. Hedblad, Michele M. Lonoconus
Permissions Assistant: Andrea Rigby

Production Director: Mary Beth Trimper
Production Assistant: Deborah Milliken

Desktop Publisher: Gary Leach
Image Database Supervisor: Randy Bassett
Imaging Specialists: Robert Duncan, Michael Logusz
Photography Coordinator: Pamela A. Reed

Library of Congress Catalog Card Number 72-27107

ISBN 0-7876-1149-2 ISSN 0276-816X

Printed in the United States of America

10 9 8 7 6 5 4 3 2 1

Contents

Authors in Forthcoming Volumes

Below are some of the authors and illustrators that will be featured in upcoming volumes of *SATA*. These include new entries on the swiftly rising stars of the field, as well as completely revised and updated entries (indicated with *) on some of the most notable and best-loved creators of books for children.

Cherie Bennett: A former Broadway actress and singer, Bennett is a popular author and advice columnist who has published scores of books for young adult readers, including the many titles comprising her "Sunset Island," "Wild Hearts," and "Surviving Sixteen" series.

Gavin Bishop: As an illustrator, New Zealander Bishop is noted for his attention to background detail in pictures that augment, often humorously, the stories they accompany. Also known as a reteller of tales, Bishop has penned many narratives that highlight the native Maori culture of his homeland.

Brian Caswell: Australian author Caswell's works for children and teens combine contemporary social issues with traditional narrative technique. His young adult novel *Asturias,* published in 1996, has been selected a Notable New Book by the International Youth Library.

Roz Chast: Best known for her humorous, off-beat cartoons for the *New Yorker,* Chast is a relative newcomer to the field of children's books. Her picture-book illustrations for young readers feature distinctive human and animal characters.

*Alexandra Day: Author and artist Day is a favorite with critics, parents, and children for her charming picture books about Carl the babysitting rottweiler and her well-known series of "Frank and Ernest" books.

Natalie Honeycutt: Honeycutt is the award-winning author of a popular quartet of books for middle-grade readers—*The All New Jonah Twist, The Best-Laid Plans of Jonah Twist, Juliet Fisher and the Foolproof Plan,* and *Lydia Jane and the Babysitter Exchange.*

Jackie Kay: Black Scottish poet and playwright Kay explores a variety of childhood experiences, ranging from imaginary friends to the pain of divorce and racism, in her collections *Three Has Gone* and *Two's Company,* the latter a winner of the Signal Poetry Award.

*Nicholasa Mohr: Author and artist Mohr draws upon her childhood to create critically acclaimed novels and short stories that offer realistic and uncompromising portraits of life in New York City's Puerto Rican barrio. She received the Hispanic Heritage Award for her body of work in 1997.

Ken Nutt: An illustrator of children's books who also works under the name Eric Beddows, Nutt is a three-time winner of the Amelia Frances Howard-Gibbon Award for Canadian illustrators. His pictures for Pam Conrad's *Rooster's Gift* earned him the Governor General's Award for Illustration from the Canada Council in 1996.

*Richard Peck: A highly regarded author of more than two dozen young adult novels, Peck explores such contemporary issues as peer pressure, single parenting, rape, censorship, suicide, and death of a loved one in titles such as *Don't Look and It Won't Hurt, Are You in the House Alone?, Father Figure* and *The Last Safe Place on Earth.*

Chris K. Soenpiet: Soenpiet is a Korean-born children's book illustrator and author whose works have been praised as warm, expressive, carefully detailed, and lively. He has received many accolades for his illustrations for the works of authors Susan Miho Nunes, Marie Bradby, and Haemi Balgassi.

Rita Williams-Garcia: In her young adult novels *Blue Tights, Fast Talk on a Slow Track,* and *Like Sisters on the Homefront,* award-winning African-American writer Williams-Garcia portrays contemporary urban youth coping with difficulties in an honest, uncontrived manner.

Introduction

Something about the Author (*SATA*) is an ongoing reference series that examines the lives and works of authors and illustrators of books for children. *SATA* includes not only well-known writers and artists but also less prominent individuals whose works are just coming to be recognized. This series is often the only readily available information source on emerging authors and illustrators. You'll find *SATA* informative and entertaining, whether you are a student, a librarian, an English teacher, a parent, or simply an adult who enjoys children's literature.

What's Inside SATA

SATA provides detailed information about authors and illustrators who span the full time range of children's literature, from early figures like John Newbery and L. Frank Baum to contemporary figures like Judy Blume and Richard Peck. Authors in the series represent primarily English-speaking countries, particularly the United States, Canada, and the United Kingdom. Also included, however, are authors from around the world whose works are available in English translation. The writings represented in *SATA* include those created intentionally for children and young adults as well as those written for a general audience and known to interest younger readers. These writings cover the entire spectrum of children's literature, including picture books, humor, folk and fairy tales, animal stories, mystery and adventure, science fiction and fantasy, historical fiction, poetry and nonsense verse, drama, biography, and nonfiction.

Obituaries are also included in *SATA* and are intended not only as death notices but also as concise overviews of people's lives and work. Additionally, each edition features newly revised and updated entries for a selection of *SATA* listees who remain of interest to today's readers and who have been active enough to require extensive revisions of their earlier biographies.

Two Convenient Indexes

In response to suggestions from librarians, *SATA* indexes no longer appear in every volume but are included in alternate (odd-numbered) volumes of the series, beginning with Volume 57.

SATA continues to include two indexes that cumulate with each alternate volume: the Illustrations Index, arranged by the name of the illustrator, gives the number of the volume and page where the illustrator's work appears in the current volume as well as all preceding volumes in the series; the Author Index gives the number of the volume in which a person's Biographical Sketch or Obituary appears in the current volume as well as all preceding volumes in the series.

These indexes also include references to authors and illustrators who appear in Gale's *Yesterday's Authors of Books for Children, Children's Literature Review,* and *Something about the Author Autobiography Series.*

Easy-to-Use Entry Format

Whether you're already familiar with the *SATA* series or just getting acquainted, you will want to be aware of the kind of information that an entry provides. In every *SATA* entry the editors attempt to give as complete a picture of the person's life and work as possible. A typical entry in *SATA* includes the following clearly labeled information sections:

- *PERSONAL:* date and place of birth and death, parents' names and occupations, name of spouse, date of marriage, names of children, educational institutions attended, degrees received, religious and political affiliations, hobbies and other interests.

- *ADDRESSES:* complete home, office, electronic mail, and agent addresses, whenever available.

■ *CAREER:* name of employer, position, and dates for each career post; art exhibitions; military service; memberships and offices held in professional and civic organizations.

■ *AWARDS, HONORS:* literary and professional awards received.

■ *WRITINGS:* title-by-title chronological bibliography of books written and/or illustrated, listed by genre when known; lists of other notable publications, such as plays, screenplays, and periodical contributions.

■ *ADAPTATIONS:* a list of films, television programs, plays, CD-ROMs, recordings, and other media presentations that have been adapted from the author's work.

■ *WORK IN PROGRESS:* description of projects in progress.

■ *SIDELIGHTS:* a biographical portrait of the author or illustrator's development, either directly from the biographee—and often written specifically for the *SATA* entry—or gathered from diaries, letters, interviews, or other published sources.

■ *FOR MORE INFORMATION SEE:* references for further reading.

■ *EXTENSIVE ILLUSTRATIONS:* photographs, movie stills, book illustrations, and other interesting visual materials supplement the text.

How a SATA Entry Is Compiled

A *SATA* entry progresses through a series of steps. If the biographee is living, the *SATA* editors try to secure information directly from him or her through a questionnaire. From the information that the biographee supplies, the editors prepare an entry, filling in any essential missing details with research and/or telephone interviews. If possible, the author or illustrator is sent a copy of the entry to check for accuracy and completeness.

If the biographee is deceased or cannot be reached by questionnaire, the *SATA* editors examine a wide variety of published sources to gather information for an entry. Biographical and bibliographic sources are consulted, as are book reviews, feature articles, published interviews, and material sometimes obtained from the biographee's family, publishers, agent, or other associates.

Entries that have not been verified by the biographees or their representatives are marked with an asterisk (*).

Contact the Editor

We encourage our readers to examine the entire *SATA* series. Please write and tell us if we can make *SATA* even more helpful to you. Give your comments and suggestions to the editor:

BY MAIL: Editor, *Something about the Author,* Gale Research, 835 Penobscot Bldg., 645 Griswold St., Detroit, MI 48226-4094.

BY TELEPHONE: (800) 347-GALE

BY FAX: (313) 961-6599

BY E-MAIL: CYA@Gale.com

Acknowledgments

Grateful acknowledgment is made to the following publishers, authors, and artists whose works appear in this volume.

ADLERMAN, DANIEL. Adlerman, Daniel (with daughter, Rachelle), photograph by Marbeth. Reproduced by permission.

ADLERMAN, KIMBERLY. Adlerman, Kimberly (with son, Joshua), photograph by Marbeth. Reproduced by permission.

ADOFF, ARNOLD. Steptoe, John, illustrator. From an illustration in *All the Colors of the Race,* by Arnold Adoff. Lothrop, Lee & Shepard Books, 1982. Illustrations © 1982 by John Steptoe. Reproduced by permission of Lothrop, Lee & Shepard Books, a division of William Morrow & Company, Inc., with the approval of the John Steptoe Literary Trust. In the British Commonwealth by Anne White. / Barbour, Karen, illustrator. From an illustration in *Street Music: City Poems,* by Arnold Adoff. HarperCollins, 1995. Text © 1995 by Arnold Adoff. Illustrations © 1995 by Karen Barbour. Reproduced by permission of HarperCollins Publishers, Inc. / Desimini, Lisa, illustrator. From an illustration in *Love Letters,* by Arnold Adoff. Blue Sky Press, 1997. Illustrations © 1997 by Lisa Desimini. Reproduced by permission of Scholastic Inc. / Adoff, Arnold, photograph by Virginia Hamilton Adoff. Reproduced by permission of Arnold Adoff.

BABER, CAROLYN STONNELL. Baber, Carolyn Stonnell, photograph. Reproduced by permission of Carolyn Stonnell Baber.

BARKLEM, JILL. Barklem, Jill, illustrator. From an illustration in *Poppy's Babies,* by Jill Barklem. HarperCollins, 1994. Text and illustrations © 1994 by Jill Barklem. Reproduced by permission. / Barklem, Jill, photograph. Reproduced by permission of Jill Barklem.

BASSIL, ANDREA. Bassil, Andrea, photograph by M. W. Ramage. Reproduced by permission of Andrea Bassil.

BEARD, DARLEEN BAILEY. Beard, Darleen Bailey, photograph. Reproduced by permission of Darleen Bailey Beard.

BETANCOURT, JEANNE. Deas, M. J., illustrator. From a cover of *My Name Is ~~Brain~~ Brian,* by Jeanne Betancourt. Apple Paperbacks, 1993. Illustration copyright © 1993 by M. J. Deas. Reproduced by permission of Scholastic Inc. / Bachem, Paul, illustrator. From a cover of *Pony Pals: The Girl Who Hated Ponies,* by Jeanne Betancourt. Little Apple Paperbacks, 1997. Illustrations copyright (c) 1997 by Scholastic, Inc. Reproduced by permission of Scholastic Inc. / Betancourt, Jeanne, photograph by Nancy Crampton. Reproduced by permission of Jeanne Betancourt.

BLAKE, QUENTIN. Blake, Quentin, illustrator. From an illustration in *The Singing Tortoise and Other Animal Folktales,* by John Yeoman. Tambourine Books, 1993, Victor Gollancz/Hamish Hamilton, 1993. Illustrations © 1993 by Quentin Blake. Reproduced by permission of Tambourine Books, a division of William Morrow & Company, Inc. In the British Commonwealth by Penguin Books Ltd. / Blake, Quentin, illustrator. From an illustration in *Clown,* by Quentin Blake. Jonathan Cape, 1995. Copyright © 1995 by Quentin Blake. Reproduced by permission of Jonathan Cape, a division of Random House UK Limited. / Blake, Quentin, illustrator. From an illustration in *The Do-It-Yourself House that Jack Built,* by John Yeoman. Atheneum Books for Young Readers, 1995. Text © 1995 by John Yeoman. Illustrations © 1995 by Quentin Blake. Reproduced by permission of Penguin Books Ltd. In the U.S. by Atheneum Books for Young Readers, a division of Simon & Schuster, Inc. / Blake, Quentin, photograph. Reproduced by permission of Quentin Blake.

BODE, JANET. Cover of *Death Is Hard to Live with,* by Janet Bode. Laurel Leaf Books, 1993. Reproduced by permission of Laurel-Leaf Books, a division of Bantam Doubleday Dell Publishing Group, Inc. / Cover of *Heartbreak and Roses: Real Life Stories of Troubled Love,* by Janet Bode and Stan Mack. Laurel-Leaf Books, 1996. Illustrations copyright 1994 by Stan Mack. Reproduced by permission of Delacorte Press, a division of Bantam Doubleday Dell Publishing Group, Inc. / Bode, Janet, photograph by Stan Mack. Reproduced by permission of Janet Bode.

BRADFORD, KARLEEN. Dodge, Bill, illustrator. From a jacket of *There Will Be Wolves,* by Karleen Bradford. Lodestar Books, 1996. Jacket illustration © 1996 by Bill Dodge. Reproduced by permission of Lodestar Books, a division of Penguin USA. / Bradford, Karleen, photograph by Donald Bradford. Reproduced by permission of Karleen Bradford.

BRANDIS, MARIANNE. Caulfield, Paul, photographer. From a cover of *The Quarter-Pie Window,* by Marianne Brandis. The Porcupine's Quill, Inc., 1985. Reproduced by permission.

BURGESS, MELVIN. Waldman, Neil, illustrator. From a cover of *The Cry of the Wolf,* by Melvin Burgess. Beech Tree Paperback Books, 1994. Reproduced by permission of Beech Tree Paperback Books, a division of William Morrow and Company, Inc. / Fiedler, Joseph Daniel, illustrator. From a jacket of *The Baby and Fly Pie,* by Melvin Burgess. Simon & Schuster Books for Young Readers, 1996. Jacket © 1996 by Simon & Schuster. Reproduced by permission of Simon & Schuster, Inc.

BURNS, MARILYN. Silveria, Gordon, illustrator. From an illustration in *The Greedy Triangle,* by Marilyn Burns. Marilyn Burns Brainy Day Books, 1994. Copyright © 1994 by Marilyn Burns Education Associates. Reproduced by permission of Scholastic Inc. / Adams, Lynn, illustrator. From a cover of *How Many Feet? How Many Tails? A Book of Math Riddles,* by Marilyn Burns. Cartwheel Books, 1996. Illustration copyright © 1996 by Scholastic Inc. Reproduced by permission of Scholastic Inc.

CALDER, MARIE DONAIS. Calder, Marie Donais, photograph. Reproduced by permission of Marie Donais Calder.

CAPEK, MICHAEL. Capek, Michael, photograph. Reproduced by permission of Michael Capek.

CARTLIDGE, MICHELLE. Cover of *Mouse Magic,* by Michelle Cartlidge. Dutton Children's Books, 1996, Macmillan Children's Books, 1996. Reproduced by permission of Dutton Children's Books, a division of Penguin USA. In the British Commonwealth by Macmillan Children's Books. / Cartlidge, Michelle, illustrator. From a jacket of *The Mice of Mousehole,* by Michelle Cartlidge. Walker Books, 1997. © 1997 Michelle Cartlidge. Reproduced by permission.

CHOCOLATE, DEBBI. Boies, Alex, illustrator. From a cover of *Imani in the Belly,* by Deborah M. Newton Chocolate. BridgeWater Books, 1994. Illustrations © 1994 by Alex Boies. Reproduced by permission of BridgeWater Books, an imprint of Troll Associates, Inc. / Ward, John, illustrator. From an illustration in *Kente Colors,* by Debbi Chocolate. Walker and Company, 1996. Text © 1996 by Debbi Chocolate. Illustrations © 1996 by John Ward. Reproduced by permission. / Chocolate, Debbi, photograph. Reproduced by permission of Debbi Chocolate.

CHWAST, SEYMOUR. Chwast, Seymour, illustrator. From an illustration in *Mathew Michael's Beastly Day,* by Deborah Johnston. Gulliver Books, 1992. Illustrations © 1992 by Seymour Chwast. Reproduced by permission of Harcourt Brace & Company. / Illustration in *The Twelve Circus Rings,* by Seymour Chwast. Harcourt Brace, 1993. Copyright © 1993 by Seymour Chwast. Reproduced by permission of Harcourt Brace & Company. / Cover of *Mr. Merlin and the Turtle,* by Seymour Chwast. Greenwillow Books, 1996. Reproduced by permission of Greenwillow Books, a division of William Morrow and Company, Inc. / Chwast, Seymour, photograph. Reproduced by permission of Seymour Chwast.

CLARK, JOAN. Clark, Joan, photograph by Kathi Robertson. Reproduced by permission of Joan Clark.

COLE, BABETTE. Cole, Babette, illustrator. From an illustration in *Dr. Dog,* by Babette Cole. Dragonfly Books, 1994. Copyright © 1994 by Babette Cole. Reproduced by permission of Random House, Inc. / Cole, Babette, illustrator. From an illustration in *Drop Dead,* by Babette Cole. Jonathan Cape, 1996. Copyright © 1996 by Babette Cole. Reproduced by permission. / Cole, Babette, photograph by Hamish Mitchell. © Hamish Mitchell. Reproduced by permission.

COONEY, BARBARA. Cooney, Barbara, illustrator. From an illustration in *Hattie and the Wild Waves,* by Barbara Cooney. Viking, 1990. Copyright © 1990 by Barbara Cooney. Reproduced by permission of Viking Penguin, a division of Penguin Books USA Inc. / Cooney, Barbara, illustrator. From a jacket of *The Remarkable Christmas of the Cobbler's Sons,* by Ruth Sawyer. Viking, 1994. Jacket illustration copyright © 1994 by Barbara Cooney. Reproduced by permission of Viking Penguin, a division of Penguin Books USA Inc. / Cooney, Barbara, illustrator. From an illustration in *Eleanor,* by Barbara Cooney. Viking, 1996. Copyright © 1996 by Barbara Cooney. Reproduced by permission of Viking Penguin, a division of Penguin Books USA Inc. / Cooney, Barbara, photograph. Reproduced by permission of Barbara Cooney.

COOPER, FLOYD. Cooper, Floyd, illustrator. From an illustration in *Laura Charlotte,* by Kathryn O. Galbraith. The Putnam & Grosset Group, 1990. Illustrations © 1990 by Floyd Cooper. Reproduced by permission. / Cooper, Floyd, illustrator. From an illustration in *Coming Home: From the Life of Langston Hughes,* by Floyd Cooper. Philomel Books, 1994. Copyright © 1994 by Floyd Cooper. Reproduced by permission.

CREIGHTON, JILL. Creighton, Jill, photograph. Reproduced by permission of Jill Creighton.

DELANEY, MICHAEL. Delaney, Michael, photograph by Molly Delaney. Reproduced by permission of Michael Delaney.

DIAZ, DAVID. Diaz, David, illustrator. From an illustration in *Smoky Night,* by Eve Bunting. Harcourt Brace and Company, 1994. Illustrations copyright © 1994 by David Diaz. All rights reserved. Reproduced by permission of Harcourt Brace & Company. / Diaz, David, illustrator. From an illustration in *Wilma Unlimited: How Wilma Rudolph Became the World's Fastest Woman,* by Kathleen Krull. Harcourt Brace, 1996. Illustrations © 1996 by David Diaz. Reproduced by permission of Harcourt Brace & Company. / Diaz, David, photograph. Reproduced by permission of David Diaz.

DURRANT, LYNDA. Durrant, Lynda, photograph. Esselburn Studio. Reproduced by permission of Lynda Durrant.

EHRLICH, AMY. Ehrlich, Amy, photograph. Reproduced by permission of Amy Ehrlich. / Jacket of *Maggie and Silky and Joe,* by Amy Ehrlich. Viking, 1994. Reproduced by permission of Viking, a division of Penguin USA.

EMORY, JERRY. Emory, Jerry, photograph by Stacy Geiken. Reproduced by permission of Jerry Emory.

FAIR, DAVID. Fair, David, photograph. Reproduced by permission of David Fair.

FLEISCHMAN, SID. Sis, Peter, illustrator. From an illustration in *The Midnight Horse,* by Sid Fleischman. Greenwillow Books, 1990. Illustrations © 1990 by Peter Sis. Reproduced by permission of Greenwillow Books, a division of William Morrow & Company, Inc. / Smith, Jos. A., illustrator. From an illustration from *Jim Ugly,* by Sid Fleischman. Greenwillow Books, 1992. Illustrations © 1992 by Jos. A. Smith. Reproduced by permission of Greenwillow Books, a division of William Morrow & Company, Inc. / Sis, Peter, illustrator. From an illustration in *The 13th Floor: A Ghost Story,* by Sid Fleischman. Greenwillow Books, 1995. Illustrations © 1995 by Peter Sis.

LARSON, KIRBY. Poydar, Nancy, illustrator. From a jacket of *Cody and Quinn, Sitting in a Tree,* by Kirby Larson. Holiday House, 1996. Reproduced by permission of the illustrator. / Larson, Kirby, photograph by Shawn Jezerinac. Reproduced by permission of Shawn Jezerinac.

LISLE, JANET TAYLOR. Halperin, Wendy Anderson, illustrator. From an illustration in *The Lampfish of Twill,* by Janet Taylor Lisle. Orchard Books, 1991. Illustrations © 1991 by Wendy Anderson Halperin. Reproduced by permission of Orchard Books, New York. In the British Commonwealth by Wendy Anderson Halperin. / Cover of *Forest,* by Janet Taylor Lisle. Apple Paperback Books, 1995. Illustration copyright © 1995 by Scholastic, Inc. Reproduced by permission of Scholastic Inc. / Shepperson, Rob, illustrator. From a jacket of *Angela's Aliens,* by Janet Taylor Lisle. Orchard Books, 1996. Jacket illustration © 1996 by Rob Shepperson. Reproduced by permission of Orchard Books, New York. In the British Commonwealth by Rob Shepperson. / Lisle, Janet Taylor, photograph by Elizabeth Lisle. Reproduced by permission of Janet Taylor Lisle.

LITTLE, DOUGLAS. Little, Douglas, photograph. Reproduced by permission of Douglas Little.

LOBEL, ANITA. Lobel, Anita, illustrator. From an illustration in *The Cat and the Cook and Other Fables of Krylov,* retold by Ethel Heins. Greenwillow Books, 1995. Illustrations © 1996 by Anita Lobel. Reproduced by permission of Greenwillow Books, a division of William Morrow & Company, Inc. / Lobel, Anita, illustrator. From an illustration in *Toads and Diamonds,* by Charlotte Huck. Greenwillow Books, 1996. Illustrations © 1996 by Anita Lobel. Reproduced by permission of Greenwillow Books, a division of William Morrow & Company, Inc. / Lobel, Anita, photograph. Reproduced by permission of Anita Lobel.

LOVE, D. ANNE. Kramer, David, illustrator. From a cover of *Dakota Spring,* by D. Anne Love. Yearling Books, 1997. Reproduced by permission of Yearling Books, a division of Bantam Doubleday Dell Publishing Group, Inc. / Love, D. Anne, photograph. Reproduced by permission of D. Anne Love.

MAYO, MARGARET. Brierley, Louise, illustrator. From an illustration in *When the World Was Young: Creation and Pourquoi Tales,* retold by Margaret Mayo. Orchard Books, 1995. Illustrations © 1995 by Louise Brierley. Reproduced by permission of Watts Publishing Group. / Ray, Jane, illustrator. From an illustration in *Mythical Birds & Beasts from Many Lands,* retold by Margaret Mayo. Orchard Books, 1996. Illustrations © 1996 by Jane Ray. Reproduced by permission of Watts Publishing Group. / Mayo, Margaret, photograph. Reproduced by permission of Margaret Mayo.

MAZILLE, CAPUCINE. Mazille, Capucine, illustration. Reproduced by permission of Capucine Mazille.

McARTHUR, NANCY. McArthur, Nancy, photograph by Ron Linek. Reproduced by permission of Nancy McArthur.

McELRATH-ESLICK, LORI. McElrath-Eslick, Lori, photograph. Reproduced by permission of Lori McElrath-Eslick.

MEEKER, CLARE HODGSON. Halsey, Megan, illustrator. From an illustration in *Who Wakes Rooster?* by Clare Hodgson Meeker. Simon & Schuster Books for Young Readers, 1996. Illustrations © 1996 by Megan Halsey. Reproduced by permission of Simon & Schuster Books for Young Readers, a division of Simon & Schuster, Inc. / Meeker, Clare Hodgson, photograph. Reproduced by permission of Clare Hodgson Meeker.

MOXLEY, SHEILA. Moxley, Sheila, illustrator. From an illustration in *Skip Across the Ocean: Nursery Rhymes from Around the World,* collected by Floella Benjamin. Orchard Books, 1995. Collection © Floella Benjamin 1995. Illustrations © Sheila Moxley 1995. Reproduced by permission of Orchard Books, New York. In the British Commonwealth by Sheila Moxley.

MURDOCH, DAVID H. Murdoch, David H., photograph. Reproduced by permission of David H. Murdoch.

MYERS, EDWARD. Natchev, Alexi, illustrator. From an illustration in *Forri the Baker,* by Edward Myers. Dial Books for Young Readers, 1995. Pictures © 1995 by Alexi Natchev. Reproduced by permission of Dial Books for Young Readers, a division of Penguin USA.

NELSON, TED W. AND SHARLENE P. Nelson, Ted W. and Sharlene P. Nelson, photograph. Reproduced by permission of Ted W. Nelson and Sharlene P. Nelson.

OLALEYE, ISAAC O. Lessac, Frane, illustrator. From an illustration in *The Distant Talking Drum: Poems from Nigeria,* by Isaac Olaleye. Wordsong, 1995. Illustrations © 1995 by Frane Lessac. Reproduced by permission. / Olaleye, Isaac O., photograph. Reproduced by permission of Isaac O. Olaleye.

PANETTA, JOSEPH N. Panetta, Joseph N. (with family), photograph. Reproduced by permission of Joseph N. Panetta.

PFEIFFER, JANET. Pfeiffer, Janet, photograph. Reproduced by permission of Janet Pfeiffer.

PIERCE, TAMORA. McDermott, Mike, illustrator. From a jacket of *Wolf-Speaker,* by Tamora Pierce. Atheneum Books for Young Readers, 1994. Jacket illustration © 1994 by Mike McDermott. Reproduced by permission of the illustrator. / Theron, illustrator. From a jacket of *Circle of Magic: Sandry's Book,* by Tamora Pierce. Scholastic, 1997. Copyright © 1997 by Tamora Pierce. Jacket painting © 1997 by Theron. Reproduced by permission of Scholastic Inc. / Pierce, Tamora, photograph by George S. Zarr, Jr. Reproduced by permission of Tamora Pierce.

PLATH, SYLVIA. McCully, Emily Arnold, illustrator. From an illustration in *The Bed Book,* by Sylvia Plath. Harper & Row,

SOMETHING ABOUT THE AUTHOR®

ADLERMAN, Daniel 1963-
(Kin Eagle, a joint pseudonym)

■ Personal

Born June 6, 1963, in Princeton, NJ; son of Mel (an insurance broker) and Gloria (a travel agent; maiden name, Katz) Adlerman; married Kimberly Hauck (an illustrator and designer), August 10, 1991; children: Rachelle, Joshua. *Education:* Boston University, B.S./ B.A. *Hobbies and other interests:* Comic books, cooking.

■ Addresses

Home and office—Kids at Our House, 47 Stoneham Pl., Metuchen, NJ 08840. *Electronic mail*—BookKids @ aol.com (America Online).

■ Career

Writer; children's publishing consultant. *Member:* Bookbinders Guild of America.

■ Writings

(With wife, Kimberly Adlerman, under joint pseudonym Kin Eagle) *It's Raining, It's Pouring,* illustrated by Rob Gilbert, Whispering Coyote Press (Danvers, MA), 1994.
Africa Calling, illustrated by Kimberly Adlerman, Whispering Coyote Press, 1996.
(Under pseudonym Kin Eagle) *Hey, Diddle Diddle,* illustrated by Rob Gilbert, Whispering Coyote Press, 1997.

Daniel Adlerman with daughter, Rachelle.

■ Sidelights

Daniel Adlerman told *SATA:* "Next to my wife and children, writing is the most gratifying aspect of my life. Artistically, I feel we have many phases. People cannot traverse to the next level until they have made at least a self-satisfying contribution to the area in which they started. I know I have some novels and adult nonfiction inside me, but I also know that I have not yet finished writing picture books.

"For example, I've been writing from the time I was a very young child. In fourth grade, it was poetry. In sixth and seventh grades, I was writing comedy bits and sketches with friends. Early in high school I discovered dialects. By the end of my high school career, college, and beyond, I wrote songs almost exclusively. It is hard for me to imagine tackling any of these categories unless I was satisfied that I had at least contributed all that I could in the phase immediately preceding it.

"As for inspiration, look around you. It's everywhere. Writing picture books feels natural to me, perhaps because my life is very much like a fairy tale. In all capacities—business, life, love, family, and books, my partner is my best friend. In my estimation, it would take hard work to become uninspired!"

*   *   *

ADLERMAN, Kimberly M. 1964-
(Kin Eagle, a joint pseudonym)

■ Personal

Born January 5, 1964, in Niagara Falls, NY; daughter of William (a chemical engineer) and Lillian (Strozewski) Hauck; married Daniel Adlerman (a writer), August 10, 1991; children: Rachelle, Joshua. *Education:* Attended Niagara County Community College; State University of New York at Buffalo, B.F.A. *Hobbies and other interests:* Tennis, gardening, baking, drawing, antiquing, "hanging out with my kids."

■ Addresses

Home and office—Kids at Our House, 47 Stoneham Pl., Metuchen, NJ 08840. *Electronic mail*—KimArts @ aol.com (American Online).

■ Career

Graphic designer, art director, and illustrator. Owner, Kids at Our House.

■ Writings

(With husband, Daniel Adlerman, under joint pseudonym Kin Eagle) *It's Raining, It's Pouring,* illustrated by Rob Gilbert, Whispering Coyote Press (Danvers, MA), 1994.
(Illustrator) Daniel Adlerman, *Africa Calling,* Whispering Coyote Press, 1996.

■ Sidelights

Kimberly M. Adlerman told *SATA:* "I've been drawing and painting for as long as I can remember. Illustrating has always been a dream of mine, but I haven't had enough confidence in myself to do something about it until recently.

"I hate to admit it, but I have horrible working habits! My husband and I have an office in our cellar, where we

Kimberly M. Adlerman with son, Joshua.

keep our computer, drawing table, and other office equipment. Although I can design there, it is extremely difficult for me to sketch or paint down there. Being a night person, with two small children, I find the best time to work is at night in our family room, after the kids have gone to bed.

"Some of my favorite artists include Eric Carle, Betsy Lewin, and Milton Glaser: Carle and Lewin for their simplicity. They can express so much with so little. Also, their work is often rife with humor. It's a characteristic that I not only appreciate, but find outstanding. If a visual can make me laugh out loud, even without the benefit of words, then I know it is effective.

"One of the main things I hope to achieve in illustrating children's books is to reach children—to help instill the love of books and reading that I have. Children are never too young to start reading. It's one of the reasons I like to make school appearances often. I want the opportunity to impress that message directly to as many children as possible."

ADOFF, Arnold 1935-

■ Personal

Born July 16, 1935, in New York, NY; son of Aaron Jacob (a pharmacist) and Rebecca (Stein) Adoff; married Virginia Hamilton (a writer), March 19, 1960; children: Leigh Hamilton (daughter), Jaime Levi (son). *Education:* City College of New York (now City College of the City University of New York), B.A., 1956; graduate studies at Columbia University, 1956-58; attended New School for Social Research, 1965-67. *Politics:* "Committed to change for full freedom for all Americans." *Religion:* "Freethinking pragmatist." *Hobbies and other interests:* History, music.

■ Addresses

Home—Yellow Springs, OH. *Office*—Arnold Adoff Agency, P.O. Box 293, Yellow Springs, OH 45387.

■ Career

Poet, writer of fiction and nonfiction, and anthologist. Teacher in New York City public schools, 1957-69; Arnold Adoff Agency, Yellow Springs, OH, literary agent, 1977—. Instructor in federal projects at New York University, Connecticut College, and other institutions; visiting professor, Queens College, 1986-87. Lecturer at colleges throughout the United States; consultant in children's literature, poetry, and creative writing. Member of planning commission, Yellow Springs. *Military service:* Served with New York National Guard.

■ Awards, Honors

Children's Books of the Year citation, Child Study Association of America, 1968, for *I Am the Darker Brother,* 1969, for *City in All Directions,* and 1986, for *Sports Pages;* Best Children's Books, *School Library Journal,* 1971, for *It Is the Poem Singing into Your Eyes,* and 1973, for *Black Is Brown Is Tan;* Notable Children's Trade Book citation, National Council for the Social Studies-Children's Book Council (NCSS-CBC), 1974, and Children's Choice citation, International Reading Association-Children's Book Council (IRA-CBC), 1985, both for *My Black Me: A Beginning Book of Black Poetry;* Art Books for Children Award for *MA nDA LA,* 1975; Books for the Teen Age citation, New York Public Library, 1980, 1981, and 1982, all for *It Is the Poem Singing into Your Eyes;* Jane Addams Children's Book Award special recognition, 1983, for *All the Colors of the Race;* Parents Choice Award (picture book) for *Flamboyan,* 1988; National Council of Teachers of English Award in Excellence in Poetry for Children, 1988.

■ Writings

POETRY, VERSE, AND PROSE POEMS FOR CHILDREN

MA nDA LA, illustrated by Emily Arnold McCully, Harper, 1971.
Black Is Brown Is Tan, illustrated by McCully, Harper, 1973.

Make a Circle Keep Us In: Poems for a Good Day, illustrated by Ronald Himler, Delacorte, 1975.
Big Sister Tells Me That I'm Black, illustrated by Lorenzo Lynch, Holt, 1976.
Tornado!, illustrated by Himler, Delacorte, 1977.
Under the Early Morning Trees, illustrated by Himler, Dutton, 1978.
Where Wild Willie, illustrated by McCully, Harper, 1978.
Eats, illustrated by Susan Russo, Lothrop, 1979.
I Am the Running Girl, illustrated by Himler, Harper, 1979.
Friend Dog, illustrated by Troy Howell, Lippincott, 1980.
OUTside/INside Poems, illustrated by John Steptoe, Lothrop, 1981.
Today We Are Brother and Sister, illustrated by Glo Coalson, Lothrop, 1981.
Birds, illustrated by Howell, Lippincott, 1982.
All the Colors of the Race, illustrated by Steptoe, Lothrop, 1982.
The Cabbages Are Chasing the Rabbits, illustrated by Janet Stevens, Harcourt, 1985.
Sports Pages, illustrated by Steven Kuzma, Lippincott, 1986.
Greens, illustrated by Betsy Lewin, Morrow, 1988.
Flamboyan, illustrated by Karen Barbour, Harcourt, 1988.
Chocolate Dreams, illustrated by Turi MacCombie, Lothrop, 1988.

ARNOLD ADOFF

Hard to Be Six, illustrated by Cheryl Hanna, Lothrop, 1990.

In for Winter, Out for Spring, illustrated by Jerry Pinkney, Harcourt, 1991.

The Return of Rex and Ethel, illustrated by Catherine Deeter, Harcourt, 1993.

Street Music: City Poems, illustrated by Karen Barbour, HarperCollins, 1995.

Slow Dance Heart Break Blues, illustrated by William Cotton, Lothrop, 1995.

Touch the Poem, illustrated by Bill Creevy, Scholastic, 1996.

Love Letters, illustrated by Lisa Desimini, Scholastic, 1997.

NONFICTION FOR CHILDREN

Malcolm X, illustrated by John Wilson, Crowell, 1970.

EDITED ANTHOLOGIES

I Am the Darker Brother: An Anthology of Modern Poems by Negro Americans, illustrated by Benny Andrews, Macmillan, 1968.

Black on Black: Commentaries by Negro Americans, Macmillan, 1968.

City in All Directions: An Anthology of Modern Poems, illustrated by Donald Carrick, Macmillan, 1969.

Black Out Loud: An Anthology of Modern Poems by Black Americans, illustrated by Alvin Hollingsworth, Macmillan, 1970.

Brothers and Sisters: Modern Stories by Black Americans, Macmillan, 1970.

It Is the Poem Singing into Your Eyes: An Anthology of New Young Poets, Harper, 1971.

The Poetry of Black America: An Anthology of the Twentieth Century (introduction by Gwendolyn Brooks), Harper, 1973.

My Black Me: A Beginning Book of Black Poetry, Dutton, 1974.

Celebrations: A New Anthology of Black American Poetry, Follett, 1977.

OTHER

Contributor of articles and reviews to periodicals.

■ Work in Progress

Day of Awe, for Lothrop; *Human, Of Course*, for Lothrop; *Once upon Time*, for Lothrop; *The Next America*, for HarperCollins.

■ Sidelights

An accomplished poet, biographer, and anthologist as well as a respected educator, Arnold Adoff is recognized as one of the first—and finest—champions of multiculturalism in American literature for children and young adults. Described by Jeffrey S. Copeland in *Speaking of Poets* as "a writer on a mission," Adoff, whose works most often reflect the African American experience, is among the first authors to consistently, accurately, and positively portray black subjects and concerns in a manner considered both specific and universal; several of his books, most notably the anthologies *I Am the*

Darker Brother and *City in All Directions*, the illustrated biography *Malcolm X*, and the picture book *Black Is Brown Is Tan*, are acknowledged as groundbreaking titles in their respective genres. For over twenty-five years, noted Copeland, Adoff "has been influencing how young readers view such matters as equality of races, sex-role stereotyping, individual rights, and ageism . . . . [He] has spent his writing career expounding the strength of family, both in terms of the individual family structure and the family of humanity." Writing in *Twentieth Century Children's Writers*, Marilyn Kaye stated that a "constant factor in Adoff's work is the imaginative expression of faith in people and their spirit. Each work, in its own way, salutes the human condition and its ability to triumph." *New York Times Book Review* contributor Ardis Kimzey called Adoff "one of the best anthologists in the world," and concluded, "With his taste and ear, it stands to reason that he should have turned to writing poetry himself, and done it well."

As a poet, Adoff characteristically utilizes free verse, vivid images, and unusual structures and sounds to express warm, affectionate family portraits; the intimate thoughts and feelings of children; and a variety of moods and tones. His poetry is noted for its invention and innovation as well as for its idiosyncratic use of capitalization and punctuation, elements that Adoff believes have a strong effect on the movement and rhythm of a poem. Adoff seeks to visually represent the

All the Colors of the Race, written by Adoff and illustrated by award-winning artist John Steptoe, features poems which express the thoughts and emotions of a girl growing up in a biracial family.

Adoff's book of poems captures various scenes and people with a distinctly urban style. (From *Street Music: City Poems,* illustrated by Karen Barbour.)

meaning of the words in his poetry by including variations of line length, type size, and letter arrangement; he uses punctuation and rhyme sparingly and sometimes incorporates black English into his verse. His collections of original poetry consist of books on a particular subject, such as eating, tornadoes, or birds; poems from the viewpoint of a particular character; and combinations of poetry and poetic prose that often focus on the duality of the fantastic and the realistic; he has also included some autobiographical material in his collections. Praised for the depth and range of subjects of his poetry as well as for its sensitivity, insight, musicality, structure, and control, Adoff is perceived as a poet whose skill with language and unexpected variances of meaning and rhythm help to make his works especially distinctive. Writing in *Twentieth Century Young Adult Writers,* Myra Cohn Livingston maintained that Adoff "strives to present a poetry of 'shaped speech' that is colloquial, that is relevant, short, and exciting." She claimed that each of Adoff's books of poetry "promises and delivers something new, fresh, and challenging.... [Always] he fulfills his own code, the 'need of the poet to help mold a complete reality through control of technique and imagination...,' in which he most assuredly excels." As an anthologist, Adoff is acknowledged for creating carefully selected poetry and prose collections that characteristically feature African American writers and focus on themes of survival, transcendence, and hope. Directing these books to young adults, Adoff includes works by such writers as Langston Hughes, Lucille Clifton, Paul Lau-

rence Dunbar, Gwendolyn Brooks, Arna Bontemps, and Nikki Giovanni as well as the creations of talented but lesser-known contributors, many of which were unavailable before their publication in Adoff's collections.

Adoff was born in New York City and grew up in a mixed working-class neighborhood in the South Bronx. His father, who operated a pharmacy, immigrated to the United States from a town near the Polish/Russian border. "In our home, as in so many others, the emphasis was on being American with a keen sense of Jewish," Adoff once told *Something about the Author* (*SATA*). Members of the Adoff family, especially the women, were deeply concerned with social justice. "There was a tradition of liberal, free-thinking females in the family," he told *SATA*. "My mother was involved in Zionist and civil rights causes. I recall when a black Baptist congregation reclaimed a derelict church in our neighborhood, my mother playing her violin, welcoming the new congregation." The Adoff family was well-read, and numerous magazines and newspapers could be found around the house—the exception being comics, which Adoff's grandmother strictly forbade as too lowbrow. Lively discussions on issues of the day were frequently exchanged. "Discussions were volatile, emotional as well as intellectual," Adoff told *SATA*. "In order to hold status within the family, you had to speak loudly ... on such burning topics as economics, socialism, the Soviet Union, and how to be assimilated into the larger society without losing one's Jewishness."

Around the age of ten, Adoff attended a neighborhood Zionist school, where, as he told *SATA,* he "studied the Old Testament and ... Zionism as well as other aspects of Jewish history and culture." His childhood reading, Adoff related in an interview in *Top of the News,* "taught me, in sum, how to walk a cultural tightrope. *Little Women* and Sholem Aleichem; *The Five Little Peppers* and *The Story of the Chanukah;* Longfellow, Riley, and Peretz...." As a teenager, Adoff read such authors as Shakespeare, Balzac, Dos Passos, Steinbeck, and De Maupassant; in addition, he was exposed to the writings of Havelock Ellis and the works of psychologists such as Menninger, Steckel, and Horney as well as, he told *Top of the News,* "Poets and poets and poets." Adoff's favorite poets, he noted, are the ones "who can sing and can control their word-songs with all-important craft"; among his most important influences are Dylan Thomas, e. e. cummings, Rilke, Marianne Moore, Gwendolyn Brooks, and Robert Hayden. Adoff attended high school in Manhattan with an early goal of becoming a doctor, but, he told *SATA,* "I felt like a fish out of water at that school because I was not a scientist in the depths of my soul." However, he developed an intense interest in jazz, an area in which his family had an influence. "Our house was filled with music," he told *SATA.* "My mother played the violin, my aunt sang, the radio played opera, gospel, and jazz." At sixteen, Adoff began writing poetry; he also began sneaking into New York City jazz clubs, becoming familiar with such jazz legends as Dizzy Gillespie, Charlie Parker, and Sarah Vaughan. Jazz demonstrated to Adoff, as he remarked to *SATA,* that "what was called 'American culture' most often did not include black or Latino culture.... By the time I graduated high school, jazz was the only music I listened to. It pushed out the boundaries of my world."

Adoff enrolled at the Columbia University School of Pharmacy, but withdrew to major in history and literature at City College. He wrote for the college newspaper and literary magazine and was politically active, participating in protests for civil liberties. At college, Adoff was introduced to writers such as James Joyce and Gertrude Stein who were especially gifted with language and wordplay. He was also greatly influenced by jazz artist Charles Mingus, who lectured before the jazz club of which Adoff was president. "Without a doubt, he was the most impressive person I had ever met," Adoff commented to *SATA.* "From then on, I went to see him wherever he played, and we got to know each other. In time, he would become my spiritual father." Later, while Adoff was substitute teaching and living in Greenwich Village, he became Mingus's manager and maintained "running chronicles of the Village club scene." Through Mingus, Adoff also met his future wife, the African American novelist and children's writer Virginia Hamilton, in 1958; the couple were married in 1960.

Adoff attended graduate school at Columbia University; although he finished the required coursework for a Ph.D. in American history, he left before completing his dissertation. While at graduate school, Adoff began teaching seventh grade social studies at a *yeshiva* in the

Brownsville section of Brooklyn. This job, he told *SATA,* "gave me confidence knowing I could stay alive outside grad school. This was important, because after two years I wanted to leave. The desire to live independently and focus on my writing had become overpowering." Adoff moved to Greenwich Village and began substitute teaching in New York City public schools; he spent the remainder of his time writing and going to jazz clubs in the Village. As he described it in *SATA,* the Village scene was "a vibrant community of painters, writers, musicians who would meet in the coffeehouses and talk art. As a poet I have been more influenced by musicians and painters than by other writers. Man Ray was an important influence, as was Picasso, the Russian Constructivists, and other painters and sculptors influenced by technology and things industrial." Shortly after Adoff and Virginia Hamilton were married, they moved to Spain and France to work on writing projects. During their stay in Europe, the Civil Rights Movement was intensifying in the United States and they decided to return. "Virginia is black, our children brown—we felt somehow it would be wrong to stay," Adoff told *SATA.* "Besides, it all seemed very exciting and we didn't want to be removed from the action. So we returned to New York, where we threw ourselves into our work and as much political work as we could handle."

Back in New York, Adoff began teaching students in Harlem and on Manhattan's Upper West Side. In addition, he told *SATA,* "I resumed collecting black literature, which I had begun in the late 1950s and early 1960s.... I would dig up old magazines like *Dial* and look for specifically black periodicals.... I'd haunt bookshops all over town...." Adoff also began to realize that there was a paucity of appropriate and relevant materials available to his students that reflected their lives. In his preface to the anthology *The Poetry of Black America,* Adoff described the exchange that resulted: "As a teacher I had students who wanted life in those dusty classrooms. They wanted pictures of themselves inside themselves.... I was the dealer. The pusher of poems and stories. Plays and paintings. Jazz and blues. And my students began to push on me. To deal their sounds and write their poems. And I was made to become serious about myself. To get my head together and attempt to go beyond the classrooms and students and schools. To go beyond the racist textbooks and anthologies that were on the shelves and in the bookstores."

Adoff began to assemble some of the poems that he had been collecting and sharing with his students. Through a friend, an editor at Macmillan, he received a positive response from the editor-in-chief of that publishing house. Adoff's first anthology, *I Am the Darker Brother: An Anthology of Modern Poems by Negro Americans,* was published in 1968, launching a number of subsequent anthologies of black poetry and prose. *The Poetry of Black America: An Anthology of the Twentieth Century* was one of the largest anthologies of black poetry ever published in the United States. Adoff told *SATA* that the volume, which contains an introduction by one of the editor's favorite poets, Gwendolyn Brooks, "contains 600 poems, although my manuscript consisted of 3000 poems that richly deserved to be included. The final choices were among the most agonizing selections I have ever had to make." Adoff faced another formidable selection task with the anthology *It Is the Poem Singing into Your Eyes,* for which the editor solicited work from young poets across the country and received over 6,000 submissions. "The tragedy ... is that I was allowed to publish only one hundred poems," he told *SATA.* "There were many, many, many poems that were absolutely superb.... The title of the volume was suggested by one of my young correspondents. I loved her statement—a poem truly does sing into your eyes and then on into your mind and soul." Among the young poets included in this collection was August Wilson, who would later become a Pulitzer Prize-winning playwright. In addition to his poetry anthologies, Adoff has compiled several collections of fiction and commentary by black writers.

In an interview with Lee Bennett Hopkins in *More Books by More People,* Adoff commented that his objective in producing black literature anthologies is to portray a truer cultural picture of literary America. "I want my anthologies of Black American writing to make Black kids strong in their knowledge of themselves and their great literary heritage—give them facts and people and power. I also want these Black books of mine to give knowledge to White kids around the country, so that mutual respect and understanding will come from mutual learning. We *can* go beyond the murder and the muddles of the present. Children have to understand that the oversimplifications they get in classrooms, along with the token non-White artists represented, are not the true American literature.... But for those who want the truth, for themselves and for their students, using an anthology is the first step to discovery. The anthology then leads to individual works of the writers." Regarding his inclusion criteria, Adoff remarked to *Top of the News* that in all of his books, "the material selected must be the finest in literary terms as well as in content/message/racial vision"; he added, "If I can lay Malcolm and DuBois on top of Sambo and Remus, will they finally die and disappear?"

During the time that Adoff was focusing on his compilations, he continued to write poetry. "The negative aspect of doing so many anthologies," he told *SATA,* "was that people came to think of me primarily as an anthologizer.... I, however, have always thought of myself as a poet first." Shortly after returning from Europe in 1965, Adoff enrolled in a class at Manhattan's New School for Social Research that was taught by the Filipino American poet Jose Garcia Villa, who would have a profound effect on Adoff's own poetry. "Jose became my second spiritual father," Adoff told *SATA.* "He talked about creating a poetry that was as pure as music.... His extremism based on an exhaustive knowledge of the art and craft of poetry set him apart." Adoff decided to create poetry in which, he says, "form and physical shape ... should serve to promote its message." In 1971, Adoff published his first book of poetry for children, *MA nDA LA,* a story poem using

Love Letters offers young readers a collection of twenty poems written in the form of valentine notes. (Illustrated by Lisa Desimini.)

only words containing the sound "ah." *MA nDA LA,* which features watercolor illustrations by Emily Arnold McCully, relates the cycle of African family life in a small village. "Logically, the poem makes no sense and is not supposed to," Adoff commented in *SATA.* Writing in *Twentieth Century Children's Writers,* Marilyn Kaye described Adoff's "sing-song verse" in *MA nDA LA* as "a simple compilation of sounds which evoke a sense of celebration." The book demonstrated Adoff's poetic principles, as he described them in *SATA:* "I use the image of invisible rubber bands pulling the reader's eye from the last letter of the last word in the first line down to the first letter of the first word in the last line.... The music of language greatly affects meaning.... Ideally, each poem should be read three times: for meaning; for rhythm; for technical tricks. My poems demand active participation."

Throughout the 1970s and 1980s, Adoff published several volumes of poetry for young people that display his characteristic use of free verse, vivid sensory images, striking word pictures, and lively rhythms while offering sensitive portrayals of family life and interior emotions. *Black Is Brown Is Tan*—modeled after Adoff's own family—is one of the first few children's books to depict interracial families; according to Kaye, it "extends the focus beyond color to encompass a family's delight in each other." A citizen's vigilante group located near New Haven, Connecticut, attacked *Black Is Brown Is Tan* because it contained no capital letters. Adoff has noted that the group was "too embarrassed to admit racist undertones"; the charges were eventually dropped. In *All the Colors of the Race*, Adoff explores the feelings of a girl with a black mother and a white father; "contemplative, jubilant, and questioning, the upbeat verses stress the young person's humanity in terms of gifts received from her forebears," wrote Ruth M. Stein in *Language Arts*. In *Where Wild Willie*, which Stein called "Adoff's paean to independence" in another review in *Language Arts*, the poet describes a child who temporarily leaves her family to go on her own adventure of learning. The poem recounts the girl's journey and is interspersed with the encouraging words of her parents. Zena Sutherland wrote in *Bulletin of the Center for Children's Books* that *Where Wild Willie* "describes with lilting fluency Willie's rambles and then the voices from home speak for themselves, an antiphonal arrangement in which the two draw closer until Willie comes home." In an essay for *Something about the Author Autobiography Series*, Adoff asserted that his best book is *OUTside/INside Poems*, a poem cycle that recreates a day in the life of a small boy and expresses his range of feelings. Adoff called this work "a great vehicle for teaching young readers to write poetry. Also, this is the one that really has the greatest element of reality/fantasy."

Adoff has said that he considers *Sports Pages*, a book of poetry for middle graders, to be "a breakthrough [because I] worked in a longer form of a combination of poetic prose and poetry and dealt with some autobiographical material using individual voice in the midst of organized activity." A reviewer in *Bulletin of the Center for Children's Books* acknowledged, "This is one of his best collections," while a critic in *Kirkus Reviews* suggested that *Sports Pages* might "easily lure the adolescent" who will enjoy Adoff's "sensitivity and acuity." With *Flamboyan*, Adoff again uses poetic prose in a picture book fantasy about a Puerto Rican girl who longs to fly with the birds who circle above her yard. Called "a magical story of a girl's yearning to be outside her own life" by a reviewer in *Publishers Weekly*, *Flamboyan* will "appeal to all who long to go beyond the ordinary." Illustrated by Karen Barbour, the book contains an unusual typographic device, a red leaf that appears in the text to provide directions for reading aloud. Ruth K. MacDonald of *School Library Journal* called *Flamboyan* a "dazzling combination of both text and illustration." Adoff's next book, *Chocolate Dreams*, is the latest collection of original poems on one of his— and children's—favorite subjects: food. Described by Betsy Hearne in *Bulletin of the Center for Children's Books* as a "rich confection of wordplay, rhythms, and unexpected twists of rhyme and meaning from a poet in his element," the poems, contended Hearne, reveal Adoff's ability to combine "invention and control, depth and delight."

In 1995, Adoff published *Street Music: City Poems*, a collection of jazzy poems in free verse that celebrates the vibrancy of city life, and *Slow Dance Heart Break Blues*, a volume of poems about the thoughts and experiences of adolescence that he directs to readers in their early teens. The latter, according to a critic in

Kirkus Reviews, "is laden with empathy," and Sharon Korbeck of *School Library Journal* concluded that "there is a great deal of depth here," challenging readers to question what poetry is and to reexamine "who and where they are in light of today's fast-moving issues and society." Writing in *Horn Book*, Robert D. Hale stated, "If the word gets out, *Slow Dance Heart Break Blues* will become a best seller. Arnold Adoff knows what teenagers are thinking and feeling, which is evident in this collection of on-target poems...." In *Love Letters*, a volume of poetry illustrated by Lisa Desimini, Adoff presents primary graders with twenty valentines written as anonymous notes. Dulcy Brainard of *Publishers Weekly* claimed that "much of the pleasure" comes from the author's and illustrator's "abilities to evoke not only ... everyday feelings but the more complicated sense of privacy and mystery they summon." Writing in *Bulletin of the Center for Children's Books*, Elizabeth Bush suggested, "When it's got to be sweet, but it can't be saccharine, drop one of these on a desktop or into a booktalk and wait for the sparks to fly."

Adoff lives and works out of Yellow Springs, Ohio, in a house he and his wife Virginia built on land behind her parents' farm. He continues to write for young people, seeing a link with his concerns for social justice. "I began writing for kids," Adoff once told *SATA*, "because I wanted to effect a change in American society. I continue in that spirit. By the time we reach adulthood, we are closed and set in our attitudes. The chances of a poet reaching us are very slim. But I can open a child's imagination, develop his appetite for poetry, and most importantly, show him that poetry is a natural part of everyday life. We all need someone to point out that the emperor is wearing no clothes. That is the poet's job." In an interview with Jeffrey S. Copeland in *Speaking of Poets*, Adoff added another perspective: "I'm still attempting to influence kids one way or another, whether it is the way they view the color of skin or reality and fantasy. I hope always to be considered perhaps controversial, perhaps dangerous, to the status quo.... It is a struggle to create something you hope is art. I work long and hard at my craft. I like to feel I have good instincts when it comes to language. All in all, I am very proud of what I've done."

■ Works Cited

Adoff, Arnold, interview in *Top of the News*, January, 1972, pp. 153-55.

Adoff, A., preface to *The Poetry of Black America: An Anthology of the Twentieth Century*, Harper, 1973.

Adoff, A., essay in *Something about the Author Autobiography Series*, Volume 15, Gale, 1993.

Brainard, Dulcy, review of *Love Letters*, *Publishers Weekly*, December 2, 1997.

Bush, Elizabeth, review of *Love Letters*, *Bulletin of the Center for Children's Books*, March, 1997, p. 239.

Copeland, Jeffrey S., interview with Adoff, *Speaking of Poets: Interviews with Poets Who Write for Children and Young Adults*, National Council of Teachers of English, 1993.

Review of *Flamboyan, Publishers Weekly,* August 26, 1988, p. 88.

Hale, Robert D., review of *Slow Dance Heart Break Blues,* in *Horn Book,* November-December, 1995, p. 770.

Hearne, Betsy, review of *Chocolate Dreams, Bulletin of the Center for Children's Books,* November, 1989, p. 49.

Hopkins, Lee Bennett, *More Books by More People: Interviews with Sixty-Five Authors of Books for Children,* Citation Press, 1974.

Kaye, Marilyn, contributor to *Twentieth Century Children's Writers,* 3rd edition, St. James Press, 1989, pp. 6-7.

Kimzey, Ardis, "Verse First, Poetry Next," *New York Times Book Review,* April 25, 1982, p. 37.

Korbeck, Sharon, review of *Slow Dance Heart Break Blues, School Library Journal,* September, 1995, p. 221.

Livingston, Myra Cohn, contributor to *Twentieth Century Young Adult Writers,* St. James Press, 1994, pp. 4-5.

MacDonald, Ruth K., review of *Flamboyan, School Library Journal,* October, 1988, p. 114.

Review of *Slow Dance Heart Break Blues, Kirkus Reviews,* July 1, 1995, p. 942.

Review of *Sports Pages, Bulletin of the Center for Children's Books,* June, 1986, p. 181.

Review of *Sports Pages, Kirkus Reviews,* May 1, 1986, p. 721.

Stein, Ruth M., review of *Where Wild Willie, Language Arts,* September, 1979, pp. 690-91.

Stein, Ruth M., review of *All the Colors of the Race, Language Arts,* April, 1983, pp. 483-84.

Sutherland, Zena, review of *Where Wild Willie, Bulletin of the Center for Children's Books,* March, 1979, p. 109.

■ For More Information See

BOOKS

Children's Literature Review, Volume 7, Gale, 1984.
Fourth Book of Junior Authors and Illustrators, Wilson, 1978.*

—Sketch by Gerard J. Senick

B

BABER, Carolyn Stonnell 1936-

■ Personal

Born April 25, 1936, in Cartersville, VA; daughter of Clayton Anderson (in lumber business) and Nellie Mae (in cattle business; maiden name, Sheldon) Stonnell; married James Pendleton Baber (a lawyer), June 14, 1958; children: Clayton Anderson, Catherine Sheperd Baber Fleischman, Courtenay James Baber Thompson. *Education:* Attended Meredith College, 1954-55; Longwood College, B.A., 1958, M.S., 1973; further graduate study at Virginia Commonwealth University, 1979, and Birmingham Southern University, 1991. *Politics:* Republican. *Religion:* Episcopal. *Hobbies and other interests:* Horseback riding, decorating, music.

■ Addresses

Home and office—Doubletree Farm, Route 2, Box 212, Cumberland, VA 23040. *Agent*—Ray Lincoln, Ray Lincoln Literary Agency, Elkins Park House, Suite 107-B, Elkins Park, PA 19117.

■ Career

Elementary schoolteacher at public schools in Cumberland County, VA, 1963-75, elementary supervisor, 1976-80; Huguenot Academy, Powhatan, VA, elementary teacher, 1985-89; Southside Livestock Markets, Inc., Blackstone, VA, president, 1993—. Stonnell Timberlands, Powhatan, Amelia, and Cumberland, VA, manager, 1979—; Gibralter Wood Corp., Cumberland, president, 1981-85. Virginia Federation of Garden Clubs, nature conservancy chairperson for Piedmont District, 1993-96. *Member:* Society of Children's Book Writers and Illustrators, Virginia Writers Club, Cartersville Garden Club (president, 1992-96).

■ Writings

Pony, illustrated by Luke T. Fleischman, Richmond Saddlery Press (Richmond, VA), 1991.
Little Billy, illustrated by Luke T. Fleischman, Jason & Nordic (Hollidaysburg, PA), 1994.

Contributor to magazines, including *Horse Talk* and *Horse Journal.*

■ Work in Progress

Three young adult titles, *Ebony King, Manitoka,* and *Lady: A Horse of War; The Family,* an adult book.

CAROLYN STONNELL BABER

10

■ **Sidelights**

Carolyn Stonnell Baber told *SATA:* "In all I have ever read or heard from professionals about writing, the one thing most emphasized for authors is to 'know your subject.' Because of my past experience as an elementary schoolteacher and administrator and my lifelong interest in and work with horses, I feel I know something of my subject: horses. In fiction, however, I am not telling facts, but exploring questions that affect the characters and readers in their daily lives. In this way, writing is a learning process for the author and certainly one for the reader.

"Because reading is such a learning experience for the young reader, I feel the facts, both historical and contemporary, must be true. Therefore, I spend much time and effort in researching the subject and, if possible, visiting the setting. For *Little Billy,* I did extensive research to learn about a little-known breed of pony called the Bashkir Curley, as well as polio, a dread disease of the time. I also visited the southwest to understand its unique atmosphere and see the country-side firsthand. I grew up in a sawmill family in Virginia during the Second World War, so the life of mill workers, both horses and men, is very familiar to me.

"My reason for writing young adult novels is that I feel young people are so vulnerable, and I can best communicate universal values to them through my characters and their experiences. In *Little Billy,* one of the main themes is the struggle of Danny, who suffers from polio, to grow up physically different from other people. The pony 'Little Billy' is also different in looks and suffers the same type of adversity as his owner and friend Danny. Starlet, another character, learns tolerance and acceptance.

"I have written other novels: *Ebony King,* a classic success story; *Manitoka,* an Indian story, which sets up the inevitable conflicts between mother and daughter; and *Lady: A Horse of War,* which illustrates that youthful love and a desire for knowledge, in this case horseback riding, can overcome even political and religious hatred.

"As to how or why I began to write, it is something that has always been with me. In high school I was complimented for my writing, but not encouraged. In college, for one brief moment during my freshman year, I was challenged to write—not because I exhibited talent but because it was simply expected of me. I have been trying to live up to this professor's expectations ever since.

"Writing has not been easy for me. I am dyslexic and, while I failed spelling tests miserably in school, was always at the end of the graph for posted grades (to my embarrassment), and had no home background for literature or the arts, I did have thorough home training in the Puritan ethic that hard work produces success. For this I am deeply indebted to my parents and my family.

"I hope this trait is visible in all my work for young people. There is no substitute for work and dedication when it comes to realizing a dream. Two of my dreams have been realized through diligence, hope, determination, and WORK.

"The first was to ride in the Ladies Five-Gaited Saddle Horse Class at the National Horse Show in Madison Square Garden in 1955. I was nineteen years old and it marked a highlight in my young life which I have never forgotten. The second dream was to be a published author. This has come later in life, but with no less excitement and gratitude for years of hope and work. I believe dreams as young people see them are the essence of an adult life worth living."

*   *   *

BAKER, Samm Sinclair 1909-1997

OBITUARY NOTICE—See index for *SATA* sketch: Born July 29, 1909, in Paterson, NJ; died following a stroke, March 5, 1997, in Port Chester, NY. Author and lecturer. Baker, a former advertising agency executive, turned to writing self-help and diet books in the 1960s. He received a bachelor's degree in economics from the University of Pennsylvania in 1929 and began his advertising career at the bottom—as a copywriter in Manhattan. But he became president of the Kiesewetter, Baker, Hagedorn and Smith agency and in 1955 became a vice president at Donahue and Coe, Inc. He began publishing books in 1955 and his first self-help book was 1959's *Casebook of Successful Ideas for Advertising and Selling.* Baker became an author full time in 1963, though he still worked as a freelance business consultant. Teaming up with experts in the fields of medicine and diet, Baker co-wrote several self-improvement books in the 1960s and 1970s including *The Doctor's Quick Weight Loss Diet* (with Doctor Irwin Stillman in 1967), *The Complete Scarsdale Medical Diet* (with Doctor Herman Tarnower in 1979) and *The Doctor's Quick Teen-Age Diet* (with Stillman in 1971). He also wrote several advice books on gardening and in 1984 penned *Erotic Focus: The New Way to Enhance Your Sexual Pleasure.* Baker's short essays were published in *McCalls, Popular Science* and *Suburbia Today.*

OBITUARIES AND OTHER SOURCES:

PERIODICALS

Los Angeles Times, March 25, 1997, p. A22.
New York Times, March 23, 1997, p. 46.
Washington Post, March 24, 1997, p. D6.

*   *   *

BARKLEM, Jill 1951-
(Gillian Gaze)

■ **Personal**

Maiden name, Gillian Gaze; born in 1951; married; children: Elizabeth, Peter.

JILL BARKLEM

■ **Addresses**

Home—Epping Forest, England.

■ **Career**

Writer and illustrator.

■ **Writings**

SELF-ILLUSTRATED

Spring Story, Philomel, 1980, new edition, HarperCollins (London), 1995.
Summer Story, Philomel, 1980.
Autumn Story, Philomel, 1980, published as *Autumn Story: Primrose Meets the Harvest Mice,* Picture Lions (London), 1995.
Winter Story, Philomel, 1980, published as *Winter Story: A Party in the Ice Palace,* Picture Lions, 1995.
The Big Book of Brambly Hedge, Philomel, 1981.
The Secret Staircase, Philomel, 1983, new edition, HarperCollins, 1996.
The High Hills, Collins, 1986, Philomel, 1986, new edition, HarperCollins, 1996.
The Four Seasons of Brambly Hedge (contains *Spring Story, Summer Story, Autumn Story,* and *Winter Story*), Collins, 1988, Philomel, 1990.
Sea Story, Collins, 1990, Philomel, 1991, published as *Sea Story: Primrose and Wilfred Sail to Sandy Bay,* Picture Lions, 1996.
The Brambly Hedge Treasury (contains *The Secret Staircase* and *The High Hills*), Collins, 1991.
The Brambly Hedge Poster Book, Collins, 1991.

Through the Hedgerow: A Three-Dimensional Pop-Up Book, Collins, 1993, published in the United States as *The World of Brambly Hedge,* Philomel, 1993.
Poppy's Babies, Collins, 1994, Philomel, 1995, published as *Poppy's Babies: Poppy and Dusty's New Family,* Picture Lions, 1996.
The Brambly Hedge Birthday Book, Philomel, 1994.
Poppy's Wedding, HarperCollins, 1995.
Primrose's Adventure: A Sliding Picture Book, HarperCollins, 1995.
The Snow Ball: A Sliding Picture Book, HarperCollins, 1995.
Wilfred's Birthday: A Sliding Picture Book, Collins, 1995.
Winter Story Sticker Book, Collins, 1996.

ILLUSTRATOR

Illustrator of the "Haffertee Hamster" books by Janet and John Perkins.

OTHER

Some of Barklem's "Brambly Hedge" books have been recorded on audiocassette. Also author and illustrator of picture books under name Gillian Gaze.

■ **Sidelights**

Jill Barklem is the author and illustrator of the "Brambly Hedge" stories, a popular series of picture books that features a society of humanized mice living in tree homes in rural England. Evoking the Victorian and Edwardian eras in her texts and pictures, Barklem presents her audience with a nostalgic and idyllic picture of country life. She also imbues her works with rural English tradition and family warmth and security, as each of her characters maintains an important role in the daily functionings and social well-being of the community. Barklem's series has sold millions of copies in England, and her creations have been marketed on china, greeting cards, and other products both there and in the United States.

Barklem began her career in 1974 by writing and illustrating books under her maiden name, Gillian Gaze; she also provided pictures for the "Haffertee Hamster" books by Janet and John Perkins and a series of collections of prayers and graces. During this period, Barklem also researched English customs, flora, and other geographical and cultural details for her "Brambly Hedge" stories. Her first four books, *Spring Story, Summer Story, Autumn Story,* and *Winter Story,* were published simultaneously in 1980 as individual volumes in a "miniature" format. *Spring Story* introduces the field mice who comprise the community of Brambly Hedge, centering on the picnic celebration of young mouse Wilfred Toadflax's birthday. *Summer Story* features a wedding; *Autumn Story,* the search for young Primrose Woodmouse, who is lost and frightened; and *Winter Story* the festivities surrounding the Snow Ball at the Ice Hall. These four works were collected in the omnibus volume *The Four Seasons of Brambly Hedge. School Library Journal* contributor Anita C. Wilson noted that these stories of normal childhood adventures

Using the Victorian- and Edwardian-style paintings characteristic of her other Brambly Hedge titles, Barklem has illustrated this tale of Dusty and his determination to provide a house for his wife, Poppy, and their children. (From *Poppy's Babies,* written and illustrated by Barklem.)

"should provide both entertainment and reassurance" to youngsters, while "the exceptional illustrations should give many hours of pleasure."

Barklem is also the creator of other "Brambly Hedge" stories, *The Secret Staircase* and *The High Hills,* which were published as full-sized volumes. The former involves the intrigue and excitement of a secret staircase and a hidden treasure discovered during preparations for the annual mid-winter celebration, while the latter is an exploration adventure in which Wilfred, in hopes of finding gold, accompanies elderly Mr. Apple on a mission of charity to deliver blankets to the voles in the High Hills of Brambly Hedge. These two works have also been published together as *The Brambly Hedge Treasury.* In *Growing Point,* Margery Fisher explained that "the plots are staples of junior adventures, used with a light tone, and the packed scenes have the perennial charm of the miniature."

Many critics have noted the resemblance between Barklem's stories and those of Beatrix Potter; most of these commentators contend, however, that while Potter remained true to animal nature when humanizing the actions of her characters, Barklem has created a world of children masquerading as mice. Further comparison between the two authors has prompted criticism for what has been described as the excessive wordiness of Barklem's text and the cluttered detail of her illustrations. Despite these comments, Barklem has garnered considerable praise from numerous reviewers who approve of the careful detail of her pictures. Crafting her illustrations with sepia ink and watercolor, Barklem is commended for offering much for young readers to discover through the patterned china, wallpaper, and fabrics, as well as the floral arrangements and other such features, with which she invests her work. Similarly,

Barklem is noted for her realistic sense of scale—for example, small blossoms make large floral arrangements for the mice—and for the authenticity of her settings. Representative of these more positive responses to Barklem's "Brambly Hedge" series is Margaret Adamson's assertion in *Reading Time* that the author has created a "delightfully intricate little world" with "charming" stories and illustrations that are "perfectly detailed representations of community living at its best, filled with colour, warmth and busyness."

■ Works Cited

Adamson, Margaret, review of *The Secret Staircase* and *The High Hills, Reading Time,* Volume 34, number 2, 1990, pp. 8, 14.

Fisher, Margery, review of *The Brambly Hedge Treasury, Growing Point,* January, 1992, pp. 5632-33.

Wilson, Anita C., review of *Autumn Story* and others, *School Library Journal,* March, 1981, p. 128.

■ For More Information See

BOOKS

Children's Literature Review, Volume 31, Gale, 1994.

PERIODICALS

Booklist, January 15, 1981, p. 695; February 1, 1984, p. 812; March 1, 1987, p. 1011; June 1, 1991, p. 1878; January 1, 1994, p. 837.

Books for Your Children, autumn-winter, 1983, p. 3.

Bulletin of the Center for Children's Books, March, 1984, p. 122.

Christian Science Monitor, April 17, 1987, p. 26.

Growing Point, January, 1981, pp. 3803-06; November, 1981, pp. 3960-61.

Horn Book Guide, Fall, 1995, p. 363.

Junior Bookshelf, February, 1981, pp. 9-10; October, 1983, p. 204; August, 1993, p. 131.
Publishers Weekly, August 29, 1980, p. 365; January 29, 1982, p. 67; January 13, 1984, p. 68.
School Librarian, December, 1983, p. 348.
School Library Journal, March, 1982, p. 128; March, 1984, p. 138; March, 1987, p. 140.
Times Educational Supplement, November 14, 1980, p. 25.
Times Literary Supplement, September 19, 1980, p. 1029.*

* * *

BASSIL, Andrea 1948-
(Anna Nilsen)

■ Personal

Born September 16, 1948, in England. *Education:* Attended Eastbourne School of Art, 1966-67; Edinburgh College of Art, Diploma in Art and Design, 1972; Moray House College of Education, Scottish Certificate of Education, 1973. *Hobbies and other interests:* Photography, travel, gardening, walking.

■ Addresses

Office—(Studio) 16 Emery St., Cambridge CB1 2AX, England. *Agent*—Rosemary Canter, Peters, Fraser & Dunlop, 503/4 The Chambers, Chelsea Harbour, London SW10 0XF, England.

■ Career

Mussleburgh Grammar School, assistant teacher of art, 1973-74; St. Margaret's School, Newington, assistant teacher of art, 1974-85; Bournemouth & Poole College of Art and Design, Bournemouth, England, Course Director in Natural History Illustration, 1985-90; Anglia Polytechnic University, Head of Graphic Arts and Illustration, 1990-94; full-time artist, writer, and illustrator, 1995—. Lamp of Lothian Art Centre, evening class lecturer, 1973-74. Pixel Magic, art director, screen designer, and games consultant, 1995-96; educational games consultant to Multimedia Corp. *Exhibitions:* Artwork exhibited in solo shows and group shows in England and Scotland. *Member:* Society of Authors.

■ Awards, Honors

Goldsmiths' Hall travelling scholarship for Paris, 1981.

■ Writings

CHILDREN'S BOOKS; UNDER PSEUDONYM ANNA NILSEN

Jungle, illustrated by Peter Joyce, Walker Books, 1994.
Farm, illustrated by Annie Axworthy, Walker Books, 1994.
Friends, illustrated by Sue Coney, Walker Books, 1994.
Wheels, illustrated by Joe Wright, Walker Books, 1994.

ANDREA BASSIL

Dinosaurs, illustrated by Annie Axworthy, Walker Books, 1994.
Terrormazia: A Hole New Kind of Maze Game, illustrated by Dom Mansell, Walker Books, 1995, Candlewick Press, 1995.
Flying High, illustrated by Tony Wells, Walker Books, 1996.
Fairy Tales, illustrated by Sue Coney, Walker Books, 1996.
Under the Sea, illustrated by Tania Hurt-Newton, Walker Books, 1996.
Drive Your Car, illustrated by Tony Wells, Walker Books, 1996, Candlewick Press, 1996.
Drive Your Tractor, illustrated by Tony Wells, Walker Books, 1996, Candlewick Press, 1996.
Where Are Percy's Friends?, illustrated by Dom Mansell, Walker Books, 1996, Candlewick Press, 1996.
Where Is Percy's Dinner?, illustrated by Dom Mansell, Walker Books, 1996, Candlewick Press, 1996.
Percy the Park Keeper Activity Book, HarperCollins, 1996.
Follow the Kite, HarperCollins, 1997.
Dig and Burrow, Zero to Ten, 1998.
Hang and Dangle, Zero to Ten, 1998.
Leap and Jump, Zero to Ten, 1998.
Swim and Dive, Zero to Ten, 1998.

OTHER

(Contributing author) *The Complete Guide to Illustration,* Quarto, 1989.
Jaguar Expedition to Belize, Royal Geographic Society, 1989.

(Illustrator) Helen Kinnier Wilson, *Cambridge Reflections,* Silent (Cambridge), 1992.

Author of *Design in Partnership,* 1989. Contributor of illustrations to *National Association of Field Study Officers' Journal.*

■ Work in Progress

Games book concepts for LEGO in collaboration with Dorling Kindersley, including *Insectoid Invasion* and *Road Mazes;* games book concepts for *Alien Alert; ABC Spelling Picture Dictionary,* for Larousse; *The Amazing Dream House,* for Walker Books; writing and illustrating *Aqua Quest LEGO* for Dorling Kindersley, scheduled for autumn, 1998; illustrating a pirates' puzzle book for Dorling Kindersley.

■ Sidelights

Andrea Bassil told *SATA:* "In 1990 Walker Books invited me to develop an 'original' concept for a puzzle book. This challenge was my first encounter with children's books, and it inspired me to produce *Terrormazia.* I had submitted an illustrated children's box for a competition run by Jonathan Cape, and it was selected for their exhibition of best entries. This had impressed my editor at Walker Books. She identified my potential as a 'deviser' of children's books. For the next five years I worked exclusively for Walker Books. In 1995 I retired as the Head of Illustration at Anglia Polytechnic University to follow a full-time career in children's books. Since then I have had books contracted with a variety of publishers.

"I also have an interest in multi-media work and have developed an educational game for the Oxford University Press *Children's Encyclopaedia* on CD-ROM. In addition, I worked as the screen designer, art director, and games consultant for a children's title, *Witches Academy.*

"As a deviser of children's books, my ideas usually start with a visual idea that incorporates an activity (mental and/or physical) around which the narrative is then woven. In this sense I am not a traditional author; normally an author would start with a written script, which is then illustrated. I find that even when developing a narrative concept, I start by sketching a series of visual images. This is due to my art college training, which included a wide range of specialties and a strong emphasis on drawing. Many of my ideas contain an educational element, probably due to the number of years I spent in the academic world. Often my aim is to provide children with an entertaining learning platform. I am interested in combining information with a game, a puzzle, or other activity to encourage children to be inquisitive about the real world. The *Aqua Quest* book, an information maze game book, is a good example. In the book, the Aquazone kits have been set in different oceans around the world, which introduces children to real fish on their maze journey around the world."

■ For More Information See

PERIODICALS

Bookseller, May 12, 1995, p. 35.
Nursery World, February 22, 1996, p. 12.
Publishers Weekly, June 3, 1996, p. 85.
School Librarian, February, 1996, p. 21.
Time Out for Kids, March-April, 1995, p. 10.

*   *   *

BEARD, Darleen Bailey 1961-

■ Personal

Born January 24, 1961; daughter of Larry (involved in greenhouse business) and Ella Holman (a homemaker) Bailey; married Danny Beard (a licensed professional counselor), March 9, 1984; children: Spencer, Karalee. *Education:* University of Oklahoma, B.A., professional writing, 1986. *Hobbies and other interests:* Flower gardening, decorating, reading, history.

■ Addresses

Home and office—6508 Diana Place, Tuttle, OK 73089. *Agent*—Ginger Knowlton, Curtis Brown Ltd., Ten Astor Pl., New York NY 10003.

DARLEEN BAILEY BEARD

■ Career

Dental assistant, Oklahoma City and Norman, OK, 1979-83; freelance writer, McGraw-Hill, School Book Division, Oklahoma City, 1989-90; part-time receptionist, Oklahoma City, 1991-95. *Member:* Society of Children's Book Writers and Illustrators, Parent-Teacher Organization.

■ Awards, Honors

Attended the Writers Workshop at Chatauqua, New York, on full scholarship from *Highlights for Children* magazine; Creme-de-la-Creme award, Oklahoma Writer's Federation, 1990.

■ Writings

The Pumpkin Man from Piney Creek, Simon & Schuster, 1995.
The Flimflam Man, Farrar, Straus, 1998.

Work represented in *Megan's Tree* and *The Barnyard Switch,* Highlights for Children Books, 1995.

■ Work in Progress

Twister, for Farrar, Straus; *Close Those Sleepy Eyes,* a picture book; a middle-grade historical novel set in Babbs Switch, Oklahoma, in 1924; *Marry Me on Recess,* an easy-to-read book; *Underwear in the Outfield,* an easy-to-read book.

■ Sidelights

Darleen Bailey Beard told *SATA:* "When I was young (or should I say young*er*) I wanted to be good at something. All my friends had things they were good at—Kathy was a good swimmer, Suzanne was a violinist, and Patty Jo was the prettiest girl in the school. So I set out on my own personal journey to find something to be good at, something to set me apart from everyone else. I knew I liked words and the way they sounded. I liked the way words created pictures in my mind and I knew I liked to tell stories so that everyone's eyes would open wide. But it wasn't until fifth grade that I realized what I was good at. Every week Mrs. Schickling would make us write stories with our spelling words. I couldn't wait to get home and start writing. Mrs. Schickling liked my stories and made me stand in front of the class and read them. Well, I was terribly shy and the first time I stood up to read I was scared silly. I shook so badly I could hardly read my story. Week after week, I stood in front of the class reading my stories and as the weeks turned into months I began to realize my search to find something that set me apart from everyone else was over. I was a writer! So right there in fifth grade, I decided that when I grew up I'd be a writer. Well, I'm not grown up yet, but I am a published writer and my first book is dedicated to Mrs. Schickling for opening up the world of writing for me.

"When I do author visits at schools I tell children about the band-aid collection I had when I was eight or nine. It all started because I was so shy and had a hard time talking to other children in school. One day, I discovered that if I wore band-aids to school kids would come up to me and ask 'What happened?' and 'Are you okay?' I'd tell them a wonderful story about how I got hurt, their eyes would open wide, and for a minute or two I wouldn't feel so shy. That's how I started my band-aid collection. And that's probably how I became a writer. I'm not as shy as I used to be. In fact, most people think I'm real out-going, the life of a party. Sometimes I am. But most times I'm quiet. I like to work at home, take care of my two kiddos and dig, dig, dig in my flower garden. I love flowers. My favorite place is my old green porch swing where I sit reading books and admiring my beautiful morning glories and daisies. I have lots of hummingbirds, too. We live on an acreage and plan to start a berry patch and plant some fruit trees."

In Beard's *Pumpkin Man from Piney Creek,* young Hattie sees a jack-o'-lantern for the first time, and tries to convince her Pa to spare one of the pumpkins he's selling. When Pa says that he's promised every pumpkin they've raised to the pumpkin man from Piney Creek, Hattie takes matters into her own hands. A writer for *Kirkus Reviews* noted that the author's first story, set in the late nineteenth century, contains "old-fashioned idioms" used "with care and taste." Teachers will find this story has "many uses in a whole-language classroom," wrote Ruth Semrau for *School Library Journal.*

■ Works Cited

Review of *The Pumpkin Man from Piney Creek, Kirkus Reviews,* October 1, 1995, p. 1424.
Semrau, Ruth, review of *The Pumpkin Man from Piney Creek, School Library Journal,* October, 1995, p. 96.

■ For More Information See

PERIODICALS

Booklist, September 15, 1995, p. 168.
Publishers Weekly, September 18, 1995, p. 90.

*   *   *

BETANCOURT, Jeanne 1941-

■ Personal

Born October 2, 1941, in Burlington, VT; daughter of Henry (a certified public accountant) and Beatrice (a secretary; maiden name, Mario) Granger; divorced first husband; married Lee Minoff (a writer and psychoanalyst), March 5, 1983; children: (first marriage) Nicole. *Education:* College of St. Joseph the Provider, B.S., 1964; New York University, M.A., 1974. *Hobbies and other interests:* "I spend my time gardening, drawing, and oil painting. I've never been good in competitive sports, probably because I have terrible eye/hand coordination; so I swim, cross-country ski, do yoga, and ride my bike around the countryside. I still love to dance."

■ Addresses

Home—New York City and Sharon, CT. *Agent*—Charlotte Sheedy, New York, NY.

■ Career

Teacher at St. Peters School, Rutland, VT, 1961-63, St. Francis deSales Academy, Bennington, VT, 1963-64, Edmunds Junior High School, Burlington, VT, 1964-65, East Islip High School, East Islip, NY, 1965-66, High School for Pregnant Teens, Bronx, NY, 1967-69, Tetard Junior High School, Bronx, 1969-70, John Jay High School, Brooklyn, NY, 1970-71, Prospect Heights High School, Brooklyn, 1971-76, and Edward R. Murrow High School, Brooklyn, 1976-80; New School for Social Research, New York City, faculty member, 1977-80; Tomorrow Entertainment/Medcom Company, New York City, director of development, 1980-81; full-time writer, 1981—. Member of preview committee of first International Film Festival, 1972, of reviewing committee of film division at Brooklyn Public Library, 1974-79, and of board of directors of the Media Center for Children, New York City, 1977-87. Developer of workshops for librarians and educators on the topic of film programming for adolescents. *Member:* New York Women in Film (president, 1981-82).

■ Awards, Honors

SMILE! How to Cope with Braces was selected an Outstanding Science Trade Book for Children by the National Science Teachers Association and the Children's Book Council, 1982; Emmy nomination for Outstanding Children's Special, 1986, for *I Want to Go Home* and *Don't Touch,* 1987, for *Teen Father,* and 1988, for *Supermom's Daughter;* Emmy nomination for Best Children's Script, 1986, and Humanitarian Award, Los Angeles Council on Assaults against Women, 1987, both for *Don't Touch;* Humanitas Award finalist, 1986, for *Don't Touch,* and 1987, for *Teen Father;* National Psychology Award for Excellence in the Media, American Psychological Association, and Nancy Susan Reynolds Award, Center for Population Options, both 1987, for *Teen Father;* Children's Choice Award, International Reading Association/Children's Book Council, 1987, for *Sweet Sixteen and Never ...;* Commendation Award, American Women in Radio and Television, and Mentor Award, National Association for Youth, both 1988, for *Supermom's Daughter.*

■ Writings

FICTION; FOR YOUNG PEOPLE

The Rainbow Kid, Avon, 1983.
Turtle Time, Avon, 1985.
Puppy Love, Avon, 1986.
Crazy Christmas, Bantam, 1988.

"PONY PALS" SERIES

I Want a Pony, Scholastic, 1995.
A Pony for Keeps, Scholastic, 1995.
A Pony in Trouble, Scholastic, 1995.

JEANNE BETANCOURT

Give Me Back My Pony, Scholastic, 1995.
Pony to the Rescue, Scholastic, 1995.
Runaway Pony, Scholastic, 1995.
The Baby Pony, Scholastic, 1996.
Circus Pony, Scholastic, 1996.
The Wild Pony, Scholastic, 1996.
Don't Hurt My Pony, Scholastic, 1996.
Good-bye Pony, Scholastic, 1996.
Keep Out Pony, Scholastic, 1996.
The Lives of Our Ponies, Scholastic, 1997.
The Girl Who Hated Ponies, Scholastic, 1997.
Pony-Sitters, Scholastic, 1997.
The Blind Pony, Scholastic, 1997.
The Missing Pony Pal, Scholastic, 1997.
Ghost Pony, Scholastic, 1997.
Pony Detective, Scholastic, 1997.

"Pony Pals" books have been translated into French and German.

NOVELS; FOR YOUNG ADULTS

Am I Normal? (film novelization), Avon, 1983.
Dear Diary (film novelization), Avon, 1983.
The Edge, Scholastic, 1985.
Between Us, Scholastic, 1986.
Sweet Sixteen and Never ..., Bantam, 1986.
Home Sweet Home, Bantam, 1988.
Not Just Party Girls, Bantam, 1988.
More than Meets the Eye, Bantam, 1991.

Kate's Turn, Scholastic, 1992.
My Name is ~~Brain~~ Brian, Scholastic, 1993.

TELEPLAYS; PRODUCED AS "ABC AFTERSCHOOL SPECIALS"

I Want to Go Home, 1985.
Don't Touch, 1985.
Are You My Mother, 1986.
Teen Father, 1986.
Supermom's Daughter, 1987.
Tattle, 1988.

NONFICTION

Women in Focus (adult), Pflaum, 1974.
SMILE! How to Cope with Braces (juvenile), illustrated by Mimi Harrison, Knopf, 1982.

OTHER

Author of feature film script *Rosie,* based on a novel by Anne Lamott; of American Broadcasting Company's movie of the week script *The Passion of Mary Francis;* and, with husband, Lee Minoff, of unproduced screenplay *Carolyn and Maggie,* based on a novel by Norma Klein. Contributor of articles and reviews to periodicals, including *Women in Film, Film Library Quarterly, Media Methods,* and *Sightlines.* Contributing editor, *Channels,* 1981-82.

■ Sidelights

Jeanne Betancourt brings an understanding of both country and city life to her books for young readers. The author of the "Pony Pals" series for elementary schoolage readers that follows the adventures of young horselovers, Betancourt is also the author of several books and "Afterschool Special" teleplays for teens that concern some of the harsh realities faced by urban kids: drug abuse, racial prejudice, cocaine addiction, homelessness, and teen parenting. "I know that my reader/viewers are either experiencing some of these difficult and challenging situations personally, through their friends and neighbors, or through the media," the author once told *Something about the Author (SATA).* "I want to show, in a story, the aspects of the 'issue' that I feel kids should be aware of. These are important issues that the media sometimes exploits. I want to explore them. I want to help kids grow stronger and wiser through the experiences of my stories, to see that they have responsibility and power. Through role models from their own age group I want to show kids what they can and should do for themselves and for others."

Betancourt was raised in rural Vermont, across the road from a dairy farm, where she spent much of her time playing, helping work in the barns, or spending time with the Swedish farm owner and his family. "Those years I never thought of being a writer," she confided to *SATA.* "I loved my tap dancing classes and wanted to be a Rockette at Radio City Music Hall."

Then, in high school, Betancourt and her family moved to the town of Burlington, where she attended a Catholic girls school. Her dreams of becoming a Rockette were

Brian's no brain... or is he?

A dyslexic sixth-grader confronts his learning disability as well as other problems of adolescence in this Betancourt novel.

finally dashed when she learned that, at five feet eight inches in height, she was too tall to be a Rockette. Betancourt transferred her energy from dreams of dancing to pursuing a religious calling that began in her junior year of high school. After graduation, she moved to Rutland, Vermont, and entered a teaching order of nuns called the Sisters of Saint Joseph. Over the next six years she earned her teaching certification and taught at high schools in Vermont. After leaving the order, she took her teaching skills to New York City; part of her new life there included getting married and having a child.

While raising her daughter, Nicole, Betancourt taught in New York's inner-city public high schools. She also found the time to pursue her interest in film and, in 1974, earned an advanced college degree in film studies from New York University that enabled her to design courses in film studies and filmmaking for secondary school students. Her first published book, 1974's *Women in Focus,* was based on her masters degree project.

"I wrote my first children's book, *SMILE! How to Cope with Braces,* when my daughter Nicole was having orthodontic treatment," recalled Betancourt. "I couldn't find the right book to help her with this new experience, so I researched and wrote one. By the time the book was published Nicole was out of braces, but her picture is on the cover of the book."

In fact, Nicole has been the inspiration for many of Betancourt's books; "But when it comes down to writing the story and getting into the head and heart of ... my characters, I have to become the character myself," the author noted. "Nicole can't do that for me." Betancourt was, however, inspired to write a series of books featuring the young protagonist Aviva Granger. She remembered, "when, at nine, Nicole first became a joint custody kid and began to split her life—two weeks at a time—with me and her father. I've given Aviva my maiden name, Granger, and set the stories in Burlington, Vermont." The four books featuring Aviva Granger—*The Rainbow Kid, Turtle Time, Puppy Love,* and *Crazy Christmas*—appeared between 1983 and 1988.

Despite having a real child on whom to base her books, Betancourt also does a great deal of research for each new book. For 1988's *Home Sweet Home,* the author tackled the subject of young Tracy Jensen's move from New York City to her Grandmother's Tilly's farm in a quiet New England country town. Tracy's feelings of alienation in her new environment are reflected by the situation of Anya, a Russian foreign exchange student she meets during her junior year in high school. "I read many books about the Soviet Union, visited dairy farms, and interviewed farmers," Betancourt said about writing the novel. And "for *Between Us*—a mystery novel that makes a connection between drugs used for medical reasons and drugs sold illegally for recreational use—I spent many mornings in the pharmacy of our local hospital in Sharon, Connecticut, learning about drugs and how a hospital pharmacy works."

Not Just Party Girls draws on the author's experiences as a nun. Sixteen-year-olds Anne, Kate, and Janet are the Party Girls, a group that arranges birthday parties for younger children in their neighborhood. When Anne becomes concerned with the meaninglessness of her life after working in a local homeless shelter, she begins to consider joining a religious order—but her new-found desire to save others ends up hurting both her friends and her family. The down-to-earth wisdom of Anne's religious guide, Sister Mary, as well as "some highly unsettling practical experiences provide a strong antidote to self-righteousness and day dreams," noted Libby K. White in her positive review of the novel for *School Library Journal.* The author's life-long love of dancing is reflected in *Kate's Turn,* in which the young teen protagonist follows her dream of becoming a ballerina to a New York dance school and learns about the real rigors of the profession first-hand.

Betancourt suffers from dyslexia, a learning disability that makes ordering letters for the correct spelling of words difficult and also makes remembering dates and names a challenge. "I also have trouble following spacial directions and am a very slow reader," she explained to *SATA.* "To compensate for my disability I have developed a sharply tuned attention to conversation (particularly the rhythms and emotional content of dialogue),

heightened visual acuity and memory, and empathy." Her personal experiences of overcoming her disability were the focus of her 1993 work, *My Name is Brain Brian.* In the novel, the sixth-grader Brian deals with his learning disability as well as all the typical problems that arise during adolescence. He begins to reexamine his long-time friendships with pals John, Rich, and Dan, as well as his relationship with his authoritarian father, his new teachers who are able to diagnose and help Brian adapt to his dyslexia, and other students at school. Even the "class brain," Isabel, gets a new impression of him after she is forced to work with Brian on a science class project. "Betancourt's depiction of Brian's emotional and psychological growth is believable and involving," noted Janice Del Negro in a *Booklist* review. A *Kirkus Reviews* contributor called the novel "a skillfully structured, entertaining story" and acknowledged that "Brian himself ... is drawn with real insight."

In *Sweet Sixteen and Never ...,* sixteen-year-old Julie is faced with a different kind of problem when she starts dating a young man with a reputation for being "fast." She knows his desire to begin a sexual relationship with

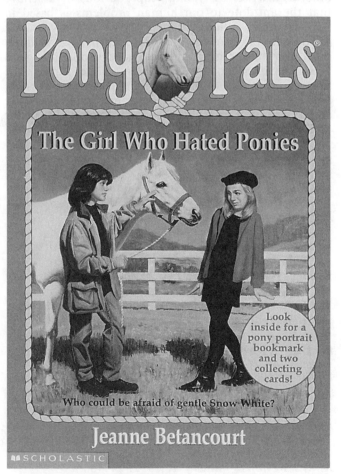

From the "Pony Pals" series for elementary school readers, *The Girl Who Hated Ponies* portrays the young horse lovers as they encounter an urban girl whose fixation on fashion and beauty alienates the equestrian group.

her is imminent, and she needs to decide how she is going to react when the time comes. Learning that her mother had a child when she was Julie's age but gave it up for adoption complicates things between mother and daughter after Julie's mother discovers birth control pills in her daughter's room. Fortunately, the lines of communication are open between each of the book's protagonists—Julie, her mom, and boyfriend Sam—and Julie is able to make the decision that is best for her. Writing in *School Library Journal,* contributor Nancy P. Reeder noted that Betancourt "effectively conveys Julie's turmoil." In a *Kliatt* review, Rita M. Fontinha applauded Betancourt's "believable plot and engaging characters," going on to say that the novel offers young girls "an excellent introduction to the real world."

"Some people think that a writer's life is lonely," Betancourt once explained to *SATA.* "When I'm writing a story I don't feel lonely because I am actively involved with lots of interesting people—the characters in my books. I love knowing that some day—in the private moment of reading—other people will get to know and care about these people too." Despite the enjoyment she gets from her work, she continues to take her responsibility as a writer for young people seriously. "I believe that the antidote to our human problems is based in human values—those little things we can do for one another to alleviate the pain. I've learned, as children must, that bad things happen to good people and good people have no choice but to become better through the process of coping. This is where the writer comes in. Samuel Johnson said it best when he wrote, 'The only end of writing is to enable the reader to enjoy life better or better to endure it.'"

■ Works Cited

Del Negro, Janice, review of *My Name is ~~Brain~~ Brian, Booklist,* April 1, 1993, p. 1430.
Fontinha, Rita M., *Sweet Sixteen and Never . . . , Kliatt,* April, 1987, p. 5.
Review of *My Name is ~~Brain~~ Brian, Kirkus Reviews,* February 11, 1993, p. 142.
Reeder, Nancy P., review of *Sweet Sixteen and Never . . . , School Library Journal,* June, 1987, p. 104.
White, Libby K., review of *Not Just Party Girls, School Library Journal,* January, 1989, pp. 90-91.

■ For More Information See

PERIODICALS

Booklist, January 15, 1988, p. 854; January 15, 1989, p. 858.
Bulletin of the Center for Children's Books, December, 1982, pp. 61-62; April, 1983, p. 143; February, 1992, p. 148; April, 1993, p. 241.
Kirkus Reviews, January 1, 1992, p. 48.
School Library Journal, August, 1982, p. 111; February, 1988, p. 84.
Voice of Youth Advocates, October, 1982, p. 53; August, 1983, p. 144; September, 1987, p. 118; April, 1988, p. 21; February, 1989, pp. 282-83; October, 1990, p. 214; April, 1992, p. 22.

BINGHAM, Sam(uel) (A.) 1944-

■ Personal

Born November 24, 1944, in Nashville, TN; son of Sam (an engineer) and Jane (a teacher; maiden name, Raoul) Bingham; married Janet Riddell (a journalist), June 12, 1971; children: Robin, S. Kevin. *Education:* Yale University, B.A., 1967. *Politics:* Democrat. *Religion:* Christian.

■ Addresses

Home and office—1757 Roslyn St., Denver, CO 80220. *Agent*—Upton Brady, Town Farm Hill #64, Hartland Four Corners, VT 05049. *Electronic Mail*—sbingham@igc.org (Econet).

■ Career

Freelance photo journalist in Vietnam and Middle East, 1967-68; *Atlantic Monthly,* Boston, MA, associate editor, 1969-70; *Newsweek,* Boston, MA, and Houston, TX, reporter, 1970-71; Rock Point Community School, Rock Point, AZ, director of bilingual education and teacher of high school biology, physics, and chemistry, 1971-84; freelance writer and agricultural consultant, 1984—. Member of World Bank team, Pastoral Pilot Project in West Africa, 1993; consultant to the World Bank Pastoral Project, 1994; instructor in Holistic Resource Management for USAID/SANREM/CRSP in Burkina Faso, 1994.

■ Writings

Between Sacred Mountains: Navajo Stories and Lessons from the Land, University of Arizona Press, 1983.
The Ultimate Wood Block Book, Sterling Press, 1986.
(Editor) Allan Savory, *Holistic Resource Management,* Island Press, 1988.
(With Allan Savory) *The Holistic Resource Management Workbook,* Island Press, 1990.
The Last Ranch: A Colorado Community and the Coming Desert, Pantheon Books, 1996.

Also co-author with Janet Bingham of textbooks for Navajo schools, including *Navajo Chapters, Slippery Rock Stories,* and *Navajo Coal,* Rock Point Community School, 1971-80. Contributor to books and magazines specializing in ecology and agriculture.

■ Sidelights

In *The Last Ranch: A Colorado Community and the Coming Desert,* Sam Bingham describes the San Luis Valley ranchers of Colorado and their struggle with an ever-shrinking pastureland. Alice Joyce, reviewing the work in *Booklist,* called *The Last Ranch* a "highly detailed, in-depth account" describing the environmental plight of grazing fields being reduced by the advancing desert. Natural vegetation barely exists now in a soil that has changed its properties because of overgrazing and a history of unsuitable farming methods. Changes in market values and the environment bring the ranchers new survival issues to wrestle with, as well as outsiders with exploitive solutions. In the *New York Times Book Review,* Keith Schneider wrote that Bingham's "command of detail is impressive" and noted that the author is equal to the task of describing divergent aspects of the landscape. A *Kirkus Reviews* commentator added that Bingham "treats with courtesy and generosity" the people in the valley, who attain "a kind of nobility" in their daily struggle that makes the book an important read.

■ Works Cited

Joyce, Alice, review of *The Last Ranch: A Colorado Community and the Coming Desert, Booklist,* September 1, 1996, p. 40.

Review of *The Last Ranch: A Colorado Community and the Coming Desert, Kirkus Reviews,* July 15, 1996, p. 1016.

Schneider, Keith, review of *The Last Ranch: A Colorado Community and the Coming Desert, New York Times Book Review,* October 20, 1996, p 19.*

*   *   *

BLAKE, Quentin (Saxby) 1932-

■ Personal

Born December 16, 1932, in Sidcup, Kent, England; son of William (a civil servant) and Evelyn Blake. *Education:* Downing College, Cambridge, M.A., 1956; University of London Institute of Education, P.G.C.E., 1956-57; attended Chelsea School of Art, 1958-59.

■ Addresses

Home—Flat 8, 30 Bramham Gardens, London SW5 0HF, England. *Agent*—(International) A. P. Watt Ltd., 20 John St., London AC IN 2DR, England.

■ Career

Author, artist, editor, and educator. Primarily an illustrator, drawing for *Punch,* beginning 1948, and other British magazines, including *Spectator,* and illustrating children's and educational books; freelance illustrator, 1957—; Royal College of Art, London, England, tutor in School of Graphic Design, 1965-78, head of Illustration Department, 1978-86, visiting tutor, 1986-89, visiting professor, 1989—, senior fellow, 1988. Has also worked as an English teacher at French Lycee in London, 1962-65. *Exhibitions:* Work has been exhibited at Workshop Gallery, 1972, 1973, 1974, 1976; at the National Theatre, 1984; at the Royal Academy, 1984, 1986, 1987; and at the London Group, England, 1987. *Military service:* Served in the Army Education Corps, 1951-53.

■ Awards, Honors

Several of Blake's books were named to the list of Child Study Association of America's Children's Books of the

Year, including *Put on Your Thinking Cap,* 1969, *Arabel's Raven,* 1974, *Custard and Company,* 1985, and *The Giraffe and the Pelly and Me,* 1986; *Guardian* Award, second prize, 1969, for *Patrick; How Tom Beat Captain Najork and His Hired Sportsmen* and *The Witches* were named Notable Books by the American Library Association; *How Tom Beat Captain Najork and His Hired Sportsmen* and *The Wild Washerwomen: A New Folktale* were named to the *Boston Globe/Horn Book* Award honor list; Hans Christian Andersen Award for illustration from the International Board on Books for Young People, 1976, for *How Tom Beat Captain Najork and His Hired Sportsmen,* 1982, for *Mister Magnolia,* and 1997, for *Clown; A Near Thing for Captain Najork* was selected one of the *New York Times* Best Illustrated Books of the Year, 1976, as was *Clown* in 1997; Kate Greenaway Medal high commendation from the British Library Association, 1980, for *The Wild Washerwomen;* Kate Greenaway Medal from the British Library Association, and Children's Book Award from the Federation of Children's Book Groups, both 1981, both for *Mister Magnolia;* Children's Book Award from the Federation of Children's Book Groups, 1982, for *The BFG;* Kurt Maschler Award runner-up from the National Book League (London), 1982, for *Rumbelow's Dance,* 1984, for *The Story of the Dancing Frog,* 1985, for *The Giraffe and the Pelly and Me,* and 1986, for *The Rain Door; The Rain Door* and *Cyril Bonhamy and Operation Ping* were exhibited at the Bologna International Children's Book Fair, 1985; Reading Magic Award, 1989, for *Quentin Blake's ABC;* Kurt Maschler Award from the National Book League, 1990, for *All Join In;* Smarties Prize (ages six to eight), 1990, for *Esio*

QUENTIN BLAKE

Trot; British Book Award (illustrated runner-up), 1990, for *Alphabeasts;* Ragazzi Award, Bologna Children's Book Fair, and Blue Ribbon citation, *Bulletin of the Center for Children's Books,* both 1996, both for *Clown.* Blake was elected a Royal Designer for Industry in 1981, awarded the Silver Pencil (Holland) in 1985, and was named an officer of the Order of the British Empire in 1988. In 1993, he received the University of Southern Mississippi Medallion for his body of work. Blake has also been the recipient of several child-selected awards.

■ Writings

SELF-ILLUSTRATED CHILDREN'S BOOKS

Patrick, Cape, 1968, Walck, 1969.
Jack and Nancy, Cape, 1969.
Angelo, Cape, 1970.
Snuff, Cape, 1973, Lippincott, 1973.
Lester at the Seaside, Collins Picture Lions, 1975.
(Compiler with John Yeoman) *The Puffin Book of Improbable Records,* Puffin, 1975, published as *The Improbable Book of Records,* Atheneum, 1976.
The Adventures of Lester, British Broadcasting Corporation (BBC), 1978.
(Compiler) *Custard and Company: Poems by Ogden Nash,* Kestrel, 1979, Little, Brown, 1980.
Mister Magnolia, Merrimack, 1980, Random Century (London), 1991.
Quentin Blake's Nursery Rhyme Book, Cape, 1983, Harper, 1984.
The Story of the Dancing Frog, Cape, 1984, Knopf, 1985.
Mrs. Armitage on Wheels, Cape, 1987, Knopf, 1988.
Quentin Blake's ABC, Knopf, 1989, Cape, 1989.
All Join In, Cape, 1990, Little, Brown, 1991.
Quentin Blake's Nursery Collection, Cape, 1991.
Cockatoos, Little, Brown, 1992, Cape, 1992.
Simpkin, Cape, 1993, Viking, 1994.
(Compiler) *The Quentin Blake Book of Nonsense Verse,* Viking, 1994, Viking Penguin, 1997.
(Compiler) *The Penguin Book of Nonsense Verse,* Penguin, 1995.
Clown, Cape, 1995, Holt, 1996.
The Quentin Blake Book of Nonsense Stories, Viking, 1996.

ILLUSTRATOR

Evan Hunter, *The Wonderful Button,* Abelard, 1961.
Frances Gray Patton, *Good Morning, Miss Dove,* Penguin, 1961.
John Moore, editor, *The Boys' Country Book,* Collins, 1961.
Rosemary Weir, *Albert the Dragon,* Abelard, 1961.
Edward Korel, *Listen and I'll Tell You,* Blackie, 1962, Lippincott, 1964.
John Moreton, *Punky: Mouse for a Day,* Faber, 1962.
Ezo, *My Son-in-Law the Hippopotamus,* Abelard, 1962.
Rupert Croft-Cooke, *Tales of a Wicked Uncle,* Cape, 1963.
Richard Schickel, *The Gentle Knight,* Abelard, 1964.
Joan Tate, *The Next-Doors,* Heinemann, 1964.
Weir, *Albert the Dragon and the Centaur,* Abelard, 1964.

Weir, *The Further Adventures of Albert the Dragon,* Abelard, 1964.
Fred Loads, Alan Gemmell, and Bil Sowerbutts, *Gardeners' Question Time,* BBC Publications, 1964, second series, 1966.
Ennis Rees, *Riddles, Riddles Everywhere,* Abelard, 1964.
James Britton, editor, *The Oxford Books of Stories for Juniors,* three volumes, Oxford University Press, 1964-66.
Rees, *Pun Fun,* Abelard, 1965.
Bill Hartley, *Motoring and the Motorist,* BBC, 1965.
Charles Connell, *Aphrodisiacs in Your Garden,* Mayflower, 1965.
Barry Ruth, *Home Economics,* Heinemann Educational, 1966.
Jules Verne, *Around the World in Eighty Days,* Chatto, 1966.
Thomas L. Hirsch, *Puzzles for Pleasure and Leisure,* Abelard, 1966.
Robert Tibber, *Aristide,* Hutchinson, 1966, Dial, 1967.
Marjorie Bilbow and Antony Bilbow, *Give a Dog a Good Name,* Hutchinson, 1967.
Tate, *Bits and Pieces,* Heinemann, 1967.
Rees, *Tiny Tall Tales,* Abelard, 1967.
Tate, *Luke's Garden,* Heinemann, 1967.
Helen J. Fletcher, *Put on Your Thinking Cap,* Abelard, 1968.
G. Broughton, *Listen and Read with Peter and Molly,* BBC, 1968.
Gordon Fraser, editor, *Your Animal Book,* Gordon Fraser, 1969.
H. P. Rickman, *Living with Technology,* Zenith Books, 1969.
Broughton, *Success with English: The Penguin Course,* Penguin, 1969.
Nathan Zimelman, *The First Elephant Comes to Ireland,* Follett, 1969.
James Reeves, *Mr. Horrox and the Gratch,* Abelard, 1969.
Rees, *Gillygaloos and the Gollywhoppers: Tall Tales about Mythical Monsters,* Abelard, 1969.
Gillian Edwards, *Hogmanay and Tiffany: The Names of Feasts and Fasts,* Geoffrey Bles, 1970.
D. Mackay, B. Thompson, and P. Schaub, *The Birthday Party,* Longman, 1970.
Elizabeth Bowen, *The Good Tiger,* Cape, 1970.
Fletcher, *Puzzles and Quizzles,* Platt, 1970.
Thomas Corddry, *Kibby's Big Feat,* Follett, 1970.
H. Thomson, *The Witch's Cat,* Addison-Wesley, 1971.
J. B. S. Haldane, *My Friend Mr. Leakey,* Puffin, 1971.
Ruth Craft, *Play School Play Ideas,* Penguin, 1971.
Aristophanes, *The Birds,* translated by Dudley Fitts, Royal College of Art, 1971.
Marcus Cunliffe, *The Ages of Man: From Sav-age to Sew-age,* American Heritage, 1971.
Broughton, *Peter and Molly,* BBC, 1972.
Natalie Savage Carlson, *Pigeon of Paris,* Blackie, 1972, Scholastic, 1975.
Norman Hunter, *Wizards Are a Nuisance,* BBC, 1973.
Julia Watson, editor, *The Armada Lion Book of Young Verse,* Collins, 1973.
R. C. Scriven, *The Thingummy-jig,* BBC, 1973.
F. Knowles and B. Thompson, *Eating,* Longman, 1973.

Clement Freud, *Grimble,* Penguin, 1974.

Dr. Seuss (pseudonym of Theodor Seuss Geisel), *Great Day for Up!,* Random House, 1974.

Bronnie Cunningham, editor, *The Puffin Joke Book,* Penguin, 1974.

Willis Hall, *The Incredible Kidnapping,* Heinemann, 1975.

Hall, *Kidnapped at Christmas,* Heinemann Educational, 1975.

Broughton, *Peter and Molly's Revision Book,* BBC, 1975.

Lewis Carroll, *The Hunting of the Snark,* Folio Society, 1976.

Sylvia Plath, *The Bed Book,* Faber, 1976.

Adele De Leeuw, *Horseshoe Harry and the Whale,* Parents Magazine Press, 1976.

Ellen Blance and Ann Cook, *Monster Books,* twenty-four volumes, Longman, 1976-1978.

Margaret Mahy, *The Nonstop Nonsense Book,* Dent (London), 1977, Margaret K. McElderry Books (New York), 1989.

Sara Brewton, John E. Brewton, and John B. Blackburn, editors, *Of Quarks, Quasars, and Other Quirks: Quizzical Poems for the Supersonic Age,* Harper, 1977.

Ted Allan, *Willie the Squowse,* McClelland & Stewart, 1977, Hastings House, 1978.

Carole Ward, *Play School Ideas 2,* BBC, 1977.

Stella Gibbons, *Cold Comfort Farm,* Folio Society, 1977.

Cunningham, editor, *Funny Business,* Penguin, 1978.

Helen Young, *What Difference Does It Make, Danny?,* Deutsch, 1980.

Evelyn Waugh, *Black Mischief,* Folio Society, 1981.

Jonathan Gathorne-Hardy, *Cyril Bonhamy v. Madam Big,* Cape, 1981.

Tony Lacey, editor, *Up with Skool!,* Kestrel, 1981.

Tim Rice and Andrew Lloyd Webber, *Joseph and the Amazing Technicolor Dreamcoat,* Holt, 1982.

Gathorne-Hardy, *Cyril Bonhamy and the Great Drain Robbery,* Cape, 1983.

Waugh, *Scoop,* Folio Society, 1983.

George Orwell, *Animal Farm,* Folio Society, 1984.

Rudyard Kipling, *How the Camel Got His Hump,* Macmillan (London), 1984, Bedrick Books, 1985.

Gathorne-Hardy, *Cyril Bonhamy and Operation Ping,* Cape, 1984.

Jeff Brown, *A Lamp for the Lambchops,* Methuen, 1985.

Mahy, *The Great Piratical Rumbustification and the Librarian and the Robbers,* Godine, 1986, Morrow, 1993.

Jan Mark, *Frankie's Hat,* Kestrel, 1986.

Dr. Pete Rowan, *Can You Get Warts from Touching Toads?: Ask Dr. Pete,* Messner, 1986.

Jeff Brown, *Stanley and the Magic Lamp,* Methuen, 1990.

Dick King-Smith, *Alphabeasts,* Gollancz, 1990, Simon & Schuster, 1992.

John Masefield, *The Midnight Folk,* Heinemann, 1991.

Hilaire Belloc, *Algernon and Other Cautionary Tales,* Cape, 1991.

John Masefield, *The Box of Delights,* Heinemann, 1992.

Hilaire Belloc, *Cautionary Verses,* Red Fox, 1995.

Charles Dickens, *A Christmas Carol,* Simon & Schuster, 1995, Pavilion (London), 1995.

Sylvia Sherry, *Elephants Have Right of Way,* Cape, 1995.

ILLUSTRATOR; ALL BY JOAN AIKEN

The Escaped Black Mamba, BBC Publications, 1973.

Tales of Arabel's Raven, Cape, 1974, published as *Arabel's Raven,* Doubleday, 1974.

The Bread Bin, BBC Publications, 1974.

Mortimer's Tie, BBC Publications, 1976.

Mortimer and the Sword Excalibur, BBC Publications, 1979.

The Spiral Stair, BBC Publications, 1979.

Arabel and Mortimer (includes *Mortimer's Tie, The Spiral Stair,* and *Mortimer and the Sword Excalibur*), Cape/BBC Publications, 1979, Doubleday, 1981.

Mortimer's Portrait on Glass, BBC Publications, 1980.

The Mystery of Mr. Jones's Disappearing Taxi, BBC Publications, 1980.

Mortimer's Cross, Cape, 1983, Harper, 1984.

Mortimer Says Nothing, Harper, 1987.

Arabel and the Escaped Black Mamba, BBC Books, 1990.

(With Lizza Aiken) *Mortimer and Arabel,* BBC Children's Books, 1992.

The Winter Sleepwalker and Other Stories, Cape, 1994.

Handful of Gold, Cape, 1995.

ILLUSTRATOR; ALL BY PATRICK CAMPBELL

Come Here Till I Tell You, Hutchinson, 1960.

Constantly in Pursuit, Hutchinson, 1962.

Brewing Up in the Basement, Hutchinson, 1963.

How to Become a Scratch Golfer, Blond, 1963.

The P-P-Penguin Patrick Campbell, Penguin, 1965.

Rough Husbandry, Hutchinson, 1965.

A Feast of True Fandangles, W. H. Allen, 1979.

ILLUSTRATOR; ALL BY ROALD DAHL (EXCEPT AS NOTED)

Danny: The Champion of the World, Cape, 1975.

The Enormous Crocodile, Knopf, 1978.

The Twits, Knopf, 1980.

George's Marvellous Medicine, Cape, 1981, published in the United States as *George's Marvelous Medicine,* Knopf, 1982.

The BFG, Farrar, Straus, 1982.

Roald Dahl's Revolting Rhymes, Cape, 1982, Knopf, 1983.

The Witches, Farrar, Straus, 1983, Random House (London), 1995.

Roald Dahl's Dirty Beasts, Cape, 1983, Penguin, 1986.

The Giraffe and the Pelly and Me, Farrar, Straus, 1985, Cape, 1985.

Matilda, Cape, 1988, Random House (London), 1994.

Rhyme Stew, Cape, 1989, Viking, 1990.

Esio Trot, Viking, 1990.

The Dahl Diary, Puffin, 1991.

Roald Dahl's Guide to Railway Safety, British Railways Board, 1991.

The Vicar of Nibbleswicke, Random Century, 1991, Viking, 1992.

My Year, Viking, 1994.
(Josie Fison and Felicity Dahl, compilers; photographs by Jan Baldwin) *Roald Dahl's Revolting Recipes*, Viking, 1994.
The Complete Adventures of Charlie and Mr. Willy Wonka (includes *Charlie and the Chocolate Factory* and *Charlie and the Great Glass Elevator*), Viking, 1995.
James and the Giant Peach, Viking, 1995.
The Magic Finger, Viking, 1995.
(Sylvia Bond and Richard Maher, compilers) *The Roald Dahl Quiz Book 2*, Puffin, 1996.
Fantastic Mr. Fox, Viking, 1996.

ILLUSTRATOR; ALL BY SID FLEISCHMAN

McBroom's Wonderful One-Acre Farm, Chatto & Windus, 1972, Greenwillow, 1992.
Here Comes McBroom!, Chatto & Windus, 1976, Greenwillow, 1992.
McBroom and the Great Race, Chatto & Windus, 1981.

ILLUSTRATOR; ALL BY NILS-OLOF FRANZEN

Agaton Sax and the Diamond Thieves, Deutsch, 1965, translated by Evelyn Ramsden, Delacorte, 1967.
Agaton Sax and the Scotland Yard Mystery, Delacorte, 1969.
Agaton Sax and the Incredible Max Brothers, Delacorte, 1970.
Agaton Sax and the Criminal Doubles, Deutsch, 1971.
Agaton Sax and the Colossus of Rhodes, Deutsch, 1972.
Agaton Sax and the London Computer Plot, Deutsch, 1973.
Agaton Sax and the League of Silent Exploders, Deutsch, 1974.
Agaton Sax and the Haunted House, Deutsch, 1975.
Agaton Sax and the Big Rig, Deutsch, 1976.
Agaton Sax and Lispington's Grandfather Clock, Deutsch, 1978.

ILLUSTRATOR; ALL BY RUSSELL HOBAN

How Tom Beat Captain Najork and His Hired Sportsmen, Atheneum, 1974.
A Near Thing for Captain Najork, Cape, 1975, Atheneum, 1976.
The Twenty Elephant Restaurant, Cape, 1980.
Ace Dragon Ltd., Cape, 1980, Merrimack, 1981.
The Marzipan Pig, Farrar, Straus, 1986.
The Rain Door, Gollancz, 1986, Crowell, 1987.
Monsters, Scholastic, 1990.

ILLUSTRATOR; ALL BY J. P. MARTIN

Uncle, Cape, 1964, Coward, 1966.
Uncle Cleans Up, Cape, 1965, Coward, 1967.
Uncle and His Detective, Cape, 1966.
Uncle and the Treacle Trouble, Cape, 1967.
Uncle and Claudius the Camel, Cape, 1969.
Uncle and the Battle for Badgertown, Cape, 1973.

ILLUSTRATOR; ALL BY MICHAEL ROSEN

Mind Your Own Business, S. G. Phillips, 1974.
Wouldn't You Like to Know?, Deutsch, 1977.
The Bakerloo Flea, Longman, 1979.
You Can't Catch Me!, Deutsch, 1981.

Quick, Let's Get Out of Here, Deutsch, 1984.
Don't Put Mustard in the Custard, Deutsch, 1986.
Under the Bed, Prentice-Hall, 1986.
Smelly Jelly Smelly Fish, Prentice-Hall, 1986.
Hard-Boiled Legs: The Breakfast Book, Prentice-Hall, 1987.
Spollyollydiddlytiddlyitis: The Doctor Book, Walker, 1987.
Down at the Doctor's: The Sick Book, Simon & Schuster, 1988.
The Best of Michael Rosen: Poetry for Kids, RDR Books, 1995.

ILLUSTRATOR; ALL BY JOHN YEOMAN

A Drink of Water and Other Stories, Faber, 1960.
The Boy Who Sprouted Antlers, Faber, 1961, revised edition, Collins, 1977.
The Bear's Winter House, World, 1969.
Alphabet Soup (poem), Faber, 1969, Follett, 1970.
The Bear's Water Picnic, Blackie, 1970, Macmillan, 1971.
Sixes and Sevens, Blackie, 1971, Macmillan, 1972.
Mouse Trouble, Hamish Hamilton, 1972, Macmillan, 1973.
Beatrice and Vanessa, Hamish Hamilton, 1974, Macmillan, 1975.

John Yeoman recounts eleven animal stories from around the world in *The Singing Tortoise and Other Animal Folktales*, illustrated by Quentin Blake.

The Young Performing Horse, Hamish Hamilton, 1977, Parents Magazine Press, 1978.

The Wild Washerwomen: A New Folktale, Greenwillow, 1979.

Rumbelow's Dance, Hamish Hamilton, 1982.

The Hermit and the Bear, Deutsch, 1984.

Our Village (Poems), Atheneum, 1988, Walker Books, 1988.

Old Mother Hubbard's Dog Dresses Up, Walker Books, 1989, Houghton, 1990.

Old Mother Hubbard's Dog Learns to Play, Walker Books, 1989, Houghton, 1990.

Old Mother Hubbard's Dog Needs a Doctor, Walker Books, 1989, Houghton, 1990.

Old Mother Hubbard's Dog Takes up Sport, Walker Books, 1989, Houghton, 1990.

The World's Laziest Duck and Other Amazing Records, Macmillan (London), 1991.

The Family Album, Hamish Hamilton, 1993.

Featherbrains, Hamish Hamilton, 1993.

The Singing Tortoise and Other Animal Folktales, Gollancz, 1993, Morrow, 1994.

Mr. Nodd's Ark, Hamish Hamilton, 1995.

The Do-It-Yourself House That Jack Built, Simon & Schuster, 1995.

Sinbad the Sailor (retelling), Pavilion, 1996.

OTHER

Also author and illustrator of *A Band of Angels* (picture book for adults), Gordon Fraser, 1969. Illustrator for "Jackanory," BBC-TV. Contributor of illustrations to periodicals, including *Punch* and *Spectator.*

■ Adaptations

"Patrick" (filmstrip), Weston Woods, 1973; "Snuff" (filmstrip with record or cassette), Weston Woods, 1975; "Great Day for Up!" (filmstrip), Random House.

■ Work in Progress

"I'm working on a book, the interim version of which was published in French by Gallimand Jeunesse in 1996 as *La Vie de la Page,* about the creative process of illustration, an autobiographical work which I hope will be interesting to children, adults, and especially to art students."

■ Sidelights

Regarded as a master artist whose line drawings and watercolors are touched with genius, Blake has written and illustrated several well-received books for children and has provided the pictures for over two hundred titles by other authors for children and adults. Considered an especially inventive and adaptable illustrator, he has created a highly recognizable style—called "calligraphic" by Brian Alderson in *Horn Book*—that ranges from the childlike to the highly sophisticated. Blake generally uses squiggly black line heightened with color to express a variety of characteristics and expressions with a minimum of strokes. Full of life and fluid movement, the humor, drama, and spirit of his illustra-

tions are thought to make them most inviting to viewers, especially children. Although these pictures may appear casual, they are acknowledged for the artistry and technical skill that the artist brings to them; in addition, Blake is praised for his keen observation of human nature as well as for the depth and pathos with which he underscores many of his works. As the creator of his own picture books and concept books and the editor of collections of stories and poems, Blake uses familiar motifs—the folktale, the cumulative tale, the alphabet book, the counting book, and the nursery rhyme—to provide his young audience with works that are considered both original and delightful. Lauded as a gifted humorist and storyteller, he invests his works with a strong theatricality and includes elements of fantasy in most of his books, which he writes in both prose and verse. Blake often uses historical settings such as the Middle Ages and the eighteenth and nineteenth centuries to introduce elements of social history along with his broadly comic yet incisive characterizations. He is often celebrated by critics as both creator and collaborator. Writing in the *Times Literary Supplement,* John Mole asserts, "[Quentin Blake's] instantly recognizable combination of sprightly pen and watery brush is a guarantee of frequent delight. He is our street-wise Ardizzone." Elaine Moss calls him "the genius who turns a difficult manuscript into a thoroughly acceptable and beckoning book," while *Times Educational Supplement* reviewer Naomi Lewis adds, "Any book which has Quentin Blake as an illustrator is in luck, for who can match his zany wit and euphoria, his engaging charm, his wild assurance of line?" Brian Alderson calls him "the laureate of happiness," and adds that "thought and graphic wizardry ... underline almost the whole of Quentin Blake's oeuvre."

The son of a civil servant and a homemaker, Blake grew up in Sidcup, a suburb of London in Kent. He once told *Something about the Author* (*SATA*), "I can remember drawing on the back of my exercise books as far back as primary school. I wasn't especially encouraged by anyone. Aside from children's comics, there wasn't a great deal of illustrated material available when I was a young boy. If you were growing up in a wealthy family, you would perhaps be conscious of Arthur Rackham. But in general, children had no notion of 'an illustrator.' Once I got past children's books, I became an omnivorous reader. I read anything and everything."

Blake began submitting prose and pictures to the *Chronicle,* the school magazine of Chiselhurst Grammar School. He told *SATA,* "My most significant experience at Chiselhurst was meeting Alfred Jackson, a cartoonist for *Punch* and other magazines. His wife, my Latin teacher, took an interest in my drawings, and arranged a meeting between us. I was fifteen at the time, and had no idea how one went about submitting drawings to magazines. After my informative meeting with Jackson, however, I began to send my work to *Punch....* [Eventually] they accepted a few small drawings. I was drawn to the work of Ronald Searle and Andre Francois. I was influenced by them, not in terms of style, but because each in his own way seemed to be absolutely

Clown, Blake's wordless picture book, documents the fortunes and misfortunes of a plucky toy in search of a loving home.

unrestricted by the conventions of illustration." When asked by Elaine Moss in *Signal* if his early success helped his parents to support Blake's leanings toward a career in humorous art, he responded that they wanted security for him, "something like banking or teaching."

After graduating from Chiselhurst, Blake served in the Army Education Corps for two years, teaching English at Aldershot and illustrating a reader for illiterate soldiers. After completing his national service, Blake went to Downing College at Cambridge University to read English. "I had decided against art school," he told *SATA,* "because I wanted an education in literature. Had I enrolled in art school I knew that I would lose the opportunity to study literature. I could still continue to draw." Blake studied for three years at Cambridge, where he drew for their undergraduate magazines as well as for *Punch.* In 1956, he went to the University of London for a year of teacher's training. "On the verge of becoming a teacher," Blake says, "I completed the training program and took the qualifications, but took no full-time job and went back to what I had always intended for myself—art and illustration."

Becoming a freelance artist, Blake was hired to do a drawing a week for *Punch* and also began working for the literary magazine *Spectator.* In addition, he became a part-time student at Chelsea College of Art, "because" he said, "I wanted to learn more about life drawing and painting." Blake enrolled at Chelsea in order to study with Brian Robb, a noted painter, illustrator, and cartoonist who taught at the school. Blake said of his art studies, "I attended Chelsea for eighteen months. The experience gained in life drawing and painting was very important, and as a result my drawings became richer. I have always liked economical, reduced drawings. A possible analogy is soup—the more ingredients you add to the broth, the better the taste. So it is with my drawings. It is my diverse background knowledge and experience that has made the simplicity of my drawings possible. I also discovered that when working in black and white, you can actually paint out or correct mistakes. That was an enormously liberating discovery and helped free me from a lot of inhibitions." Blake also kept up his connection with instructor Brian Robb, who, he says, "did influence my attitude toward work, especially toward book illustration. He later left Chelsea for the Royal College of Art where he became head of the illustration department. Years later, he invited me to teach there."

Blake's early cartoons, he said, "were funny, which was their main objective. I was not at all interested in political satire, which is probably why my career developed more in the direction of book illustration than cartooning. I was drawn to the drama of illustration and the theatricality of it. Books offered a continuity of narrative, which was very important to me. I was interested in storytelling and in showing how people react, how they move, and how they're placed in a scene. I was fascinated with the way one could tell a story by visually portraying the action of the characters. Of course, I didn't identify this as a motive at the time, but

it certainly had a lot to do with my development in the direction of book illustration."

"For *Punch* I had to think up funny things and invent visual jokes. Whereas for the *Spectator* I was briefed once a week when I went to the office and expected to come up with something by the next day. One week it was Kruschev, the next it was French cooking. I liken this kind of work, and the versatility it demands, to repertory acting: one week you're Ophelia and the next Macbeth."

At the age of thirty-six, Blake created his first children's book, *Patrick,* a picture book fantasy about a young man who fiddles his way through Ireland on a magical violin. Years earlier, he had begun illustrating books for other authors. Throughout his career, Blake has provided the pictures for writers such as Lewis Carroll, Sylvia Plath, Rudyard Kipling, Dr. Seuss, Jules Verne, Margaret Mahy, George Orwell, John Masefield, Joan Tate, Evelyn Waugh, and Aristophanes. He is especially well known for his illustrations for the children's books of Joan Aiken, Michael Rosen, Sid Fleischman, J. P. Martin, and Nils-Olof Franzen. However, Blake's greatest success as an illustrator is perhaps reserved for the works of Roald Dahl, Russell Hoban, and John Yeoman, the latter a friend with whom Blake attended Cambridge and with whom he has cowritten some texts. Blake sees his work as an illustrator as a collaboration with text and author: "The first collaboration is with the story. If you're the right illustrator for the text, you get a rush of ideas and feelings from the story itself. Then you can go to the author and confer. If you're not the right illustrator, I don't believe the collaboration will ever be fruitful." In an essay he wrote for *Horn Book,* Blake adds, "I'm certainly not one of those children's illustrators who like to illustrate only their own ideas, and one of the aspects of the job in which my interest has developed and continues to develop is that of working not so much with authors as with their manuscripts." He told *SATA,* "I work in different ways with different authors. I know John Yeoman very well; he is an old friend, and I would call our working relationship a collaboration." Blake also told *SATA* about taking drawings to the late Roald Dahl for his reaction: "'What you've drawn is what I wrote,' Dahl [would] say. 'But it might be better if we did it another, less literal way.' That is collaboration."

Beginning in the late 1960s, Blake began to intersperse his original picture books, comic fantasies, concept books, and compilations with the books for which he provided illustrations. One of his most acclaimed works is *Mister Magnolia,* the story of how the cheerful, dashing title character searches for and is presented with a boot to match the one he is wearing. Called "Blake's masterpiece" by Brian Alderson, *Mister Magnolia* is the author's own favorite among his books; Blake told *SATA,* "it's not autobiographical, but reflects the things I like in *pictures.* " Blake tells a rhyming nonsense tale in which flute, newt, hoot, rooty-toot and other words guide the story. *Growing Point* reviewer Margery Fisher added that his "typically active line and emphatic

A farcical reworking of the traditional verses of "The House that Jack Built," *The Do-It-Yourself House that Jack Built*
features typically whimsical illustrations by Quentin Blake. (Written by John Yeoman.)

colour and his comic detail" were never better. Writing in *Book Window*, Margaret Walker claimed that Blake "has excelled himself" and urged all: "Do buy it." Perhaps the book that best demonstrates Blake's sensitivity and understanding of the human condition is *The Story of the Dancing Frog*. Recounted as family history by a mother to her small daughter, the tale describes how Great Aunt Gertrude, who has recently been widowed, is prevented from drowning herself by the sight of a frog dancing on a lilypad. Gertrude and the frog, which she names George, become increasingly successful on the strength of George's talent; they travel the world before retiring to the south of France. At the end of the story, the child asks, "Are they dead now, then?" Her mother, whom Blake implies is herself widowed, replies, "That was a long time ago, so I suppose they must be." Writing in *The Signal Selection of Children's Books*, Jane Doonan noted, "The light touch with pen and paint catches the humor and hints at the sadness." She concluded: "It is Blake at his best." In his book *The Telling Line: Essays on Fifteen Contempo-*

rary Book Illustrators, Douglas Martin called *The Story of the Dancing Frog* "storytelling and illustrative book designing at its most accomplished."

Blake continues to write and illustrate books of his own while compiling collections of prose and verse and providing pictures for the works of other authors. *Simpkin* is a picture book with a rhyming text that is noted for expressing the duality of a small boy's nature while explaining the concept of opposites; in his review in *Junior Bookshelf*, Marcus Crouch asserted, "This artist grows more assured with every book." *The Singing Tortoise and Other Animal Folktales* is a collection of international cautionary tales from the nineteenth and early twentieth centuries collected by John Yeoman which Blake decorates with, according to *Publishers Weekly*, "[his] inimitably puckish art." With *Clown*, Blake has created a story that is considered to have the panache of such works as *The Story of the Dancing Frog*. In his wordless picture book, the artist outlines how a discarded toy clown searches for a home for himself and his stuffed animal friends, all of whom have been discarded in a trash can in a tough urban neighborhood. Thrown through the window of a run-down apartment where a crying baby is being cared for by her older sister, the clown cheers up the girl and the infant with juggling tricks, helps with the dishes, sweeps, and even changes the baby. After rescuing the other toys, he returns back to the apartment, where the children's tired mother returns to find a clean house and smiling offspring. *Horn Book* reviewer Ann A. Flowers maintained, "Only Quentin Blake's remarkable skill as an artist could produce such a touching, endearing story . . . ." Writing in *School Library Journal,* Carol Ann Wilson commented, "Blake succeeds admirably in presenting a multilayered and thought-provoking tale that will capture readers' imaginations." Jim Gladstone of the *New York Times Book Review* noted the "pitch-perfect details and often unsettling undertones" of the story; Blake, Gladstone continued, "draws up serious underlying questions that go on to follow Clown . . . . Is it really better to be owned or on one's own?" He concluded that the author "delivers a Dickensian happy ending that can easily be read as very unhappy, uniting the city's underclass: the children, the poor, and the wide-eyed toys." Blake, in fact, has illustrated a book by Charles Dickens, an edition of *A Christmas Carol* that was, like *Clown,* published in 1995. *Horn Book* reviewer Ann A. Flowers wrote, "everything is handsome about this edition . . . . It would be hard to think of a more quintessentially Dickensian illustrator."

Blake has said of his own writing, "Most of the books I've written are really just sequences of drawings with text added for necessary explanations. My urge is to draw, and the story is worked out later. The illustrations are, so to speak, *leading* the story. *The Story of the Dancing Frog* was my only book not written like this. Illustrating it was a bit like working on someone else's manuscript. I'm delighted that I can do both, but if I had to give up one, I would give up writing.

"Working on my own books is often more of a headache. When you illustrate someone else's text, that text is well defined when you start. You get the manuscript, you start, you find the structure, think about the mood, the characters and how to fit them into the illustration. You want to do well by the story, but there are limits. When you work on your own text, however, you can change the pictures, or change the text at will. Everything is up for negotiation. The possibilities are infinite. It's like swimming in mud; all I can think about is, 'Where's the shore?'"

Writing in *Horn Book,* Blake commented, "I embrace the simplicity of both the story and the pictures, in which there may not seem to be, for the grownup, much to talk about. To ease that frustration, it would be quite possible for me to invoke a range of stylistic references—I have extensive knowledge of my drawing's genealogy—but at the present moment I would rather invite the spectator of whatever age to believe that I have never spoken in any other language and that these pictures are simply happening."

Blake has won several prestigious awards for his works. "I do cherish," he told *SATA,* "the Kate Greenaway Medal for *Mister Magnolia.* My favorite, however, was the Children's Book Award from the Federation of Children's Book Groups, which is actually awarded by children—their vote decides the winner. What you win is not a medal or money, but a book filled with their own writing and drawing, all in response to your books. Quite a marvelous prize indeed!"

"I don't have children, but am still in touch with the child in me, and this has been immensely important to me as an artist. Part of keeping one's child-self alive is not being embarrassed to admit it exists."

Blake offered the following advice to young artists: "You must want to draw all the time, because that is the only way you can get good at it. You can study a certain amount of technique, but *doing it* is the key element. Beyond that, I am disinclined to prescribe anything because one of the main aspects of being an illustrator or children's author is that you are a hybrid, a mixture of many elements . . . . I tend to be concerned with people—the faces they make and the way they move. If you have the instinct to want to draw and to tell stories in pictures, there are many ways to approach illustration and many different things one might contribute. Look at other artists' work but don't be too influenced by them. Go on drawing, go on doing the job, and you will find out what you really like, and what you have to contribute. In this sense, there are no rules. Everybody's got to find out for himself."

■ Works Cited

Alderson, Brian, "All Join In: the Generous Art of Quentin Blake," *Horn Book,* September-October, 1995, pp. 562-71.

Blake, Quentin, "Wild Washerwomen, Hired Sportsmen, and Enormous Crocodiles," *Horn Book,* October, 1981, pp. 505-13.

Crouch, Marcus, review of *Simpkin, Junior Bookshelf,* February, 1994, pp. 12-13.

Doonan, Jane, review of *The Story of the Dancing Frog, The Signal Selection of Children's Books,* 1984, p. 8.

Fisher, Margery, review of *Mister Magnolia, Growing Point,* May, 1980, p. 3708.

Flowers, Ann A., review of *A Christmas Carol, Horn Book,* January-February, 1996, p. 73.

Flowers, Ann A., review of *Clown, Horn Book,* July-August, 1996, p. 444.

Gladstone, Jim, review of *Clown, New York Times Book Review,* September 22, 1996, p. 28.

Lewis, Naomi, "Once Upon a Line," *Times Educational Supplement,* November 19, 1982, p. 32.

Martin, Douglas, "Quentin Blake," *The Telling Line: Essays on Fifteen Contemporary Book Illustrators,* Julia MacRae Books, 1989, p. 253.

Mole, John, "Space to Dance," *Times Literary Supplement,* November 9, 1984, p. 1294.

Moss, Elaine, "Quentin Blake," *Signal,* January, 1975, pp. 33-39.

Review of *The Singing Tortoise and Other Animal Folktales, Publishers Weekly,* May 16, 1994, p. 64.
Walker, Margaret, review of *Mister Magnolia, Book Window,* Spring, 1980, p. 12.
Wilson, Carol Ann, review of *Clown, School Library Journal,* May, 1996, p. 84.

■ For More Information See

BOOKS

Children's Literature Review, Volume 31, Gale, 1994.
Holtze, Sally Holmes, editor, *Fifth Book of Junior Authors and Illustrators,* H. W. Wilson, 1983.
Kingman, Lee, and others, compilers, *Illustrators of Children's Books: 1957-1966,* Horn Book, 1968.
Kingman, Lee, and others, compilers, *Illustrators of Children's Books: 1967-1976,* Horn Book, 1968.
Peppin, Brigid and Lucy Micklethwait, *Book Illustrators of the Twentieth Century,* Arco, 1984.

PERIODICALS

Artist's and Illustrator's Magazine, April, 1987, pp. 14-17.
Folio, autumn, 1976.
Graphis (children's book edition), September, 1975.
New Statesman, October 31, 1969; November 9, 1973; November 21, 1980.
New York Times Book Review, November 3, 1974; January 15, 1989.
Observer, April 15, 1990.
Punch, December 15, 1965.
Spectator, December 5, 1970; April 16, 1977.
Times (London), July 29, 1989; April 21, 1990.
Times Educational Supplement, March 28, 1980; October 31, 1980; June 9, 1989, p. B9.
Times Literary Supplement, November 26, 1982, p. 1303; May 6, 1988, p. 513; July 7, 1989, p. 757.
Washington Post Book World, October 14, 1990, p. 10.

—Sketch by Gerard J. Senick

* * *

BODE, Janet 1943-

■ Personal

Surname is pronounced *Boe*-dy; born July 14, 1943, in Penn Yan, NY; daughter of Carl J. (a writer and professor) and Margaret (Lutze) Bode. *Education:* University of Maryland, B.A., 1965; graduate study at Michigan State University and Bowie State College.

■ Addresses

Home—New York, NY.

■ Career

Writer, since 1972. Has worked in Germany, Mexico, and the United States as personnel specialist, program director, community organizer, public relations direc-

tor, and teacher. *Member:* PEN, National Writers Union, Authors Guild.

■ Awards, Honors

Outstanding Social Studies Book Award, National Council for the Social Studies (NCSS), for *Rape: Preventing It; Coping with the Legal, Medical and Emotional Aftermath;* Notable Children's Trade Book in the Field of Social Studies, NCSS, Best Books for Young Adults Citation, American Library Association (ALA), and Books for the Teen Age selection, New York Public Library (NYPL), 1981 and 1982, all for *Kids Having Kids: The Unwed Teenage Parent;* Best Books for Young Adults selection, ALA, Outstanding Merit Book, NCSS, and Books for the Teen Age selection, NYPL, 1990, all for *New Kids on the Block: Oral Histories of Immigrant Teens;* Best Books for Young Adults selection, ALA, Books for the Teen Age, NYPL, 1991, Blue Ribbon Book, *Bulletin of the Center for Children's Books,* Best Books citation, *School Library Journal,* and Editor's Choice, *Booklist,* all for *The Voices of Rape;* Best Books for Young Adults selection, ALA, Books for the Teen Age, NYPL, 1992, and Recommended Books for Reluctant Young Adult Readers, Young Adult Library Services Association (YALSA), all for *Beating the Odds: Stories of Unexpected Achievers;* Notable Children's Trade Book in the Field of Social Studies, NCSS, and Books for the Teen Age, NYPL, 1993, both for *Kids Still Having Kids: People Talk about Teen Pregnancy;* Quick Picks—Best Books for Reluctant Readers selection, YALSA, Books for the Teen Age, NYPL, 1993, and Young Adults' Choice for 1995, International Reading Association, all for *Death Is Hard to Live With: Teenagers Talk about How They Cope with Loss;* Best Books for Young Adults selection, ALA, and Books for the Teen Age, NYPL, 1995, both for *Heartbreak and Roses: Real Life Stories of Troubled Love;* Quick Picks—Best Books for Reluctant Readers, YALSA, and Books for the Teen Age, NYPL, 1995, both for *Trust and Betrayal: Real Life Stories of Friends and Enemies;* Best Books for Young Adults selection, ALA, Top Ten Quick Picks—Best Books for Reluctant Readers, YALSA, and Books for the Teen Age, NYPL, 1997, all for *Hard Time: A Real Life Look at Juvenile Crime and Violence.*

■ Writings

Kids School Lunch Bag (on the National School Lunch Program), Children's Foundation, 1972.
View from Another Closet: Exploring Bisexuality in Women, Hawthorn, 1976.
Fighting Back: How to Cope with the Medical, Emotional and Legal Consequences of Rape, Macmillan, 1978.
Rape: Preventing It; Coping with the Legal, Medical and Emotional Aftermath (young adult), F. Watts, 1979.
Kids Having Kids: The Unwed Teenage Parent (young adult), F. Watts, 1980.
Different Worlds: Interracial and Cross-Cultural Dating, F. Watts, 1989.

JANET BODE

New Kids on the Block: Oral Histories of Immigrant
    Teens, F. Watts, 1989, reprinted by Scholastic as
    New Kids in Town.
The Voices of Rape, F. Watts, 1990.
Truce: Ending the Sibling War, F. Watts, 1991.
Beating the Odds: Stories of Unexpected Achievers,
    graphic stories by Stan Mack, F. Watts, 1991.
Kids Still Having Kids: People Talk about Teen Pregnan-
    cy, graphic stories by Stan Mack, F. Watts, 1992.
Death Is Hard to Live With: Teenagers Talk about How
    They Cope with Loss, graphic stories by Stan Mack,
    Delacorte, 1993.
Heartbreak and Roses: Real Life Stories of Troubled
    Love, graphic stories by Stan Mack, Delacorte,
    1994.
Trust and Betrayal: Real Life Stories of Friends and
    Enemies, Delacorte, 1995.
(With Stan Mack) Hard Time: A Real Life Look at
    Juvenile Crime and Violence, Delacorte, 1996.
Food Fight: A Guide to Eating Disorders for Pre-Teens
    and Their Parents, Simon & Schuster, 1997.

Co-author of "Women against Rape" (television documentary film), 1975. Contributor of articles to periodicals, including New York Times, Cosmopolitan, Redbook, New York, and Mademoiselle.

■ **Adaptations**

Different Worlds: Interracial and Cross-Cultural Dating
was made into a CBS-TV Schoolbreak Special entitled
Different Worlds: A Story of Interracial Love.

■ **Sidelights**

I just graduated from high school. I feel we had a curse on
my class. Six people died. The worst was Shannon, my
best friend. She was free-spirited, the last person you'd
expect to die.

One day she's great.

The next day she's dead.

I wasn't prepared for it.

Leticia, age seventeen, the narrator in a chapter entitled
"Death Hurts" in Janet Bode's book Death Is Hard to
Live With: Teenagers Talk about How They Cope with
Loss, tells about the death of her friend Shannon. She
was killed by a hit-and-run driver who stole a car and hit
her and a group of pedestrians. "Actually, Tommy, the
one driving, went to elementary school with us," Leticia
explains.

The story that Leticia tells is not really Shannon's story but Leticia's own. She goes on to tell about how she put her life back in shape after the death of her best friend. Leticia is a survivor, the sort of person that Bode's book celebrates. "Some of you don't want to think about death," Bode writes in her introduction, entitled "Death Is Not Optional." "You want to forget that everything alive must die. Plants, ants, snakes, fish, dogs, cats—and people. You want to believe that you and those you love are somehow going to live forever."

"This book," the author continues, "is a place to start sorting out your emotions and making sense of your world. Think of it as a survival guide. This book will help answer the question: How do I cope with the death of someone special? Wherever that person is, whether there's a soul, eternity, reincarnation—you're still here. How do you deal with your conflicting emotions and get on with your life? To help you on your own journey, teenagers from across the country recount how they face these questions head on."

Issues like those described in *Death Is Hard to Live With* are the sort of problems that Janet Bode confronts in her award-winning books. Titles such as *Kids Having Kids:*

In this 1993 work, Bode shares advice given by teenagers who have experienced the death of a friend or relative.

The Unwed Teenage Parent, Different Worlds: Interracial and Cross-Cultural Dating, Heartbreak and Roses: Real Life Stories of Troubled Love, and *Hard Time: A Real Life Look at Juvenile Crime and Violence* look at problems faced by modern teens and suggest solutions, often through the wisdom of other teenagers. Bode's work is often presented with the illustrations of cartoonist Stan Mack, which also present the stories of teens in crisis. "Bode uses the young adults' own words as much as possible and the discussions throughout Bode's books have an honest ring that create immediate connections with readers," writes Hollis Lowrey-Moore in *Twentieth-Century Young Adult Writers.* "Expert interviews which sometimes follow teen's stories are never preachy or arrogant but provide information and differing viewpoints, and offer practical suggestions for help."

Several of Bode's books have teen pregnancy as their topic. *Kids Having Kids: The Unwed Teenage Parent,* for example, traces the difficulties and responsibilities of teenage parenthood. Bode carefully describes the potential health problems that can arise from unprotected sex (and from birth control, which can have its own separate set of problems), explains the options that are available to sexually active teens, and uses the stories of other teenagers to show how they react to the new responsibilities of caring for an infant. *School Library Journal* contributor Joan Scherer Brewer explains that the book can be read in many different ways, depending on the interests of the reader: it can be used as a guide for teens who think they might be pregnant, and its extensive bibliography directs researchers to other helpful sources. Bode also gives historical perspectives to attitudes on teenage sex and pregnancy, Brewer states, "making this useful for term papers as well as personal guidance."

Kids Still Having Kids: People Talk about Teen Pregnancy, a sequel to *Kids Having Kids,* also confronts issues of sexuality, pregnancy, and parenting. It expands the scope of the earlier book by concentrating on feelings and attitudes toward sexuality. "It touches not only on teenage pregnancy and related issues of abortion and adoption, but also on teenage sex, foster care, and parenting," states *Booklist* contributor Stephanie Zvirin. "For balance and insight Bode includes the perspectives of adults who work with teens." "The discussion of options is generally fair-minded in terms of pros and cons," Libby K. White declares in her *School Library Journal* review of the book. "While Bode appears to be pro-choice, she urges those who believe abortion to be morally wrong to reject it as an option for them." "This book," concludes *Voice of Youth Advocates* contributor Barbara Flottmeier, "is a compendium of excellent information concerning the facts of teenage pregnancy, the emotional effects of that pregnancy and the help that is available for the pregnant teenage mother and father."

Reviewers comment on Bode's no-nonsense approach to the subject of death in *Death Is Hard to Live With: Teenagers Talk about How They Cope with Loss.* Susan R. Farber states in her *Voice of Youth Advocates* review that the author "goes beyond platitudes and the 'happy, happy, joy, joy' religious approach to dealing with the

Teenagers relate their experiences with romance in hopes that others will learn from their situations. (Cover illustration by Stan Mack.)

aftermath of death." "She interviews teenagers about the deaths of friends or relatives," explains a *Publishers Weekly* reviewer, "and she also calls on professionals (doctors, funeral directors, clergymen as well as therapists)." *School Library Journal* contributor Celia A. Huffman calls the volume "a thorough approach to the topic that encourages readers to talk about their personal experiences involving death, let go of the pain, grieve, and move on, allowing it to be a lesson about life." "*Death Is Hard to Live With* has its flaws," Farber concludes, " ... but overall it's an important book, a book to help teens survive a traumatic time in their lives."

Bode has also written several books about the subject of rape and how it affects both victims and perpetrators. The earliest of these were *Fighting Back: How to Cope with the Medical, Emotional and Legal Consequences of Rape* and *Rape: Preventing It; Coping with the Legal, Medical and Emotional Aftermath. Fighting Back* was intended for adult women, but *Rape* was directed specifically at teenagers and other young adults. In the

latter book, explains a *Kirkus Reviews* contributor, "she emphasizes that the decision to report or prosecute is up to the victim (though a medical exam is a must) and points out the variety of problems—from finding the guy to finding a non-sexist jury—which frequently stand in the way of conviction." "Laced with colloquialisms and street adjectives," states *School Library Journal* reviewer Denise L. Moll, "Bode's book strives to break down the myths and misconceptions that surround the topic of rape."

The book that broke new ground on the topic, however, was *The Voices of Rape,* in which Bode allowed victims and perpetrators of the crime to speak for themselves. "In an effort 'to educate, to help, and to bring the human element to the issue,' she turns most of her platform over to a carefully chosen group of teenagers and specialists," writes Stephanie Zvirin in *Booklist,* "each of whom views rape from a different vantage point—rapist, survivor, police officer, mental health professional, lawyer, nurse." Carolyn Polese, writing in *School Library Journal,* notes that several points of view have been omitted: "[Discussion] of incest or child sexual abuse is negligible, and some of the most disturbing and ambiguous monologues—such as one by a boy who casually participated in several 'gang bangs'—are presented without interpretation or comment." Several reviewers, however, praised Bode's work for just such editorial restraint. Bode, states *Voice of Youth Advocates* contributor Judy Sasges, "survived a robbery and gang rape. Her reassuring yet realistic tone will appeal to readers. Some sentences are choppy and poorly constructed, but Bode acknowledges that 'the language you read is the language I heard—not always perfect ... but always clear.'" "Choosing not to intrude in the interviews," Zvirin explains, "[Bode] lays the burden of interpretation on her reading audience, and while that's a lot to demand from some teens, she gives them honesty and respect in return."

In *Hard Time: A Real Life Look at Juvenile Crime and Violence,* Bode examines the problems faced by young people who commit crimes. She cites Georges Benjamin, M.D., chairman of the trauma care, violence and injury control committee of the American College of Emergency Physicians in Washington, D.C. Dr. Benjamin compares modern hospital emergency rooms to "MASH units in war zones." "We're treating gunshot violence, domestic violence, drug- and alcohol-related violence," the doctor continues. "And the victims of violence I see are younger and younger. Many of you teenagers know this. You've been going to more funerals than proms. It's the adults who often don't seem to understand that everyone's kid is at risk. Even theirs." Dr. Benjamin recommends learning mediation and anger-management skills to counter some of the worst problems. "Violence-free is a goal," the doctor concludes. "If you don't know where you're going, you won't get there."

"Through poems, narrative prose, and cartoon strips," writes a reviewer for *Bulletin of the Center for Children's Books,* "we hear a diversity of voices, including those of

Sean, a seventeen-year-old who killed his mother; Randall Watson, the project coordinator who teaches writing workshops to teens in prison; and Tanya, the fifteen-year-old whose letter to the author describes her decision to lead a straight life." "One 17-year-old girl is in [prison] for 'participating in the murder of my best friend. She said she was going to steal my boyfriend,'" explains Carolyn Noah in *School Library Journal*. "*Hard Time* both shocks the reader and provides a glimmer of hope," declares Anne O'Malley in *Booklist*, "stemming from the few success stories inside the grim walls." "That people from urban, suburban, poor, and middle-class environments are represented," Noah concludes, "reinforces the validity of the book." "Bode says the book is a 'wake-up call'; it is not for the faint-hearted," states a *Kirkus Reviews* contributor, "but it should be available to all those in similar situations—whether perpetrators or victims."

Heartbreak and Roses: Real Life Stories of Troubled Love is one of the few nonfiction books aimed at young adults that deals with the subject of romance. "All of the young people in Bode's stories are trying to come to grips with their sexuality," states Evelyn Carter Walker in *School Library Journal*, "and each one portrays a troubled relationship." Bode explains in her introduction to the book that it is a series of twelve short stories that tell of love and pain and the relationship between the two. "Some tell of love gone wrong—violent love, obsessive love, tormented love leading to suicide attempts," Bode writes. "Others speak of bittersweet love—battles for love fought against outside forces." She reminds readers that these are true stories of real teenagers. "As in life, and especially life in the teen years, the course of love in these stories is turbulent. They may upset you. They may comfort you. They may also help you see your own love problems more clearly." She hopes that the stories and the interspersed fact boxes "may give you a little more insight into your own love life."

Like the rest of Bode's work, *Heartbreak and Roses* lets young men and women speak for themselves. "While sex is a concern common to many of the stories," a *Publishers Weekly* contributor says, "the collection explores a wide variety of other issues—coping with a disability, violence, interracial dating, self-acceptance, co-dependence and breaking up among them. Unobtrusive onlookers who offer neither answers nor judgments, Bode and Mack relay each story as if merely transcribing the words of its narrator." "Whether it's a disabled teen talking about the practicalities of having sex, someone involved in an abusive relationship, or a gay youth whose first lover pretends their intimacy never happened, the stories are candid—about love, about pain, and about sex," states Stephanie Zvirin in *Booklist*. "And as in real life, they often have no satisfying conclusion."

All of Bode's books are rooted in the idea that young adults, armed with appropriate information and knowledge, will be able to find their own ways to gain control over their lives. "Bode's abilities to communicate honestly with young adults," writes Lowery-Moore, "and to provide information and help in a way that teens find palatable make her books a valuable tool for teens, parents, teachers, and librarians. Bode's works also provide snapshots and insights into some of society's most pressing issues and impart a sense of certainty that today's teens will find solutions to many of the ills they have inherited."

■ Works Cited

Bode, Janet, *Death Is Hard to Live With: Teenagers Talk about How They Cope with Loss*, Delacorte, 1993.

Bode, Janet, *Heartbreak and Roses: Real Life Stories of Troubled Love*, Delacorte, 1994.

Bode, Janet, and Stan Mack, *Hard Time: A Real Life Look at Juvenile Crime and Violence*, Delacorte, 1996.

Brewer, Joan Scherer, review of *Kids Having Kids: The Unwed Teenage Parent*, *School Library Journal*, February, 1981, p. 73.

Review of *Death Is Hard to Live With: Teenagers Talk about How They Cope with Loss*, *Publishers Weekly*, August 9, 1993, p. 480.

Farber, Susan R., review of *Death Is Hard to Live With: Teenagers Talk about How They Cope with Loss*, *Voice of Youth Advocates*, April, 1994, p. 43.

Flottmeier, Barbara, review of *Kids Still Having Kids: The Unwed Teenage Parent*, *Voice of Youth Advocates*, February, 1993, p. 364.

Review of *Hard Time: A Real Life Look at Juvenile Crime and Violence*, *Bulletin of the Center for Children's Books*, May, 1996, pp. 293-94.

Review of *Hard Time: A Real Life Look at Juvenile Crime and Violence*, *Kirkus Reviews*, December 15, 1995, p. 1767.

Review of *Heartbreak and Roses: Real Life Stories of Troubled Love*, *Publishers Weekly*, June 27, 1994, p. 79.

Huffman, Celia A., review of *Death Is Hard to Live With: Teenagers Talk about How They Cope with Loss*, *School Library Journal*, August, 1993, p. 192.

Lowrey-Moore, Hollis, "Janet Bode," *Twentieth-Century Young Adult Writers*, St. James Press, 1994, pp. 62-63.

Moll, Denise L., review of *Rape: Preventing It; Coping with the Legal, Medical and Emotional Aftermath*, *School Library Journal*, February, 1980, p. 63.

Noah, Carolyn, review of *Hard Time: A Real Life Look at Juvenile Crime and Violence*, *School Library Journal*, April, 1996, p. 161.

O'Malley, Anne, review of *Hard Time: A Real Life Look at Juvenile Crime and Violence*, *Booklist*, April 1, 1996, p. 1351.

Polese, Carolyn, review of *The Voices of Rape*, *School Library Journal*, October, 1990, p. 146.

Review of *Rape: Preventing It; Coping with the Legal, Medical and Emotional Aftermath*, *Kirkus Reviews*, November 1, 1979, p. 1268.

Sasges, Judy, review of *The Voices of Rape*, *Voice of Youth Advocates*, February, 1991, pp. 371-72.

Walker, Evelyn Carter, review of *Heartbreak and Roses: Real Life Stories of Troubled Love, School Library Journal,* July, 1994, p. 116.

White, Libby K., review of *Kids Still Having Kids: People Talk about Teen Pregnancy, School Library Journal,* March, 1993, p. 226.

Zvirin, Stephanie, review of *The Voices of Rape, Booklist,* October 1, 1990.

Zvirin, Stephanie, review of *Kids Still Having Kids: People Talk about Teen Pregnancy, Booklist,* January 1, 1993.

Zvirin, Stephanie, review of *Heartbreak and Roses: Real Life Stories of Troubled Love, Booklist,* October 1, 1994, p. 315.

■ For More Information See

PERIODICALS

ALAN Review, winter, 1996.
Booklist, September 15, 1991; March 1, 1995, p. 1234.
Bulletin of the Center for Children's Books, February, 1991, p. 138; June, 1995, pp. 538-39.
Kirkus Reviews, February 15, 1995, p. 221; May 15, 1997, p. 797.
New York Times Book Review, March 12, 1995, p. 20.
Publishers Weekly, January 2, 1995, p. 78.
School Library Journal, June, 1991, p. 129; November, 1991, p. 138; July, 1994, p. 116; February, 1995, p. 115; April, 1996, p. 161.*

—*Sketch by Kenneth R. Shepherd*

* * *

BRADFORD, Karleen 1936-

■ Personal

Born December 16, 1936, in Toronto, Ontario, Canada; daughter of Karl H. (an accountant) and Eileen (a homemaker; maiden name, Ney) Scott; married James C. Bradford (a Canadian foreign service officer), August 22, 1959; children: Donald, Kathleen, Christopher. *Education:* University of Toronto, B.A., 1959. *Hobbies and other interests:* Flying, scuba diving, reading.

■ Addresses

Office—c/o Writers' Union of Canada, 24 Ryerson Ave., Toronto, Ontario M5T 2P3, Canada.

■ Career

T. Eaton Co., Toronto, Ontario, advertising copywriter, 1959; West Toronto Young Women's Christian Association, Toronto, social worker, 1959-63; writer, 1963—. *Member:* International Board on Books for Young People, Writers Union of Canada (curriculum chairperson, 1984-85), Canadian Authors Association, Canadian Society of Children's Authors, Illustrators, and Performers, PEN.

KARLEEN BRADFORD

■ Awards, Honors

Grant from Ontario Arts Council, 1977; first prize in juvenile writing, Canadian Authors Association, 1978, for short story "A Wish about Freckles"; first prize, CommCept Canadian KiddLit Competition, 1980, for *The Other Elizabeth;* grants from Canada Council, 1983, 1985, 1996; second prize in juvenile writing, Canadian Authors Association, 1984; Max and Greta Ebel Award, 1990; Young Adult Book Award, Canadian Library Association, 1993, for *There Will Be Wolves.*

■ Writings

A Year for Growing, illustrated by Charles Hilder, Scholastic, 1977, revised edition published as *Wrong Again, Robbie,* 1983.
The Other Elizabeth, illustrated by Deborah Drew-Brook, Gage, 1982.
I Wish There Were Unicorns, illustrated by Greg Ruhl, Gage, 1983.
The Stone in the Meadow, illustrated by Ruhl, Gage, 1984.
The Haunting at Cliff House, Scholastic, 1985.
The Nine Days Queen, Scholastic, 1986.
Write Now!, Scholastic, 1988.
Windward Island, Kids Can Press, 1989.
There Will Be Wolves, HarperCollins (Toronto), 1992, Dutton, 1996.
The Thirteenth Child, HarperCollins, 1994.
Shadows on a Sword (sequel to *There Will Be Wolves*), HarperCollins, 1996.

Also author of *Animaux Heroes,* translated into English as *Animal Heroes,* Scholastic; author of short stories represented in anthologies, including *Beyond Belief,* Clarke, Irwin, 1980; contributor to newspapers and magazines, including *Cricket, Canadian Children's Magazine, Jabberwocky,* and *Instructor.* Editor of *Our*

Books in the Curriculum, three volumes, Writers' Union of Canada, 1985; *Canadian Authors Association Newsletter,* Ottawa Branch, 1984-85; and *American College Women's Newsletter,* Manila, Philippines, 1978-79.

■ Work in Progress

A third book on the crusades, titled *Lionheart's Scribe.*

■ Sidelights

Canadian children's author Karleen Bradford has combined her experiences living around the world with her interests in both young people and the past to produce a series of award-winning historical novels that profile teens from various times and places in difficult situations. Among her historical novels, the most ambitious—*There Will Be Wolves* and its sequel, *Shadows on a Sword*—depict life in the eleventh century, particularly the religious crusades in which Europeans, filled with religious zeal as well as human greed and avarice, journeyed to the holy lands of the Middle East with the intention of wresting the territory from non-Christians.

Born in Ontario, Canada, Bradford spent her teen years in Argentina before returning to her own country to attend college in Toronto. Married in 1959 to an officer in the Canadian foreign service, she spent many more years on foreign soil, "travelling from country to country—an experience that has proven to be wonderfully stimulating for me both as a person and as a writer," Bradford once told *Something about the Author* (*SATA*). She and her family have lived in Southeast Asia, South America, Germany, and England, the last country having perhaps the greatest influence on her career as an author. "During the time we lived there we found that two of our favourite places were Cornwall and Wales, and two of my books take place in those locales: *The Stone in the Meadow* (Cornwall) and *The Haunting at Cliff House* (Wales)."

Several of Bradford's books have what she calls a "back to the past" theme. "In *The Stone in the Meadow* a young Canadian girl visiting her uncle is magically transported back to 300 B.C., a time when Britain was occupied by warring tribes of Celts and their Druid priests," the author noted. "In *The Other Elizabeth,* a modern-day girl enters an old building in Upper Canada Village—a pioneer village [museum] in Ontario—and suddenly finds herself back in the year 1813, during the war between the United States of America and Canada. *The Haunting at Cliff House* concerns a Canadian girl who has accompanied her father, a novelist and university professor, on his sabbatical to a small town in Wales. They move into an old house on the coast which he has inherited, and the heroine finds that it is haunted by the ghost of another girl who lived there over a hundred years before. [These novels are] concerned with events that happened in the past, and the possibility of altering those events in such a way that the future, as well, is altered. It's a theme that has fascinated me for a long time."

KARLEEN BRADFORD

There Will Be Wolves

Set in 1096, Bradford's historical novel features a young healer who escapes execution for witchcraft by joining the People's Crusade, where she witnesses savagery in the guise of religious fervor. (Cover illustration by Bill Dodge.)

Historical research is another of Bradford's fascinations. A series of Canada Council grants have enabled her to visit historic sites in which she has set several of her historical novels. In 1983 she traveled to England to research *Nine Days Queen,* a fictional portrait of Lady Jane Grey, who was Queen of England for nine days when she was fifteen years old before being executed on Tower Green. Such first-hand, in-depth research was not always Bradford's forte, however, as she recalled in an essay in *Canadian Children's Literature:* "I began writing historical novels by accident, and research, to me, was an intimidating and boring word.... [But] a funny thing happened while I was doing it. It suddenly stopped being an intimidating and boring word and became an exciting and fascinating pursuit. In fact, I became positively enamoured of the activity to the extent that I created a new problem for myself: digging into the past became so interesting and exciting—not to mention so much easier than actually writing—that it was very hard to stop and get to work on the book itself."

Nine Days Queen required weeks of study in the British Museum, where Bradford read histories of the Tudor period, Lady Jane's surviving letters, and accounts of people who remembered the one-time queen of England. The novel recalls the brief life of Queen Jane, from her privileged childhood through her love affair with young King Edward VI, her arranged marriage with Guilford Dudley, the son of the duke of Northumberland, and the political turmoil that led to her short-lived reign as queen and then the deaths of both herself and her husband by order of Queen Mary in 1554. Praising Bradford's ability to present the political facets of Lady Jane's situation clearly, Sara Ellis noted in *Canadian Materials* that "Karleen Bradford will be a writer to watch as she expands her writing horizons." And in *Canadian Children's Literature*, Marjory Body applauded the way the author "makes history come alive." "The broad palette of this well-written novel with its lurid factual events ... will be of great interest to children," stated Body, who concluded that *Nine Days Queen* is an entertaining book for "those of us, children at heart, who simply enjoy a good story."

The People's Crusade of the eleventh century has also provided Bradford with the opportunity for extensive research. Beginning with her novel, *There Will Be Wolves,* she has tackled a compelling chapter in European and religious history—the Christian pilgrimage from Cologne, Germany, to the holy city of Jerusalem during which Christian zealots slaughtered many Jews and pillaged their homes under the guise of liberating the holy city from Turkish infidels. The book's protagonist, Ursula, is a young healer living with her ailing father in Cologne when the religious figure Peter the Hermit calls upon Christians to march to Jerusalem. Ursula, who has been harassed by the church for her supposed practice of witchcraft, is allowed to join Peter's followers to cleanse herself of sin in lieu of being burned at the stake. Accompanied by her father, who dies along the way, and befriended by a young stonecutter named Bruno, she is soon a witness to what Barbara L. Michasiw called "an unholy progress of greed, blood lust, and violence" by the crusading soldiers. While noting that Ursula's inner feelings are impenetrable, Michasiw described *There Will Be Wolves* as "gripping" and found the novel's "insights into human nature uncompromising." Hilary Turner similarly noted in *Canadian Children's Literature* that "Bradford makes no attempt to sanitize the unpleasant truth that ... faith alone cannot sustain the needs of the body, or that greed and self-interest frequently masquerade as piety." Bradford continued the story of Ursula and Bruno in 1996's *Shadows on a Sword,* the second of four projected novels on the period.

Other novels by Bradford, including *Wrong Again, Robbie* and *I Wish There Were Unicorns,* take place in present-day Canada and focus on such issues as learning to get along with others and coping with new and trying circumstances. *I Wish There Were Unicorns* concerns thirteen-year-old Rachel's move from the bustle of urban Toronto to a rural farm in Canada after her parents' divorce. At first angry and resentful, Rachel's feelings about her family change after her younger sister runs away in order to protect an abused dog that she has befriended. Although noting that some of the novel's characters are too upbeat to be believable, Frieda Wishinsky observed in *Quill and Quire* that Bradford "succeed[s] in portraying a young girl's confused feelings without sounding pedantic, which, in itself, is an accomplishment."

Published in 1989, *Windward Island* takes places on the southern coast of Nova Scotia, a world of lighthouse keepers and Atlantic shoreline fishermen. Research began for Bradford four years before the release of the book, in the spring of 1985; she was able to spend several weeks living on a small lighthouse island in the area. "There I found a peace and a strength that I have not found anywhere else, and I want[ed] very much to write about it," she admitted to *SATA*. The novel that resulted—the story of teens Caleb and Loren and their feelings about leaving their island home and moving to the Nova Scotia mainland—was hailed by *Canadian Children's Literature* reviewer Gordon Moyles as "readable, entertaining and exciting." Moyles also lauded the author's "ability to make the action of her novel reveal the emotional dilemma of her characters." Roger Burford Mason, writing in *Quill and Quire,* appreciated the way that *Windward Island* presents "the timeless aspirations, fears, jealousies, and problems of young people growing up."

Another of Bradford's stories set in modern times is *The Thirteenth Child,* a 1994 novel for young readers about a girl who lives in a fantasy world in order to avoid the harsh realities of her own life. Kate has watched as her father's alcoholism has destroyed her once-stable family, leading her mother to take refuge in front of the television to avoid his abusive behavior and forcing Kate to work long hours at her family's small restaurant and gas station when she is not in school. Writing romantic fantasies is Kate's way of coping with her problems, but fantasy becomes reality when she becomes drawn to Mike, a loner in town who strikes her as both "dangerous" and fascinating. "Bradford is touching on a most disquieting aspect of the lives of girls and women—the dangerousness, as well as the attractiveness, of men," declared Sandy Odegard in *Canadian Children's Literature,* adding that the novel stopped short of providing hope for avoiding the situations encountered by its female protagonists. Celia Barker Lottridge also felt that *The Thirteenth Child* was not a complete success, commenting in *Quill and Quire* that "the power of this novel could lie in the impact of [its] three vulnerable [protagonists] on each other. Instead, a hectic series of sensational events keep the characters occupied." But *Canadian Materials* contributor Margaret Mackey praised the novel's "tight" plot and maintained that "the reactions of the characters are believable for the most part."

"I've often been asked why I write for children rather than adults," Bradford told *SATA*. "In fact, I was once asked why a thirteen-year-old who could read at an adult level would need a 'children's' book at all. My answer to that particular question was that a thirteen-year-old who was capable of reading at an adult level did not necessarily *want* to read about adults and adult concerns all of the time. Often, that young person would like to read about other young people of the same age, with the same interests and concerns. For that reason I write for them—in an adult manner, but about *them*, about the problems and complexities that face *them*. And I hope that through my writing I can offer these young people—if not solutions—at least understanding, perhaps some ideas of how to cope, and most important of all, a sense of humor about the whole business."

■ Works Cited

Body, Marjorie, review of *The Nine Days Queen, Canadian Children's Literature,* Volume 48, 1987, pp. 85-86.

Bradford, Karleen, commentary in *Canadian Children's Literature,* Volume 83, 1996, pp. 75-77.

Ellis, Sarah, review of *The Nine Days Queen, Canadian Materials,* January 1988, p. 5.

Lottridge, Celia Barker, review of *The Thirteenth Child, Quill and Quire,* September 1994, pp. 73-74.

Mackey, Margaret, review of *The Thirteenth Child, Canadian Materials,* November/December 1994, p. 229.

Mason, Roger Burford, review of *Windward Island, Quill and Quire,* October 1989, pp. 14, 16.

Michasiw, Barbara L., review of *There Will Be Wolves, Quill and Quire,* December 1992, p. 27.

Moyles, Gordon, review of *Windward Island, Canadian Children's Literature,* Volume 62, 1991, p. 110.

Odegard, Sandy, review of *The Thirteenth Child, Canadian Children's Literature,* Volume 77, 1995, pp. 88-89.

Turner, Hilary, review of *There Will Be Wolves, Canadian Children's Literature,* Volume 73, 1994, p. 71.

Wishinsky, Frieda, review of *I Wish There Were Unicorns, Quill and Quire,* July 1983, p. 60.

■ For More Information See

PERIODICALS

Books in Canada, November, 1992, p. 38.

Bulletin of the Center for Children's Literature, October, 1996, p. 50.

Canadian Materials, March, 1990, p. 70; November, 1992, p. 304.

Kirkus Reviews, July 1, 1996, p. 964.

Publishers Weekly, June 24, 1996, p. 62.

Voice of Youth Advocates, April, 1997, p. 27.

*   *   *

BRANDIS, Marianne 1938-

■ Personal

Born October 5, 1938, in Amersfoort, The Netherlands. *Education:* Attended University of British Columbia, 1956-58, and St. Francis Xavier University, 1958-59; McMaster University, B.A., 1960, M.A., 1964.

■ Addresses

Home—10 Lamport Ave., Apt. #206, Toronto, Ontario M4W 1S6, Canada.

■ Career

Canadian Broadcasting Corporation, writer of promotional material, 1964-66; Ryerson Polytechnic, Toronto, Ontario, instructor in English, 1967-89; writer. *Member:* Writers Union of Canada.

■ Awards, Honors

"Our Choice/Your Choice" book designation by the Canadian Children's Book Centre, 1982-85, for *The Tinderbox,* and 1986-89, for *The Quarter-Pie Window;* Violet Downey award, Imperial Order of the Daughters of the Empire, and Young Adult Canadian Book Award, Saskatchewan Library Association, both 1986, for *The Quarter-Pie Window;* Geoffrey Bilson Award for Historical Fiction, Canadian Children's Book Centre, 1991, for *The Sign of the Scales,* and 1996, for *Rebellion: A Novel of Upper Canada.*

■ Writings

This Spring's Sowing (novel), McClelland & Stewart, 1970.

A Sense of Dust (short story), illustrated by Gerard Brenner a Brandis, Brandstead, 1972.

The Tinderbox (novel), illustrated by Brenner a Brandis, Porcupine's Quill, 1982.

The Quarter-Pie Window (novel), illustrated by Brenner a Brandis, Porcupine's Quill, 1985.

Elizabeth, Duchess of Somerset: A Novel in Two Volumes, Porcupine's Quill, 1989.

The Sign of the Scales (novel), Porcupine's Quill, 1990.

Special Nests (novel), Netherlandic Press, 1990.

Fire Ship (novel), Porcupine's Quill, 1992.

Rebellion: A Novel of Upper Canada, illustrated by Brenner a Brandis, Porcupine's Quill, 1996.

Also contributor to *Family Circle.*

■ Sidelights

Canadian writer Marianne Brandis is noted for her ability to convincingly recreate the Canada of the early nineteenth century—particularly in and around the city of Toronto—for young readers. As Jeanette Lynes and S. R. MacGillivray noted in *Canadian Children's Literature,* "Brandis provides ... meticulous research in recreating the lives of ordinary people caught up in extraordinary historical events." In novels such as her "Emma" series—*The Tinderbox, The Quarter-Pie Window,* and *The Sign of the Scales*—Brandis gives her teen protagonists multi-layered pasts, complex personalities, and challenging problems to overcome. "I do not see myself as specifically a children's writer," she once told *Something about the Author (SATA).* "I write for adults as well and find that there is a great deal of common ground."

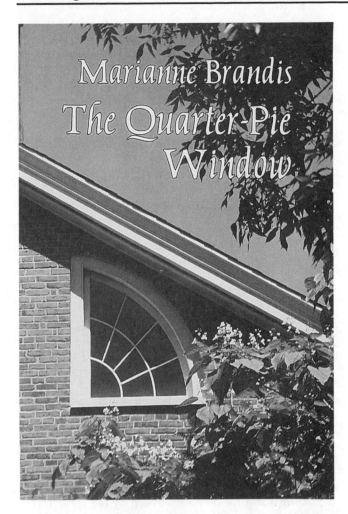

Set in the nineteenth-century city of York, now Toronto, Marianne Brandis's historical novel follows the lives of newly orphaned Emma and John, who are pressed into servitude by their guardian aunt. (Cover photo by Paul Caulfield.)

Brandis was born in The Netherlands, but moved to Canada at the close of World War II. "English is my second (though now most comfortable) language," she explained to *SATA.* "We came to Canada just before my ninth birthday, and as part of the process of learning English I read a great deal. Knowing more than one language meant that I was aware of the various ways in which different languages work; therefore I was constantly exploring alternative ways of saying things. That, I have found, is a very useful habit for a writer to have."

Brandis began writing as a way to channel her imagination. As she told *SATA,* "I began writing because I wanted to do what my favourite writers did—create imaginary worlds and explore the real one." During college she enrolled in a creative writing course; "the most important thing it taught me," Brandis recalled, "was how to read other people's books so as to learn from them. For the rest, I have learned by trial and error, and by means of useful criticism from my friends and readers."

Writing and researching her novels takes up most of Brandis's time. She admitted, "my hobbies and other activities are mostly connected with writing. I read a great deal, and most of what I read is relevant to the subjects or style of my own work. I am very interested in history; when I travel I make a point of visiting museums and historical places. For me it is impossible to distinguish 'hobby' from 'research.' My novels are concerned with the way people actually lived in the past, or with the more private side of the lives of prominent people. Wherever I go, and in whatever I read, I look for facts and insights which illuminate this."

Brandis's first novel for young adults, 1982's *The Tinderbox,* recounts the adventures of fourteen-year-old Emma Anderson and her younger brother, John, who live in the nineteenth-century city of York, now known as Toronto. The story follows the two siblings as they lose the rest of their family members in a tragic fire and have to decide what to do next. *The Tinderbox* was followed three years later by *The Quarter-Pie Window.* In this work, newly orphaned Emma and John are forced to depend on their wits and ability to survive after being taken in by their hostile guardian Aunt MacPhail, who takes advantage of her niece and nephew and uses them as servants in her hotel. Emma is initially angry about her difficult new life in which she is burdened both by the responsibility of caring for John and her mixed-up emotions regarding her parents' death. But she gradually draws upon her inner strength and compassion and is finally able both to accept her parents' failings and to take responsibility for her own situation. "The fine research and authentic flavour that characterized *The Tinderbox* are present in this work as well," Anneli Pekkonen noted of *The Quarter-Pie Window,* although adding in her *Books in Canada* review that certain characters lacked development. William Blackburn, writing in *Canadian Children's Literature,* lauded the psychological aspects of the novel, stating that Brandis "succeeds in putting meaningful adventure well within the grasp of her intended audience."

The Sign of the Scales further continues the story of Emma and John, this time following Emma—now sixteen—to her new job at a general store in town. While learning the ropes as a shopkeeper, Emma begins to suspect that not all business transacted at the store is legal. She bravely decides to confront the smuggling operation she discovers, despite consequences that might threaten a love interest. Reviewing the 1990 novel in *Canadian Children's Literature,* Diane Watson commented that while the protagonist's overly judgmental attitudes might prove off-putting to some readers, "Brandis has achieved a good balance of narrative and historical detail." Callie Israel was even more enthusiastic in her *Quill & Quire* review, maintaining that Brandis's "prose is rich with pungent descriptions and authentic details." Israel added, "Emma is a believable and engaging heroine whose feelings and actions will ring true with contemporary young adults."

Brandis returned to the early nineteenth century in 1992's *Fire Ship,* a coming-of-age novel that takes place during the War of 1812. Thirteen-year-old Daniel Dobson and his family have moved from the United States to York, Upper Canada, where the men in his family go to work helping to build a British frigate. At first excited by the possibility of going to war aboard the completed ship, the *Sir Isaac Brock,* Daniel's attitude changes after he witnesses the brutality of war first-hand by working alongside a local surgeon to treat those who are wounded in the American invasion of the city later known as the Battle of York. Praising *Fire Ship* as "a good novel," Anne Kelly added in her *Canadian Materials* review that "the issues it raises—from name calling to the realization that not all dreams come true—are real and of interest to young readers."

Brandis considers her 1996 novel, *Rebellion: A Novel of Upper Canada,* to be perhaps the most difficult book she has written because of the complexity of both its story line and character development. She also found it a challenge to seamlessly weave fact and fiction in the tale using actual men and women from history. The story centers on fourteen-year-old Adam Wheeler, an emigrant from England whose arrival in the city of Toronto coincides with the Rebellion of 1837. While noting that the small-scale rebellion has rarely been taken seriously by modern historians, Brandis explained in *Canadian Children's Literature* that "wars are always frightening to the people who live where they take place, and especially to children. However the events are assessed by later historians, to the children who endure them they are violent, incomprehensible, and terrifying, the stuff of life-long anxieties and nightmares. Developing these ideas into a novel that would work as a story and at the same time give insight into history and human lives required much research, recollection, reflection—and revision." In the course of the novel, the author unveils, through Adam's eyes, the politics of the time and contrasts the class unrest that prompted the rebellion with the situation in England during the same period. "Though he recognizes … that power resides with the rich and privileged in Upper Canada as in England, Adam nonetheless is encouraged to believe that class divisions are less strictly drawn in his new country," observed a *Canadian Children's Literature* critic. The reviewer noted that by the end of the novel Adam has expectations of "a future undreamt of in the hard land he left behind."

■ Works Cited

Blackburn, William, "Even Parents Are People" (review of *The Quarter-Pie Window*), *Canadian Children's Literature,* Volume 46, 1987, pp. 76-77.

Brandis, Marianne, "*Rebellion:* The Back of the Tapestry," *Canadian Children's Literature,* Vol. 84, 1996, pp. 80-82.

Israel, Callie, review of *The Sign of the Scales, Quill & Quire,* July, 1990, p. 38.

Kelly, Anne, review of *Fire Ship, Canadian Materials,* January, 1993, p. 15.

Lynes, Jeanette, and S. R. MacGillivray, review of *Fire Ship, Canadian Children's Literature,* Vol. 79, 1995, pp. 76-77.

Pekkonen, Anneli, review of *The Quarter-Pie Window, Books in Canada,* April, 1988, pp. 23-24.

Review of *Rebellion: A Novel of Upper Canada, Canadian Children's Literature,* Vol. 84, 1996, p. 105.

Watson, Diane, review of *The Sign of the Scales, Canadian Children's Literature,* Vol. 61, 1991, pp. 85-87.

■ For More Information See

PERIODICALS

Books in Canada, October, 1990, p. 29.
Canadian Materials, September, 1990, pp. 219-20.
Quill & Quire, December, 1992, p. 28; September, 1996, p. 74.

* * *

BRANSCUM, Robbie (Tilley) 1937-1997

OBITUARY NOTICE—See index for *SATA* sketch: Born February 17, 1937, in Big Flat, AR; died of a heart attack, May 24, 1997, in San Pablo, CA. Farmer and author of children's books. Raised in poverty on small farms in rural Arkansas, Branscum recalled her childhood in novels for children and young adults. She painted vivid word pictures using the distinctive dialogue of the Arkansas hills where she grew up, detailing stories of youngster's struggles and joys in overcoming hard times and situations. After her father died when she was four years old, Branscum and her siblings were sent to live with her strict, hardworking grandparents. Branscum's zest for reading was fed by the local library and by the surroundings in her own home, which was wallpapered in newspapers, a common practice in area homes. She dropped out of school and married at fifteen. Her writing career began when she submitted a story to a church newspaper; not only was the story accepted, the newspaper asked for more. Branscum left her husband after fifteen years of marriage to pursue her writing career. Two years later, her first novel, *Me and Jim Luke,* was published. More than twenty novels followed, many set in the backwoods of Arkansas and featuring children triumphing over adversity. Among Branscum's titles were two series of coming-of-age books. She published *Johnny May* in 1975, *The Adventures of Johnny May* in 1984, and *Johnny May Grows Up* in 1987. Another series of books was sparked by *Toby, Granny and George,* which won the Friends of American Writers Award in 1977. *Toby Alone* and *Toby and Johnny Joe* both followed in 1978. Other novels of note were the semi-autobiographical *The Girl* and Branscum's mystery *The Murder of Hound Dog Bates,* winner of the 1993 Edgar Allan Poe Award.

OBITUARIES AND OTHER SOURCES:

BOOKS

Something about the Author Autobiography Series, Volume 17, Gale, 1994, pp. 17-26.

PERIODICALS

Publishers Weekly, June 16, 1997, p. 31.

BURGESS, Melvin 1954-

■ Personal

Born April 25, 1954, in Twickenham, Surrey, England; son of Christopher (an educational writer) and Helen Burgess; married to Avis von Herder (marriage ended); married to Judith Liggett; children: Oliver von Herder, Pearl Burgess. *Politics:* Left.

■ Addresses

Home—4 Hartley St., Garby, Lancashire BB8 GNL, England.

■ Career

Writer. *Member:* Society of Authors.

■ Awards, Honors

Carnegie Medal runner-up, British Library Association, 1991, for *The Cry of the Wolf,* and 1993, for *An Angel for May;* Carnegie Medal, British Library Association, and Guardian Award for Children's Fiction, *The Guardian,* both 1997, both for *Junk.*

■ Writings

The Cry of the Wolf, Andersen (London), 1990, Tambourine Books, 1992.
Burning Issy, Andersen, 1992, Simon & Schuster, 1994.
An Angel for May, Andersen, 1992, Simon & Schuster, 1995.
The Baby and Fly Pie, Andersen, 1993, Simon & Schuster, 1996.
Loving April, Andersen, 1995.
Earth Giant, Andersen, 1995, Putnam, 1997.
Junk, Andersen, 1996.
Tiger, Tiger, Andersen, 1996.
Kite, Andersen, 1997.

■ Work in Progress

City of Light.

■ Sidelights

Melvin Burgess is the author of several novels for middle-graders and teenage readers that combine fantasy with down-to-earth stories of young protagonists attempting to cope with various problems. Beginning his career as a young adult author in 1990 with *The Cry of the Wolf,* British-born Burgess has produced a series of titles that showcase his creative and unique views on the experience of adolescence. As Burgess told *Something about the Author* (*SATA*), "My books are about anything that interests me, but they nearly all have this in common: they are life seen from the under-side, not (usually) from on top."

Taking place in Surrey, England, *The Cry of the Wolf* features a young boy who inadvertently threatens the

A hunter, determined to slaughter the last wolves in England, faces a dauntless prey in Melvin Burgess's ecological thriller. (Cover illustration by Neil Waldman.)

wolf population near his home. Ten-year-old Ben tells a stranger identified only as "the Hunter" about a wolf pack that lives in the forest nearby; the Hunter, on a mission to gain notoriety for killing the last of the wolves surviving in the wild in England, arms himself with a crossbow and hunts them down. "This is indeed a powerful first novel, and sinister too," noted a reviewer in *Junior Bookshelf.* Calling the novel "a dramatic and horrifying tale of the tragedy of extinction," Susan Oliver added in *School Library Journal* that *The Cry of the Wolf* is "an ecological thriller that will draw nature lovers and horror fans alike."

Tiger, Tiger recalls Burgess's first novel in its focus on the plight of animals. The story revolves around a Chinese businessman's attempts to use several hundred square miles in Yorkshire as a safari park featuring Siberian tigers, rare animals which are said to have magical properties. When one of the great cats—a female called Lila—escapes and encounters several children living in a nearby village, a merger between cat and human on both physical and intellectual levels is the result. "The adroit combination of fact and fantasy is expertly managed with no concession to the tenderhearted," explained a *Junior Bookshelf* critic, who also noted the story's use of the folklore of werewolves and human-to-animal shape shifting. Linda Newbery praised the work in *School Librarian,* declaring that *Tiger, Tiger* "ends with a poignant reflection on the status of wild animals in the modern world."

An Angel for May, first published in England in 1992, finds Tam, a twelve-year-old upset over his parents' recent divorce, spending a great deal of time roaming through the moors and the charred ruins of a farmhouse near his country home. On one of his rambles, Tam's chance encounter with an unusual bag lady named Rosey draws him fifty years into the past—the World War II era—where he meets a young retarded child named May. May helps the boy to put his own family situation into perspective and he, in turn, becomes an important, caring presence in her life. Calling the novel "a sad, strange little story," a *Junior Bookshelf* reviewer stated that Burgess's book "hits the right note throughout" and is written "with a restraint which is all the more moving for its quietness." Merri Monks, in a *Booklist* assessment, lauded Burgess's tale as "a story of courage, moral development, friendship, and love."

In *Burning Issy,* also a 1992 work, Burgess draws readers into the seventeenth century, depicting the life of a young orphaned woman who befriends both white and black witches. She is eventually accused of witchcraft amid an era of superstition, when witch hunters and the church persecuted herbal healers and others with supposed "magical" powers. As the story unfolds, Issy, who was badly burned as a small child, realizes that her recurrent nightmares of fire are actually recollections of almost being burned alongside her mother, a convicted witch who was burned at the stake. When she herself is imprisoned, Issy is determined to escape, whatever the cost. Helen Turner, in a review in *Voice of Youth Advocates,* called the book "a riveting exploration into some dark corners of history." *Burning Issy* was also hailed by *Horn Book* contributor Nancy Vasilakis as "a compelling story with a thoughtful message on the destructive force of superstition."

From the distant past, Burgess moves ahead to the not-so-distant future in his novel *The Baby and Fly Pie.* The book's unusual title comes from the two main characters: Fly Pie, an orphaned teen surviving on London streets as one of the scavenging "Rubbish Kids," and the infant daughter of a wealthy family that Fly Pie and his friend Sham intercept during a kidnapping attempt gone awry. When the kidnapper dies of his wounds, the teens find themselves surrogate parents and must decide whether to return infant Sylvie to her distraught parents or hold out for ransom. While some reviewers felt the novel was too bleak to interest teens, the book received high marks from several critics. A *Junior Bookshelf* commentator noted that the novel's "topical theme and its sympathetic treatment, its social message and its refusal to compromise with the harsh reality of shanty

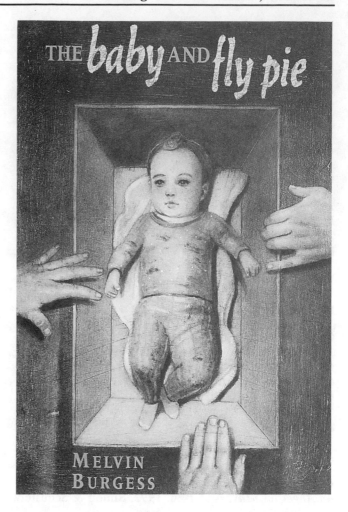

Three street kids living in a futuristic London struggle with a moral dilemma when they find a kidnapped baby whose ransom could make them instantly rich. (Cover illustration by Joseph Daniel Fiedler.)

town economy make it strong meat for early teenagers." *Booklist* contributor Anne O'Malley maintained: "The stunning characterizations, fascinating scenario, well-plotted, virtually nonstop action, and mounting suspense pull the reader right in from start to tragic end."

Winner of the 1997 Carnegie Medal and the Guardian Children's Fiction Award, *Junk* follows the story of two fourteen-year-old runaways, Tar and Gemma. Fleeing disturbing home environments, the pair find their place among the squatters in Bristol and embark on a delinquent lifestyle which eventually includes shoplifting, prostitution, and heroin addiction. Critics praised Burgess for offering without condescension an accurate depiction of teen drug abuse. Writing in *Observer,* reviewer Neil Spencer noted the "absence of adult finger-wagging" in the book. He went on to praise Burgess for leaving the book's ending open, but with "a sense of hope rather than despair" for the characters. Calling the novel "complex, multifoliate, and tremendously powerful," a contributor to *Books for Keeps* applauded the author's ability to capture the "addicts' self-deluding psychobabble," saying "the chill authenticity of their ramblings is frightening."

"I wanted to write ever since I was fourteen," Burgess told *SATA*, "and never went into adult education as I felt I'd get more from doing other things. I think to write well you need to have lived at least three different lives and been at least three different people."

■ Works Cited

Review of *An Angel for May, Junior Bookshelf,* February, 1993, pp. 26-27.
Review of *The Baby and Fly Pie, Junior Bookshelf,* April, 1994, p. 64.
Review of *The Cry of the Wolf, Junior Bookshelf,* February, 1991, pp. 29-30.
Review of *Junk, Books for Keeps,* May, 1997, p. 27.
Monks, Merri, review of *An Angel for May, Booklist,* May 1, 1995, pp. 1571-72.
Newbery, Linda, review of *Tiger, Tiger, School Librarian,* August, 1996, p. 117.
Oliver, Susan, review of *The Cry of the Wolf, School Library Journal,* September, 1992, p. 250.
O'Malley, Anne, review of *The Baby and Fly Pie, Booklist,* May 15, 1996, p. 1586.
Spencer, Neil, review of *Junk, Observer,* March 30, 1997, p. 17.
Review of *Tiger, Tiger, Junior Bookshelf,* August, 1996, pp. 153-54.
Turner, Helen, review of *Burning Issy, Voice of Youth Advocates,* April, 1995, pp. 19-20.
Vasilakis, Nancy, review of *Burning Issy, Horn Book,* March-April, 1995, p. 193.

■ For More Information See

PERIODICALS

Booklist, October 15, 1992, p. 428.
Bulletin of the Center for Children's Books, July, 1995, pp. 378-79; May, 1996, pp. 294-95.
Junior Bookshelf, June, 1992, pp. 117-18; August, 1995, pp. 142-43; August, 1996, p. 146.
Kirkus Reviews, October 15, 1992, p. 1307; October 1, 1997, p. 1529.
School Librarian, November, 1992, pp. 156-57; May, 1993, p. 59.
School Library Journal, December, 1994, p. 106; June, 1995, p. 108.
Voice of Youth Advocates, August, 1996, p. 154.

*   *   *

BURNS, Marilyn 1941-

■ Personal

Born 1941.

■ Addresses

Home—Sausalito, CA.

■ Career

Writer and educator.

■ Awards, Honors

Outstanding Science Books for Children award, National Science Teachers Association/Children's Book Council, 1975, for *The I Hate Mathematics! Book.*

■ Writings

NONFICTION; FOR CHILDREN

The Hanukkah Book, illustrated by Mary Weston, Four Winds, 1981.
The Hink Pink Book: Or, What Do You Call a Magician's Extra Bunny?, illustrated by Weston, Little, Brown, 1981.
The $1.00 Word Riddle Book, illustrated by Weston, Math Solutions, 1990.
How Many Feet? How Many Tails? A Book of Math Riddles, illustrated by Lynn Adams, Scholastic, 1996.

Designer of math activities for "Hello Math Reader" series, Scholastic, 1997—.

NONFICTION; "BROWN PAPER SCHOOL" SERIES

The I Hate Mathematics! Book, Little, Brown, 1975.
The Book of Think: Or, How to Solve a Problem Twice Your Size, Little, Brown, 1976.
I Am Not a Short Adult! Getting Good at Being a Kid, Little, Brown, 1977.
Good for Me! All about Food in 32 Bites, Little, Brown, 1978.
This Book Is about Time, Little, Brown, 1978.
Math for Smarty Pants: Or, Who Says Mathematicians Have Little Pig Eyes, Little, Brown, 1982.

FICTION; FOR CHILDREN

The Greedy Triangle, illustrated by Gordon Silveria, Scholastic, 1994.
Spaghetti and Meatballs, illustrated by Debbie Tilley, Scholastic, 1997.

NONFICTION; FOR ADULTS

A Collection of Math Lessons: Grades 3-6, Math Solutions, 1987.
(With Bonnie Tank) *A Collection of Math Lessons: Grades 1-3,* Math Solutions, 1988.
(With Cathy Humphreys) *A Collection of Math Lessons: Grades 6-8,* Math Solutions, 1990.
Math by All Means: Multiplication, Grade 3, Math Solutions, 1991.
About Teaching Mathematics: A K-8 Resource, Marilyn Burns Education Associates (Sausalito), 1992.
Math and Literature: K-3, Math Solutions, 1992.
Writing in Math Class: A Resource for Grades 2-8, Math Solutions, 1995.
Fifty Problem-solving Lessons, Addison Wesley, 1995.

■ Sidelights

Author and math teacher Marilyn Burns is noted for her many books that instill an interest and enthusiasm for the world of numbers into her school-age readers. In addition to such works as *The I Hate Mathematics!*

Still, the triangle's favorite thing was to slip into place when people put their hands on their hips. "That way I always hear the latest news," it said, "which I can tell my friends."

Introducing math concepts in an entertaining fashion, Marilyn Burns takes a dissatisfied triangle through a variety of geometric metamorphoses in her instructional picture book. (From *The Greedy Triangle,* illustrated by Gordon Silveria.)

Book, which was published as part of the "Brown Paper School" series, and *The Greedy Triangle,* Burns has also produced a number of teaching guides for math instructors in the elementary grades, all based on the concept of teaching math as a subject that is part of students' daily lives rather than an abstract concept.

The I Hate Mathematics! Book, with section titles that include "Infinity Is Not in Vermont" and "Fathead," has a direct appeal to the non-math student. A humorously illustrated selection of riddles, brain teasers, and other puzzles involving number calculations based on real-life examples are included in a mix that *Horn Book* reviewer Mary M. Burns dubbed "educationally sound and exciting."

From mathematics fun, the "Brown Paper School" series extends to other concerns of the elementary-age set. In *I Am Not a Short Adult! Getting Good at Being a Kid,* youngsters can learn through statistics, questions, and other relevant information that they are a lot like other kids. Burns also provides her young readers with an understanding of the history of "childhood," as well as an overview of the legal aspects of being underage. Straightforward experiments and tests readers can give themselves provide young readers with "some new insights into why the world is the way it is," stated Ann A. Flowers in a *Horn Book* review. *This Book Is about Time,* published in 1978, includes activities like how to

make a sundial as it discusses clocks, timepieces, and the way humans have marked the passage of time throughout history. And in *Good for Me! All about Food in 32 Bites,* Burns uses interesting facts, quizzes, cartoon dialogue, and hands-on projects to present a guide to nutrition that highlights how foods are made and how they fuel the body. A *Booklist* reviewer praised *Good for Me!* as an "upbeat, informative book."

The Greedy Triangle, a work of math-related fiction, is an enthusiastic, playful look at the world of geometric shapes for young students. Through the antics of the title character, a spunky triangle with beady black eyes and a mischievous grin, the book shows how the world is full of geometry. The Greedy Triangle has many jobs in the book, such as "holding up roofs, supporting bridges, making music in a symphony orchestra, catching the wind for sailboats." After turning itself into a slice of pie, or resting in the crook of the elbow of someone standing with their hands on their hips, the Greedy Triangle, true to its name, decides to become a "shape shifter" and grow a few more angles. It becomes a quadrilateral and shadows a television screen and a book page; from there, it continues to sprout more

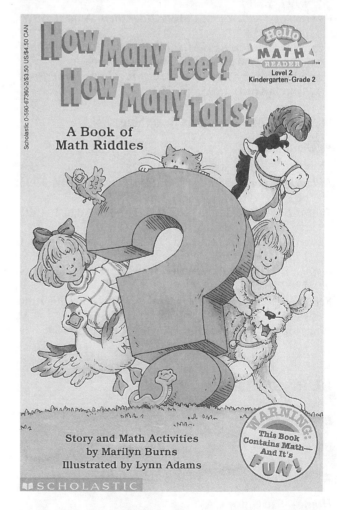

This collection of riddles centers on two children who, while walking with their grandfather, must use math skills to solve puzzles about animals. (Cover illustration by Lynn Adams.)

angles, changing into a pentagon, then a hexagon, a septagon, and so on. Soon it has so many angles that it has become almost round, and the Greedy Triangle decides that being a triangle was work enough and returns to its original three-sided, three-angled form. While Susan Dove Lempke, a reviewer in *The Bulletin of the Center for Children's Books*, maintained that the triangle's changing shapes "surely will make children wonder what happened to all of the things that were triangle-shaped after the triangle became a quadrilateral," a *Publishers Weekly* reviewer noted that readers "come away from [*The Greedy Triangle*] noticing and naming the shapes of the objects around them."

In addition to her mathematics-based books, Burns has also written a history of Hanukkah, which is designed to enable Jewish children to learn about their own history and become more comfortable dealing with questions that highlight their cultural differences. Beginning with a short history of the holiday starting during the reign of Alexander the Great of Macedonia, *The Hanukkah Book* then focuses on the ways that the holiday is now celebrated around the world. Recipes for holiday foods, including potato latkes, are included alongside descriptions of holiday prayers, games, songs, crafts, and other traditional activities. Of special interest is the book's final section, where Burns focuses on the feelings of not "fitting in" that Jewish children sometimes experience when facing the inevitable question, "What did you get for Christmas?" In a review of the volume in the *Bulletin of the Center for Children's Books*, Zena Sutherland noted that while *The Hanukkah Book* "is capably organized," it may attempt to cover too much information. *School Library Journal* critic Jean Hammond

Zimmerman was more enthusiastic about the book, declaring, "If you can only buy one Hanukkah book, this should be it."

■ Works Cited

Burns, Marilyn, *The Greedy Triangle*, Scholastic, 1994.

Burns, Mary M., review of *The I Hate Mathematics! Book, Horn Book,* April 1976, p. 177.

Flowers, Ann A., review of *I Am Not a Short Adult! Getting Good at Being a Kid, Horn Book,* April, 1978, p. 175.

Review of *Good for Me! All about Food in 32 Bites, Booklist,* November 15, 1978, pp. 542-43.

Review of *The Greedy Triangle, Publishers Weekly,* January 2, 1995, p. 77.

Lempke, Susan Dove, review of *The Greedy Triangle, Bulletin of the Center for Children's Books,* March, 1995, p. 230.

Sutherland, Zena, review of *The Hanukkah Book, Bulletin of the Center for Children's Books,* December, 1981, pp. 64-65.

Zimmerman, Jean Hammond, review of *The Hanukkah Book, School Library Journal,* October, 1981, p. 157.

■ For More Information See

PERIODICALS

Booklist, October 15, 1975, p. 297.

Horn Book, February, 1979, p. 76.

Kirkus Reviews, October 15, 1977, p. 1099; January 1, 1979, p. 8; October 15, 1981, p. 1297.

School Library Journal, February, 1979, p. 53.

C

MARIE D. CALDER

CALDER, Marie D(onais) 1948-

■ Personal

Born January 6, 1948, in Antler, Saskatchewan, Canada; daughter of Edmond Joseph Donais (a farm implement dealer) and Frances Louise (a cook; maiden name, Peters) Donais Muldoon; married Darcy Ronald Calder (a retailer and landlord), October 21, 1967; children: Nicole, Chantelle, Kari-Lynn. *Education:* University of Regina, B.Ed., 1980. *Hobbies and other interests:* Travel, gardening, reading, spending time with family.

■ Addresses

Home—413 Maple Bay, Estevan, Saskatchewan, Canada S4A 2E6.

■ Career

Teacher at elementary and junior high schools in Prince Albert, Saskatchewan, 1971-74; kindergarten teacher at schools in Thompson, Manitoba, 1976-78, and Estevan, Saskatchewan, 1978-80; Estevan Rural Schools, Estevan, teacher of kindergarten and French, 1980—. Workshop leader. *Member:* Estevan Toastmasters Club, Estevan Writers Club, Saskatchewan Early Childhood Association.

■ Awards, Honors

Competent Toastmaster Award, Toastmasters International, 1997.

■ Writings

Humpty Dumpty Is a Friend of Mine, Winston-Derek (Nashville, TN), 1997.

Also author of a parent/caregiver's resource package and a teacher's resource package for *Humpty Dumpty Is a Friend of Mine,* both published by Nicharitay Publications (Estevan, SK), 1997.

■ Work in Progress

Little Miss Muffet Isn't Frightened Anymore; Jack and Jill and the Block Parent Sign; One Little Ladybug Going for a Snack; In My Apple House; and a series about Evelyn, including *Friends for Mandy Dandelion, Evelyn's Carrot,* and *Evelyn's Allergy.*

■ Sidelights

Marie D. Calder told *SATA:* "My early years were full of experiences that nurtured my imagination. My family lived in a tiny village, Tilston, Manitoba, Canada, where the great outdoors provided our playground even in the dead of winter. In the summer we learned to cooperate as we built our playhouses with old blankets and sheets supplied by our parents. Everyone contributed what they could to the playhouse so that it was completely furnished. We found the challenges we sought as we climbed the highest trees and explored the local ponds for the biggest frogs (I was so proud when my older brother Ed was proclaimed the best frog collector—he could ride his bike with no hands too!). Winter brought new challenges as the temperature plummeted far below zero. We were not to be deterred by old man winter, however, as we played soccer in the snow and skated at the local rink. Jam-can curling was another event that kept us busy in those wonderful years. Springtime was trumpeted in with the sightings of crocuses in the pastures. We readied ourselves for the track-and-field meets at which our village fared well. Tilston provided me with the richest childhood a person could ask for.

"My parents were always patient and supportive. My mother taught me the intricacies of mathematical computations at the kitchen table as she peeled potatoes. I was a preschooler so she gave me toothpicks to manipulate and had me find answers to endless mathematical equations. I loved this activity. My father, I'm sure, gritted his teeth with revulsion when I proudly set a cake I baked for him at his place at the supper table. He was not a man for desserts so my cakes, with their bright turquoise and/or purple icings, must have been quite a test for his palate! He did not waiver in his praise and, as far as I know, he ate the generous portions I served up for him.

"My parents taught me that I could do most anything I set my mind to. My father had such faith in my abilities that he invited me to assist him with his office duties at his implement dealership. I was only eleven years old that summer but I answered the phones and worked on the business books. I was such a proud little girl when I spent time in my dad's office. I was not made to work. I could go in whenever I wanted. It was like another opportunity to role play and I learned how valuable I was to my dad.

"Summer Saturday evenings were often spent on our wrap-around veranda as my sister Joan, myself, and our friends performed concerts for my parents. We thought we were the best singers in the world in those preteen years. Our parents were a captive and enthusiastic audience. Winter Saturday evenings were spent watching Hockey Night in Canada. Dad would give my little sister and me a quarter and off we would go to the local cafe. We'd buy licorice plugs for Dad and whatever else we wanted for ourselves. A quarter went a long way in the 1950s.

"My childhood was comfortable and filled with love—until my father died in a car accident. I was only eleven years old, but my childhood had come to an abrupt end. Gone was the carefree nature of my existence. It had been replaced by a world full of despair and anxiety. My

writing reflected this change as I moved from silly limericks to expressing my grief. I was not even aware that I was writing until many years later, when one of my kindergarten students, Taylor Hanson, was diagnosed with cancer. The next month one of my young colleagues was diagnosed with leukemia. Two months later my step-dad died of cancer. This combination was almost too much for me to handle. My writing began in earnest as I relived the horror of my father's death through these devastating experiences. I am an author because of my mom, my dad, and Taylor. All three, each in their own way, led me into this wonderful world of authorship.

"I believe that the reason I write for children is twofold. First, I teach kindergarten, and I often want to teach a certain concept. My imagination usually comes to my rescue, and a new story is born. Second, when I was a child, books were scarce. I was reading the Dick and Jane books before I started school and thirsted for more literature. Our tiny school had a library to match its size. I had read all of the books in our classroom within a few weeks of beginning school. We had no access to a public library so I grew up with a hunger for literature. My parents gave me the book *Little Women* for Christmas when I was nine years old. I read and re-read that book until it fairly fell apart. I have made certain that my three daughters grew up with books galore and that they were read to every day of their childhood. My parents would have done the same for me, had it been possible.

"Our daughters and my students have taught me more about children than any university could hope to do. I have published two resource books to accompany my children's picture book, *Humpty Dumpty Is a Friend of Mine.* One resource book is for early childhood teachers. It is designed to accommodate the varying levels of readiness and abilities of the children within our classrooms. It is a complete and integrated package based on the nursery rhyme character Humpty Dumpty. The theme focuses on friendship and on the concept of eggs. It is designed for the busy classroom teacher so that he or she can concentrate on the *teaching* of a theme, rather than the planning for it. The second resource package is for parents and caregivers. The activities in it guide the facilitator through the stages from birth to age seven. Since fifty percent of a child's learning is said to take place by the age of four, I believe that the caregivers of preschool children will find this resource helpful in enhancing their children's optimal early learning experiences."

* * *

CAPEK, Michael 1947-

■ Personal

Born September 19, 1947, in Covington, KY; son of Harold (in business) and Naomi (Larken) Capek; married Terri Richardson (a teacher), June 14, 1969; children: Christopher, Kari Jo. *Education:* Cumberland

College, B.A., 1969; Eastern Kentucky University, M.A., 1976. *Hobbies and other interests:* Photography, nature.

■ **Addresses**

Home—5965 Tipp Dr., Taylor Mill, KY 41015.

■ **Career**

Walton-Verona High School, Walton, KY, teacher of English, 1969—. *Member:* Society of Children's Book Writers and Illustrators.

■ **Awards, Honors**

Merit Honor Award, Society of Children's Book Writers and Illustrators, 1993, for the article "Artistic Trickery," which appeared in *Cricket* magazine.

■ **Writings**

Artistic Trickery: The Trompe L'Oeil Tradition (nonfiction), Lerner Publications, 1995.
Murals: Cave, Cathedral, to Street (nonfiction), Lerner Publications, 1996.

Contributor to *Heath Middle Level Literature: Grade 8,* D.C. Heath, 1994, and other textbooks. Contributor of numerous stories and articles to periodicals, including *Highlights for Children, Ranger Rick, Short Story Digest, Images, Cricket,* and *Adventure;* contributor of devotionals to *Encounter!* and *Essential Connection.*

■ **Work in Progress**

A young adult biography of cartoonist/animator Winsor McCay; nonfiction titles on Jamaica and sculpture.

■ **Sidelights**

Retired teacher and author Michael Capek has contributed numerous stories, poems, devotionals, and articles to children's magazines. In addition, he has issued two books, *Artistic Trickery: The Trompe L'Oeil Tradition* and *Murals: Cave, Cathedral, to Street,* both of which educate his readers about art styles and history.

Capek's first book, *Artistic Trickery,* written for readers aged ten and above, is an overview of the decorative art style known as *trompe l'oeil* ("fool the eye") and of the artists who created it, from the Roman Empire to the present day. *Trompe l'oeil* is a technique that artists employ to achieve a result that is so realistic that it appears to be the actual subject depicted, or a photograph of it, rather than a painting. As Capek's title implies, many *trompe l'oeil* artists have used their talents to create visual tricks that amuse and fool the eye. Capek's volume includes reproductions of *trompe l'oeil* art, profiles of many artists in the tradition, and chapters devoted to common subjects of this type of artwork, including food, doors, people, and money. *Artistic Trickery* was generally well-received by critics,

MICHAEL CAPEK

among them a *Publishers Weekly* reviewer who praised Capek's "clear, comprehensive text." The reviewer remarked that in this book "one of the more oddball traditions in art gets a well-deserved spotlight." Julie Yates Walton of *Booklist* lauded Capek for writing so "engagingly" and "appreciatively of his subject."

Similarly, *Murals: Cave, Cathedral, to Street* is, according to Carolyn Phelan of *Booklist,* an "informative history" of an art form that dates as far back as prehistorical man. Capek begins by discussing modern-day murals that can be found on buildings, and works backward to explore the important muralists of the 1930s and 1940s, classical works such as Leonardo da Vinci's *The Last Supper,* and the prehistoric cave paintings that have been found in France. By providing information on how artistic styles have changed over the years, Capek has written a book that serves as "a good starting point for the student who want to learn more about art," Jeanne M. McGlinn noted in *Voice of Youth Advocates.*

Capek once commented: "What authors inspire and influence me? All of them. I've never read anything in my life that did not change me in some way. Skilled wordsmiths—Thoreau, St. Paul, Steinbeck, Keats, and many others—always dismantle and reconstruct my thinking every time I read them. Even insipid or stupid writers show me what not to do.

"My main motivation in writing for children is always to excite and influence readers' thinking in some way, the way I was aroused and influenced as a child by the books I read—and I read *everything,* trash and treasure, while I was growing up. Invariably, when I write, it's for the child-self that hides deep inside me. It's hard to please that child and even harder to move him. He's incredibly innocent, but brutally honest. And unless I'm quick about it, I'll lose him. He's got better things to do than listen to some windbag of an adult ramble on. If I can make him laugh or make him think or make him care, I've succeeded. My entire writing life is dedicated to pleasing that child.

"I've always written a lot of fiction, but for sheer challenge there's nothing like nonfiction. I love it—to paraphrase John F. Kennedy—not because it's easy, but because it's hard to do well. Besides, often fact is stranger and infinitely more fascinating than fiction anyway. To write nonfiction that compels like fiction, that's a noble goal, in my opinion.

"I cannot imagine ever having a research assistant. Perhaps I'll change my mind someday, but I adore research, positively dote on it. After all, one of the reasons I became a writer was the sensuous appeal of books: smelling them, touching them, hefting them onto my lap. Intoxicating! If I couldn't go to the library, get lost in the stacks for hours, I'd feel bereft. Much of my passion for writing derives from the burning lust I have to lay hands on bound volumes. Why should I pay someone else to have all the fun?

"By nature I am a teacher. I've done it for nearly thirty years, professionally, in one rural public high school. Even before I started getting paid for it, though, I was a teacher. I used to teach kids in the neighborhood where I grew up how to do all sorts of things—play basketball, find fossils, fish, whittle, spit, fight, whistle. You name it. So many people I knew as kids, when they see me, still preface conversations with, 'Do you remember the time you taught me...?' Usually, I don't remember. There were too many of them. I do know, though, that this need to instruct, which I've always felt, is directly related to why I write."

■ Works Cited

Review of *Artistic Trickery: The Trompe L'Oeil Tradition*, *Publishers Weekly*, May 8, 1995, p. 298.
McClinn, Jeanne M., review of *Murals: Cave, Cathedral, to Street*, *Voice of Youth Advocates*, October, 1996, pp. 226-27.
Phelan, Carolyn, review of *Murals: Cave, Cathedral, to Street*, *Booklist*, June 1 and 15, 1996, p. 1687.
Walton, Julie Yates, review of *Artistic Trickery: The Trompe L'Oeil Tradition*, *Booklist*, June 1 and 15, 1995, p. 1758.

■ For More Information See

PERIODICALS
Bulletin of the Center for Children's Books, July-August, 1995, p. 379.
Kirkus Reviews, April 1, 1996, p. 527.
School Library Journal, July, 1995, p. 84; October, 1996, p. 154.

Scientific American, December, 1996, p. 120.

* * *

CAPUCINE
See MAZILLE, Capucine

* * *

CARTLIDGE, Michelle 1950-

■ Personal

Born October 13, 1950, in London, England; daughter of Haydn Derrick (director of transportation) and Barbara (a gallery director; maiden name, Feistmann) Cartlidge; married Richard Cook (an artist), June 25, 1982 (divorced, 1994); children: Theo. *Education:* Attended Hornsey College of Art, 1967-68, and Royal College of Art, 1968-70. *Hobbies and other interests:* Travel abroad.

■ Addresses

Agent—Laura Cecil, 17 Alwyne Villas, London N1 2HG, England.

■ Career

Artist, 1970—; writer and illustrator of books for children, 1978—. *Member:* Society of Authors.

■ Awards, Honors

Mother Goose Award, Books for Your Children Booksellers, 1979, for *Pippin and Pod.*

■ Writings

MOUSE BOOKS; SELF-ILLUSTRATED

Pippin and Pod, Pantheon, Heinemann, 1978.
A Mouse's Diary, Lothrop, 1981, Dutton, 1994.
Mousework, Heinemann, 1982.
Welcome to Mouseville, Methuen, 1982.
Baby Mouse, Heinemann, 1984, Penguin, 1986.
Mouse's Christmas Tree, Penguin, 1985.
Little Mouse Makes a Garden, Walker, 1986.
Little Mouse Makes a Mobile, Walker, 1986.
Little Mouse Makes Cards, Walker, 1986.
Little Mouse Makes Sweets, Walker, 1986.
A House for Lily Mouse, Prentice-Hall, 1986, Methuen, 1987.
Mouse House, Dutton, Campbell, 1990.
Baby Mice, Heinemann, 1991.
Clock Mice, Campbell, 1991.
Mouse in the House, Dutton, 1991.
Mouse Time, Dutton, 1991.
Mouse's Christmas House: A Story/Activity Book, Andrews and McMeel, 1991.
Mouse Theater, Dutton, 1992, published in England as *Theatre Mice*, Campbell, 1992.
Baby Mice at Home, Dutton, 1992.

Mouse Letters, Dutton, 1993.

The Mouse Wedding: A Press-Out Model Book, Andrew and McMeel, 1993.

Mouse Birthday, Dutton, 1994, published in England as *Birthday Mouse,* Campbell, 1994.

Mouse's Scrapbook, Dutton, Campbell, 1995.

Mouse Christmas, Dutton, Campbell, 1996.

Mouse Magic, Dutton, 1996, published in England as *Magic Mouse,* Campbell, 1996.

The Mice of Mousehole: A Movable Picture Book, Candlewick Press, 1997, Walker, 1997.

School Mouse, Campbell, 1997.

BEAR AND TEDDY BOOKS; SELF-ILLUSTRATED

The Bears' Bazaar: A Story-craft Book, Lothrop, Heinemann, 1979.

Teddy Trucks, Lothrop, Heinemann, 1981.

Dressing Teddy (cut-out book), Heinemann, 1983, Penguin, 1986.

Teddy's Holiday, Heinemann, 1984.

Teddy's Birthday Party, Penguin, 1985.

Bear's Room: No Peeping, Methuen, 1985.

Teddy's Dinner, Simon & Schuster, 1986.

Teddy's Garden, Simon & Schuster, 1986.

Teddy's House, Simon & Schuster, 1986.

Teddy's Toys, Simon & Schuster, 1986.

Teddy's Christmas, Simon & Schuster, Walker, 1986.

Hello, Teddy, Heinemann, 1991.

Bear in the Forest, Dutton, 1991.

Bears on the Go, Dutton, 1992.

Good Night, Teddy, Candlewick Press, Walker, 1992.

Teddy's Friends, Walker, Candlewick Press, 1992.

Teddy's Cat, Walker, Candlewick Press, 1996.

BUNNY BOOKS; SELF-ILLUSTRATED

Playground Bunnies, Walker Books, 1987.

Seaside Bunnies, Walker Books, 1987.

Toy Shop Bunnies, Walker Books, 1987.

Birthday Bunnies, Walker Books, 1987.

Little Bunny's Picnic, Dutton, 1990.

Bunny's Birthday, Dutton, 1992.

OTHER; SELF-ILLUSTRATED

Little Boxes (cut-out book), Heinemann, 1983.

Munch and Mixer's Puppet Show: Presenting the Magic Lollipop, Prentice-Hall, Heinemann, 1983.

Little Shops, Heinemann, 1985.

Gerry's Seaside Journey, Heinemann, 1988.

Rabbit's Party, Heinemann, 1991.

Duck in the Pond, Dutton, 1991.

Elephant in the Jungle, Dutton, 1991.

Doggy Days, Heinemann, 1991, Dutton, 1992.

The Cats That Went to the Sea, PictureLions, 1992.

Fairy Letters, Campbell, 1993.

Michelle Cartlidge's Book of Words, Dutton, 1994.

OTHER; ILLUSTRATED BY KIM RAYMOND AND RUTH BLAIR

Bella's Birthday Party, Heinemann, 1994.

Boss Bear's Boat, Heinemann, 1994.

Gerry Kicks Off, Heinemann, 1994.

Gerry's Big Nose, Heinemann, 1994.

Some of Cartlidge's works have been translated and published in Spanish, Japanese, French, German, Portuguese, and Welsh.

■ **Sidelights**

When her first book, *Pippin and Pod,* was published in 1978, Michelle Cartlidge was honored with the Mother Goose Award as the "most exciting newcomer to children's book illustration." Since that time, Cartlidge has created a number of picture books featuring anthropomorphized mice, bears, and bunnies that wear clothes, live in houses, and do the everyday things real children do. Cartlidge's books usually contain few words; they are known for her finely-detailed, delicate line drawings and warm pastel watercolors. While some critics have described her characters as static or have complained that it is difficult to tell them apart, many are charmed by the simple plots and cuddly animals Cartlidge portrays.

Cartlidge told *Something about the Author* (*SATA*) that she began her career as an artist at an early age. She was just fourteen when she left school to work in a pottery studio. Later, Cartlidge studied pottery at the Hornsey School of Art and then the Royal College of Art. When she was twenty years old, she decided that her pottery "was becoming so fragile that I was the only person who could touch it with safety." Cartlidge began to devote her efforts to drawing. "To support myself, I did odd jobs, waitressing and washing up, but had the opportu-

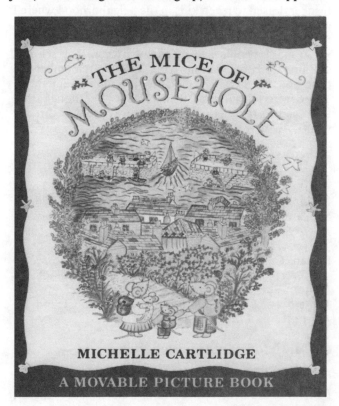

Flaps and tabs allow the reader to explore every corner of Cartlidge's highly detailed Cornish village of mice inhabitants.

nity to show publisher and illustrator Jan Pienkowski a selection of cards I'd produced for my family and friends. This resulted in a commission to design a series of cards for Gallery Five."

Cartlidge's *Pippin and Pod,* featuring "dainty line and watercolor" illustrations according to a *Kirkus Reviews* critic, was published in 1978. Set in Cartlidge's childhood neighborhood of Hampstead, London, the book follows the afternoon adventures of two mice. While their mother shops, the brothers wander through a colorfully rendered market, construction site, playground, and park. Then, as a critic for *Publishers Weekly* noted, the "wee mice suddenly realize they're lost and want to go home." The mice finally find their mother and all ends well. Barbara Elleman of *Booklist* complemented Cartlidge's illustrations in the book, stating that the pictures give "a warm feeling to this simply told tale."

The Bears' Bazaar, Cartlidge's next book, presents craft ideas and instructions within a tale about a bear sister and brother. Together with their parents, they make a mobile, painted paperweights, paper dolls, gingerbread bears, and mustard men. Then they take their completed project to school, which, Cartlidge told *SATA,* she modeled after her own primary school. The book comes complete with directions in an appendix. A *Publishers Weekly* reviewer lauded the book as "a buoyant story with ideas for projects that can involve the whole family." Although a *Junior Bookshelf* critic voiced some concerns about the presentation of the projects, the reviewer described the overall work as "attractive, with seemingly inexhaustible detail." Writing in *Growing Point,* Margery Fisher called *The Bears' Bazaar* "the most attractive craft-book of last year."

After *The Bears' Bazaar,* Cartlidge continued to produce books about tiny mice or soft-looking bears, all with simple plots or scenes. *A Mouse's Diary* features a mouse girl who writes in her diary about such activities as going to the park, to ballet class, and on a nature walk. As a *Junior Bookshelf* critic observed, the mousegirl's life is very human; that is, she lives like "a small girl." Yet the mouse-girl's house, and all her things, from ballet slippers to books, are tiny. A critic for *Growing Point* appreciated how Cartlidge rendered fully detailed scenes with "bright paint and a strong sense of composition." In a *Publishers Weekly* assessment of the book, a commentator stated that the story "rolls along effortlessly."

Cartlidge combined her fictional realms of bears and mice in *Bear's Room: No Peeping.* While Bear is busy working in the kitchen, bedroom, workroom, and bathroom, the mice do their best to spy on him. Readers, of course, are let in on the secret of bear's activities. In "crowded strip pictures," as a *Junior Bookshelf* critic described them, Cartlidge portrayed the large, dressed bear preparing treats, painting a mural in his room, and then taking a bath. At the end of the story, Bear invites the mice into his room for a party, and they take delight in the seesaw he has crafted for them.

Award-winning illustrator Michelle Cartlidge created this movable book with pull-tabs that enable the magician mouse to perform tricks.

Cartlidge told *SATA* that she does her "best to create a world that a child will recognize, the kind of book he or she can step into to mingle with the characters portrayed." Throughout her career, Cartlidge has created picture books which provide activities, see-through windows, or movable parts, so that children "who have enjoyed reading about" her "characters can meet them again in active play." *Little Bunny's Picnic,* for example, has windows on every other page that give children a peek at the next scene. Liza Bliss of *School Library Journal* described this as "a fun gimmick." *Mouse Birthday, Mouse Time, Mouse Theater, Mouse's Scrapbook,* and *Mouse Letters* are movable books; in the latter two books, attached envelopes contain letters and mementos relating to the story. For her younger fans, Cartlidge creates board books with watercolor teddy bears engaged in daily activities, from playing to eating lunch. While these books, which include *Teddy's Friends, Teddy's House, Teddy's Toys, Teddy's Garden,* and *Teddy's Dinner,* do not move, according to *School Library Journal* contributor Linda Wicher in a review of *Teddy's Friends,* they are "easy for young hands to hold."

Michelle Cartlidge's Book of Words, published in 1994, features a watercolor-rendered mouse family in a number of detailed everyday scenes on double-page spreads. As the mice get dressed, go to school, go grocery shopping, visit the playground and have fun at a birthday party, Cartlidge presents over 300 common words young children and beginning readers may want to see or hear. A *Kirkus Reviews* critic questioned the "conventional picture of mouse family life portrayed" in the book, and noted that the female mice were placed in some stereotypical female roles. Similarly, Patricia Pearl Dole of *School Library Journal* pointed out that the female characters were all in dresses, but observed that chores were "shared by both sexes."

Cartlidge once explained to *SATA* how she goes about creating her books. "When planning a book, I like to decide on a location, do lots of sketches, and develop the story from them. The amount of detail I include appeals to children, and Theo, my small son, takes a lively and useful interest in my work. I find him a most useful critic."

■ Works Cited

"Animal Postures," *Growing Point,* November, 1981, p. 3960.

Review of *The Bears' Bazaar, Junior Bookshelf,* June, 1980, p. 114.

Review of *The Bears' Bazaar, Publishers Weekly,* March 28, 1980, p. 49.

Review of *Bear's Room: No Peeping, Junior Bookshelf,* October, 1985, p. 211.

Bliss, Liza, review of *Little Bunny's Picnic, School Library Journal,* August, 1990, p. 126.

Dole, Patricia Pearl, review of *Michelle Cartlidge's Book of Words, School Library Journal,* January, 1995, pp. 82-83.

Elleman, Barbara, review of *Pippin and Pod, Booklist,* October 1, 1978, pp. 290-91.

Fisher, Margery, review of *The Bears' Bazaar, Growing Point,* May, 1980, p. 3704.

Review of *Michelle Cartlidge's Book of Words, Kirkus Reviews,* November 15, 1994, p. 1524.

Review of *A Mouse's Diary, Junior Bookshelf,* April, 1982.

Review of *A Mouse's Diary, Publishers Weekly,* July 16, 1982, p. 78.

Review of *Pippin and Pod, Kirkus Reviews,* October 1, 1978, p. 1065.

Review of *Pippin and Pod, Publishers Weekly,* September 25, 1978, p. 141.

Wicher, Linda, review of *Teddy's Friends, School Library Journal,* October, 1992, p. 85.

■ For More Information See

PERIODICALS

Growing Point, March, 1983, p. 4046.
Horn Book Guide, fall, 1994, p. 267.
Publishers Weekly, October 28, 1983, p. 70.
School Library Journal, April, 1982, p. 56.

*　　　*　　　*

CHOCOLATE, Debbi 1954-
(Deborah M. Newton Chocolate)

■ Personal

Born January 25, 1954, in Chicago, IL; daughter of Steve (a mailman) and Alma L. (Robinson) Newton; married Robert Chocolate, Sr. (an accountant) December 31, 1980; children: Robert Jr., Allen Whitney. *Education:* Spelman College, B.A., 1976; Brown Univer-

DEBBI CHOCOLATE

sity, M.A., 1978. Currently attending the School of the Art Institute of Chicago on scholarship. *Religion:* Baptist. *Hobbies and other interests:* Reading, traveling, playing basketball, collecting baseball cards, writing for children.

■ Addresses

Agent—Jane Jordan Browne, 410 South Michigan Ave., Suite 724, Chicago, IL 60605.

■ Career

Writer. Riverside Publishing Company, Chicago, IL, editor, 1978-90; Triton College, River Grove, IL, English instructor, 1990-92. Oak Park Public Schools, writing workshop leader at Youth Author's Conference, 1985-95; AYA African Arts Festival, storyteller, 1990 and 1991. Affiliated with Illinois Young Author's Conference hosted by the Illinois State Board of Education, 1992, 1995, and 1997. *Member:* Children's Reading Roundtable of Chicago.

■ Awards, Honors

Reader's Digest Journalism Scholar, 1975; creative writing fellow from Brown University, 1976-78; Smith Scholar from the School of the Art Institute of Chicago, 1990-97; grant from City of Chicago Cultural Arts, 1991 and 1992; Parent's Choice Award, for *Talk, Talk: An Ashanti Legend;* Notable Book selection, Children's Book Council, for *On the Day I Was Born;* Pick of the Lists, American Booksellers Association, for *Imani in the Belly;* Book of the Month Club selections for *My*

First Kwanzaa Book, A Very Special Kwanzaa, and *Kente Colors;* Top 100 Books, *Booklist,* for *NEATE to the Rescue!*

■ Writings

NEATE to the Rescue!, illustrated by Melodye Rosales, Just Us Books (East Orange, NJ), 1992.
Elizabeth's Wish, Just Us Books, 1994.
On the Day I Was Born, illustrated by Melodye Rosales, Scholastic, 1995.
A Very Special Kwanzaa, Scholastic, 1996.
Kente Colors, illustrated by John Ward, Walker, 1996.
The Piano Man, illustrated by Eric Velasquez, Walker, 1998.

UNDER NAME DEBORAH M. NEWTON CHOCOLATE

Kwanzaa, illustrated by Melodye Rosales, Children's Press, 1990.
My First Kwanzaa Book, illustrated by Cal Massey, Scholastic, 1992.
Spider and the Sky God: An Akan Legend, illustrated by Dave Albers, Troll, 1993.
Talk, Talk: An Ashanti Legend, illustrated by Dave Albers, Troll, 1993.
Imani in the Belly, illustrated by Alex Boies, BridgeWater, 1994.

■ Work in Progress

Writing a screenplay adaptation of *A Very Special Kwanzaa;* research for *Black Images of Dignity: The Art of Charles White.*

■ Sidelights

Debbi Chocolate has commented: "I grew up in Chicago, the youngest of five children. My father was a mailman and my mother was a housewife. My grandmother danced in stage shows; my grandfather was a musician.

"My mother was always fond of books. I like to think that she passed her love of books, music, and theater along to me. I learned to read when I was only three years old. By the time I was seven, when I wasn't reading, painting, or drawing, I was busy recreating my mother's childhood memories of the theater into my own stories. The 'Mary Poppins' books were the most memorable reading for me back in those days.

"I always knew I would do something in the arts when I grew up. When I was eight years old, my mother bought me my first oil paint set. At that time, I thought I would become a painter.

"Music came later. I turned into a serious band musician by the age of thirteen and was quite accomplished before I graduated from high school. Sandwiched in between painting and music came my love of film. I was nine years old when my mother bought me an eight millimeter film projector with a limited collection of feature length and animated films. On Saturday after-

noons in late autumn and early winter, when the weather was too cold for my friends and I to play outside, I'd set up folding chairs in my basement, pop popcorn, and sell tickets to my 'movie theater' to all the kids in the neighborhood. Even though I showed the same films every Saturday, my friends didn't seem to mind. They kept coming back every week.

"As I grew older, I found myself writing stories more often than I found myself painting, playing music, or showing movies to my friends. Now that I am a professional writer, I realize that what I had discovered was a way to put all my loves onto paper.

"Before I became a writer, I worked as an editor of children's books. As an editor, I read so many books that I found it easy to sit down and create my own storybook. The first book I wrote was published right away. The publisher said they had been looking for a book just like the one I'd written. I felt very lucky.

"I still get my ideas from movies, paintings, music, and the theater. The children I meet and my own two little boys often provide the foundation for an interesting character.

"My purpose is always the same: I write to entertain. And, more often than not, I write to share my vision of life's hope, its beauty and its promise.

"What do I like most about being a writer? Meeting children who love to read, and who have enjoyed reading books that I have written. For those who want to be writers, my advice is to keep reading. Reading is what makes a writer."

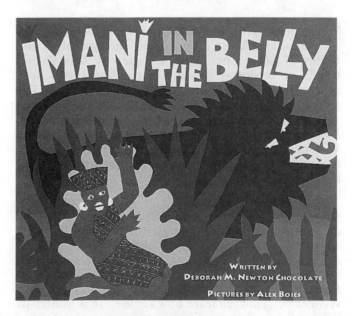

In this retelling of a Swahili folktale, Imani relies on her faith and courage to rescue her children from the stomach of the lion Simba. (Cover illustration by Alex Boies.)

RED, YELLOW, BLUE—
BLACK AND GOLD.

Verse text explains the significance of the West African fabric, kente, and delineates the meaning of its colors and patterns. (From *Kente Colors,* written by Chocolate and illustrated by John Ward.)

My First Kwanzaa Book, Chocolate's sequel to her debut children's book, *Kwanzaa,* is a guide for young readers through the seven days of Kwanzaa. The book illustrates such traditions as lighting candles, dressing in African clothing, and gift-giving between family and friends. Through Chocolate's words and illustrator Cal Massey's creativity, *My First Kwanzaa Book* "effectively conveys the spirit of the holiday," commented Jane Marino, a reviewer for *School Library Journal. Bulletin of the Center for Children's Books* contributor Roger Sutton called *My First Kwanzaa Book* "a pleasant introduction to the holiday."

With similar African-enriched themes, *On the Day I Was Born* and *Kente Colors* depict the symbolism and beauty of African heritage. Prompted by Alex Haley's television version of *Roots, On the Day I Was Born* celebrates the arrival of an African-American baby. The grown-up boy narrates the story, recalling the warmth and love expressed by his family on his special day. *School Library Journal* contributor Barbara Osborne Williams praised the colorful illustrations that "complement the text," calling the book "an excellent collaboration."

One Day I Was Born also describes the symbolic use of the kente cloth given to the narrator as a baby. Presented with a special kente at birth, the young narrator tells readers that he must save this cloth to celebrate his twelfth birthday. This traditional item is the subject of *Kente Colors* as well. Through the rhythmic text and vivid colors, children learn how kente cloth is utilized in West African culture. Chocolate even explains what each color means. *School Library Journal* contributor Carol Jones Collins praised *Kente Colors* as "the first [children's book] to convey an understanding of kente cloth's history and cultural significance."

Chocolate captures the spirit of folktales in *Spider and the Sky God: An Akan Legend* and *Imani in the Belly. Spider and the Sky God* is about a spider named Ananse who announces that he can present the Sky God with species that are much larger than him. Although it seems utterly impossible, Ananse achieves this feat with the help of his wife. In retelling this folktale taken from the West African Akan culture, Chocolate adds "a nice combination of narrative patterns, colloquial speech, and descriptions of a genius web spinner," asserted a *Wilson Library Bulletin* contributor.

Imani in the Belly is Chocolate's 1994 retelling of a Swahili folktale. Imani is a grieving mother whose children are swallowed by a lion. After receiving guidance from her own mother in a dream, Imani risks her life by going into the lion's stomach to get her children. She heroically saves her children and several others by starting a fire inside the lion. Advocating spirituality and faith, *Imani in the Belly* is an "exuberant retelling" of an old story, according to a *Publishers Weekly* contributor.

Two more well-known books by Chocolate are *NEATE to the Rescue!* and *Elizabeth's Wish.* Both follow the lives of NEATE members—Naimah, Elizabeth, Anthony, Tayesha, and Eddie. The first book of the series, *NEATE to the Rescue!,* focuses on Naimah Jackson whose mother, Shannon Gordon, is campaigning to maintain her seat on the local city council. Mrs. Gordon's opponent is a prejudiced ex-police officer whose son happens to be challenging Naimah for student council president. NEATE members imperil Mrs. Gordon's chances when they conflict with supporters of her opponent and end up in jail. Naimah and her friends regroup and facilitate a plan to encourage people to vote for her mother. *Booklist* contributor Quraysh Ali praised *NEATE to the Rescue!* as a "positive" book with characters who have "clearly defined personalities." *Elizabeth's Wish,* Chocolate's second book in the series, centers on Elizabeth's entrance into a citywide music competition. Other sub-plots surrounding NEATE members include prejudice, a Vietnamese refugee shelter's possible closure, a father/son conflict, and a debate on rap versus heavy-metal music. Praising the "natural" dialogue, *School Library Journal* contributor Elaine E. Knight considered the book "emotionally satisfying."

■ Works Cited

Ali, Quraysh, review of *NEATE to the Rescue!, Booklist,* March 15, 1993, p. 1319.

Chocolate, Debbi, author comments in a Troll publicity flyer, c. 1997.

Collins, Carol Jones, review of *Kente Colors, School Library Journal,* June, 1996, p. 114.

Review of *Imani in the Belly, Publishers Weekly,* October 3, 1994, p. 69.

Knight, Elaine E., review of *Elizabeth's Wish, School Library Journal,* April, 1995, p. 130.

Marino, Jane, review of *My First Kwanzaa Book, School Library Journal,* October, 1992, p. 38.

Review of *Spider and the Sky God: An Akan Legend, Wilson Library Bulletin,* September, 1993, p. 87.

Sutton, Roger, review of *My First Kwanzaa Book, Bulletin of the Center for Children's Books,* February, 1993, p. 171.

Williams, Barbara Osborne, review of *On the Day I Was Born, School Library Journal,* January, 1996, p. 77.

■ For More Information See

PERIODICALS

Booklist, September 1, 1992, p. 62; October 15, 1994, p. 429; December 15, 1995, p. 707; February 15, 1996, p. 1023.

Bulletin of the Center for Children's Books January, 1993, p. 142; March, 1993, p. 207; February, 1995, p. 194.

Kirkus Reviews, September 15, 1992, p. 1196; February 15, 1996, p. 293.

Publishers Weekly, September 7, 1992, p. 65; November 30, 1992, p. 56; October 23, 1995, p. 68.

School Library Journal, December, 1994, p. 72.

*   *   *

CHOCOLATE, Deborah M. Newton
See CHOCOLATE, Debbi

*   *   *

CHWAST, Seymour 1931-

■ Personal

Born August 18, 1931, in the Bronx, NY; son of Aaron Louis (a file clerk and waiter) and Esther (Newman) Chwast; married Jacqueline Weiner (an artist), 1952 (divorced, 1971); married Paula Scher (a designer), 1973 (divorced, 1979, re-married, 1989); married Barbara Wool, 1980 (divorced, 1982); children: (with Weiner) Eve, Pamela. *Education:* Cooper Union Art School, diploma, 1957.

■ Addresses

Home—Manhattan, NY. *Office*—c/o Pushpin Group, Inc., 18 East 16th Street, New York, NY 10003.

■ Career

Graphic artist, designer, and illustrator, 1956—; *New York Times,* New York City, junior designer; worked variously for *Esquire, House and Garden,* and *Glamour;* Push Pin Studios, New York City, founding partner, originator and director of studio publication, *Push Pin Graphic,* 1956-80, studio director, 1975-82; Pushpin, Lubalin, Peckolick, Inc., New York City, partner, 1982-86; Pushpin Group, president and director, 1982—. Cooper Union Art School, New York City, instructor of design and illustration, 1975-81; Parsons School of Design, visiting lecturer. American Institute of Graphic Arts, vice-president and member of board of directors; New York Art Directors Guild, member of board of directors. *Exhibitions:* Musee Des Arts Decoratif, the Louvre, Paris, 1971, 1973; "A Century of American Illustration," Brooklyn Museum, 1973; American Institute of Graphic Arts; Art Directors Club of New York; Society of Illustrators; Type Directors Club of New York; Art Directors Club of Chicago; Lincoln Center for the Performing Arts, New York; California State University; Galerie Delpire, Paris. One-man shows include: Cooper Union, New York, 1986; Jack Gallery, New York, 1987; Lustrare Gallery, New York, 1991; Bradley Gallery, Milwaukee, 1992; GGG Gallery, Tokyo, 1992, Recruit Gallery, Osaka, 1992; Michael Kisslinger Gallery, New York, 1994. Works are held in the Museum of

SEYMOUR CHWAST

Modern Art, New York, the Cooper-Hewitt Museum, the Brooklyn Museum, the Whitney Museum of American Art, and the Smithsonian Institute. *Member:* Alliance Graphique Internationale, Art Directors Club, American Institute of Graphic Arts.

■ Awards, Honors

Best Illustrated Book of the Year, *New York Times,* 1969, for *Sara's Granny and the Groodle,* and 1970, for *Finding a Poem;* American Institute of Graphic Arts' Fifty Books selections, 1969, for *Still Another Alphabet book,* 1972, for *Still Another Children's Book* and *The Pancake King,* and 1973, for *The House That Jack Built;* Children's Book Showcase selection, 1972, for *Rimes de la Mere Oie: Mother Goose Rendered into French;* St. Gavden's Medal, Cooper Union; Hall of Fame, New York Art Directors Club, 1984; Gold Medal, American Institute of Graphic Arts, 1985; Parents' Choice picture book award, 1988, and Jewish Book Council award for illustration, 1989, both for *Just Enough Is Plenty: A Hanukkah Tale;* Parents' Choice picture book award, 1991, for *The Alphabet Parade;* Cooper Union Citation for Excellence; honorary Ph.D., Parsons School of Design, 1992; Master Series Award, the School of Visual Arts, 1997.

■ Writings

CHILDREN'S BOOKS; SELF-ILLUSTRATED

(With Martin Stephen Moskof) *Still Another Alphabet Book,* McGraw, 1969.
(With Moskof) *Still Another Number Book,* McGraw, 1971.
Bushy Bride: Norwegian Fairy Tale, Creative Education, 1983.
Tall City, Wide Country: A Book to Read Forward and Backward, Viking, 1983.
The Alphabet Parade, Harcourt Brace Jovanovich, 1991.
Paper Pets: Make Your Own Three Dogs, Two Cats, One Parrot, One Rabbit, One Monkey, Harry N. Abrams, 1993.
The Twelve Circus Rings, Harcourt Brace Jovanovich, 1993.
Mr. Merlin and the Turtle, Greenwillow Books, 1996.

Also author and illustrator of *Still Another Children's Book* (with Martin Stephen Moskof), *Flip-Flap Limerickricks,* and *Flip Flap Mother Goooooose,* all 1972.

CHILDREN'S BOOKS; ILLUSTRATOR

Joan Gill, *Sara's Granny and the Groodle,* Doubleday, 1969.
Eve Merriam, *Finding a Poem,* Atheneum, 1970.
Phyllis La Farge, *The Pancake King,* Delacorte, 1971.
(With Milton Glaser and Barry Zaid) Ormande deKay Jr., translator, *Rimes de la Mere Oie: Mother Goose Rendered into French,* Little, Brown, 1971.
The House That Jack Built, Random House, 1973.
Steven Kroll, *Sleepy Ida and Other Nonsense Poems,* Pantheon Books, 1977.
Dan Weaver, adaptor, *The Little Theater Presents "A Christmas Carol": A Play in Three Acts Adapted*

Merlin becomes bored with his pet turtle and turns him into several animals by means of reader-manipulated flaps in Chwast's humorous picture book.

from the Story by Charles Dickens, Viking Kestrel, 1986.
Harriet Ziefert, *Keeping Daddy Awake on the Way Home from the Beach,* Harper and Row, 1986.
Ziefert, *My Sister Says Nothing Ever Happens When We Go Sailing,* Harper and Row, 1986.
Barbara Diamond Goldin, *Just Enough Is Plenty: A Hanukkah Tale,* Viking Kestrel, 1988.
Harriet Ziefert, *Harry's Bath,* Bantam Books, 1990.
Deborah Johnston, *Mathew Michael's Beastly Day,* Harcourt Brace Jovanovich, 1992.
Out of the Bag: The Paper Bag Players (plays), Hyperion Books for Children, 1996.

OTHER

(Designer) *The Illustrated Cat,* compiled by Jean-Claude Suares and edited by William E. Maloney, Harmony Books, 1976.
(Designer) Emily Blair Chewning, *The Illustrated Flower,* Harmony, 1977.
(Editor with Jean-Claude Suares) *The Literary Cat,* Windhover Books, 1977.
(Editor and compiler with Steven Heller) *The Art of New York,* Abrams, 1983.
(Illustrator) Erica Heller and Vicki Levites, *300 Ways to Say No to a Man,* Simon & Schuster, 1983.
(With D. J. R. Bruckner and Steven Heller) *Art against War: 400 Years of Protest in Art,* Abbeville Press, 1984.
(Self-illustrated) *The Left-Handed Designer,* edited by Steven Heller, Abrams, 1985.

(Self-illustrated) *Happy Birthday Bach,* Doubleday, 1985.

(Illustrator with Alkan Cober and Guy Billout) *Everybody's Business: A Fund of Retrievable Ideas for Humanizing Life in the Office,* edited by Malcolm Clark and William Houseman, Herman Miller Research Corporation, 1985.

(With Donald Barthelme) *Sam's Bar,* Doubleday, 1987.

(Compiler and editor with Barbara Cohen and Steven Heller) *New York Observed: Artists and Writers Look at the City, 1650 to the Present,* H. N. Abrams, 1987.

(Illustrator) Steven Heller, *Design Career: A Handbook for Illustrators and Graphic Designers,* Van Nostrand Reinhold, 1987.

(Illustrator) *Visions of Peace,* edited by Vito Perrone, North Dakota Quarterly Press, 1988.

(With Steven Heller) *Graphic Style: From Victorian to Post-Modern,* Abrams, 1988.

(With Barbara Cohen and Steven Heller) *Trylon and Perisphere: The 1939 New York World's Fair,* Abrams, 1989.

(Editor with Steven Heller) *Sourcebook of Visual Ideas,* Van Nostrand Reinhold, 1989.

(With Vicki Gold Levi and Steven Heller) *You Must Have Been a Beautiful Baby: Baby Pictures of the Stars,* Hyperion, 1992.

(Self-illustrated) *Bra Fashions by Stephanie,* Warner Books, 1994.

(With Steven Heller) *Jackets Required: An Illustrated History of the American Book Jacket 1920-1950,* Chronicle Books, 1995.

(With James Fraser and Steven Heller) *Japanese Modern: Graphic Design between the Wars,* Chronicle Books, 1996.

(Illustrator) D. K. Holland, *Illustration America: 25 Outstanding Portfolios,* Rockport Publishers, 1996.

Author of *The Book of Battles,* privately published, 1957; designer of *Connoisseur Book of the Cigar,* 1967. Also creator of illustrations, posters, typographic designs and animated commercials for print and television advertising, book jackets, record albums, packages, brochures and magazines, and art for theatrical productions.

■ Adaptations

The Twelve Circus Rings was adapted as a CD-ROM in 1996.

■ Sidelights

Seymour Chwast is considered among the most influential commercial artists of the twentieth century in the United States. Some of his works are held in major U.S. museums, and he is known for his innovations in graphic design around the world. Since the mid-1950s he has expressed his political perspective in cartoons rendered in pen and ink, on posters designed with

Chwast illustrates Deborah Johnston's story about a young boy who imagines that he can change into animals to reflect his surroundings. (From *Mathew Michael's Beastly Day,* written by Deborah Johnston and illustrated by Chwast.)

In the ninth circus ring, my sister saw with me nine jugglers juggling, eight bears performing, seven clowns a-clowning, six acrobats, five dogs a-barking, four aerialists zooming, three monkeys playing, two elephants, and a daredevil on a high wire.

Using the repetitious pattern of "The Twelve Days of Christmas," *Twelve Circus Rings* **introduces numbers through the sights and sounds of the big top.** (Written and illustrated by Chwast.)

woodcuts, and, more recently, in steel sculptures. As Chwast explained to Steven Heller in *Innovators of American Illustration,* he is a "nonconformist" who recognizes that "art has to establish its own order and authority while attacking the existing one." Chwast added: "Therefore I try to use my assignments as platforms for whatever I have to say." Chwast's contribution has not been limited, however, to adult audiences. He is the author or illustrator of over twenty books for children, many of which feature his unmistakable cartoon style.

Chwast lived some of his childhood years on Coney Island, where he spent a great deal of time drawing. When he entered high school in New York City, his talent for art was apparent, and he was encouraged by his art teacher. Chwast later attended Cooper Union Art School, where he studied printmaking, woodcut techniques, and typography. Upon graduating from that institution, Chwast teamed up with other Cooper Union-trained artists to publish *The Push Pin Almanac.* Chwast, Milton Glaser, and Edward Sorel formed the Push Pin Studios in 1954.

The Push Pin group, in some organizational form or another, challenged traditional, sentimental illustration and graphic design for decades, earning its members admiration and respect. They also renewed styles popu-

lar in years past. Chwast explained to Heller in *Innovators in American Illustration,* "I found that around 1950 designers had come to the end of a period of evolving style. We came to that point because extensive publishing allowed us to observe and digest everything that had been done before. We started borrowing from the past, and that seemed to progress chronologically." Some of the styles that Chwast and his partners have worked in include Victoriana, art nouveau and art deco.

In addition to his work with the Push Pin Group, Chwast has taken on a number of other projects over the years. He told Heller in *Innovators of American Illustration,* "I'm always working on half a dozen things simultaneously. While I'm working on drawings, I might be conceptualizing and designing with other members of my studio." Chwast created his first children's books with Martin Stephen Moskof in the late 1960s. Their first collaboration, the 1969 work *Still Another Alphabet Book,* was praised by critics for its originality, colorful pictures with hidden words, and gaiety. The illustrations in the volume, according to Zena Sutherland of the *Bulletin of the Center for Children's Books,* are "a graphic triumph over tedium." A *Publishers Weekly* critic wrote that the book was "to be looked at with the greatest happiness." Similarly, *Still Another Number Book,* published in 1971, was described as "absolutely glorious" by a *Publishers Weekly* commentator. Zena Sutherland, in a *Bulletin of the Center for Children's Books* appraisal, called it an "imaginative introduction to numbers."

In the early 1980s, Chwast created *Tall City, Wide Country: A Book to Read Forward and Backward*. This book has what Ann A. Flowers of *Horn Book* described as an "ingenious format." Double-page, horizontal illustrations present country life, and vertical illustrations (which require the reader to turn the book ninety degrees) capture city life. "Chwast's bright, wobbly cartoons are still droll," wrote a *Kirkus Reviews* critic. *The Alphabet Parade*, published in 1991, showcases marchers and floats representing every letter of the alphabet in sequence. The people watching the parade also contribute to the fun. The book was lauded as "cheerfully inventive" by a *Kirkus Reviews* critic. Joanne Oppenheim, writing in the *New York Times Book Review*, similarly praised the book as "truly playful."

Chwast's 1993 picture book, *The Twelve Circus Rings*, gives the familiar verses of "The Twelve Days of Christmas" a new twist. On double-page, light-blue colored spreads, circus clowns and monkeys, jugglers and elephants and horseback riders present themselves in a variety of permutations. A *Publishers Weekly* critic applauded the "cumulative counting book," particularly its "glossy, simply outlined figures" that help children identify mathematical patterns. Deborah Abbott of *Booklist* praised the overall work as "an entertaining package."

After more than forty years as a designer and illustrator, Chwast continues to please adults and children alike with his graphic style. *Mr. Merlin and the Turtle*, a 1996 book, was written and illustrated by Chwast in pen, ink, and color film. The result, in the words of a *Publishers Weekly* critic, is a "clever lift-the-flap volume." The story concerns Mr. Merlin, who becomes bored with his pet turtle and decides to turn him into a bird. Mr. Merlin finds fault with the bird, however, and soon changes it into a monkey. The transformations continue through a camel and elephant before Mr. Merlin realizes that his old turtle wasn't so bad after all. Readers participate in the story by using various flaps to transform the turtle into the different animals. A *Kirkus Reviews* contributor commented favorably on the story's illustrations, stating that, like comic strips, they remain "perfectly balanced between telling a story and telling a joke."

■ Works Cited

Abbott, Deborah, review of *The Twelve Circus Rings*, *Booklist*, March 15, 1993, p. 1352.
Review of *The Alphabet Parade*, *Kirkus Reviews*, August 15, 1991, p. 1096.
Chwast, Seymour, interview with Steven Heller, *Innovators of American Illustration*, edited by Heller, Van Nostrand Reinhold, 1986.
Flowers, Ann A., review of *Tall City, Wide Country: A Book to Read Forward and Backward*, *Horn Book*, August, 1983, p. 429.
Review of *Mr. Merlin and the Turtle*, *Kirkus Reviews*, June 15, 1996, p. 896.
Review of *Mr. Merlin and the Turtle*, *Publishers Weekly*, June 24, 1996, p. 60.
Oppenheim, Joanne, "Books to Play With," *New York Times Book Review*, November 10, 1991, p. 32.
Review of *Still Another Alphabet Book*, *Publishers Weekly*, August 25, 1969, p. 284.
Review of *Still Another Number Book*, *Publishers Weekly*, July 15, 1971, p. 50.
Sutherland, Zena, review of *Still Another Alphabet Book*, *Bulletin of the Center for Children's Books*, July, 1970, pp. 173-74.
Sutherland, Zena, review of *Still Another Number Book*, *Bulletin of the Center for Children's Books*, September, 1971, p. 2.
Review of *Tall City, Wide Country*, *Kirkus Reviews*, June 1, 1983, p. 617.
Review of *The Twelve Circus Rings*, *Publishers Weekly*, March 1, 1993, p. 56.

■ For More Information See

BOOKS

Chwast, Seymour, *The Left-Handed Designer*, Abrams, 1985.
Naylor, Colin, editor, *Contemporary Designers*, St. James Press, 1990.
Siegel, RitaSue, *American Graphic Designers*, McGraw-Hill, 1984.

PERIODICALS

Booklist, June 1, 1995, p. 1715.
Esquire, June, 1987, p. 42.
Horn Book, November-December, 1988, p. 763.
Publishers Weekly, September 20, 1985.
School Library Journal, January, 1993, p. 80; April, 1993, p. 94; October, 1996, p. 85.

*   *   *

CLARK, Joan 1934-

■ Personal

Born October 12, 1934, in Liverpool, Nova Scotia, Canada; daughter of W. I. and Sally (Dodge) Mac-Donald; married Jack Clark (a geotechnical engineer), 1958; children: Tim, Tony, Sara. *Education:* Acadia University, B.A., 1957; attended University of Alberta, 1960.

■ Addresses

Home—6 Dover Place, St. John's, Newfoundland A1B 2P5, Canada. *Office*—c/o Writers' Union of Canada, 24 Ryerson Ave., Toronto M5T 2P3, Canada.

■ Career

Writer. Teacher in Sussex, New Brunswick, 1957-58, Edmonton, Alberta, 1960-61, Calgary, Alberta, 1962-63, and Dartmouth, Nova Scotia, 1969-70; co-founder and co-editor of *Dandelion* (magazine), 1974-81. *Member:* Writers' Union of Canada, PEN International, Writers' Guild of Alberta (president, 1983-84), Writers' Alliance of Newfoundland and Labrador.

■ Awards, Honors

Alberta Book Award, 1983; Alberta Culture Award, 1985; Bologna International Children's Book Fair, 1985, and runner-up, Canadian Library Association Book of the Year for Children, 1986, both for *Wild Man of the Woods;* Canada Council 'B' Award, 1988; Governor General's Fiction Award Shortlist, 1989; W. H. Smith/Books Canada Award Shortlist, 1989; Canadian Authors Association Award for Fiction, 1989, for *The Victory of Geraldine Gull;* Geoffrey Bilson Award for Historical Fiction, Canadian Children's Book Centre, 1995, and Mr. Christie's Book Award, Christie Brown and Co., 1996, both for *The Dream Carvers.*

■ Writings

FOR YOUNG PEOPLE

Girl of the Rockies, Ryerson Press, 1968.
Thomasina and the Trout Tree, illustrated by Ingeborg Hiscox, Tundra Books, 1971.
The Hand of Robin Squires, illustrated by William Taylor and Mary Cserepy, Clarke, Irwin, 1977.
The Leopard and the Lily (fable), illustrated by Velma Foster, Oolichan Books, 1984.
Wild Man of the Woods, Penguin Books Canada, 1985.
The Moons of Madeleine, Viking Kestrel, 1987.
Eiriksdottir: A Tale of Dreams and Luck, illustrated by Joe Lobo, Macmillan of Canada, 1994.
The Dream Carvers, Viking, 1995.
Leaving Home, illustrated by Cherrisa Bonine, Your Book, 1996.

OTHER

From a High Thin Wire (short stories), NeWest Press, 1982.
The Victory of Geraldine Gull (novel), Macmillan of Canada, 1988.
Swimming toward the Light (short stories), Macmillan of Canada, 1990.

Contributor to anthologies, including *CBC Anthology, Alberta Anthology, Doublebound, Glass Canyons, Calgary Stories,* and *Prairie Fire.* Contributor of short stories to magazines, including *Canadian Fiction, Waves, Dalhousie Review, Saturday Night, Journal of Canadian Fiction,* and *Wascana Review.*

■ Sidelights

Joan Clark populates her historical fiction with young heroes and heroines who are confronted with real, modern-day problems as well as adventures of the kind

JOAN CLARK

often found in myths and folklore. Sorting through the research necessary to tell these stories, Clark takes what history she perceives to be the most factual and builds her books from there, integrating fiction in a manner that prevents the facts from overwhelming the story. Clark explained in an essay for *Canadian Children's Literature* that she is "guided by the words that the Icelandic novelist, Halldor Laxness, wrote in *Christianity in Glacier,* '... the closer you try to approach history through facts, the deeper you sink into fiction.'"

Clark herself did not sink into the writing of fiction until after she married and moved from the eastern part of Canada to Winisk in northern Ontario. It was here that Clark began to write poetry, and she continued to write in this genre after another move to Calgary. "I like the energy in the West," Clark explained in an interview with Nancy Robb for *Quill and Quire.* "It was very much the frontier, while the Maritimes were very traditional—and enclosed. Just walking down the street in Halifax, or any of the small towns I lived in, you can see the leaves leaning overhead, and you're kind of in a tunnel. It was almost like I was breaking out when I went west. Anything was possible."

Clark's first book for young readers, *Girl of the Rockies,* is the story of a girl and a bear cub in the mountains. "I just naturally slid into the young girl's point of view," Clark remembered in her interview with Robb. After scribbling out a rough draft, she bought a typewriter and finished the manuscript, sending it off to Ryerson Press, where it was quickly accepted. "I was so surprised when *Girl of the Rockies* was published, but I could see the glaring flaws," she maintained in her *Quill and Quire* interview. "That's when I knew I was serious about writing."

Since then, Clark has published several more books for young readers as well as novels and short stories for adults that have appeared both in magazines and as collections. Writing was not always an easy task for Clark as her three children were growing up, however. "There were long periods when I couldn't write at all," she related to Robb. "They'd all come down with chicken pox at the same time, or something like that." In addition, Clark also found herself dealing with the tension created by the conflicts she felt between being a mother and being a writer. "I was always a bit too tired, and I thought that to be a good writer, I should do it full-time," she explained to Robb, adding: "But I knew I had my priorities straight."

As her children grew older and more independent, Clark became more active in the publishing world. In 1974 she became a co-founding editor of *Dandelion,* a literary magazine to which she contributed for seven years. At the same time, her writing career flourished with such novels as *The Hand of Robin Squires, Wild Man of the Woods,* and *The Moons of Madeleine.* Based on historical accounts of searches for treasure on Oak Island off Nova Scotia between 1795 and 1971, *The Hand of Robin Squires* follows the adventures of nineteen-year-old Robin Squires as he travels from England to Oak Island with his Uncle Edward after his father's death. His father had invented a pump to use in mine shafts during flooding, which Uncle Edward wants Robin to build in conjunction with a huge vault on Oak Island to hide the Spanish treasure he seized during the battle of Vigo Bay. Robin's "first-person narration invites immediate reader-identification and his blend of visual detail, conversations, and action creates a sense of time present," maintained John Smallbridge in *Canadian Children's Literature.* Smallbridge added that "each chapter advances the plot significantly and contains sufficient foreshadowing and suspense to impel the reader to finish the book 'at one sitting.'"

More time may be needed for Clark's companion novels *Wild Man of the Woods* and *The Moons of Madeleine,* which she originally conceived as one story. Realizing how differently boys and girls handle conflict, though, Clark opted for two separate books about cousins as they travel to each other's houses for the summer. Stephen leaves Calgary to visit his aunt, uncle, and cousin Louie in Inverary in the Rockies, while Madeleine, Louie's sister, visits Stephen's family back in Calgary. For both, the summer is filled with experiences that raise them to higher levels of maturity. Stephen must deal with being bullied, which he does through the use of a mythical mask that brings about a violent climax. Madeleine, on the other hand, is dealing with her grandmother's illness as well as her own maturation into womanhood through a mythical escape to the cave of the First Woman, which offers her insight into the continuity of the circle of life. In a *Canadian Children's Literature* review of both *Wild Man of the Woods* and *The Moons of Madeleine,* Barbara Michasiw pointed out that "the stories are self-contained, and the truths the protagonists discover are profoundly different; but each complements the other.... For both cousins, the month will bring experience, testing, a symbolic death, and a rebirth into a new stage of maturity."

Much of the same is in store for Freydis Eiriksdottir, the illegitimate daughter of Eirik the Red in Clark's *Eiriksdottir: A Tale of Dreams and Luck.* Eiriksdottir organizes an expedition in 1015 to Leifsbudir, the Viking outpost in Newfoundland established by her brother Leif Eiriksson. Determined that luck and good fortune will be hers, Freydis endures many hardships during her journey, which continue even after she settles in her new home. "With the characters and conditions of the voyage very firmly established, Clark diversifies both plot and narrative, bringing the adventure to life," maintained Kathleen Hickey in *Quill and Quire.* Eva Tihanyi, in a review for *Books in Canada,* concluded that *Eiriksdottir* "leaves one slightly startled, as if one had been listening to a long and intricate tale unfolded gradually over a hundred winter nights...; here is a meditation on the nature of the human spirit, its courage and treachery, its quest for material wealth and sensory adventure, but above all, its quest for meaning of its own self."

Using the same time period and places for its setting, *The Dream Carvers* centers on the kidnapping of fourteen-year-old Thrand when he accompanies his father from their Greenland home to Leif Ericsson's colony on the northern tip of Newfoundland. Captured by the Osweet people to replace a young man in the tribe killed by Greenlanders, Thrand at first tries to escape, but eventually adapts to his new culture and comes to respect the traditions and lifestyle of the Osweets. "On the whole, Clark uses and invents from her source material with skill and tact," observed Frances Frazer in *Canadian Children's Literature.* Describing *The Dream Carvers* as "an exciting adventure story," *Quill and Quire* contributor Barbara Greenwood praised Clark's use of "language that is poetic and reflective."

Clark's penchant for historical fiction is something the author herself cannot fully explain. "While I am conceiving a story, be it historical or not, I seldom understand why I am attracted to it," she commented in *Canadian Children's Literature.* "Part of the process of writing the story is figuring out the attraction. I like to think this adds to the mysteriousness, the indefinable quality of a story, that which helps lift it from the page. The reason for writing any story, amorphous as the initial impulse might be, is simply that it is there. The fact that the impulse (or, if you like, inspiration) comes from the past makes it no less real."

■ Works Cited

Clark, Joan, "What Is History?," *Canadian Children's Literature,* number 83, 1996, pp. 78-81.

Frazer, Frances, review of *The Dream Carvers, Canadian Children's Literature,* winter, 1995, p. 80.

Greenwood, Barbara, review of *The Dream Carvers, Quill and Quire,* March, 1995, p. 75.

Hickey, Kathleen, review of *Eiriksdottir: A Tale of Dreams and Luck, Quill and Quire,* May, 1994, pp. 22-23.

Michasiw, Barbara, review of *Wild Man of the Woods* and *The Moons of Madeleine, Canadian Children's Literature,* number 50, 1988, pp. 86-87.

Robb, Nancy, interview with Joan Clark, *Quill and Quire,* December, 1986, pp. 12-13.

Smallbridge, John, "Two Mysteries: Pirate Treasure and Wisdom," *Canadian Children's Literature,* number 14, 1979, pp. 73-75.

Tihanyi, Eva, "Heroic Quests," *Books in Canada,* September, 1994, pp. 48-49.

■ For More Information See

PERIODICALS

Books in Canada, December, 1985.
Canadian Children's Literature, winter, 1991, pp. 238-40.
Growing Point, January, 1980, pp. 3619-23.
Junior Bookshelf, April, 1980, p. 79.
Maclean's, June 27, 1988, pp. 52-53.
Quill and Quire, December, 1985, p. 30; May, 1988, p. 26; June, 1990, p. 30.
School Library Journal, September, 1986, p. 132.*

*   *   *

COLE, Babette 1949-

■ Personal

Born September 10, 1949, in Jersey, Channel Islands, England; daughter of Fred (a director) and Iris (a homemaker; maiden name, Fosbray) Cole. *Education:* Canterbury College of Art, B.A. (with honors), 1974.

■ Addresses

Home and office—Ivy Cottage, Wingmore Lane, Wingmore, Elham, North Canterbury, Kent CT4 6LS, England.

■ Career

Author and illustrator of children's books, 1973—. *Exhibitions:* Bologna International Children's Book Fair, 1985-89; Salon International du Livre, Switzerland, 1988.

■ Awards, Honors

Nungu and the Hippopotamus was selected a Children's Book of the Year, Child Study Association of America,

BABETTE COLE

1980; *The Wind in the Willows Pop-Up Book* was selected a New York Public Library's Children's Books, 1983; Kate Greenaway Medal Commendation, The Library Association, 1986, for *Princess Smartypants;* Annabell Fargeon Award, The Library Association, 1986, for *Princess Smartypants,* and 1987, for *Prince Cinders;* Kate Greenaway Medal, The Library Association, 1987, for *Prince Cinders;* Kurt Mascher Award, Book Trust, 1996, for *Drop Dead.*

■ Writings

SELF-ILLUSTRATED JUVENILES

Basil Brush of the Yard, Purnell, 1977.
Promise Solves the Problem, Kaye and Ward, 1977.
Nungu and the Hippopotamus, McDonald, 1978, McGraw-Hill, 1979.
Nungu and the Elephant, McGraw-Hill, 1980, MacDonald, 1980.
Promise and the Monster, Granada, 1981.
Don't Go Out Tonight: A Creepy Concertina Pop Up, Hamish Hamilton, 1981, Doubleday, 1982.
Nungu and the Crocodile, McDonald, 1982.
Beware of the Vet, Hamish Hamilton, 1982.
The Trouble with Mum, Kaye and Ward, 1983, published as *The Trouble with Mom,* Putnam, 1984.
The Hairy Book, Cape, 1984, Random House, 1985.
The Trouble with Dad, Heinemann, 1985, Random House, 1986.
The Slimy Book, Cape, 1985, Random House, 1986.
Princess Smartypants, Hamish Hamilton, 1986, Putnam, 1987.

The Trouble with Gran, Putnam, 1987, Heinemann, 1988.

Prince Cinders, Hamish Hamilton, 1987, Putnam, 1988.

The Smelly Book, Cape, 1987, Simon & Schuster, 1988.

The Trouble with Grandad, Putnam, 1988, Heinemann, 1988.

King Change-a-lot, Hamish Hamilton, 1988, Putnam, 1989.

Three Cheers for Errol!, Heinemann, 1988, Putnam, 1989.

The Silly Book, Cape, 1989, Doubleday, 1990.

Cupid, Hamish Hamilton, 1989, Putnam, 1990.

(With Ron Van der Meer) *Babette Cole's Beastly Birthday Book,* Heinemann, 1990, Doubleday, 1991.

Hurray for Ethelyn, Little, Brown, 1991, published in England as *Hurrah for Ethelyn!,* Heinemann, 1991.

Tarzanna!, Heinemann, 1991, Putnam, 1992.

Supermoo!, Putnam, 1992, BBC Books, 1992.

The Trouble with Uncle, Little, Brown, 1992, Heinemann, 1992.

Mommy Laid an Egg!; or, Where Do Babies Come From?, Chronicle Books, 1993, published in England as *Mummy Laid an Egg!; or Where Do Babies Come From?,* Cape, 1993.

Winni Allfours, BridgeWater Books (Mahwah, NJ), 1993, Hamish Hamilton, 1993.

(With Van der Meer) *The Bible Beasties,* Harper, 1993, Marshall Pickering, 1993.

Dr. Dog, Knopf, 1994, Cape, 1994.

Babette Cole's Cats, Warner Books, 1995, Heinemann, 1995.

Babette Cole's Dogs, Warner Books, 1995, Heinemann, 1995.

Babette Cole's Fish, Warner Books, 1995, Heinemann, 1995.

Babette Cole's Ponies, Warner Books, 1995, Heinemann, 1995.

The Bad Good Manners Book, Hamish Hamilton, 1995, Dial, 1996.

Drop Dead, Cape, 1996, Knopf, 1997.

Brother, Heinemann, 1997.

Dad, Heinemann, 1997.

Mother, Heinemann, 1997.

Sister, Heinemann, 1997.

ILLUSTRATOR

Joan Tate, *Your Dog,* Pelham, 1975.

Annabel Farjeon, *The Unicorn Drum,* 1976.

Joan Aiken, *Mice and Mendelson,* Cape, 1978.

Oliver Postgate, *A Flying Bird,* Kaye and Ward, 1978.

Postgate, *The Narrow Boat,* Kaye and Ward, 1978.

Jim Slater, *Grasshopper and the Unwise Owl,* Granada, 1979, Holt, 1980.

Slater, *Grasshopper and the Pickle Factory,* Granada, 1980.

Norman Hunter, *Sneeze and Be Slain and Other Incredible Stories,* Bodley Head (London, England), 1980.

Hunter, *Count Bakwerdz on the Carpet and Other Incredible Stories,* Bodley Head, 1981.

Slater, *Grasshopper and the Poisoned River,* Granada, 1982.

Willis Hall, *The Last Vampire,* Bodley Head, 1982.

Lesley Young, *Hocus Pocus,* Hamish Hamilton, 1983.

Kenneth Grahame, *The Wind in the Willows Pop-Up Book,* Holt, 1983.

Hall, *The Inflatable Shop,* Bodley Head, 1984.

Hall, *The Vampire's Holiday,* 1992.

Also illustrator of *The Eye of Conscience,* Follett (River Grove, IL), and *The Bird Whistle,* Kaye and Ward, 1977.

■ Sidelights

Adjectives such as quirky, goofy, zany and anarchic are often employed when discussing the fiction and illustrations of the English children's writer, Babette Cole. In some three dozen self-illustrated picture books, Cole has managed to turn fairy tales—both contemporary and ancient—on their heads, poke fun at family dynamics, take an irreverent look at the normally serious subject of health and reproduction, and generally entertain her young readers with fanciful situations in which text and pictures work together in harmony. Cole once told *Something about the Author* (*SATA*) that people keep telling her, in spite of her steady sales, "'You obviously write alternative children's books.' I guess it's because I tend to be a little eccentric. My books get nominated for all the prizes and are consistently named runner-up (they don't like anarchic books for prizes)." However, she eventually captured top billing, winning England's Kurt Mascher Award in 1996 for her book, *Drop Dead.*

Cole's course to becoming a children's writer and illustrator was a long and convoluted one. Born in Jersey, one of England's Channel Islands, she spent much of her youth exploring the island with her pony. Animals made up for a dearth of childhood friends, and her love of animals—horses in particular—has contin-

Then we went to school.

Two feisty grandparents relate their life stories to their grandchildren in Cole's witty saga of the aging process. (From *Drop Dead,* written and illustrated by Cole.)

Dr. Dog went to a conference in Brazil to give a talk about bone marrow.

Hygiene and health lessons are offered through the tale of the Gumboyle family as they are treated for various illnesses by their pet beagle, who is also a physician. (From *Dr. Dog,* written and illustrated by Cole.)

ued throughout her life. Books also informed her youth. "We spent lots of time reading Lewis Carroll and Edward Lear," Cole recalled in *SATA.* "If I didn't like a book, I'd rewrite it and re-draw the pictures." She also wrote poetry as a young girl, and one of her early efforts which won a prize was, significantly, a piece of nonsense verse. Cole attended a convent school, and when she wasn't in school she was with her horse. She also began to draw and sculpt—albeit in mud—as a youth.

An early ambition was to be a vet, but she finally gave that up, realizing her strength did not lie in the sciences. With her love of horses, she thought she would like to be a professional show horse owner, but large quantities of money were required to fulfill such a dream. Thus, Cole took to illustration as a means to support her ambition. Denied admission to an art school in Bristol, she worked for a time in an advertising agency, "one of the darkest periods of my life," as she noted in *SATA.* But this practical experience gave her the courage to re-apply to art school, and this time she was accepted at Canterbury College of Art where she studied graphics and printmaking.

Art school was not a happy experience for her, however, as the other students and faculty did not respond to her idiosyncratic style. "As frustrated and unhappy as I was in art school, I got a lot out of the experience as a whole," Cole told *SATA.* Out of art school, Cole made a living illustrating greeting cards and books. She also formed a twelve-year relationship with a social anthropologist, which at one point took her to Africa for nine months. "Water had to be dug up and boiled before drinking," Cole recalled of those days in *SATA,* "food was in shortage, and animals lay dying of starvation." But the drawings she did during her stay later resulted in a trio of books about "Nungu," based on myths she heard while in Africa. In *Publishers Weekly,* a reviewer

called *Nungu and the Hippopotamus* an "enchanting make-believe" and noted that Cole's "paintings are vivid, realistic views of African landscapes, but these serve as backgrounds for funny impossibilities."

Moving to Wales and on her own again, Cole concentrated on her work and animals. The result was the inception of her popular "The Trouble With" series, which takes a humorous look at various members of the family. In the first book in the series, *The Trouble with Mom,* Cole presents an exaggerated case of the school child's fear of his or her parent being different from the other parents. In this case, the mother is a witch who brings the child to school via a broomstick. It's the father's turn next with *The Trouble with Dad,* when that parent decides to seek relief from his boring job by inventing robots. The only trouble is that the robots do not operate as they are meant to. *The Trouble with Gran* has an extraterrestrial grandmother liven up a trip to the seashore, and in *The Trouble with Grandad,* the grandfather's enormous vegetables get him into a spot of trouble with the local police. More distant relatives are not safe in the series, either. *The Trouble with Uncle* features a peculiar uncle who is a pirate and eventually marries a mermaid. Reviewing the first title in the series, Rebecca Jennings in *School Library Journal* noted that Cole's "detailed watercolor and pen-and-ink illustrations fill the page with humor and originality." Reviewing *The Trouble with Dad* in *Publishers Weekly,* a critic commented that "Cole plays fast and loose with her suitably droll text and comic pictures," and a contributor to *Kirkus Reviews* called the book "hilarious," with humor both in the text and illustrations. Ann F. Flowers concluded in a *Horn Book* review of *The Trouble with Gran* that the book was "Zany, very British illustrations ... and a mad, cheerful story line." In *Publishers Weekly* a critic summed up a review of the third title in the series with, "one hopes other offbeat relatives wait in the wings." They were. Lauralyn Persson, writing in *School Library Journal*, commended *The Trouble with Grandad* as a "good example of words and pictures working together to make a nicely-blended whole." And *The Trouble with Uncle* was described as a "wonderfully wacky universe where ordinary rules don't apply," by a contributor to *Publishers Weekly*. "An outstanding addition to Cole's oeuvre," the reviewer concluded.

Cole has also produced several fractured fairy tales and myths, including *Princess Smartypants*, *Prince Cinders*, *King Change-a-Lot*, and *Cupid*. In the first-mentioned, a princess acts in contravention of the usual roles: she goes about in dungarees and never wants to be married. In *Kirkus Reviews* a critic called it a "modern fairy tale with a feminist theme," and a reviewer in *Publishers Weekly* noted that "Cole's characteristic wacky humor sparks this fable." *Prince Cinders* is a reworking of the Cinderella fable, with a young male taking the role of drudge persecuted by three older brothers. A contributor to *Publishers Weekly* dubbed it a "jaunty, contemporary version" of the old tale. A spoof fairy tale is at the center of *King Change-a-Lot*, in which the regent only needs to rub his potty to bring forth a magic genie to help put his land to rights. Lori A. Janick noted in *School Library Journal* that "Cole's illustrations have spontaneous humor." With *Cupid*, Cole turned her hand to mythology, updating the story of the matchmaker as he comes to Earth for the Miss Universe contest.

Cole lives in a five-hundred-year-old Tudor house in Kent, and has plenty of land now for her horses and other animals. She insists upon researching her books thoroughly, even going to Greece for the background on *Cupid*. She is also very particular about her work. "My work is very hard to reproduce," she told *SATA*. "The tones get muddled. So I go to the scannings and sit with the scanner telling him exactly which buttons to push and which knobs to turn .... I do most of my illustrations with dyes, the same things that most people use with airbrushes. I, however, paint with them. It's extremely demanding, because you cannot make a mistake."

Many of Cole's books feature animals caught in interesting and amazing situations. She has even been able to make a rat sympathetic. In *Three Cheers for Errol!*, she presents a rodent with not much in the brain department, but a very determined athlete, chosen by his school to run in the International Ratathlon. In *Junior Bookshelf* a reviewer commented that "the pictures are lively and full of action," and of the book's sequel, *Hurray for Ethelyn*, the story of a brainy ratlet, Denise Krell in *School Library Journal* noted that it was a "light, action-packed adventure with clever dialogue, humorous illustrations, and brains winning out in the end." With *Supermoo!*, Cole created a bovine Superman spin-off, with the heifer out to protect mother Earth from eco-disasters. A contributor to *Junior Bookshelf* commented that "Lively illustrations add further details to the brief text which would be suitable for beginner readers and for reading aloud to younger children." Another superhero comes in for some laughs with

Tarzanna!, the story of a female Tarzan who commandeers a male Jane in the form of one Gregory, who takes her to London with him where she promptly sets free the animals in the zoo. Cassie Whetstone, writing in *School Library Journal*, called the book a "funny tale," and concluded that the story was "an imaginative yarn bound to please." In *Winni Allfours*, Cole turns the traditional tale of a young girl who desperately wants a horse upside down. In Cole's rendering, the girl herself turns into a horse after eating loads of vegetables, and as a horse wins the Grand National race. In *Junior Bookshelf* a reviewer felt that this was "an ideal book for any child obsessed by horses," while Deborah Stevenson in *Bulletin of the Center for Children's Books* concluded that this was a "fantasy taken to a degree that [young readers] may not have dared and will deeply appreciate."

Health and the workings of the body also take their hits from Cole, in her *Mommy Laid an Egg!; Or Where Do Babies Come From?* and *Dr. Dog*. In a *Publishers Weekly* review of *Mommy Laid an Egg!*, a critic commented that Cole "unleashes her endearingly loony sense of humor on the subject of the birds and the bees, and the result is, as expected, hilarious." When parents begin to tell their children about sex in metaphors, the kids—better informed—get into the act and do a series of drawings that educate the parents. A contributor to *Kirkus Reviews* labeled the book a "fresh, matter-of-fact approach." *Dr. Dog* also takes a humorous look at health with a family dog explaining the risks of smoking and how body lice and worms are transmitted. The humor here is broader than in many Cole titles, though a few reviewers found some of the doggie explanations ("Never scratch your bum and suck your thumb,") to be one step beyond good taste. However, a reviewer, writing in *Junior Bookshelf*, noted that the "illustrations, and the text, are very amusing and, at first, children will probably not realise how much information they have been given."

Cole's earthy humor comes into play in all of her books, but perhaps most acutely in *The Bad Good Manners Book* and the award-winning *Drop Dead*. With the former title, Cole does not bother with the subtleties of please and thank you, but with the bad form of clogging a toilet with too much toilet paper or of calling your mom fat. Reviewing *The Bad Good Manners Book* in *Booklist*, Stephanie Zvirin noted that "*Goofy* is probably not a potent enough adjective to describe Cole's books." Of award-winning *Drop Dead*, which irreverently explores the cycle of life, an older couple recall to their grandchildren the mischief they shared through the years. Still full of adventure and good-humor, the pair fully intend to continue living life to the fullest until they "drop dead." In *Kirkus Reviews* a critic commented that Cole "proves she can fracture more than Emily Post in this eccentric tale" which deals with birth and death in a humorous manner. While admitting the book may not "suit all tastes," a contributor to *Publishers Weekly* applauded Cole's "comical imagery and matter-of-fact voice" in talking about such a sensitive topic.

Over the years, Cole's book production has not slowed, nor has her zany humor been tempered. "Sometimes I wish I could spend all my time with my horses," she concluded in *SATA*. "Just to keep my hand in, I'd do one book a year. But I keep getting ideas and wake up in the middle of the night to jot things down and make drawings. I've got a drawer so thick with files I could do books forever. And I must admit, it's not such a bad feeling."

■ Works Cited

Cole, Babette, *Dr. Dog*, Knopf, 1994.

Review of *Dr. Dog, Junior Bookshelf*, August, 1994, pp. 127-8.

Review of *Drop Dead, Kirkus Reviews*, March 1, 1997, p. 378.

Flowers, Ann A., review of *The Trouble with Gran, Horn Book*, January-February, 1988, p. 51.

Janick, Lori A., review of *King Change-a-Lot, School Library Journal*, August, 1989, p. 118.

Jennings, Rebecca, review of *The Trouble with Mom, School Library Journal*, May, 1984, p. 63.

Krell, Denise, review of *Hurray for Ethelyn, School Library Journal*, March, 1992, p. 212.

Review of *Mommy Laid an Egg, Publishers Weekly*, June 7, 1993, p. 68.

Review of *Mommy Laid an Egg, Kirkus Reviews*, June 15, 1993, p. 783.

Review of *Nungu the Hippopotamus, Publishers Weekly*, February 26, 1979, p. 183.

Persson, Lauralyn, review of *The Trouble with Grandad, School Library Journal*, April, 1989, p. 78.

Review of *Prince Cinders, Publishers Weekly*, March 2, 1992, p. 66.

Review of *Princess Smartypants, Kirkus Reviews*, February 15, 1987, p. 296.

Review of *Princess Smartypants, Publishers Weekly*, May 13, 1991, p. 77.

Stevenson, Deborah, review of *Winni Allfours, Bulletin of the Center for Children's Books*, May, 1994, p. 283.

Review of *Supermoo!, Junior Bookshelf*, April, 1993, p. 57.

Review of *Three Cheers for Errol!, Junior Bookshelf*, August, 1989, p. 159.

Review of *The Trouble with Dad, Kirkus Reviews*, March 15, 1986, p. 468.

Review of *The Trouble with Dad, Publishers Weekly*, May 30, 1986, p. 64.

Review of *The Trouble with Gran, Publishers Weekly*, August 28, 1987, p. 78.

Review of *The Trouble with Uncle, Publishers Weekly*, July 27, 1992, p. 62.

Whetstone, Cassie, review of *Tarzanna!, School Library Journal*, June, 1992, p. 90.

Review of *Winni Allfours, Junior Bookshelf*, June, 1994, p. 93.

Zvirin, Stephanie, review of *The Bad Good Manners Book, Booklist*, June 1, 1996, p. 1725.

■ For More Information See

BOOKS

Twentieth-Century Children's Writers, 4th edition, edited by Laura Standley Berger, St. James Press, 1995, pp. 231-2.

PERIODICALS

Books for Keeps, July, 1997, pp. 6-7.

Bulletin of the Center for Children's Books, June, 1987, p. 185; April, 1988, p. 152; May, 1989, p. 219; March, 1990, p. 155.

Horn Book, August, 1984, p. 455; July, 1987, p. 493; July, 1993, p. 490.

Junior Bookshelf, October, 1982, p. 179; April, 1986, p. 59; June, 1988, p. 129; October, 1988, p. 229; June, 1993, p. 91.

Publishers Weekly, June 10, 1996, p. 99, March 17, 1997, p. 83.

School Librarian, February, 1997, p. 18.

School Library Journal, August, 1994, p. 127; November, 1994, p. 95; August, 1995, p. 166; July, 1996, p. 77.

Times Educational Supplement, April 8, 1988, p. 21; July 29, 1988, p. 21; November 8, 1991, p. 42; February 2, 1996, p. 12; July 12, 1996, p. 6.

—Sketch by J. Sydney Jones

*   *   *

CONDY, Roy 1942-

■ Personal

Born August 11, 1942, in Dagenham, Essex, England; son of Reginald Kenneth and Olive Hannah (Roberts) Condy; married Margaret Mary Thormin (a writer), October 3, 1965. *Education:* Attended Ecole des Beaux Arts, Montreal, Quebec. *Religion:* None. *Hobbies and other interests:* Making wooden balancing toys.

■ Addresses

Home and office—1562 Alwin Circle, Pickering, Ontario, Canada L1V 2W2.

■ Career

Freelance cartoonist and illustrator of children's books, television graphics for children's programs, and animated characters, 1972—. *Member:* Canadian Society of Children's Authors, Illustrators, and Performers (CAN-SCAIP).

■ Illustrator

Nancy Hazbry, *How to Get Rid of Bad Dreams*, Scholastic Canada, 1983.

Itah Sadu, *Christopher, Please Clean up Your Room!*, Firefly Books, 1993.

(And author) *Shark Attacks and Spider Snacks* (nonfiction), Scholastic Canada, 1996.

Itah Sadu, *Christopher Changes His Name,* Scholastic Canada, 1996.

■ For More Information See

PERIODICALS

Quill and Quire, February, 1996, p. 41.*

* * *

COONEY, Barbara 1917-

■ Personal

Born August 6, 1917, in Brooklyn, NY; daughter of Russell Schenck (a stockbroker) and Mae Evelyn (an artist; maiden name, Bossert) Cooney; married Guy Murchie (an author and war correspondent), December, 1944 (divorced, March, 1947); married Charles Talbot Porter (a physician), July 16, 1949; children: (first marriage) Gretel Goldsmith, Barnaby; (second marriage) Charles Talbot, Jr., Phoebe. *Education:* Smith College, B.A., 1938; also attended Art Students League, 1940. *Politics:* Independent.

■ Career

Freelance author and illustrator, 1938—. *Military service:* Women's Army Corps, World War II, 1942-43; became second lieutenant. *Exhibitions:* Cooney's works are held in the Kerlan Collection at the University of Minnesota; the de Grummond Collection at the University of Southern Mississippi; the Northeastern Children's Literature Collection at the University of Connecticut; in museums at Rutgers University and Bowdoin College; and in the public libraries of Gary, Indiana; Philadelphia, Pennsylvania; and Milwaukee, Wisconsin.

■ Awards, Honors

New York Herald Tribune's Children's Spring Book Festival Honor Book, 1943, for *Green Wagons,* and 1952, for *Too Many Pets;* American Library Association Notable Book citation, 1948, for *American Folk Songs for Children in Home, School and Nursery School,* 1958, for *Chanticleer and the Fox,* and 1974, for *Squawk to the Moon, Little Goose;* Caldecott Medal from the American Library Association, 1959, for *Chanticleer and the Fox,* and 1980, for *Ox-Cart Man;* Chandler Book Talk Award of Merit, 1964; Child Study Association of America Children's Books of the Year, 1969, for both *Christmas Folk* and *The Owl and the Pussy-Cat,* 1971, for both *Hermes, Lord of Robbers* and *Book of Princesses,* 1973, for *Down to the Beach,* 1974, for *Squawk to the Moon, Little Goose,* 1975, for *Lexington and Concord, 1775,* and 1986, for *The Story of Holly and Ivy, The Little Fir Tree, Christmas in the Barn,* and *Emma; Squawk to the Moon, Little Goose* was included on *School Library Journal*'s Best Books List, 1974; *New York Times* Outstanding Books of the Year, 1974, for *Squawk to the Moon, Little Goose,* 1975, for *When the Sky Is Like Lace,* and 1979, for *Ox-Cart Man;* Silver

BARBARA COONEY

Medallion from the University of Southern Mississippi, 1975, for outstanding contributions to the field of children's books; Medal from Smith College, 1976, for her body of work; *Ox-Cart Man* was selected one of *New York Times* Best Illustrated Books of the Year, 1979; Notable Children's Trade Book in the Field of Social Studies, National Council for the Social Studies and Children's Book Council, 1982, for *Tortillitas para Mama and Other Nursery Rhymes,* and 1986, for *The Story of Holly and Ivy;* American Book Award for Hardcover Picture Book from the Association of American Publishers, 1983, and *New York Times* Best Book of the Year, 1983, both for *Miss Rumphius;* Notable Children's Book, Association for Library Services to Children, American Library Association, 1984, for *Spirit Child; Boston Globe-Horn Book Award* honor list, 1989, for *Island Boy;* Ph.D., Fitchburg State College, 1988; Keene State College Children's Literature Festival Award, 1989; McCord Children's Literature Citation, 1990; Lupine Award, 1990, for *Hattie and the Wild Waves;* Kerlan Award, 1992, for body of work; honorary doctorates from the University of Maine at Machais, Westbrook College, and Bowdoin College, in 1994, 1995, and 1996, respectively; proclaimed an official state treasure of Maine, 1996.

■ Writings

FOR CHILDREN; SELF-ILLUSTRATED, EXCEPT AS NOTED

The King of Wreck Island, Farrar & Rinehart, 1941.
The Kellyhorns, Farrar & Rinehart, 1942.
Captain Pottle's House, Farrar, 1943.
(Adapter) Geoffrey Chaucer, *Chanticleer and the Fox,* Crowell, 1958.
The Little Juggler: Adapted from an Old French Legend, Hastings House, 1961, new edition, 1982.

(Adapter) *The Courtship, Merry Marriage, and Feast of Cock Robin and Jenny Wren: To Which Is Added the Doleful Death of Cock Robin,* Scribner, 1965.

(Adapter) Jacob Grimm and Wilhelm Grimm, *Snow White and Rose Red,* Delacorte, 1966.

Christmas, Crowell, 1967.

(Editor) *A Little Prayer,* Hastings House, 1967.

A Garland of Games and Other Diversions: An Alphabet Book, Holt, 1969.

Miss Rumphius, Viking, 1982.

(Reteller) J. Grimm, *Little Brother and Little Sister,* Doubleday, 1982.

Island Boy, Viking, 1988.

Hattie and the Wild Waves, Viking, 1990.

The Story of Christmas, illustrated by Loretta Krupinski, HarperCollins, 1995.

Eleanor, Viking, 1996.

ILLUSTRATOR

Bertil Malmberg, *Ake and His World,* Farrar & Rinehart, 1940.

Frances M. Frost, *Uncle Snowball,* Farrar & Rinehart, 1940.

Oskar Seidlin and Senta Rypins, *Green Wagons,* Houghton, 1943.

Anne Molloy, *Shooting Star Farm,* Houghton, 1946.

Phyllis Crawford, *The Blot: Little City Cat,* Holt, 1946.

Nancy Hartwell, *Shoestring Theater,* Holt, 1947.

L. L. Bein, *Just Plain Maggie,* Harcourt, 1948.

Lee Kingman, *The Rocky Summer,* Houghton, 1948.

Ruth Crawford Seeger, *American Folk Songs for Children in Home, School and Nursery School: A Book for Children, Parents and Teachers,* Doubleday, 1948, Linnet, 1993.

Child Study Association of America, *Read Me Another Story,* Crowell, 1949.

Rutherford George Montgomery, *Kildee House,* Doubleday, 1949, Walker, 1994.

Lee Kingman, *The Best Christmas,* Doubleday, 1949, reprinted, Peter Smith, 1985.

Phyllis Krasilovsky, *The Man Who Didn't Wash His Dishes,* Doubleday, 1950.

Ruth Crawford Seeger, *Animal Folk Songs for Children: Traditional American Songs,* Doubleday, 1950.

Nellie M. Leonard, *Graymouse Family,* Crowell, 1950.

Child Study Association of America, *Read Me More Stories,* Crowell, 1951.

Rutherford George Montgomery, *Hill Ranch,* Doubleday, 1951.

Elisabeth C. Lansing, *The Pony That Ran Away,* Crowell, 1951.

Lee Kingman, *Quarry Adventure,* Doubleday, 1951, published in England as *Lauri's Surprising Summer,* Constable, 1957.

Elisabeth C. Lansing, *The Pony That Kept a Secret,* Crowell, 1952.

Mary M. Aldrich, *Too Many Pets,* Macmillan, 1952.

Margaret Wise Brown, *Where Have You Been?,* Crowell, 1952, reprinted, Scholastic Book Services, 1966.

Barbara Reynolds, *Pepper,* Scribner, 1952.

Miriam E. Mason, *Yours with Love, Kate,* Houghton, 1952.

Margaret Wise Brown, *Christmas in the Barn,* Crowell, 1952.

Catherine Marshall, *Let's Keep Christmas,* Whittlesey House, 1953.

Ruth Crawford Seeger, *American Folk Songs for Christmas,* Doubleday, 1953.

Nellie M. Leonard, *Grandfather Whiskers, M. D.: A Graymouse Story,* Crowell, 1953.

Lee Kingman, *Peter's Long Walk,* Doubleday, 1953.

Elisabeth C. Lansing, *A Pony Worth His Salt,* Crowell, 1953.

Jane Quigg, *Fun for Freddie,* Oxford University Press, 1953.

Margaret Sidney, *The Five Little Peppers,* Doubleday, 1954.

Margaret Wise Brown, *The Little Fir Tree,* Crowell, 1954, reissued, 1985.

Margaret G. Otto, *Pumpkin, Ginger, and Spice,* Holt, 1954.

Helen Kay (pseudonym of Helen C. Goldfrank), *Snow Birthday,* Farrar, Straus, 1955.

Louisa May Alcott, *Little Women; or, Meg, Jo, Beth, and Amy,* Crowell, 1955.

Louise A. Kent, *The Brookline Trunk,* Houghton, 1955.

Catherine S. McEwen, *Away We Go! One-Hundred Poems for the Very Young,* Crowell, 1956.

Catherine Marshall, *Friends with God: Stories and Prayers of the Marshall Family,* Whittlesey House, 1956.

H. Kay, *City Springtime,* Hastings House, 1957.

Neil Anderson (pseudonym of Jerrold Beim), *Freckle Face,* Crowell, 1957.

Henrietta Buckmaster, *Lucy and Loki,* Scribner, 1958.

Harry Behn, *Timmy's Search,* Seabury, 1958.

Margaret G. Otto, *Little Brown Horse,* Knopf, 1959.

Elizabeth George Speare, *Seasonal Verses Gathered by Elizabeth George Speare from the Connecticut Almanack for the Year of the Christian Era, 1773,* American Library Association, 1959.

Le Hibou et la Poussiquette (French adaptation of *The Owl and the Pussycat* by Edward Lear), translated by Francis Steegmuller, Little, Brown, 1961.

Walter de la Mare, *Peacock Pie: A Book of Rhymes,* Knopf, 1961.

Noah Webster, *The American Speller: An Adaptation of Noah Webster's Blue-Backed Speller,* Crowell, 1961.

Margaret G. Otto, *Three Little Dachshunds,* Holt, 1963.

Sarah Orne Jewett, *A White Heron: A Story of Maine,* Crowell, 1963.

Virginia Haviland, *Favorite Fairy Tales Told in Spain,* Little, Brown, 1963.

Papillot, Clignot, et Dodo (French adaptation of *Wynken, Blynken, and Nod* by Eugene Field), translated by F. Steegmuller and Norbert Guterman, Farrar, Straus, 1964.

Hugh Latham, translator, *Mother Goose in French,* Crowell, 1964.

Anne Molloy, *Shaun and the Boat: An Irish Story,* Hastings House, 1965.

Jane Goodsell, *Katie's Magic Glasses,* Houghton, 1965.

Samuel Morse, *All in a Suitcase,* Little, Brown, 1966.

Aldous Huxley, *Crowns of Pearblossom,* Random House, 1967.

Alastair Reid and Anthony Kerrigan, *Mother Goose in Spanish*, Crowell, 1968.

Edward Lear, *The Owl and the Pussy-Cat*, Little, Brown, 1969.

Natalia M. Belting, *Christmas Folk*, Holt, 1969.

Eugene Field, *Wynken, Blynken and Nod*, Hastings House, 1970.

William Wise, *The Lazy Young Duke of Dundee*, Rand McNally, 1970.

Homer, *Dionysus and the Pirates: Homeric Hymn Number 7*, translated and adapted by Penelope Proddow, Doubleday, 1970.

Felix Salten (pseudonym of Siegmund Salzman), *Bambi: A Life in the Woods*, Simon & Schuster, 1970.

Book of Princesses, Scholastic Book Services, 1971.

Homer, *Hermes, Lord of Robbers: Homeric Hymn Number Four*, translated and adapted by Penelope Proddow, Doubleday, 1971.

Homer, *Demeter and Persephone: Homeric Hymn Number Two*, translated and adapted by Penelope Proddow, Doubleday, 1972.

John Becker, *Seven Little Rabbits*, Walker, 1972.

May Garelick, *Down to the Beach*, Four Winds, 1973.

Robyn Supraner, *Would You Rather Be a Tiger?*, Houghton, 1973.

Dorothy Joan Harris, *The House Mouse*, Warne, 1973.

Edna Mitchell Preston, *Squawk to the Moon, Little Goose*, Viking, 1974.

Zora L. Olsen, *Herman the Great*, Scholastic Book Services, 1974.

Elinor L. Horwitz, *When the Sky Is Like Lace*, Lippincott, 1975.

Jean Poindexter Colby, *Lexington and Concord, 1775: What Really Happened*, Hastings House, 1975.

Edna Mitchell Preston, *The Sad Story of the Little Bluebird and the Hungry Cat*, Four Winds, 1975.

Marjorie Weinman Sharmat, *Burton and Dudley*, Holiday House, 1975.

M. Jean Craig, *The Donkey Prince*, Doubleday, 1977.

Aileen Fisher, *Plant Magic*, Bowmar, 1977.

Ellin Greene, compiler, *Midsummer Magic: A Garland of Stories, Charms, and Recipes*, Lothrop, 1977.

Donald Hall, *Ox-Cart Man*, Viking, 1979.

Delmore Schwartz, *I Am Cherry Alive, the Little Girl Sang*, Harper, 1979.

Norma Farber, *How the Hibernators Came to Bethlehem*, Walker, 1980.

Wendy Ann Kesselman, *Emma*, Doubleday, 1980.

Margot C. Griego and others, selectors and translators, *Tortillitas para Mama and Other Nursery Rhymes: Spanish and English*, Holt, 1982.

John Bierhorst, translator, *Spirit Child: A Story of the Nativity*, Morrow, 1984.

Rumer Godden, *The Story of Holly and Ivy*, Viking, 1985.

Sergei Prokofiev, *Peter and the Wolf: A Mechanical Book*, Viking, 1985.

Toni de Gerez, reteller, *Louhi, Witch of North Farm*, Viking, 1986.

Elinor L. Horwitz, *When the Sky Is Like Lace*, Lippincott, 1987.

Gloria Houston, *The Year of the Perfect Christmas Tree: An Appalachian Tale*, Dial, 1988.

Alice McLerran, *Roxaboxen*, Lothrop, 1991.

Michael Bedard, *Emily*, Doubleday, 1992.

Jane Yolen, *Letting Swift River Go*, Little, Brown, 1992.

Ruth Sawyer, *The Remarkable Christmas of the Cobbler's Sons*, Viking, 1994.

Opal Whiteley, *Only Opal: The Diary of a Young Girl*, selected and adapted by Jane Boulton, Philomel, 1994.

OTHER

Twenty-Five Years A-Graying: The Portrait of a College Graduate, a Pictorial Study of the Class of 1938 at Smith College, Northampton, Massachusetts, Based on Statistics Gathered in 1963 for the Occasion of Its 25th Reunion, Little, Brown, 1963.

Contributor of illustrations to periodicals.

■ Adaptations

Chanticleer and the Fox was adapted as a sound filmstrip by Weston Woods, 1959; *Wynken, Blynken and Nod* was adapted as a sound filmstrip by Weston Woods, 1967; *Owl and the Pussycat* was adapted as a sound filmstrip, 1967; *The Man Who Didn't Wash His Dishes* was adapted as a sound filmstrip by Weston Woods, 1973; *Squawk to the Moon, Little Goose* was adapted as a sound filmstrip by Viking, 1975; *Miss Rumphius* was adapted as a filmstrip with cassette by Live Oak Media, 1984; *Ox-Cart Man* was adapted as a filmstrip with cassette by Random House and as a videocassette by Live Oak Media; *How the Hibernators Came to Bethlehem* was adapted as a filmstrip with cassette by Random House; *American Folk Songs for Children* was adapted as a cassette.

■ Sidelights

Described by Kay E. Vandergrift in *Twentieth Century Children's Writers* as "one of the most prolific and most versatile author/illustrators in the children's book field," Barbara Cooney is recognized as a writer, artist, and reteller who brings dignity, delicacy, sensitivity, and technical skill to over a hundred books—mostly for children—in a career that has spanned more than fifty years. Praised for her diversity, insight, thorough research, and attention to detail as well as for the love of nature and strong sense of place in her works, Cooney is the creator of picture books, retellings, fiction, and nonfiction; she is best known for her adaptations of European tales and for her picture books with American settings. Several of these latter works are set in the nineteenth or early twentieth centuries and include autobiographical background information. In these books, which are often regarded as superior social histories, Cooney expresses the continuity and interconnectedness of generations; she often depicts young children and the elderly as characters, especially those who are considered somewhat different and who are in tune with the natural world. Cooney underscores her works with her affection for New England, particularly for her adopted state of Maine, and her books are often noted for their authenticity and accurate depiction of lifestyle. As a reteller, Cooney is acknowledged for bringing freshness, wit, and accessibility to stories that come from historical sources. As an artist, she is well known for creating a recognizable style while using a variety of mediums as well as for developing a scratch-board technique and the craft of color separation. She went from using black-and-white line drawings, a medium with which she was initially forced to stay by her publishers, to drawing in charcoal, working with collage, and painting in watercolor and in bright hues with acrylics on fiber; she is also interested in photography, a medium that influences her art. Celebrated for her evocation of landscapes and exteriors, Cooney is often acknowledged for her success in matching her illustrations, which reflect primitive and folk art as well as medieval designs and cultural details from her international travels, to the texts of the books she illustrates. In honor of her talents as an artist, Cooney was twice awarded the Caldecott Medal, for her *Chanticleer and the Fox* in 1959 and for *Ox-Cart Man,* a book by Donald Hall for which she provided the pictures, in 1980. Lee Bennett Hopkins, a writer with four books illustrated by Cooney, wrote of her in *Books Are By People,* "Her work . . . is interrelated with her life. Her books are gay, entertaining, and simple, yet complex. Is it any wonder that children young and old enjoy books by Barbara Cooney?"

Born in Brooklyn, New York, Cooney comes from a long line of artists. Her great-grandfather, a German immigrant who settled in Manhattan, was a commercial artist, making cigar-store Indians for a living and painting oils on canvas "by the yard," Cooney said in the *Horn Book Magazine.* She continues, "My grandmother, when she was little, sometimes helped him 'putting in the skies.' In my mind's eye I see that little girl, named Philippina Krippendorf, painting away, making yards and yards of fluffy clouds and sunsets and storms with clouds and rainbows." Cooney's mother, Mae Evelyn Bossert, was an amateur impressionist painter in oils and watercolors. "She was," notes Cooney, "also very generous. I could mess with her paints and brushes all I wanted. One condition, that I kept my brushes clean." Cooney once told *Something about the Author* (*SATA*), "I've been drawing pictures for as long as I can remember. It's in the blood . . . . My favorite days were when I had a cold and could stay home from school and draw all day long." Cooney related in *Horn Book,* "I was no more talented . . . than any other child. I started out ruining the wallpaper with crayons, like everybody else, and making eggs with arms and legs. Most children start this way, and most children have the souls of artists. Some of these children stubbornly keep on being children even when they have grown up. Some of these stubborn children get to be artists . . . . I became an artist because I had access to materials and pictures, a minimum of instruction, and a stubborn nature."

Cooney's second grandmother had a home in Waldboro, Maine, where Barbara spent nearly every summer. Her father, Russell Schenck Cooney, she told *SATA,* "was a stockbroker and we lived for the most part in suburbia, which I didn't like as much as Maine. I attended boarding school and, although I was always considered the 'class artist,' I was truly terrible. We had very little in the way of art education. Perhaps because I wasn't exposed to strict formal training, I probably didn't have proper respect for what that could be. I never seriously considered going to art school, for example. Now I wish I had gone. But I wanted a liberal arts education, and so went to Smith College . . . . In art, I was way behind technically, and what I've learned I have had to teach myself. To this day, I don't consider myself a very skilled artist." At Smith, Cooney took courses mainly in art history. "As graduation neared," she told *SATA,* "I realized I had to decide what to do with myself in the 'real world.' Book illustration, I thought, might be a way to use what little talent I judged I had." Cooney began receiving instruction in etching and lithography at the Art Students League in New York, "not so much," she confided to *SATA,* "because I wanted to work in those mediums but because I thought they would help my black-and-white drawing skills. After not too long, I put together a portfolio, trudged it around to art directors and landed some work."

With the outbreak of the Second World War, Cooney joined the Women's Army Corps (WACS), because, she said, "I felt I wanted to do something to contribute . . . . I was in Officer's Candidate School, went through basic training, and to this day make my bed the way I was taught in the army." Although she became a second lieutenant, Cooney notes, "My military career didn't last long." Marriage and her first pregnancy pushed her into leaving the military and turning to more domestic matters.

"The first twenty years of my life," Cooney wrote in *Children's Literature Association Quarterly,* "I spent growing up. The next twenty years I was busy getting married and having children, staying home and taking care of my family, and decorating books. I drew what was near at hand—children—over and over again. Children—and animals. It sometimes seemed that the number of jobs offered was in direct proportion to the quality of the fur I drew." Throughout her career as an illustrator, Cooney has provided the pictures for the works of such authors as Margaret Wise Brown, Edward Lear, Margaret Sidney, Delmore Schwartz, Louisa May Alcott, Walter de la Mare, Elizabeth George Speare, Sarah Orne Jewett, Eugene Field, Rumer Godden, Homer, Jane Yolen, Felix Salten, Virginia Haviland, Noah Webster, Ruth Sawyer, and Aldous Huxley. Soon after beginning work as an illustrator, Cooney began writing and illustrating books of her own. Although she received positive reviews for her first three books, all stories for middle graders, the picture book *Chanticleer and the Fox* was recognized as a work of special merit. A retelling of the fable from Geoffrey Chaucer's *Canterbury Tales* in which a handsome rooster nearly loses his life through the flattery of a sly fox, *Chanticleer* is lauded both for its contemporary flavor and for the beauty of its illustrations, line drawings with five-color overlays. A reviewer in the *Chicago Tribune* described the book as a volume "destined by its design and superb illustrations to be a modern classic" and claimed that many children will "love and recognize this book as a treasure. Many adult collectors will claim it for their own." Margaret Sherwood Libby of the *New York Times Book Review* echoed this praise, calling *Chanticleer* a "book for all ages to cherish," while Aldren A. Watson of *Horn Book* maintained, "To lure, coax, or lead the reader to take part in such a story is an art, but to have combined art and artistry in such an ancient and repeatedly published tale as that of Chanticleer is an achievement. It has the look of having appeared now for the first time." Cooney began *Chanticleer,* she said in her Caldecott Medal acceptance speech, because "I just happened to want to draw chickens." Searching for a vehicle, she found her inspiration when she was sick in bed one day with the grippe—"I do seem to get my best ideas when I'm slightly feverish," she noted—and read "The Nun Priest's Tale" in Chaucer's *Canterbury Tales* collection. She spent months researching the Middle Ages at the Cloisters and at the New York Public and Morgan libraries. "I tried to convey in my pictures," she related, "what Chaucer conveys in his words: that people—in this case, chickens—can be beautiful and loveable even when they are being ridiculous. There is another reason, too, for *Chanticleer and the Fox,* and that is, I do think Chaucer is possible for children . . . . [They] have a greater capacity of accepting the world as it is than is generally supposed." Cooney does not think children "should read only about things they understand." Instead, she feels that "'a man's reach should exceed his grasp.' So should a child's. For myself, I will never talk down to—or *draw* down to—children. Much of what I put into my pictures will not be understood . . . Yet if I put enough detail in my pictures, there may be something for everyone. Not all will be understood, but some will be understood now and maybe more later. That is good enough for me."

Writing in *Children's Literature Association Quarterly,* Cooney said, "It was not until I was in my forties, in the fifth decade of my life, that the sense of place, the *spirit* of place, became of paramount importance to me. It was

Based on the experiences of Cooney's mother, *Hattie and the Wild Waves* **shares a turn-of-the-century story about a young girl's childhood experiences and her awakening artistic talents. (Written and illustrated by Cooney.)**

Award-winner Cooney illustrated this Tyrolean folktale of a goblin king whose visit magically transforms the Christmas holiday for a poor cobbler and his sons.

then that I began my travels, that I discovered, through photography, the quality of light, and that I gradually became able to paint the mood of place." When she began to work on her story *The Little Juggler,* a retelling of the legend of the juggler of Notre Dame, Cooney went to France. She wrote in *Horn Book,* "And what unconsciously happened was that my characters began to be no longer isolated from their backgrounds. More and more they became part of the landscape, part of their environment. Perhaps a certain humility was born . . . ." Shortly thereafter, her editor asked Cooney to illustrate *Mother Goose in French* and *Mother Goose in Spanish;* the artist moved her family to both France and Spain and began traveling to several other countries. Cooney has illustrated a number of folktales, nursery rhymes, and myths from around the world. Quoted in *Horn Book,* she said, "I often go to great lengths to get authentic backgrounds for my illustrations. I climbed Mount Olympus to see how things up there looked to Zeus. I went down into the cave where Hermes was born. I slept in Sleeping Beauty's castle." Cooney added in *Children's Literature*

Association Quarterly, "After travelling to many places, both physically and in my head, I finally came home again. I built a house on the coast of Maine, and there . . . I finally painted New England in full color. The pictures for Donald Hall's *Ox-Cart Man* were the first I did in the new house. They show the passage of the seasons in the New Hampshire hills."

Ox-Cart Man, a picture book about a nineteenth-century New Hampshire farmer who makes the long journey from his inland home to a coastal market, is illustrated with art that evokes early American primitive wood paintings while depicting the cycle of working and growing. Writing in the *New York Times Book Review,* Harold C. K. Rice called *Ox-Cart Man* "remarkable in any season," adding "It's the pictures that knock you out." *Horn Book* reviewer Mary M. Burns stated, "Like a pastoral symphony translated into picture book format, the stunning combination of text and illustrations recreates the mood of nineteenth-century rural New England." *Junior Bookshelf* reviewer Marcus Crouch claimed, "This book is a winner.... Here is a whole way of life set down and preserved in all its integrity and beauty." After she received her second Caldecott Medal for *Ox-Cart Man,* Cooney felt that she had finished her apprenticeship as an author and illustrator; the award, she determined, gave her the freedom and assurance to do the books she wanted to do in the manner in which she wanted to do them. "After that book," declared Cooney in *Children's Literature Association Quarterly,* "came *Miss Rumphius,* which is so much my heart that I cannot see it clearly. It is many places, and all of them are part of me.... They are all part of me—and I am part of them." A picture book inspired by a real woman—Hilda the Lupine Lady—who had went about planting flower seeds, *Miss Rumphius* addresses the theme of bequeathing beauty as a legacy. In Cooney's story, Alice Rumphius promises her grandfather as a young girl that she will make the world more beautiful when she grows up. After becoming an international traveler, she comes back to her home town in Maine as an elderly woman to live by the ocean and to create something of beauty before she dies. Alice fulfills her promise to her grandfather by scattering five bushels of lupine seeds around the countryside. "Of all the books I have done," Cooney once said, "*Miss Rumphius* has been, perhaps, the closest to my heart. There are, of course, many dissimilarities between me and Alice Rumphius, but, as I worked, she gradually seemed to become my *alter ego.* Perhaps she had been that right from the start." In an interview with Julia Smith in *Instructor,* the author said that the creation of Miss Rumphius was a major development in her art because, claimed Cooney, "she has a *real* soul." Smith concluded, "*Miss Rumphius* is the story of an artist's challenge. Wanting to add to the beauty of the world, an artist must search for the right means of adding to the beauty that already surrounds us. Miss Rumphius finds her answer and challenges the artist in all of us to find ours." A *Publishers Weekly* critic noted, "With the publication of this book Cooney will have to make room for more awards...." *Miss Rumphius* won the American Book Award in 1983 and was selected as a *New York Times* Best Book of the Year in the same year. In 1989, the Children's and Young Adults' Services Section of the Maine Library Association created the Lupine Award in honor of Cooney and *Miss Rumphius.*

With her next original picture book, *Island Boy,* Cooney creates a hymn to self-reliance and the continuity of life by describing the life and death of a nineteenth-century man on a remote New England island; loosely based on the story of John Gilley, who was born on a lonely Maine island in the nineteenth century, the story is noted for sensitively presenting death to the picture book audience. "Cooney's flawless transitions between the generations and between third-person points of view always maintain a child's perspective," wrote Ginny Moore Kruse in *School Library Journal,* while a *Kirkus Reviews* critic claimed that Cooney's illustrations for "this tribute to self-reliance and an ideal America are as lovely as the ones for *Miss Rumphius* and as evocative of their setting as those in *Ox-Cart Man.*" Writing in the *New York Times Book Review,* Rebecca Lazear-Okrent

concluded that *Island Boy* "is an invitation to our budding rocket scientists and corporate moguls to consider and vicariously enjoy another sort of successful life. For them, Ms. Cooney has created a book in which every word and picture fits her story and its themes." In an interview with Robert D. Hale in *Horn Book,* Cooney dubbed *Island Boy* her favorite work, for reasons she called "obvious."

Cooney's next work as an author/illustrator, *Hattie and the Wild Waves: A Story from Brooklyn,* is a picture book about her mother's childhood in New York City at the turn of the century. While describing Hattie's comfortable life in a Manhattan mansion, a summer house on Rockaway Beach, a Long Island estate, and a Brooklyn hotel, Cooney focuses on her character's decision to become an artist. "Cooney is at her best here," maintained Zena Sutherland in *Bulletin of the Center for Children's Books,* while Ilene Cooper of *Booklist* commented, "Cooney sets out to capture an era, and at this she succeeds, but the heart of the story is a girl's determination to follow her dream." With *The Story of Christmas,* an informational book for primary graders, Cooney traces the origins of a variety of global facts, legends, and customs that helped to define the celebration; the book is a revised edition of the author's earlier *Christmas* (1967). Although some reviewers questioned the reduction of Christian references in the revision, a reviewer in *Publishers Weekly* asserted that Cooney does "a commendable job" of bringing together biblical stories, legends of pagan festivals, and modern customs. *Eleanor* is a picture biography of Eleanor Roosevelt that describes Roosevelt's life from her unhappy childhood through her graduation from an English boarding school at the age of eighteen, an experience that she said "opened the world" for her. According to Maria B. Salvadore in *Horn Book,* Cooney includes illustrations in *Eleanor* that "use a palette of reds and deep pinks to reflect Eleanor's growth in self-confidence...." Barbara Kiefer of *School Library Journal* stated, "Cooney once again brings her unique vision to biography," while Leslie Bennetts of the *New York Times Book Review* commented that "Ms. Cooney's tale is affecting; any child will find it easy to relate to this classic account of an ugly duckling...." In an interview with Julie Yates Walton in *Publishers Weekly,* Cooney said: "I've done a lot of books based on history, but they were not totally factual. I loved writing this book because somehow I felt that I had done what I had never been able to do before: to write exact truth. Every word is researched and true, every sentence I tried to whittle down to its true meaning. I think that *Eleanor* is the nicest thing I've ever written."

Responding in *Horn Book* to queries as to why she became an illustrator, Cooney said, "The answer is that I love stories. Lots of artists have loved stories. The sculptors and vase-painters of ancient Greece were forever illustrating Homer. The Byzantine and Romanesque and Gothic artists spent their lives illustrating the Bible. Stories from the Ramayana were the basis for much of the great art in the Orient. Like all these artists, I love illustrating a good story." As to why she decided

Cooney's self-illustrated biography explores the difficult childhood of First Lady Eleanor Roosevelt. (From *Eleanor.*)

to make picture books for children, Cooney declared, "[In] the world of illustration, the picture-book field is far and away the most exciting. And ... I am *not* making picture books for children. I am making them for *people.*"

Cooney told *SATA,* "As I look back on the decades I've been making books for children, I feel extremely grateful. I've been able to do the books I wanted in the way I wanted. And I have enjoyed some of the 'trappings' that accompany what we tend to think of as 'success.' But the trappings are of relatively minor importance. What counts is the mark on the page."

■ Works Cited

Bennetts, Leslie, review of *Eleanor, New York Times Book Review,* December 8, 1996, p. 78.

Burns, Mary M., review of *Ox-Cart Man, Horn Book Magazine,* February, 1980, pp. 44-45.

Review of *Chanticleer and the Fox, Chicago Tribune— Books,* November 2, 1958, p. 11.

Cooney, Barbara, "The Spirit Place," *Children's Literature Association Quarterly,* winter, 1984-85, pp. 152-53.

Cooney, Barbara, "Caldecott Award Acceptance," *Horn Book Magazine,* August, 1959, pp. 310-14.

Cooney, Barbara, "Caldecott Medal Acceptance," *Horn Book Magazine,* August, 1980, pp. 378-82.

Cooper, Ilene, review of *Hattie and the Wild Waves: A Story from Brooklyn, Booklist,* November 1, 1990, p. 528.

Crouch, Marcus, review of *Ox-Cart Man, Junior Bookshelf,* December, 1980, pp. 283-84.

Hale, Robert D., interview with Barbara Cooney, *Horn Book Magazine,* January-February, 1994, pp. 110-11.

Hopkins, Lee Bennett, *Books Are by People,* Citation Press, 1969, pp. 42-43.

Review of *Island Boy, Kirkus Reviews,* October 1, 1988, p. 1467.

Kiefer, Barbara, review of *Eleanor, School Library Journal,* September, 1996, pp. 195-96.

Kruse, Ginny Moore, review of *Island Boy, School Library Journal,* October, 1988, pp. 116-17.

Lazear-Okrent, Rebecca, review of *Island Boy, New York Times Book Review,* December 4, 1968, p. 40.

Libby, Margaret Sherwood, review of *Chanticleer and the Fox, New York Times Book Review,* November 2, 1958, p. 2.

Review of *Miss Rumphius, Publishers Weekly,* July 9, 1982, p. 49.

Rice, Harold C. K., review of *Ox-Cart Man, New York Times Book Review,* November 11, 1979, p. 51.

Salvadore, Maria B., review of *Eleanor, Horn Book,* September-October, 1996, pp. 610-11.

Smith, Julia, "Barbara Cooney's Award-Winning Picture Books ... 'Make the World More Beautiful,'" *Instructor,* March, 1985, pp. 94-96.

Review of *The Story of Christmas, Publishers Weekly,* September 18, 1995, p. 103.

Sutherland, Zena, review of *Hattie and the Wild Waves: A Story from Brooklyn, Bulletin of the Center for Children's Books,* December, 1990, pp. 81-82.

Vandergrift, Kay E., entry on Barbara Cooney, *Twentieth Century Children's Writers,* Fourth edition, St. James Press, 1995.

Walton, Julie Yates, "Portrait of a First Lady to Be," *Publishers Weekly,* October 14, 1996, pp. 31-32.

Watson, Aldren A., review of *Chanticleer and the Fox, Horn Book Magazine,* October, 1960, pp. 386-87.

■ For More Information See

BOOKS

Children's Literature Review, Gale, Volume 23, 1991.

Colby, Jean Poindexter, *Writing, Illustrating, and Editing Children's Books,* Hastings House, 1967.

Field, Elinor W., *Horn Book Reflections,* Horn Book, 1969.

Fuller, Muriel, editor, *More Junior Authors,* H. W. Wilson, 1963, pp. 53-54.

Georgiou, Constantine, *Children and Their Literature,* Prentice-Hall, 1969.

Hurlimann, Bettina, *Picture-Book World,* World Publishing, 1969.

Klemin, Diana, *The Art of Art for Children's Books,* C. N. Potter, 1966.

Roginski, Jim, compiler, *Newbery and Caldecott Medalists and Honor Book Winners,* Libraries Unlimited, 1982.

PERIODICALS

Booklist, February 1, 1994, pp. 980, 984; March 15, 1995, p. 348.

Bulletin of the Center for Children's Books, November, 1996, pp. 93-94.

Horn Book Magazine, August, 1980, pp. 383-87; November, 1988, pp. 769-70; September, 1992, p. 581; May, 1994.

Junior Bookshelf, December, 1989, p. 262.

Kirkus Reviews, October 15, 1995, p. 1488.

Los Angeles Times Book Review, November 20, 1988, p. 8.

New York Times Book Review, April 25, 1982, p. 42; November 14, 1982, p. 43; December 4, 1988, p. 40; January 6, 1991, p. 26.

Publishers Weekly, March 23, 1959; July 29, 1988, p. 138; June 29, 1990, p. 68; March, 1991, pp. 194-95; April 12, 1991, p. 57.

School Library Journal, October, 1995, p. 36.

Washington Post Book World, May 9, 1982, p. 16; November 6, 1988, p. 14.

—*Sketch by Gerard J. Senick*

*   *   *

COOPER, Floyd

■ Personal

Education: University of Oklahoma, B.F.A.

■ Addresses

Home—East Orange, NY.

■ Career

Author and illustrator. Worked in advertising and for a greeting card company in Missouri; freelance illustrator, 1984—.

■ Awards, Honors

Notable Book selection, American Library Association, for *Grandpa's Face*, written by Eloise Greenfield; Parents' Choice Award, Parents' Choice Foundation, 1990, for *Laura Charlotte*, written by Kathryn Osebold Galbraith; Coretta Scott King Honor citation for Illustration, American Library Association, 1995, for *Meet Danitra Brown*.

■ Writings

SELF-ILLUSTRATED

Coming Home: From the Life of Langston Hughes, Philomel, 1994.
Mandela: From the Life of the South African Statesman, Philomel, 1996.
Cumbayah, Morrow, in press.

ILLUSTRATOR

Margaret Davidson, *The Story of Jackie Robinson, Bravest Man in Baseball*, Dell, 1988.
Eloise Greenfield, *Grandpa's Face*, Philomel, 1988.
Elizabeth Fitzgerald Howard, *Chita's Christmas Tree*, Bradbury Press, 1989.
Kathryn O. Galbraith, *Laura Charlotte*, Philomel, 1990.
Jacqueline Woodson, *Martin Luther King Jr. and His Birthday*, Silver-Burdett, 1990.
Karen Lynn Williams, *When Africa Was Home*, Orchard Books, 1991.
Deborah Eaton, *Petey*, Silver Burdett, 1992.
Denise Burden-Patmon, *Imani's Gift at Kwanzaa*, Modern Curriculum Press, 1992.
Jean Merrill, *The Girl Who Loved Caterpillars: A Twelfth-century Tale from Japan*, Philomel, 1992.
Virginia M. Fleming, *Be Good to Eddie Lee*, Philomel, 1993.
Joyce Carol Thomas, *Brown Honey in Broomwheat Tea: Poems*, HarperCollins, 1993.
Wade Hudson, selector, *Pass It On: African-American Poetry for Children*, Scholastic, 1993.
Sandra Belton, *From Miss Ida's Porch*, Four Winds Press, 1993.
Gerald Hausman, reteller, *Coyote Walks on Two Legs: A Book of Navajo Myths and Legends*, Philomel, 1993.
Judith Gorog, *Tiger Lily*, Philomel, 1994.
Nikki Grimes, *Meet Danitra Brown*, Lothrop, 1994.
Kathryn D. Jones, *Happy Birthday, Dr. King*, Modern Curriculum Press, 1994.
Candy Dawson Boyd, *Daddy, Daddy, Be There*, Philomel, 1995.
Joyce Carol Thomas, *Gingerbread Days: Poems*, HarperCollins, 1995.

Elizabeth Fitzgerald Howard, *Papa Tells Chita a Story*, Simon & Schuster, 1995.
Wade and Cheryl Hudson, selectors, *How Sweet the Sound: African-American Songs for Children*, Scholastic, 1995.
Carol J. Farley, *King Sejong's Secret*, Lothrop, 1995.
James Haskins and Kathleen Benson, *African Beginnings*, Lothrop, 1995.
Virginia Hamilton, *Jaguarundi*, Blue Sky Press, 1995.
Jane Kurtz, *Pulling the Lion's Tale*, Simon & Schuster, 1995.
Monalisa DeGross, *Arabbin' Man*, Hyperion, 1996.
Nikki Grimes, *Danitra Brown Leaves Town*, Lothrop, 1996.
Virginia L. Kroll, *Faraway Drums*, Little, Brown, 1996.
Alan Schroeder, *Satchmo's Blues*, Doubleday, 1996.
Nancy Lamb, *One April Morning: Children Remember the Oklahoma City Bombing*, Lothrop, 1996.
Patricia C. McKissack, *Ma Dear's Aprons*, Atheneum, 1997.
J. C. Collins, *I Have Heard of a Land*, HarperCollins, 1997.
Jane Yolen, *Miz Berlin Walks*, Philomel, 1997.

■ Sidelights

Author and illustrator Floyd Cooper has brought to life many stories, poems, songs, and works of nonfiction detailing centuries of African-American experience. Beginning his career as a children's book illustrator with his work on the 1988 picture book *Grandpa's Face* after spending several years in the advertising field and working for a greeting card company, Cooper has since been hailed by critics for what a *Publishers Weekly* reviewer called his "painterly, sun-drenched portraits" and Lois F. Anderson lauded as "reveal[ing] keen observations of people and neighborhood" in a *Horn Book* review.

Grandpa's Face, written by Eloise Greenfield, is the sensitive portrait of a young girl named Tamika who sees her grandfather's expression become scary; unaware that he is practicing for the part of an angry character in a play, she purposefully misbehaves to see if he could get angry enough at her to wear such a mean expression. Illustrating the work in muted pastel tones of gold and rich warm brown, Cooper's work was praised by a *Publishers Weekly* critic for "reinforc[ing] in the pictures the feelings of warmth and affection that exist between generations." Such feelings were also kindled in his artwork for Kathryn Galbraith's *Laura Charlotte*, as a young girl's fear of the dark at bedtime is diminished with the story of how her favorite stuffed animal—an elephant who once belonged to her mother—came to be. Cooper's grainy, "somber-toned illustrations envelop the reader in their warmth as they capture the mood of summer nights and cozy bedrooms," noted a *Publishers Weekly* commentator.

Sandra Belton's *From Miss Ida's Porch* evokes an earlier age as elderly residents of a city's African American neighborhood gather in the early evening hours and recall musical idols Duke Ellington and Marian Anderson. As a counterpoint to Belton's lyrical prose, Cooper's oil wash illustrations "add to the warmth and sense of community," according to *School Library Journal* reviewer Elizabeth Hanson. A *Publishers Weekly* commentator noted that Cooper's pictures "affectingly capture the fading light on the young and old faces and complement the nostalgic quality of the story." Cooper opens a similar window to the past in Patricia C. McKissack's *Ma Dear's Aprons,* as young David tells the story of how he can always tell what day of the week it is by the apron his widowed mother, a domestic servant, wears to work each day. "The love between the mother and son is palpable," noted Maeve Visser Knoth in a *Horn Book* review, "and the composition and colors of the illustration emphasize the strength of the relationship; Ma Dear leans toward or touches David Earl in each picture." Also praising Cooper's oil-wash artwork, Hazel Rochman commented in *Booklist* that his illustrations "show the exhausting work, as well as the proud and loving bonds of family." In addition to stories—both of the African-American experience and of other cultures, such as twelfth-century Japan in his highly praised work for Jean Merrill's *The Girl Who Loved Caterpillars*—Cooper has illustrated several collections of verse for younger children, including two volumes by poet Joyce Carol Thomas. Thomas's first collection, *Brown Honey in Broomwheat Tea,* features watercolor illustrations that a *Publishers Weekly* reviewer characterized as "essentially realistic but enveloped in a haze of light," and that *Booklist* contributor Janice Del Negro noted "invite the viewer to participate in the family gatherings and ritual tea brewing that take place." In Thomas's *Gingerbread Days,* the twelve poems featured—one for each month of the calendar year—are "made even stronger by Floyd Cooper's glowing golden illustrations," in the opinion of Martha V. Parravano in *Horn Book.* And praising the illustrator's work for Wade Hudson's compilation *Pass It On: African-American Poetry for Children,* Jane Marino remarked upon Cooper's characteristic "glowing colors and skillfully drawn faces" in her *School Library Journal* review.

In his self-illustrated picture-book biography of Langston Hughes, Cooper explores the lonely childhood of this celebrated African-American writer.

Featuring the artwork of Floyd Cooper, *Laura Charlotte* illustrates how a young girl, comforted by a stuffed elephant that once belonged to her mother, overcomes her fear of the dark. (From *Laura Charlotte,* written by Kathryn O. Galbraith.)

In addition to picture books and poetry for young readers, nonfiction works have also benefitted from Cooper's artistic talents. In response to the tragedy that occurred in Oklahoma City in 1995, during which nineteen young people were among the many victims, Nancy Lamb and Cooper produced *One April Morning: Children Remember the Oklahoma City Bombing.* According to a *Publishers Weekly* reviewer, Cooper's "softly focused renderings of children ... effectively serve as all-purpose, emotion-laden backdrops to the disquieting but ultimately life-affirming text." *Booklist* critic Kay Weisman asserted that Cooper's "muted pastel illustrations convey the intense emotion of the survivors from a discrete distance." In 1996's *Satchmo's Blues,* the early life of trumpeter Louis Armstrong is fictionalized through Alan Schroeder's text and what *Booklist* contributor Bill Ott called "some of [Cooper's] best work." Ott continued: "His soft-focus, two-page spreads ... use hazy browns and golds to capture the shimmering heat and pulsing rhythm of New Orleans' streets."

In 1994, Cooper published his first work as both author and illustrator: *Coming Home: From the Life of Langston Hughes.* Focusing on the poet's lonely childhood and his search for a stable home despite his parents' extended absences, Cooper tells of the writer's early years "in a warm and intimate tone that conveys both the deprivations and sources of strength" in Hughes's

youth, according to *Bulletin of the Center for Children's Books* critic Roger Sutton. And Cooper's "writing proves equal to his artwork in highlighting elements that convey the emotion and important events" from Hughes's youth, Louise L. Sherman maintained in *School Library Journal.*

Continuing to pursue an interest in biography, Cooper has also written of another black leader in 1996's *Mandela: From the Life of the South African Statesman.* Retaining a focus on his subject's youth, Cooper illuminates the South African leader's philosophical origins as a child growing up in a Transkai village, and outlines the basis of the character that enabled Mandela to withstand personal difficulties—including an almost thirty-year prison term—during decades of fighting to end apartheid in his homeland. Praising Cooper's artwork, *Publishers Weekly* deemed the volume "a forceful, credible picture of a strong and deeply devoted statesman."

■ Works Cited

Anderson, Lois F., review of *Coming Home: From the Life of Langston Hughes, Horn Book,* September/October, 1994, pp. 604-05.

Review of *Brown Honey in Broomwheat Tea, Publishers Weekly,* October 11, 1993, p. 87.

Del Negro, Janice, review of *Brown Honey in Broomwheat Tea, Booklist,* September 15, 1993, p. 115.

Review of *From Miss Ida's Porch, Publishers Weekly,* July 26, 1993, p. 73.

Review of *Grandpa's Face, Publishers Weekly,* October 28, 1988, p. 78.

Hanson, Elizabeth, review of *From Miss Ida's Porch, School Library Journal,* November, 1993, p. 76.

Knoth, Maeve Visser, review of *Ma Dear's Aprons, Horn Book,* May-June, 1997, p. 310.

Review of *Laura Charlotte, Publishers Weekly,* February 9, 1990, p. 60.

Review of *Mandela: From the Life of the South African Statesman, Publishers Weekly,* August 26, 1996, p. 98.

Marino, Jane, review of *Pass It On: African-American Poetry for Children, School Library Journal,* May, 1993, pp. 99-100.

Review of *One April Morning: Children Remember the Oklahoma City Bombing, Publishers Weekly,* April 15, 1996, p. 69.

Ott, Bill, review of *Satchmo's Blues, Booklist,* September 15, 1996, p. 251.

Parravano, Martha V., review of *Gingerbread Days, Horn Book,* March-April, 1996, p. 219.

Review of *Pass It On: African-American Poetry for Children, Publishers Weekly,* January 18, 1993, p. 471.

Rochman, Hazel, review of *Ma Dear's Aprons, Booklist,* February 15, 1997, p. 1027.

Sherman, Louise L., review of *Coming Home: From the Life of Langston Hughes, School Library Journal,* November, 1994, pp. 95-96.

Sutton, Roger, review of *Coming Home: From the Life of Langston Hughes, Bulletin of the Center for Children's Books,* January, 1995, p. 162.

Weisman, Kay, review of *One April Morning: Children Remember the Oklahoma City Bombing, Booklist,* May 15, 1996, p. 1583.

■ **For More Information See**

PERIODICALS

Booklist, September 1, 1992, p. 54; December 15, 1994, p. 753; September 15, 1996, p. 243.

Horn Book, March-April, 1989, p. 197; November-December, 1993, pp. 743-44; September-October, 1995, pp. 626-27.

Kirkus Reviews, September 15, 1994, p. 1269; August 1, 1996, pp. 1148-49.

New York Times Book Review, February 12, 1995, p. 13; June 18, 1995, p. 25.

Publishers Weekly, October 12, 1992, p. 78; October 10, 1994, p. 70; January 20, 1997, p. 401.

School Library Journal, April, 1990, p. 90; December, 1990, p. 22; September, 1992, p. 269; November, 1993, p. 103; December, 1994, p. 75; June, 1995, p. 87; January, 1996, p. 107; September, 1996, p. 191.

* * *

CREIGHTON, Jill 1949-

■ **Personal**

Born December 2, 1949, in London, Ontario, Canada; daughter of Peter James Arnold (a sales manager) and Pamela Mary Hughes (a teacher); married Robert Creighton (an artist and teacher), December 10, 1977; children: Tom, Anna. *Education:* McMaster University, B.A. *Hobbies and other interests:* Walking, gardening, reading, quilting.

■ **Career**

Writer. Brant County Board of Education, Brantford, Ontario, Canada, teacher, 1988—. Carnegie Gallery, Dundas, Ontario, Canada, director, 1984-86. Member of Lynden community choir.

■ **Awards, Honors**

White Ravens Award, International Youth Library, 1992, for *The Weaver's Horse.*

■ **Writings**

Maybe a Monster, illustrated by Ruth Ohi, Annick, 1989.

One Day There Was Nothing to Do, illustrated by Ruth Ohi, Annick, 1990.

The Weaver's Horse, illustrated by Robert Creighton, Annick, 1991.

Where the Sky Begins, illustrated by Sue Harrison, Annick, 1992.

JILL CREIGHTON

Eight O'Cluck, illustrated by Pierre-Paul Pariseau, Scholastic, 1995.

The Great Blue Grump, illustrated by Kitty Macaulay, Annick, 1997.

■ **Sidelights**

Jill Creighton told *Something about the Author (SATA)*: "I started writing because I had loved books since I was young, and longed to try writing one myself. Only as time went by did I realize that one day I'd be an old lady rocking away and thinking, I didn't have the courage to try. So I reworked a story I'd begun at a university creative writing course, and that became *Maybe a Monster.* The initial idea was based on my then small children, as was the idea for *One Day There Was Nothing to Do.*" Published in 1990, *One Day There Was Nothing to Do* captures the creativity of three children trying to free themselves of boredom. Their mother advises them to conjure up a fun activity and they amusingly do just that, pulling their mother into a series of fictitious situations involving animals battling against her superhuman persona. *Quill and Quire* contributor Ann Gilmore praised Creighton for the "humour and imaginative quality of the text." Pearl Herscovitch, writing in *Canadian Materials,* described *One Day There Was Nothing to Do* as "a warm and satisfying portrayal of family life." "Most of my ideas have some basis in personal experience," Creighton told *SATA.* "My background in weaving and a love of horses (though I don't ride) went into *The Weaver's Horse,* a medieval legend. My husband suggested setting it in the Middle Ages, since he wanted to try illustrations in the style of the Tres Riches Heures of the Duc de Berry. It was exciting to see our work together."

The Weaver's Horse is about a lord who must leave his valuables in the hands of his younger sibling while he goes off to war. Upon Lord Henry's return, he discovers that his brother has impermissibly acquired his castle and sold his beloved horse, Lily. Instead of contending with his brother, Henry leaves to become a talented weaver and to search for his horse. He eventually finds Lily again, but she is taken away when Henry refuses to weave a tapestry of horses for a powerful man. Calling *The Weaver's Horse* an "interesting story," *Canadian Materials* contributor Adele M. Fasick suggested that Henry's decision to "renounce fighting" would be an appropriate discussion topic for older children. *Books in Canada* reviewer Phil Hall added that the book is "sure to enchant its audience."

"The setting for *Where the Sky Begins* came from a fishing village on the north shore of St. Lawrence River in Quebec, where I taught school for two years (1973-75)," Creighton continued. "It was a hauntingly barren place, a difficult place, with a wonderful mosaic of people. I tried to capture the loneliness, the beauty, the hardiness of the people in my story. And I had fun working through the characters and finding out what they were going to do."

Where the Sky Begins involves three children who are inadvertently left on their own after an accident involving a sibling, causing the oldest brother, Jenkin, to feel responsible. The children are unwillingly placed in the custody of their alcoholic uncle, whose unpredictable behaviour prompts them to run away from home. The story's ending brings about a resolution of Jenkin's difficult search for his own personal strength. Praising *Where the Sky Begins* for telling a "compelling story," *Quill and Quire* contributor Fred Boer said the book has "well-developed characters, natural dialogue, and an interesting setting." *Books in Canada* reviewer Heather Kirk called the language "fresh" and commented that the book "illuminates life."

"My background is British and we were required to speak 'properly' growing up," Creighton related to *SATA*. "My parents talked a lot and laughed, and I was always conscious of the sound and shape of words, of how a tone of voice or a look could change meaning. A rich voice, an evocative poem, a simple but powerful story, are like compelling forces of nature to me. So I suppose I write because I want to see if I can do it. But also I want to say something about the magical complexity of the world, about the heroism of ordinary people. Sometimes things seem so funny and silly to me, and I love to capture that feeling of absurdity and play by trapping it in words.

"I'm fascinated by imagination. How can I fit an elephant inside my head? How is it that I can conjure up another world just by saying so, where animals talk or make-believe people stagger through doorways?

"I write in pencil first because I can think and see better that way, and I'm not tied to a machine. Then I type it up on the computer to see how it looks. Then I rewrite on the print-out. At times it's easy, usually it isn't. Words and sentences and ideas run through my head most of the time. I don't always catch them, especially at times like now when my job has taken over my life, but I keep trying."

■ Works Cited

Boer, Fred, review of *Where the Sky Begins, Quill and Quire,* November, 1992, p. 34.

Fasick, Adele M., review of *The Weaver's Horse, Canadian Materials,* November, 1991, p. 353.

Gilmore, Anne, review of *One Day There was Nothing to Do, Quill and Quire,* July, 1990, p. 36.

Hall, Phil, review of *The Weaver's Horse, Books in Canada,* October, 1991, p. 53.

Herscovitch, Pearl, review of *One Day There was Nothing to Do, Canadian Materials,* July, 1990, p. 179.

Kirk, Heather, review of *Where the Sky Begins, Books in Canada,* summer, 1993, p. 31.

■ For More Information See

PERIODICALS

Quill and Quire, August, 1991, p. 24; October, 1995, p. 44; November, 1995, pp. 44-45.

D

DELANEY, Michael 1955-

■ Personal

Born April 7, 1955; son of Thomas (a stockbroker) and Antoinette (an author and illustrator of children's books; maiden name, Barrett) Delaney; married Christine Hauck (a graphic artist), September 24, 1988; children: Emma. *Education:* New York University, B.A., English, 1977.

■ Addresses

Home—25 Sherwood Place, Greenwich, CT 06830. *Agent*—Wendy Schmalz, Harold Ober Associates, 425 Madison Ave., New York, NY 10017. *Electronic mail*—chauck@discovernet.net.

MICHAEL DELANEY

■ Career

Writer and illustrator. *Gourmet* magazine, freelance illustrator, 1981-96; J. Walter Thompson, advertising copywriter, 1985-90.

■ Writings

The Marigold Monster, Unicorn Books, 1983.
Henry's Special Delivery, Dutton, 1984.
Not Your Average Joe, Dutton, 1990.

SELF-ILLUSTRATED

Deep Doo Doo, Dutton, 1996.

OTHER

Cartoons and illustrations published in the *New York Times, National Lampoon,* and *Saturday Review.*

■ Work in Progress

A children's novel.

■ Sidelights

Michael Delaney told *SATA:* "I began writing because I'm really not a very articulate person and I tend to say things that, later, I wish I'd said better and in a funnier way. Writing allows me to show that I am not quite the dunderhead I often think I sound.

"I strive to create books that readers, both young and old, enjoy reading. My hope, my dream, is to write a book that one day finds its way into the 'Classics' section of the Children's Books department of the bookstore. (Ideally, I'd like it to be put there by an employee of the bookstore, rather than by some customer who happened to misplace it.)

"When I work I have a fairly regular (my wife would say boring) routine. I rise at dawn, jog, return home, shower, dress, make breakfast for my daughter, and pack her lunch. After she goes off to preschool and my wife goes off to work, I sit down to write.

"While writing *Deep Doo Doo,* I wanted to create a world in which the adults have made a real mess of things (in this case, politics) and children save the day. My other goal was to write a book that was fun to read. My writing has been influenced by, among others, F. Scott Fitzgerald and E. B. White.

"In addition to these outside influences, I come from a family of children's book authors and illustrators, all of whom, I am happy to say, are still very much on the scene. My mother has written and illustrated several picture books as well as illustrated for *Sesame Street.* My older brother, Ned, has written and illustrated dozens of picture books. And my sister, Molly, has written and illustrated a picture book. If only I had a sibling who was a children's book reviewer for the *New York Times,* I'd be all set."

In Delaney's amusing story, *Deep Doo Doo,* two inventive twelve-year-olds, Bennet and Pete, create an electronic apparatus that will interrupt the televised speech of a gubernatorial candidate. They replace the incumbent's image with film footage of Pete's dog, adding a voice-over script revealing the hypocrisy of the candidate. This disruption leads to the demise of the governor. Linda Perkins, writing for *Booklist,* declared that the "adults are caricatures [and] the premise farfetched," but the characters of the boys make the story "believable and very funny." A critic for *Publishers Weekly* asserted that young readers would enjoy this story's "swift action and political puns." Finally, a critic in *Bulletin of the Center for Children's Books* gave the story a thumbs up for its "generous helping of political satire."

■ Works Cited

Review of *Deep Doo Doo, Bulletin of the Center for Children's Books,* February, 1997.
Review of *Deep Doo Doo, Publishers Weekly,* November 18, 1996, pp. 75-76.
Perkins, Linda, review of *Deep Doo Doo, Booklist,* January 1 & 15, 1997, pp. 858-59.

*   *   *

DIAZ, David 1958-

■ Personal

Born in Fort Lauderdale, FL, 1958; married; wife's name, Cecelia (an artist); children: Jericho, Ariel, Gabrielle. *Education:* Attended Fort Lauderdale Art Institute. *Hobbies and other interests:* Ceramics, music.

■ Addresses

Home—California.

DAVID DIAZ

■ Career

Graphic artist and illustrator. Worked variously as a newspaper illustrator, designer, and graphic artist in California, 1980—.

■ Awards, Honors

Caldecott Medal, American Library Association, 1995, for *Smoky Night.*

■ Illustrator

Gary Soto, *Neighborhood Odes,* Harcourt, 1992.
Len Cabral, *Anansi's Narrow Waist,* Addison-Wesley, 1994, translated as *La Cinturita de Anansi,* 1995.
Eve Bunting, *Smoky Night,* Harcourt, 1994.
Eve Bunting, *Going Home,* HarperCollins, 1996.
Marybeth Lorbiecki, *Just One Flick of a Finger,* Dial, 1996.
Eve Merriam, *The Inner City Mother Goose,* 3rd edition, Simon & Schuster, 1996.
Joseph A. Citro, *Passing Strange: True Tales of New England Hauntings and Horrors,* Chapters, 1996.
Kathleen Krull, *Wilma Unlimited: How Wilma Rudolph Became the World's Fastest Woman,* Harcourt, 1996.
Eve Bunting, *December,* Harcourt, 1997.

■ Sidelights

David Diaz is an illustrator whose career has progressed in a rather topsy-turvy way: he was awarded one of the most prestigious illustration honors in the United States—the American Library Association's 1995 Caldecott Medal—for only his second book project, a child's-eye view of the 1992 Los Angeles riots entitled *Smoky Night.* Commenting on Diaz's illustrations, Caldecott Award Selection Committee chair Grace W. Ruth was quoted in *School Library Journal* as saying: "*Smoky Night* is dramatic and groundbreaking. Diaz uses thickly textured, expressionistic acrylic paintings to portray a night of urban rioting from a child's perspective." And reviewer Hazel Rochman characterized Diaz's artwork in *Booklist* as "powerful—pulsating and crowded; part street mural, part urban collage."

Smoky Night, written by Eve Bunting, depicts a young boy's reaction to rioting on the streets below his family's apartment in an ethnically diverse large-city neighborhood. Although then undertaking his very first illustration assignment for a major publisher (Gary Soto's *Neighborhood Odes* for Harcourt), Diaz was also given the job of illustrating Bunting's text on the strength of a book he had designed that interspersed found objects

Diaz won the 1995 Caldecott Medal for his illustrations for Eve Bunting's *Smoky Night,* a story about the 1992 riots in Los Angeles told from a child's point of view.

Diaz's sepia-toned illustrations grace Kathleen Krull's picture-book biography of Olympic great Wilma Rudolph, who overcame a childhood bout with polio to win three gold medals as a sprinter. (Illustration from *Wilma Unlimited: How Wilma Rudolph Became the World's Fastest Woman.*)

and drawings to reflect a summer spent in Brazil. That style would find its way into *Smoky Night;* in his illustrations for the story, Diaz mixed his heavily outlined acrylic paintings incorporating soothing blue, purple, and green tones with collages of photographs of common objects. In the series of illustrations depicting the looting of a grocery store, for instance, his artwork is layered over a photographed backdrop of spilled cereal. As Diaz recalled of his first encounter with Bunting's text in his Caldecott Medal acceptance speech, as printed in *Horn Book:* "Eve Bunting had taken a timely subject and had handled it in a truly sensitive and thoughtful way. I felt the book could have a positive effect and help erode barriers of prejudice and intolerance. And above all, it was a book that could be part of the post-riot healing process."

Diaz's attempts to make his work part of the "post-riot healing process" were noted by several critics. Commenting on the illustrator's deliberate efforts to make characters of diverse ethnic backgrounds appear physically similar, a *Publishers Weekly* critic asserted that "even the artwork here cautions the reader against assumptions about race." Likewise, Ellen Fader observed in *Horn Book* that "Diaz's bold artwork is a perfect match for the story.... Because each double-page spread is so carefully designed, because the pictorial elements work together harmoniously, the overall effect is that of urban energy, rather than cacophony. Both author and illustrator insist on an headlong confrontation with the issue of rapport between different races, and the result is a memorable, thought-provoking book."

While many commentators found much to praise in *Smoky Night,* its status as 1995 Caldecott Medal recipient left some critics bewildered. As Cathy Collison

noted in the *Detroit Free Press,* "'Smoky Night' is hardly well known, even among those who regularly peruse the children's shelves, and its appeal to children is debatable." One of the book's most outspoken critics, Michael Patrick Hearn, commented in an essay in *Teaching and Learning Literature* that *Smoky Night* was not an appropriate choice for the award. While acknowledging that "David Diaz is certainly a brilliant jacket and cover designer, one of the best in the business," Hearn added: "Taken individually, the rugged, flat designs in heavy outline and simple contour and raw color are indeed striking, but after a while their stylized, detached imagery is a bit numbing. There is a terrible sameness from spread to spread.... I never imagined a riot could appear quite so benign as this." Similarly, while praising Diaz for "tak[ing] up the gauntlet boldly" to illustrate a challenging text, *New York Times Book Review* contributor Selma G. Lanes maintained that committees have a "tendency to reward flashiness over substance. Often such glitzy illustrations accompany subject matter that is of the moment, politically fashionable, and decidedly correct.... *Smoky Night* falls into this ... category of knock-'em-dead artwork for an *au courant* if less than riveting story."

In addition to the award-winning *Smoky Night,* Diaz has illustrated several other picture books that feature urban settings and social problems. In *The Inner City Mother Goose,* Eve Merriam's poetic reflection on the problems of the inner city is republished for a young adult audience and imbued with new life through Diaz's bold use of color and line. Carolyn Phelan praised the artist's work in a *Booklist* review, noting that his "small, intense paintings create portraits rich in composition, color, and gesture." Phelan added: "The images, almost mythic in their sense of representing more than individual people, seem to move with the rhythm of the verse."

And in Marybeth Lorbiecki's *Just One Flick of the Finger*, urban teen violence is explored as a young man's act of taking a gun to school to ward off a local bully is portrayed by Diaz in his characteristic heavy style against a "background [that] evokes a kind of feverish excitement with neon-lit graffiti, peeling walls, flashing color," according to *Booklist* reviewer Hazel Rochman.

Less "message-oriented" books for children have also been graced by Diaz's unique artwork. Poet Gary Soto's highly acclaimed *Neighborhood Odes* features woodcut silhouettes that complement the collection's twenty-one poems in what *Booklist*'s Carolyn Phelan called "an unobtrusive, playful way." Diaz and *Smoky Night* author Eve Bunting collaborated again on *Going Home*, a 1996 picture book featuring a migrant worker family returning to the Mexican town of their birth. Calling the work a "veritable treat for the eyes," a *Publishers Weekly* reviewer added that Diaz "sets his artwork within photographic backdrops that show gaily painted pottery, folk art figurines, Mexican Christmas decorations, festive flowers and other shiny holiday trinkets." "Bunting conveys her message softly, leaving the major role to Diaz," maintained Barbara Kiefer in *School Library Journal*. "His distinctive style is well suited to the setting and the mood of the book." And *Wilma Unlimited: How Wilma Rudolph Became the World's Fastest Woman* is graced by "richly colored, stylized illustrations that—though painted—have the look and permanence of wood carvings" and a font of Diaz's own design, according to *Booklist* reviewer Michael Cart. In illustrating the story of the black child who battled polio to become a three-time gold medalist at the 1960 Olympic Games, Diaz uses watercolor, gouache, and acrylic in sepia tones in his characteristic stylized manner to "artfully capture [Rudolph's] physical and emotional determination," in the words of *Horn Book*'s Ellen Fader, "as well as the beauty of her body in motion."

■ Works Cited

Cart, Michael, review of *Wilma Unlimited: How Wilma Rudolph Became the World's Fastest Woman, Booklist*, May 1, 1996, p. 1503.

Collison, Cathy, "View of Urban Riots Wins Children's Book Illustration Award," *Detroit Free Press*, February 7, 1995, p. C1.

Diaz, David, "Caldecott Medal Acceptance," *Horn Book*, July-August, 1995, pp. 430-33.

Fader, Ellen, review of *Smoky Night, Horn Book*, May-June, 1994, p. 309.

Fader, Ellen, review of *Wilma Unlimited: How Wilma Rudolph Became the World's Fastest Woman, Horn Book*, September-October, 1996.

Review of *Going Home, Publishers Weekly*, September 23, 1996, p. 76.

Hearn, Michael Patrick, "After the Smoke Has Cleared," *Teaching and Learning Literature*, September-October, 1995, pp. 54-56.

Kiefer, Barbara, review of *Going Home, School Library Journal*, September, 1996, p. 171.

Lanes, Selma G., "Violence from a Distance," *New York Times Book Review*, May 21, 1995, p. 25.

"Newbery, Caldecott Medals Go to New Creators," *School Library Journal*, March, 1995, p. 108.

Phelan, Carolyn, review of *Neighborhood Odes, Booklist*, June 15, 1992, p. 1838.

Phelan, Carolyn, review of *The Inner City Mother Goose, Booklist*, April 15, 1996, p. 1432.

Rochman, Hazel, review of *Smoky Night, Booklist*, March 1, 1994, pp. 1266-67.

Rochman, Hazel, review of *Just One Flick of the Finger, Booklist*, June 1, 1996, p. 1718.

Review of *Smoky Night, Publishers Weekly*, January 31, 1994, p. 89.

■ For More Information See

PERIODICALS

American Spectator, July, 1995, pp. 64-65.
Booklist, October 1, 1996, p. 357.
Horn Book, May-June 1992, pp. 352-53.
Publishers Weekly, March 23, 1992, p. 74; April 29, 1996, p. 73; August 19, 1996, p. 67.
School Library Journal, May, 1992, p. 128; May, 1994, p. 89; May, 1996, p. 142; June, 1996, pp. 116-17; September, 1996, p. 204.

*   *   *

DURRANT, Lynda 1954-

■ Personal

Born December 17, 1954, in Cleveland, OH; daughter of Oliver (an engineer) and Shirley (a teacher; maiden name, Petersen) Durrant; married Wesley Lemmon (an executive), May 27, 1989; children: Jonathan. *Education:* University of Washington, Seattle, B.A., 1979, M.A., 1982. *Politics:* "Moderate." *Religion:* Congregationalist. *Hobbies and other interests:* Horses.

■ Addresses

Home and office—P.O. Box 123, Bath, OH 44210.

■ Career

Writer and teacher.

■ Writings

Echohawk, Clarion, 1996.

■ Work in Progress

Beaded Moccasins: The Story of Mary Campbell; a sequel to *Echohawk;* a novel about Elizabeth Zane.

■ Sidelights

Lynda Durrant told *SATA:* "Even when I was a young reader, I knew that I wanted to write for young readers. I write to a child's enthusiasm, curiosity, and more than

LYNDA DURRANT

anything else, a child's willingness to suspend his disbelief. A children's book could seem outlandish, even repulsive, in any other medium. Children give the writer the benefit of the doubt. That's what makes children's books so special."

■ For More Information See

PERIODICALS

Booklist, September 1, 1996, p. 118.
Bulletin of the Center for Children's Books, October, 1996, p. 56.
Publishers Weekly, September 9, 1996, p. 84.
School Library Journal, September, 1996, p. 201.

DUSSLING, Jennifer 1970-

■ Personal

Born May 8, 1970, in Lima, PA; daughter of John and Ricky (Pfeifer) Dussling. *Education:* University of Delaware, B.A.; College of William and Mary, M.A.

■ Addresses

Home—Highland Park, NJ.

■ Career

Writer.

■ Writings

Finger Painting, illustrated by Carrie Abel, Grosset, 1995.
In a Dark, Dark House, illustrated by Davy Jones, Grosset, 1995.
Under the Sea, illustrated by Marcos Monteiro, Grosset, 1995.
Bossy Kiki, illustrated by Matthew Fox, Grosset, 1996.
Stars, illustrated by Mavis Smith, Grosset, 1996.
Creep Show, illustrated by Jeff Spackman, Grosset, 1996.
A Very Strange Dollhouse, illustrated by Sonja Lamut, Grosset, 1996.
Don't Call Me Names!, illustrated by Tom Brannon, Grosset, 1996.
Muppet Treasure Island, Grosset, 1996.
Top Knots!: The Ultimate Bracelet and Hair-Wrapping Kit, illustrated by Edward Heins, Grosset, 1996.
The Bunny Slipper Mystery, illustrated by Joe Ewers, Grosset, 1997.
A Simple Wish, Grosset, 1997.
Bug Off!, illustrated by Amy Wummer, Grosset, 1997.

■ For More Information See

PERIODICALS

Bulletin of the Center for Children's Books, July, 1996, p. 368.
School Library Journal, August, 1996, pp. 121, 134.

E

EAGLE, Kin
  See ADLERMAN, Daniel and
  ADLERMAN, Kimberly M.

  *   *   *

EHRLICH, Amy 1942-

■ Personal

Born July 24, 1942, in New York, NY; daughter of Max
(a television writer and novelist) and Doris (Rubenstein)
Ehrlich; married Henry Ingraham (a college professor),
June 22, 1985; children: Joss. *Education:* Attended
Bennington College, 1960-62 and 1963-65.

■ Addresses

Home—Box 73, RFD 3, St. Johnsbury, VT 05819.

■ Career

Writer. Early jobs for short periods include teacher in
day-care center, fabric colorist, and hospital receptionist. Freelance writer and editor for publishing companies; roving editor at *Family Circle* magazine; senior
editor at Delacorte Press, 1977-78; Dial Books for
Young Readers, New York City, senior editor 1978-82,
executive editor, 1982-84; Candlewick Press, Cambridge, MA, vice-president, editor-in-chief, 1991-96,
consulting editor, 1996—.

■ Awards, Honors

New York Times Outstanding Book of the Year, 1972,
School Library Journal Best Book of the Year, and *ALA
Children's Books of Exceptional Interest* citations, all for
Zeek Silver Moon; Children's Choice citation, Interna-
tional Reading Association-Children's Book Council
(IRA-CBC), for *The Everyday Train;* "Pick of the Lists"
citation, American Booksellers Association (ABA), Kan-
sas State Reading Circle, and Editor's Choice, *Booklist,*
all for *Leo, Zack, and Emmie;* Editor's Choice, *Booklist,*
Children's Choice, IRA-CBC, Children's Book of the

AMY EHRLICH

Year, Child Study Association, and "Pick of the Lists"
citation, ABA, all for *Thumbelina;* Children's Book of
the Year citation, *Redbook,* 1987, for *The Wild Swans;*
"Pick of the Lists" citation, ABA, and Editor's Choice
citation, *Booklist,* both for *The Snow Queen;* "Pick of
the Lists" citation, ABA, Child Study Association
Children's Book of the Year, and Kansas State Reading
Circle citations, all for *Cinderella;* Young Adult Reviewer's Choice and Best of the Decade citations, *Booklist,*

and Dorothy Canfield Fisher Award, 1990, all for *Where It Stops, Nobody Knows;* Editor's Choice citation, *Booklist*, 1993, for *Parents in the Pigpen, Pigs in the Tub.*

■ Writings

Zeek Silver Moon, illustrated by Robert Andrew Parker, Dial, 1972.

(Adapter) Dee Brown, *Wounded Knee: An Indian History of the American West* (from Brown's *Bury My Heart at Wounded Knee*), Holt, 1974.

The Everyday Train, illustrated by Martha Alexander, Dial, 1977.

(Reteller) Hans Christian Andersen, *Thumbelina,* illustrated by Susan Jeffers, Dial, 1979.

(Reteller) Hans Christian Andersen, *The Wild Swans,* illustrated by Susan Jeffers, Dial, 1981.

Leo, Zack, and Emmie, illustrated by Steven Kellogg, Dial, 1981.

(Reteller) Hans Christian Andersen, *The Snow Queen,* illustrated by Susan Jeffers, Dial, 1982.

(Adapter) *Annie* (storybook from John Huston's movie of the same title), Random House, 1982.

Annie Finds a Home, illustrated by Leonard Shortall, Random House, 1982.

Annie and the Kidnappers, Random House, 1982.

(Editor and adapter) *The Random House Book of Fairy Tales,* illustrated by Diane Goode, Random House, 1985.

(Adapter) *The Ewoks and the Lost Children* (storybook from the George Lucas television film), Random House, 1985.

(Adapter) *Bunnies All Day Long,* illustrated by Marie H. Henry, Dial, 1985.

(Adapter) *Bunnies and Their Grandma,* illustrated by Marie H. Henry, Dial, 1985.

(Adapter) *Bunnies on Their Own,* illustrated by Marie H. Henry, Dial, 1986.

(Adapter) *Bunnies at Christmastime,* illustrated by Marie H. Henry, Dial, 1986.

Leo, Zack, and Emmie Together Again, illustrated by Steven Kellogg, Dial, 1987.

Buck Buck the Chicken, illustrated by R. W. Alley, Random House, 1987.

Emma's New Pony, photographs by Richard Brown, Random House, 1988.

Where It Stops, Nobody Knows (young adult novel), Dial, 1988.

(Adapter) *Pome and Peel,* illustrated by Laszlo Gal, Dial, 1989.

The Story of Hanukkah, illustrated by Ori Sherman, Dial, 1989.

(Adapter) Brothers Grimm, *Rapunzel,* illustrated by Kris Waldherr, Dial, 1989.

Lucy's Winter Tale, illustrated by Troy Howell, Dial, 1991.

The Dark Card (young adult novel), Viking, 1991.

Parents in the Pigpen, Pigs in the Tub, illustrated by Steven Kellogg, Dial, 1993.

Maggie and Silky and Joe, illustrated by Robert Blake, Viking, 1994.

(Editor) *When I Was Your Age: Original Stories about Growing Up,* Candlewick Press, 1996.

Hurry up, Mickey, illustrated by Miki Yamamota, Candlewick Press, 1996.

■ Sidelights

Amy Ehrlich is a writer and editor whose work for children encompasses both original picture books and critically acclaimed young adult novels. Her YA novel, *Where It Stops, Nobody Knows,* was cited among *Booklist* magazine's "Best of the Decade," and many of her picture books have also topped the awards lists. Her works are noted for their innovative story lines and language that challenges the reader. From her first book published in 1972, *Zeek Silver Moon,* it was apparent that Ehrlich would take a different slant on life, and would explore themes that matter to young readers.

"I always wanted to write, even from the time I was a young child," Ehrlich once noted in an interview for *Something about the Author* (*SATA*). Interestingly, Ehrlich was raised in a writer's household. Her father, Max Ehrlich, was a television writer and novelist. Though a distant father, deeply involved in his own work, he influenced his daughter to follow a writing life. "I did read some of his books," Ehrlich told *SATA,* "and I think in a way that had a big influence on me as a writer. He was always proud of my writing." As a young child, Ehrlich would make up a story at night in bed, continuing and building on the tale in her imagination each night. She was also a serious reader, absorbing everything from Laura Ingalls Wilder to Mary Poppins and *Babar.* The first adult novel she tackled was Betty Smith's *A Tree Grows in Brooklyn.* The wonder of books for her was that they "romanticized a very completely drawn alternate reality," as she told *SATA.* "I do really believe in the power of the story in books—not only in children's books, but also adult books."

Growing up in New York and Connecticut, Ehrlich did relatively well in school, but as she noted in *SATA,* she "always felt like a misfit. Inside I always felt different— alienated and out of step." A bright patch in this loneliness was the winning of an award for a short story in the ninth grade, the first time she ever felt special in a truly positive sense. With her parent's divorce, Ehrlich's mother left the role of housewife and started what became a successful travel agency. As a junior in high school, Ehrlich wanted to leave public school, where she felt an outsider, and her mother sent her to a Quaker boarding school in Poughkeepsie, New York. "That was a very good experience because I was in an advanced English class in my senior year, and the teacher was very good," Ehrlich explained to *SATA.* Also, the entire atmosphere of the school, with its emphasis on academic and intellectual achievement, was a match for Ehrlich and prepared her for the rigors of a college education.

Ehrlich attended Bennington College from 1960 to 1962 and again from 1963 to 1965, but "never quite finished.... The 1960s were wild and I was a classic case," she told *SATA.* Throughout the 1960s and early

1970s, Ehrlich lived a roving life, taking jobs as a teacher in a day care center, as a fabric colorist, and as a receptionist. Eventually, she gravitated to freelance and part-time work in publishing, writing copy and working with children's books as an editorial assistant. During this time she would generally spend the summers on a commune in Vermont, then return to New York in the fall and find freelance work again.

"I had wanted to write a children's book for a long time and my boss encouraged me to write one," Ehrlich told *SATA.* "I was writing a lot of copy and she'd always say, 'Oh, your copy's so good—why don't you write a book?'" Ehrlich tried, but had trouble initially finding the right material. Then some friends of hers in California had a baby and Ehrlich wanted to send a little story as a present. "I sat down and started writing this thing. After I got to the second page I realized I was writing a book." The text for *Zeek Silver Moon* took a weekend of nonstop work to complete, and was published exactly as written. The winner of the *New York Times* Outstanding Book of the Year award, among others, *Zeek Silver Moon* was representative of the manner in which parents were bringing up children at the time, tracing the everyday childhood events of the first five years of a boy's life.

Ehrlich then took a break from books, spending a year in Jamaica with a friend, and then in 1973, after returning to the United States, she had a son. "After my son was born," Ehrlich told *SATA,* "my view of life changed dramatically." Moving back to New York City, Ehrlich continued with her writing, adapting Dee Brown's *Bury My Heart at Wounded Knee* for young readers. Ehrlich's *Wounded Knee* was thus an overview of the conquest of the Indians of the American West by European settlers, ending with the carnage of Wounded Knee. A single parent, Ehrlich also took various editorial jobs, eventually ending up at Dial for six years. In 1977, she published *The Everyday Train,* a picture book story of a little girl who loves to watch the freight train pass her house each day. Ehrlich's 1979 retelling of the Hans Christian Andersen story, *Thumbelina,* also garnered a favorable response, as did her *Leo, Zack, and Emmie,* an easy-to-read title about how the new girl in Leo and Zack's class affects their friendship. There followed more retellings, based on both fairy tales and movies, as with Ehrlich's *Annie* books, based on the movie about Little Orphan Annie.

Much of Ehrlich's time, however, was devoted to the corporate world of publishing, and this executive life was not to her liking. Conventions and sales conferences were a strain, and when her sister became ill in Vermont, Ehrlich went to take care of her. She initially planned to be gone a matter of months; instead, she never returned. She began writing more and then met a man who eventually became her husband. More picture books and adaptations followed, including *Cinderella,* for which Ehrlich teamed up with the illustrator Susan Jeffers, with whom she had worked on several other adaptations. A *Publishers Weekly* reviewer commented that the pair's collaboration on *Cinderella* "surpasses

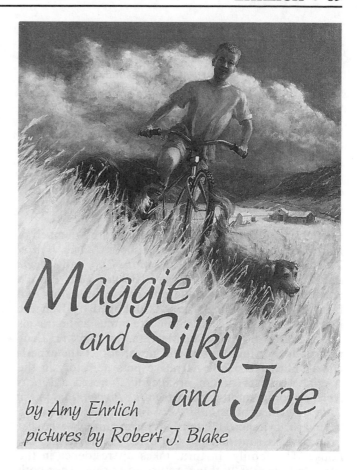

Joe has had a life-long relationship with his two pet dogs and must deal with heartbreaking loss when one of them dies.

them all." A *Bulletin of the Center for Children's Books* critic noted that "Ehrlich's simplified adaptation ... makes this edition particularly appropriate for reading aloud."

Reviewing Ehrlich's retelling of the Grimm fairy tale *Rapunzel, Horn Book* contributor Carolyn K. Jenks wrote that this "elegant, spare retelling" is "more distanced from the reader, creating a feeling of mysterious beauty." Ehrlich also retold a Venetian fairy tale with her *Pome and Peel,* the story of Peel, who risks his life to save his brother Pome's bride from her father's curse. "Young readers will be entranced by this Venetian fairy tale, with its many classic ingredients," noted a *Publishers Weekly* critic, while Betsy Hearne of the *Bulletin of the Center for Children's Books* concluded that the "total effect is sophisticated enough to appeal beyond the older picture book crowd to romantic fairy tale readers."

Despite the favorable response to her retellings, Ehrlich began to leave adaptations behind, concentrating more and more on original picture books and young adult novels. Her subjects for picture books are wide-ranging, from the daily lives of second-graders, to the loss of a pet, to contemporary fairy tales, to the story of Hanukkah. Ehrlich returned to the world of Leo, Zack, and Emmie with her *Leo, Zack, and Emmie Together Again,* set during the winter amid a flurry of snowballs, valentines, and a bout of chicken pox. Lauralyn Persson, writing in *School Library Journal*, concluded that the "expert blend of picture and story makes this a book that will be a popular and worthwhile choice for the easy-reader shelves." Ehrlich teamed with illustrator Ori Sherman for *The Story of Hanukkah*, a "notable Hanukkah picture book that combines both cohesive storytelling and distinguished art," according to Betsy Hearne in *Bulletin of the Center for Children's Books*. A *Kirkus Reviews* critic commented that the origin of the Festival of Lights is "retold in clear, well-cadenced, biblically formal language."

Ehrlich's rural Vermont life is also mirrored in much of her work, including the picture books *Lucy's Winter Tale, Parents in the Pigpen, Pigs in the Tub*, and *Maggie and Silky and Joe*. With *Lucy's Winter Tale*, Ehrlich created something of a modern fairy tale—the story of a farm girl named Lucy who is kidnapped by Ivan the juggler and placed in his miniature circus as he travels on in search of his love, Martina. In the end, Lucy returns to her family, but will never forget the experience. "Ehrlich's poetic narrative puts her story in the special world of dream or allegory," noted a *Kirkus Reviews* commentator. *Parents in the Pigpen, Pigs in the Tub*, described by a *Publishers Weekly* reviewer as "a barnyard switcheroo," tells of farm animals who get tired of their routine lives and decide to move into the house. The family, in turn, takes up residence in the barn, but eventually things return to normal when both parties get tired of the new arrangement. "Ehrlich and [illustrator Steven] Kellogg ... invest the naively accommodating family with a goofy cheerfulness that provides much of the book's humor," the *Publishers Weekly* writer added. Vanessa Elder, writing in *School Library Journal*, concluded that the book was "squeaky clean fun that's bound to get the children guffawing."

More somber of tone is *Maggie and Silky and Joe*, the story of a young farm boy who grows up with the family's cow dog, Maggie. When a stray puppy, Silky, comes to the farm, Maggie helps to train the younger dog. But Maggie grows old, and one day, taking refuge under the back porch during a thunder storm, she dies, and young Joe must learn to deal with loss. A *Publishers Weekly* commentator called the book a "tender story of the death of a beloved pet," noting that it managed to avoid sentimentality by "letting honest facts speak for themselves." *Booklist*'s Hazel Rochman similarly asserted that "kids will feel Joe's sorrow, the physicality of his loss."

Though she has written only two young adult novels, Ehrlich is perhaps better known for these than for her many picture books, retellings, and easy-readers. *Where It Stops, Nobody Knows* remains a popular title a decade after it was written, while *The Dark Card* broke new ground in subject matter for YA novels. Inspired by the real-life experience of her son's friend, *Where It Stops, Nobody Knows* is the story of a young adolescent, Nina, and her mother Joyce, who together continually move from place to place. There is a mystery surrounding these moves, for Nina can never let her friends know where she is going. Is it about the $16,000 that Joyce has hidden or perhaps stolen? Is Joyce her mother's real name? Clue is laid upon clue until the ending, "which proves surprising when it is finally revealed," according to a *Kirkus Reviews* critic, who added that "the narrative is taut enough to hold attention until its believable, unsentimental conclusion." Zena Sutherland, reviewing the novel in *Bulletin of the Center for Children's Books*, concluded that it was "trenchant and touching." Awards committees agreed, and *Where It Stops, Nobody Knows* earned several honorary citations.

With *The Dark Card*, Ehrlich again explored the life of a young girl in difficult circumstances. Trying to come to terms with her mother's death, seventeen-year-old Laura is lured into the glitzy world of Atlantic City's casinos. Dressing in her mother's clothes and jewelry, she assumes a new identity by night at the casinos, becoming involved with a slick gambler named Ari, who in one startling scene induces Laura to strip for him. Eventually Laura escapes from what becomes a dangerous situation for her, though as Robert Strang noted in *Bulletin of the Center for Children's Books*, her escape is "a relief rather than a victory." Strang added: "Laura's story is sad, but more significant, it's scary." A *Kirkus Reviews* critic commented that even "minor characters here are well drawn ... while relationships are deftly portrayed," and concluded that the book was a "well-structured cautionary tale ... that also thoughtfully explores the complicated feelings that can follow the loss of a flawed parent."

"I feel very strongly about the books that I'm writing and about the market in general," Ehrlich told *SATA*. "My books shouldn't preach or offer simple answers." Despite some criticism for the edgy situations depicted in her YA novels, Ehrlich feels that her first job as a writer is to provide a story. "I don't think kids have any trouble with any of it; I just think that some adults do." As she once remarked, books need to reach young readers. "Basically I do feel that the best book (at least for children) is the most readable and entertaining book. The writer's job as far as I am concerned is first and foremost to tell a good story about characters the readers will care about." And the editor in Ehrlich made her add: "Good editing is terribly important for writers. A good editor is as valuable as the financial terms of a contract or the promotion budget for a book—much *more* valuable, come to think about it."

■ Works Cited

Review of *Cinderella, Bulletin of the Center for Children's Books*, October, 1985, p. 35.

Review of *Cinderella, Publishers Weekly*, September 27, 1985, p. 96.

Review of *The Dark Card, Kirkus Reviews*, March 1, 1991, p. 317.

Elder, Vanessa, review of *Parents in the Pigpen, Pigs in the Tub, School Library Journal*, October, 1993, p. 98.

Hearne, Betsy, review of *The Story of Hanukkah, Bulletin of the Center for Children's Books,* December, 1989, p. 82.

Hearne, Betsy, review of *Pome and Peel, Bulletin of the Center for Children's Books,* September, 1990, p. 6.

Jenks, Carolyn K., review of *Rapunzel, Horn Book,* November-December, 1989, p. 779.

Review of *Lucy's Winter Tale, Kirkus Reviews,* August 15, 1992, p. 1060.

Review of *Maggie and Silky and Joe, Publishers Weekly,* July 25, 1994, p. 55.

Review of *Parents in the Pigpen, Pigs in the Tub, Publishers Weekly,* August 16, 1993, p. 102.

Persson, Lauralyn, review of *Leo, Zack, and Emmie Together Again, School Library Journal,* October, 1987, pp. 110-11.

Review of *Pome and Peel, Publishers Weekly,* December 22, 1989, p. 56.

Rochman, Hazel, review of *Maggie and Silky and Joe, Booklist,* July, 1994, p. 1954.

Review of *The Story of Hanukkah, Kirkus Reviews,* July 15, 1989, p. 1074.

Strang, Robert, review of *The Dark Card, Bulletin of the Center for Children's Books,* April, 1991, pp. 190-91.

Sutherland, Zena, review of *Where It Stops, Nobody Knows, Bulletin of the Center for Children's Books,* January, 1989, p. 120.

Review of *Where It Stops, Nobody Knows, Kirkus Reviews,* November 1, 1988, p. 1603.

■ For More Information See

BOOKS

Seventh Book of Junior Authors and Illustrators, Wilson, 1996, pp. 95-96.

Twentieth-Century Young Adult Writers, edited by Laura Standley Berger, St. James Press, 1994, pp. 198-200.

PERIODICALS

Booklist, October 1, 1987, pp. 325-26; July, 1992, p. 1942; January 1, 1993, p. 818; September 15, 1993, p. 150; April 15, 1996, p. 1437.

Horn Book, January, 1994, p. 62.

Junior Bookshelf, June, 1986, pp. 103-4; December, 1989, pp. 291-92; December, 1991, pp. 272-73.

New York Times Book Review, December 17, 1989, p. 29.

Publishers Weekly, February 22, 1991, p. 219; August 10, 1992, p. 70; March 4, 1996, p. 66.

School Library Journal, July, 1990, p. 76; April, 1991, p. 141; September, 1992, p. 202; September, 1994, p. 184; August, 1996, p. 152.

—*Sketch by J. Sydney Jones*

EMORY, Jerry 1957-

■ Personal

Born June 24, 1957, in Stanford, CA; married Jeannie Lloyd, 1985; children: Sarah Melendez, Samantha Frances. *Education:* Stanford University, B.A., 1979; University of California-Berkeley, M.A., 1984.

■ Addresses

Home—740 Summit Ave., Mill Valley, CA 94941. *Electronic Mail*—jemory @ hooked.net.

■ Career

Writer. Golden Gate Audubon Society, Berkeley, CA, executive director, 1979-81; Mono Lake Coalition, San Francisco, CA, steward, 1981-85; Charles Darwin Research Station/The Nature Conservancy, Galapagos Islands, Ecuador, director of public relations, 1985-86; Conservation International, Quintana Roo, Mexico, communications consultant, spring, 1987; columnist, "Pacific Beat," for *Pacific Discovery,* California Academy of Sciences, San Francisco, 1988-90.

■ Awards, Honors

California State Graduate Fellowship, 1981-85; Tinker Travel Grant, Latin American Studies, University of

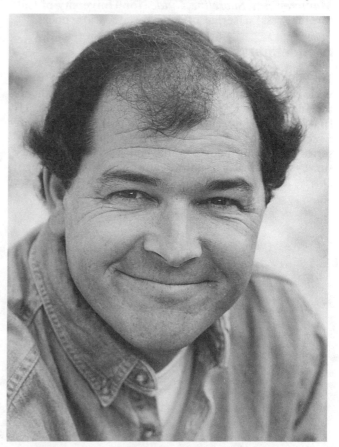

JERRY EMORY

California-Berkeley, 1983; Distinguished Teaching Award, University of California-Berkeley, 1985; Hubert Herring Award for Best Masters Thesis, Pacific Coast Council on Latin American Studies, 1985; Individual Artists Grant for Creative Writing, Marin (County) Arts Council, 1989.

■ Writings

"GREENPATCH" SERIES; NONFICTION FOR YOUNG ADULTS

Nightprowlers: Everyday Creatures under Every Night Sky, illustrated by Annie Cannon with Renee Menge, Harcourt Brace, 1994.

Dirty, Rotten, Dead? A Worm's Eye View of Death, Decomposition ... and Life, illustrated by Taylor Bruce, Harcourt Brace, 1996.

OTHER

San Francisco Bay Shoreline Guide, University of California Press, 1995.

Has written over sixty articles for *National Geographic Magazine, National Geographic World, Coast & Ocean, Travel & Leisure, Orion, Islands, Pacific Discovery, Runner's World, Wilderness,* and other periodical publications.

■ Work in Progress

Monterey Bay Shoreline Guide, for University of California Press; a series of marine education books.

■ Sidelights

Jerry Emory is a writer and environmentalist whose various works share an overarching concern with preserving the environment and endangered species. His first book, *Nightprowlers: Everyday Creatures under Every Night Sky,* a contribution to the "Greenpatch" series for young people published by Harcourt Brace, surveys the night sky and creatures that roam at night. *Dirty, Rotten, Dead? A Worm's Eye View of Death,* *Decomposition ... and Life,* another "Greenpatch" book, shares with Emory's earlier title an oversized format studded with glossy pictures. *Dirty, Rotten, Dead?* provides readers with the science behind death and decomposition in the natural world. Each title contains instructions for related activities, and encourages the reader to join Greenpatch or another environmental group for young people. Short biographies of children who are already Greenpatch members are also part of each title.

The focus of *Nightprowlers* is broad, providing information on phases of the moon, tides, evolutionary theory, and constellations, as well as common nocturnal animals. *Booklist* contributor Janice Del Negro described the presentation of science in *Nightprowlers* as "the 'sound-byte' approach," which, although far from being in-depth in its coverage, is nonetheless "pleasant to browse and may spark a science project from an otherwise reluctant student." Reviewing *Dirty, Rotten, Dead?* for the *Bulletin of the Center for Children's Books,* Deborah Stevenson found the breadth of coverage "appealing," adding that the format "is alluring, as is the book's forthright attitude towards gross subjects."

■ Works Cited

Del Negro, Janice, review of *Nightprowlers: Everyday Creatures under Every Night Sky, Booklist,* November 15, 1994, pp. 592-93.

Stevenson, Deborah, review of *Dirty, Rotten, Dead? A Worm's Eye View of Death, Decomposition ... and Life, Bulletin of the Center for Children's Books,* May, 1996, pp. 298-99.

■ For More Information See

PERIODICALS

Appraisal, autumn, 1995, pp. 58-59.
California Classroom Science, May, 1996.
Publishers Weekly, November 7, 1994, p. 80.
School Library Journal, August, 1996, p. 152.
Science Books & Films, January, 1995, p. 21.

F

FAIR, David 1952-

■ Personal

Born July 20, 1952, in Coldwater, MI; son of Jerry (an architect) and Ann (a teacher; maiden name, Robinson) Fair; married Susan Thomas (a library page) August 23, 1986; children: Robinson. *Education:* Thomas Jefferson College, Ph.B.

■ Addresses

Home—14825 Harrisville Rd., Mt. Airy, MD 21771.

■ Career

Carroll County Public Library, Westminster, MD, librarian and bookmobile head, 1977—. Performer in rock 'n' roll bands, including Half Japanese and Coo Coo Rockin' Time.

■ Writings

The Fabulous Four Skunks, illustrated by Bruce Koscielniak, Houghton, 1996.

■ Sidelights

David Fair told *SATA:* "I grew up in Michigan with three brothers and one sister. We lived at a lake every summer and moved into town during the winter months. In college I took courses in childhood education, switched to filmmaking, and ended up with a bachelor of philosophy. After graduation I moved to California with friends and spent a year writing songs, painting, and shooting super 8 film. When my savings ran out I relocated to the east coast and became a librarian. For a while I lived in my parents' attic and spent all my money on guitars and amplifiers. Along with my brother Jad, I formed a rock and roll band called Half Japanese and recorded several albums.

"I intended to quit rock and roll when I turned thirty but found it difficult to leave behind. I lingered a few

DAVID FAIR

extra years. Eventually I found something I loved even more and in 1986 I got married. In 1989 my son, Robinson, was born. At that point I switched from song writing to story writing.

"I spent many years playing rock and roll music and my book *The Fabulous Four Skunks* is about this experience. Although I didn't start playing until I was in college, the 'four skunks' were much younger. The story was actually based on a band my youngest brother, Peter, had when he was in junior high school.

"Other writers I admire are Paul Rhymer, Mark Twain, Robert Louis Stevenson, Dylan Thomas, Daniel Pinkwater, Bailey White, Ernie Bushmiller, James Marshall, Maira Kalman, and A. A. Milne."

In Fair's humorous *The Fabulous Four Skunks,* Stinky, Smelly, Reeky, and Stenchy form a rock band and get a booking to play at the local teen center even though the manager says they stink. The night of their gig they play for a bunch of animals who turn up their noses, faint away, or leave in disgust when the four skunks play their music. This "stinking" problem is taken care of when the manager hands out clothespins for everyone to wear on their noses so they can enjoy the truly talented musicians without skunk odor getting in the way. A *Publishers Weekly* critic declared that Fair's "gags and double entendres are likely to grab kids." In *Booklist,* Ilene Cooper maintained that the clothespin gag "falls flat," but added that the rest of the story is "laugh-out-loud funny."

■ Works Cited

Cooper, Ilene, review of *The Fabulous Four Skunks, Booklist,* February 1, 1996, p. 937.
Review of *The Fabulous Four Skunks, Publishers Weekly,* January 15, 1996, p. 461.

■ For More Information See

PERIODICALS

Kirkus Reviews, January 1, 1996, p. 67.
School Library Journal, April, 1996, p. 108.

* * *

FLEISCHMAN, (Albert) Sid(ney) 1920-
(Carl March)

■ Personal

Born March 16, 1920, in Brooklyn, NY; son of Reuben and Sadie (Solomon) Fleischman; married Betty Taylor, January 25, 1942; children: Jane, Paul, Anne. *Education:* San Diego State College (now University), B.A., 1949. *Hobbies and other interests:* Magic, gardening.

■ Addresses

Home and office—305 Tenth St., Santa Monica, CA 90402.

■ Career

Writer for children and adults. Is also a screenwriter and has been a professional magician. Worked as a magician in vaudeville and night clubs, 1938-41; traveled with Mr. Arthur Bull's Francisco Spook Show (magic act), 1939-40; *Daily Journal,* San Diego, CA, reporter and rewrite man, 1949-50; *Point* (magazine), San Diego, associate editor, 1950-51; full-time writer, 1951—. Author of scripts for television show *3-2-1 Contact,* 1979-82. *Military service:* U.S. Naval Reserve, 1941-45; served as yeoman on destroyer escort in the Philippines, Borneo, and China. *Member:* Authors Guild, Authors

SID FLEISCHMAN

League of America, Writers Guild of America West, Society of Children's Book Writers and Illustrators (SCBWI).

■ Awards, Honors

New York Herald Tribune's Children's Spring Book Festival Award Honor Book and *Boston Globe-Horn Book* Award Honor Book, both 1962, both for *Mr. Mysterious & Company;* Spur Award from the Western Writers of America, Southern California Council on Literature for Children and Young People Award, and Boys' Clubs of America Junior Book Award, all 1964, George C. Stone Center for Children's Books Recognition of Merit Award, 1972, and Friends of Children and Literature (FOCAL) Award from the Los Angeles Public Library, 1983, all for *By the Great Horn Spoon!;* Commonwealth Club of California Juvenile Book Award, 1966, for *Chancy and the Grand Rascal;* Lewis Carroll Shelf Award, 1969, for *McBroom Tells the Truth; Longbeard the Wizard* was selected one of the American Institute of Graphic Arts Children's Books, 1970; Honor Book, Children's Spring Book Festival Award, *Book World,* and Notable Books selection, American Library Association, both 1971, both for *Jingo Django;* Southern California Council on Literature for Children and Young People Award, 1972, for "Comprehensive Contribution of Lasting Value to the Literature for Children and Young People"; Honor Book, Golden Kite Award, Society of Children's Book Writers, 1974, for *McBroom the Rainmaker;* Mark Twain Award, Missouri Association of School Libraries, and Charlie May Simon Children's Book Award, Arkansas Elementary School Council, both 1977, and Young Hoosier Award, Association for Indiana Media Educators, 1979, all for *The Ghost on Saturday Night;* National Book Award finalist and *Boston Globe-Horn Book* Award for Fiction, both 1979, both for *Humbug Mountain;* Newbery Medal, American Library Association, and Children's Books of the Year selection, Child Study Association of America, both 1987, both for *The Whipping Boy;* Paul A. Witty Award, International Reading Association, and Children's Picturebook Award, *Redbook,* 1988, both for *The Scarebird;* Parents Choice Award, 1990, for *The Midnight Horse,* and 1992, for *Jim Ugly;* Nene Award, 1992, for *The Whipping Boy.* Several of Fleischman's books were named Junior Literary Guild selections in their respective years of publication.

■ Writings

FOR CHILDREN AND YOUNG ADULTS

Mr. Mysterious & Company, illustrated by Eric von Schmidt, Little, Brown, 1962, Greenwillow, 1997.

By the Great Horn Spoon!, illustrated by E. von Schmidt, Little, Brown, 1963, published as *Bullwhip Griffin,* Avon, 1967.

The Ghost in the Noonday Sun, illustrated by Warren Chappell, Little, Brown, 1965, new edition illustrated by Peter Sis, Greenwillow, 1989.

Chancy and the Grand Rascal, illustrated by E. von Schmidt, Little, Brown, 1966, Greenwillow, 1997.

McBroom Tells the Truth, illustrated by Kurt Werth, Norton, 1966, new edition illustrated by Walter Lorraine, Little, Brown, 1981.

McBroom and the Big Wind, illustrated by K. Werth, Norton, 1967, new edition illustrated by W. Lorraine, Little, Brown, 1982.

McBroom's Ear, illustrated by K. Werth, Norton, 1969, new edition illustrated by W. Lorraine, Little, Brown, 1982.

Longbeard the Wizard, illustrated by Charles Bragg, Little, Brown, 1970.

Jingo Django, illustrated by E. von Schmidt, Little, Brown, 1971, Dell, 1995.

McBroom's Ghost, illustrated by Robert Frankenberg, Grosset, 1971, new edition illustrated by W. Lorraine, Little, Brown, 1981.

McBroom's Zoo, illustrated by K. Werth, Grosset, 1972, new edition illustrated by W. Lorraine, Little, Brown, 1982.

The Wooden Cat Man, illustrated by Jay Yang, Little, Brown, 1972.

McBroom's Wonderful One-Acre Farm (includes *McBroom Tells the Truth, McBroom and the Big Wind,* and *McBroom's Ghost*), illustrated by Quentin Blake, Chatto & Windus, 1972, Greenwillow, 1992.

McBroom the Rainmaker, illustrated by K. Werth, Grosset, 1973, new edition illustrated by W. Lorraine, Little, Brown, 1982.

The Ghost on Saturday Night, illustrated by E. von Schmidt, Little, Brown, 1974, reprinted with illustrations by Laura Cornell, Greenwillow, 1997.

Mr. Mysterious's Secrets of Magic (nonfiction), illustrated by E. von Schmidt, Little, Brown, 1975, published as *Secrets of Magic,* Chatto & Windus, 1976.

McBroom Tells a Lie, illustrated by W. Lorraine, Little, Brown, 1976.

Here Comes McBroom (includes *McBroom Tells a Lie, McBroom the Rainmaker,* and *McBroom's Zoo*), illustrated by Q. Blake, Chatto & Windus, 1976, Greenwillow, 1992.

Kate's Secret Riddle Book, F. Watts, 1977.

Me and the Man on the Moon-Eyed Horse, illustrated by E. von Schmidt, Little, Brown, 1977, published in England as *The Man on the Moon-Eyed Horse,* Gollancz, 1980.

Humbug Mountain, illustrated by E. von Schmidt, Little, Brown, 1978.

Jim Bridger's Alarm Clock and Other Tall Tales, illustrated by E. von Schmidt, Dutton, 1978.

McBroom and the Beanstalk, illustrated by W. Lorraine, Little, Brown, 1978.

The Hey Hey Man, illustrated by Nadine Bernard Westcott, Little, Brown, 1979.

McBroom and the Great Race, illustrated by W. Lorraine, Little, Brown, 1980.

The Bloodhound Gang in the Case of the Flying Clock, illustrated by William Harmuth, Random House/ Children's Television Workshop, 1981.

The Bloodhound Gang in the Case of the Cackling Ghost, illustrated by Anthony Rao, Random House, 1981.

The Bloodhound Gang in the Case of Princess Tomorrow, illustrated by Bill Morrison, Random House, 1981.

The Bloodhound Gang in the Case of the Secret Message, illustrated by W. Harmuth, Random House, 1981.

The Bloodhound Gang's Secret Code Book, illustrated by Bill Morrison, Random House, 1982.

The Bloodhound Gang in the Case of the 264-Pound Burglar, illustrated by B. Morrison, Random House, 1982.

McBroom's Almanac, illustrated by W. Lorraine, Little, Brown, 1984.

The Whipping Boy, illustrated by Peter Sis, Greenwillow, 1986.

The Scarebird, illustrated by P. Sis, Greenwillow, 1988.

The Ghost in the Noonday Sun, illustrated by P. Sis, Greenwillow, 1989.

The Midnight Horse, Greenwillow, 1990.

Jim Ugly, illustrated by Jos. A. Smith, Greenwillow, 1992.

The 13th Floor: A Ghost Story, illustrated by P. Sis, Greenwillow, 1995.

The Abracadabra Kid: A Writer's Life (nonfiction), Greenwillow, 1996.

NOVELS; FOR ADULTS

The Straw Donkey Case, Phoenix Press, 1948.

Murder's No Accident, Phoenix Press, 1949.

Shanghai Flame, Fawcett Gold Medal, 1951.

Look behind You, Lady, Fawcett Gold Medal, 1952, published in England as *Chinese Crimson,* Jenkins, 1962.

Danger in Paradise, Fawcett Gold Medal, 1953.

Counterspy Express, Ace Books, 1954.
Malay Woman, Fawcett Gold Medal, 1954, published
     as *Malaya Manhunt,* Jenkins, 1965.
Blood Alley, Fawcett Gold Medal, 1955.
Yellowleg, Fawcett Gold Medal, 1960.
The Venetian Blonde, Fawcett Gold Medal, 1963.

SCREENPLAYS

Blood Alley, starring John Wayne and Lauren Bacall,
     Batjac Productions, 1955.
Goodbye, My Lady (based on a novel by James Street),
     Batjac Productions, 1956.
(With William A. Wellman) *Lafayette Escadrille,* War-
     ner Brothers, 1958.
The Deadly Companions (based on his novel *Yellowleg*),
     starring Maureen O'Hara, Carousel Productions,
     1961.
(With Albert Maltz) *Scalawag,* starring Kirk Douglas,
     Byrna Productions, 1973.
(Under pseudonym Max Brindle) *The Whipping Boy,*
     starring George C. Scott, Disney, 1994.

OTHER

Between Cocktails, Abbott Magic Company, 1939.
(Under pseudonym Carl March) *Magic Made Easy,*
     Croydon, 1953.
(Contributor) Paul Heins, editor, *Crosscurrents of Criti-
     cism,* Horn Book, 1977.
The Charlatan's Handbook, L and L Publishing, 1993.

Fleischman's books have been translated into sixteen
languages.

■ Adaptations

By the Great Horn Spoon! was filmed as *Bullwhip Griffin*
by Walt Disney, 1967; *The Ghost in the Noonday Sun,*
starring Peter Sellers, was filmed by Cavalcade Films,
1974. *The 13th Ghost* was released as an audio recording
in 1996.

■ Sidelights

Regarded as a master of the tall tale as well as one of the
most popular humorists in American children's literature, Fleischman is noted for writing action-filled adventure stories that weave exciting plots, rollicking wit,
and joyous wordplay with accurate, well-researched
historical facts and characterizations that reveal the
author's insight into and understanding of human
nature. He is perhaps best known as the author of *The
Whipping Boy,* a Newbery Medal-winning story that
features a spoiled prince and the stoical lad who takes
his punishment, and a comic series of tall tales about
blustery Iowa farmer Josh McBroom and his amazingly
productive one-acre farm. Compared to such writers as
Mark Twain, Charles Dickens, and Leon Garfield,
Fleischman is praised for his ingenuity, vigorous literary
style, polished craftsmanship, and keen sense of humor.
His works, which often draw on American folklore and
pioneer history and utilize backgrounds such as the
California Gold Rush, seventeenth-century piracy, and
rural life from Ohio to Vermont, are consistently

**Orphaned Touch fights his menacing great-uncle with
the help of The Great Chaffalo, a magician ghost, in
Fleischman's tale of danger and intrigue. (From** *The
Midnight Horse,* **illustrated by Peter Sis.)**

acknowledged for their diversity of subjects and settings. Formerly a professional magician, Fleischman
fills his books with mystery, elements of surprise, and
quick-witted characters. His young protagonists, who
are regarded as figures with whom young readers can
quickly identify, often embark on quests, noted Emily
Rhoads Johnson in *Language Arts,* "for land or treasure
or missing relatives," where "the heroes meet up with
every imaginable kind of trouble, usually in the form of
villains and cut-throats, impostors and fingle-fanglers."
In his *Written for Children,* John Rowe Townsend
asserted that, like Garfield, Fleischman "is fond of
flamboyant, larger-than-life characters, and of mysteries
of origin and identity; a recurrent Fleischman theme is
the discovery of a father or father-substitute." Although
he frequently styles his stories as farces, Fleischman
underscores his works with a positive attitude toward
life and a firm belief in such values as courage, loyalty,
and perseverance. The author's love of language—an
attribute for which he is often lauded—is evident in the
flamboyant names he gives to his characters, his use of
wild metaphors and vivid images, and the colorful
expressions that dot his stories. Johnson explains that
Fleischman's "words don't just sit there on the page;
they leap and cavort, turn somersaults, and sometimes
just hang suspended, like cars teetering at the top of a
roller coaster." Acknowledged as exceptional to read

aloud, Fleischman's works are often considered effective choices for reluctant readers.

Reviewers usually provide Fleischman with a warm critical reception. Johnson noted that he has "produced some of the funniest books ever for children," while Jane O'Connor claimed in the *New York Times Book Review,* "When it comes to telling whopping tall tales, no one can match Sid Fleischman." Writing in the same publication, Georgess McHargue said that Fleischman "can put more action into 32 pages than some authors of 'explosive best sellers' can put into 75 turgid chapters." Writing in the *Horn Book Magazine,* Mary M. Burns added that although Fleischman's books are expectedly funny, his "transforming setbacks into comic situations and seeing possible triumphs where others with lesser gifts see only disasters ... [is perhaps] what makes his books so popular...." Observing that Fleischman's characters care deeply about each other, Johnson noted, "this, I feel, is what gives his books their substance and strength. To know Sid Fleischman, in person or through his work, is to experience an affirmation of life." In *Twentieth Century Children's Writers,* Jane Yolen concluded that Fleischman "has made the particular voice of the tall tale so much his own that, if any one author could be said to be master of the genre, it is he.... [He has made] highly original contributions to the literature of childhood, at least in this critic's opinion."

Born in Brooklyn, New York, Fleischman was raised in San Diego, California. He credits his father Reuben, a Russian Jewish immigrant whom his son calls "an airy optimist with nimble skills," and his mother Sadie, a "crackerjack penny ante card player," with fostering his interest in storytelling. "My earliest literary memories," wrote Fleischman in *Horn Book,* "were funny ones. I remember most vividly the woodman's wife with the link sausages attached to her nose in 'The Three Wishes.' That had me rolling in the aisles—or on the living-room carpet. A little later came Lewis Carroll's Cheshire Cat and the Mad Hatter." Fleischman recalls *Aesop's Fables* and *Uncle Tom's Cabin* being read to him by his mother; however, the book that he claims affected him most profoundly was *Robin Hood,* which he calls "my first great reading experience, and my favorite of those early years." As a minority in San Diego due to his faith, Fleischman developed an identity with underdogs. "I can see this," he told *Language Arts,* "in the dynamics of my choice of characters to write about. The butler in *By the Great Horn Spoon!* The gypsies in *Jingo Django.* And children, of course, are every generation's underdogs." As a small boy, Fleischman developed a strong interest in magic, voraciously reading books on the subject, perfecting tricks to perform, and creating inventions of his own. At the age of seventeen, he decided to write a book of his original tricks, *Between Cocktails;* published when Fleischman was nineteen, the book was still in print over fifty years later. "When I saw my name on the cover," Fleischman recalls, "I was hooked on writing books."

After graduating from high school, Fleischman traveled around the country with stage acts—such as Mr. Arthur Bull's Francisco Spook Show—during the last days of vaudeville. This experience, during which he heard folktales and folk speech in small towns throughout America, is often thought to have influenced the improvisational quality of the author's works; Fleischman's son, Paul, himself a Newbery Award-winning writer, called his father "a prestidigitator of words" in *Horn Book,* while Fleischman referred to his own writing as "sleight-of-mind" in an interview with Sybil S. Steinberg in *Publishers Weekly.* During the Second World War, Flesichman served in the U. S. Naval Reserve on a destroyer escort in the Philippines, Borneo, and China. In 1942, he married Betty Taylor; the couple have three children: Jane, Paul, and Anne. After the war, Fleischman began writing detective stories, suspense tales, and other pulp fiction for adults, learning, he says, "to keep the story pot boiling, to manage tension and the uses of surprise." In 1949, he graduated from San Diego State College and began working as a reporter for the San Diego *Daily Journal.* A year later, Fleischman became associate editor of *Point* magazine, a position he held

Twelve-year-old Jake and his part-wolf dog, Jim Ugly, undertake a perilous journey through the frontier West to track down Jake's missing father. (From *Jim Ugly,* written by Fleischman and illustrated by Jos. A. Smith.)

until 1951 when he became a full-time writer. In 1955, he began a continuing career as a screenwriter when his novel *Blood Alley* was adapted to film.

When his children were young, Fleischman related in *Publishers Weekly,* they "didn't understand what I did for a living. So one day I sat down and wrote a story for children and read it by them." This book, *Mr. Mysterious & Company,* which includes Fleischman and his family as characters, became his first published book for children. Describing the warm relationship of the Hackett family, *Mr. Mysterious* includes the concept of Abracadabra Day, an annual event where children are allowed to be as bad as they want to be without fear of reproach. "A marvelous institution that may well sweep the country," wrote Dorothy M. Broderick in the *New York Times Book Review,* while *Horn Book* reviewer Ruth Hill Viguers called *Mr. Mysterious* "wholly delightful . . . . It is hard to imagine a child who would not enjoy it." The McBroom series about the Iowan and his fertile farmland was prompted during the writing of *Chancy and the Grand Rascal,* a story about a young boy and his "coming-and-going" uncle that Jane Yolen

In this characteristically buoyant Fleischman tale, twelve-year-old Buddy Stebbins is transported back in time and finds himself fighting pirates and witchhunters. (From *The 13th Floor: A Ghost Story,* illustrated by Peter Sis.)

called a "perfect blend of one part quest story and two parts tall tale" in the *New York Times Book Review.* "For all readers who adore braggadocio and consider Paul Bunyan and Pecos Bill the apogee of American humor," Yolen continued, "*Chancy and the Grand Rascal* is a godsend." While coming up with two tall tales for *Chancy,* Fleischman was so amused by his initial invention that he turned it into the first McBroom book, *McBroom Tells the Truth.* Although he did not intend to write another story about McBroom, Fleischman has currently written nearly a dozen books about the folksy character who entertains young readers with a succession of wild impossibilities on, as Zena Sutherland described it in *Bulletin of the Center for Children's Books,* "the marvelous McBroom farm, where instantaneous growth from superfertile soil and blazing Iowa sun provide magnificent crops of food and stories"; in addition to his tales about the farmer and his eleven children, Fleischman has written a compendium of McBroom's homespun advice in almanac format. McBroom's shaggy dog stories are usually considered to be as funny as they are unlikely. In *Now upon a Time: A Contemporary View of Children's Literature,* Myra Pollack Sadker and David Miller Sadker noted that "Fleischman has created a tall tale hero who delights younger independent readers and also provides a grand vehicle for storytelling and reading aloud." Another of Fleischman's most popular series features the Bloodhound Gang, a team of three multiethnic junior detectives. Based on Fleischman's scripts for the *3-2-1 Contact* television show for the Children's Television Workshop, the books are fast-paced, fun-to-solve mysteries directed to middle graders and early adolescents that include short chapters filled with plenty of action. In each book, as Judith Goldberger noted in *Booklist,* "a neatly worked out plot is based on simple, believable gimmicks."

With *The Whipping Boy,* Fleischman departs from his characteristic yarns with American settings to write a story, in the words of *Horn Book* reviewer Ethel L. Heins, in "the manner of Joan Aiken and Lloyd Alexander [that is] set in an undefined time and place." Reminiscent of *The Prince and the Pauper* and written in a style that harkens back to that of nineteenth-century melodramas, *The Whipping Boy* describes how spoiled Horace, nicknamed Prince Brat because of his behavior, runs away with Jemmy, the street-smart orphan who takes the punishment for the things that the prince refuses to do, like learn to read. When they are kidnapped by villains Cutwater and Hold-Your-Nose Billy, the boys switch roles; after escaping the scoundrels in an exciting chase through a rat-filled sewer, Horace and Jemmy return to the palace as friends. Jemmy has learned to sympathize with the prince's restricted life and to admire his courage while realizing his own desire for knowledge, while Horace, who takes a whipping for Jemmy, discovers his personal strength and ability to change. "Like much of the author's writing," maintained Heins, "beneath the surface entertainment the story also speaks of courage, friendship, and trust." Janet Hickman of *Language Arts* concurred, noting that besides "its lively entertainment value and stylistic polish, the story has much to say about human nature and the vagaries of justice." Writing in the *New York Times Book Review,* Martha Saxton concluded, "This is indisputably a good, rollicking adventure, but in its characterizations *The Whipping Boy* offers something special." Frances Bradburn of *Wilson Library Bulletin* added, "The importance of education, the true meaning of friendship, and the need for understanding and compassion for all people are enclosed within the covers of this book—but not so obviously that children will find them offensive. Rather, they are such an integral part of the story that there would be no story without them."

It took almost ten years for Fleischman to write *The Whipping Boy.* The initial idea for the book came to the author from some historical research he was doing for another book. In his Newbery Medal acceptance speech printed in *Horn Book,* Fleischman said, "I stumbled across the catapulting idea for *The Whipping Boy* .... I checked the dictionary. 'A boy,' it confirmed, 'educated with a prince and punished in its stead.'" Fleischman thought he could write the book quickly, but "after about eighteen months," he recalled in *Horn Book,* "I was still trying to get to the bottom of page five." Eventually, Fleischman realized the problem. "My original concept for the story was wrong," he explained. "Wrong, at least, for me. I saw *The Whipping Boy* as a picture book story." One day he read over the manuscript and discovered that his work needed to be much longer: "Once I took the shackles off, the story erupted. Scenes, incidents, and characters came tumbling out of a liberated imagination. Within a few months I had it all on paper." When told that *The Whipping Boy* had won the Newbery Medal, Fleischman was elated. "I don't happen to believe in levitation, unless it's done with mirrors, but for a few days I had to load my pockets with ballast. The Newbery Medal is an enchantment. It's bliss. It should happen to everyone."

Following *The Whipping Boy,* Fleischman published *The Scarebird,* which contains illustrations by Peter Sis, who has also provided the pictures for several of the author's other works. The story and pictures describe how Lonesome John, whose sole companion is the scarecrow in his yard, slowly makes friends with Sam, an orphan looking for work who comes to John's farm. In her review in *Bulletin of the Center for Children's Books,* Betsy Hearne stated, "In a period of thin picture books, this has much to teach about the substance of story and the complement of illustration." With *The Midnight Horse,* Fleischman returns to the adventure story genre with a novel that is, in the worlds of Ethel R. Twichell of *Horn Book,* "a mixture of tall tale, folk tale, and downright magic." The story outlines how Touch, an orphan boy who comes to the town of Cricklewood, New Hampshire—where the entry sign reads "Population 217. 216 Fine Folks and 1 Infernal Grouch"—reclaims his rightful inheritance from his wicked great-uncle with the help of a ghostly magician. "The enjoyment of the book," Twichell concluded, "lies in Fleischman's exuberant narrative flow and his ingenuity in dispatching his scoundrels." A *Publishers Weekly* critic

called *The Midnight Horse* a "deftly told tale of innocence and villainy." Fleischman's next novel, *Jim Ugly,* is a parody set in the Old West that includes such thinly disguised movie stars of the time as Mary Pickford, Douglas Fairbanks, Mae West, and W. C. Fields. In this story, twelve-year-old Jake discovers that the father that he thought he had buried is alive and is accused of stealing some missing diamonds; with his father's dog—which Jake describes as "part elkhound, part something else, and a large helping of short-eared timber wolf"—as companion, Jake and Jim Ugly travel by baggage car from town to town, trying to escape a villainous bounty hunter; in the end, Jake and his father are reunited in San Francisco and the mystery of the diamonds is solved. In *Bulletin of the Center for Children's Books,* Zena Sutherland wrote: "Lively, clever, and humorous, this must have been as much fun to write as it is to read," while *School Library Journal* contributor Katherine Bruner added, "With a little silent-movie piano accompaniment, this rollicking parody of Western melodrama would effortlessly unfold across any stage." With *The 13th Floor: A Ghost Story,* Fleischman makes his first contribution to the time travel genre of fantasy literature. In this work, twelve-year-old Buddy and his lawyer sister Liz are left penniless when their parents are killed in a plane crash. Liz disappears after meeting a client on the thirteenth floor of an old building, and the client turns out to be their ancestor, a young girl accused of witchcraft in Puritan Boston. When Buddy goes after Liz, he is taken by magic elevator to a pirate ship captained by another ancestor and, after being cast adrift, is reunited with Liz, who defends—and acquits—ten-year-old Abigail in court; at the end of the book, the siblings return safely to the twentieth century with a treasure in hand. *Publishers Weekly* advised, "Hold on to your hats—there's never a dull moment when Fleischman is at the helm." "An easy, light-hearted adventure," maintained Ann A. Flowers in *Horn Book,* "yet the author's note also points out the serious consequences of ignorance and superstition."

The Abracadabra Kid: A Writer's Life is Fleischman's autobiography for young readers. Considered as lively and eminently readable as his fiction, *The Abracadabra Kid* includes Fleischman's personal information as well as his advice on writing; each chapter is introduced with quotes from children's letters to the author, ended with a cliff-hanging episode from his life, and illustrated with black and white family photographs. "Sid Fleischman is a pro," asserted Betsy Hearne in *Bulletin of the Center of Children's Books,* "and it shows in this autobiography as much as it does in his fiction." *Kirkus Reviews* claimed that Fleischman "offers a gold mine of interesting reflections of writing," from one who has "lived adventurously and thoughtfully." Writing in *Voice of Youth Advocates,* Candace Deisley commented, "The reader is rewarded with an appreciation for the author's art, and spurred with the desire to read more of his works." Carolyn Phelan of *Booklist* concluded, "From cover to cover, a treat."

■ Works Cited

Review of *The Abracadabra Kid, Kirkus Reviews,* July 1, 1996, p. 967.

Bradburn, Frances, review of *The Whipping Boy, Wilson Library Bulletin,* April, 1987, p. 48.

Broderick, Dorothy M., review of *Mr. Mysterious & Company, New York Times Book Review,* May 13, 1962, p. 30.

Bruner, Katherine, review of *Jim Ugly, School Library Journal,* April, 1992, pp. 113-14.

Burns, Mary M., review of *The Abracadabra Kid: A Writer's Life, Horn Book,* November-December, 1996, p. 759.

Deisley, Candace, review of *The Abracadabra Kid: A Writer's Life, Voice of Youth Advocates,* April, 1997, pp. 52, 54.

Fleischman, Paul, "Sid Fleischman," *Horn Book,* July-August, 1987, pp. 429-432.

Fleischman, Sid, "Laughter and Children's Literature," *Horn Book,* October, 1976, pp. 465-70.

Fleischman, Sid, "Newbery Medal Acceptance," *Horn Book Magazine,* July-August, 1987, pp. 423-28.

Flowers, Ann A., review of *The 13th Floor: A Ghost Story, Horn Book,* November-December, 1995, pp. 741-42.

Goldberger, Judith, review of *The Bloodhound Gang in the Case of the Cackling Ghost* and *The Bloodhound Gang in the Case of Princess Tomorrow, Booklist,* April 15, 1981, p. 1159.

Hearne, Betsy, review of *The Abracadabra Kid, Bulletin of the Center for Children's Books,* September, 1996, pp. 11-12.

Hearne, Betsy, review of *The Scarebird, Bulletin of the Center for Children's Books,* September, 1988, pp. 6-7.

Heins, Ethel L., review of *The Whipping Boy, Horn Book,* May-June, 1986, pp. 325-26.

Hickman, Janet, review of *The Whipping Boy, Language Arts,* December, 1986, p. 822.

Johnson, Emily Rhoads, "Profile: Sid Fleischman," *Language Arts,* October, 1982, pp. 754-59, 772.

McHargue, Georgess, review of *The Hey Hey Man, New York Times Book Review,* January 20, 1980, p. 30.

Review of *The Midnight Horse, Publishers Weekly,* August 10, 1990, p. 445.

O'Connor, Jane, review of *Me and the Man on the Moon-Eyed Horse, New York Times Book Review,* September 11, 1977, p. 32.

Phelan, Carolyn, review of *The Abracadabra Kid: A Writer's Life, Booklist,* September 1, 1996, p. 126.

Sadker, Myra Pollack and David Miller Sadker, *Now Upon a Time: A Contemporary View of Children's Literature,* Harper, 1977, p. 327-28.

Saxton, Martha, review of *The Whipping Boy, New York Times Book Review,* February 22, 1987, p. 23.

Steinberg, Sybil S., "What Makes a Funny Children's Book?: Five Writers Talk about Their Method," *Publishers Weekly,* February 27, 1978, pp. 87-90.

Sutherland, Zena, review of *McBroom's Ear, Bulletin of the Center for Children's Books,* May, 1970, p. 143.

Sutherland, Zena, review of *Jim Ugly, Bulletin of the Center for Children's Books,* March, 1992, p. 179.

Review of *The 13th Floor: A Ghost Story, Publishers Weekly,* October 9, 1995, p. 86.

Townsend, John Rowe, *Written for Children: An Outline of English Language Children's Literature,* revised edition, Lippincott, 1974.

Twichell, Ethel R., review of *The Midnight Horse, Horn Book,* November-December, 1990. p. 744.

Viguers, Ruth Hill, review of *Mr. Mysterious & Company, Horn Book,* June, 1962, p. 279.

Yolen, Jane, review of *Chancy and the Grand Rascal, New York Times Book Review,* November 6, 1966, p. 40.

Yolen, Jane, entry on Sid Fleischman, *Twentieth Century Children's Writers,* Fourth edition, St. James Press, 1995.

■ For More Information See

BOOKS

Cameron, Eleanor, *The Green and Burning Tree,* Atlantic-Little, Brown, 1969.

Cart, Michael, *What's So Funny: Wit and Humor in American Children's Literature,* HarperCollins, 1995.

Children's Literature Review, Volume 15, Gale, 1988.

Huck, Charlotte S. and Doris Young Kuhn, *Children's Literature in the Elementary School,* second edition, Holt, 1968.

Meigs, Cornelia and others, editors, *A Critical History of Children's Literature,* revised edition, Macmillan, 1969.

PERIODICALS

Bulletin of the Center for Children's Books, October, 1995, p. 53.

Horn Book, October, 1976, pp. 465-70; September-October, 1996, p. 567.

Kirkus Reviews, April 1, 1992, p. 463; October 1, 1995, p. 1427.

New York Times Book Review, October 17, 1971.

—Sketch by Gerard J. Senick

*　　*　　*

FORTH, Melissa D(eal)

■ Personal

Born July 3 in Nashville, TN; daughter of Gustavus Waller (a florist) and Evelyn (a seed analyst; maiden name, Prenzel) Tidwell; married Christopher Jackson Deal (a musician; died, 1982). *Education:* Attended Belmont College. *Religion:* Methodist. *Hobbies and other interests:* Horses, snow skiing, reading, antiques.

■ Addresses

Home and office—18 Hale Lane, Darien, CT 06820. *Electronic mail*—MDF7@aol.com (America Online).

■ Career

RC Square Corp., Nashville, TN, manager of the personal offices of musicians and songwriters, including Rodney Crowell and Rosanne Cash; Criterion Music Corp., Nashville, creative director, 1983-86; American Artists Film Corp., Atlanta, GA, 1986-94, began as production assistant and assistant to the director, became associate producer; writer of children's books, 1994—. Associate producer of the television specials, *Angels: Mysterious Messengers* and *Angels II: Beyond the Light,* aired by National Broadcasting Co.; guest on television and radio programs, including *The Oprah Winfrey Show* and *The Rolonda Watts Show.*

■ Writings

The Heavenly Seven: Stories of the Mighty Archangels, illustrated by Robert Schwalb, Andrews & McMeel, 1996.

■ Work in Progress

The Adventures of the Heavenly Seven and *Through the Window in Time,* sequels to *The Heavenly Seven;* a screenplay and film treatment for *The Adventures of the Heavenly Seven; The Ghost of Giggleswick,* for young adults; research in Yorkshire, England.

■ Sidelights

Melissa Deal Forth told *SATA:* "*The Heavenly Seven* is a fresh, new, first-of-its kind adventure story. It is a lively tale of the mightiest angels in the heavens, the original superheroes who were present at the beginning of the world. Michael, Gabriel, Raphael, Uriel, Metatron, Raziel, and Haniel witness the birth of man and the doom of Lucifer. Soon after receiving their superpowers, they form an army of goodness and set out for Earth, weaving themselves into our human history and mythology as they pursue Lucifer and his evil followers Hate, Greed, Ignorance, Fear, Prejudice, and Death. It is a magical, spiritual, and uplifting journey with seven powerful, nonviolent superheroes who guide, inspire, and transform us all with the power, light, and love of God.

"The adventure series was written in hopes of introducing children and young adults, no matter what their religion, color, nationality, or economic status, to a new set of role models—those who teach love, faith, truth, kindness, and hope. I feel the superheroes that saturate children's literature and media today are but metaphors for these truly powerful, super beings that are in constant pursuit of good and war against evil. With these books I hope not only to express the splendor and glory of the angels, but to instill in children a sense of hope and security, even when faced with life's most desperate situations.

"The belief in angels is one of the strongest common threads that bind mankind today. I believe that by introducing angels as role models for our youth, we are making positive steps toward bringing spirituality into their lives early, when values are first established. Who better for our children to imitate than the archangels, the original superheroes?

"My books remind children that they are loved and not alone in this world, that when they are afraid or lonely or scared, there is always an angel nearby, a personal friend who loves them, who hears them, who is there to help and hold them. Today's children are faced with scary times. We must teach them to be kind to one another, themselves, the animals, and the earth. We must teach them to believe in miracles, to hold tight to their dreams, no matter how bleak the situation, for they, themselves, are a miracle and have a right and a purpose to be here!"

■ For More Information See

PERIODICALS

Time, December 27, 1993, pp. 61-62.*

G

GAL, Laszlo 1933-

■ Personal

Born February 18, 1933, in Budapest, Hungary; came to Canada in 1956, naturalized in 1961; son of Istvan and Anna (Gemes) Gal; married Armida Romano Gargarella, January 20, 1962; children: Anna Maria, Raffaella. *Education:* Attended Academy of Dramatic Arts, Budapest, Hungary, 1951-52; Superior School of Pedagogy, Budapest, diploma, 1955. *Religion:* Roman Catholic.

LASZLO GAL

■ Addresses

Home—Toronto, Ontario, Canada.

■ Career

Author and illustrator of books for children. Teacher of art to children in grades five to eight in Budapest, Hungary, for three years; freelance artist beginning in the 1950s; *Globe and Mail,* Toronto, Ontario, Canada, artist of political portraits, c. 1956; Eaton's (department store), Toronto, layout artist, c. 1957; Canadian Broadcasting Company (CBC), Toronto, graphic designer, 1958-65, 1977—; Arnoldo Mondadori Editore, Verona, Italy, illustrator, 1965-69; freelance illustrator, Toronto, 1969-77. *Member:* Royal Canadian Academy of Arts.

■ Awards, Honors

Children's Book of the Year Award, Canadian Library Association (CLA), 1971, for *Cartier Discovers the St. Lawrence;* Children's Books of the Year, Child Study Association of America, 1971, for *The Moon Painters, and Other Estonian Folk Tales;* Best Children's Book of the Year designations, Imperial Order of the Daughters of the Empire, 1978, for *My Name Is Not Odessa Yarker, The Shirt of the Happy Man/La camicia dell' uomo felice,* and *Why the Man in the Moon Is Happy, and Other Eskimo Creation Stories,* and 1980, for *The Twelve Dancing Princesses: A Fairy Story;* Governor General's award for illustration, 1979, and Amelia Frances Howard-Gibbon Illustrator's Medal, CLA, 1980, both for *The Twelve Dancing Princesses: A Fairy Story;* Amelia Frances Howard-Gibbon Illustrator's Award runner-up, and Governor General's award for illustration, both 1984, both for *Hans Christian Anderson's "The Little Mermaid";* nominated for the Hans Christian Andersen Award, 1984; *Canadian Fairy Tales* and *The Willow Maiden* were included in the exhibition at the Bologna International Children's Book Fair, 1985.

■ Writings

SELF-ILLUSTRATED

(Compiler) Hans C. Andersen, *Fiable de Andersen,* Mondadori (Verona), 1967.

(Reteller) *Prince Ivan and the Firebird: A Russian Folktale,* McClelland & Stewart (Toronto), 1991.

(Reteller) *East of the Sun and West of the Moon,* McClelland & Stewart, 1993.

Merlin's Castle, Stoddart (Toronto), 1995.

(Reteller, with Raffaella Gal) *The Parrot: an Italian Folktale,* Douglas & McIntyre, 1997.

ILLUSTRATOR

Maria Luisa Gefaell de Vivanco, reteller, *Le gesta del Cid,* Mondadori, 1965, translated as *El Cid: Soldier and Hero,* Golden Press, 1968.

M. L. Gefaell de Vivanco, *I Nibelunghi,* Mondadori, 1966, translated as *Siegfried: The Mighty Warrior,* McGraw, 1967.

M. L. Gefaell de Vivanco, *Chason de Roland* (title means "Song of Roland"), Mondadori, 1966.

M. L. Gefaell de Vivanco, *Orlando paladino di Francia,* Mondadori, 1968.

M. L. Gefaell de Vivanco, reteller, *Aeneid,* Mondadori, 1969.

Roland Melzack, reteller, *Raven, Creator of the World,* Little, Brown (Boston), 1970.

William Toye, *Cartier Discovers the St. Lawrence,* Walck, 1970.

Selve Maas, reteller, *The Moon Painters, and Other Estonian Folk Tales,* Viking, 1971.

Leslie M. Frost, *Forgotten Pathways of the Trent,* Burns & MacEachern (Ontario), 1973.

Nancy Cleaver, *How the Chipmunk Got Its Stripes,* Clarke, Irwin (Toronto), 1973.

Mary Alice Downie, *Scared Sarah,* Nelson (Toronto), 1974.

Marion Ralston, *Comparative Mythology,* Heath (Toronto), 1974.

Bert Williams, *Sword of Egypt,* Scholastic-TAB, 1976.

Edith Fowke, *Folklore of Canada,* McClelland & Stewart (Toronto), 1976.

Mariella Bertelli, *The Shirt of the Happy Man/La camicia dell' uomo felice,* Kids Can Press (Toronto), 1977.

Marian Engle, *My Name Is Not Odessa Yarker,* Kids Can Press, 1977.

Ronald Melzack, reteller, *Why the Man in the Moon Is Happy and Other Eskimo Creation Stories,* McClelland & Stewart, 1977.

Janet Lunn, reteller, *The Twelve Dancing Princesses: A Fairy Story,* Methuen (Toronto), 1979.

Catherine Ahearn, *Cristobel: A Story for Young People,* Golden Dog Press (Ottawa), 1982.

Margaret Crawford Maloney, reteller, *Hans Christian Andersen's "The Little Mermaid,"* Methuen, 1983.

Eva Martin, reteller, *Canadian Fairy Tales,* Douglas & McIntyre (Vancouver), 1984.

Meghan Collins, *The Willow Maiden,* Dial (New York City), 1985.

Eva Martin, reteller, *Tales of the Far North,* Dial, 1986.

Robert D. San Souci, reteller, *The Enchanted Tapestry: A Chinese Folktale,* Dial, 1987.

Margaret Crawford Maloney, reteller, *The Goodman of Ballengiech,* Methuen, 1987.

Marianna Mayer, *Iduna and the Magic Apples,* Macmillan, 1988.

P. K. Page, *A Flask of Sea Water,* Oxford University Press, 1989.

Marianna Mayer, *The Spirit of the Blue Light,* Macmillan, 1990.

Amy Ehrlich, reteller, *Pome and Peel: A Venetian Tale,* Dial, 1990.

Joanne Robertson, *Sea Witches,* Oxford University Press (Toronto), 1991, Dial, 1991.

Donia Blumenfeld Clenman, *The Moon and the Oyster,* Orca Book Publishers (Victoria, BC), 1992.

Anne Smythe, *Islands,* Douglas & McIntyre (Vancouver, BC), 1995.

Margaret Shaw-MacKinnon, *Tiktala,* Stoddart (Toronto), 1996, Holiday House (New York City), 1996.

Tim Wynne-Jones, reteller, *Dracula,* Key Porter Books (Toronto), 1997.

Several books illustrated by Gal have been made available in braille editions.

OTHER

Sziklaevek: hatrahagyott versek 1969-1975 (collected works), Forum (Ujvidek), 1983.

■ Sidelights

Hungarian-born illustrator and author Laszlo Gal works in Canada, where he produces intricate drawings and paintings that bring to life the works of both legendary folk and fairy tales and the works of modern children's authors. In addition to his more than three decades illustrating retellings of such classical works as the tales of Hans Christian Andersen, Gal has also lately turned author as well as illustrator: his versions of the Russian folktale *Prince Ivan and the Firebird* and Norway's *East of the Sun and West of the Moon* have been praised by critics as well-told and beautifully illustrated volumes that provide young readers with an appealing introduction to traditional folklore. His continued work on behalf of Canadian authors has made Gal one of that country's most highly esteemed illustrators.

Gal was born in Budapest, Hungary, in February of 1933, the youngest in a family of six children. Gal's parents felt that providing an artistic home environment was important; they encouraged each of their children to develop their natural talents in both drawing and music. While one of his brothers would go on to become a successful opera singer, Gal demonstrated an interest in art and a talent for drawing. By the time he was nine years old, he had determined to work toward becoming an illustrator; scarcely four years later the thirteen-year-old artist was in Paris, exhibiting some of his works in an international exhibition of youth art.

A few years after he had established his reputation as a talented young artist, Gal's aspirations turned to acting.

He was accepted into Budapest's prestigious Academy of Dramatic Arts, and began study there in 1951. However, when he was cut from the program the following year, he returned home, convinced that his talents lay elsewhere. After revolts against the country's communist leadership resulted in a dramatic reduction in personal freedom under Hungary's Soviet regime, career choices for young people suddenly became very limited. Despite his wish to become an illustrator, the communist government determined that Gal should use his artistic abilities for the good of the state—as a teacher. He was enrolled at the Superior School of Pedogogy in Budapest and, in 1955, received an Art Education Diploma enabling him to teach art to children.

A year later, political revolution again swept Hungary, and twenty-three-year-old Gal took this opportunity to leave the country and emigrate to Canada. Settling in the city of Toronto, he found odd jobs like washing dishes, waiting tables, and painting signs to keep the bills paid until he was able to put his artistic skills to use. Soon the miscellaneous odd jobs gave way to opportunities to utilize his skills as an artist: Gal worked as a political cartoonist for the Toronto-based *Globe and Mail*, where his work appeared on the editorial page, then as a layout designer for Eaton's department store. By 1958, little more than two years after arriving in North America, he was employed as a graphic designer for the Canadian Broadcasting Company (CBC). Gal

In his self-illustrated retelling *East of the Sun and West of the Moon*, Laszlo Gal follows the traditional Norwegian folktale of a woodcutter's daughter who courageously rescues a prince from danger.

worked for CBC until 1965, later returning to his position in 1977.

In 1962 Gal married Armida Romano Gargarella, a young woman of Canadian and Italian heritage, with whom he would eventually have three children. On a vacation to Italy with his wife in 1963, Gal presented his portfolio to the Verona offices of publisher Arnoldo Mondadori, who was impressed and encouraged the young artist to create illustrations for a text of the Spanish twelfth-century epic poem *El Cid*. The work—over sixty separate illustrations—took the conscientious illustrator more than twelve months to complete, but it was worth it. In 1965 Gal signed a contract with Mondadori to illustrate two full-color books each year. He and his family then moved to Italy, where Gal spent the next four years working as a book illustrator. In addition to his work on Maria Luisa Gefaell de Vivanco's retelling *El Cid: Soldier and Hero*, which was published in 1965, Gal provided illustrations for both de Vivanco's *Siegfried: The Mighty Warrior* and *Chason de Roland*, as well as for Italian translations of the tales of Hans C. Andersen and Virgil's *Aeneid*, the latter published in 1969.

Unfortunately, working as a staff book illustrator didn't provide sufficient income for Gal and his family, and in 1969 the artist returned to Canada. Once again in Toronto, he circulated his portfolio and, with several published books now to his credit, was able to find enough freelance assignments to make ends meet. In 1977 he returned to his graphic designer post at CBC, but has continued to work on illustration projects on the side. He makes time for these efforts during lunch hours, in the evenings, and on weekends. Although Gal tries to maintain a regular schedule, sometimes life intercedes: "I have to put away an illustration for two or three weeks and I have to start it all over again," Gal explained. "If you aren't practicing constantly, you lose the touch."

While Gal prefers to illustrate using a full range of colors, Canadian publishers often require him to design in one or two colors in order to reduce production expenses. Even with these restrictions, Gal seeks perfection in his work. "When I have the final drawing then I think I know what I am doing; but when I start to paint, I always find it isn't the way I thought it would be," he explained to Virginia Van Vliet in *Profiles 2: Actors and Illustrators*. "As I work on each painting my eyes become so critical that as each day passes I want to make it better and better and better. Although I might have liked it the day before yesterday and thought 'That's pretty good,' when I see it the next day in a different surrounding I decide it is not good."

Gal's high standards have not gone unnoticed. In 1978 he won Toronto's Imperial Order of the Daughters of the Empire award for his black and white illustrations in the books *My Name Is Not Odessa Yarker, The Shirt of the Happy Man,* and *Why the Man in the Moon is Happy*. Among his other award-winning books is 1979's *The Twelve Dancing Princesses*, in which Gal invoked a

In order to learn the spirits of the animals, Tiktala is changed into a seal by her spirit guide. (From *Tiktala*, written by Margaret Shaw-MacKinnon and illustrated by Laszlo Gal.)

sense of the Renaissance beauty of Verona that impressed him deeply while living there. The book, which took more than two years to complete, is also a personal favorite of the artist because his daughters, Anna Maria and Raffaella, served as models. As Gal later recalled to Van Vliet, "I said when I finished that if I don't get any results with this book I will never touch another one. One has to be very dedicated or just simply crazy to work for two years for practically nothing as I did for this book. That's why you don't find illustrators in this country because nobody makes sacrifices for what sometimes seems a hopeless cause."

Other books illustrated by Gal include 1990's *A Flask of Sea Water*, which he illustrated in the style of Persian miniatures in tones of gold and deep blue to beautifully complement the text of poet P. K. Page. Margaret Shaw-MacKinnon's *Tiktala*, which recounts the search of a young Inuit artist for spiritual guidance for her art, also benefits from Gal's artistry. As Elizabeth S. Watson noted in *Horn Book*, Gal's "interpretation supports the fantasy and helps make the mystical story accessible to younger children." And his work for Anne Smythe's gently told nature story *Islands* was praised by *Booklist* reviewer Carolyn Phelan, who asserted that "Gal's beautiful artwork, evidently done in oil pastels, gleams with warm tones under the blues and greens of ice, snow, trees, and water."

In more recent years, Gal has begun to illustrate his own texts. *Prince Ivan and the Firebird*, Gal's colorful retelling of the story collected by nineteenth-century folklorist Alexander Afanasyev, was praised as "fluent and sure" by a *Canadian Materials* reviewer, who also noted that his "beautifully rendered details of architecture and costume convey both the flavour of the Russian setting and a touch of fantasy." Gal's story, which concern's the search by the tsar's youngest son for the bird that flew off with rare golden apples from the royal garden, was also praised by Ruth Bennett in *Quill and Quire* as being told "in a leisurely, flowing style," with his pastel and watercolor illustrations "a glorious reflection on and enlargement of the exciting tale." *East of the Sun and West of the Moon* is the tale of a woodcutter's daughter, who is sent to live with a huge white bear by her father, who receives riches in return for his child. Similar in theme to *Beauty and the Beast,* the folk legend is "retold and illustrated ... in fine style," according to Gillian Martin Noonan in *Canadian Materials.*

■ Works Cited

Bennett, Ruth, review of *Prince Ivan and the Firebird, Quill and Quire,* November, 1991, p. 26.

Noonan, Gillian Martin, review of *East of the Sun and West of the Moon, Canadian Materials,* May, 1994, p. 80.

Phelan, Carolyn, review of *Islands, Booklist,* December 1, 1996, pp. 669-70.

Review of *Prince Ivan and the Firebird, Canadian Materials,* May, 1992, p. 158.

Van Vliet, Virginia, "Laszlo Gal," *Profiles 2: Actors and Illustrators,* edited by Irma McDonough, Canadian Library Association, 1982.

Watson, Elizabeth S., review of *Tiktala, Horn Book,* July/August, 1996, p. 456.

■ For More Information See

PERIODICALS

Booklist, July, 1996, p. 1838.

Books in Canada, April, 1992, p. 45; February, 1994, p. 49.

Canadian Materials, March, 1985, p. 71; May, 1992, p. 158.

Horn Book, January-February, 1990, p. 60; May-June, 1990, pp. 366-68.

Publishers Weekly, November 8, 1991, p. 64.

School Library Journal, November, 1991, p. 112; July, 1992, p. 68; May, 1996, p. 98.

*   *   *

GARDELLA, Tricia 1944-

■ Personal

Born July 10, 1944, in San Francisco, CA; daughter of Theodore R. (an attorney and judge) and Gloria June (a homemaker; maiden name, Whitehouse) Vilas; married Jack Gardella (a cattleman), August 3, 1963; children:

TRICIA GARDELLA

Gina (deceased), Michelle Keefe, Jodi Richey, John Gardella. *Education:* Attended Holy Names College. *Politics:* "Nonpolitical." *Religion:* "Raised Catholic."

■ **Addresses**

Home—8931 Montezuma, Jamestown, CA 95327. *Electronic mail:* trigar @ mlode.com.

■ **Career**

Homemaker, rancher, and author. *Member:* Society of Children's Book Writers and Illustrators (regional advisor for North Central California).

■ **Awards, Honors**

Just Like My Dad was listed as one of the Children's Books of the Year, 1993, by the Child Study Children's Book Committee.

■ **Writings**

Just Like My Dad (picture book), illustrated by Margot Apple, HarperCollins, 1993.
Casey's New Hat (picture book), illustrated by Margot Apple, Houghton Mifflin, 1997.

■ **Work in Progress**

Unnamed cookbook, to be published by Boyds Mills Press, that collects favorite recipes from childhood of children's authors and illustrators. Research for the book *Weird Beard: A Pictorial History of Facial Hair.*

■ **Sidelights**

Tricia Gardella's picture books draw on her intimate knowledge of life on a ranch and have earned praise in part for their rare depiction of modern-day cowboys who still round up cattle, mend fences, and spin yarns as in years gone by. In *Just Like My Dad,* Gardella's first book, a young boy puts on chaps, spurs, and his cowboy hat for his first day working alongside his father on the family ranch. In her next book, *Casey's New Hat,* a young girl searches for the perfect new cowboy hat as she and her father run errands to the feed store, a clothing store, and to the veterinarian.

At the center of Gardella's *Just Like My Dad* is the warm relationship between the boy narrator and his rancher father, noted several admiring reviewers. As the boy and his father perform their chores, including mending fences and roping and branding cattle, the boy constantly looks to his father as his model and inspiration. *Just Like My Dad* ends with a very tired little cowboy being tucked into bed by his parents at the end of a long day's work. A reviewer for *Quarter Horse Journal* felt that the idea of "being a cowboy and being with their dad all day" would strike a chord with young readers. Margaret A. Bush, writing in *Horn Book,* lauded the "appealing" way in which the book combines a "strong parent-child relationship" with a portrayal of ranch life. Similarly, Kathy Nowicki in the *Daily Hampshire Gazette* contended, "This book is an education in itself about ranch life as well as a tender story of love between a father and son."

A warm, loving relationship between a child and her family is also the subtext for Gardella's second picture book, *Casey's New Hat.* In this story, a young girl discovers that she is outgrowing her treasured hat. On her father's suggestion, she looks for a new hat while the two run errands associated with the family ranch. Casey's careful search is "an act of self-assertion that even the youngest readers will understand," wrote Lisa S. Murphy in *School Library Journal.* None of the many hats she tries is just right until she spies Grandpa's old hat hanging in the back of the pickup truck. Grandpa tells Casey some of the stories associated with the hat, as if to warn her of the dangerous adventures she might have should she become its owner. According to a reviewer for *Publishers Weekly,* the resulting story is "a good-humored little yarn."

Tricia Gardella told *SATA:* "I was born in San Francisco during World War II. My parents were married shortly before my father, a lieutenant in the navy, was shipped overseas. I was an unexpected surprise. My dad and I met when I was sixteen months old. After the war my father took a job as Assistant District Attorney in Sonora, California, where my mother had graduated from high school. I have lived my life here in the heart of the Mother Lode. I left Tuolumne County for one year to attend college, but dropped out to marry my high school sweetheart, and the town girl moved onto a ranch.

"I've been a voracious reader since I could hold a book. I always thought about writing, but that was something you do 'someday.' Babies, ranching, a ceramics business, teaching myself all the fiber arts, designing, developing and marketing my 'Drimble' line, all kept me busy through 1985. Then one day I said it's time to write. That's actually how it happened. I hadn't a clue where to begin, but I dove in anyway.

"Through Anna Grossnickle Hines, who spoke at a creative writing class I was taking, I discovered the Society of Children's Book Writers and Illustrators (SCBWI). I attended my first conference in the summer of 1986, where I met Judith Ross Enderle and Stephanie Gordon Tessler, who took time, and still take time, for a know-nothing. I sold my first magazine story that same year and then sold more magazine stories in 1987 and my first picture book, *Just Like My Dad,* to Harper and Row in June of 1988. Although I lost my editor there, the book was published in 1993. In the meantime, I sold more magazine stories, but couldn't sell another book until after *Dad* came out. *Casey's New Hat* was sold to Scribners in the fall of 1993. This time, not only did I lose my editor, but Scribners was erased in the Macmillan restructuring. *Casey* was sent to Atheneum, then back to me in April 1994 with a 'Sorry.' It was resold to Houghton Mifflin in June of 1994.

"In 1991 I began writing a weekly picture book review column called 'Picture This' for *The Union Democrat.* It is a great joy. I've never missed a week. I also do reviews for other publications from time to time. I became the regional advisor for the new SCBWI region in North

"Casey, are you coming?" Dad sounded ready.
Casey stood in the center of her room and slowly turned around. That's when she saw it. A red-and-white cord dangling over the edge of her toy basket.
Casey tugged her hat from under the horse trailer Grandpa had given her for her birthday. The trailer came with it.

When Casey outgrows the hat she finds essential to her life on the ranch, she searches for a new one that will be just right for her. (From *Casey's New Hat,* written by Gardella and illustrated by Margot Apple.)

Central California, organized the first Author Days for our county, and taught my first writing for children class at our local community college, all that same year. It only took four years for me to realize all this writing stuff was eating into my writing. I'm in the process of cutting back.

"One of the reasons I began to write was to make sense of the 1970s. In 1970 we lost our oldest daughter to cancer. In that same decade I lost a four-day-old niece, an eighteen-month-old nephew, my twenty-five-year-old brother, and my fifty-six-year-old mother to ventricular arrhythmias, then I was diagnosed with the same condition. I thought I might write about dealing with death. But I also wanted to share what it was like to live on a ranch. What it was like to be a real cowboy. And that's the direction my writing took. Writing—like knitting, weaving, spinning, and all the other fiber arts—keeps my attention because there is so much to learn, so much to explore, and I want to learn it all.

"Lois Lowry was the featured speaker at my first SCBWI conference. Eve Bunting headed our table at the ice-breaker. Liz Gordon was the editor. Oh, how I wanted to be both Lois and Eve. And they made me believe that I could. I also wanted to send a story to Liz Gordon, but knew that every one of the more than two hundred conferees were feeling exactly the same, so I held off sending to her. And when I finally did ... she bought! I thought I'd arrived. I thought I knew it all.

"Luckily, in 1989 I was accepted into Jane Yolen's first master class at Centrum. Here I discovered how little I knew. Here I began to learn to write. And here I began collecting my dearest writer friends. Centrum was the incubating place of my Write Sisters. Since 1991, seven of us—Ann Whitford Paul, Dian Curtis Regan, Helen Ketteman, Kirby Larson, Mary Nethery, Vivian Sathre, and I—from four states, have gathered in Los Angeles for two days of intense critiquing before the National SCBWI conference. We are all now successfully published.

"The more I learn about writing, the more I know what I don't know. I may not sit down to write at a computer every day, but I'm always writing in my head. This blends well with my other passion, fiber arts, which allows for a lot of thinking time. By the time a story has 'stewed,' and I put my fingers to the keyboard, my story is usually pretty close to done. Some stories take only hours to 'cook,' some have been simmering for years. And best of all, over the past three years another rich resource has been added to my idea file. Seven grandbabies! So many stories, so little time."

■ Works Cited

Bush, Margaret A., review of *Just Like My Dad, Horn Book*, July 1993, p. 442.

Review of *Casey's New Hat, Publishers Weekly*, February 3, 1997, p. 106.

Review of *Just Like My Dad, Quarter Horse Journal*, October 1993, p. 92.

Murphy, Lisa A., review of *Casey's New Hat, School Library Journal*, April, 1997, p. 102.

Nowicki, Kathy, review of *Just Like My Dad, Daily Hampshire Gazette*, August 28, 1993, p. 17A.

■ For More Information See

PERIODICALS

Booklist, May 1, 1993, p. 1602; April 15, 1997.

Publishers Weekly, May 3, 1993, p. 304.

School Library Journal, September, 1993, pp. 207-08.

*   *   *

GAVIN, Jamila 1941-

■ Personal

Born August 9, 1941, in Mussoorie, India; daughter of Terence (a retired Indian civil servant) and Florence Jessica (a teacher; maiden name, Dean) Khushal-Singh; married Barrie Gavin (a television producer) in 1971 (divorced, 1990); children: Rohan Robert, Indra Helen. *Education:* Trinity College of Music, L.T.C.L. in piano performance and drama instruction; studied piano in Paris; attended Hochschul fur Musik, Berlin, Germany. *Politics:* Labour Party. *Hobbies and other interests:* Theater.

JAMILA GAVIN

■ Addresses

Home—"The Laurels," All Saints Road, Uplands Stroud, Gloucestershire GL5 1TT, England. *Agent*—Jacqueline Korn, David Higham Associates, 5-8 Lower John St., Golden Square, London W1R 4HA, England.

■ Career

Freelance writer and lecturer. British Broadcast Corporation (BBC), London, radio studio manager, then television production assistant, 1964-71. Member, Stroud Town Council; member of advisory committee, Cheltenham Literary Festival. Writer and co-director, Taynton House Children's Opera Group; affiliated with Children's Drama Group, Niccol Center, Cirencester. *Member:* PEN, West of England Writers, Writers Guild.

■ Awards, Honors

Guardian award (runner up), 1993, for *The Wheel of Surya; Guardian* award (special runner up) and Carnegie Medal nomination, both 1995, both for *The Eye of the Horse.*

■ Writings

The Magic Orange Tree and Other Stories, illustrated by Ossie Murray, Methuen, 1979.
Double Dare and Other Stories, illustrated by Simon Willby, Methuen, 1982.
Kamla and Kate, illustrated by Thelma Lambert, Methuen, 1983.
Digital Dan, illustrated by Patrice Aitken, Methuen, 1984.
Ali and the Robots, illustrated by Sally Williams, Methuen, 1986.
Stories from the Hindu World, illustrated by Joanna Troughton, Macdonald, 1986, Silver Burdett, 1987.
The Hideaway, illustrated by Jane Bottomley, Methuen, 1987.
(Reteller) *Three Indian Princesses: The Stories of Savitri, Damayanti, and Sita,* illustrated by Govinder Ram, Methuen, 1987.
The Singing Bowls, Methuen, 1989.
I Want to Be an Angel, Methuen, 1990.
Kamla and Kate Again, illustrated by Rhian Nest-James, Methuen, 1991.
Deadly Friend, Heinemann, 1994.
A Fine Feathered Friend, illustrated by Carol Walters, Heinemann, 1996.
The Mango Tree, illustrated by Rhian Nest-James, Heinemann, 1996.
Presents, illustrated by Nest-James, Heinemann, 1996.
Who Did It?, illustrated by Nest-James, Heinemann, 1996.
The Wormholers, Methuen, 1996.
(Contributor with James Riordan and Margaret Nash) *The Wolf and the Kids; The Straw House; Lake of the Stars; The Ugly Duckling,* 4 vols., Heinemann Educational, 1996.
Grandma's Surprise, illustrated by Nest-James, Heinemann, 1996.

Our Favourite Stories: Children Just Like Me Storybook, Dorling Kindersley, 1997.
Out of India: An Anglo-Indian Childhood (memoir), Pavilion, 1997.

"SURYA" SERIES

The Wheel of Surya, Methuen, 1992.
The Eye of the Horse, Methuen, 1994.
The Track of the Wind, Methuen, 1997.

"GRANDPA CHATTERJI" SERIES

Grandpa Chatterji, illustrated by Mei-Yim Low, Methuen, 1993.
Grandpa's Indian Summer, illustrated by Yow, Methuen, 1995.

Also author of the books *The Temple by the Sea,* Ginn; *The Demon Drummer,* Pavillion; *Pitchou; The Girl Who Rode on a Lion,* Ginn; *Forbidden Dreams,* Mammoth; *All Aboard,* Heinemann; *A Singer from the Desert,* Pavillion; *Forbidden Clothes,* Methuen; and *Just Friends,* Mammoth. Also author of the musical *The Green Factor,* music by Nigel Stephenson.

■ Adaptations

The Demon Drummer was adapted as a play, Cheltenham Literary Festival, 1994; *Grandpa Chatterji* was adapted for television, 1996; six-part adaptation of *The Wheel of Surya,* BBC-TV, 1996.

■ Work in Progress

Starchild on Clark Street for Oxford University Press.

■ Sidelights

Jamila Gavin brings her understanding of the special concerns of children of mixed parentage to her stories and novels for young readers. Born in India of an Indian father and a British mother, Gavin has focused on her Indian heritage in such books as *Three Indian Princesses: The Stories of Savitri, Damayanti, and Sita,* as well as in her highly praised epic trilogy that begins with the 1992 novel *The Wheel of Surya.* In addition to her novels and short fiction for middle school readers, Gavin, who has worked in television and in theater for many years, has also authored plays for younger viewers. Several of her works have been adapted for broadcast on British television. "I began writing to be published, rather than for fun in 1979, when I realised how few books for children reflected the multicultural society in which they lived," Gavin explained to *Something about the Author* (*SATA*). "As someone of mixed Indian and British origins, I wanted to see my mirror image, and felt that every child, no matter what their race or colour, was entitled to see their mirror image."

Among Gavin's first books was *Kamla and Kate,* a collection of short stories featuring a young girl named Kate who gains a best friend when six-year-old Kamla and her family move from India to Kate's boy-dominated street. While engaging together in tasks and activities common to young British children, Kate joins her new friend in celebrating the Indian Festival of Light, or Diwali. The book reflects the author's belief that "people with different customs and beliefs [need] to find common ground," while also celebrating their differences, according to Margery Fisher of *Growing Point.* The two best friends return in *Kamla and Kate Again,* a second collection of stories that *School Librarian* contributor Julie Blaisdale cited as showing "with sensitivity and understanding" the many ways in which young people can "share in and celebrate a diversity of cultural influences."

Other books by Gavin are steeped in Indian culture and tradition. In *The Singing Bowls,* a mixed Anglo-Indian teen named Ronnie delves into the mystery surrounding three wooden bowls that have mystical properties rooted in Tibetan history. The sixteen-year-old hopes that the bowls can help him find his Indian father, who disappeared ten years ago; after letters passed on to Ronnie by his dying grandfather shed new light on his father's absence and one of the bowls is found to have disappeared as well, Ronnie takes it as a sign and travels to his father's birthplace to begin a search for his roots. While noting that the writing is "slightly uneven," a *Junior Bookshelf* reviewer praised *The Singing Bowls* for evoking "the dust, heat and beauty of India" and presenting a "revealing and thought-provoking" portrait of the multi-layered generations of Indian society. Indian culture also plays a significant role in *Grandpa Chatterji,* a collection of stories about Sanjay and Neeta, sisters who get to know their Indian grandfather when he makes a long-awaited visit from his home in Calcutta. A man of traditional, old-fashioned values, "Grandpa Chatterji is a wonderful character ... with his warmth and enthusiasm for life," according to *School Librarian* contributor Teresa Scragg; a reviewer for *Junior Bookshelf* agreed, noting that Gavin's "charming" book paints the portrait of a family with strong ties to two diverse cultures "and offers the hope that its members will draw the best from both."

First published in England in 1992, Gavin's *Wheel of Surya* is the first book of her "Surya" trilogy. Taking place in a small Indian village in the Punjab on the eve of India's war for independence, the novel follows the adventures of Marvinder and Jaspal Singh, siblings whose mother decides to bring the family to England to join her husband, who has been absent for many years in an effort to further his education. During the trip the children's mother and grandmother both die, but the brother and sister remain determined to find the father whom they hardly remember. With little money, the pair find their way to Bombay, and stow away aboard an ocean liner bound for England. When at last they find their father, Govind, he is not at all the person they expected to find—he has married an Irishwoman and has a son—and the two children must adjust to both a new family and a new culture. In a review of *The Wheel of Surya* for *School Librarian,* Linda Saunders praised Gavin for "the power of her descriptions and her portrayal of two different societies." A *Junior Bookshelf* critic called the novel "a tribute to the stubbornness of

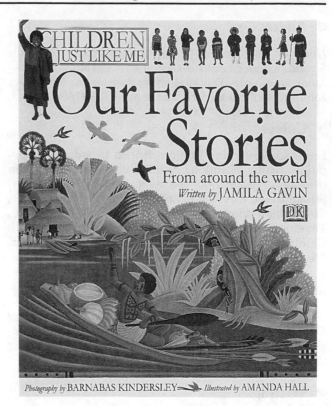

Gavin has penned this collection in which real children from around the world introduce favorite stories from their native land. (Cover illustration by Barnabas Kindersley and Amanda Hall.)

children the world over whose instinct is for survival first and prosperity second."

In the sequels to *The Wheel of Surya—The Eye of the Horse* and *The Track of the Wind*—readers continue to follow the adventures of Mavinder and her brother Jaspal. *The Eye of the Horse* finds the children's father released from jail after a conviction for dealing in stolen goods; on the heels of his release, now abandoned by his Irish wife, Govind gathers his children together and returns to his native India, which is now free of British domination. The story threads in and out of many historic events of the 1940s, including the death of Mahatma Gandhi and the religious and political turmoil that racked India during the decade. In a review for *Books for Your Children,* Val Bierman dubbed the novel a "powerful book of betrayal, sadness and anger" that also reveals the "power of healing and forgiveness," and in his *School Librarian* review, Peter Hollindale praised it as "an immensely readable, exciting story."

Gavin is often asked by readers if books such as the "Surya" trilogy are autobiographical. "The answer is yes and no," she explained to *SATA.* "Yes, that I couldn't have written them had I not been born in India into the period leading up to the Second World War, independence, and partition; yes, that as a child I lived both in a palace in the Punjab and in a drab flat in a war-damaged London street; yes, that music, sea voyages, schools, friends were all part of my rich Anglo-Indian existence.

But no—in any accurate sense to do with plots or events as described in the books. Everything I experienced simply became material with which I could overlay a complete fantasy. As a child can turn a table into a house or two chairs into a train, I turned my life into a fiction in which any resemblance to characters living or dead is purely coincidental—as they say in the movies."

Of her more recent works, Gavin told *SATA:* "Perhaps, of all my books, *The Wormholers* represents my exploration of the inner world, but inspired by the glorious theories and astro-physical world of the physicist Stephen Hawking. That is the joy of writing; that there are so many doors waiting to be opened and be a source of inspiration."

■ Works Cited

Bierman, Val, review of *The Eye of the Horse, Books for Your Children,* spring, 1995, p. 12.

Blaisdale, Julie, review of *Kamla and Kate Again, School Librarian,* November, 1991, p. 144.

Fisher, Margery, review of *Kamla and Kate, Growing Point,* May, 1983, p. 4089.

Review of *Grandpa Chatterji, Junior Bookshelf,* June, 1993, pp. 96-97.

Hollindale, Peter, review of *The Eye of the Horse, School Librarian,* November, 1994, p. 165.

Saunders, Linda, review of *The Wheel of Surya, School Librarian,* November, 1992, pp. 157-58.

Scragg, Teresa, review of *Grandpa Chatterji, School Librarian,* August, 1993, p. 108.

Review of *The Singing Bowls, Junior Bookshelf,* October, 1989, p. 237.

Review of *The Wheel of Surya, Junior Bookshelf,* August, 1992, p. 153.

■ For More Information See

PERIODICALS

Books for Keeps, May, 1986, p. 20; March, 1989; May, 1991; January, 1996.

Books for Your Children, summer, 1986, p. 8; summer, 1989, p. 12; summer, 1993, p. 10.

Growing Point, September, 1979, p. 3578; September, 1982, p. 3943.

Junior Bookshelf, October, 1979, p. 271; April, 1988, p. 93; April, 1992, p. 62; August, 1994, p. 134; February, 1995, pp. 35-36.

School Librarian, February, 1988, p. 20; November, 1989, p. 160.

Times Educational Supplement, August 26, 1983, p. 20.

*   *   *

GAZE, Gillian
See BARKLEM, Jill

GOULD, Alberta 1945-

■ Personal

Born December 10, 1945, in Skowhegan, ME; daughter of Ray O. (a woodsman and farmer) and Pedita H. (Fenderson) Dickinson; married Raymond A. Gould (a carpenter), December 16, 1963 (died, 1991); married Mitchell E. Cole (a wastewater superintendent), February 24, 1994; children: (first marriage) Melony R. Gould Harter, Holly L. Gould Pierce. *Education:* Attended high school in Skowhegan, ME. *Religion:* Protestant. *Hobbies and other interests:* Gardening, bird watching, reading.

■ Addresses

Home—Madison, ME. *Office*—c/o Heritage Publishing Co., P.O. Box 792, Farmington, ME 04938.

■ Career

Bloomfield Elementary School, Skowhegan, ME, reading teacher, 1986—. Also served as town clerk, Cornville, ME. *Member:* Maine Writers and Publishers Alliance.

■ Writings

First Lady of the Senate: A Life of Margaret Chase Smith, Windswept House (Mount Desert, ME), 1989, 2nd edition, 1995.

ALBERTA GOULD

In Search of Peace: George Mitchell, Heritage Publishing (Farmington, ME), 1996.

■ Work in Progress

Bear Brothers, historical fiction about Native Americans; a biography of William S. Cohen, former Maine senator and U.S. Secretary of Defense.

■ Sidelights

Alberta Gould told *SATA:* "I am an avid student of history. I love books that tell stories through the perspective of a person of the time. Because I am a reading teacher, I attempt to write in a simple, direct style that can be clearly understood by older students as well as adults.

"I also like to draw blueprints for homes. I have done this for more than twenty-five years. Many of my home designs were built by my late husband, who was a carpenter. I have pounded nails, shingled houses, painted, and hung doors. Some of my other occupations include owning and working as the superintendent for six apartment houses and my partnership with my husband in a handcrafted furniture business.

"In 1991 my first husband died. I have since remarried, and my second husband and I have built a new home overlooking the Longfellow Mountain Range. My hobby is gardening, and I am presently designing a bird nesting and feeding habitat around our home.

"I enjoy music and the *Nutcracker* ballet. When I have the opportunity to read for pleasure, some of my favorite writers for adults are David McCullough, author of *Truman,* and the late James Herriot, author of *All Things Wise and Wonderful, All Things Bright and Beautiful,* and *All Creatures Great and Small.* My favorite children's book authors are Barbara Winslow, author of *Dance on a Sealskin;* Barbara Cooney, who wrote *Island Boy, Eleanor,* and *Miss Rumphius;* Russell Freedman, author of *Lincoln: A Photobiography* and *Eleanor Roosevelt;* and Alan Baker, author of concept books for very young children. I buy books for my extensive library at lawn sales and at every book store I can find.

"I enjoy going to schools to talk with students about writing, publishing, and the subjects of my books. I am currently working on a series of biographies of Maine politicians, including Edmund S. Muskie. After completing this political biography series, I have plans for many other books."

* * *

GRANFIELD, Linda 1950-

■ Personal

Born November 22, 1950, in Medford, MA; moved to Canada, 1974, maintaining dual U.S./Canadian citizen-

ship; daughter of Joseph J. (an attorney) and Barbara H. (Boyd) Granfield; married Cal Smiley, 1978; children: Devon Marie, Brian Lindsay. *Education:* Studies at Oxford University, 1971; Salem State College, B.A., 1972; Northeastern University, M.A., 1974; attended University of Toronto, 1974-76. *Hobbies and other interests:* Reading, gardening, needlework, art.

■ Addresses

Home and office—40 Hardwick Court, Etobicoke, Ontario, Canada, M9C 4G6. *Electronic mail*—gransmil @ interlog.com.

■ Career

Writer. *Member:* International Board on Books for Young People (IBBY-Canada), Writers' Union of Canada, Canadian Society of Children's Authors, Illustrators and Performers, The Canadian Children's Book Centre, Friends of the Osborne and Lillian H. Smith Collections—Toronto Public Library.

■ Awards, Honors

Best Books selection, Ontario Library Association, 1988, and Best Nonfiction for Children, Canadian

LINDA GRANFIELD

Library Association, 1989, both for *All about Niagara Falls;* Frances E. Russell award, IBBY-Canada, 1991; "Pick of the Lists," American Booksellers Association, 1994, for both *Cowboy* and *The Make Your Own Button Book;* Information Book Award, Canadian Children's Literature Roundtables, 1994, for *Cowboy;* Information Honor Book, Canadian Children's Literature Roundtables, 1994, for *Extra! Extra!;* Notable Children's Trade Book in the Field of Social Studies, National Council for the Social Studies-Children's Book Council (NCSS-CBC), 1994, for *Cowboy;* "Quick Picks for Young Adults" selection, American Library Association, 1995, for *Cowboy;* Honor Book, Canadian Library Association and Children's Literature Roundtables Information Book Award, both 1996, both for *In Flanders Fields;* regional Silver Birch Award, Ontario Library Association, and Best Books selection, Internationale Jugendbibliothek, both 1997, both for *In Flanders Fields.*

■ Writings

All about Niagara Falls: Fascinating Facts, Dramatic Discoveries, illustrated by Pat Cupples, Kids Can Press, 1988, Morrow, 1989.

Canada Votes: How We Elect Our Government, illustrated by Bill Slavin, Kids Can Press, 1990, revised edition, 1992.

Extra! Extra!: The Who, What, When, Where, and Why of Newspapers, illustrated by Bill Slavin, Kids Can Press, 1993, Orchard Books, 1994.

(With Andrea Wayne-Von Konisgslow) *The Make-Your-Own-Button Book,* illustrated by Andrea Wayne-Von Kongislow, Hyperion Books for Children, 1994.

Cowboy: An Album, Douglas & McIntyre, 1993, Ticknor & Fields, 1994.

In Flanders Fields: The Story of the Poem by John McCrae, illustrated by Janet Wilson, Lester Publishing, 1995, Bantam, 1996.

Amazing Grace: The Story of the Hymn, illustrated by Janet Wilson, Tundra Books, 1997.

Silent Night: The Song from Heaven, illustrated by Nelly and Ernst Hofer, Tundra, 1997.

Postcards Talk, illustrated by Mark Thurman, Pembroke, 1997.

Circus, Douglas & McIntyre, 1997, published as *Circus: An Album,* DK Ink, 1998.

"THE YEAR I WAS BORN" SERIES; ILLUSTRATED BY BILL SLAVIN

The Year I Was Born—1987, Kids Can Press, 1994.
The Year I Was Born—1988, Kids Can Press, 1995.
The Year I Was Born—1984, Kids Can Press, 1996.

Contributor to magazines, including *Cottage Life, Quill & Quire, Owl,* and *Books in Canada.* Also contributor to *Terrific Titles for Young Readers* and *Reading: Lifelong Adventure.*

■ Work in Progress

Research on projects about pandas, workhorses, poppies, Irish immigrants to North America, World War II, and the Vietnam War; research for the "Year I Was Born" books.

■ Sidelights

As a child growing up in New England, award-winning author Linda Granfield was continuously exposed to the region's rich history. Her love of the subject was complemented by her desire to write. She told *SATA,* "I knew I wanted to be a writer after reading Louisa May Alcott's *Little Women* when I was ten years old. I wanted to be Jo March. My parents took me to her home in Concord, Massachusetts—the visit only made the bug bite harder!" As an adult living in Canada, Granfield has achieved her goal, writing in illuminating detail about the subject she loves most—history. Her nonfiction books "for anyone aged 10 through 100" present a wealth of historical and biographical information to readers, even when they deal with contemporary subjects. Granfield has won praise for her thorough research and for her presentation of material in an entertaining and engaging fashion. She revealed to *SATA* that she takes particular satisfaction in helping "young readers make connections between their personal family histories and the history of mankind."

Primarily educated in Massachusetts, Granfield began her career during her doctoral studies at the University of Toronto in Canada, where she met her husband and found work reviewing children's books. Granfield was invited to write her first book on a topic familiar to United States and Canadian citizens alike: the amazing natural attraction, Niagara Falls. *All about Niagara Falls* presents young tourists, researchers, or casual readers with information about the geography and history of the area, along with interesting stories, facts, and activities. According to Carolyn Phelan of *Booklist,* the work is "inviting" and entertains readers as it educates them. A *Kirkus Reviews* critic noted that the book should be "valuable for school assignments."

The success of *All about Niagara Falls* bolstered Granfield's career. She continued her work as an editor, consultant, and reviewer while beginning new projects of her own. She began research for the "Year I Was Born" series and also for a craft book, a book about voting, and another about newspapers. The result of this latter effort won special praise from critics. *Extra! Extra!: The Who, What, When, Where, and Why of Newspapers,* is a "clever, gossipy, idea-packed volume," according to Judie Porter in *School Library Journal.* The book explains how newspapers are made, from the way reporters collect stories to the business of operations. *Extra! Extra!* also provides related activities to help children publish their own newspapers or creatively recycle newspapers. A glossary helps readers understand the newspaper person's vocabulary. Trina Preece, writing in *Canadian Materials,* noted that Granfield does "a thorough, clear and fascinating job" with *Extra! Extra!,* while describing the work as "dynamic and fact-packed." *Quill & Quire* contributor John Lorinc asserted that "*Extra! Extra!* is clearly a useful reference book for school libraries."

Granfield's account of the famous poem "In Flanders Fields" includes facts about World War I and details of the true-life circumstances that led an army doctor to write the inspirational verse. (From *In Flanders Fields: The Story of the Poem by John McCrae*, illustrated by Janet Wilson.)

Published the same year as *Extra! Extra, Cowboy: An Album* was described by *Kirkus Reviews* as an "affectionate tribute to cowboys, in myth and reality." Readers learn why cowboys were needed in the American and Canadian West, and are helped to understand the way they lived. Granfield includes women, Native Americans, and African Americans in her account. According to Deborah Stevenson of the *Bulletin of the Center for Children's Books,* the "organization is good and the text generally clear." Generously enhanced by scores of photographs, paintings, illustrations, charts, and maps, *Cowboy,* in the words of *Quill & Quire* contributor Patty Lawlor, "belongs ... in birthday giftwrap."

Some of Granfield's most highly praised works detail the histories of contemporary cultural artifacts and customs. "In Flanders Fields" is a brief but beloved poem written by Canadian poet and doctor John McCrae. The poem, which communicates the horror and sadness of World War I, is known to school children around the world. Granfield, along with illustrator Janet Wilson, set out to make its message even more accessible; *Quill & Quire* contributor Sarah Ellis maintained that the pair "succeed admirably." *In Flanders Fields* provides more than information about the poem; it tells of McCrae's life, describes the conditions of the war on the battlefield and in the hospital, relates how McCrae conceived the poem, explains how the poem affected Canadian society and the Canadian armed forces, and reveals how it led to the poppy tradition observed on Remembrance Day. In a starred review, Carolyn Phelan of *Booklist* described *In Flanders Fields* as a "fine introduction to the poem, the man, and the war." Ellis concluded in her *Quill & Quire* review that it is "hard to imagine this clearly conceived and well-designed book being bettered."

Granfield continues to live and work in Canada, where her days are busy. She spends a great deal of time in libraries conducting research, in schools presenting children with her work, and in meetings with publishers. "Everything is related to my books," she explained to *SATA.* "Sometimes I have to 'fight' for the actual time to write!" Still, Granfield finds time to relax by reading biographies, magazines, and novels by "nineteenth-century English and French authors" and "current novelists like Jane Urquhart." She told *SATA* that she reads "everything from scholarly books to the backs of potato chip bags" and advises aspiring young writers to follow her example. "Keep reading. The more you read, the more you develop your own style."

■ Works Cited

Review of *All about Niagara Falls, Kirkus Reviews,* April 15, 1989, p. 624.

Review of *Cowboy: An Album, Kirkus Reviews,* February 1, 1994, p. 143.

Ellis, Sarah, review of *In Flanders Fields, Quill & Quire,* December, 1995, p. 38.

Lawlor, Patty, review of *Cowboy: An Album, Quill & Quire,* October, 1993, p. 42.

Lorinc, John, review of *Extra! Extra!: The Who, What, When, Where, and Why of Newspapers, Quill & Quire,* July, 1993, pp. 57-58.

Phelan, Carolyn, review of *All about Niagara Falls, Booklist,* July, 1989, p. 1902.

Phelan, Carolyn, review of *In Flanders Fields, Booklist,* November 1, 1996, p. 496.

Porter, Judie, review of *Extra! Extra!: The Who, What, When, Where, and Why of Newspapers, School Library Journal,* March, 1994, pp. 228-29.

Preece, Trina, review of *Extra! Extra!: The Who, What, When, Where, and Why of Newspapers, Canadian Materials,* January, 1994, pp. 20-21.

Stevenson, Deborah, review of *Cowboy: An Album, Bulletin of the Center for Children's Books,* March, 1994, pp. 222-23.

■ For More Information See

BOOKS

Writing Stories, Making Pictures, Canadian Children's Book Centre, 1994.

PERIODICALS

Books in Canada, February, 1997.
Booklist, February, 1994, p. 1004.
Horn Book, Fall, 1994, p. 396.
Quill & Quire, July, 1994, p. 62; February, 1997.
Publishers Weekly, December 6, 1993, p. 74.
School Library Journal, May, 1989, p. 118; January, 1994, p. 121; December, 1996, p. 129.
Wilson Library Bulletin, June, 1994, p. 127.

H

HAAS, Irene 1929-

■ Personal

Born June 5, 1929, in New York City; married Philip Clark (a banker); children: James, Jo Ann. *Education:* Attended Black Mountain College, Pratt Institute, and Art Students League.

■ Addresses

Home—New York City.

■ Career

Illustrator. Scenic designer for summer stock theater; designer of patterns for china, fabrics, and wallpaper; freelance illustrator for magazines, record album covers, posters, and advertisements; illustrator of children's books, 1954—. *Exhibitions:* Works have been exhibited by the American Institute of Graphic Art.

■ Awards, Honors

Best Illustrated Children's Books of the Year, *New York Times*, 1955, for *A Little House of Your Own*, and 1956, for *Was It a Good Trade?*; *Horn Book* Honor List citation, 1961, for *There Is a Dragon in My Bed*, 1963, for *Tatsinda*, and 1967, for *Emily's Voyage;* Irma Siminton Black Award, 1975, for *The Maggie B.;* Owl Prize, 1977, for *The Maggie B.*, and 1980, for *Carrie Hepple's Garden.*

■ Writings

SELF-ILLUSTRATED

The Maggie B., Atheneum, 1975.
The Little Moon Theater, Atheneum, 1981.
A Summertime Song, McElderry, 1997.

ILLUSTRATOR

Richard Banks, *Mysterious Leaf*, Harcourt, 1954.
Beatrice Schenk de Regniers, *A Little House of Your Own*, Harcourt, 1955.
Beatrice Schenk de Regniers, *Was It a Good Trade?*, Harcourt, 1956.
Paul Kapp, *Cat Came Fiddling*, Harcourt, 1956.
Beatrice Schenk de Regniers, *Something Special*, Harcourt, 1958.
Sesyle Joslin, *There Is a Dragon in My Bed*, Harcourt, 1961.
Sesyle Joslin, *Dear Dragon, and Other Useful Letter Forms*, Harcourt, 1962.
Elizabeth Enright, *Tatsinda*, Harcourt, 1963.
Elizabeth Enright, *Zeee*, Harcourt, 1965.
Emma Smith, *Emily's Voyage*, Harcourt, 1966.
Myra Cohn Livingston, *Come Away*, Atheneum, 1974.
Ruth Craft, *Carrie Hepple's Garden*, Atheneum, 1979.

■ Sidelights

Irene Haas once told *SATA:* "I don't know if it is true for other illustrators or writers for children, but I honestly believe that my style and taste stem from and are an extension of what I liked as a child. I loved pictures I could 'live' in, literally for hours. They were completely conceived by the artist, full of atmosphere and detail. It was wonderful to discover something new, no matter how minute. Realizing how gratifying these illustrations were—and still are—and how much they enriched my life, it is a great joy to find that I am able to make more of these alive little worlds for children."

Irene Haas's childhood fascination with intricately detailed illustrations is evident in her award-winning picture books for children. In *The Maggie B.*, a little girl wishes upon a star, and when her wish comes true she is the captain of a ship named for her. The magical boat is filled with a miniature garden, a net full of lobsters, various animals, and Maggie's baby brother to keep her company. A reviewer for *Junior Bookshelf* called *The Maggie B.* "one of the most outstanding picture books to be seen this year." The same reviewer noted that Haas's first self-illustrated book is "a truly child-centred book, sensitive and not to be missed." Zena Sutherland of the *Bulletin of the Center for Children's Books* remarked that "the writing is on the sentimental side, but it's imbued with sensuous images."

Irene Haas was praised for her lush illustrations accompanying her story book *A Summertime Song,* in which young Lucy attends a magical birthday party on a moonlit summer night.

Several years later, Haas produced a second solo effort, *The Little Moon Theater,* an episodic fantasy with a complex structure. A little girl named Jo Jo and her dog and cat comprise the Little Moon Theater, a traveling troupe that goes from town to town, telling stories and singing songs that magically solve the problems of the children they meet. A critic for *Publishers Weekly* praised Haas's charming story and watercolor illustrations, asserting: "Haas has infused this fairy tale with beauty, gentle humor and magnetism."

Haas's third self-illustrated picture book was published in 1997. Like her earlier solo efforts, *A Summertime Song* is a fantasy showcasing the artist's highly regarded illustrations. In this work, a frog invites a little girl to a birthday party where, upon her acceptance of a magic party hat, she is transformed into miniature size. The two ride off in a bird-nest taxi and pick up other partygoers along the way. The rhyming text also introduces a threatening owl, but he is disarmed by the news that the party is for him. A reviewer for *Publishers Weekly* admired *A Summertime Song,* raving about Haas's "gorgeous illustrations whose sumptuous imagery and sultry compositions virtually define romance and mystery." At the same time, Roger Sutton of *Horn Book* found Haas's story slight but noted of the illustrations that "each ... is a virtuoso's display of silky lines and rich color accentuated and deepened by the midnight black of the background."

In addition to illustrating her own works for children, Haas is widely recognized as the illustrator of a number of award-winning picture books by other authors. Included among these works are *A Little House of Your Own* and *Was It a Good Trade?* by Beatrice Schenk de Regniers, *Emily's Voyage* by Emma Smith, and *Carrie Hepple's Garden* by Ruth Craft.

■ Works Cited

Review of *The Little Moon Theater, Publishers Weekly,* October 16, 1981, p. 79.

Review of *The Maggie B., Junior Bookshelf,* April, 1977, pp. 77-78.

Review of *A Summertime Song, Kirkus Reviews,* April 1, 1997, p. 556.

Review of *A Summertime Song, Publishers Weekly,* March 24, 1997, p. 82.

Sutherland, Zena, review of *The Maggie B., Bulletin of the Center for Children's Books,* May, 1976, p. 145.

Sutton, Roger, review of *A Summertime Song, Horn Book,* May, 1997, p. 307.

■ For More Information See

BOOKS

Illustrators of Children's Books: 1967-1976, compiled by Lee Kingman, Grace Allen Hogarth, and Harriet Quimby, Horn Book, 1978.

PERIODICALS

Booklist, November 15, 1975, p. 453; December 15, 1981, p. 548.

Bulletin of the Center for Children's Books, September, 1997, p. 12.

Growing Point, December, 1976, p. 3029.

New York Times Book Review, September 28, 1975, p. 12; October 18, 1981, p. 49.

Publishers Weekly, August 4, 1975, p. 57.

School Library Journal, November, 1975, p. 62; October 18, 1981, p. 129.*

HAHN, Emily 1905-1997

OBITUARY NOTICE—See index for SATA sketch: Born January 14, 1905, in St. Louis, MO; died February 18, 1997, in New York, NY. Adventurer, author. Hahn gained acclaim as the prolific author of more than fifty books on topics ranging from diamonds to apes. After short stints as a mining engineer, Hollywood screen writer, and travel guide in New Mexico, Hahn began a long career as a freelance writer for *The New Yorker*. She traveled throughout the world and chronicled her adventures for *The New Yorker* and in numerous volumes of prose. She wrote about her exploits with the Red Cross while she was in Africa in *Congo Solo: Misadventures Two Degrees North*. She also spent several years in China and Hong Kong, where she became acquainted with the Soong family; one of her daughters became the wife of Chiang Kai-shek; another the wife of Sun Yatsen. Her experiences in China are chronicled in *The Soong Sisters, China Only Yesterday, 1850-1950: A Century of Change*, and *China to Me: A Partial Autobiography*. Her other works include *Once Upon a Pedestal: An Informal History of Women's Lib, On the Side of the Apes: A New Look at the Primates, The Men Who Study Them and What They Have Learned, Eve and the Apes, Chiang Kai-shek: An Unauthorized Biography*, and *The Emily Hahn Reader*. Hahn also penned a number of books for young people, among them *China A to Z, Francie, First Book of India*, and *Julie Finds a Way* for Franklin Watts, and *Mary Queen of Scots* and *Leonardo da Vinci* for Random House.

OBITUARIES AND OTHER SOURCES:

PERIODICALS

New York Times, February 19, 1997, p. B7.
Times (London), February 25, 1997, p. 19.
Washington Post, February 22, 1997, p. C4.

*   *   *

HANSEN, Ann Larkin 1958-

■ Personal

Born June 25, 1958, in Minneapolis, MN; married; children: three. *Education:* College of St. Thomas, B.A. (summa cum laude).

■ Addresses

Home—19351 165th St., Bloomer, WI 54724. *Electronic mail*—shansen @ win.bright.net (Internet).

■ Career

Farmer and writer.

■ Writings

"THE FARM" SERIES, PUBLISHED BY ABDO AND DAUGHTERS

All Kinds of Farms, 1996.

Crops on the Farm, 1996.
Farm Kids, 1996.
Farm Machinery, 1996.
Farmers, 1996.
Seasons on the Farm, 1996.

"FARM ANIMALS" SERIES; PUBLISHED BY ABDO AND DAUGHTERS

Cattle, 1996.
Chickens, 1996.
Goats, 1997.
Pigs, 1997.
Sheep, 1997.
Uncommon Farm Animals, 1997.

"POPULAR PET CARE" SERIES; PUBLISHED BY ABDO AND DAUGHTERS

Birds, 1997.
Cats, 1997.
Dogs, 1997.
Fish, 1997.
Hamsters and Gerbils, 1997.
Turtles, 1997.

OTHER

Contributor to business magazines and art journals.

■ Sidelights

Ann Larkin Hansen told SATA: "Writing is a winter activity for me. In the summer I'm busy with the chickens, garden, hay-making, and kids. I'm a city girl, but I'd always dreamed of being a farmer and writer. The two seem to go together. With my husband's encouragement, I have been raising beef cattle for about three years and writing for about ten. I have written for business and art magazines, public relations firms, and private corporations. Doing a series of kids' books on farming was the most fun assignment I've ever had. After my series on pet care, I am looking forward to writing about more of my favorite topics in the future: farms, animals, the environment, science, and history."

*   *   *

HILL, Lee Sullivan 1958-

■ Personal

Born September 2, 1958, in Hartford, CT; daughter of Philip Richard Sullivan (a physician) and Nancy Doyle Lee (a systems manager; maiden name, Doyle); married Gary William Hill (a construction purchasing manager), May 8, 1982; children: Adam Doherty, Colin James. *Education:* Lafayette College, A.B., Engineering, 1980. *Politics:* Registered Democrat. *Religion:* Episcopalian.

■ Career

Office of Robert Cameron, Dedham, MA, member of land surveying crew, 1978; Ford Motor Co., Steel Division, Dearborn, MI, summer intern, 1979; Turner Construction Co., Washington, DC, 1980-87, began as field engineer for the construction of a wastewater treatment plan, became senior estimator; Turner Construction Co., Shelton, CT, part-time estimator, 1995-96; writer, 1996—. Riding teacher, Woodland Horse Center, Silver Spring, MD; trainer and exerciser, Something Extra Arabian Farm, Salisbury, CT. Volunteer at local schools and libraries. *Member:* Society of Children's Book Writers and Illustrators, Foundation for Children's Books, Children's Reading Round Table, National Trust for Historic Preservation, Nature Conservancy.

■ Writings

"BUILDING BLOCK BOOKS"; PUBLISHED BY CAROLRHODA

Bridges Connect, 1997.
Roads Take Us Home, 1997.
Towers Reach High, 1997.
Dams Give Us Power, 1997.
Canals Are Water Roads, 1997.
Farms Feed the World, 1997.
Parks Are to Share, 1997.
Libraries Take Us Far, 1998.
Schools Help Us Learn, 1998.

■ Work in Progress

Six volumes in the series "Get Around Books," including *Get Around in the City, Get Around in the Country, Get Around in Air and Space, Get Around on Water, Get Around for Fun,* and *Get Around with Cargo,* publication by Carolrhoda expected in fall, 1998; several nonfiction books; a folk tale; a historical novel.

■ Sidelights

Lee Sullivan Hill told *SATA:* "I write because I love putting thoughts on paper, creating beautiful books. I love to share my dreams and ideas and knowledge with people everywhere—especially children. The more I write, the more I want to write.

"I began to write because I loved to read—and to save my sanity. I had taken a leave of absence from my construction estimating job when my first child was born, and I continued to stay at home with my second. I enjoyed my babies, but felt my brain power slipping away. So I began to write. Once I started, I found I couldn't stop!

"I can't remember a time without books. I was born in Hartford, Connecticut, but that was a fluke. My parents lived there for a year while my father completed his medical training. I am actually from the Boston area. As a child I never said, 'I want to be a writer when I grow up.' I always planned to be an architect or a veterinarian, but I did adore reading. My list of favorite authors included Robert Louis Stevenson, P. D. Eastman, Laura Ingalls Wilder, J. R. R. Tolkien, C. S. Lewis ... the list could go on and on.

LEE SULLIVAN HILL

"It's not that I couldn't write; the thought of writing as a profession just didn't occur to me. In fact, a teacher at Wellesley High School once wrote a note on a fairy tale I had written, 'Lee, have you ever considered a career writing books for children?' At the time, I laughed, pleased with the grade of 'A plus.' But write? You know the old saying, to write what you know. I couldn't imagine that anyone would want to read about my boring life. How could I write?

"So I lived my life. I went off to Lafayette College, planning to major in French and go to veterinary school. My roommate was an engineering student. I kept helping her with homework. Engineering? It was another profession I had never considered, but what fun it was! I switched into Lafayette's interdisciplinary program that combined liberal arts and engineering. During summer breaks I worked in a steel mill for one year and for a land surveyor another. After college, I went into construction management. I worked on job sites, then in the office. Life was getting interesting—and I got to be a mother, too!

"When I became serious about my writing, I took a class and joined the Society of Children's Book Writers and Illustrators, whose conferences gave me the specialized knowledge to compete in the field of children's literature. By the way—there was never any question for whom I would write. Stories for children just came naturally to me. I could even see the books in my hands.

"I didn't have to wait long to see a real book. The first piece I submitted to editors was accepted on the third try. *Bridges Connect* expresses my love of structures, my love of engineering. Carolrhoda Books recognized this. In fact, the publisher decided to launch a whole series that became the 'Building Block Books.'

"I have other projects in the works: a chapter book, a historical novel, and an art series. The more I write, the more I love to write."

* * *

HUGHES, Sara
    See SAUNDERS, Susan

I–J

INNOCENTI, Roberto 1940-

■ Personal

Born 1940, in Bagno a Ripoli, Italy. *Education:* Self-educated illustrator.

■ Career

Worked as an illustrator in animation studio, Rome, Italy; worked as a film and theater poster designer and a book designer, Florence, Italy; book illustrator, 1970—. Worked in a steel foundry, 1953-58.

■ Awards, Honors

Golden Apple, Biennale of Illustrators Bratislava, 1985, Notable Book citation, American Library Association (ALA), Honor Book citation, *Boston Globe-Horn Book,* and Mildred L. Batchelder Award, ALA, all 1986, all for *Rose Blanche;* Kate Greenaway Medal "Highly Commended" citation, British Library Association, 1988, for *The Adventures of Pinocchio;* Best Illustrated citation, *New York Times,* Kate Greenaway Medal "Commended" citation, British Library Association, both 1990, and Golden Apple, Biennale of Illustrators Bratislava, 1991, all for *A Christmas Carol.*

■ Illustrator

Alberto Manzi, *La Luna Nelle Baracche,* Salani, 1974.
Seymour Reit, *All Kinds of Planes,* Golden Press, 1978.
Reit, *All Kinds of Ships,* Golden Press, 1978.
Reit, *All Kinds of Trains,* Golden Press, 1978.
Reit, *Sails, Rails, and Wings* (contains *All Kinds of Planes, All Kinds of Ships,* and *All Kinds of Trains,*) Golden Press, 1978.
Charles Perrault, *Cinderella,* Creative Education, 1983.
Christophe Gallaz and Roberto Innocenti, *Rose Blanche,* translated by Martha Coventry and Richard Graglia, Creative Education, 1985.
Carlo Collodi, *The Adventures of Pinocchio,* Knopf, 1988.

Charles Dickens, *A Christmas Carol,* Creative Editions/Harcourt Brace, 1990.
E. T. A. Hoffmann, *Nutcracker,* Creative Editions/Harcourt Brace, 1996.

Innocenti's illustrated books for children have been translated into several languages, including German, French, Norwegian, Japanese, and Chinese.

■ Sidelights

Italian illustrator Roberto Innocenti is known for his highly detailed, painterly style and his devotion to realistic representation in such classic works as *Cinder-*

ROBERTO INNOCENTI

From *Rose Blanche,* **written by Christophe Gallaz and illustrated by Innocenti.**

ella, The Adventures of Pinocchio, A Christmas Carol, and *Nutcracker.* He is also the illustrator of an original Holocaust tale, *Rose Blanche,* highly publicized throughout Europe and the United States. Innocenti's illustrations are unmistakable, demonstrating a delicacy of palette as well as a refinement of line, both of which are surprising in light of the fact that Innocenti is completely self-trained in his art.

Born in a small town near Florence, Italy, just after the outbreak of World War II, Innocenti left school at thirteen to help support his family by working in a steel foundry. By age eighteen he had moved to Rome and found work in an animation studio, a move that would influence his future career. He began to learn the trade of illustration and soon moved back to Florence. There he illustrated posters for movies and the theater in addition to designing books. In 1970 Innocenti met an American artist, John Alcorn, who convinced him to try his hand at book illustration.

Innocenti's early work for a North American audience appeared in Golden Books with text by Seymour Reit. The "All Kinds" series looked at transport from three perspectives: planes, ships, and trains. Each picture book gave a short history of the vehicle in question, accompanied by pictures of a variety of types. *All Kinds of Ships,* for example, introduced children to the history of sailing, from the early boats hollowed out of logs to the large supertankers that sail on the water today.

One of Innocenti's early major works was illustrating the classic tale *Cinderella* by Charles Perrault. Instead of

setting the tale of rags to riches in some remote fairy tale kingdom, Innocenti decided to plant it firmly in the twentieth century, locating Cinderella in an English village during the Roaring Twenties. He chose this time and place so that he would not be influenced by all the illustrations of the story that had come before, and also as he has explained, in order to make Cinderella live more as a universal archetype not limited by her time. Patty Campbell noted in the *New York Times Book Review* that *Cinderella* was "a witty flapper era" rendition that "has been widely admired." *Cinderella* was but the first of several classic tales that Innocenti has illustrated, yet his next book would be far from the realm of fairy tales.

Rose Blanche, written by Innocenti and Christophe Gallaz, is set in World War II, the time of illustrator Innocenti's childhood. It tells of the horrors of that time as seen through the eyes of a young girl who is not yet old enough to fully understand the events surrounding her. Rose Blanche is a young German girl who, witnessing a strange scene in her village one day, is thrust face to face with the reality of the Holocaust. The heroine's name is also that of the youthful German resistance group which tried to sabotage the Nazi war effort, often losing their lives in the conflict. Rose Blanche, seeing the mayor of her town handing over a small boy to the soldiers, follows the tracks of the truck that has taken the boy away. Deep in the woods she discovers a barbed-wire compound. Inside are small children in striped uniforms bearing a yellow star. Rose Blanche feels sympathy for these children and brings them scraps of food she steals, only to be shot by a soldier just as the war is ending. She, like the resistance group of the same name, has given her life for principle, becoming "a symbol of goodness in a dark world," according to *Quill and Quire* reviewer Susan Perren. Partly inspired by Innocenti's own experiences during the war, *Rose Blanche* was widely praised by reviewers for its avoidance of sentimentality and its hard-edged message. Lorraine Douglas, writing in *School Library Journal,* noted that the "oppression of Fascism is shown through the powerful and realistic paintings" within which Rose Blanche "is the only brightly colored individual." Perren, continuing in her review of *Rose Blanche,* dubbed Innocenti "a modern-day Breughel," and a reviewer in *Publishers Weekly* concluded that "This is a stunning book and a forceful argument for peace." In *Junior Bookshelf,* Marcus Crouch posed the rhetorical question of how suitable such a book was for young readers of picture-book age, and answered, "Why not? There is no hatred in the book, only sadness and love and a shred of hope."

The tale of Pinocchio, the wooden puppet full of mischief and tricks who wants desperately to become a real boy, was the subject for Innocenti's next illustration effort. Set in 19th-century Italy, the book is rich in the atmosphere of Florence, the native city of both Innocenti and Carlo Collodi, the creator of *The Adventures of Pinocchio.* Mary M. Burns, writing in *Horn Book,* noted that "Innocenti must now be considered the foremost interpreter of Pinocchio. The full-color paintings are marvels of content, composition, color, and perspective." In *Publishers Weekly* a critic called Innocenti's work a "luminous interpretation," and Faith McNulty in *The New Yorker* commented that this "must surely be the most beautiful edition of 'Pinocchio' ever seen."

Innocenti has also turned his hand to famous Christmas stories, illustrating both *A Christmas Carol* by Charles Dickens and *Nutcracker* by E. T. A. Hoffmann. Innocenti turned Scrooge's tale into a loving depiction of London and of interiors filled with activity and warmth. A contributor to *School Library Journal* noted that Dickens's text "is superbly served by Innocenti's paintings of London," and that the book was a "handsome example of the bookmaster's art." Writing in *Publishers Weekly* a reviewer felt that "Few of the many interpretations of Dickens's holiday parable can match this handsome edition for atmosphere, mood and sheer elegance," while in *Horn Book*, Ann A. Flowers commented on Innocenti's "subdued palette of browns and grays" and his "striking perspective," concluding that Innocenti's *A Christmas Carol* was a "magnificent edition." With *Nutcracker*, Innocenti serves Hoffmann as well as he did Dickens, meticulously detailing the story of the little girl who transforms her toy nutcracker into a handsome prince.

Through such works, Innocenti has developed a loyal following among readers and critics alike. As was noted by Amy J. Meeker in *Children's Books and Their Creators*, "Innocenti's remarkable ability to create drama and story through visually eloquent yet unsentimental paintings" is in evidence throughout his works, and these illustrations "have gained notice in fine arts journals as well as in the field of children's literature."

■ Works Cited

Review of *The Adventures of Pinocchio*, *Publishers Weekly*, September 30, 1988, p. 69.

Burns, Mary M., review of *The Adventures of Pinocchio*, *Horn Book*, March-April, 1989, p. 209.

Campbell, Patty, review of *Rose Blanche*, *New York Times Book Review*, July 21, 1985, p. 14.

Review of *A Christmas Carol*, *Publishers Weekly*, October 12, 1990, p. 63.

Review of *A Christmas Carol*, *School Library Journal*, October, 1990, p. 36.

Crouch, Marcus, review of *Rose Blanche*, *Junior Bookshelf*, April, 1986, pp. 62-3.

Douglas, Lorraine, review of *Rose Blanche*, *School Library Journal*, October, 1983, p. 172.

Flowers, Ann A., review of *A Christmas Carol*, *Horn Book*, March-April, 1991, p. 198.

McNulty, Faith, review of *The Adventures of Pinocchio*, *The New Yorker*, December 12, 1988, p. 156.

Meeker, Amy J., *Children's Books and Their Creators*, edited by Anita Silvey, Houghton Mifflin, 1995, pp. 344-5.

Perren, Susan, review of *Rose Blanche*, *Quill and Quire*, May, 1991, p. 24.

Review of *Rose Blanche*, *Publishers Weekly*, May 10, 1985.

■ For More Information See

BOOKS

Brezzo, Steven L., *Roberto Innocenti: The Spirit of Illustration*, with an essay by Leonard S. Marcus, Art Services International, 1996.

PERIODICALS

Booklist, November 1, 1985, p. 408; September 15, 1986, p. 138; March 1, 1987, p. 1396; November 1, 1991, p. 510.

Emergency Librarian, January, 1992, p. 52.

Five Owls, March, 1988, p. 62; May, 1988, p. 68; November, 1992, p. 29.

Los Angeles Times Book Review, March 31, 1991, p. 1.

Publishers Weekly, August 19, 1996, p. 69.

School Library Journal, January, 1988, p. 37; February, 1989, p. 66.

—Sketch by J. Sydney Jones

*   *   *

JENNINGS, Patrick 1962-

■ Personal

Born February 25, 1962; son of Richard Jennings and Patricia Ann Utley; married Alison Kaplan (a bookbinder), August 2, 1997. *Education:* Arizona State University, B.F.A., 1985; attended San Francisco State University, 1987-91.

■ Addresses

Home—P.O. Box 1377, Bisbee, AZ 85603. *Agent*—Ruth Cohen, P.O. Box 7626, Menlo Park, CA 94025.

■ Career

Educator in San Francisco, CA, San Cristobal de las Casas, Chiapas, Mexico, and Bisbee, AZ, 1991-96; writer, Bisbee, AZ, 1991—; Copper Queen Library, library technician, 1994—.

■ Awards, Honors

Booklist Editors' Choice selection, 1996, for *Faith and the Electric Dogs*.

■ Writings

Faith and the Electric Dogs, Scholastic Press, 1996.

■ Sidelights

Patrick Jennings told *SATA:* "When I was ten, I wrote a play. I convinced my teacher to allow me to stage it (with me as director and star) and, with his consent, 'The Half-True Story of Jesse James' was presented to the student body of South Ward Elementary School, Crown Point, Indiana. It closed after only one performance. I kept writing after that. I wrote essays and

PATRICK JENNINGS

stories and reviews and screenplays. (This was done in seats of higher learning, not in South Ward's.) I learned a lot about writing and a lot about what I do and don't like to do. I learned so much in fact, that I left film school and took a job as a preschool teacher. I chose preschool because I love kids. I mean that seriously. I have always loved to be around them. They know how to do what they like. Kids paint pictures then paint over them. They say memorable things, like 'I've hidden a whisper bomb in everybody's house.' They think screaming is exercise. They look at the bookshelf and never say, 'I really should read more.' You've got to like that.

"I read a lot of children's books at preschool. My exposure to children's literature up to then amounted to the small collection of books I had as a child (Pooh, Dr. Seuss, Charlie Brown), the books I'd checked out of the Crown Point Public Library (Cleary, Dahl, E. B. White, Meindert DeJong, Paddington Bear, the Mushroom Planet), and the books I'd studied in seats of higher learning (Huck Finn, Alice, *The Little Prince*, etc.). Consequently, I was unprepared for the great big happy bright world of books for children. *The Amazing Bone* stunned me, as did *The Night Kitchen*, not to mention *The Runaway Bunny, Madeline, The Tale of Peter Rabbit, A Hole Is To Dig,* and *Harold and the Purple Crayon.* Beyond their virtues of perfect pitch, rhythm,

balance, and humor, these books *worked.* Children loved them, chanted them, used them in their play. (Alas, I discovered not all writers for children understand childhood so well. Some books read more like primers for adulthood than books for kids.)

"I began to read kid's books at home—just for my own pleasure! I reread Milne, White, Cleary, Seuss, Carroll, and Cameron. My books on deconstructionist filmmaking gathered dust. Then one day, as I read how James' parents were gobbled up by a rhinoceros, I decided to start a story of my own. The voice came first, just a whisper in my ear—a dog's voice. Then came the rocket ship and the rocket girl. Later, when I moved to Mexico, the story moved with me. The dog became electric, his narration, multilingual. Language became a key element of the story. Until I taught preschool, I labored under the typical adult delusion that children consider reading and writing to be chores tantamount to, say, yardwork. Nothing could be further from the truth. Language to children is like twittering is to birds, roaring to lions, grunting to pigs, barking to dogs. Kids chant and warble and make up very silly things to say. They bask in the sound of their voices. They smile when understood. And they adore stories—to tell, to hear, to look at, to read. Children love language, whether they are aware of it or not. This is why I write books for them.

"I continue to spend lots of time with kids. I'm not teaching at the moment, but I love visiting them in their schools, or reading stories to them at the local library, or inviting them (and their parents) over for dinner. We have a lot of things in common. We like to laugh. We like to fool around. We like books. We like kids."

In Jennings's *Faith and the Electric Dogs,* Faith is saved from bullies by a stray dog she names Edison (a stray dog in Mexico is called un perro corriente, or "electric dog"). But she doesn't like living in Mexico and wants to return to San Francisco. This unhappy ten-year-old, with Edison as humorous, multilingual narrator and companion, proceeds to build a rocketship that takes the pair to a desert island. A *Kirkus Reviews* critic described Edison as "a witty ambassador of languages and cultures," and Susan Dove Lempke, writing in *Booklist,* attributed both "charm and substance" to Jennings's first book.

■ Works Cited

Review of *Faith and the Electric Dogs, Kirkus Reviews,* September 15, 1996, pp. 1402-03.
Lempke, Susan Dove, review of *Faith and the Electric Dogs, Booklist,* December 1, 1996, p. 653.

■ For More Information See

PERIODICALS

Publishers Weekly, October 28, 1996, p. 82.

JOOSSE, Barbara M(onnot) 1949-

■ Personal

Born February 18, 1949, in Grafton, WI; daughter of Robert Elmer (a banker) and M. Eileen (Hutmacher) Monnot; married Peter Clifford Joosse (a psychiatrist), August 30, 1969; children: Maaike Sari, Anneke Els, Robert Collin. *Education:* Attended University of Wisconsin-Stevens Point, 1966; University of Wisconsin-Madison, B.A., 1970; Attended University of Wisconsin-Milwaukee, 1977-80. *Hobbies and other interests:* Reading, walking, biking, baking.

■ Addresses

Home and office—W61 N764 Riveredge Dr., Cedarburg, WI 53012.

■ Career

Writer. Associated with Stephan & Brady, Madison, WI, 1970-71; Waldbillig & Besteman, Madison, copywriter, 1971-74. *Member:* Society of Children's Book Writers and Illustrators, Author's Guild, Council for Wisconsin Writers.

■ Awards, Honors

Picture Book Award, Council of Wisconsin Writers, 1983, for *The Thinking Place,* 1985, for *Fourth of July,* and 1997, for *I Love You the Purplest; Fourth of July* was exhibited at the Bologna International Children's Book Fair, 1985; Golden Kite Award (Picture-Illustration), 1991, for *Mama, Do You Love Me?;* Best Books, *Child* Magazine and *Parents* Magazine, both 1996, both for *I Love You the Purplest.*

■ Writings

The Thinking Place, illustrated by Kay Chorao, Knopf, 1982.
Spiders in the Fruit Cellar, illustrated by Chorao, Knopf, 1983.
Fourth of July, illustrated by Emily Arnold McCully, Knopf, 1985.
Jam Day, illustrated by McCully, Harper, 1987.
Anna, The One and Only, illustrated by Gretchen Will Mayo, Lippincott, 1988.
Better with Two, illustrated by Catherine Stock, Harper, 1988.
Dinah's Mad, Bad Wishes, illustrated by Emily Arnond McCully, Harper, 1989.
Pieces of the Picture, Lippincott, 1989.
Mama, Do You Love Me?, illustrated by Barbara Lavallee, Chronicle, 1991.
The Pitiful Life of Simon Schultz, HarperCollins, 1991.
Nobody's Cat, illustrated by Marcia Sewall, HarperCollins, 1991.
Anna and the Cat Lady, illustrated by Gretchen Will Mayo, HarperCollins, 1992.
Wild Willie and King Kyle Detectives, illustrated by Sue Truesdell, Clarion, 1993.

The Losers Fight Back: A Wild Willie Mystery, illustrated by Truesdell, Clarion, 1994.
Snow Day!, illustrated by Jennifer Plecas, Clarion, 1995.
The Morning Chair, illustrated by Sewall, Clarion, 1995.
I Love You the Purplest, illustrated by Mary Whyte, Chronicle, 1996.
Nugget and Darling, illustrated by Sue Truesdell, Clarion, 1997.
Lewis and Papa: Adventure on the Santa Fe Trail, illustrated by Jon Van Zyle, Chronicle, 1998.
Ghost Trap: A Wild Willie Mystery, illustrated by Truesdell, Clarion, 1998.

Contributor of fiction to *Cricket* and contributor of adult humor to *Milwaukee* and *Chicago Tribune.*

■ Sidelights

The everyday incidents of childhood occupy the pages of Barbara M. Joosse's children's stories. These events are a mixture of the trials and tribulations Joosse remembers from her own childhood in Wisconsin and those she endured later as a mother of three children. "I like to write about real children," she related in an article for *Milwaukee* magazine. "Children do so many heroic things every day. When a child does something that's very difficult for her to do, she is a hero. I like to dramatize that 'every day heroism' in my stories."

BARBARA M. JOOSSE

How long?

I'll love you until
the umiak flies
into the darkness,
till the stars turn
to fish in the sky,
and the puffin howls at the moon.

Set in the Inuit culture of Northern Alaska, *Mama, Do You Love Me?* revolves around the questions a young girl asks to test the limits of her mother's love. (Written by Joosse and illustrated by Barbara Lavallee.)

Joosse's childhood in Grafton, Wisconsin, was stable and secure; she lived in the same house until high school and when the family moved it was to a house only two blocks away. "My parents were always *there.* Forever, without question," she related in *Milwaukee.* Joosse's early ambition to pursue a career as a creative writer was sidetracked by her experiences in college, where she received conflicting opinions on her work from college professors; she became an advertising copywriter instead, readily leaving that job behind after the birth of her first child.

Jumping into motherhood, Joosse soon realized that she needed other activities to add more balance to her life. "The days were incredibly long," she commented in *Milwaukee.* "I didn't allow myself to watch soap operas, but 'Star Trek' became the light at the end of my daily tunnel. I rocked and rocked and rocked. Maaike cried, I clenched my teeth. I loved her dearly, but I couldn't adjust to the lack of adult contact, ideas and lunches out." These emotions and the changes in Joosse's life were so strong that the only medium she could express them in was poetry. Realizing that this poetry meant something only to her, however, Joosse soon decided to channel her energies into children's writing.

"I decided to be a children's writer with all the naivete of a child deciding to be an astronaut or à cowboy," Joosse continued in *Milwaukee.* "I was blissfully unaware of how few writers succeed in this field. I've been told, probably by the amorphous 'they,' that children's literature is the most difficult field to break into." Because of the difficulty of the field, Joosse formed a plan to accomplish her goal of becoming a writer for children; she enrolled in creative writing at the University of Wisconsin-Milwaukee, hired a babysitter to come two mornings a week, researched publishers, and got started early each day. During the course of the next

year Joosse wrote ten stories and sent them out to publishers, rewriting each one and re-sending it once it had returned four times. There were several editors who held onto the manuscripts and considered them, until finally an editor at Knopf helped Joosse publish her first book.

The Thinking Place is where young Elisabeth is sent after putting candy corn in the dishwasher. At the beginning of her punishment Elisabeth is sorry to be standing in the corner, but not sorry for what she did. Her mind begins to wander, filling with fantasies of her friend Melissa coming by with tea and cookies, a Gila monster who is after her for his dinner, and a witch who almost gets her to write on the wall with lipstick. Stopping herself just in time, Elisabeth apologizes to her mother before going to bed to fight off some imaginary sharks. "Elisabeth's attitudes and fantasies are accurately rebellious and scary," Nancy Palmer wrote in *School Library Journal.* A *Publishers Weekly* commentator asserted that *The Thinking Place* "deserves a warm welcome" and that Joosse "writes with quiet humor" in her first book.

With *The Thinking Place* Joosse introduced what would become the main focus of her body of work—everyday incidents in the lives of very realistic children. "My stories are about children you know," she maintained in *Milwaukee.* "They dramatize the fears and battles, the wisdom and triumphs that mark growing up as surely as the penciled 'growth lines' on the kitchen wall. I try to write with humor, while maintaining dignity, because, to a child, these events are very serious matters." Joosse knows this because her own childhood was filled with just such events. "Because I wasn't ill, or constantly moving, or enduring a family separation, I was free to concentrate on the meaty issues of growing up: braving the spiders in the fruit cellar, competing with a neighbor whose white tennis shoes stayed white, coping with the disappointment of hard-earned 'jumping shoes' that didn't work," Joosse recalled in *Milwaukee*. "These are the things—monumental incidents—that I write about. And, because my childhood memories are not overshadowed by major traumas, I am able to recall them with clarity."

These recollections, along with the experiences of her own children, provide Joosse with the material for most of her books. For instance, young Elisabeth in *Spiders in the Fruit Cellar* must face her fears of spiders while helping her mother with "grown-up" tasks. Finally braving the fruit cellar to fetch some peaches, she drops the jar in her rush to escape the spiders she fears, which prompts a confession from her mother of similar fears when she was little. The story is filled with "delicately delineated vignettes of Elisabeth," Reva S. Kern declared in her *School Library Journal* review, adding that Joosse sustains "just enough apprehension for young readers who will share in her struggle for courage."

Five-year-old Ross wants to be more grown-up in Joosse's *Fourth of July*. Told by his parents that he has to wait until he is six before he can have sparklers and cross the street alone, Ross sets out to prove just how responsible he is by marching in the Fourth of July parade. He makes it through the long march, holding the banner at the head of the parade until the very end, and is rewarded with a snow cone and permission to set off sparklers in celebration of the holiday. "Joosse perfectly portrays the feelings of a small child who is longing to be bigger, and children will find in Ross a kindred spirit," asserted Lucy Young Clem in *School Library Journal*. And a *Publishers Weekly* reviewer commented of *Fourth of July* that "children will love it."

Quiet time with his mother in their favorite chair is one thing that remains the same when young Bram moves from Holland to New York City. (From *The Morning Chair*, written by Joosse and illustrated by Marcia Sewall.)

Another young girl in search of approval and love from her mother occupies the pages of *Mama, Do You Love Me?* Set in the culture of the Inuits of Northern Alaska, this story revolves around the question posed in the title, as well as several other questions a young girl asks to test the limits of her mother's love. A *Publishers Weekly* reviewer described *Mama, Do You Love Me?* as a "striking volume, which uses a timeless culture to convey a timeless message." Carolyn K. Jenks similarly

A mother expresses the uniqueness of her love for each of her sons when they try to make a contest out of winning her affection. (From *I Love You the Purplest*, written by Joosse and illustrated by Mary Whyte.)

concluded in *Horn Book:* "The book is a beautiful combination of a rich culture and a universal theme."

Another foreign culture provides the setting for Joosse's tale of immigration—*The Morning Chair.* Moving with his family from Holland to New York City, young Bram finds his new surroundings harsh, loud, and overwhelming; the streets are filled with hurrying people speaking a language that Bram doesn't understand. The arrival of the family's furniture, including Bram's morning chair, adds some familiarity to their new home; he can now spend his usual morning quiet time with his mother in their chair while they share tea and Dutch cookies. And it is in this setting that they discuss their likes and dislikes about their new home while they settle in to listen to the morning sounds of their new neighbors. *School Library Journal* contributor Martha Rosen noted that in *The Morning Chair,* "the complexity of the emigration experience is conveyed to young readers in all the simplicity of the warm text." Kathleen Krull pointed out in the *New York Times Book Review* that "immigrant stories have a certain pattern to them, but Ms. Joosse has chosen a generous way of telling this one that should give it a long life."

The bond Joosse describes between young Bram and his mother is just the kind she hopes to create with her own stories. "Of special interest to me is the bond between the 'reader' and the 'listener' of picture books," she explained in *Milwaukee.* "Picture books are often read aloud by someone a child cares about very much. I want these two—through a shared reading experience—to understand each other better, and love each other more."

■ Works Cited

Clem, Lucy Young, review of *Fourth of July, School Library Journal,* August, 1985, p. 55.

Review of *Fourth of July, Publishers Weekly,* March 22, 1985, p. 59.

Jenks, Carolyn K., review of *Mama, Do You Love Me? Horn Book,* November-December, 1991, p. 729.

Joosse, Barbara, "How Do You Print So Small?," *Milwaukee,* May, 1984.

Kern, Reva S., review of *Spiders in the Fruit Cellar, School Library Journal,* August, 1983, pp. 52-53.

Krull, Kathleen, review of *The Morning Chair, New York Times Book Review,* October 8, 1995, p. 31.

Review of *Mama, Do You Love Me? Publishers Weekly,* August 9, 1991, p. 56.

Palmer, Nancy, review of *The Thinking Place, School Library Journal,* April, 1982, p. 59.

Rosen, Martha, review of *The Morning Chair, School Library Journal,* June, 1995, pp. 88-89.

Review of *The Thinking Place, Publishers Weekly,* March 19, 1982, p. 70.

■ For More Information See

PERIODICALS

Booklist, May 1, 1993, p. 1590; June 1, 1995, p. 1786; October 15, 1996, p. 436.

Bulletin of the Center for Children's Books, September, 1987, p. 11; February, 1989, pp. 149-50; June, 1989, p. 253; December, 1991, pp. 94-95; February, 1992, p. 158.

Horn Book, September-October, 1989, p. 612; November-December, 1991, pp. 745-46; May-June, 1995, pp. 325-26.

Kirkus Reviews, November 15, 1988, pp. 1675-76; April 1, 1989, p. 548; December 15, 1991, p. 1592; April 1, 1993, p. 458; October 15, 1994, p. 1408; July 1, 1995, p. 947.

Publishers Weekly, June 12, 1987, p. 83; March 24, 1989, pp. 68-69; September 16, 1996, p. 82; February 24, 1997, p. 91.

School Library Journal, December, 1988, p. 104; April, 1989, p. 102; July, 1989, p. 67; November, 1991, p. 98; March, 1992, p. 238; June, 1993, p. 83; November, 1994, pp. 82-83; September, 1995, pp. 179-80.*

K

KALBACKEN, Joan 1925-

■ Personal

Born June 30, 1925, in Chicago, IL; daughter of Leslie (a farmer) and Bertha (Andreen) Formell; married Norman M. Kalbacken (a registered seed analyst); children: Teryl Kalbacken Engel, Scott. *Education:* University of Wisconsin—Madison, B.S., 1947; Coe College, teaching certificate, 1965; University of Toulouse, teaching certificate, 1966; Illinois State University, M.A., 1968, supervisory degree, 1984.

■ Addresses

Home and office—903 Ruston Ave., Normal, IL 61761-2817.

■ Career

Lincoln Junior High School, Beloit, WI, mathematics teacher, 1947-48; Pekin Community High School, Pekin, IL, algebra teacher, 1958-60; McLean County Unit Five Schools, Normal, IL, teacher of mathematics and French and foreign language supervisor, 1960-85; author of children's books, 1988—. Member, Illinois Council on the Teaching of Mathematics, 1965-72, Friends of the Normal Public Library, and As You Like It Heritage Club (past president); hostess, McLean County Retired Teachers, 1985—. *Member:* American Association of University Women, American Association of Teachers of French, Delta Kappa Gamma (chairperson of International Educational Foundation, 1992—, and State Foundation for Educational Studies, 1994—), Phi Delta Kappa (vice-chairperson), Phi Delta Phi (life member), Kappa Delta Pi.

■ Awards, Honors

Distinguished Illinois Author Award, Illinois Reading Council, 1994.

■ Writings

(With Emilie U. Lepthien) *Recycling,* Childrens Press, 1991.
White-Tailed Deer, Childrens Press, 1992.
(With Emilie U. Lepthien) *Wetlands,* Childrens Press, 1993.
(With Emilie U. Lepthien) *Foxes,* Childrens Press, 1993.
The Menominee, Childrens Press, 1994.
Peacocks and Peahens, Childrens Press, 1994.

JOAN KALBACKEN

Isle Royale National Park, Grolier, 1996.
Badgers, Grolier, 1996.
Sheepskin and Morning Star, illustrated by Bill Muzzy, Aegina Press (Huntington, WV), 1996.

Contributor of articles and poems to periodicals.

■ **Work in Progress**

The Food Guide Pyramid, Food Safety, and *Vitamins and Minerals,* all for Grolier; two picture books; three additional nonfiction manuscripts.

■ **Sidelights**

Joan Kalbacken told *Something about the Author* (*SATA*): "I was raised on a dairy farm in northwestern Wisconsin with three sisters, one brother, a pet lamb, two dogs, many cats, and cows. Helping with the farm chores—milking cows, haying, and planting—were all a big part of my early years. I attended a two-room schoolhouse.

"Writing has been a big part of my life since I was in elementary school. I had excellent teachers who encouraged me to write poetry. In the seventh grade, I won a children's writing competition sponsored by the *Superior Telegram,* a Wisconsin newspaper. Ever since, I have enjoyed trying to have poems and stories published. In college, I wrote poetry in the French language and was praised by my French professors. Positive reinforcement kept me writing, and I have always been an avid reader.

"I taught for twenty-nine years and retired to take care of my ill husband. I enjoyed my teaching and missed the students. Consequently, I started writing manuscripts for children's books. Emilie Lepthien, a retired Chicago principal, encouraged me to submit my manuscripts to Childrens Press in Chicago. This resulted in six books. Now I am happily working with the Children's Press Division at Grolier and submitting work to other publishers as well.

"My interests, besides my family, are reading good literature, rose gardening, and writing poetry for fun. I have had numerous requests to speak to school children about the importance of good reading and writing. I love getting back into the classroom with students, but I am unable to do so as often as asked due to my husband's illness."

■ **For More Information See**

PERIODICALS

School Library Journal, October, 1991, p. 110.

KALMAN, Maira 1949-

■ **Personal**

Born in Tel Aviv, Israel, 1949; came to United States in 1953; married Tibor Kalman (a graphic designer); children: Alexander, Lulu. *Education:* New York University, B.A.

■ **Career**

Writer and illustrator of children's books, 1986—. Designer, M & Co., New York City.

■ **Awards, Honors**

Parents' Choice Award for Picture Books, Parents' Choice Foundation, 1989, for *Hey Willy, See the Pyramids; New York Times* Best Illustrated Children's Books of the Year citation, *New York Times,* 1991, for *Ooh-la-la (Max in Love).*

■ **Writings**

Roarr: Calder's Circus, photographs by Donatella Brun, Whitney Museum of American Art, 1991.
(Illustrator) David Byrne, *Stay up Late,* Viking, 1987.

SELF-ILLUSTRATED

Hey Willy, See the Pyramids, Viking, 1988.
Sayonara, Mrs. Kackleman, Viking, 1989.
Max Makes a Million, Viking, 1990.
Ooh-la-la (Max in Love), Viking, 1991.
Max in Hollywood, Baby, Viking, 1992.
Chicken Soup, Boots, Viking, 1993.
Swami on Rye: Max in India, Viking, 1995.
Max Doll, Viking, 1995.
Max Deluxe, Viking, 1996.

■ **Sidelights**

Maira Kalman is a writer and illustrator of picture books noted not only for appealing to children, but often their parents as well. Lauded for her witty, stream-of-consciousness prose, Kalman is also known for her animated illustrations that are full of parodies of famous painters, wild colors, and geometric shapes. Her books frequently deal with the dreamlike adventures of children and animals in exotic locales. From the outset, Kalman's books were intended to entertain both children and adults, a point not overlooked by Ilene Cooper when she reviewed Kalman's first book, *Stay up Late,* with lyrics by David Byrne of the music group Talking Heads. Cooper noted in her *Booklist* review that Kalman's "zesty . . . totally New Wave" artwork is "filled with numerous asides that parents and kids will find amusing, each on their own level." It is that very ability for entertaining two audiences at once that has graced her work since then.

Kalman was born in Tel Aviv, Israel in 1949. When she was four years old, her family moved to the United States, and she was brought up in Riverdale, a section of the Bronx. At an early age, Kalman was introduced to the arts. As she explained in a *Publishers Weekly* interview with Elizabeth Devereaux, "My mother decided that we had to have culture—all good girls have to have culture," which meant hours of piano and dance lessons, and attendance at "a million concerts and a million museums." After attending the High School of Music and Art, Kalman went to New York University (NYU), studying literature and also indulging a long-held desire to become a writer. It was at NYU in 1968 that Kalman met her future husband, Tibor Kalman, then a student of graphic design. Just as she had given up music after high school, Kalman decided to give up writing after college, concentrating instead on drawing. When her husband became creative director of Barnes and Noble, a national book store chain, in the early 1970s, Kalman would help him with his ad campaigns or graphics. Later, when he founded the graphic design firm, M & Co., she collaborated with him, creating album covers, textile designs, and movie titles.

But Kalman had not really given up writing; in fact she slowly began to se the possibilities of putting both her drawing and writing together. As she quipped to Devereaux in *Publishers Weekly:* "Oh, you can do both together. It's called a book!" Her first project was taken from the song "Stay up Late" written by her friend David Byrne, a member of the musical group Talking Heads. Noting that baby boomers like themselves were beginning to have children and that traditional nursery rhymes from another generation were not speaking to these new parents, Byrne and Kalman decided to experiment with the form. "It was and still is a good time to do children's books because the baby-boom generation is interested in new forms of art," Kalman told Jennet Conant in an interview for *Harper's Bazaar.* "And our generation has had such a prolonged adolescence that our taste is much closer to our kids' than our parent's was." At the outset, then, Kalman made a choice: "The books I am going to do are going to be for adults *and* for children," she told Devereaux in *Publishers Weekly.*

The simple lyrics of Byrne's song have a bite to them that would appeal to both adults and children: "Mommy had / a little baby. / There he is / fast asleep. / He's just / a little plaything. / Why not / wake him up?" While the parents are busy celebrating the arrival of the new baby, they do not notice his two siblings merrily, and mischievously, keeping the baby awake. Kalman complemented the lyrics with naif paintings in a style inspired by two of her painterly idols, Henri Matisse and Marc Chagal, employing flamboyant colors and irregular typeface, all designed by M & Co. The lyrics seem to dance around the "colorful, funny pictures that make you want to put crayon on paper," noted Conant in *Harper's Bazaar.* Writing in *Booklist,* Cooper commented that the book was "Strictly for the hippest families ... wild and woolly excitement." In an extended review of the book, Nicholas Paley, writing in *Journal of Youth Services in Libraries,* commented on the postmodernist edge to *Stay up Late,* concluding that this "is a picture book that zooms around in its own

Lulu tells her little brother fanciful bedtime stories in Kalman's self-illustrated *Hey Willy, See the Pyramids.*

orbit, leaving a collection of question marks and exclamation points scattered in its quirky path." However, not all reviewers were so enthusiastic. *Publishers Weekly* noted a "mean-spirited edge" to Kalman's art that came from the lyrics themselves, and concluded that the book "has a definite appeal for hip adults, but it's not for the literal-minded child." Tobi Tobias, in a 1995 overview of Kalman's work in the *Los Angeles Times Book Review,* dubbed this first effort "irresistible" and noted that it contained all of Kalman's essential themes: "life's giddy abundance, rules gleefully bent."

Kalman's first solo effort, *Hey Willy, See the Pyramids,* came a year later, featuring a brother and sister, Lulu and Alexander, inspired by her own children. Patient Lulu tells her little brother nonsense stories when he wakes up in the middle of the night, brief vignettes that include people from their own family. These stories "make sense in the way that images sliding across the mind as you fall asleep make sense," noted a reviewer for *Kirkus Reviews,* who concluded that the book is "outlandish, but born of genuine creativity and understanding." Kalman dished up her usual mixture of childlike figures and folk art, along with seemingly chaotic movement in the illustrations, to accompany the almost surreal tales. Roger Sutton, writing in *Bulletin of the Center for Children's Books,* commented on the "new-wave cornucopia of narrative and visual fragments" which comprised the book, and felt that "younger readers won't appreciate the hipper-than-thou tone." *Booklist*'s Cooper, however, concluded that "children will probably respond more to the book's wild feel than to the actual content. In any case, for the right child, this could be a mind-stretcher."

Lulu and Alexander continue their adventures in *Sayonara, Mrs. Kackleman,* detailing their adventures touring Japan. Lulu presents the reader with fanciful and realistic recollections of slurping "oodles and poodles of noodles," of being packed onto the Tokyo subway like "marshmallows all stuffed together in a bag," and of visits to an outdoor bath and a Noh play, among other activities. In the *New York Times Book Review,* John Burnham Schwartz noted that Kalman "has captured perfectly the child's sense of wonder and has created a funny, exuberant, and inventive introduction to Japan for people of all ages." Schwartz went on to comment that Kalman "fills the page—and our minds—with a wild assortment of colorful images" to create a "picture book that is in perfect harmony with the way children think, speak, and fantasize." In a *Five Owls* review, Cathryn A. Camper echoed this sentiment, noting that "this surrealistic travelogue is actually very close to how a real child might record his or her experiences when visiting a foreign country." And Sutton, writing in *Bulletin of the Center for Children's Books,* was more impressed with this effort than with earlier ones, concluding in his review: "Dreams and reality collide in witty ways, and underneath all the zaniness is a true and affectionate portrait of Japan."

After two books centered on character spin-offs of her own children, Kalman decided that she would give them a rest and take them out of the spotlight. For her next book she used a friendly beagle named Max who had made a cameo appearance in *Hey Willy, See the Pyramids.* Max is not just any old dog—he has literary aspirations. In *Max Makes a Million,* the canine sells his book of poetry and is finally able to fulfill his lifelong dream of leaving New York and going to Paris. But meanwhile, there is still New York for Max to visualize. Bill Ott lauded Kalman's writing and illustrations in a *Booklist* review, saying: "In a perfect blending of words and pictures, Kalman creates pages that jump with the syncopated rhythms and Day-Glo colors of city life." Ott called Kalman's "wonderfully witty, remarkable detailed paintings" a "battleground of competing colors," going on to say that "this is definitely a book for children—and for adults with enough courage and energy to look at life the way Max does." A reviewer in *Publishers Weekly* remarked: "Banter that rings with sophistication is well matched by the esoteric illustrative approach readers have come to expect from Kalman."

Max has become something of a cottage industry for Kalman, who has sent him to Paris and romance in *Ooh-la-la (Max in Love),* to Hollywood on the search for stardom accompanied by poodle friend, Crepe Suzette, in *Max in Hollywood, Baby,* and off to India in search of enlightenment in *Swami on Rye: Max in India.* It is in this series that Kalman has staked out her main themes: the lure of the exotic and the safety of home and the nest. But as Tobi Tobias noted in the *Los Angeles Times Book Review,* the "fine thing about Kalman's texts is

Poet-dog Max, protagonist of several Kalman picture books, travels to Paris and finds romance in *Oh-la-la (Max in Love).* (Written and illustrated by Kalman.)

that they present no problems and no moral—except for a gentle nudge in the direction of accepting human nuttiness." For Tobias, the fact that the books are "rampant flights of fancy" is a plus: they avoid the usual "instructive" mode of much of children's literature. David Small, however, himself a writer and illustrator of children's books, in a *New York Times Book Review* of *Swami on Rye,* felt that Kalman "leaves most young readers out of the joke more often than not," and despite being "beautifully illustrated," her "children's stories are grounded in almost nothing that a child can relate to." Other reviewers note that Kalman's work appeals to both children and adults because of the variety of elements in her books, making the books appealing to a wide audience of readers. In a *School Library Journal* review of *Max in Hollywood, Baby,* Heide Piehler remarked that while children might miss Kalman's "mocking of the Golden Age of Hollywood," they would "be caught up in the frenetic rhythms and rhymes of the text."

Reviewers often have trouble in placing Kalman's work: Is she a children's writer and illustrator who appeals to adults, or vice-versa? Linda Wertheimer, reviewing *Ooh-la-la (Max in Love)* in the *New York Times Book Review,* observed that the book was "clever and it's silly and seems loony enough to attract children, if not to all the nonsense, at least to the sound of the words." Reviewing *Max in Hollywood, Baby* in the *New York Times Book Review,* Kurt Andersen noted that Kalman's books were not just chic: "They are smart and funny and high-spirited, dense with irony and strangeness in the manner of some hopped-up late-night Dr. Seuss." Andersen also commented on the typography employed, with "different sizes and fonts in a single sentence, and blocks of text teased into zany, occasionally confusing shapes." But Andersen also conceded that it is probably the parents rather than the children who "dote on Maira Kalman's books." *Max in Hollywood, Baby* has been optioned for television.

Kalman has also written and illustrated a book about the world of work in *Chicken Soup, Boots,* which Sutton in *Bulletin of the Center for Children's Books* found "more authentically childlike than her Max the Dog books." Lolly Robinson in *Horn Book* concluded that the "full-page art shows people and other subjects painted in a way that manages to be irreverent and loving at the same time." It is this irreverence and love that form the poles of much of Kalman's work. "Good writing," Kalman told Devereaux in *Publishers Weekly,* "liberates you, it takes you out of the mundane and to an extremely inspiring and creative level.... It inspires you rather than depresses you.... To me, ninety-nine percent [of children's books] don't inspire you at any level. They're comforting, and they're nice, but they aren't books that take you over the top in some way."

■ Works Cited

Andersen, Kurt, review of *Max in Hollywood, Baby, New York Times Book Review,* December 6, 1992, p. 90.

Byrne, David, *Stay up Late,* illustrated by Maira Kalman, Viking, 1987.

Camper, Cathryn A., review of *Sayonara, Mrs. Kackleman, Five Owls,* September-October, 1989, p. 8.

Conant, Jennet, "Dream Weaver," *Harper's Bazaar,* March, 1992, pp. 179, 191-92.

Cooper, Ilene, review of *Stay up Late, Booklist,* October 1, 1987, pp. 390-91.

Cooper, Ilene, review of *Hey Willy, See the Pyramids, Booklist,* February 1, 1989, p. 939.

Devereaux, Elizabeth, "Maira Kalman's Many Muses," *Publishers Weekly,* September 27, 1991, pp. 32-33.

Review of *Hey Willy, See the Pyramids, Kirkus Reviews,* October 15, 1988, pp. 1528-29.

Kalman, Maira, *Sayonara, Mrs. Kackleman,* Viking, 1989.

Review of *Max Makes a Million, Publishers Weekly,* October 12, 1990, p. 60.

Ott, Bill, review of *Max Makes a Million, Booklist,* October 1, 1990, p. 343.

Paley, Nicholas, "Postmodernist Impulses and the Contemporary Picture Book: Are There Any Stories to These Meanings?," *Journal of Youth Services in Libraries,* Winter, 1992, pp. 151-61.

Piehler, Heide, review of *Max in Hollywood, Baby, School Library Journal,* November, 1992, pp. 71-72.

Robinson, Lolly, review of *Chicken Soup, Boots, Horn Book,* March-April, 1994, p. 191.

Schwartz, John Burnham, review of *Sayonara, Mrs. Kackleman, New York Times Book Review,* November 12, 1989, pp. 25, 49.

Small, David, "Max Gets a Guru," *New York Times Book Review,* November 12, 1995, p. 48.

Review of *Stay up Late, Publishers Weekly,* September 11, 1987, p. 89.

Sutton, Roger, review of *Hey Willy, See the Pyramids, Bulletin of the Center for Children's Books,* September, 1988, pp. 11-12.

Sutton, Roger, review of *Sayonara, Mrs. Kackleman, Bulletin of the Center for Children's Books,* November, 1989, p. 63.

Sutton, Roger, review of *Chicken Soup, Boots, Bulletin of the Center for Children's Books,* January, 1994, p. 157.

Tobias, Tobi, "Talking Pictures," *Los Angeles Times Book Review,* December 24, 1995, pp. 6-7.

Wertheimer, Linda, "An American Dog in Paris," *New York Times Book Review,* November 10, 1991, p. 31.

■ For More Information See

BOOKS

Children's Literature Review, Volume 32, Gale, 1994, pp. 176-186.

Seventh Book of Junior Authors and Illustrators, Wilson, 1996, pp. 161-63.

PERIODICALS

Booklist, October 15, 1991, p. 449; October 15, 1995, p. 404.

Kirkus Reviews, October 15, 1992, p. 1310; October 1, 1993, p. 1275.

Publishers Weekly, September 18, 1995, p. 130.

School Library Journal, December, 1990, pp. 80-81; November, 1991, pp. 98, 100.

—*Sketch by J. Sydney Jones*

* * *

KATZ, Welwyn Wilton 1948-

■ Personal

Born June 7, 1948, in London, Ontario, Canada; daughter of Robert and Anne (Taylor) Wilton; married Albert N. Katz, 1973 (separated 1989); children: Meredith Allison. *Education:* University of Western Ontario, B.S., 1970. *Hobbies and other interests:* Playing the flute, reading myths and legends, finding recipes that incorporate the herbs she grows, knitting.

■ Addresses

Home and Office—549 Ridout St., N., Unit 502, London, Ontario, Canada, N6A 5N5.

■ Career

Writer; South Secondary School, London, Ontario, Canada, teacher, assistant head of mathematics, 1970-77. Past refugee coordinator, Amnesty International; treasurer and member of the steering committee, Lon-

WELWYN WILTON KATZ

don Children's Literature Round Table; former researcher, Girls' Group Home of London. *Member:* Writers' Union of Canada, Canadian Society of Children's Authors, Illustrators and Performers.

■ Awards, Honors

Book of the Year Runner-up, Canadian Library Association, 1985, for *Witchery Hill,* 1987, for *Sun God, Moon Witch,* 1988, for *False Face,* and 1989, for *The Third Magic;* Ruth Schwartz Award Finalist, 1987, for *False Face,* and 1988, for *The Third Magic;* International Children's Fiction Prize, Governor-General's Award Finalist, Max and Greta Ebel Award, and Trillium Award Finalist, all 1987, and *School Library Journal* Best Books citation and *American Bookseller* Pick of the List citation, both 1988, all for *False Face;* Governor-General's Award, 1988, for *The Third Magic;* Young Adult Honour Book Award, Canadian Library Association, 1996, for *Out of the Dark. False Face* was a Junior Literary Guild selection.

■ Writings

The Prophecy of Tau Ridoo, illustrated by Michelle
    Desbarats, Tree Frog Press, 1982.
Witchery Hill, Atheneum, 1984.
Sun God, Moon Witch, Douglas & McIntyre, 1986.
False Face, Douglas & McIntyre, 1987, Macmillan,
    1988.
The Third Magic, Douglas & McIntyre, 1988, Macmillan, 1989.

Whalesinger, Douglas & McIntyre, 1990, Macmillan,
    1991.
Come Like Shadows, Viking, 1993.
Time Ghost, Simon & Schuster/Margaret K. McElderry,
    1995.
Out of the Dark, Groundwood, 1996.

■ Sidelights

For Welwyn Wilton Katz, it was the books of J. R. R. Tolkien that changed everything. As she once stated in *Something about the Author* (*SATA*), "I found that it was possible, using words alone, to create a whole world, a marvellously complex and unreal world that other people could believe in." Katz has used her interest in myths, legends, and the supernatural to weave stories that incorporate both current problems most teenagers face—insecurity, parental divorce to name just two—and timeless mythological themes that play out the conflict between good and evil. Whether on their home turf or transported to another time or planet, her characters deal with evil outside themselves or within, when the protagonist becomes the unwitting prey of evil powers.

Katz, a fifth-generation Canadian, was born June 7, 1948, in London, Ontario, Canada. She credits her Scottish and Cornish ancestors with her abiding interest in Celtic myths. Unlike many writers, Katz does not recall writing very much when she was young. One exception was a high school final exam in which she was asked to write for three hours on one of five topics. "I spent two hours trying to decide which of those awful topics I would choose," she told *SATA,* "and the remaining hour 'taking dictation' from some inspired part of my brain, the words simply flowing out of me . . . . It was one of the most exciting experiences I've ever had." But even with the excellent grade she earned and the thrill of this feeling, it took a long time for Katz to try her hand at writing again.

An honors student in mathematics, Katz became a high school teacher, a position she held until she was twenty-eight. She found it difficult to adjust to being in the classroom, though she liked her students and made a good salary. She tried several makeovers—pierced ears, contact lenses, new clothes—but still felt awkward in her chosen profession. Uninspired, Katz worried that her whole life would continue on this steady, dull course and, as she told *SATA,* "it gave me the creeps."

It was at this point that she read Tolkien; the immediate effect was that Katz decided to write an adult fantasy novel. Initially, she devoted evenings and summers to her writing, but found that part-time writing didn't suit her. A year's leave of absence was followed by another, and by then she had finished her first draft, a hefty 750 pages. The ambitious story took place in a different world and had a huge cast of characters, whose complex setting demanded long, detailed exposition. By 1979, she had resigned as a teacher and used another year to rewrite the manuscript.

Katz sent it out to several publishers but none expressed interest. "When there was no one left to send it to, I cried a little—okay, a lot!—and then put the book on my top shelf. There it sits to this day," she admitted to *SATA*. But Katz made a very important discovery: she wanted to write. Furthermore, she learned about writing itself from doing the work, honing her technique and style. Among her characters were several children, and Katz thought she might try a children's book next.

Her breakthrough came in 1982, when her first novel *The Prophecy of Tau Ridoo* appeared. In it, the five Aubrey siblings find themselves in the strange and threatening world of Tau Ridoo, controlled by the terrifying Red General. He sends his deputies after the children, who become separated from each other. Cooky, a sorceress, comes to their aid and together they manage to defeat the evil General and to be reunited.

Witchery Hill's protagonist is Mike, whose parents have recently divorced. Along with his journalist father, Mike travels to Guernsey (one of the English Channel Islands) for a summer visit with the St. Georges, family friends. Mike's friendship with the eldest daughter, Lisa, reveals surprising turmoil beneath the apparently calm surface of her family life. Diabetic and fiercely attached to her father, Lisa suspects her stepmother is not only a witch, but trying to gain control of the local coven. Vanquishing the evil powers set loose on the island and destroying the coven fall to Mike, who must also reconcile himself to a less-than-perfect relationship with his father. A contributor in *Publishers Weekly* lauded Katz for holding the reader in "thrall," concluding that *Witchery Hill* "is a knockout, with each character deftly delineated and a socko finish." John Lord, writing in *Voice of Youth Advocates,* echoed this view, praising Katz's use of the setting, with its Stonehenge-like standing stones and its invitation to adventure in a world of facts interwoven with fantasy. "For the reader who needs action and intrigue," Lord stated, "this book is definitely 'IT.'"

Witchery Hill sprang out of a series of coincidences connected to Katz's chance visit to Guernsey, whose ferry docked in the small town where she dropped off a rental car. A randomly chosen hotel happened to be staffed by a woman with an interest in the island's folklore. Katz found references to witchcraft on the island as late as 1967 and came upon a manual of witchcraft in a bookstore. She decided to set her story on the island and to use a very powerful book of sorcery as the source of the witches' strife.

Historical facts were the inspiration for *Sun God, Moon Witch* as well. Katz read widely on dowsers (also known as water-witchers), who often reported strong electrical shocks when they came into contact with standing stones like those in the stone circles in England. Katz also recalled a family story about a dowser who had discovered a spring on their farm, and she knitted the two together. In *Sun God, Moon Witch,* Thorny McCabe is underwhelmed by the idea of summering with her cousin Patrick in an English village. But she soon discovers that the village is engaged in a controversy over the ancient stone circle of Awen-Ur. Like *Witchery Hill, Sun God, Moon Witch* revolves around the protagonist's struggle to keep evil from taking over the world.

False Face tackles a different kind of ethical dilemma—the appropriate handling of cultural artifacts—as played out against a difficult family drama. Protagonist Laney McIntyre finds an Indian mask in a bog near her London, Ontario, home. The tensions in her house following her parents' recent divorce are symbolized by their different reactions to Laney's find: as a successful antiques dealer, her mother encourages her to profit by it, but her father, a professor, encourages her to donate it to a museum. Meanwhile, the mask itself appears to be emitting corrupting powers that only she and her Indian friend Tom seem able to stop. *Voice of Youth Advocates*'s Rosemary Moran pointed out that the novel is "steeped in Canadian lore" and that the characters embodied the difficulties of dealing with different cultures "with enough suspense to keep the reader involved until the climax." A *Publishers Weekly* review-

In Katz's time-travel adventure, Sara and Dani suddenly find themselves in an earlier era when the earth was green and developers were just beginning the destructive processes which the girls know will lead to irreversible pollution.

Welwyn Wilton Katz

OUT OF THE DARK

After his mother's death, Ben Elliot becomes absorbed in fantasies in which he relives Viking mythology and history.

er found that Katz "welds the supernatural element onto the family's conflicts with grace and competence."

Katz changed direction a bit with *Whalesinger,* which looks at the relationships between humans, animals, and nature. Set in spectacular Point Reyes National Seashore in northern California, *Whalesinger* features two teenagers with problems, both of whom are involved in a summer marine conservation program. Nick is an angry young man eager to blame the team leader for Nick's older brother's death in a shipboard explosion, and Marty is a learning-disabled, lonely girl who has an empathic bond with a gray whale and her calf. Katz uses the coastline as emblematic of nature's power—the action climaxes in an earthquake—and history—there are references to an accident that occurred centuries before when Sir Francis Drake visited the area. A critic in *Publishers Weekly* chided Katz for a "veritable bouillabaisse of fishy plot developments," finally determining that she "has gone overboard." *School Library Journal's* Patricia Manning applauded Katz for her "complex pattern of science, personalities, a lost treasure, and a whale mother with an ailing baby" and pronounced the book "intriguing."

With her interest in the supernatural, it's no surprise that Katz would find herself drawn to *Macbeth*—and making full use of the play's reputation among theater people for being cursed. Teenaged Kinny O'Neill, the protagonist of *Come Like Shadows,* has a summer job with the director of the Stratford, Canada, Shakespeare festival. When she finds the perfect mirror prop, Kinny has no idea that it contains the spirit of the eleventh-century witches that destroyed the real Macbeth. The company travels to perform in Scotland, the witches by now in modern dress and using the apparently helpless Kinny to further their plot to renew their coven. Barbara L. Michasiw wrote of the book in *Quill and Quire* that "*Come Like Shadows* is difficult to reconcile with reality . . . . This is a challenging story that will probably not be comfortably accessible" to all readers. Lucinda Snyder Whitehurst of the *School Library Journal* also found the alternating points of view, from Kinny to Macbeth, a little difficult to follow, but felt that it would be "appreciated by drama and Shakespeare enthusiasts." Reviewing the book for *Voice of Youth Advocates,* Mary Jane Santos declared it "an intriguing mystery-fantasy with well developed characters and realistic dialogue."

Again and again, reviewers point to Katz's ability to use landscape and location to great advantage in her work. She proved herself especially adept in her 1995 novel, *Time Ghost,* which is set in the polluted world fifty years hence. Along with their friends—brother and sister Josh and Dani—Sara and her brother Karl accompany their grandmother to the North Pole. An argument between Sara and her grandmother catapults Sara and Dani back in time, to the late twentieth century before nature was irrevocably ruined. In *Booklist,* Carolyn Phelan predicted that readers would be drawn to the "flow of action and emotion, the deft descriptions of the natural world, and the sympathetic characters." Susan L. Rogers of *School Library Journal* was impressed with Katz's "absorbing story" that delivers "a serious ecological message," sentiments echoed by a *Publishers Weekly* critic, who also noted the ecological message and found it "stifles neither characters nor the plot."

After a break from myths, Katz returned to the ancient Norse tales for *Out of the Dark,* which *Children's Reader* reviewer Janet Wynne-Edwards termed "satisfying." Thirteen-year-old Ben, his younger brother Keith and their father move from Ottawa to start a new life in Newfoundland, in the town of Ship Cove, where his father grew up. Before her death, Ben's mother told him many of the Viking stories, and in her honor he begins to carve a knarr (a Viking ship), the myths and historical details helping him to deal with his own problems. As Wynne-Edwards wrote, "The young reader is not subjected to an anthropological checklist of artifacts and so may well retain this history."

Despite plots that sometimes strike reviewers as too complex, Katz consistently provides her readers with strong writing, compelling characters, and believable dialogue. She manages to work in her environmental concerns and her own fascination with ancient tales without overloading the story, earning her many awards and an enthusiastic, loyal following.

■ Works Cited

Review of *False Face, Publishers Weekly,* July 29, 1988, p. 234.

Lord, John, review of *Witchery Hill, Voice of Youth Advocates,* April, 1985, p. 48.

Manning, Patricia, review of *Whalesinger, School Library Journal,* May, 1991, p. 111.

Michasiw, Barbara L., review of *Come Like Shadows, Quill and Quire,* February, 1993, p. 36.

Miles, Margaret, review of *The Third Magic, Voice of Youth Advocates,* June, 1989, p. 116.

Moran, Rosemary, review of *False Face, Voice of Youth Advocates,* February, 1989, p. 286.

Phelan, Carolyn, review of *Time Ghost, Booklist,* May 1, 1995, p. 1573.

Rogers, Susan L., review of *Time Ghost, School Library Journal,* May, 1995, p. 108.

Santos, Mary Jane, review of *Come Like Shadows, Voice of Youth Advocates,* October, 1993, p. 228.

Strang, Robert, review of *The Third Magic, Bulletin of the Center for Children's Books,* February, 1989, p. 150.

Review of *Whalesinger, Publishers Weekly,* December 21, 1990, p. 57.

Whitehurst, Lucinda Snyder, review of *Come Like Shadows, School Library Journal,* December, 1993, p. 134.

Review of *Witchery Hill, Publishers Weekly,* November 2, 1984, p. 77.

Wynne-Edwards, Janet, "The Mythical Presence of Here: Recent Canadian Children's Fiction" in *The Children's Reader,* Winter, 1995-96.

■ For More Information See

BOOKS

Twentieth-Century Children's Writers, edited by Laura Standley Berger, St. James, 1995, pp. 503-04.

PERIODICALS

Publishers Weekly, July 15, 1996, pp. 74-75.

—*Sketch by Megan Ratner*

*   *   *

KELLER, Emily

■ Personal

Daughter of Anthony (a politician and insurance broker) and Jennie (an artist and seamstress; maiden name, Oliwiecki) Keller; married Thad A. Malec, 1960 (divorced, 1973); children: Tammyanne Malec Capone, Barbie Jean Malec Glambra. *Education:* Attended Niagara University; State University of New York at Buffalo, B.A., 1965, M.A., 1969. *Politics:* Republican. *Religion:* Roman Catholic. *Hobbies and other interests:* Art, gardening, history, culinary arts, and nature.

EMILY KELLER

■ Addresses

Home—9354 Rivershore Dr., Niagara Falls, NY 14304.

■ Career

Math Association of America, started as editorial assistant, became chief copyeditor, 1977-84; high school English teacher, Buffalo and Niagara Falls, NY, 1960-90; Erie County Community College, Buffalo, instructor, 1989-91; Niagara County Community College, Niagara Falls, NY, writing instructor, 1990-91. American Legion Auxiliary, president, 1992-93; Echo Society of Niagara Falls, director, 1997. *Member:* Association of Professional Women Writers.

■ Awards, Honors

Scribbler's Prize, State University of New York at Buffalo, 1965; New York Poetry Forum, 1980; poetry fellowship, University of Rochester Conference, 1981; *Writers Digest* Honorable Mention Award, for poetry, 1982; March Society Essay Award, 1983; poetry fellowship, Virginia Center of Creative Arts and Writers, 1984; Nonfiction Honor list, *Voice of Youth Advocates,* 1997, for *Margaret Bourke-White: A Photographer's Life.*

■ Writings

Margaret Bourke-White: A Photographer's Life, Lerner, 1996.

Work represented in *Anthology of Magazine Verse & Yearbook of American Poetry,* 1984; poems published in various journals.

■ Work in Progress

Poems and feature articles.

■ Sidelights

Emily Keller told *SATA:* "I have always wanted to be a writer. As a child, my greatest pleasure, aside from climbing trees, was reading, anything, from my brothers' comic books, to Einstein's theories, and then to the classics. I was an English major from kindergarten through graduate school. Five years of piano lessons gave me a love of classical music, but I was more interested in reading the composers' lives than in practicing. In college my interest in history and poetry flowered. Not only did the humorists, Dickens and Twain, delight me when I was young, but also the Brontes, Jane Austen, George Eliot, as well as Russian, French, and Roman writers. I took five years of Latin in school and 'Arma virumque cano' from Virgil's Aeneid still sings in my memory. I admired the poetry of Yeats, Emily Dickinson, Wordsworth, Frost, and Dylan Thomas. Later, my interests included reading Thomas Hardy, Proust, and the mysteries of Agatha Christie, as well as traveling, sketching, and snow and water skiing.

"In the 1970s and 1980s, raising my two daughters Tammyanne and Barbie Jean added joy, but left little time for writing. I did begin publishing poems in local papers and national literary magazines. Thereafter followed articles and interviews.

"*Margaret Bourke-White: A Photographer's Life* is my first book. As a child I found few good biographies of women who could inspire young girls. I realized later that many women excelled in the arts, but few were allowed to excel in other fields. Therefore, I decided to concentrate on writing about women who have succeeded in nontraditional professions. As a feminist, I'd like to write a series of books on strong successful women.

"I see books as treasures, so the artistic appearance of a book inside and out is very important to me. As I wrote the life of this photographer, I obtained photos from her estate at Syracuse University and asked my publisher, The Lerner Group, to use as many as possible and I would cover the cost. Twenty of these photos have never been seen before in any known biography.

"I find morning hours best for writing; it's quiet with no distractions. I write or research almost every day when I'm not babysitting my three grandsons, Joseph, Anthony, and Paul.

"Today I prefer reading biographies and history, short stories, and poetry by Joyce Carol Oates, John Updike, Maxine Kumin, Tess Gallagher, et al.

"I would advise aspiring writers to study books in their genre and publications where they'd like their work to appear and to read their work first in writers' workshops and finally, to believe in themselves and persevere."

Keller's *Margaret Bourke-White: A Photographer's Life* describes the remarkable life and work of *Life* Magazine's first woman photographer. Breaking boundaries for women's traditional working roles, Bourke-White captured black-and-white images that are memorable for their adroit coverage of historical events and people. Her well-known photos include portraits of Joseph Stalin and Mohandas Gandhi, coverage of the powerful steel industry, and her stark portrayal of poverty in America during the Depression. Hazel Rochman, reviewing the biography in *Booklist,* noted that Keller's narrative would give readers reason for further research. *School Library Journal* contributor Carol Schene offered a favorable estimation of Keller's "carefully researched account," concluding the book "well-balanced, insightful and sensitive."

■ Works Cited

Rochman, Hazel, review of *Margaret Bourke-White: A Photographer's Life, Booklist,* June 1 & 15, 1996, p. 1690.

Schene, Carol, review of *Margaret Bourke-White: A Photographer's Life, School Library Journal,* August, 1996.

■ For More Information See

PERIODICALS

Bulletin of the Center for Children's Books, September, 1996, p. 18.

* * *

KING, Thomas 1943-

■ Personal

Born April 24, 1943, in Sacramento, CA; son of Robert Hunt and Kathryn K. King; married Kristine Adams, 1970 (marriage ended, 1981); married Helen Hoy; children: Christian, Benjamin Hoy, Elizabeth. *Education:* Chico State College (now California State University, Chico), B.A., 1970, M.A., 1972; University of Utah, Ph.D., 1986. *Hobbies and other interests:* Photography.

■ Addresses

Home—St. Paul, MN. *Agent*—Denise Bukowski, Bukowski Agency, 182 Avenue Rd., Suite 3, Toronto M5R 2J1, Ontario, Canada.

■ Career

Novelist and editor. Photojournalist in Australia and New Zealand; Boeing Aircraft, tool designer; University of Utah, Salt Lake City, director of Native Studies, 1971-73; California State University, Humboldt, associate dean for student services, 1973-77; University of Utah, coordinator of History of the Indians of the Americas Program, 1977-79; University of Lethbridge, Alberta, Canada, assistant professor of Native Studies, 1979-89; University of Minnesota, Twin Cities, MN, associate professor of American and Native Studies, 1989—, chairperson of Native Studies.

■ Awards, Honors

PEN/Josephine Miles Award winner, and Commonwealth Writer's Prize nominee, both for *Medicine River;* Canadian Governor General's Award, 1992, for *A Coyote Columbus Story.*

■ Writings

FOR CHILDREN

A Coyote Columbus Story, illustrated by William K. Monkman, Groundwood, 1992.

OTHER

(Editor, with Cheryl Dawnan Calver and Helen Hoy) *The Native in Literature: Canadian and Comparative Perspectives* (criticism), illustrated by Jay Belmore, ECW Press, 1987.
Medicine River (novel), Viking, 1990.
(Editor and author of introduction) *All My Relations: An Anthology of Contemporary Canadian Native Fiction,* McClelland and Stewart, 1990, University of Oklahoma Press, 1992.
Green Grass, Running Water (novel), Houghton, 1993.
One Good Story, That One (short stories), Harper, 1993.

Also author of the teleplay *Medicine River,* broadcast by CBC-TV, 1993, and the radio drama *Medicine River,* CBC-Radio, 1993. Contributor of poems to periodicals, including *Canadian Literature, Soundings, Whetstone,* and *Tonyon Review.* Editor of *Canadian Fiction,* 1988.

■ Sidelights

Thomas King is a writer of Greek, German, and Native American heritage whose writings and edited works center on Native Americans. As a novelist for adults, King is best known for his works which utilize comedy and irony to expose the continuing domination of Native American Indians and their culture by the white world. *Medicine River* and *Green Grass, Running Water* are examples of these works. King has also written a children's book, *A Coyote Columbus Story,* that shares with the writer's adult works an irreverent approach to reality as it is traditionally perceived by the white world. Although King was born in California and bears a Cherokee heritage from a father who abandoned his family when King was five, the author is often dubbed a Native-Canadian writer, for he has lived and taught extensively in Canada, and writes primarily about Natives of the Blackfoot tribe who reside on or near reservations in the Canadian province of Alberta.

Medicine River, King's first novel, describes a half-Blackfoot Indian named Will who returns to the reservation where his mother lived and, courtesy of a trickster figure named Harlan Bigbear, finds himself becoming involved in the lives of those around him. Similarly, *Green Grass, Running Water,* King's second novel, features characters in often comical situations where the underlying theme is a serious attempt to explore Indian identity. The title alludes to the standard phrasing of Indian treaties that the land will be theirs "as long as the grass is green and the water runs." Central to the novel, ironically, is a dam which threatens to stop the water and dry up the grass. Four mystical elderly Indians named Hawkeye, Ishmael, Robinson Crusoe, and Lone Ranger escape from a mental institution determined to intervene. Woven throughout the narrative is a talking coyote who tells a creation myth. Lauding the work in *Newsweek,* Malcolm Jones, Jr. asserted: "Successfully mixing realism and myth, comedy and tragedy ... King has produced a novel that defies all our expectations about what Native American fiction should be. It is a first-class work of art."

A Coyote Columbus Story is a novel for children that combines a humorous version of the creation myth with the story of the "discovery" of America by Columbus told from the perspective of the Native Americans who already lived there. "This is an entertaining story, great fun to read aloud because the language is crisp, colloquial, and very expressive," wrote Celia Lottridge in *Quill & Quire.* "It is also extremely thought-provoking." Coyote, a trickster figure found in traditional Native lore, creates the world and then begins populating it in the hopes of putting together a team to play baseball. After a while, however, neither the animals nor the humans want to play because Coyote is constantly changing the rules so that she always wins. Coyote then creates a new group of potential players, Christopher Columbus and his crew, who only want to work and make money, and go off in search of things to buy and sell. Part of what they find to sell are members of the first race of humans, whom they enslave. Like King's novels for adults, *A Coyote Columbus Story* sets aside the restraints of linear storytelling, and achieves some of its comic effects from surprising and anachronistic juxtapositions. Sarah Ellis, writing in *Horn Book,* noted that King's comedy does not hide the fact that his sympathy lies with the values of the first nation of humans, whose Native American speech patterns dominate the narrative. Furthermore, added Ellis, "what *Coyote* captures—a quality I've often heard in native storytelling, but less often seen expressed in print—is the spirit of cheekiness, a bold, outrageous iconoclastic energy that incorporates warmth and inclusiveness."

The exclusion of Native Americans from white society, history, and culture is a prevalent theme in much of King's writing. "I think of myself as a serious writer,"

King told Malcolm Jones Jr. of *Newsweek.* "Tragedy is my topic. Comedy is my strategy."

■ Works Cited

Ellis, Sarah, review of *A Coyote Columbus Story, Horn Book,* September, 1993, pp. 637-38.

Jones, Malcolm, Jr., review of *Green Grass, Running Water, Newsweek,* April 12, 1993, p. 60.

Lottridge, Celia, review of *A Coyote Columbus Story, Quill & Quire,* July, 1992, p. 44.

■ For More Information See

BOOKS

Contemporary Literary Criticism, Volume 89, Gale, 1996, pp. 74-102.

Native North American Literature, Gale, 1994, pp. 373-82.

PERIODICALS

Kirkus Reviews, January 1, 1993, p. 14.
Publishers Weekly, March 8, 1993, pp. 56-57.
Quill & Quire, April, 1990, p. 26; March, 1993, p. 46.
School Library Journal, April, 1991, p. 154.*

* * *

KITTINGER, Jo S(usenbach) 1955-

■ Personal

Born October 7, 1955; son of Donald (an owner of a pest control business) and Vivian (a university office manager) Susenbach; married Richard Joel Kittinger (a computer analyst), December 28, 1974; children: Michael, Robert, Rebecca. *Education:* University of Montevallo, B.F.A., 1977. *Politics:* Conservative. *Religion:* Evangelistic Christian. *Hobbies and other interests:* Pottery, photography, collecting McDonald's Happy Meal toys, theatre, animals, nature.

■ Addresses

Home and Office—1612 Colesbury Circle, Hoover, AL 35226.

■ Career

Wood & the Works (fine crafts gallery), Alabaster, AL, co-owner and resident potter, 1977-80; freelance crafts designer, 1978-91. Secretary to the board of directors, Mental Retardation and Developmental Disabilities Health Care Authority of Jefferson County, Inc., 1994—; member of task force and legislative committee supporting the developmentally disabled, 1996—. *Member:* Society of Children's Book Writers and Illustrators (conference coordinator, 1995—), Alabama Mineral and Lapidary Society, Shades Valley Community Church (drama team).

JO S. KITTINGER

■ Writings

Dead Log Alive!, Franklin Watts, 1996.
A Look at Rocks: From Coal to Kimberlite, Franklin Watts, 1997.

Contributor to *Child Times of Alabama.*

■ Work in Progress

The Joy of Cats for Meadowbrook Press; *Treasure Underfoot: Minerals, Stone Cones and Other Plant Fossils,* and *Stone Bones and Other Animal Fossils,* all for Franklin Watts.

■ Sidelights

Jo S. Kittinger told *Something about the Author (SATA):* "I have always loved books, the written word. I was on my high school yearbook staff and became editor my senior year. In college I pursued art with a minor in biology. My art and interest in publishing led to freelance crafts designs which appeared in numerous books and magazines. But my desire was to see a book with my name on the cover. I decided to take some classes being offered locally by a published children's author. The class led to a critique group. I have to confess, without the support, encouragement, and prayers of fellow writers I would have quit before ever realizing my dream. I began with writing fiction and received many rejection slips. A speaker at a conference of the Society of Children's Book Writers and Illustrators suggested nonfiction was perhaps a quicker road to publication. As one of those people who always loved school and learning, this appealed to me. Research was even more enjoyable than I expected. My first nonfiction query netted a contract for *Dead Log Alive!*

"I try to write every day but keep my family as a higher priority. When the kids are out of school, the time spent with them is valuable fodder as a children's author. Every event and activity becomes more material that I can incorporate in my writing. It is important for authors to remember that a great deal of writing goes on in our heads and in our hearts, not only in our computers. Freelance writing and/or illustrating can help writers get experience, income, and encouragement in the face of frequent rejection. I write, illustrate, and take photos for a local parenting publication, *Child Times of Alabama.*

"I seek to use, to the best of my ability, the gifts God has given me. I want children to enjoy learning through my books. I want them to run to a friend and say, 'Did you know....'"

*   *   *

KNIGHT, Christopher G. 1943-

■ Personal

Born January 10, 1943, in Cleveland, OH; son of Charles L. (a landscape architect) and Lillian (Balboni) Knight; married Kathryn Lasky (a writer), May 30, 1971; children: Maxwell B., Meribah G. *Education:* Dartmouth College, B.A. (magna cum laude); Harvard Graduate School of Design, M.Arch., 1969.

■ Addresses

Home—7 Scott St., Cambridge, MA 02138.

■ Career

Documentary film producer, photographer. Founded The New Film Company, Inc., 1969.

■ Awards, Honors

Boston Globe-Horn Book nonfiction award, 1981, Notable Book citation, American Library Association (ALA), New York Academy of Science Honor Book, 20 Best Science Books for Children, *Scientific American,* all for *The Weaver's Gift;* Notable Book, ALA, *New York Times* Thirteen Best Children's Books, 1983, and Newbery (Honor), 1984, all for *Sugaring Time;* Editors' Choice, *Booklist,* 1985, for *Puppeteer;* Reading Magic Award, *Parenting* Magazine, Parent's Choice Honor Book, Best Books, *Booklist,* 1990, Notable Book, ALA, 1990, John Burroughs Outstanding Nature Books, 1990, all for *Dinosaur Dig;* Notable Book, ALA, 1993, for

Surtsey; Editors' Choice, *Booklist,* 1995, for *Days of the Dead.*

■ Illustrator

FOR CHILDREN; ALL WRITTEN BY KATHRYN LASKY

I Have Four Names for My Grandfather, Little, Brown, 1976.
Tugboats Never Sleep, Little, Brown, 1977.
The Weaver's Gift, F. Warne, 1980.
Dollmaker: The Eyelight and the Shadow, Scribner, 1981.
Sugaring Time, Macmillan, 1983.
(Written by Lasky as Kathryn Knight, with Maxwell B. Knight) *A Baby for Max,* Scribner, 1984.
Puppeteer, Macmillan, 1985.
Dinosaur Dig, Morrow Junior Books, 1990.
Surtsey: The Newest Place on Earth, Hyperion, 1992.
(With Jack Swedberg) *Think Like an Eagle: At Work with a Wildlife Photographer,* Little, Brown, 1992.
Monarchs, Harcourt Brace, 1993.
(With Meribah Knight) *Searching for Laura Ingalls: A Reader's Journey,* Macmillan, 1993.
Days of the Dead, Hyperion, 1994.
The Most Beautiful Roof in the World: Exploring the Rainforest Canopy, Harcourt Brace, 1997.
Shadows in the Dawn: The Lemurs of Madagascar, Harcourt Brace, 1998.

OTHER

Kathryn Lasky, *Tall Ships,* illustrated by Christopher G. Knight, Scribner, 1978.
Kathryn Lasky Knight, *Atlantic Circle* (adult travelogue), illustrated by Christopher G. Knight, Norton, 1985.

Also the photographer of pictures for numerous articles written by Kathryn Lasky for *Sail Magazine.*

■ Sidelights

Christopher G. Knight is a photographer who, together with his wife, Kathryn Lasky, has produced several nonfiction books for children and young adults showcasing such arresting sights as the world's newest land mass, the celebration of the Days of the Dead in Mexico, and the migration of the monarch butterfly. Knight and Lasky have gained a reputation for producing books that combine a clear, well-written text with photographs that many commentators have found stunningly beautiful. "We expect good things from the husband-and-wife team of Lasky and Knight," wrote Stephanie Zvirin at the head of her starred review of *Surtsey: The Newest Place on Earth* in *Booklist.*

Lasky and Knight and their two children participated in the adventure that is at the heart of *Dinosaur Dig,* which chronicles their experiences the summer they joined a paleontological dig in Montana. "The exquisite full-color photos, like the text, stimulate all senses," remarked Cathryn A. Camper in *School Library Journal,* "capturing the dusty smells, the gritty sands, and the subtle colors of the harsh Montana Badlands." Another family vacation provided the setting for *Searching for Laura Ingalls: A Reader's Journey,* in which Lasky and daughter Meribah Knight, an ardent fan of the Laura Ingalls Wilder books, share the narrative, detailing the family's journey to the places where the classic children's author once lived. Illustrated by "Knight's crisp color photos [which] accurately portray the sites and local color of these areas," according to Kay Weisman in *Booklist, Searching for Laura Ingalls* was dubbed "a natural for Wilder followers" by Elizabeth S. Watson in *Horn Book.*

Knight and Lasky visited Iceland for their book *Surtsey: The Newest Place on Earth,* an award-winning portrait of a tiny volcanic island that emerged from the ocean in 1963. In pictures and text, the book offers a view of the short-lived island that emphasizes the miraculous development of life there, a living science experiment. *Surtsey* is "well organized, finely tooled, and beautifully designed—a treat for inquiring minds and eyes," Patricia Manning asserted in *School Library Journal.* Knight and Lasky's collaboration on *Monarchs* also produced a book which reviewers recommended for young scientists. In this work, photos and text teach the reader about the development and migration of monarch butterflies from Canada and the United States to Mexico. "There is much to learn, enjoy, and ponder in this beautiful book," Margaret A. Bush remarked in *Horn Book,* while *School Library Journal* contributor Susan Oliver asserted of *Monarchs:* "Vibrant description melds with fascinating full-color photographs in a book that strikes a perfect balance between science and humanity."

Knight and Lasky returned to Mexico to research *Days of the Dead,* an investigation into the celebration of the Mexican national holiday honoring the spirits of the dead. "Busy, vivid pictures capture the customs associated with the holiday, celebrated around the time of our Halloween," noted Francine Prose in the *New York Times Book Review.* Both text and pictures center on how one family participates in the festivities, a focus which "contribute[s] a sense of immediacy and intimacy to their description of how and why the Days of the Dead are celebrated in a Mexican village," critic Zvirin remarked. Although *Days of the Dead* was not as enthusiastically received as some of Knight and Lasky's earlier works, it was dubbed by *School Library Journal* contributor Jessie Meudell "a good resource for reports as well as an interesting and appealing selection for pleasure reading."

Born in Cleveland, Ohio, Knight first became interested in photography at age thirteen. Years later, while in college, he combined his interest in boating with his love for photography by kayaking from Alaska to Seattle, Washington, with his brother, photographing the trip along the way. Knight once told *SATA* that in 1964 he "paddled a canoe down the Danube River with a group of other students, visiting seven countries and photographing a forty-seven-page article for *National Geographic.* This lucky break began a career in photography, which resulted in stories for *National Geographic* on Alaska, Japan, and Romania, plus numerous other magazine articles." Since then, as Knight explained to *SATA,* he and his family have made "a series of sailing voyages, including two crossings of the Atlantic, and cruising in Scandinavia, inland Europe via the canals, the Mediterranean, and the Caribbean."

In addition to photographing pictures for children's books, Knight runs a film company that produces documentary films. "This company," as he explained to *SATA,* "has produced films ranging from a theatrical feature starring Joan Baez to television programs on aging, single-handed sailing, the reintroduction of bald eagles, a solo canoe voyage to the Arctic Ocean, and 'Yankee in Kamchatka,' the story of an expedition to Siberia." Many of these works have aired on the PBS television programs *Adventure* and *Nova.*

■ Works Cited

Bush, Margaret A., review of *Monarchs, Horn Book,* November, 1993, p. 755.

Camper, Cathryn A., review of *Dinosaur Dig, School Library Journal,* May, 1990, p. 98.

Manning, Patricia, review of *Surtsey: The Newest Place on Earth, School Library Journal,* February, 1993, p. 100.

Meudell, Jessie, review of *Days of the Dead, School Library Journal,* October, 1994, p. 135.

Oliver, Susan, review of *Monarchs, School Library Journal,* September, 1993, p. 244.

Prose, Francine, review of *Days of the Dead, New York Times Book Review,* October 23, 1994, p. 30.

Watson, Elizabeth S., review of *Searching for Laura Ingalls: A Reader's Journey, Horn Book,* March, 1994, pp. 224-25.

Weisman, Kay, review of *Searching for Laura Ingalls: A Reader's Journey, Booklist,* October 15, 1993, p. 436.

Zvirin, Stephanie, review of *Days of the Dead, Booklist,* October 15, 1994, p. 421.

Zvirin, Stephanie, review of *Surtsey: The Newest Place on Earth, Booklist,* January 1, 1993, p. 805.

■ For More Information See

PERIODICALS

Booklist, November 15, 1993, p. 618; April 1, 1997, p. 93.

New York Times Book Review, June 24, 1990, p. 28.

Publishers Weekly, January 12, 1990, p. 63.

School Library Journal, April, 1992, p. 138; October, 1993, p. 144.

Scientific American, December, 1990, p. 134A; December, 1993, p. 133.*

KOEHLER-PENTACOFF, Elizabeth 1957-

■ Personal

Born November 30, 1957, in Milwaukee, WI; daughter of Elmer (a spray painter in a factory) and Helen (a bookkeeper) Koehler; married Robert Pentacoff (a civil engineer), June 20, 1981; children: Christopher. *Education:* California State University, Fresno, B.A. (liberal studies), B.A. (children's theater), and teaching credentials. *Politics:* Democrat. *Religion:* Roman Catholic. *Hobbies and other interests:* Theater, the beach, playing the piano, reading, dogs, chocolate, old movies.

■ Addresses

Electronic mail—lizbooks @ aol.com (America Online).

■ Career

California State University, Hayward, Education/Extension Department, teacher of drama to educators. Has also worked as an elementary schoolteacher and director of children's plays and drama programs in northern California. *Member:* National Organization for Women, Society of Children's Book Writers and Illustrators, Authors Guild, American Association of University Women, California Writers Club.

ELIZABETH KOEHLER-PENTACOFF

■ Writings

Curtain Call (drama games), Incentive Publications (Nashville, TN), 1989.
Explorers (for teachers), Frank Schaffer (Torrance, CA), 1994.
Louise the One and Only, illustrated by R. W. Alley, Troll, 1995.
Wish Magic, illustrated by R. W. Alley, Troll, 1996.
Help!: My Life Is Going to the Dogs, Troll, 1997.

Contributor of articles and reviews to magazines.

■ Work in Progress

A humorous picture book, a chapter book, and a novel for the middle grades.

■ Sidelights

Elizabeth Koehler-Pentacoff told *SATA:* "After I had my son, I stopped teaching to stay home with him. I discovered that I needed a creative outlet, so I enrolled in a writing class. The teacher taught us how to submit our articles and short stories to newspapers and magazines. I freelanced for a while and got hooked.

"When my son was a toddler, I used to make deals with him. If he would play quietly while I typed a page, then I would play with him. One day he came home from preschool and said that the teacher had asked the students what their parents did for a living. He had told them, 'My mommy is a typist, and my daddy drives trains.' That motivated me to write a picture book for my son, *Too Tall Tofer,* so he would understand what I did. Several more Tofer stories followed, and a publisher bought them. (Problems with the illustrations have delayed their publication.)

"*Louise the One and Only* originated on a soccer field. I overheard a mother (who is also a teacher) telling another mother that all of her kindergarten students wanted to change their names. A little voice popped into my head, saying 'I'm not Louise.' From that moment, Louise wouldn't leave me alone. I volunteered in my son's kindergarten classroom, so many details and ideas began there.

"*Wish Magic* is a fantasy about a girl who suddenly finds her wishes coming true. Her brainy brother, Morris, has secretly sprinkled a magic potion on her doughnut. The character of Morris grew out of my cousin, who liked to play tricks on me, and out of my own son, who is scientific and smart. I wrote a 'trick' ending, so the reader must pay attention to both written and illustrated clues.

"*Help!: My Life Is Going to the Dogs* is based on anecdotes of my early life. I grew up in Wisconsin during the sixties, and we didn't have much money. Our old Chevy had survived many years of wet Wisconsin summers and below-zero winters. Rust framed the car, and the lower side and bottom occasionally flaked away, leaving less and less car. The roof was liberally sprinkled with holes. Driving in wet weather became an event our visitors would never forget.

"Once, an elderly, large woman squeezed into the back seat. Her high heels went right through the floor boards. I was six or seven at the time, and I remember yanking her feet out. My mother passed an umbrella to us, while opening hers. Between my mother and father on the front seat was a bucket. Raindrops plunked from the ceiling to the umbrella and into the pail, creating a staccato rhythm. Although this was an everyday occurrence for us, our visitor was amazed.

"By using my life, observing others and using my imagination, I create fiction."

■ For More Information See

PERIODICALS

Booklist, July, 1996, p. 1826.
School Library Journal, August, 1996, p. 125.

*   *   *

KOWALSKI, Kathiann M. 1955-

■ Personal

Born December 27, 1955, in Mineola, NY; daughter of Edward S. (a civil engineer) and Julianna L. (a teacher and assistant principal of an elementary school) Kowalski; married Michael G. Meissner (an attorney), June 16, 1979; children: Christopher Michael, Laura Kathryn, Bethany Lynn. *Education:* Hofstra University, B.A. (summa cum laude), 1976; Harvard University, J.D. (cum laude), 1979. *Religion:* Roman Catholic.

■ Addresses

Home and office—21255 South Park Dr., Fairview Park, OH 44126. *Electronic mail*—im448 @ cleveland.freenet.edu.

■ Career

Squire, Sanders & Dempsey (law firm), Cleveland, OH, associate, 1979-88, partner, 1988-94; freelance writer, 1994—. *Member:* Society of Children's Book Writers and Illustrators; St. Angela Merici Home and School Association (member of board of directors, 1994-97; president, 1995-96); Fairview Park Junior Women's Club; Phi Beta Kappa; Cleveland Council on World Affairs; Footpath Dance Company, past member of board of directors; Starfire Baton Corps; St. Augustine Academy Parents' Guild; St. Ignatius High School Loyola Society.

■ Awards, Honors

Outstanding Book Award, science category, Society of School Librarians International, 1996, for *Hazardous Waste Sites*.

KATHIANN M. KOWALSKI

■ Writings

Hazardous Waste Sites, Lerner Publications (Minneapolis, MN), 1996.

Contributor of nearly fifty articles, stories, and photographs to magazines, including *Cobblestone, Straight, R-A-D-A-R, Youth Update, Girls' Life,* and *Odyssey.*

■ Work in Progress

Alternative Medicine, for Enslow Publishers (Hillside, NJ); *Campaign Politics: What's Fair? What's Foul?,* for Lerner Publications; various magazine articles and stories.

■ Sidelights

Kathiann M. Kowalski told *Something about the Author* (*SATA*): "In contrast to the dry, 'textbook' stuff that lined library shelves when I was younger, today's nonfiction for children and teens is really exciting. You not only get information you need, but you also get a fun reading experience.

"My writing aims both to entertain and to inform young readers. To do this, I learn as much as possible and find key facts that interest and excite me. Often I'll start with reading whatever children's books are already available on a topic. Then I'll move on to 'adult' works and, wherever possible, primary sources. Besides reading primary documentary sources (historical materials, first-hand studies and reports, judicial cases, and so forth), I really enjoy contacting experts and getting their comments and input.

"Once I am both knowledgeable and excited about a topic, then it is time to write, so the reader can experience that enthusiasm and excitement. This means drawing upon all my creative writing skills to make a subject come alive. True-life anecdotes, specific details, and hard-hitting quotations all add drama to a piece. A light tone where appropriate and a sense of humor pique the interest of teens and children. I like to challenge readers to develop informed opinions on difficult issues.

"*Hazardous Waste Sites* developed from my experiences as a lawyer practicing environmental law. In the course of representing private and public clients, I appreciated firsthand that citizen and neighbor groups, private corporations, and government agencies all have different approaches and outlooks on how best to address scientific and social problems relating to hazardous waste sites. Nonetheless, most of the books my own children were exposed to at school took a one-sided, simplistic approach to the issue. If everything were that simple, the problems would have been solved long ago!

"Working in law has taught me to keep probing and searching until all my questions are answered, and it has trained me to be a stickler for accuracy. These traits have certainly come in handy, even on subjects that don't seem to have much to do with law at all.

"Yes, freelance writing requires discipline and determination. It also provides the freedom to focus on new and different issues and to grow in my own understanding of the world around me. That's just the sense of curiosity and wonder I hope to inspire in my readers."

*　　　*　　　*

KREMER, Marcie
See SORENSON, Margo

*　　　*　　　*

KRIEGER, Melanie

■ Personal

Education: Douglass College/Rutgers University, A.B., 1965; California State Polytechnic University, M.A., 1967.

■ Addresses

Home—5 Deacon Court, Melville, NY 11747.

■ Career

Ward Melville High School, Melville, NY, teacher, 1979-86, academic teams coordinator, 1985—, research director for West Prep, 1986—; Stony Brook University, Stony Brook, NY, adjunct professor, 1984-96, co-director of Stony Brook High School Summer Research Institute and creator of mentor program linking high school students with college professors, 1984-96; American representative for the Summer Research Program and the Science Olympieda Competition at Technion University, Haifa, Israel, 1992—.

■ Awards, Honors

Teacher of the Year, Three Village School District, 1983, 1985; Woman of the Year in Education, Village Times Newspapers, 1987; MIT Excellence in Teaching Award, 1991; Outstanding Teacher of the Year in the Metropolitan New York Region, 1991; Distinguished Teaching Award, Ward Melville High School, 1995; Tandy Technology Scholar Teacher of the Year, 1997.

■ Writings

How to Excel in Science Competitions, Franklin Watts, 1991.
Means & Probabilities: Using Statistics in Science Projects, Franklin Watts, 1996.

■ Work in Progress

How to Start Your Own Science Research Course.

MELANIE KRIEGER

■ Sidelights

Melanie Krieger told *Something about the Author* (*SATA*): "I am the program coordinator for West Prep, a course in independent research in math and science at Ward Melville High School. In the course, students work on major independent science, math, and social science projects to enter in various competitions. During the course, students are taught science research, how to write a research paper, how to present a research paper, and statistics. The premier competition is the Westinghouse Science Talent Search. In the past ten years, Ward Melville, under my direction, has produced seventy-three semifinalists and twelve finalists. In 1997, Ward Melville High School had more finalists than any other school in the United States. In addition, I work on similar projects with high school students at Stony Brook University. I am interested in showing that students can win major scholarships through academics rather than athletics."

Krieger's *How to Excel in Science Competitions* guides high school students through the step-by-step process for entering an independent research project into a major science competition. From the initial stage of choosing a topic, to presenting the research, to learning what to expect from the judges, Krieger's expertise is evident in her use of "clear, concise text" and "practical advice and guidance," according to *Booklist*'s Karen Hutt. Karen Perry of *Voice of Youth Advocates* found the appendices, which include, among other things, a sample entry form from Westinghouse, rules for judging, and lists of major competitions, "most interesting" and recommended the book as an "excellent resource" for the serious secondary science student.

■ Works Cited

Hutt, Karen, review of *How to Excel in Science Competitions, Booklist,* December 15, 1991, p. 757.

Perry, Karen, review of *How to Excel in Science Competitions, Voice of Youth Advocates,* April, 1992, p. 57.

■ For More Information See

PERIODICALS

School Library Journal, February, 1992, p. 114.

*   *   *

KRYKORKA, Vladyana 1945-

■ Personal

Born June 29, 1945, in Prague, Czechoslovakia; married, husband's name Paul; children: Zuzanna, Ian. *Education:* Attended Ontario College of Art. *Hobbies and other interests:* Volleyball, skiing, theatre, painting on silk, and designing calendars, greeting cards, and logos.

■ Addresses

Home—153 Sherwood Ave., Toronto, Ontario, Canada M4P 2A9.

■ Career

Illustrator.

■ Awards, Honors

Ruth Schwartz Picture Book Award, Ontario Arts Council and Canadian Booksellers Association, 1994, Notable Book, Canadian Library Association (CLA), and Amelia Frances Howard-Gibbon Illustrator's Honour Book, Canadian Association of Children's Librarians, all for *Northern Lights: The Soccer Trails.*

■ Illustrator

David Carefoot, *The Big Yellow Frog,* Three Trees Press (Toronto, Ontario), 1978.

Patricia Quinlan, *Planting Seeds,* Annick, 1988.

Michael A. Kusugak and Robert Munsch, *A Promise is a Promise,* Annick, 1988.

Joyce Zemke, *An Animal Alphabet,* Ginn (Scarborough, Ontario), 1989.

Gail Chislett, *Whump,* Annick, 1989.

Michael A. Kusugak, *Baseball Bats for Christmas,* Annick, 1990.

Michelle B. Goodman, *Vanishing Cookies: Doing OK When a Parent Has Cancer,* Benjamin Family Foundation (Downsview, Ontario), 1990.

Nancy Crystal, *Are We There Yet?,* North Winds (Richmond Hill, Ontario), 1991.

Michael A. Kusugak, *Hide and Sneak,* Annick, 1992.

Allen Morgan, *Megan and the Weather Witch: Two Stories,* Oasis (Toronto, Ontario), 1992.

Rafe Martin, *Dear as Salt,* Scholastic Canada, 1993.

Rafe Martin, *Le Chandelier Geant,* Scholastic Canada, 1993.

Michael A. Kusugak, *Northern Lights: The Soccer Trails,* Annick, 1993.

Allen Morgan, *Celebrate the Season—Winter: A Story Collection,* Oasis (Toronto, Canada), 1994.

Ty Hochban, *Hear My Roar: A Story of Family Violence,* Annick, 1994.

Eliza Clark, *Butterflies and Bottlecaps,* HarperCollins, 1996.

Michael A. Kusugak, *My Arctic 1,2,3,* Annick, 1996.

Rosalind Kerven, *The Weather Drum,* Cambridge University Press, 1996.

■ Sidelights

When assessing her career as an illustrator, Vladyana Krykorka commented in a publicity release for Annick Press: "It's the most wonderful profession I can think of.... I want to keep on doing this for the rest of my life."

Krykorka grew up in Prague, Czechoslovakia, as an only child who studied art for many years. Her greatest

STORY·MICHAEL ARVAARLUK KUSUGAK
ART·VLADYANA KRYKORKA

With pictures by Vladyana Krykorka, *Baseball Bats for Christmas* illustrates the ingenuity of a young Inuit boy who decides to fashion baseball bats from donated Christmas trees. (Written by Michael Arvaarluk Kusugak.)

influence may have come from her "very artistic" parents who sent her to art classes. Krykorka later lent her skills to a position as an art director before she began illustrating picture books professionally.

Krykorka furnished the pictures for Michael A. Kusugak's well-known picture book *Baseball Bats for Christmas,* about a young boy living in Repulse Bay (located along the northwest coast of the Hudson Bay in Canada) in 1955. The boy, Arvaarluk, and his community are perplexed when their supply pilot, Rocky Parsons, gives them six Christmas trees or "standing-ups," as the Arctic people call trees. Since no one understands the relationship between the trees and Christmas, Arvaarluk and his friends use them to make baseball bats. Calling *Baseball Bats for Christmas* a "stand-out season winner," *Quill and Quire* contributor Kenneth Oppel praised Krykorka's "colourful, lively illustrations." Sarah Ellis, a reviewer for *Horn Book,* described Krykorka's images as "naturalistic."

Krykorka again collaborated with Kusugak to create illustrations for *Hide and Sneak,* which also encompasses the familiar Arctic surroundings of *Baseball Bats for Christmas* but is set during the summer season. The story finds Allashua innocently playing hide and seek until she is captured by a leprechaun named Ijiraq. Her adventure brings Inuit folktales and artifacts into the present-day as Allashua escapes with the help of an "inuksugaq." "The illustrations are realistic ... and attractive, with the subtle beauty of the barrens in summer carefully rendered," noted *Canadian Children's Literature* reviewer Stan Atherton. *Quill and Quire* contributor Sarah Ellis stated that "emotions are clear" from Krykorka's drawings.

Krykorka adds her artistic expertise to another Kusugak work entitled *Northern Lights: The Soccer Trails.* Highlighting some customs of the Inuit people, like rubbing noses and playing soccer with a caribou-skin ball, the story focuses on Kataujaq, a young girl who loses her mother to tuberculosis. Kataujaq's grandmother helps her cope with the loss by telling her the tale of the northern lights, which, according to Inuit lore, represent the souls of loved ones who continue to play soccer after death. "Krykorka's illustrations are luminous and aptly evoke the shimmering lights of the North," asserted *Quill and Quire* contributor Linda Granfield. *Canadian Materials* contributor Patricia Fry commented that readers could become "mesmerized by some of these pictures."

■ Works Cited

Atherton, Stan, review of *Hide and Sneak, Canadian Children's Literature,* Vol. 72, 1993, p. 84.

Ellis, Sarah, review of *Baseball Bats for Christmas, Horn Book,* May, 1991, p. 366.

Ellis, Sarah, review of *Hide and Sneak, Quill and Quire,* March, 1992, p. 65.

Fry, Patricia, review of *Northern Lights: The Soccer Trails, Canadian Materials,* January, 1994, pp. 21-22.

Granfield, Linda, review of *Northern Lights: The Soccer Trails, Quill and Quire,* September, 1993, p. 67.

Krykorka, Vladyana, author comments in an Annick Press publicity release, c. 1995.

Oppel, Kenneth, review of *Baseball Bats for Christmas, Quill and Quire,* October, 1990, p. 14.

■ For More Information See

PERIODICALS

Books in Canada, summer, 1992, p. 36.

Canadian Children's Literature, Vol. 53, 1989, p. 55; Vol. 61, 1991, pp. 61-63.

School Library Journal, February, 1989, p. 74; March, 1990, p. 189; May, 1995, pp. 197-98.*

L

KIRBY LARSON

LARSON, Kirby 1954-

■ Personal

Born August 17, 1954, in Seattle, WA; daughter of David Neil (a mechanical contractor) and Donna Marie (a bookkeeper; maiden name, Brown) Miltenberger; married Neil Edwin Larson (a certified public accountant), September 6, 1975; children: Tyler Kenton, Quinn

Lois. *Education:* Western Washington State College, B.A., 1976; University of Washington, M.A., 1980. *Hobbies and other interests:* Reading, quilting, traveling.

■ Addresses

Home—8523 Northeast 147th Place, Bothell, WA 98011. *Electronic mail*—Kirlane @ aol.com.

■ Career

Children's book author and homemaker. Northshore Public Education Foundation, board of trustees, 1995—; Northshore Performing Arts Center Foundation, co-founder and member of board of trustees, 1995—. Moorlands Elementary PTA, co-president, 1991-94; Northshore School District, board of directors, 1994—, president, 1995—. *Member:* Author's Guild, Society of Children's Book Writers and Illustrators, PTA.

■ Awards, Honors

Golden Acorn Award, 1994, for PTA Service.

■ Writings

Second-Grade Pig Pals, illustrated by Nancy Poydar, Holiday House, 1994.
Cody and Quinn, Sitting in a Tree, illustrated by Nancy Poydar, Holiday House, 1996.

"SWEET VALLEY KIDS" BOOKS

Scaredy-Cat Elizabeth, Bantam Doubleday Dell, 1995.
Elizabeth Hatches an Egg, Bantam Doubleday Dell, 1996.

■ Work in Progress

Water Baby, a story about a second grader who is afraid of the water; *Red, White and Blueberry,* an easy reader; *Slug Sisters,* a story about friendship and slugs; and *Grummie's Dummies,* a story about a bossy girl who has mix-ups with math. "I am always studying new things!

Current topics of interest include parakeets and old hats."

■ Sidelights

Kirby Larson has published two chapter books for young people that critics find good humored and accurate reflections of the problems and fixations of childhood. In Larson's first book, *Second-Grade Pig Pals,* Quinn is the only student in her class who has not thought of some way to contribute to the celebration of National Pig Day. Quinn tries to befriend Manuela, a new student, but is briefly foiled by Annie May, who captures Manuela's attention first. Susan Dove Lempke, in the *Bulletin of the Center for Children's Books,* remarked that young readers might have fun "reading [about Quinn's] travails as she agonizes, in true-to-life second-grade fashion, over the pigs and Manuela." Quinn's solution to her dilemma, which involves the two girls working together to write a limerick about pigs, provides the book with a "whole-hoggedly satisfying ending," according to Janet M. Bair in *School Library Journal.* And *Booklist*'s Mary Harris Veeder noted that Quinn solves her own problem without the help of adults—"a nice, realistic touch."

Larson's heroine shows up again in her second book, *Cody and Quinn, Sitting in a Tree,* a story about how the class bully, with his relentless taunting, tries to ruin Quinn's friendship with a boy. "Larson's second-graders act out this typical school story with a generous measure of humor and sensitivity," stated Pat Mathews in *Bulletin of the Center for Children's Books.* Kay Weisman declared in *Booklist* that "Larson has an accurate sense of seven-year-olds' preoccupations and a good ear for dialogue," adding that *Cody and Quinn, Sitting in a Tree* is likely to be "a popular choice for beginning readers."

Larson told *SATA:* "Once upon a time, there was a little girl with a funny name and blue cats-eye glasses. Her family moved around a lot; nearly every fall, she was the new kid in school. Sometimes she was lonely but she never worried about making friends—she had two brothers and a sister to play with and hundreds of companions in the books she read. When she wasn't reading, the girl liked to build cushion forts in the living room or put on plays for her parents. She never broke any bones or world records, except maybe for reading. The girl loved to read so much that sometimes even her teachers complained!

"When the little girl grew up, she did many things— went to college, worked at a radio station; she even made those annoying sales calls people hang up on. Along the way, she met a handsome prince (maybe not a prince, but definitely handsome), got married and had two children, a boy and a girl. Those babies loved being read to! Which was good because, even though she was grown up, the girl still loved to read. She especially loved to read about George and Martha, Frog and Toad, dear little Frances and anything by Betsy Byars. The girl

Larson's chapter book for primary graders relates the story of a friendship between a boy and a girl and how the class bully tries to ruin their relationship. (Cover illustration by Nancy Poydar.)

loved these children's books so much that she wanted to write one herself. So she did.

"And it was awful. She wrote another one and it was worse. And no fairy godmother showed up to help her, either. She kept writing. Some of it was still bad. But some of it was getting better! The girl didn't give up and, one day, one of her stories was published.

"You've no doubt guessed that this fairy tale is about me. Everything's absolutely true—except for the part about not having a fairy godmother. Actually, I have many! They are fellow children's book writers who tell me when my story needs work and give me good ideas about how to fix it. We cry over each other's rejections and rejoice over each other's good news. In *Charlotte's Web,* E. B. White wrote: 'It is not often that someone comes along who is a true friend and a good writer.' That is why I so treasure all my fairy godmothers.

"In *Second-Grade Pig Pals,* Nancy Poydar drew a picture of the main character, Quinn, hop-skipping with happiness. That picture exactly captures my feelings about making books for children! I love recreating those school-age feelings, thoughts, and actions in a believable way; writing dialogue that sounds like real kids talking—I even love revising (despite all my grumbling). My favorite part is coming to the end of the story and finding out how my main character will solve the story problem.

"Recently I was visiting a school and a young girl asked me, 'Do you feel lucky to be writing children's books?' I answered with an enthusiastic, 'Yes, I do!' In fact, as long as I can write children's books, I'll live 'happily ever after.'"

■ Works Cited

Bair, Janet M., review of *Second-Grade Pig Pals, School Library Journal,* November 1994, p. 84.

Lempke, Susan Dove, review of *Second-Grade Pig Pals, Bulletin of the Center for Children's Books,* December, 1994, p. 1334.

Mathews, Pat, review of *Cody and Quinn, Bulletin of the Center for Children's Books,* September, 1996, p. 19.

Veeder, Mary Harris, review of *Second-Grade Pig Pals, Booklist,* November 1, 1994, p. 497.

Weisman, Kay, review of *Cody and Quinn, Booklist,* April 1, 1996, p. 1366.

■ For More Information See

PERIODICALS

School Library Journal, April, 1996, p. 113.

*　　*　　*

LISLE, Janet Taylor 1947-

■ Personal

Born February 13, 1947, in Englewood, NJ; daughter of Alden (in insurance) and Janet (an architect) Taylor; married c. 1970 (divorced); married Richard Lisle (in international banking), 1976; children: Elizabeth. *Education:* Smith College, B.A., 1969; Attended Georgia State University.

■ Addresses

Home—Rhode Island. *Agent*—Gina Maccoby, P.O. Box 60, Chappaqua, NY 10514.

■ Career

Writer. Has worked as a journalist in Georgia and New York; VISTA (Volunteers in Service to America), volunteer, Atlanta, GA, c. 1970.

■ Awards, Honors

Best Books for Young Adults, American Library Association (ALA), Best Books, *School Library Journal,* Editors' Choice, *Booklist,* all 1985, Parent's Choice Award, Parent's Choice Foundation, 1986, and Best of the '80s, *Booklist,* all for *Sirens and Spies;* Golden Kite Honor Book for Fiction, Society of Children's Book Writers, Best Children's Books, *Parent's Magazine,* and Editors' Choice, *Booklist,* all 1987, all for *The Great Dimpole Oak;* Best Books, *School Library Journal,* Editors' Choice, *Booklist,* and Parent's Choice, all 1989, and Newbery Honor Book, ALA, 1990, all for *Afternoon of the Elves;* Best Books, *School Library Journal, New York*

JANET TAYLOR LISLE

Times Book Review, Boston Globe, and *Parent's Magazine,* all 1991, all for *The Lampfish of Twill;* Best Books, *School Library Journal,* "Pick of the Lists," American Booksellers Association (ABA), and Best Books, Bank Street Child Study Children's Books Committee, for *Forest;* Notable Books selection, Bank Street Child Study Children's Books Committee, 1994, for *The Gold Dust Letters,* and 1995, for *Looking for Juliette;* Best Books, *School Library Journal,* 1995, for *A Message from the Match Girl.*

■ Writings

FOR CHILDREN

The Dancing Cats of Applesap, illustrated by Joelle Shefts, Bradbury, 1984.

Sirens and Spies, Bradbury, 1985.

The Great Dimpole Oak, illustrated by Stephen Gammell, Orchard, 1987.

Afternoon of the Elves, Orchard, 1989.

The Lampfish of Twill, illustrated by Wendy Anderson Halperin, Orchard, 1991.

Forest, Orchard, 1993.

The Gold Dust Letters, Orchard, 1994.

Looking for Juliette, Orchard, 1994.

A Message from the Match Girl, Orchard, 1995.

Angela's Aliens, Orchard, 1996.

■ Sidelights

Janet Lisle is the author of young adult and juvenile novels that explore the relationships and boundaries between the miraculous and the quotidian. Blending humor and realistic character development, Lisle creates worlds full of both fantasy and fact. She revels in dancing cats, backyard elves, and forests shared by squirrels and humans leading parallel lives. Set primarily in the northeastern United States where Lisle was raised and continues to live, early Lisle titles such as *Sirens and Spies, The Great Dimpole Oak,* and *Afternoon of the Elves* were all award-winners and garnered the author a wide readership. Later titles include the four companion volumes of the "Investigators of the Unknown" series. Whatever the topic or setting, "Lisle's books are uniformly delightful," according to Andrea Cleghorn in an essay in *Children's Books and Their Creators.* And if she employs elements of fantasy in her books, it is in order to delve more deeply into the hidden recesses of human life. As Lisle noted in an essay for *Something about the Author Autobiography Series* (*SAAS*), "the investigation of reality, both the inward and outward sort, is at the core of the stories I like to write."

Lisle has been writing stories since she was a child. The only daughter of five children, she grew up in rural Rhode Island and Connecticut. She enjoyed her special position as the sole girl in the family, and she as well as her brothers were avid readers from an early age, consuming Tolkien and Robert Louis Stevenson until they felt "in a trance" from the stories, as she recalled in *SAAS.* Her tranquil childhood in Farmington, Connecti-

An old fisherman leads Eric through a whirlpool into an ancient and glorious world at the center of the earth in Lisle's fantasy. (From *The Lampfish of Twill,* illustrated by Wendy Anderson Halperin.)

cut, changed radically when she went to a private school in the sixth grade. "I was a new girl," Lisle wrote in *SAAS,* "an outsider, and even though I recognized some of the students in my class from home, I felt shy and out of place." Worse, she began to have academic troubles, something that had never occurred before. Math, particularly, was a weak spot, but she soon compensated with a talent for soccer that won her friends and recognition. Yet always throughout school, English classes were her safe haven. From the age of ten, Lisle was composing stories both at school and increasingly on her own at home. When her teachers became more concerned with such things as spelling and sentence structure over content, Lisle turned to "secret writing," as she called it in *SAAS.*

Attending Smith College, Lisle majored in English, but her study of the great writers daunted her with the high benchmark they set. "I did not take a single writing class at Smith College," Lisle noted in *SAAS.* "In a completely unforeseen way, my education had silenced me." Out of college, she married and worked as a volunteer for VISTA (Volunteers in Service to America) for a time. Then she returned to school and earned a degree in journalism. Thereafter she worked for a decade as a journalist, writing both hard news and features. The daily grind of deadline writing was another kind of school for Lisle, and helped give her a facility for speedy organization. A new marriage and the birth of her child put Lisle on a different path, however.

In 1981 she gave up journalism and started writing for children. A writer's workshop helped with this decision, and the inspiration of some childhood memories resulted in her first book, *The Dancing Cats of Applesap,* the story of a shy ten-year-old girl who manages to save her town's drugstore and soda fountain by bringing some amazing cats together. As Ilene Cooper noted in a *Horn Book* article about Lisle, the story was "an utterly original fantasy," about cats that dance in a drugstore after hours to the guitar strums of the owner. Melba Morris, the protagonist of the book, brings Applesap, New York, notoriety when she helps spread the news about the cats in Mr. Jiggs's old-fashioned drugstore. This notoriety, in turn, saves the drugstore. "This story has elements found in the most enduring works of children's fiction: humor, inventiveness, and a message gently relayed," Cooper wrote in *Booklist.* Anne Osborn, in *School Library Journal,* called the book a "gentle but rewarding story" and "not so much a cat fantasy as a novel of character development and growth."

Lisle followed this initial publication with a more realistic young adult novel, *Sirens and Spies,* the story of two sisters and their secret-bearing violin teacher. As Lisle explained in *SAAS,* "I contrived to place a pair of sisters at the center of the story so that I could experience a little of the doubleness of sisterhood," the doubleness she was missing in her own youth surrounded by four younger brothers. Mary and Elsie take violin lessons from Miss Fitch, with Elsie being the favorite. It is therefore surprising to Mary when her sister turns against the aged teacher, accusing her of being a collaborator with the Germans during the Second World War in her native France. But when Miss Fitch is injured in her home by an intruder, Mary helps to unravel the secret in the teacher's past. Nancy Choice, writing in *Voice of Youth Advocates,* called the book a "moving story about friendship, forgiveness, and the awful power of secrets." Zena Sutherland of *Bulletin of the Center for Children's Books* noted that *Sirens and Spies* is a "truly sophisticated book," while David A. Lindsey in *School Library Journal* dubbed it "a piece of quality fiction."

Lisle wrote a quartet of fanciful novels for children and young adults from 1987 to 1993, including *The Great Dimpole Oak, Afternoon of the Elves, The Lampfish Twill,* and *Forest.* Something of a technical tour de force, *The Great Dimpole Oak* cuts back and forth from Paris to Bombay to small town America where a majestic oak tree is weaving its subtle magic over all concerned. Everyone who comes into contact with the tree is affected in this "feat of originality and plotting," according to a critic in *Publishers Weekly,* who concluded: "A beautifully orchestrated novel, this is short yet deeply satisfying." Anita Silvey, writing in *Horn Book,* found everything about the book, from writing to cover art, "marked by exquisite taste," and concluded that

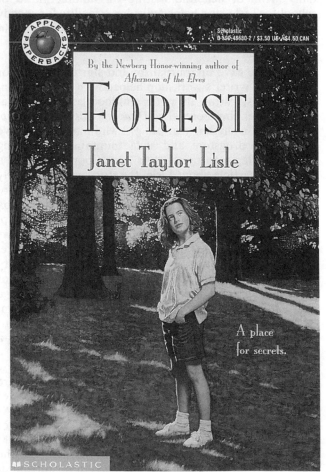

Twelve-year-old Amber battles to save the precious woodlands near her home, especially after she befriends a sentient squirrel named Woodbine.

Lisle's third novel "contains no echoes of other creators' voices."

"A fascinating portrayal of a manipulative yet touching friendship" is how Annette Curtis Klause summed up Lisle's next book, *Afternoon of the Elves,* in *School Library Journal.* The outcast, Sara-Kate, befriends the younger, more popular Hillary by showing her an elf village in her back yard, but Hillary also discovers the truth about Sara-Kate: that she is alone caring for her sick mother and desperately trying to cope with domestic duties and unpaid bills. Neither Hillary nor the reader are ever quite sure of the reality of the elves, but once social services intervenes and takes Sara-Kate from her mother, Hillary sets the tiny village up in her own yard. In *Bulletin of the Center for Children's Books,* Betsy Hearne described *Afternoon of the Elves* as "a carefully developed story focused on two children who influence each other in realistic, subtle stages." With *The Lampfish of Twill,* the magic is underwater. An old fisherman leads Eric down via a whirlpool into an ancient and glorious world at the center of the Earth. A *Publishers Weekly* contributor compared *The Lampfish of Twill* favorably to other classics of the imagination such as *Wrinkle in Time* and *The Lion, the Witch, and the Wardrobe,* and noted that it "tickles the imagination and challenges preconceived notions about reality and illusion." A *Kirkus Reviews* commentator called it "a splendid, unique fantasy" in which "fantastical creatures help convey truths that transcend the harsh realities of a world whose rituals and prejudices are all too familiar."

With *Forest,* the magic is more traditional, involving the exploits of twelve-year-old Amber and a sentient squirrel named Woodbine. Amber unwittingly sets off a war between humans and the other forest animals when she builds a tree house too deep in the forest. Carol Fox, reviewing the book in *Bulletin of the Center for Children's Books,* concluded that "Lisle has created a world of innocence marked with heartache, truth infused with absurdity, and wisdom relinquished to recklessness—all in the guise of animal fantasy." In *Publishers Weekly* a reviewer noted that this "expertly crafted promotion of open-mindedness and tolerance is sure to hold its audience's attention."

Lisle has also written a series of four middle-grade novels titled collectively "Investigators of the Unknown." The stories, which include *The Gold Dust Letters, Looking for Juliette, A Message from the Match Girl,* and *Angela's Aliens,* recount a year in the lives of four 9-year-olds who, while investigating magic, begin to discover truths about themselves and their families. In the initial volume, Angela receives letters, covered in gold dust, from a lonely, old-fashioned fairy. Investigating these letters with her friends, Georgina and Poco, helps to take Angela's mind off her strained relationship with her father. "Lisle celebrates the imagination's power to help ease wounds," maintained a *Publishers Weekly* critic in a starred review of *The Gold Dust Letters.* Starr LaTronica noted in *School Library Journal* that the author had created a "multifaceted novel to be

When Angela returns from Mexico significantly changed, her friends begin to believe her story of an alien encounter. (Cover illustration by Rob Shepperson.)

appreciated on many levels." The magic and reality-checks continued with the second novel in the series, *Looking for Juliette,* in which Angela moves to Mexico for the year, leaving her cat, Juliette, with Poco. But when Juliette turns up missing, Poco and Georgina blame the elderly Miss Bone, who is caretaking Angela's house. Walter, another classmate, introduces a Ouija board to the hunt. Ellen Fader noted in *School Library Journal* that the book "is well plotted, and replete with humor, interesting characters, and enough shivers and surprises to satisfy readers." Ilene Cooper called the book "a magical mix" in her *Booklist* review. With the third work in the series, *A Message from the Match Girl,* Georgina and Poco try to help Walter, an orphan who believes he is being haunted by, and receiving messages from, his dead mother. A contributor to *Kirkus Reviews* called the book "a tantalizing mystery of mother love," and a *Publishers Weekly* critic called it a "poignant story." The series was rounded off with the return of Angela from Mexico in *Angela's Aliens.* Because she seems to have become a different person—taller and more adult and somber—after being away, Poco, Georgina and Walter suspect that Angela has been abducted by aliens and then returned in an altered state. In

Publishers Weekly a reviewer noted that Lisle's magic would work on even the "most down-to-earth readers," and that as with all the books in the series—indeed, with all of Lisle's books—*Angela's Aliens* is more concerned with "opening the door to possibilities in human relationships than on solving supernatural mysteries."

"I believe in the unknown," Lisle once commented. "There is a great deal we don't know about our world, like how big the universe is or what makes our brains work." And as she concluded in *SAAS,* "What we know and believe must always be qualified by what we don't know yet. New facts are arriving daily, however, new ways of thinking and seeing.... The stories are there to be told, and unless there's some unseen system at work that's set on preventing me, I expect to keep on writing them."

■ Works Cited

Review of *Angela's Aliens, Publishers Weekly,* September 16, 1996, p. 84.

Choice, Nancy, review of *Sirens and Spies, Voice of Youth Advocates,* December, 1985, p. 320.

Cleghorn, Andrea, "Janet Taylor Lisle," *Children's Books and Their Creators,* edited by Anita Silvey, Houghton Mifflin, 1995, p. 410.

Cooper, Ilene, review of *The Dancing Cats of Applesap, Booklist,* July, 1984, p. 1550.

Cooper, Ilene, "New Voices, New Visions: Janet Taylor Lisle," *Horn Book,* November-December, 1988, pp. 755-58.

Cooper, Ilene, review of *Looking for Juliette, Booklist,* September 15, 1994, p. 136.

Fader, Ellen, review of *Looking for Juliette, School Library Journal,* August, 1994, p. 158.

Review of *Forest, Publishers Weekly,* August 30, 1993, p. 97.

Fox, Carol, review of *Forest, Bulletin of the Center for Children's Books,* January, 1994, p. 160.

Review of *The Gold Dust Letters, Publishers Weekly,* January 10, 1994, p. 62.

Review of *The Great Dimpole Oak, Publishers Weekly,* October 9, 1987, p. 88.

Hearne, Betsy, review of *Afternoon of the Elves, Bulletin of the Center for Children's Books,* October, 1988, p. 37.

Klause, Annette Curtis, review of *Afternoon of the Elves, School Library Journal,* September, 1989, p. 254.

Review of *The Lampfish of Twill, Kirkus Reviews,* October 1, 1991, p. 1288.

Review of *The Lampfish of Twill, Publishers Weekly,* September 13, 1991, p. 80.

LaTronica, Starr, review of *The Gold Dust Letters, School Library Journal,* April, 1994, pp. 128-29.

Lindsey, David A., review of *Sirens and Spies, School Library Journal,* August, 1985, p. 78.

Lisle, Janet, essay in *Something about the Author Autobiography Series,* Volume 14, Gale, 1992, pp. 157-66.

Review of *A Message from the Match Girl, Publishers Weekly,* September 25, 1995, p. 57.

Review of *A Message from the Match Girl, Kirkus Reviews,* October 1, 1995, p. 1432.

Osborn, Anne, review of *The Dancing Cats of Applesap, School Library Journal,* October, 1984, p. 159.

Silvey, Anita, review of *The Great Dimpole Oak, Horn Book,* January-February, 1988, p. 64.

Sutherland, Zena, review of *Sirens and Spies, Bulletin of the Center for Children's Books,* June, 1985, pp. 188-89.

■ For More Information See

BOOKS

Dictionary of American Children's Fiction, Greenwood Press, 1993.

Sixth Book of Junior Authors and Illustrators, Wilson, 1989.

Twentieth-Century Children's Writers, Fourth edition, edited by Laura Standley Berger, St. James Press, 1995.

PERIODICALS

Booklist, February 1, 1994, p. 1007; November 1, 1996, p. 498.

Bulletin of the Center for Children's Books, July, 1984, pp. 208-09; December, 1994, p. 136; November, 1995, p. 98.

Horn Book, September, 1989, p. 622; March, 1994, pp. 199-200.

New York Times Book Review, December 13, 1987, p. 36; November 12, 1989, p. 28; November 10, 1991, p. 31; November 14, 1993, p. 47.

School Library Journal, November, 1996, p. 108.

Wilson Library Bulletin, September, 1989, p. 254; May, 1994, p. 82.

—Sketch by J. Sydney Jones

*   *   *

DOUGLAS LITTLE

LITTLE, Douglas 1942-

■ Personal

Born September 6, 1942; son of Albert (a motor body builder) and Willetta (a dressmaker) Little; married Patricia Ann, July 8, 1963; children: Lisa Frances Stallard, Zoe Justine Allen, Nicholas Freestone. *Education:* University of New South Wales, B. Arch., 1966; attended National Art School. *Religion:* Christian Science. *Hobbies and other interests:* Bush regeneration, sports, church work, printmaking, letter writing.

■ Addresses

Home and Office—2/355 Maroubra Rd., Maroubra, Australia 2035.

■ Career

Self-employed architect, Sydney, New South Wales, 1966—; Arts Administration, manager of architectural competitions and national awards; AFS student exchange program, chapter president, 1985-88; guest speaker at primary schools, 1996—. *Member:* Writer Centre of New South Wales.

■ Awards, Honors

Honour Book, Children's Book Council of Australia, 1996, for *Ten Little-Known Facts About Hippopotamuses.*

■ Writings

Ten Little-Known Facts About Hippopotamuses, illustrated by David Frances and Donna Rawlins, Houghton, 1995, Ashton Scholastic (Australia), 1995.

■ Work in Progress

When Pieter Bruegel the Elder Was Younger, an art book for children; *Prince Richard the Ready,* a story set in the Middle Ages.

■ Sidelights

Douglas Little told *SATA:* "From ages two through nine I lived in a very small house on Tent Road. But it didn't matter that our house was small, we only went inside to eat meals or to sleep. The rest of the time we roamed free under the sky. We had a huge back yard with a vegetable garden, poultry, and a cow. After our yard there was a seemingly, endless paddock and occasionally we—my brother, two sisters and I—would visit what we called 'the far corner.'

"Television came late to our town and to me. Not counting the times I watched it through a shop window, I was eighteen before I saw it regularly. I was partly educated by listening to the radio. I loved to listen to British comedy. Such shows as 'Much-Binding-in-the-Marsh,' 'Take it from Here,' and the 'Goon Show' were my teachers and refined my love of humour. My literary heroes are Antoine de Saint-Exupery (*The Little Prince* and *Wind, Sand, and Stars*), J. D. Salinger (especially *Franny and Zooey*), and Garrison Keillor, especially his radio show 'The Prairie Home Journal.' I didn't start to write until age forty-six, but I am grateful to have begun and to have sent some ideas out into the world on the backs of a herd of hippopotamuses."

Little's *Ten Little-Known Facts about Hippopotamuses* mixes fact and fiction about animals, birds, and reptiles in a zany and humorous way. His format is unique; for example, while anteaters crawl through the text, sharing the page with a row of pineapples, the author describes the difference between the two. Little spices correct information with outlandish misinformation, making it confusing for librarians to index the book. A critic for *Appraisal* declared that this "wry and often funny" book is best shelved with humor rather than science. In *Kirkus Reviews*, a contributor also noted Little's "lively imagination" and keen humor but was concerned that children would find it hard to tell fact from fiction. In *School Library Journal*, Amy Addler responded to the indexing dilemma of this "offbeat" book. She declared it a "science carrot that librarians" can hold "in front of reluctant nonfiction readers."

■ Works Cited

Addler, Amy, review of *Ten Little-Known Facts about Hippopotamuses, School Library Journal*, November, 1995, p. 113.
Review of *Ten Little-Known Facts about Hippopotamuses, Appraisal*, winter-spring, 1996.
Review of *Ten Little-Known Facts about Hippopotamuses, Kirkus Reviews*, July 1, 1995, p. 949.

*   *   *

LOBEL, Anita (Kempler) 1934-

■ Personal

Surname is pronounced "*Lo*-bel"; born June 3, 1934, in Cracow, Poland; immigrated to the United States, 1952; naturalized citizen, 1956; daughter of Leon and Sofia (Grunberg) Kempler; married Arnold Stark Lobel (an author and illustrator) April, 1955 (died December 4, 1987); children: Adrianne, Adam. *Education:* Pratt Institute, B.F.A., 1955; attended Brooklyn Museum Art School, 1975-76.

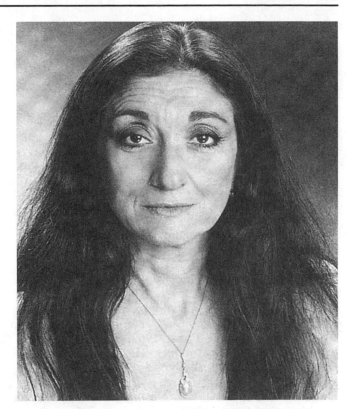

ANITA LOBEL

■ Addresses

Home—New York, NY.

■ Career

Freelance textile designer, 1957-64; writer and illustrator of children's books, 1964—. *Exhibitions:* Lobel's art and papers are included in the Kerlan Collection at the University of Minnesota.

■ Awards, Honors

Best Illustrated Book selection, *New York Times*, 1965, for *Sven's Bridge*, and 1981, for *Market Street;* Spring Book Festival Award (picture book), 1972, for *Little John;* Children's Book Showcase Award, 1974, for *A Birthday for the Princess*, and 1977, for *Peter Penny's Dance;* Outstanding Book selection, *New York Times*, 1976, for *Peter Penny's Dance*, 1977, for *How the Rooster Saved the Day*, and 1981, for *On Market Street;* Boston Globe/Horn Book Award (illustration), 1981, for *On Market Street*, and 1984, for *The Rose in My Garden;* Caldecott Honor Book Award, and American Book Award finalist, both 1982, both for *On Market Street*.

■ Writings

SELF-ILLUSTRATED

Sven's Bridge, Harper, 1965, Greenwillow, 1992.
The Troll Music, Harper, 1966.
Potatoes, Potatoes, Harper, 1967.
The Seamstress of Salzburg, Harper, 1970.

Under a Mushroom, Harper, 1970.

A Birthday for the Princess, Harper, 1973.

(Reteller) *King Rooster, Queen Hen,* Greenwillow, 1975.

(Reteller) *The Pancake,* Greenwillow, 1978.

(Adapter) *The Straw Maid,* Greenwillow, 1983.

Alison's Zinnia, Greenwillow, 1990.

The Dwarf Giant, Holiday, 1991.

Pierrot's ABC Garden, Western, 1992.

Away from Home, Greenwillow, 1994.

ILLUSTRATOR; BY HUSBAND, ARNOLD LOBEL

How the Rooster Saved the Day, Greenwillow, 1977.

A Treeful of Pigs, Greenwillow, 1979.

On Market Street, Greenwillow, 1981.

The Rose in My Garden, Greenwillow, 1984.

ILLUSTRATOR

Paul Kapp, *Cock-a-Doodle Doo! Cock-a-Doodle Doo!,* Harper, 1966.

Meindert De Jong, *Puppy Summer,* Harper, 1966.

The Wishing Penny and Other Stories (anthology), Parents Magazine Press, 1967.

F. N. Monjo, *Indian Summer,* Harper, 1968.

Alice Dalgliesh, *The Little Wooden Farmer,* Macmillan, 1968.

Benjamin Elkin, *The Wisest Man in the World,* Parents Magazine Press, 1968.

Barbara Borack, *Someone Small,* Harper, 1969.

Doris Orgel, *The Uproar,* McGraw, 1970.

Mirra Ginsburg, editor, *Three Rolls and One Doughnut: Fables from Russia,* Dial, 1970.

B. Elkin, *How the Tsar Drinks Tea,* Parents Magazine Press, 1971.

Theodore Storm, *Little John,* retold by D. Orgel, Farrar, 1972.

John Langstaff, editor, *Soldier, Soldier, Won't You Marry Me?,* Doubleday, 1972.

Cynthia Jameson, *One for the Price of Two,* Parents Magazine Press, 1972.

Elizabeth Shub, adapter, *Clever Kate,* Macmillan, 1973.

Carolyn Meyer, *Christmas Crafts: Things to Make the Days Before Christmas,* Harper, 1974.

Janet Quin-Harkin, *Peter Penny's Dance,* Dial, 1976.

Penelope Lively, *Fanny's Sister,* Dutton, 1980.

Jane Hart, compiler, *Singing Bee! A Collection of Favorite Children's Songs,* Lothrop, 1982, published in England as *Sing a Song of Sixpence! The Best Song Book Ever,* Gollancz, 1983.

Clement Clarke Moore, *The Night Before Christmas,* Knopf, 1984.

Harriet Ziefert, *A New Coat for Anna,* Knopf, 1986.

B. P. Nichol, *Once: A Lullaby,* Greenwillow, 1986.

Steven Kroll, *Looking for Daniela: A Romantic Adventure,* Holiday House, 1988.

Charlotte S. Huck, reteller, *Princess Furball,* Greenwillow, 1989.

Charlotte Zolotow, *This Quiet Lady,* Greenwillow, 1992.

Ethel L. Heins, reteller, *The Cat and the Cook and Other Fables of Krylov,* Greenwillow, 1995.

C. S. Huck, reteller, *Toads and Diamonds,* Greenwillow, 1995.

Charlotte Pomerantz, *Mangaboom,* Greenwillow, 1997.

■ Adaptations

The Little Wooden Farmer was adapted as a filmstrip with cassette by Threshold Filmstrips, 1974; *Peter Penny's Dance* was adapted as a filmstrip with cassette by Weston Woods, 1978; *A New Coat for Anna* was adapted as a filmstrip with cassette by Random House, 1987; A *Treeful of Pigs* and *On Market Street* have been adapted as filmstrips with audiocassettes by Random House; *King Rooster, Queen Hen* and *The Rose in My Garden* have been adapted as audiocassettes by Random House; *On Market Street* has been adapted as a videocassette by Random House.

■ Sidelights

Celebrated as both a talented artist and the creator of charming texts, Lobel is the author and illustrator of picture books, fantasies, retellings, and concept books that have as their hallmarks a theatrical approach and a keen sense of design. She has also provided the pictures for more than twenty-five texts by writers such as Meindert De Jong, Doris Orgel, Clement Clarke Moore, Penelope Lively, John Langstaff, and Charlotte Zolotow. Several of Lobel's works, both as author/illustrator and illustrator, are considered tour de forces. As an artist, Lobel is well known for creating evocative, detailed paintings in line-and-wash or watercolor and gouache that reflect her signature style of richly patterned landscapes, opulent costumes and tapestries, and colorful flowers. As a writer, Lobel characteristically uses the traditions of the folk and fairy tale, such as "once-upon-a-time" settings and happy endings, to structure her stories, which are usually filled with humor; however, she underscores several of her works with serious themes, such as the nature of war and the results of parental neglect. As a creator of concept books, Lobel is credited for her originality and inventiveness, especially in her contributions to the alphabet book genre. Four of Lobel's works were created with her late husband Arnold; their third collaboration, *On Market Street* (1981), received several prizes, including the *Boston Globe/Horn Book Award* for illustration and designation as a Caldecott Medal honor book. Writing of Anita Lobel's career in *Twentieth Century Children's Writers,* Jacqueline L. Gmuca concludes, "Lobel ably illustrates the meaning of a statement she made to *Publishers Weekly* in 1971: 'It's nice to tell a tale that is pleasant for a child to read, be diverting, and at the same time have some kind of substance to it.' Her books are clearly informed by the pleasant, substantial spirit of which she speaks."

Born in Cracow, Poland, Lobel, as she told Lee Bennett Hopkins in *Books Are by People,* "was born into a relatively comfortable merchant family. Hitler put a stop to those comforts. My parents separated for practical reasons, believing we would all have better chances for survival, which proved to be true. My brother and I were left in the care of a Polish woman with whom we stayed and drifted around Poland for the next four and one half years."

Lobel has illustrated a collection of tales originally penned by renowned nineteenth-century Russian poet and fabulist Ivan Andreevich Krylov. (From *The Cat and the Cook and Other Fables of Krylov,* retold by Ethel Heins.)

"I had a wonderful nanny and when ... I was five years old ... the nanny took me and my younger brother into the Polish countryside—which was primitive, nasty, raw, and Catholic. That was on one side and the Nazis on the other. Aside from the fact that there was an outside force that hated us and chased us, I always felt my brother and I were protected by this person who chose to protect us. I loved her and she loved us, and I think that this was very important. I really feel Nanny's affection colors my work, because I don't feel I have to portray the awful bleakness of the time."

"Toward the end of the war, my brother and I were captured and sent to a concentration camp in Germany, from which we were rescued in 1945." Lobel and her brother were rescued by the Swedish Red Cross and, after two years, were reunited with their parents through the efforts of a relief organization based in Stockholm. Lobel continues, "I did not go to school until I was thirteen, but was taught how to read and write. I came from Sweden to New York against my will because my parents wanted to reclaim some long-lost relatives they had in this country." Lobel and her family moved to New York in 1952; after graduating from high school, she entered Pratt Institute to study for her B.F.A. in Fine Arts. Although she had received encouragement to become an artist, Lobel was also interested in the theater, and took part in school plays at Pratt. She met her future husband Arnold when she was cast in a play he was directing; the couple were married in 1955.

"For several years after graduation," Lobel related in *Junior Library Guild,* "I worked as a textile designer. Then Susan Hirschman, who had 'discovered' Arnold, asked me to do a book. I thought I couldn't, but Susan and Arnold encouraged me and I came through with *Sven's Bridge.*" Published in 1965, Lobel's first book as an author/illustrator grew from an idea that came to her about a goodhearted man; the story also includes examples of Swedish folk designs that the illustrator remembered from her childhood. *Sven's Bridge,* Lobel stated in the *Third Book of Junior Authors,* "started with pictures and the words followed." In contrast, the illustrations followed the text in her fourth book, *The Seamstress of Salzburg* (1970). "At first, I thought only of illustrating stories by other authors but found, with a little effort, I, too, could supply a story to go with the pictures," she told *Books Are by People,* adding, "When I begin a book, I have a specific style in mind, for instance a historical period." Lobel also incorporates a love of embroidery and tapestry and drawing flowers and large figures into her work. *The Troll Music* (1966), she says, "was mainly inspired by the bottom parts of medieval tapestries with all the vegetation and little animals running around."

Lobel's third book, *Potatoes, Potatoes* (1967), is considered one of her most affecting works. The story, which was inspired, Lobel says, "partly from childhood memories in Poland," describes how two brothers who become enemies in war are brought together by their mother, who refuses to give the boys something to eat until they and their comrades stop fighting. As Jacque-line L. Gmuca describes her in *Twentieth Century Children's Writers,* the mother "not only serves to protect her sons from joining in the fighting for a number of years but also functions as a peacemaker when she reminds them, and the opposing armies they lead, of their former lives of contentment." A reviewer in the *Times Literary Supplement* calls the book "beautifully executed," while *New York Times Book Review* critic Barbara Wersba remarks, "Lobel's illustrations ... [are] excellent picture-book fare, finely drawn and colored." Lobel told *Books Are By People,* "I like *Potatoes, Potatoes* because of its theme. But I do not take it as seriously as some of the reviewers have."

For many years, Lobel and her husband worked from nine in the morning until late afternoon and then, after spending time with their two children, returned to their work until 2:00 a.m. Unlike many husband and wife teams, the Lobels did not initially collaborate on their books. Anita told *Publishers Weekly,* "I think maybe we take ideas from each other, but it is not a conscious thing. Whenever germs of ideas start with each of us, they are entirely different.... I must have been influenced by old fairy tales, tales that have a logical beginning, a middle, and then retribution in the end for someone and happiness for someone else."

The Lobels first combined their talents on *How the Rooster Saved the Day* (1977), a book written by Arnold. Their second collaboration, *A Treeful of Pigs* (1979), was, Anita told *Junior Library Guild,* "written specifically for me to illustrate, the way an author might write a star part for an actress. There were a few noises of objection coming in my direction during the execution of the pictures. The nice thing about having the illustrator and the author together in the same studio is that we can decide to change or rethink little details while the work is in progress. For many years we tried to keep our work separate but, when we discovered this extra bonus, we nodded and bowed graciously to each other and giggled with a sense of a new discovery. That discovery, I felt, is especially a gift to me." Before Arnold's death in 1987, the Lobels collaborated on a total of four books.

Lobel's first book as an author and illustrator since the death of her husband is *Alison's Zinnias* (1990), which Caroline Ward of *School Library Journal* describes as a "luscious-looking alphabet book." The text links a girl's name with a verb and a flower, all starting with a letter of the alphabet, before coming back to the beginning; each page features a painting and a line of type, below which is a large letter and a smaller storyboard that shows the flower chosen by each child. Zena Sutherland of *Bulletin of the Center for Children's Books* calls *Alison's Zinnias* "an unusual alphabet book" and a "dazzling display of floral painting"; *Horn Book Magazine* reviewer Mary M. Burns calls it, "a book to brighten the dreariest of days.... What could have been just another clever idea becomes ... a tour de force." Lobel's next book, *The Dwarf Giant* (1991), is a story set in ancient Japan in which an evil dwarf, intending to take over a peaceful kingdom, is defeated by the resourcefulness of the country's princess after her husband is bewitched; although the dwarf is stopped, the story ends in a minor key with other visitors waiting outside the palace. *Kirkus Reviews* calls *The Dwarf Giant* "a deeply felt variant on a classic theme that more often ends in tragedy," and adds that Lobel's illustrations, graceful paintings that reflect Japanese art and architecture, reveal a new direction "for this fine illustrator, their allusive power reinforcing the Faustian subtext...."

With *The Quiet Lady* (1992), Lobel provides the illustrations for a tender picture book by Charlotte Zolotow in which a little girl looks at photographs of her mother in the various stages of her life; the book ends with the birth and baby picture of the young narrator. Each of Lobel's double-page spreads includes a small, darkly hued painting of the little girl and richly colored paintings of her mother. Writing in *Publishers Weekly,* a critic calls *The Quiet Lady* an "excellent choice for quiet mother-child sharing [that is] sure to invite genealogy lessons filled with fond memories," while *Booklist* reviewer Carolyn Phelan notes, "The exceptional talents of Zolotow and Lobel combine in this celebration of life.... Lobel's sense of design and her signature use of costume and flowers find apt expression in this series of portraits." Lobel's next book as an author/illustrator is *Pierrot's ABC Garden* (1993), an alphabet book in which Pierrot the clown packs a huge basket with alphabetically gathered produce—both familiar and exotic—and musical instruments for a picnic with his friend Pierrette. Described by *Kirkus Reviews* as "another enchanting alphabet from the illustrator," *Pierrot's ABC Garden*—a new edition of a Little Golden Book—is called "simple and pleasing" by Carolyn Phelan in *Booklist,* who concludes that preschoolers will love it, "whether or not they care about the ABCs or vegetables." Lobel's next book, *Away from Home* (1994), is also an alphabet book; a companion piece to *Alison's Zinnias,* the volume focuses on little boys rather than little girls and, in the words of a *Publishers Weekly* reviewer, "takes the reader on a globe-trotting adventure as Lobel sets the stage—literally—to introduce letters and various world cities as well." On each page, a small boy stands under the spotlight before a child audience, who responds to alliterative sentences like "Adam arrived in Amsterdam" and "Henry hoped in Hollywood." A *Publishers Weekly* contributor commends the accuracy, romanticism, and informativeness of the illustrations, while *Booklist* reviewer Hazel Rochman notes that "an all-male cast pulls you into imagining each character's story and making the journey to each exciting place."

With *The Cat and the Cook and Other Fables of Krylov* (1995), Lobel illustrates twelve Russian fables retold by Ethel L. Heins, several of which are prose versions of poems by popular fabulist Ivan Andreevich Krylov. The artist paints vigorous folk-art paintings that are noted both for their theatrical quality and evocation of the works of Marc Chagall. In her *Booklist* review, Julie Corsaro claims that Lobel "outdoes herself" with "paintings that are brilliantly colored and wonderfully composed." *School Library Journal* reviewer Cheri Estes adds, "the artist adeptly captures the essence of

Lobel illustrated Charlotte Huck's tale of two stepsisters—one kind and one unkind—who are bestowed with magical gifts perfectly matched to their dispositions. (From *Toads and Diamonds.*)

each tale.... [The] paintings will entice youngsters to read this collection independently." *Toads and Diamonds* (1996) is a retelling of a classic French folktale by Charlotte S. Huck, whose popular *Princess Furball* (1989) is also illustrated by Lobel. In *Toads and Diamonds,* lovely Renee lives with her nasty stepmother and stepsisters, who treat her as a lowly servant. When Renee goes to the well, she brings water to an old woman, who rewards her with flowers and jewels every time she speaks; she wins the heart of a handsome prince, who appreciates her for herself and not for her jewels. "Full of life, color, and grace, Lobel's paintings create a sense of magic within everyday reality," writes Carolyn Phelan in *Booklist,* while Maria B. Salvadore of the *Horn Book Magazine* concludes, "This is some of Anita Lobel's best work, each picture in close harmony with the text to move quickly to a satisfying conclusion...."

In 1968, Lobel wrote in *Illustrators of Children's Books: 1957-1966,* "I feel very strongly that an artist working in the field of children's book illustration should by no means compromise on the graphic design quality of his work. Our senses are bombarded by so much ugliness from our earliest days that it is to be hoped that picture books do open a child's eyes and start at least a germ for a future aesthetic sense. I have always loved to draw flowers and I love needlework and tapestries as well as embroidery. During my years as an art student, I spent most of my time drawing and painting monumental figures. When I had to make a living, I became a textile designer. Picture books have opened to me an opportunity to bring back some of my old fat friends and put them in landscapes filled with floral design! I usually plan a book as a play. The pictures become 'scenes' with 'principals' and 'chorus' grouped and regrouped according to what is then happening in the story."

As she alludes above, the theme perhaps most prevalent in Lobel's character as an artist and creator of children's books is her great affection for the theater. She told *Books Are by People,* "I wanted to be in the theatre at one time. When I am illustrating a manuscript, I do it as if it might be a stage play." She told John F. Berry in *Book World,* "Picture books are like screenplays. How do you translate very terse text into some kind of visual context? Really and truly, if you don't know anything about the theatre, it is very difficult to illustrate children's books." She comments in *Twentieth Century Children's Writers,* "Writing and illustrating books for children is a form of drama for me. I approach the construction of a picture book as if it were a theatre piece to be performed, assigning dialogue, dressing the characters, and putting them into an appropriate setting. Some books take the form of zany farces (*King Rooster, Queen Hen,* and *The Pancake*). Others, like *Peter Penny's Dance,* are a bit like *Around the World in Eighty Days,* a sort of movie or musical. *The Seamstress of Salzburg* and *A Birthday for the Princess* are more like operettas. *On Market Street* was constructed like a series of solos in a ballet, held together by a prologue and epilogue, with an implied divertimento for the score."

Lobel has been able to modify her schedule so that she can finish studio work by 2:00 p.m., then put her energy into other interests, such as the theater. As a result, she has landed roles in several Off-Broadway shows. "My ideal day now," she told John F. Berry in *Book World,* "is to work from nine until two in the afternoon at my drawing desk, then go to rehearsal—if I'm lucky enough to have a part."

■ Works Cited

Review of *Away from Home, Publishers Weekly,* July 4, 1994, pp. 60-61.

Berry, John F., "The Lobels: A Marriage of Two Drawing Boards," *Washington Post Book World,* June 13, 1982.

Bragg, Pamela, "Authors & Editors," *Publishers Weekly,* May 17, 1971, pp. 11-13.

Burns, Mary M., review of *Alison's Zinnia, Horn Book Magazine,* November-December, 1990, p. 730.

Corsaro, Julie, review of *The Cat and the Cook and Other Fables of Krylov, Booklist,* March 15, 1995, p. 1330.

Review of *The Dwarf Giant, Kirkus Reviews,* April 15, 1991, p. 537.

Estes, Cheri, review of *The Cat and the Cook and Other Tales of Krylov, School Library Journal,* April, 1995, pp. 142-43.

Gmuca, Jacqueline L., entry on Anita Lobel, *Twentieth Century Children's Writers,* 4th edition, St. James Press, 1995.

Hopkins, Lee Bennett, editor, *Books Are by People,* Citation Press, 1969.

Junior Library Guild, March, 1979.

Lobel, Anita, in *Illustrators of Children's Books: 1957-1966,* edited by Lee Kingman and others, Horn Book, 1968.

Lobel, Anita, entry in *Third Book of Junior Authors,* edited by Doris de Montreville and Donna Hill, Wilson, 1972, pp. 180-81.

Lobel, Anita, interview in *Twentieth Century Children's Writers,* 2nd edition, St. Martin's Press, 1983.

Lobel, Anita, interview in *Twentieth Century Children's Writers,* 4th edition, St. James Press, 1995.

Phelan, Carolyn, review of *This Quiet Lady, Booklist,* May 1, 1992, p. 1599.

Phelan, Carolyn, review of *Pierrot's ABC Garden, Booklist,* November 15, 1993, p. 632.

Phelan, Carolyn, review of *Toads and Diamonds, Booklist,* November 1, 1996, p. 496.

Review of *Pierrot's ABC Garden, Kirkus Reviews,* October 1, 1993, p. 1276.

Review of *Potatoes, Potatoes, Times Literary Supplement,* June 26, 1969.

Rochman, Hazel, review of *Away from Home, Booklist,* August, 1994, p. 2054.

Salvadore, Maria B., review of *Toads and Diamonds, Horn Book Magazine,* November-December, 1996, p. 751.

Sutherland, Zena, review of *Alison's Zinnia, Bulletin of the Center for Children's Books,* October, 1990, p. 36.

Review of *This Quiet Lady, Publishers Weekly,* June 1, 1992, p. 61.

Ward, Caroline, review of *Alison's Zinnia, School Library Journal,* October, 1990, p. 96.

Wersba, Barbara, review of *Potatoes, Potatoes, New York Times Book Review,* October 1, 1967.

■ For More Information See

BOOKS

Contemporary Authors New Revision Series, Vol. 33, Gale, 1991.

Cummins, Julie, editor, *Children's Book Illustration and Design,* PBC International, 1992.

Illustrators of Children's Books, 1967-1976, edited by Lee Kingman and others, Horn Book, 1978.

Lanes, Selma G., *Down the Rabbit Hole,* Atheneum, 1971.

Major Authors and Illustrators for Children and Young Adults, Gale, 1993.

Silvey, Anita, editor, *Children's Books and Their Creators,* Houghton Mifflin, 1995.

Twentieth-Century Children's Writers, 3rd edition, edited by Tracey Chevalier, St. Martin's, 1989.

PERIODICALS

Booklist, April 1, 1991.
Horn Book Magazine, February, 1971; August, 1981;
    July-August, 1995.
New York Times Book Review, October 1, 1967; April
    26, 1981; April 1, 1984.
Publishers Weekly, March 20, 1995; July 24, 1996.
School Library Journal, May, 1991; June, 1992; Septem-
    ber, 1996.

—*Sketch by Gerard J. Senick*

* * *

LOVE, D. Anne 1949-

■ Personal

Born January 12, 1949, in Selmer, TN; daughter of
Oscar W. and Elsie M. (Boleyn) Catlett; married Ronald
W. Love, June 8, 1974. *Education:* Lamar University,
B.S., 1972; University of North Texas, M.Ed., 1976,
Ph.D., 1984. *Politics:* Independent. *Religion:* Protestant.
Hobbies and other interests: Jazz music, travel.

■ Addresses

Home—LeMars, IA. *Office*—c/o Holiday House, Inc.,
425 Madison Ave., New York, NY 10017.

■ Career

Writer. School administrator in Richardson, TX, 1974-
88; University of North Texas, Denton, professor, 1989-
91; Western Hills Area Education Agency, Sioux City,
IA, consultant, 1994-96. *Member:* Society of Children's
Book Writers and Illustrators.

■ Awards, Honors

Prize for Juvenile Fiction, Friends of American Writers,
for *My Lone Star Summer,* 1997.

■ Writings

Bess's Log Cabin Quilt, illustrated by Ronald Himler,
    Holiday House, 1995.
Dakota Spring, illustrated by Ronald Himler, Holiday
    House, 1995.
My Lone Star Summer, Holiday House, 1996.

Contributor to magazines and newspapers.

■ Work in Progress

Three against the Tide, a novel of the Civil War.

■ Sidelights

A writer of historical fiction for young adults, D. Anne
Love once commented: "I left public school administration in order to devote more time to writing and
teaching at the university level. For me, the writing

D. ANNE LOVE

process usually begins with visualizing the last scene and
working backward. I am a collector of information and
often find that a postcard, brochure, or photograph
collected somewhere along the way can spark story
ideas. Inspiration flows from my love of history and a
strong sense of place."

Love's novels typically feature strong female protagonists who rise to the occasion when faced with severe
challenges. *Bess's Log Cabin Quilt* tells the story of a
ten-year-old girl who single-handedly comes to the
rescue of her pioneer family. When her father fails to
return from his work on the Oregon Trail and her
mother falls ill, Bess must handle the incursions of
Indians and a money-lender who threatens to seize the
family farm. Melissa McPherson, a contributor to *Voice
of Youth Advocates,* applauded Love's detailed description of frontier life, going on to claim that "readers of
historical fiction will definitely enjoy this."

Dakota Spring, Love's second novel, was widely admired by critics. In this story, Caroline and her brother
are left to manage their Dakota farm with the help of
just one neighbor after their father breaks his leg. Their
straitlaced grandmother arrives shortly to help out, and
the children must learn to deal with her cold personality
and their shared grief over her daughter's, and their
mother's, untimely death. Susan Steinfirst compared
Dakota Spring to the classic children's story, *Sarah,
Plain and Tall,* in her review in *Voice of Youth Advocates,* adding that Love's book "should appeal to kids
who love these tame wild west sagas." *Booklist* contributor Carolyn Phelan recommended the book strongly,

In Love's historical novel, Caroline and Jess learn to admire their standoffish grandmother when the three of them endure several hardships. (Cover illustration by David Kramer.)

praising Love's "well drawn and intriguing" characters, consistent point of view, and strong sense of place and historical period. "This book will please youngsters looking for good historical fiction," Phelan concluded.

In her first work of contemporary fiction, *My Lone Star Summer,* Love focuses on twelve-year-old Jill, who has visited her grandmother's ranch each summer, enjoying her time spent with B. J., her best friend in Texas. B. J. insists on being called Belinda this year, however, and has started wearing make-up and flirting with boys, leaving little time for Jill. "This is a fairly standard girl-coming-of-age novel for the youngest of YAs," Alice F. Stern remarked in *Voice of Youth Advocates.* Deborah Stevenson of the *Bulletin of the Center for Children's Books* admitted that "the story's a bit formulaic," but praised Love's strong characterizations, adding "the narration is unforced, honest, and touching in its examination of the gains and losses of growing up."

■ Works Cited

McPherson, Melissa, review of *Bess's Log Cabin Quilt, Voice of Youth Advocates,* October, 1995, p. 220.
Phelan, Carolyn, review of *Dakota Spring, Booklist,* November 15, 1995, p. 560.
Steinfirst, Susan, review of *Dakota Spring, Voice of Youth Advocates,* April, 1996, p. 27.
Stern, Alice F., review of *My Lone Star Summer, Voice of Youth Advocates,* October, 1996, pp. 211-12.
Stevenson, Deborah, review of *My Lone Star Summer, Bulletin of the Center for Children's Books,* July, 1996, pp. 378-79.

■ For More Information See

PERIODICALS

Booklist, May 1, 1996, pp. 1506-07.
Publishers Weekly, April 17, 1995, p. 60.
School Library Journal, June, 1995, p. 111; March, 1996, p. 196.

*   *   *

LUCAS, Victoria
See PLATH, Sylvia

M

MAJURE, Janet 1954-

■ Personal

Surname is pronounced like "major"; born November 22, 1954, in Topeka, KS; daughter of Oliver Davis (an artist) and Betty Lou (Tucker) Majure; children: Susan Elizabeth Lee. *Education:* University of Kansas, B.S., 1976, M.B.A., 1981. *Politics:* Democrat. *Religion:* United Methodist. *Hobbies and other interests:* Reading, cooking, sewing, travel.

■ Addresses

Home—Lawrence, KS. *Office*—P.O. Box 1161, Lawrence, KS 66044-0161. *Electronic mail*—majure @ sunflower.com.

■ Career

Arizona Daily Star, Tucson, copy editor, 1976; *Denver Post,* Denver, CO, copy editor, 1976-78; *Arizona Republic,* Phoenix, copy editor, 1978-79; W. R. Grace, Memphis, TN, financial analyst, 1981-82; *Kansas City Star,* Kansas City, MO, began as copy editor, became bureau chief, assistant city editor, and business writer, 1983-89; *Lawrence Observer,* Lawrence, KS, owner, publisher, and editor, 1989; freelance writer and editor, 1990—. Spencer Museum of Art, member of board of directors, Friends of the Art Museum, 1993-96; United Way of Douglas County, past committee co-chairperson; member of local conservation, environmental, and social issue organizations; Girl Scout leader, 1995—. *Member:* International Association of Culinary Professionals, Association of Food Journalists, Mid-America Publishers Association, Old West Lawrence Association.

■ Writings

Elections, Lucent Books (San Diego, CA), 1996.
Recipes Worth Sharing, Breadbasket Publishing, 1997.

OTHER

Also contributor to *Kansas Storms,* edited by Diane Silver, Hearth Publishing, 1991, and *Fodor's USA,* Fodor's Travel Publications, 1993-95.

■ Work in Progress

AIDS, for Enslow Publishing.

■ Sidelights

Janet Majure told *SATA:* "Sometime in high school, I learned that I was good with words, and I thought that language was fascinating. Nevertheless, I couldn't imagine being a writer when I grew up—dilettantes and oddballs make careers as writers, and I was pretty normal (at least I thought). Consequently, I headed for journalism. I wanted to use my skills while working for a worthwhile social purpose, and daily news journalism seemed an appropriate field.

"Although my first interest was reporting, I found editing more suited to my insecure late-adolescent self. After college, I had a good, three-year newspaper career as a copy editor before, frustrated with career limitations, I headed back to school. After earning a master's degree in business administration, I tried my hand as a financial analyst in the fertilizer division of a big conglomerate; I became bored. I returned to my childhood place, the Kansas City area, and to newspapers. At the *Kansas City Star,* I worked as a copy editor, then suburban bureau chief, and finally as an assistant city editor before motherhood.

"Wanting a less-demanding position, I became a reporter for the first time since my college days. I liked the work and meeting people, but I still itched for something more. That urge led me two years later to start a weekly newspaper in Lawrence, Kansas, where I had moved after marriage. That frustrating, satisfying, and draining experience lasted six months.

"I have been freelancing as a writer and editor ever since. The market's constant evolution and consolidation has made the job ever-changing as publishers' needs change and as publishers buy out each other.

"Now in my early forties, I am returning to the point where I started my career planning. I do want to be a writer. I've taken satisfaction in the books I have written, and I've treasured the compliments I have received as a writer. With two books in print, another written, and a novel just under way, I can see writing as something I *can* do as a grown-up. Thanks in part to my journalism background, I'm good at taking complex issues and explaining them in a way anyone can understand, and I enjoy doing that. Now I am challenging myself to examine social issues more creatively and more personally through fiction. I am not sure where my efforts will take me, but I feel at last I'm on the right road."

■ For More Information See

PERIODICALS

Voice of Youth Advocates, October, 1996, p. 234.

*   *   *

MARCH, Carl
See FLEISCHMAN, (Albert) Sid(ney)

*   *   *

MAYO, Margaret (Mary) 1935-

■ Personal

Born May 10, 1935, in London, England; daughter of William John and Anna (maiden name, Macleod) Cumming; married Peter Robin Mayo (a university lecturer), July 28, 1958; children: Roderick, Katrina, Andrew. *Education:* University of Southampton, B.Sc. (with honors), 1956, certificate in education, 1957.

■ Addresses

Home—85 Peacock Lane, Brighton, Sussex BN1 6WA, England.

■ Career

Writer, 1974—. Teacher at numerous schools in England, 1957-61, 1969-71, 1973-75, and 1975-80.

■ Awards, Honors

Aesop Accolade, Children's Folklore Society of the American Folklore Society, for *When the World Was Young: Creation and Pourquois Tales,* 1996.

MARGARET MAYO

■ Writings

FOLKTALE COLLECTIONS PUBLISHED BY KAYE & WARD

(Compiler) *If You Should Meet a Crocodile and Other Verse,* illustrated by Carol Barker, 1974.

(Reteller) *The Book of Magical Horses,* illustrated by Victor Ambrus, 1976, published in the United States by Hastings House, 1977.

(Reteller) *The Book of Magical Birds,* illustrated by Fiona French, 1977.

(Reteller) *The Book of Magical Cats,* illustrated by Victor Ambrus, 1978.

Saints, Birds, and Beasts, illustrated by Cara Lockhart Smith, 1980.

The Italian Fairy Book, illustrated by Smith, 1981.

Fairy Tales from France, illustrated by Smith, 1983.

OTHER FOLKTALE COLLECTIONS

(Reteller) *The Orchard Book of Magical Tales,* illustrated by Jane Ray, Orchard, 1993, published in the United States as *Magical Tales from Many Lands,* Dutton, 1993.

(Reteller) *How to Count Crocodiles,* illustrated by Emily Bolam, Orion, 1994, published in the United States as *Tortoise's Flying Lesson: Animal Stories,* Harcourt Brace, 1995.

(Reteller) *First Fairy Tales,* illustrated by Selina Young, Orchard, 1994, published in the United States by Barnes and Noble Books, 1996.

(Reteller) *The Orchard Book of Creation Stories,* illustrated by Louise Brierley, Orchard, 1995, published in the United States as *When the World Was Young: Creation and Pourquois Tales,* Simon & Schuster, 1996.

(Reteller) *The Orchard Book of Mythical Birds and Beasts,* illustrated by Jane Ray, Orchard, 1996, published in the United States as *Mythical Birds and Beasts from Many Lands,* Dutton, 1997.

OTHER WORKS FOR CHILDREN

Little Mouse Twitchy Whiskers, illustrated by Penny Dann, Orchard, 1992.

■ **Work in Progress**

First Bible Stories.

■ **Sidelights**

Margaret Mayo's contribution to children's literature comes in a familiar form: the folktale collection. Yet Mayo's work is distinguished by her careful selection of little-known but delightful tales from around the world, by her talent for engaging narration, and by her passion for her work. As she once told *SATA,* Mayo is intent on preserving the oral tradition of storytelling and unique stories that merit attention from contemporary children. She selects "stories that have passed the most difficult of tests—the test of time," she explained, tales that "can still entertain and satisfy emotionally like no others. They are a precious part of our common heritage, and if our children are also to share it, then the tales must be told afresh to them."

Mayo began her career as a writer for children in the mid-1970s with *If You Should Meet a Crocodile and Other Verse.* This book is a compilation of short rhymes, poems, and limericks written by both famous and anonymous poets. According to a critic writing in *Growing Point,* this book was "designed for the very young." Mayo's first book for older readers contains thirteen fairytales about horses. *The Book of Magical Horses* tells of an enchanted mule, a winged horse, and even a water horse. A reviewer for *Junior Bookshelf* described the stories as "typically vigorous and full of action," and a *Booklist* contributor wrote that they are "told in an assured, conventional style." Mayo spent the last years of the seventies working on similar collections featuring magical birds and cats for Kaye and Ward publishers.

Mayo's *Saints, Birds, and Beasts* was published in 1980. This book tells the stories of sixteen saints with an emphasis on their relationships with animals. St. Jerome deals with a lion, St. Ailbe is raised by a wolf, and St. George fights his fabled dragon. In addition to the tales, Mayo provides brief biographies of the saints. According to a *Junior Bookshelf* contributor, the work displays "Mayo's considerable gifts as a storyteller." Mayo published two other children's books for Kaye and Ward during the 1980s: *The Italian Fairy Book* and *Fairy Tales from France.*

Magical Tales from Many Lands, which includes fourteen folktales and comes complete with endnotes citing origins and sources, appeared in 1993. The emphasis in this work is the magic that works wonders for people around the world, from Arabians and Australians to Zulus. There is a story about a king from the Caribbean, a Baba Yaga tale from Russia, a Native American tale about the morning star, a story from Peru and another from China. "The stories read aloud well," observed Carolyn Phelan in a *Booklist* review. A critic writing in *Kirkus Reviews* described the book as a "remarkably felicitous collection" and lauded Mayo's story selection: "Mayo has chosen splendidly." A *Publishers Weekly* contributor appreciated Mayo's "lively vocabulary" and "fine sense of theater." According to this critic, the collection is "a winner" whether read piece by piece or all at once. "Mayo's book will work its magic on all who open it," asserted Barbara Chatton in *School Library Journal. How to Count Crocodiles,* like Mayo's earlier work, *If You Should Meet a Crocodile and Other Verses,* is a collection for young children. In the words of *Magpies* contributor Nola Allen, these stories are told with "exuberance." Eight stories, from Africa, Indonesia, Japan, and other countries, feature a monkey, an eagle, a tortoise, crocodiles, rabbits, elephants, a hippopotamus, bears, a lion, and other animals. The tales,

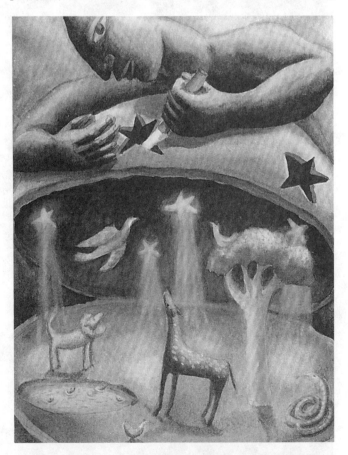

This multicultural compendium of ten retellings incorporates explanations of creation and familiar aspects of life on Earth. (From *When the World Was Young: Creation and Pourquoi Tales,* retold by Mayo and illustrated by Louise Brierley.)

Mayo's folklore collection offers ten tales of fantastic creatures from dragons to unicorns. (From *Mythical Birds and Beasts from Many Lands,* illustrated by Jane Ray.)

reported a *Junior Bookshelf* critic, "include many amusing incidents, animal noises, tricks and games." The collection, published in the United States as *Tortoise's Flying Lesson: Animal Stories,* "brims with both vigor and cheer," wrote a contributor to *Publishers Weekly.* "What an engaging collection!" exclaimed Harriett Fargnoli in a *School Library Journal* review.

Mayo's *When the World Was Young: Creation and Pourquois Tales* received similar attention. This book, published in 1996, provides ten retold tales which explain some familiar aspect of life on Earth. Like Mayo's other collections, this one is multicultural. There is a Native American story that explains how fire gets in trees, a Polynesian story about the sun, a tale from Ghana about human skin color, a tale from Iceland about salt in the sea, and one from Egypt which tells how the moon came to the sky. The work comes with a foreword and source notes. According to Susan Hepler in a *School Library Journal* review, Mayo speaks to her audience and offers "connections for today's youngsters." Writing in *Publishers Weekly,* a reviewer described Mayo's retellings as "lively" and "suspenseful" and called her a "masterful" storyteller.

Mythical Birds and Beasts from Many Lands provides ten tales of fantastic creatures from dragons to unicorns. A Thunderbird from Native American folklore and an ancient Aztec Quetzalcoatl are featured along with mermaids, serpents, and familiar creatures from Greek mythology. Once again, Mayo's storytelling talents were praised by critics. "Mayo lends the oral cadence of a storyteller's voice to these tales of enchantment," wrote a *Kirkus Reviews* contributor. In a *Publishers Weekly* review, a critic stated, "Mayo's energetically paced versions possess a lively intensity that never fails to entertain."

■ Works Cited

Allen, Nola, review of *How to Count Crocodiles, Magpies,* May, 1995, p. 29.

Review of *The Book of Magical Horses, Booklist,* November 15, 1977, p. 552.

Review of *The Book of Magical Horses, Junior Bookshelf,* August, 1976, p. 207.

Chatton, Barbara, review of *Magical Tales from Many Lands, School Library Journal,* September, 1993, p. 226.

Fargnoli, Harriett, review of *Tortoise's Flying Lesson: Animal Stories, School Library Journal,* May, 1995, p. 101.

Hepler, Susan, review of *When the World Was Young, School Library Journal,* December, 1996, p. 116.

Review of *How to Count Crocodiles, Junior Bookshelf,* June, 1995, p. 101.

Review of *If You Should Meet A Crocodile and Other Verse, Growing Point,* April, 1975, p. 2605.

Review of *Magical Tales from Many Lands, Kirkus Reviews,* September 1, 1993, p. 1148.

Review of *Magical Tales from Many Lands, Publishers Weekly,* September 6, 1993, p. 91.

Review of *Mythical Birds and Beasts from Many Lands, Kirkus Reviews,* May 1, 1997, p. 725.

Review of *Mythical Birds and Beasts from Many Lands, Publishers Weekly,* April 14, 1997, p. 73.

Phelan, Carolyn, review of *Magical Tales from Many Lands, Booklist,* November 1, 1993, p. 517.

Review of *Saints, Birds, and Beasts, The Junior Bookshelf,* February, 1981, p. 23.

Review of *Tortoise's Flying Lesson: Animal Stories, Publishers Weekly,* May 1, 1995, pp. 58-59.

Review of *When the World Was Young, Publishers Weekly,* October 21, 1996, p. 85.

■ For More Information See

PERIODICALS

Booklist, September 1, 1996, pp. 122-23.
Growing Point, November, 1977, p. 3203.
Horn Book, January-February, 1994, pp. 77-78.
Junior Bookshelf, December, 1978, p. 302.
School Library Journal, May, 1993, p. 57.
Times Educational Supplement, September 30, 1983, p. 48.

* * *

MAZILLE, Capucine 1953-
(Capucine)

■ Personal

Born December 23, 1953, The Hague, Netherlands; daughter of Charles (a painter and illustrator) and Sophie Burki; married Michel Mazille (a silkscreen printer), October 20, 1973; children: Julien, Joris, Chloe. *Education:* Attended Royal Academy of Arts, The Hague.

■ Addresses

Home—Orbessy-bas, St. Eusebe 74150 Rumilly, France. *Agent*—David Bennett, TLA, 72 Glengowan Rd., Toronto, Ontario, Canada M4N 1G4.

■ Career

Artist.

■ Illustrator

Catherine Dexter, *A Is for Apple, W Is for Witch,* Candlewick Press (Cambridge, MA), 1996.

Contributor of illustrations to *Realms of Tolkien,* HarperCollins, 1996, and *Tolkien's Hobbit,* HarperCollins, 1997.

FRENCH WORKS

Claude Clement, *Le monstre de Crock'fess,* Fleurus (France), 1988.
Un concert imprevu, Editions du Jasmin (France), 1997.
Une journee chargee, Editions du Jasmin, 1997.
Une etrange maladie, Editions du Jasmin, 1997.

CAPUCINE MAZILLE, self-portrait.

Illustrator of postcards and calendars for the Dutch company Art Unlimited, 1996-97, and postcards for Rossat-Mignod in France. Contributor of illustrations to magazines in Europe. Some works appear under the name Capucine.

■ Work in Progress

Illustrating *The Poet's Kitchen*, a volume of poems, and three books for small children at the Editions du Jasmin.

■ Sidelights

Capucine Mazille told *SATA:* "Being the daughter of an artist, I grew up among pencils and brushes and never thought about anything else than becoming a painter. It was obvious to go to art school after secondary school, when I was eighteen. Two years later I went on holidays—hitchhiking to France—and stopped in front of the castle (house, in fact) of my fairy-tale prince! We married, had three children, and lived happily ever after.

"Of course I continue to play with brushes and pencils and paint all day. Once or twice a year I exhibit my paintings (watercolors), and I love illustrating books. I read a lot of books and even run a library, together with some friends in our little village. We live in the French Alps (Haute-Savoie) in a small house in the country, with a garden full of old roses and hundreds of other plants. I love gardening. I also love drawing animals, strange creatures, monsters, and humans, but I hate straight lines, cars, and machines (specialties of my father)."

■ For More Information See

PERIODICALS

Booklist, September 15, 1996, p. 238.
School Library Journal, July, 1996, p. 84.

* * *

McARTHUR, Nancy

■ Personal

Born in Cleveland, OH; daughter of W. R. (in sales) and Irene (a homemaker) McArthur. *Education:* Baldwin-Wallace College, B.A.

■ Addresses

Home and office—P.O. Box 296, Berea, OH 44017-0296. *Agent*—Susan Cohen, Writers House, Inc., 21 West 26th St., New York, NY 10010.

■ Career

Freelance writer. Baldwin-Wallace College, part-time lecturer in journalism; also worked in public relations connected with the performing arts. *Member:* Society of Children's Book Writers and Illustrators, Authors Guild, Mystery Writers of America, Sisters in Crime.

■ Writings

How to Do Theatre Publicity, Good Ideas (Berea, OH), 1978.

(Contributor) *Stories for Free Children,* McGraw, 1982.

Megan Gets a Dollhouse, illustrated by Megan Lloyd, Scholastic, 1988.

Pickled Peppers, illustrated by Denise Brunkus, Scholastic, 1988.

The Plant That Ate Dirty Socks, Avon, 1988.

The Return of the Plant That Ate Dirty Socks, Avon, 1990.

The Adventure of the Buried Treasure, illustrated by Irene Trivas, Scholastic, 1990.

The Adventure of the Backyard Sleepout, illustrated by Trivas, Scholastic, 1992.

The Escape of the Plant That Ate Dirty Socks, Avon, 1992.

The Secret of the Plant That Ate Dirty Socks, Avon, 1993.

NANCY McARTHUR

More Adventures of the Plant That Ate Dirty Socks, Avon, 1994.

The Plant That Ate Dirty Socks Goes Up in Space, Avon, 1995.

Mystery of the Plant That Ate Dirty Socks, Avon, 1996.

The Plant That Ate Dirty Socks Gets a Girlfriend, Avon, 1997.

The Adventure of the Big Snow, illustrated by Mike Reed, Scholastic, in press.

■ Work in Progress

Adapting *The Plant That Ate Dirty Socks* as a play.

■ Sidelights

Nancy McArthur told *SATA:* "I got interested in being a writer when I was about ten or eleven. My first published writing was in my high school newspaper.

"People ask me how I got the idea for my most popular book, *The Plant That Ate Dirty Socks.* One day I thought of the title, jotted it down, and threw it into my idea files. I write down any ideas, even if I don't know what I could possibly do with them. It is amazing how many random ideas turn out to be useful.

"To make up stories, I often ask myself questions. If I have an action in mind, to start developing a character I ask 'What kind of person would do this?' If I start with a character, I wonder 'What would this person do in such-and-such a situation?' So I thought, 'Who would really want a plant that eats dirty socks?' A very messy kid, of course. I remembered that when I was a kid, I was the messy one in the family. My brother and sister were very neat. So I gave my messy-boy character a neatness-nut little brother to drive him crazy. That funny conflict gave me the start for my story.

"In addition to using my imagination and experience, I also do research for realistic details to make my settings and characters lifelike. My books begin with a very messy rough draft, slowly constructed, while I figure out the story. Although I start with some ideas, many more emerge as I write."

■ For More Information See

PERIODICALS

Booklist, September 15, 1988, p. 169.
School Library Journal, December, 1988, p. 89.

*   *   *

McCORD, David (Thompson Watson) 1897-1997

OBITUARY NOTICE—See index for *SATA* sketch: Born November 15, 1897, in New York, NY; died April 13, 1997, in Boston, MA. Editor, executive, educator, poet, and author. McCord is best remembered for his children's poetry that appeared in works such as *Far and Few: Rhymes of the Never Was and Always Is, Every*

Time I Climb a Tree, The Star in the Pail, One at a Time, and *Mr. Bidery's Spidery Garden.* McCord's poetry ranges from pure nonsense to emotional yet restrained lyricism. Writing about nature, childhood, and timeless joys like climbing trees, holidays, and make-believe, McCord enthusiastically invited his audience to explore and appreciate their world. The National Council of Teachers of English acknowledged his contributions to children's verse by giving him its first national award for excellence. McCord had a varied career, first serving as associate editor and later editor of the *Harvard Alumni Bulletin.* During a subsequent five-year stint with the *Boston Evening Transcript,* he also completed the first of nearly forty years with the Harvard Fund Council as its executive director. He also found time to work as Phi Beta Kappa poet at schools like Tufts College, Massachusetts Institute of Technology, and Colby College. In addition to his children's poetry, McCord wrote verse for adults that appeared in works such as *Odds Without Ends, And What's More, The Crows,* and *Remembrance of Things Passed.* He edited books, including *What Cheer: An Anthology of American British Humorous and Witty Verse,* and penned nonfiction works such as *The Language of Request: Fishing with a Barbless Hook* and *The Fabric of Man: Fifty Years of the Peter Bent Brigham Hospital.* The recipient of numerous honorary degrees, McCord was the first to be awarded Harvard's honorary doctor of humane letters.

OBITUARIES AND OTHER SOURCES:

BOOKS

Twentieth-Century Children's Writers, 4th edition, St. James Press, 1995.

PERIODICALS

New York Times, April 16, 1997, p. D22.
Publishers Weekly, May 12, 1997, p. 36.
Washington Post, April 20, 1997, p. B6.

* * *

McELRATH-ESLICK, Lori 1960-

■ Personal

Born May 29, 1960, in Muskegon, MI; married Golman Eslick (a teacher); children: Camille. *Education:* Attended Kansas City Art Institute; Kendall School of Design, A.A. *Hobbies and other interests:* Painting "just for me," camping, swimming, and cross-country skiing.

■ Addresses

Home—1621 Mills Ave., North Muskegon, MI 49445.

■ Career

Children's book illustrator. Volunteer for HOSTS (Help One Student to Succeed), a literacy program. *Exhibitions:* Bologna Fair Children's Book Illustration in Bologna, Italy and Japan, Muskegon (Michigan) Muse-

LORI McELRATH-ESLICK

um of Art, and in many annual art shows. *Member:* Society of Children's Book Writers and Illustrators.

■ Illustrator

Lynne Deur, *Nishnawbe: A Story of Indians in Michigan,* River Road (Spring Lake, MI), 1981.
Carolyn Nystrom, *The Lark Who Had No Song,* Lion Publishing, 1991.
Nancy White Carlstrom, *Does God Know How to Tie Shoes?,* Eerdmans, 1993.
Nancy White Carlstrom, *I Am Christmas,* Eerdmans, 1995.
Vashanti Rahaman, *Read for Me, Mama,* Boyds Mills Press, 1997.
Nancy White Carlstrom, *Glory,* Eerdmans, 1998.
(Reteller) Margaret Scrogin Chang and Raymond Chang, *Da Wei's Treasure: A Chinese Tale,* McElderry, 1998.

Illustrations have appeared in *Highlights for Children, National Wildlife, Cricket,* and *Ladybug and Spider Magazine.*

■ Sidelights

Lori McElrath-Eslick is an illustrator noted for her vibrant oil paintings. In Nancy White Carlstrom's *Does God Know How to Tie Shoes?,* the author "deftly juxtaposes an adult metaphysical sensibility ... against a child's hands-on approach to spirituality," according to a reviewer for *Publishers Weekly.* Thus, on each double-page spread, McElrath-Eslick illustrates a child's question about God's clothing, pets, or feelings and the adult's corresponding answer, which draws upon language taken from the Bible. The illustrator garnered positive comments for her use of bright colors, bold brush-strokes, and a strong sense of composition.

"While there are many illustrated Bible stories available, there is nothing else that attempts to explain God to this age group," noted Jane Gardner Connor in *School Library Journal.*

A similar Bible-inspired text is at the center of Carlstrom's *I Am Christmas,* in which the story of the first Christmas is retold in language that is drawn from a variety of biblical sources, all outlined at the end of the book. McElrath-Eslick utilized a rich and varied palette of colors in her accompanying illustrations, according to Jane Marino in *School Library Journal.* Marino concluded that McElrath-Eslick's paintings "elucidate the traditional story with far greater resonance and feeling" than the text.

Drawing upon her experience as a volunteer for the learning-to-read program HOST (Help One Student to Succeed) in Michigan, McElrath-Eslick used richly colored oil paints to illustrate the large picture book *Read for Me, Mama.* In this 1997 work, Joseph continually begs his single working mother to read to him, not knowing that she is unable to read. Joseph's mother, frustrated and embarrassed by her illiteracy, finally attends a vocational school recommended by a friend at her church. By story's end she is able to read, especially to her son. "Painterly illustrations by McElrath-Eslick work in harmony with the text, showing the warmth between Joseph and his mother, as well as their humble, homey surroundings," asserted a *Kirkus Reviews* commentator.

■ Works Cited

Connor, Jane Gardner, review of *Does God Know How to Tie Shoes?, School Library Journal,* March, 1994, pp. 190-91.

Review of *Does God Know How to Tie Shoes?, Publishers Weekly,* July 5, 1993, p. 72.

Marino, Jane, review of *I Am Christmas, School Library Journal,* October, 1995, pp. 35-36.

Review of *Read for Me, Mama, Kirkus Reviews,* January 1, 1997.

■ For More Information See

PERIODICALS

Booklist, December 1, 1993, p. 692; September 1, 1995, p. 54.

* * *

MEEKER, Clare Hodgson 1952-

■ Personal

Born February 7, 1952, in Huntington, NY; daughter of Amherst W. and Barbara H. Meeker; married Daniel Grausz (an attorney), July 30, 1978; children: Sarah, Sam. *Education:* Boston University, B.A. (music), 1975; Hofstra Law School, J.D., 1980. *Hobbies and other interests:* Member of the singing group "The Righteous Mothers."

CLARE HODGSON MEEKER

■ Addresses

Home and office—9520 Southeast 61st Pl., Mercer Island, WA 98040.

■ Career

Lawyer and writer. KCTS/9, Seattle, WA, manager of planned giving, 1982-85; Washington Volunteer Lawyers for the Arts, Seattle, director, 1986-1988; Seattle University, Seattle, WA, grant writer, 1988-90. Teaches creative writing workshops in K-12 schools. *Member:* Society of Children's Book Writers and Illustrators, Washington Bar Association.

■ Awards, Honors

First place award, Pacific Northwest Writer's Contest, 1993, for *Who Wakes Rooster?*

■ Writings

A Tale of Two Rice Birds: A Folktale from Thailand, illustrated by Christine Lamb, Sasquatch Books (Seattle, WA), 1994.

Who Wakes Rooster?, illustrated by Megan Halsey, Simon and Schuster, 1996.

Partner in Revolution: The Life of Abigail Adams, Marshall Cavendish, (Tarrytown, NY), 1997.

The sun shines and Rooster crows.

Meeker's story of the rooster's early-morning wake-up call in the barnyard helps young readers identify the sounds of farm animals. (From *Who Wakes Rooster?*, illustrated by Megan Halsey.)

■ Work in Progress

A middle-grade book and a nonfiction picture book.

■ Sidelights

Clare Hodgson Meeker told *SATA:* "I started to write picture books when my two children were young. Inspired by such authors as Robert McCloskey, Barbara Cooney, and Barbara Helen Berger, I write stories about people and places I've known or have learned about using words that are lyrical and fun to read out loud."

A Tale of Two Rice Birds, Meeker's first book, introduces children to Thai culture and the Buddhist belief in reincarnation. Based on a folktale from Thailand, the story begins with two rice birds who lose their babies in a terrible fire. The mother bird, blaming the father for being away from the nest when the accident occurred, decides to take her own life and vows never to speak to a man again. The father bird follows her, determined to reunite with his wife in the next life. The mother bird is reborn as a princess who does not speak to any men and the father bird as a farmer's son. When the king offers his daughter's hand in marriage to the man who can make her speak, the farmer's son is determined to meet the challenge. Janice Del Negro of *Booklist* asserted that *A Tale of Two Rice Birds* is "gracefully written," with a storyline that is "thought-provoking." *School Library Journal* reviewer Diane S. Marton said that the book

would be "a pleasant addition to multicultural collections."

"I am also a lawyer and a musician," Meeker continued. "These skills are important in my writing. For instance, I listen to how each sentence sounds as I'm writing and read my work out loud. Does a story need a gentle, flowing rhythm or a snappy tone? I am careful about each word I choose to make sure it gives the right effect."

Published in 1996, *Who Wakes Rooster?* commences with farm animals uncharacteristically sleeping just after sunrise. They are still at rest because the sun is hidden behind dark clouds, causing the rooster not to crow. When the sun finally does show through the clouds, the rooster shouts his eye-opening cock-a-doo-dle-do, setting off a domino effect of noisily awakening animals. Through vivid pictures, alliterative text, and repetition, the book helps children learn to read by identifying certain animals with their sounds. Calling *Who Wakes Rooster?* "engaging," *Booklist* contributor Leone McDermott said the book is a "sure choice for the young." Praising Meeker's use of animal shapes and noises, *School Library Journal* contributor Virginia Opocensky claimed that *Who Wakes Rooster?* would be "a winner for preschool story times."

"I also love research," Meeker added. "In my newest book, *Partner In Revolution: The Life of Abigail Adams,* I reviewed American Revolutionary War history through the eyes of Abigail Adams and the women of her time.

"Each book has challenged me to write for a different age group. I have not yet written a middle grade novel but would like to. Perhaps it will be a dude ranch story, inspired by our favorite family vacations. But my first love will always be the picture book, for its clear storylines and emphasis on poetic use of language."

■ Works Cited

Del Negro, Janice, review of *A Tale of Two Rice Birds: A Folktale from Thailand, Booklist,* January 15, 1995, p. 920.

Marton, Diane S., review of *A Tale of Two Rice Birds: A Folktale from Thailand, School Library Journal,* November, 1994, p. 100.

McDermott, Leone, review of *Who Wakes Rooster?, Booklist,* November 1, 1996, p. 508.

Opocensky, Virginia, review of *Who Wakes Rooster?, School Library Journal,* September, 1996, p. 185.

■ For More Information See

PERIODICALS

Kirkus Reviews, July 15, 1996, p. 1052.
Publishers Weekly, October 3, 1994, p. 69.

* * *

MOON, Nicola 1952-

■ Personal

Born June 16, 1952, in Bristol, England; daughter of J. Watt and M. (Walker) Watt; married Philip Moon (an electronic products manager), 1974; children: Kate, Ben. *Education:* Bristol University, B.Sc. (with honors), 1973.

■ Addresses

Agent—Murray Pollinger, 222 Old Brompton Rd., London 2W5 OB2, England.

■ Career

Research assistant in cancer research, London, England, 1973-74; secondary schoolteacher, Wilshire, England, 1974-79; writer.

■ Writings

At the Beginning of a Pig, illustrated by Andy Ellis, Kingfisher, 1994.
Jodie's Colours, illustrated by Lizzie Sanders, Pavillion (England), 1994.
Lucy's Picture, illustrated by Alex Ayliffe, Dial, 1995.
Mouse Finds a Seed, illustrated by Anthony Morris, Trafalgar Square, 1996.
Something Special, illustrated by Alex Ayliffe, Peachtree Publishers, 1997.

Penguins in the Fridge, illustrated by Peter Day, Trafalgar Square, 1997.

■ Sidelights

Nicola Moon once commented: "Books were very much a part of my own childhood, an interest which was reawakened in the early 1980s when I was able to share the enjoyment with my own two children. In addition to reading to them, I wrote stories for them—something I had never done before. Once the children were both at school, and health problems (rheumatoid arthritis) ruled out a return to teaching, I decided to try writing for publication—with the aim of success before my fortieth birthday! This I achieved (just!), signing my first contract, for *At the Beginning of a Pig* (Kingfisher), in 1992.

"Having always had an interest in education, I feel very strongly that learning to read is one of the most important and basic skills a child can master. If a child is familiar with and enjoys books from an early age, the first step toward literacy has been taken."

In *Lucy's Picture,* Moon describes how her young character Lucy "builds" a picture for her blind grandfather. While at school, Lucy gathers twigs, leaves, feathers, and other items to assemble a collage for her grandfather. Cutting a piece of her own hair, she even fashions a golden retriever's coat to resemble her grandfather's seeing-eye dog. A reviewer for *Publishers Weekly* wrote that Moon tells an "affecting story" through her "straightforward prose." Mary Harris Veeder, reviewing the work in *Booklist,* stated that children will "enjoy the story of picture making at school."

■ Works Cited

Review of *Lucy's Picture, Publishers Weekly,* January 2, 1995, p. 76.
Veeder, Mary Harris, review of *Lucy's Picture, Booklist,* January 15, 1995, p. 938.

■ For More Information See

PERIODICALS

Kirkus Reviews, February 15, 1995.*

* * *

MOXLEY, Sheila 1966-

■ Personal

Born September 10, 1966 in Bournemouth, England; daughter of Alan Moxley (a solicitor). *Education:* Bournemouth and Poole College of Art & Design, Diploma of Foundation Studies, 1985-86; St. Martin's School of Art, B.A. (honors), Graphic Design, 1986-89. *Hobbies and other interests:* Stained glass.

■ Addresses

Home—181 Stroud Green Rd., Finsbury Park, London N43PZ, England. *Office*—Unit 8B Huguenot Place, 17A Heneagest, London E1 5LN. *Agent*—Rosemary Sandberg, 6 Bayley St., London WC1B 3HB.

■ Career

Sadie Fields Production Ltd., London, design work and construction of pop-up books, 1987-92; self-employed illustrator, London, England, 1989—; Bournemouth and Poole College of Art and Design, guest lecturer, 1990-92; The Designers Guild, London, textile design work, 1995. *Exhibitions:* "Spirit of London," The Royal Festival Hall, London, 1988; "Artist '89'," London Contemporary Art, 1989; "Affairs of the Heart," The Heffer Gallery, Cambridge, 1990; "The Tram Depot Open," London, 1991, 1992; "The Art of Science," Plymouth City Museum and Art Gallery, 1991; "The Art of Protest," The Watershed, Bristol, 1991; "The Vortex," Stoke Newington, London, 1992; "The Blue Legume," Stoke Newington, 1995; "Martin X," St. Martin's School of Art, London, 1995.

■ Awards, Honors

The Royal Academy/Save the Children Fund Christmas Card Competition prize, 1988; *Elle Magazine* Talent Contest citation, 1989; first prize, Charity Christmas Card of the Year Award, 1991.

■ Illustrator

(And author) *The Christmas Story,* Dial, 1993, Tango Books (United Kingdom), 1993.
Stan Cullimore, reteller, *The Turtle and the Crane,* Longman (United Kingdom), 1994.
Grace Hallworth, reteller, *Anansi at the Pool,* Longman, 1994.
Pratima Mitchell, *Bhaloo the Greedy Bear,* Longman, 1994.
Wendy Body, *Our Favourite Stories from around the World,* Longman, 1994.
Neil Philip, *The Arabian Nights,* Orchard Books, 1994.
Floella Benjamin, compiler, *Skip Across the Ocean: Nursery Rhymes from around the World,* Orchard Books, 1995, Frances Lincoln (United Kingdom), 1995.
Andrew Matthews, *How the World Began,* MacDonald Young Books (United Kingdom), 1996.
Pomme Clayton, *The Orchard Book of Stories from the Seven Seas,* Orchard Books (United Kingdom), 1996.
Andrew Matthews, *Marduk the Mighty & Other Stories of Creation,* Millbrook Press, 1997.

Some of Moxley's books have been published in Germany, France, and Denmark.

■ Work in Progress

Joy to the World, a multicultural book of Christmas.

■ Sidelights

Sheila Moxley told *SATA:* "For as long as I can remember, I've always been interested in illustration and publishing. As a child I used to make magazines which I would distribute to my friends. I think I was lucky to know from an early age what I wanted to do, so later, when it came to choosing a career, going to art school was the natural option. I did a one-year foundation course in Bournemouth, England, followed by a three-year degree course at St. Martin's School of Art in London.

"After leaving college, the majority of my work was commissioned by magazines. I also started doing illustrations for cards and wrapping paper. I was then approached by publishing companies who had seen my work, and they commissioned me to do work for children's books.

"Most of my children's book work has dealt with folktales and mythological subjects, this being a personal interest of mine. Travel is another major theme of my work. I have been inspired by visits to India, Spain, and North Africa. These trips helped to develop a stronger sense of colour and decoration. Imagery and information gathered whilst travelling has been invaluable. Working with the translucent colours of stained glass also inspires and influences my work."

Featuring illustrations by Sheila Moxley, *Skip Across the Ocean* **presents favorite children's rhymes and lullabies from around the world. (Collected by Floella Benjamin.)**

Moxley's vibrant acrylic illustrations form the backdrop for folklorist Neil Phillip's enthusiastic narratives in *The Arabian Nights.* Her colorful and energetic paintings augment the adventurous stories of 'Aladdin,' 'Ali Baba and the Forty Thieves,' and 'The Anklet.' A *Publishers Weekly* commentator maintained that Moxley's illustrations enhance the stories, "conveying a fairy-tale wonder." Cheri Estes of *School Library Journal* added that Moxley's "jewel-toned acrylics are as rich as the king's treasure," while Carolyn Phelan, a reviewer for *Booklist,* asserted that Moxley's illustrations "glow with warm colors and bold highlights."

■ Works Cited

Review of *The Arabian Nights, Publishers Weekly,* October 31, 1994, pp. 62-63.
Estes, Cheri, review of *The Arabian Nights, School Library Journal,* December, 1994, pp. 116-17.
Phelan, Carolyn, review of *The Arabian Nights, Booklist,* December 15, 1994, pp. 749-50.*

*　　*　　*

MURDOCH, David H. 1937-

■ Personal

Born November 11, 1937, in Wallasey, Cheshire, England; son of Hamilton Ball (a captain in the merchant navy) and Doris (a homemaker; maiden name, Lovatt) Murdoch. *Education:* Sidney Sussex College, Cambridge, B.A., 1959, M.A., 1969. *Politics:* "Conservative (nostalgic Thatcherite)."

■ Addresses

Office—Department of History, University of Leeds, Leeds, West Yorkshire LS2 9JT, England.

■ Career

University of Leeds, Leeds, England, assistant lecturer, 1964-67, lecturer, 1967-91, senior lecturer in history, 1991-95, principal teaching fellow, 1995—. Queens College of the City University of New York, visiting professor, summers, 1968-71; Northern Universities American Studies Group, member, 1976-87; consultant to British Broadcasting Corporation Television, 1984, 1986; National Association of Foreign Study Advisers, USA, 1987. *Member:* Royal Historical Society (fellow), British Association of American Studies.

■ Awards, Honors

Fellow of the Royal Historical Society, 1980. Books for the Teen Age nomination, New York Public Library, 1995, for *North American Indian.*

DAVID H. MURDOCH

■ Writings

(Editor) *Rebellion in America: A Contemporary British Viewpoint, 1765-1783,* American Bibliographical Center-Clio Press (Santa Barbara, CA), 1979.
Cowboy, illustrated with photographs by Geoff Brightling, Knopf (New York City), 1993.
North American Indian, illustrated with photographs by Lynton Gardiner, Knopf, 1995.
The American West: The Invention of a Myth, International Specialized Book Services, 1996.

■ Work in Progress

Research on the mythology of the American West.

■ Sidelights

David H. Murdoch told *SATA:* "Two things captivated me when I was a boy: history and Western movies—history because the past seemed so much more absorbing than the boring present of 1950s Britain, and Westerns because I found that their images and stereotypes, their rituals and implicit world-view were mesmeric. My enthusiasm for history made it inevitable that it became my degree subject at university, where I discovered American history and how extraordinarily different it was from the past of Britain and Europe. This is why it became my central interest when I became a university teacher myself.

"Perhaps because it seemed logical to link my British background with my fascination for America, I first concentrated on the era of the Revolution, probably with a notion of demonstrating how perverse Americans were in abandoning the British Empire. Gradually, however, I found myself considering in general, as a key to understanding their past, how Americans think about themselves. This, of course, was not meant to involve my passion for Westerns, which I had managed to keep a secret vice, but eventually it did so. In following a well-trodden path in trying to perceive relationships between politics, culture, and ideas, I had to contend with the obvious: that Americans have assigned to their nineteenth-century conquest of the West a special historical significance, because it is held to define a special experience. I became, not so much a scholarly explorer of the West itself, but the mythology that surrounds it. Today, the course I most enjoy teaching involves a study of the origins of that mythology and, by analyzing a selection of Western movies, how and for what purpose the myths have been used by Americans over the last fifty years."

■ For More Information See

PERIODICALS

Booklist, October 1, 1994, p. 336.
School Librarian, February, 1994, p. 26.
School Library Journal, November, 1994, p. 131; September, 1995, p. 213.

*   *   *

MYERS, Edward 1950-

■ Personal

Born April 1, 1950, in Denver, CO; son of Francis Milton (a college professor) and Estela (a college professor; maiden name, Montemayor) Myers; married Edith Poor (a writer and writing consultant), June 29, 1985; children: two. *Education:* Attended Grinnell College, 1968-70, and University of Denver, 1973-75. *Religion:* "Theologically polymorphous."

■ Addresses

Home—Maplewood, NJ. *Agent*—Faith Hamlin, Sanford J. Greenburger Associates, 55 Fifth Ave., New York, NY 10003.

■ Career

Worked variously as a bricklayer, language instructor, greenhouse worker, baker, librarian, hospital orderly, secretary, administrator at two mental health clinics, editor, proofreader, and cabinetmaker; full-time writer, 1982—.

■ Writings

FOR YOUNG ADULTS

The Mountain Made of Light (fantasy; first novel in "The Mountain Trilogy"), NAL/Dutton, 1992.
Fire and Ice (fantasy; second novel in "The Mountain Trilogy"), NAL/Dutton, 1992.

The Summit (fantasy; third novel in "The Mountain Trilogy"), NAL/Dutton, 1994.
Climb or Die (young adult novel), Hyperion, 1994.
Forri the Baker (picture book), illustrated by Alexi Natchev, Dial, 1995.
Hostage (young adult novel), Hyperion, 1996.

FOR ADULTS

The Chosen Few (nonfiction), And Books, 1982.
When Parents Die: A Guide for Adults, Viking, 1986.
Mind Movies (fiction), American Health Foundation, 1986.
(With Jane Greer) *Adult Sibling Rivalry: Understanding the Legacy of Childhood* (nonfiction), Crown, 1992.
Spirit Writer Asks, rev. ed., Country Press, 1996.

■ Sidelights

Edward Myers is a writer who started out writing nonfiction titles for adults. Myers's first work of fiction for young adults appeared in the early 1990s as *Mountain Made of Light,* an adventure/fantasy novel that is the first installment in the author's Mountain Trilogy. Though some of Myers's books for young adults are better known for their relentless pacing and tension-filled plots than for their insightful characterizations, the novels in the Mountain Trilogy were often highly praised for their sensitive treatment of the "lost race" theme.

Mountain Made of Light introduces the character of Jesse O'Keefe, an anthropology student in the Peruvian Andes climbing and doing field work in the 1920s. He is told about expert local climbers by an old man who leads him to discover the airy, alpine realm of the Rixtirra. "There is a strange quality to this book early on, a wistful innocent thirst for knowledge," reviewer Scott Winnett commented in *Locus,* praising this novel's "wonderful sense of place" that illuminates "both culture and character." Involving himself in the conflicts of the civilization he finds, O'Keefe befriends a lovely native named Aeslu. When a new climber—the spoiled, upper-class Forster Beckwith—intrudes, the two outsiders unwittingly fulfill an ancient prophecy that tells of two strangers: one who will lead Rixtirra to salvation on the Mountain Made of Light, the other to calamity. "Myers's viewpoint is a refreshing change from the British imperialism of his models, Rudyard Kipling and H. Rider Haggard," remarked a reviewer in *Publishers Weekly,* adding praise for the author's sympathetic portrayal of the Rixtirra people.

In *Fire and Ice,* the second novel of the Mountain Trilogy, rival adventurers Jesse and Forster both fall in love with Aeslu as they play out their predestined roles in the mountaintop world's mythology. One Rixtirran faction favors the playboy Forster and the other Jesse, so they compete to be the first to reach the top of the Mountain of Light. Reviewer Faren Miller, writing in *Locus,* was intrigued that "despite Forster's frequent caddishness, the roles of hero and villain are not entirely clear-cut" and that "the rival factions ... also resist being categorized." This ability to present more than

The two forces faced each other for a long moment.

Forri the baker is ostracized by his fellow townspeople because of his oddly shaped bread until he equips them with loaves in the shape of weapons to scare off invaders. (From *Forri the Baker,* written by Edward Myers and illustrated by Alexi Natchev.)

one point of view, says Miller, "allows Myers a degree of subtlety unusual in a Lost Race adventure." The third volume in the trilogy is *The Summit.*

Myers has also published two adventure novels for young adults. In *Climb or Die,* two young teenagers, Danielle and Jake, must save the life of their parents by climbing to a mountaintop rescue station during a blizzard after their car crashes in the storm. "Climb or die, says the title, and that basically sums up the story," noted Roger Sutton in *Bulletin of the Center for Children's Books.* "It isn't subtle but it moves fast." "Characterization is a bit obvious, but this is an adventure story," concurred Joel Shoemaker in *School Library Journal,* adding praise for Myers's "crisp and clear" writing, which places the "emphasis on action." Indeed, *Climb or Die* is a "suspenseful survival story that younger YAs of both sexes will enjoy," averred Merri Monks in *Booklist. Hostage,* Myers's second adventure novel for young adults, satisfied the critics somewhat less than his earlier effort. In this book, two teenagers are taken hostage by a fossil thief through the desert in Dinosaur National Monument. Critics faulted the plot as contrived and predictable, though Sutton allowed that, like *Climb or Die, Hostage* "does have lots of action and a pair of resourceful young heroes."

Myers's venture in the picture-book genre in the form of *Forri the Baker* received complementary reviews. Set during medieval times, the story centers on an innova-

tive baker whose unusually shaped loaves—resembling keys, fish, roses, and pens—leads to the townspeople ostracizing him. Then, when the town is about to be attacked by a group of barbarians, Forri arms the villagers with weapons made of bread, which in the dim light of dawn scare off the invading army. "Myers's traditional, well-crafted narrative is tinged with humor and embellished with spry imagery," contended the reviewer for *Publishers Weekly. Forri the Baker* is "a superb book in both word and art," averred the critic for *Kirkus Reviews,* praising the author's good humor and adding, "it's nice to see the underdog pull one off."

Myers's books for adults include *The Chosen Few,* which is "a study of the so-called survivalist movement in the United States," as the author once said. "Based on interviews with men and women of greatly differing backgrounds and orientations, the book explores their plans and preparations for surviving nuclear war and other disasters," Myers continued. Similarly, Myers's *When Parents Die* is a nonfiction work intended for an adult audience. In this book, Myers offers information on resources and advice to adults whose parents are dying. "Because I feel that a book like this should be useful in tangible ways, *When Parents Die* contains chapters about dealing with both the emotional and practical consequences of experiencing the loss of a parent," the author remarked. "My hope is that *When Parents Die* will help Americans come to terms with one of the most complex issues of our time: the aging of the older generation."

Myers is a professional writer whose works include nonfiction titles for adults and fiction titles for young adults and children. Among his fiction works, his Mountain Trilogy, including *Mountain Made of Light, Fire and Ice,* and *The Summit,* is a highly regarded treatment of the Lost Race theme, in which (unlike the works of Myers's precursors in this vein) the interior lives of both Western and non-Western protagonists are imagined. Myers's adventure novels for young adults, including *Climb or Die* and *Hostage,* are considered exciting, plot-driven stories that will satisfy younger YAs or reluctant readers.

■ Works Cited

Review of *Forri the Baker, Kirkus Reviews,* February 15, 1995, p. 230.

Review of *Forri the Baker, Publishers Weekly,* March 20, 1995, p. 60.

Miller, Faren, review of *Fire and Ice, Locus,* November, 1992, p. 17.

Monks, Merri, review of *Climb or Die, Booklist,* December 1, 1994, p. 664. Review of *Mountain Made of Light, Publishers Weekly,* January 13, 1992, p. 52.

Shoemaker, Joel, review of *Climb or Die, School Library Journal,* January, 1995, pp. 108-9.

Sutton, Roger, review of *Climb or Die, Bulletin of the Center for Children's Books,* December, 1994, pp. 140-41.

Sutton, Roger, review of *Hostage, Bulletin of the Center for Children's Books,* February, 1996, p. 198.

Winnett, Scott, review of *Mountain Made of Light, Locus,* December, 1991, p. 33.

■ For More Information See

PERIODICALS

Booklist, January 1, 1992, p. 811.
Kirkus Reviews, January 15, 1996, p. 139.*

N-O

NELSON, Sharlene (P.) 1933-

■ Personal

Born August 27, 1933, in Los Angeles, CA; daughter of William O. (a coach and teacher) and Katherine (an office manager; maiden name, Bailey) Patten; married Ted William Nelson (a forester), July 17, 1955; children: Gregg, Janise Nelson Gates. *Education:* University of California, Berkeley, B.A., 1955. *Politics:* Republican. *Religion:* Congregational. *Hobbies and other interests:* Sailing, backpacking with her grandchildren, skiing, writing.

■ Addresses

Home and office—824 South Marine Hills Way, Federal Way, WA 98003.

■ Career

Freelance writer, 1956—. *Pacific Search,* staff writer, 1966-72; *Oregonian,* correspondent, 1973-82. Has worked with a number of historical societies, including the Washington County Historical Society of North Carolina, for which she served as president, 1969-1970. *Member:* Society of Children's Book Writers and Illustrators, U.S. Lighthouse Society, Pacific Northwest Writers Conference, Oregon Historical Society, Washington State Historical Society, Washington Trail Association, Tacoma Yacht Club, Tacoma Women's Sailing Association, Lewis and Clark Trail Heritage Foundation.

■ Awards, Honors

Second place award, children's nonfiction book category, Pacific Northwest Writers Conference, 1972, for a submission titled "Gray Whale."

■ Writings

ALL WITH HUSBAND, TED NELSON

(With Joan LeMieux) *Cruising the Columbia and Snake Rivers: Eleven Cruises in the Inland Waterway,* Pacific Search Press (Seattle, WA), 1981, revised edition, 1986.

The Umbrella Guide to Washington Lighthouses, Umbrella Books (Friday Harbor, WA), 1990.

The Umbrella Guide to California Lighthouses, Epicenter Press (Seattle), 1993.

The Umbrella Guide to Oregon Lighthouses, Epicenter Press, 1994.

Bull Whackers to Whistle Punks: Logging in the Old West, F. Watts (Danbury, CT), 1996.

Sharlene and Ted Nelson.

The Umbrella Guide to Exploring the Columbia-Snake River Inland Waterway, Epicenter Press, 1997.

Mount St. Helens National Volcanic Monument, Children's Press (Danbury), 1997.

Olympic National Park, Children's Press, 1997.

Hawaii Volcanoes National Park, Children's Press, in press.

Mount Rainier National Park, Children's Press, in press.

Author of booklets about forestry.

■ **Work in Progress**

Nonfiction articles for children.

■ **Sidelights**

Sharlene and Ted Nelson told *SATA:* "Little did we suspect that a college assignment would lead to our working together as co-authors many years later. In 1953 Sharlene was given a course assignment to write a children's story or review one hundred children's books. She chose to write a story about Smokey Bear, a then well-known symbol for forest fire prevention. Her fiance, Ted, agreed to do the illustrations. We produced the hand-printed book with watercolor illustrations and had it bound in hardcover. The assignment yielded an 'A.' The story was submitted later to publishers, and Sharlene received her first rejection slip. Now and then, we pull the original from the bookshelf and read it to our grandchildren, who ask, 'Who is Smokey Bear?'

"After our marriage, Ted pursued a career in forestry, and we developed an affinity for the outdoors, an interest in local history, and an enjoyment of research. Sharlene patiently pursued her interest in writing, despite numerous rejection slips.

"In 1977 we moved from the Oregon coast to Longview, Washington, and began sailing on the nearby Columbia River. Sharlene learned of a publisher who wanted to produce a boaters' guide to the Columbia River, and she volunteered. When Ted heard of the project, he exclaimed, 'That river is twelve-hundred miles long, and we've only sailed thirty miles of it!' We got busy. The publisher agreed to a book covering only the 465-mile-long inland waterway, a navigable portion of the lower Snake and Columbia Rivers that follows the western end of the Lewis and Clark Trail. After traveling every mile by water, doing interviews and research, our first book, *Cruising the Columbia and Snake Rivers,* was published in 1981.

"In 1989, then living on Washington's Puget Sound, we had an urge to write another book. Learning of a publisher who was looking for regional guidebooks, we began brainstorming ideas. One morning Ted looked out of the window and across the sound at the flashing light of a lighthouse. 'How about a book about lighthouses?' he asked. We knew little about lighthouses, but we had enjoyed seeing them when sailing. *The Umbrella Guide to Washington Lighthouses* was published in 1990.

"For *Bull Whackers to Whistle Punks,* we drew on our experiences living in a remote logging camp in northern California. While the other books used mostly photographs taken by Ted, this book used mostly historic photographs. Ted was able, however, to provide drawings for the chapter art.

"The bull whackers book led to an assignment for books on three national parks and the Mount St. Helens National Volcanic Monument. We had backpacked the trails of Olympic and Mount Rainier National Parks and hiked trails at the Hawaii Volcanoes National Park. When Mount St. Helens erupted, we were living in Longview, only thirty-five miles away.

"We have an ability to work closely together. Our shared experiences and mutual interests have gotten us through the times when there were writing commitments and only a blank page before us. Sharlene likes the quotation, 'When you want to know a subject, write a book about it.'"

■ **For More Information See**

PERIODICALS

Booklist, August, 1996, p. 1899.
Library Journal, June 1, 1990, p. 158.
School Library Journal, July, 1996, p. 94.

*   *   *

NELSON, Ted (W.) 1931-

■ **Personal**

Born June 22, 1931, in McCloud, CA; son of DeWitt (a forester) and Sadiebelle (a lecturer; maiden name, Friedley) Nelson; married Sharlene Patten (a writer), July 17, 1955; children: Gregg, Janise Nelson Gates. *Education:* Attended Pomona College, 1949-51; University of California, Berkeley, B.S., 1954; University of Michigan, M.F., 1957. *Politics:* Republican. *Religion:* Methodist. *Hobbies and other interests:* Sailing, backpacking, skiing, oil painting, playing the banjo.

■ **Addresses**

Home and office—824 South Marine Hills Way, Federal Way, WA 98003.

■ **Career**

Diamond Match Co., Lyman Springs, CA, resident forester, 1957-64; Weyerhaeuser Co., Tacoma, WA, position at retirement: vice-president Timberlands, Washington Division, 1964-91; writer, 1991—. Member of board of directors, China Relations Council, Japan-America Society, and World Affairs Council; trustee, Washington Forest Protection Association. *Military service:* U.S. Army, Infantry, 1954-56; became first lieutenant. *Member:* Forest History Society (member of board of directors, 1992—), Society of American Foresters, Society of Children's Book Writers and Illustrators,

U.S. Lighthouse Society, Washington Forest Protection Association (honorary trustee, 1991), Tacoma Yacht Club, National Maritime Historical Society, Oregon Historical Society, Washington State Historical Society.

■ Writings

ALL WITH WIFE, SHARLENE NELSON

(With Joan LeMieux) *Cruising the Columbia and Snake Rivers: Eleven Cruises in the Inland Waterway,* Pacific Search Press (Seattle, WA), 1981, revised edition, 1986.

The Umbrella Guide to Washington Lighthouses, Umbrella Books (Friday Harbor, WA), 1990.

The Umbrella Guide to California Lighthouses, Epicenter Press (Seattle), 1993.

The Umbrella Guide to Oregon Lighthouses, Epicenter Press, 1994.

Bull Whackers to Whistle Punks: Logging in the Old West, F. Watts (Danbury, CT), 1996.

The Umbrella Guide to Exploring the Columbia-Snake River Inland Waterway, Epicenter Press, 1997.

Mount St. Helens National Volcanic Monument, Children's Press (Danbury), 1997.

Olympic National Park, Children's Press, 1997.

Hawaii Volcanoes National Park, Children's Press, in press.

Mount Rainier National Park, Children's Press, in press.

Author of booklets about forestry.

■ Work in Progress

Nonfiction articles for children.

■ Sidelights

For discussion of Ted Nelson's life and career, please see "Sidelights" essay on Sharlene Nelson in this volume.

■ For More Information See

PERIODICALS

Booklist, August, 1996, p. 1899.
Library Journal, June 1, 1990, p. 158.
School Library Journal, July, 1996, p. 94.

* * *

NILSEN, Anna
See BASSIL, Andrea

* * *

OLALEYE, Isaac O. 1941-

■ Personal

Born May 17, 1941, in Erin, Nigeria; son of Joseph Oluroye (a farmer) and Comfort Fayiluka (a trader) Olaleye. *Education:* Institute of Transport, Essex, En-

gland, graduated, 1970. *Religion:* Jehovah's Witnesses. *Hobbies and other interests:* Photography, jogging, soccer.

■ Addresses

Home and office—P.O. Box 1241, Keyser, WV 26726.

■ Career

Writer. Worked for Department of Public Prosecutions, Lagos, Nigeria, as a messenger, and as a clerk in a clothing store in Ibadan, Nigeria; Pan American Airways, sales agent, 1970-71; a house painter, proprietor of drapery business, and other odd jobs, 1972-92; full-time writer, 1993—.

■ Awards, Honors

Outstanding Books for 1995 selection, Parent Council Limited, for *Bitter Bananas;* Notable Children's Trade Book, National Council for the Social Studies and the Children's Book Council, Children's Book of Distinction, *Hungry Mind Review,* and Notable Book citation, American Library Association, all 1996, all for *The Distant Talking Drum.*

■ Writings

FOR CHILDREN

Bitter Bananas, illustrated by Ed Young, Boyds Mills Press, 1994.

ISAAC O. OLALEYE

The Distant Talking Drum: Poems from Nigeria, illustrated by Frane Lessac, Boyds Mills Press, 1995.
Two Boys and a Big Snake, Boyds Mills Press, 1998.
In the Rainfield, illustrated by Ann Grifalconi, Scholastic, 1999.
Duro's Dream, Boyds Mills Press, in press.
The Foolish Archerfish, Scholastic, in press.
When There Were No Mountains, Boyds Mill Press, in press.

OTHER

Did God Make Them Black? (for adults), Winston-Derek, 1990.

Also author of *Did God Create the World in Six Days?,* 1997. Contributor to *Highlights for Children.*

■ Work in Progress

The Human Race and Development (nonfiction), *A Country without Crooks* (fiction), *Who Made God?* (nonfiction), and several children's and adults' books.

■ Sidelights

Isaac O. Olaleye told *SATA:* "I took to writing because I had always wondered why some cultures are developed technologically and scientifically while other cultures are not so developed.... Writing—for both adults and children—was like, in my case, diving into a pool without knowing how to swim. I am not a good swimmer yet. But it does seem I am not going to drown. 'Lifeguards' have had to 'rescue' me. If I feel I am getting water inside of me, into my lungs, I know where the lifeguards are! I hope to share knowledge, challenge, entertain and inspire through my books. I work eight to ten hours or longer a day when I write. Ashley Montagu of Yale University inspired me with his book—*Man's Most Dangerous Myth—The Fallacy of Race.* Dr. Seuss has, to a small degree, influenced me. I read one or two of his books before I began writing children's books. In my growing up years, I had access to only one book that was not a textbook. To aspiring writers: keep plugging. The labor may be bitter, but the fruit will be sweet. The winner never quits, the quitter never wins."

Olaleye is a writer who has drawn upon his childhood in Nigeria for material to create his award-winning children's books. The fifth of seven children, Olaleye saw his already large family double in size when his father took a second wife, with whom he also had seven children. "I certainly did not have a shortage of children to play with, fight with, be adventurous with, or get into massive mischief with," the author explained in an essay for *Something about the Author Autobiography Series* (*SAAS*). The family was poor, and could only afford to send Olaleye through primary school. After leaving home and working a series of jobs, he was able to travel to England, where he earned an Advanced Certificate of Education, the equivalent of a junior college diploma, in law, economics, and biblical studies. Olaleye attended Thurrock Technical College in Essex, England, where he became a graduate of the Institute of

Transport. He briefly returned to Nigeria where he worked for Pan American Airways, and then moved to the United States.

Olaleye's first book for children is an adaptation of a story told him by his father about how a man solved the problem of baboons stealing his palm sap. After several attempts, Olaleye decided to alter the bloody resolution of the original story, and *Bitter Bananas* was born. In Olaleye's version "it takes patience, ingenuity, and several trials before Yusuf outwits his forest rivals" by tainting the tree sap with foul-tasting wormwood, Elizabeth Bush noted in *Bulletin of the Center for Children's Books.* Critics singled out the author's effective use of repeated refrains of "Oh no! Oh no!" and "Oh yes! Oh yes!" in his story. "Olaleye's eminently readable text naturally calls for audience participation," noted Janice Del Negro in *Booklist.*

For his second children's book, Olaleye was asked by an editor at Boyds Mills Press to write a series of poems about what it was like to grow up in Nigeria. *The Distant Talking Drum: Poems from Nigeria* is a collection of fifteen poems, each describing a different aspect of life in the rain forest, such as washing clothes in a stream, listening to stories, dancing, and going to school. "Readers will gain new information from the collection as well as a feeling of shared humanity" with the Nigerian children pictured in Olaleye's book, Maeve Visser Knoth remarked in *Horn Book. School Library*

A Nigerian farming village is described in Olaleye's series of poems evoking different aspects of life in a tropical rain forest. (From *The Distant Talking Drum: Poems from Nigeria,* illustrated by Frane Lessac.)

Journal contributor Dot Minzer praised Olaleye's "eloquent free verse," noting that the author evokes the way of life in his homeland "with an ease of expression that celebrates everyday life." A reviewer for *Publishers Weekly* concluded that these "rhythmic, detailed, musical poems provide a welcome and informed look at the customs and people" of the rain forest.

"Socrates said that all knowledge begins with the knowledge of oneself," Olaleye wrote in his autobiographical essay for *SAAS*. "And the knowledge of oneself certainly ranks high in terms of our reasons for writing. In our writing we reveal to the world the inner self, the secret person of our hearts. This is shown in different ways, but especially in the way we portray our characters. So it can be said that writing is partially a process of self-discovery, the way we think, the way we want the world to be, the way we would want others to act, and what we would like to see happen to good and evil. I discover myself through the pages of my writing."

■ Works Cited

Bush, Elizabeth, review of *Bitter Bananas, Bulletin of the Center for Children's Books,* October, 1994, p. 61.

Del Negro, Janice, review of *Bitter Bananas, Booklist,* September 15, 1994, p. 144.

Review of *The Distant Talking Drum: Poems from Nigeria, Publishers Weekly,* December 19, 1994, p. 54.

Knoth, Maeve Visser, review of *The Distant Talking Drum: Poems from Nigeria, Horn Book,* March, 1995, p. 211.

Minzer, Dot, review of *The Distant Talking Drum: Poems from Nigeria, School Library Journal,* February, 1995, p. 92.

Olaleye, Isaac O., essay in *Something about the Author Autobiography Series,* Volume 23, Gale, 1997, pp. 211-25.

■ For More Information See

PERIODICALS

Booklist, January 1, 1995, p. 824; March 15, 1996, p. 1289.

Publishers Weekly, July 18, 1994, p. 245; January 1, 1996, p. 71.

School Library Journal, August, 1994, pp. 141-42.

Wilson Library Bulletin, October, 1994, p. 110.

P

Joseph N. Panetta with family.

PANETTA, Joseph N. 1953-

■ Personal

Born October 24, 1953, in Philadelphia, PA; son of Nicholas (a firefighter) and Concetta (a homemaker; maiden name, Vernacchio) Panetta; married Gina Angelucci (an emergency room technician), 1978; children: Nicholas, Louis, Judith, Joseph. *Education:* La Salle College, B.A., 1975. *Politics:* Republican. *Religion:* Roman Catholic.

■ Addresses

Home and office—Philadelphia, PA.

■ Career

Naval Inventory Control Point, Philadelphia, PA, disposal specialist, 1981—. Self-employed electrical contractor, 1989—. Also worked as a high school teacher of Spanish and Italian. *Member:* Lawncrest Athletic Association (youth coach).

■ Writings

Bluedevils, American Literary Press (Baltimore, MD), 1996.

Author of the poem "The Comet," 1997.

■ Work in Progress

A high school reminiscence.

■ Sidelights

Joseph N. Panetta told *SATA:* "As a former teacher, I enjoy writing books that teach a lesson. I like to target the teenage reader. *Bluedevils* is a reminiscence of my years as the coach of a boys' soccer team. The message in the book is the rewards of effort regardless of victory. My current work deals with the problems of growing. It involves teenage drinking, dating, and trying to 'fit in.' I hope to find an entertaining way to get my message across to the reader."

PFEIFFER, Janet (B.) 1949-

■ Personal

Born February 23, 1949, in Brooklyn, NY; daughter of Clayton L. (an electrician) and Rae I. (a secretary; maiden name, Sole) Pfeiffer; married Richard Mazzacca (divorced, April, 1984); married Kenneth R. MacDougall, October 13, 1996; children: (first marriage) Richard, Tonia Mazzacca DeMarco, Christopher, Donna. *Education:* Englewood Cliffs College (now St. Peter's College), A.A., 1969. *Religion:* Roman Catholic. *Hobbies and other interests:* Race-walking, photography, music, hiking.

■ Addresses

Home and office—182 Schoolhouse Road, Oak Ridge, NJ 07438.

■ Career

Anger management consultant, motivational speaker, and writer; guest on television and radio programs. Home Maintenance Service, owner. Volunteer with Youth Group Ministries, Rainbows for All God's Children, Visions (adult singles group), Chilton Hospital, Habitat for Humanity, committee member and keynote speaker for the Week without Violence, sponsored by the national YWCA, 1997.

■ Awards, Honors

First place awards, Garden State Writer's Challenge, 1994, for *The Angel and the Gift,* and 1995, for *The Orchids of Gateway Lane;* honorable mention Garden State Writer's Challenge, 1996, for *Jordan's Promise;* photography awards; athletic awards include gold medal from a New Jersey state race-walking competition, 1994, as well as gold, silver, and bronze medals in national marathons, 1994-95.

■ Writings

The Seedling's Journey, Fairway Press, 1994.
The Angel and the Gift: A Second Chance, Winston-Derek (Nashville, TN), 1996.
The Orchids of Gateway Lane: Galen's Message of Peace, Winston-Derek, 1996.
Jordan's Promise, Winston-Derek, 1998.

■ Work in Progress

Clayton's Symphony (tentative title).

■ Sidelights

Janet Pfeiffer told *SATA:* "When I was thirty-three years old, after thirteen years of marriage, my husband left me with four young children to raise on my own. Needing an income, but also needing to be at home with my children, I began a very successful business that I ran from home.

JANET PFEIFFER

"During the years that followed my divorce, my life became increasingly difficult. I began a nine-year battle with bulimia, my ex-husband legally blackmailed me out of a substantial amount of money, then seriously damaged my relationship with my children (to the extent that they have not spoken to me for various periods of time). My self-esteem was so low that my life almost ended as a result of it.

"My faith in God and the ever-present goodness that surrounds us got me through all of this. For more than twenty years I have been in and out of therapy, attended workshops and lectures on everything from spirituality to holistic healing to physical fitness, psychic development, and anger management. Not sure of my purpose in life, I continually searched for answers. I wrote *The Seedling's Journey* in 1993. It is the story of a little seedling that ends up inside the crevice of a rock. He complains that life is unfair, but soon learns to be thankful for what he has and to 'grow where he is planted.' At this point, my purpose in life became very clear: God was directing me to where he wanted me to be.

"After *The Seedling's Journey* was released, I began to do a lot of promotional work and talked extensively about how my life paralleled that of the young seedling. I began lecturing on anger management, conflict resolution, forgiveness, goal-setting, and random acts of kindness. I now have a very successful career as a consultant and motivational speaker.

"I believe that there is good in everyone and everything, and that life is a series of lessons to be learned. Our greatest teacher is pain. The more painful the situation, the greater the lesson. When we learn that lesson, we emerge stronger, wiser, more patient, more loving, and much more understanding.

"Through all of the pain, I learned more about myself than I ever imagined possible. I learned that there was an incredible amount of untapped potential within me and that I needed to discover, develop, and share it with the world. I became excited about creating a very new and successful life for myself.

"I continued my writing and am working on a series of inspirational books for young people and adults. All contain valuable lessons and messages of hope in various aspects of life: cherishing relationships, defeating the enemy by making him your friend, being able to feel a sense of peace and hope when death takes a loved one, and *celebrating* (not merely accepting) the uniqueness and differences within each one of us. All of my stories are taken from my own personal experiences in life that have taught me lessons; all are messages from God.

"I have lived life with a new-found sense of enthusiasm and self-power. In addition to my career in lecturing and writing, I also co-hosted my own radio talk show on personal growth issues, facilitated couples in divorce negotiations, and I present ongoing workshops on anger management. I have won awards in writing and photography, and I am a former state and national medalist on race-walking competitions. I just celebrated my fifteen-year anniversary of walking no less than twelve miles a day every single day of the year.

"Two of the most influential books in my life have been Mandino's *The Greatest Salesman in the World* and Barbara Sher's *I Can Do Anything If Only I Know What That Is*. These books have helped me to gain control over my own life by making conscious choices to be happy, healthy, peaceful, and successful. I believe, as Barbara puts it, that we are all created with certain gifts and talents and that, when we develop and use these talents for the good of all, we find happiness and success. I believe that God allowed me to experience serious pain and loss in my life so that I could learn the lessons that I now share with many others through my writing and lecturing. I would not trade my life for anyone's."

PIERCE, Tamora 1954-

■ Personal

Born December 13, 1954, in Connellsville, PA; daughter of Wayne Franklin and Jacqueline S. Pierce. *Education:* University of Pennsylvania, B.A., 1976.

■ Addresses

Agent—Craig R. Tenney, Harold Ober Associates, 425 Madison Ave., New York, NY 10017.

■ Career

City of Kingston, NY, tax data collector, 1977-78; towns of Hardenburgh and Denning, NY, tax clerk, 1978; McAuley Home for Girls, Buhl, ID, social worker and housemother, 1978-79; Harold Ober Associates, New York City, assistant to literary agent, 1979-82; creative director of ZPPR Productions, Inc. (radio producers), 1982-86; Chase Investment Bank, New York City, secretary, 1985-89; freelance writer, 1990—. Former instructor, Free Woman's University, University of Pennsylvania. *Member:* Authors Guild, Science Fiction and Fantasy Writers of America.

TAMORA PIERCE

■ Awards, Honors

Author's Citation, Alumni Association of the New Jersey Institute of Technology, 1984, for *Alanna: The First Adventure;* Schuler-Express ZDF Preis (Germany), 1985, and South Carolina Children's Book Award nomination, 1985-86, both for *In the Hand of the Goddess;* Children's Paperbacks Bestseller, *Australian Bookseller and Publisher,* 1995, for *Wolf-Speaker;* Best Books for Young Adults list, Hawaii State Library, Best Science Fiction, Fantasy and Horror list, *Voice of Youth Advocates,* both 1995, and Best Books for Young Adults list, American Library Association, 1996, all for *The Emperor Mage;* Best Science Fiction, Fantasy and Horror list, *Voice of Youth Advocates,* 1996, and Best Books for the Teen Age list, New York Public Library, 1997, both for *The Realms of the Gods.*

■ Writings

"SONG OF THE LIONESS" SERIES; PUBLISHED BY ATHENEUM

Alanna: The First Adventure, 1983.
In the Hand of the Goddess, 1984.
The Woman Who Rides like a Man, 1986.
Lioness Rampant, 1988.

"THE IMMORTALS" SERIES; PUBLISHED BY ATHENEUM

Wild Magic, 1992.
Wolf-Speaker, 1994.
The Emperor Mage, 1995.
The Realms of the Gods, 1996.

"CIRCLE OF MAGIC" SERIES; PUBLISHED BY SCHOLASTIC

Sandry's Book, 1996.
Tris's Book, 1998.
Daja's Book, 1998.
Briar's Book, in press.

OTHER

(Contributor) Steve Ditlea, editor, *Digital Deli,* Workman, 1984.
(Contributor) Douglas Hill, editor, *Planetfall,* Oxford University Press, 1985.

Author of radio scripts aired on National Public Radio, 1987-89. Contributor to periodicals, including *Christian Century* and *School Library Journal.* Pierce's works have been translated into German, Danish, and Spanish.

■ Sidelights

Tamora Pierce's fantasy novels for young readers are noted for their strong female protagonists and their imaginative, well-drawn plots. In her "Song of the Lioness" quartet, Pierce features the character Alanna, a young woman who disguises herself as a man in order to train as a knight, and then uses her physical strength and her capabilities as a healer to serve Prince Jonathan and engage in numerous medieval adventures. "I enjoy

Fourteen-year-old Daine and her mentor, the mage Numair, help a wolf pack roust the humans who have invaded and pillaged the land in their attempts to mine precious opals. (Cover illustration by Mike McDermott.)

writing for teenagers," Pierce once explained to *Something about the Author* (*SATA*), "because I feel I help to make life easier for kids who are like I was."

Alanna is introduced to readers in *Alanna: The First Adventure,* published in 1983. The first novel in the "Song of the Lioness" series, *Alanna* focuses on the title character's determination to avoid the traditional fate of young women her age—life in a secluded convent. Instead, she cuts her hair, binds her breasts, and, as "Alan," changes identities with her brother and begins training to become a knight in the service of her country's king. During her grueling education, she becomes close friends with Prince Jonathan, who does not know that his favorite knight-in-training is, in fact, a young woman. Only during a battle in the forbidding Black City does the prince discover Alanna's true gender; on the pair's return to the palace he makes her his squire regardless.

In Pierce's second novel, the highly praised *In the Hand of the Goddess,* Alanna, now a squire, struggles to master the skills she will need to survive her test for knighthood in the Chamber of the Ordeal. She goes to war against a neighboring country and clashes repeatedly with Duke Roger, an urbane and devious mage who is determined to usurp the throne from his cousin, Prince Jonathan. Successful in her efforts to protect Jonathan despite the duke's attempts to get rid of her, she eventually decides to leave royal service and journey out into the world in search of further adventures. In a *School Library Journal* review, Isabel Soffer praised Pierce's books about Alanna as "sprightly, filled with adventure and marvelously satisfying."

In *The Woman Who Rides like a Man*, the third installment of "Song of the Lioness," Alanna is on her own. With her servant Coram Smythesson and Faithful, her cat, she encounters a tribe of desert warriors called the Bazhir. Proving her worth in physical combat, she is accepted by the Bazhir and ultimately becomes their shaman, or wizard. Alanna broadens the outlook of these desert people, raising a few women of the tribe to an equal level with the men before moving on to other adventures. And in the final volume of the quartet, *Lioness Rampant*, the stubborn heroine has become legendary for her skills in battle and for her magical powers; now she goes on a quest for the King of Tortall. Ascending to the Roof of the World after encountering numerous trials and challenges, she attempts to claim the Dominion Jewel, a precious stone said to give its bearer the power to do good. In addition to adventure, she also encounters love in the person of Liam, a warrior known far and wide as the Shang Dragon; however, his dislike of her magical powers makes their relationship a fragile one. Calling Pierce "a great story-teller," a *Junior Bookshelf* reviewer praised the series' inventive characters in particular, noting that the multi-talented heroine's "sword, her companion and her cat will always be ready to rise to any emergency."

Pierce followed her popular "Song of the Lioness" novels with a second series, "The Immortals," which began in 1992 with the novel *Wild Magic*. Although Alanna makes an appearance in the novel, the new protagonist is thirteen-year-old Daine, an orphaned teen who has an unexplained empathy with wild creatures and a second sense that allows her to foresee danger. In fact, she is in danger of reverting to a wild creature herself until the wizard Numair teaches her to control and channel her "wild magic." Daine then uses her powers to stop evil humans from coercing the newly arrived Immortals—dragons, griffins, spidrens, and Stormwings—to help them accomplish destructive purposes. Called "a dynamic story sure to engross fantasy fans" by Sally Estes in *Booklist, Wild Magic* was praised by Anne A. Flowers, who maintained in her *Horn Book* review that readers will "find in Daine a strong heroine whose humble beginning makes her well-deserved rewards even more gratifying."

Wolf-Speaker continues the adventures of Daine as the fourteen year old and her mentor, the mage Numair, join a wolf pack that are at odds with humans. Men, working for an evil wizard named Tristan, have discovered opals in the wolves' hunting lands in Dunlath

The first "Circle of Magic" story in a projected four-volume series, *Sandry's Book* introduces readers to four young people who learn to use their fantastic powers when they are placed in a disciplined temple community.

Valley. The scramble for the precious gems resulted in mine pollution and a destroyed ecosystem. Hunted by Stormwings controlled by Tristan, Daine and her companions must use all their powers, including shape changing, to stop the impending ecological catastrophe. "Daine is a super new heroine who makes this action-packed fantasy a joy to read," Mary L. Adams wrote in *Voice of Youth Advocates,* while Bonnie Kunzel added in her *School Library Journal* article that *Wolf-Speaker* "is a compulsively readable novel that YAs won't be able to put down until the final battle is over and good triumphs. Pierce's faithful readers as well as any action-adventure or animal fantasy fans will be delighted with this new series." Daine's adventures continue in other "Immortals" novels, which include *The Emperor Mage,* published in 1995, and 1996's *The Realms of the Gods,* the concluding novel of the series in which Pierce's young female protagonist convinces dragons and other Immortal creatures to fight on her side against the powers of evil.

Magic once again plays an important role in Pierce's most recent fantasy series, "Circle of Magic." In *San-*

dry's Book, "a rich and satisfying read," according to a *Kirkus Reviews* critic, Sandry, Daja, Briar, and Trisana—four young people from various walks of life—meet and become friends while living in a temple community. As the four protagonists overcome the negative aspects of their lives, they learn a variety of crafts as well as the use of their unique powers, including magic.

"I owe my career as a writer and my approach to writing to people like my writing mentor, David Bradley, who taught me that writing is not an arcane and mystical process, administered by the initiate and fraught with obstacles, but an enjoyable pastime that gives other people as much pleasure as it does me," Pierce once told *SATA*. "I enjoy telling stories, and, although some of my topics are grim, people get caught up in them."

A woman with wide-ranging interests, Pierce continues to focus her research in specific areas, many of which eventually become incorporated into her fantasy novels for teens. "I am interested in medieval customs, life, and chivalry," she told *SATA*. "I study Japanese, Central Asian, and Arabic history and culture; wildlife and nature; crime; the American Civil War; and the conflicts between Islam and Christianity in the Middle Ages and the Renaissance. Occasionally I rescue hurt or homeless animals in a local park ... visit schools as often as I can, and read, read, read. I belong to the Science Fiction and Fantasy Writers of America (SFWA) and the Authors Guild, have an internet webpage, and belong to two online computer services. I even have an online fan club!"

■ Works Cited

Adams, Mary L., review of *Wolf-Speaker, Voice of Youth Advocates,* August, 1994, p. 159.
Estes, Sally, review of *Wild Magic, Booklist,* October 15, 1992, p. 419.
Flowers, Anne A., review of *Wild Magic, Horn Book,* January-February, 1993, p. 93.
Kunzel, Bonnie, "The Call of the Wild: YAs Running with the Wolves," *School Library Journal,* August, 1995, pp. 37-38.
Review of *Sandry's Book, Kirkus Reviews,* July 15, 1997.
Soffer, Isabel, review of *In the Hand of the Goddess, School Library Journal,* December, 1984, p. 94.
Review of *The Woman Who Rides like a Man, Junior Bookshelf,* October, 1989, p. 243.

■ For More Information See

BOOKS

The Encyclopedia of Fantasy, St. Martin's Press, 1997.
Seventh Book of Junior Authors and Illustrators, H. W. Wilson, 1995.
Speaking for Ourselves II: More Autobiographical Sketches by Notable Authors of Books for Young Adults, National Council of Teachers of English, 1993.
Twentieth-Century Young Adult Writers, St. James Press, 1994.

PERIODICALS

Booklist, March 15, 1994, p. 1344; June 1-15, 1995, p. 1757; October 15, 1996, p. 414.
Bulletin of the Center for Children's Books, November, 1984, p. 53; April, 1986, p. 156; November, 1997, pp. 97-98.
Horn Book, May-June, 1986, pp. 333-34; March-April, 1989, p. 234; September-October, 1994, p. 613; July-August, 1995, p. 485.
Kirkus Reviews, August 1, 1988, pp. 1154-55; October 15, 1992, p. 1314.
School Library Journal, July, 1995, p. 80; November, 1996, p. 124.
Voice of Youth Advocates, April, 1985, p. 56; December, 1988, p. 248; April, 1995, p. 14.

*   *   *

PLATH, Sylvia 1932-1963
(Victoria Lucas)

■ Personal

Born October 27, 1932, in Jamaica Plain (now part of Boston), MA; committed suicide, February 11, 1963, in London, England; buried in Heptonstall, Yorkshire, England; daughter of Otto Emil (a professor) and Aurelia (a teacher; maiden name, Schober) Plath; married Ted Hughes (a poet), June 16, 1956 (separated, 1962); children: Frieda Rebecca, Nicholas Farrar. *Edu-*

SYLVIA PLATH

cation: Attended Harvard University, summer, 1954; Smith College, B.A. (summa cum laude), 1955; Newnham College, Cambridge, M.A., 1957. *Religion:* Unitarian Universalist. *Hobbies and other interests:* Beekeeping, horseback riding.

■ Career

Poet and novelist. While in college, worked as a volunteer art teacher at the People's Institute, Northampton, MA; Smith College, Northampton, English instructor, 1957-58. Guest editor for *Mademoiselle* magazine, summer, 1953.

■ Awards, Honors

Mademoiselle College Board contest winner in fiction, 1953; Irene Glascock Poetry Prize, Mount Holyoke College, 1955; Bess Hokin Award, *Poetry* magazine, 1957; first prize, Cheltenham Festival, 1961; Eugene F. Saxton fellowship, 1961; Pulitzer Prize in poetry, 1982, for *Collected Poems.*

■ Writings

FOR CHILDREN

The Bed Book, illustrated by Emily Arnold McCully, Harper, 1976.

The It-Doesn't-Matter Suit, illustrated by Rotraut Susanne Berner, St. Martin's, 1996.

POETRY

The Colossus, Heinemann, 1960, published with alternate selection of poems as *The Colossus, and Other Poems,* Knopf, 1962.

(Editor) *American Poetry Now* (supplement number two to *Critical Quarterly*), Oxford University Press, 1961.

Uncollected Poems (booklet), Turret Books (London), 1965.

Ariel, edited by Ted Hughes and Alwyn Hughes, Faber, 1965, published with alternate selection of poems, Harper, 1966.

Wreath for a Bridal, limited edition, Sceptre Press, 1970.

Million Dollar Month, Sceptre Press, 1971.

Child, Rougemont Press, 1971.

Crossing the Water: Transitional Poems, edited by Ted Hughes, Faber, 1971, published with alternate selection of poems, Harper, 1971.

Crystal Gazer and Other Poems, limited edition, Rainbow Press (London), 1971.

Lyonnesse, limited edition, Rainbow Press, 1971.

Winter Trees, edited by Ted Hughes, Faber, 1971, published with alternate selection of poems, Harper, 1972.

Pursuit with an Etching and Drawing by Leonard Baskin, Rainbow Press, 1973.

Two Poems, Sceptre Press, 1980.

The Collected Poems, edited by Ted Hughes, Harper, 1981.

Dialogue over a Ouija Board: A Verse Dialogue, Rainbow Press, 1981.

The Green Rock, Embers Handpress, 1982.

Stings: Original Drafts of the Poem in Facsimile, Reproduced from the Sylvia Plath Collection at Smith College, essay by Susan R. Van Dyne, Smith College, 1982.

Sylvia Plath's Selected Poems, edited by Ted Hughes, Faber, 1985.

Has had poetry published in anthologies, including *The New Yorker Book of Poems,* Viking, 1969. *Early Poems,* a collection of Plath's work, was published as the May, 1967, issue of *Harvard Advocate;* fifty of her early unpublished poems appeared in the *Times Literary Supplement,* July 31, 1969.

NOVELS

(Under pseudonym Victoria Lucas; and illustrator) *The Bell Jar,* Heinemann, 1963, published under Plath's real name, Faber, 1965, Harper, 1971.

OTHER

Three Women: A Monologue for Three Voices (radio play; broadcast on British Broadcasting Corp. in 1962), limited edition, Turret Books, 1968.

Letters Home: Correspondence, 1950-1963, selected and edited with a commentary by Plath's mother, Aurelia Schober Plath, Harper, 1975.

Johnny Panic and the Bible of Dreams: And Other Prose Writings, edited by Ted Hughes, Faber, 1977, published as *Johnny Panic and the Bible of Dreams: Short Stories, Prose, and Diary Excerpts,* Harper, 1979.

A Day in June: An Uncollected Short Story, Embers Handpress, 1981.

The Journals of Sylvia Plath, edited by Frances McCullough and Ted Hughes, Dial, 1982.

Above the Oxbow: Selected Writings, Catawba Press (Northampton, MA), 1985.

Contributor to *Seventeen, Christian Science Monitor, Mademoiselle, Harper's, Nation, Atlantic, Poetry, London Magazine,* and other publications. Significant collections of Plath's manuscripts, journals, and other papers are kept at Indiana University and Smith College.

■ Adaptations

The Bell Jar was adapted into a film directed by Larry Peerce, Avco Embassy Pictures, 1978; *Letters Home* was adapted into a play by Rose Leiman Goldemberg and staged in 1979; a recording of Plath reading poems collected in *The Colossus, Ariel, Crossing the Water, Collected Poems,* and *Letters Home* is available from Caedmon.

■ Sidelights

Poet and novelist Sylvia Plath is remembered not only for her dark and confessional poems but also for her tragic death, which cut short a promising literary career. Plath grew up in the 1950s, a time when many women struggled to assert their identities in a society that did not as yet recognize women as equals. This struggle is reflected in her only novel, the autobiographical *Bell Jar,* which critics generally believe is based on Plath's own experience. Popular with young adult audiences, *The Bell Jar* allows the reader to better understand the poet's personal conflicts, which inspired her famous confessional poetry and ultimately led to her death. Plath's often angry verse and the circumstances surrounding her death, a suicide, have led people to associate her with the darker side of life. Nevertheless, Plath also created two lighthearted books for young children, both published after her death.

Plath was born in 1932 in Jamaica Plain, Massachusetts, at a time when women had limited options as to what they were allowed to do with their lives. But instead of accepting the traditional role of housewife and mother, Plath desired a career in a male-dominated field. The resistance she met in pursuing this goal and her battles with more private demons caused the poet to suffer recurring depression and several breakdowns. In an article in *Contemporary Literature,* Marjorie G. Perloff wrote that it's "beautifully ironic that Sylvia Plath, who never heard of Women's Liberation ... has written one of the most acute analyses [*The Bell Jar*] of the feminist problem that we have in contemporary fiction." In a discussion of Plath's verses, Joyce Carol Oates also commented in an article that appeared in *Southern Review:* "All of this appears to be contemporary, but Sylvia Plath's poems are in fact the clearest, most precise (because most private) expression of an old moral predicament that has become unbearable now in the mid-twentieth century." The author summarized her desires more poetically in *The Bell Jar:* "The last thing I wanted," she wrote, "was ... to be the place an arrow

Marilyn Hassett starred as protagonist Esther Greenwood in the film production of *The Bell Jar,* Plath's autobiographical novel of a brilliant young woman's spiraling descent into madness.

shoots off from. I wanted ... to shoot off in all directions myself."

Plath was the first child born to Aurelia Schober and Otto Emil Plath. Days after her eighth birthday, her father died as a result of complications due to a long-undiagnosed case of diabetes mellitus. It was a loss that would profoundly influence the future poet. "The death of her father when Sylvia was only eight sadly altered [the stability of her family life]," wrote Elaine Kendall in a *Los Angeles Times Book Review* article, "and despite the best efforts of her extended family, that early loss would remain the central trauma of an otherwise happy girlhood." After her husband's death, Plath's mother took her daughter and son Warren with her to Wellesley, Massachusetts, where they lived with Plath's grandparents. Once there, Plath's mother took on teaching jobs to support the family.

Although her new life in Wellesley was not a bad one, Plath would forever maintain idyllic memories of those first years spent near the sea while her father was still alive. Kendall observed that, contrary to what one might expect, "the immediate result [of Plath's father's death] was not despair but achievement. No adolescence is entirely tranquil, but there is little in Sylvia Plath's history to presage her mental breakdown and early suicide." In fact, it was at the age of eight—around the same time as her father's death—that Plath's first published poem appeared in the *Boston Traveller.* She wrote steadily throughout her childhood and once described her early work, as A. Alvarez recalled in a radio obituary published in *TriQuarterly,* as being mostly about "birds, bees, spring, fall—all those subjects which are absolute gifts to the person who doesn't have any interior experience to write about." Plath published her first "mature" work while still a teenager. In 1950 the *Christian Science Monitor* accepted an essay she co-wrote with a classmate. That same day, she received an acceptance letter from *Seventeen,* to which she had submitted the story "And Summer Will Not Come Again."

After graduating summa cum laude from Smith College in Northampton, Massachusetts, Plath accepted a Fulbright scholarship to Cambridge University, where she earned a master's degree and met and married poet Ted Hughes. While Plath had had individual poems published in various periodicals for years, her first collection was not accepted by a publisher until 1960. That collection, *The Colossus,* is often critically measured against her later work, posthumously published in *Ariel, Crossing the Water,* and *Winter Trees.* The earlier poems are generally considered to be more painstakingly written, controlled, emotionally restrained, and written with a concern for technique. Plath was influenced by such poets as Robert Lowell—whose seminar at Boston University Plath audited in 1959—Marianne Moore, Elizabeth Bishop, William Butler Years, Theodore Roethke, and Ted Hughes, and she diligently strove to learn from their work. According to an essay by J. D. McClatchy published in Harold Bloom's *Sylvia Plath: Modern Critical Edition,* the young Plath was "an

From *The Bed Book*, written by Plath and illustrated by Emily Arnold McCully.

assiduous apprentice," who "put herself resolutely through the traditionalist paces." McClatchy quoted from an early interview Plath gave to Lee Anderson: "Technically," said the poet, "I like [poetry] to be extremely musical and lyrical, with a singing sound.... At first I started in strict forms [such as the sonnet and villanelle]—it's the easiest way for a beginner to get music ready-made.... I lean very strongly toward forms that are, I suppose, quite rigid in comparison certainly to free verse. I'm much happier when I know that all my sounds are echoing in different ways throughout the poem." Most of the poems included in *The Colossus* were written between 1956 and 1959, the first three years of her marriage to Hughes.

After *The Colossus,* Plath began to find her own voice in her poetry. "It is generally thought to be the poems in the posthumous *Ariel* [Plath's second collection] that are her most significant," according to Betty Abel in *Contemporary Review.* Alicia Ostriker wrote in *Language and Style* that Plath's work represents "the startling phenomenon of a poet finding her own voice in the space of a very few years." But in a more disturbing interpretation of Plath's growth, Paul West pointed out that the more intense and personal her poems became, the closer Plath crept toward depression and suicide. The verses she wrote toward the end of her life, West observed in *Book World,* "tell us how close you can go before you fall in."

Plath's most common themes include the tension between order and chaos, male-female relationships—especially as they relate to her father, pain, birth, rebirth, and death. Violence becomes an overriding element as her work progresses, but the issue of control is paramount throughout her writings from *The Bell Jar* to *Ariel.* In a 1962 interview quoted in *The Poet Speaks: Interviews with Contemporary Poets,* Plath herself said that she believed "one should be able to control and manipulate experiences, even the most terrifying, like madness, being tortured, this kind of experience, and one should be able to manipulate these experiences with an informed and an intelligent mind. I think that personal experience is very important, but certainly it shouldn't be a kind of shut-box and mirror-looking, narcissistic experience.... [It] should be *relevant,* and relevant to the larger things ... such as Hiroshima and Dachau and so on."

Though it is for her poetry that Plath is most often admired and written about, her sole novel has generated much critical attention as well, not to mention a large audience that includes many teenage readers. Critics generally believe that *The Bell Jar* echoes the significant events and personal encounters in Plath's life during the summer of her junior year at Smith College. It was at that time that she won a one-month guest editorship at *Mademoiselle* magazine in New York City, along with eleven other winners from colleges and universities all over the United States. The brief editorship was extremely stressful on Plath, who found herself doubting her abilities because she was unable to satisfy her "capricious and demanding" senior editor, as Kendall

described Plath's supervisor. Her feelings of inadequacy were further exacerbated after she returned home to Massachusetts and learned that she had been denied admission to a summer fiction writing program at Harvard. Plath became severely depressed and underwent electro-shock treatments that did little or nothing to relieve her condition. Her subsequent attempt to commit suicide by swallowing sleeping pills failed, however, and she was sent to a therapist until she was well enough to return to college.

In the novel, Plath becomes Esther Greenwood, a college student who has just arrived in New York with several other young women to work at *Ladies Day* magazine "for a month, expenses paid, and piles and piles of free bonuses, like ballet tickets and passes to fashion shows and hair stylings at a famous expensive salon and chances to meet successful people in the field of our desire and advice about what to do with our particular complexions." Indeed, Plath received similar perks while working at *Mademoiselle,* including the chance to interview novelist and short story writer Elizabeth Bowen and poet Marianne Moore. But to Plath the whole experience was an overwhelming whirlwind of new activities, including a frantic night life, a bout of ptomaine poisoning—suffered by all who consumed the crabmeat salad at an ad agency's luncheon—and the drudge work of a guest managing editor, all of which is described in the novel, though some parts are more fictionalized than others.

Throughout the novel, Esther worries about her looks and ability to attract men and constantly compares herself to other women around her. She feels ambivalent about her intellectual and creative ambitions and entertains doubts about whether they will get in the way of her finding a husband, which is what the society she lives in ultimately expects a nice, intelligent young woman to do. Critics point to this conflict as a major theme in all of Plath's writing. And the conflict between living and creating art—a popular theme among artists in general—is even more intense because she is a woman. As Pamela J. Annas wrote in *A Disturbance in Mirrors: The Poetry of Sylvia Plath,* "to identify oneself as a woman poet ... was to admit that you did not expect to be taken seriously. Even the most cursory survey of American literary criticism yields examples of negative and patronizing pronouncements based on [gender]. Yet the themes of Plath's strongest poetry are clearly based on her experience as a woman poet trying to do creative work ... in a world which did not take women's creativity seriously."

The novel that fictionalizes these occurrences wasn't written by Plath until 1961, about seven years after the events it recounts. There were a number of factors that kept her from writing her novel. After marrying Ted Hughes and earning her master's degree at Cambridge, she and her new husband returned to the United States, where Plath taught freshman English at Smith College. They then moved to Boston before returning to England at the end of 1959. In addition to her frequent moves, Plath's life was filled with the duties of being a new mother, and she also suffered from poor health. In the course of only a couple of years, the poet suffered from a miscarriage, an appendectomy, and constant bouts with sinusitis. Still, she managed to continue publishing her poetry, all the while delaying work on her novel.

Early reviews of *The Bell Jar* reflected a variety of reactions. One of the most common was to compare it to J. D. Salinger's novel of a young man's attempt to reconcile himself with the world, *The Catcher in the Rye*. Saul Maloff, in a 1971 *New Republic* review, saw the novel as incomplete without considering her poetry, suggesting that together they compose a sort of autobiography: "She laid out the elements of her life, one after the other, and left to the late poems the necessary work of imagining and creating it." But some reviewers felt the novel was a weak effort. For example, *Prairie Schooner* critic Linda Ray Pratt preferred the later poems, calling *The Bell Jar* an "early and unsatisfactory novel which never gets below the surface of its real materials." On the other hand, Howard Moss wrote in a *New Yorker* article: "Its material, after all, is what has been transcended. It is a frightening book, and if it ends on too optimistic a note as both fiction and postdated fact, its real terror lies elsewhere. Though we share every shade of feeling that leads to Esther's attempts at suicide, there is not the slightest insight ... into suicide itself. That may be why it bears the stamp of authority. Reading it, we are up against the raw experience of nightmare, not the analysis or understanding of it."

Plath suffered a major emotional blow when Hughes, the poet she once thought would make the ideal spouse, left her for another woman. Separated from her husband and living with her two young children in a London flat in which William Butler Yeats once resided, Plath spent the final two months of her life completing *The Bell Jar*, beginning a second novel, and writing most of the poems later included in *Ariel* and *Winter Trees*. Abandoning her careful and technically precise style for spur-of-the-moment writing, the poet poured her soul into her final poems. Alvarez quoted Plath's note to the BBC in 1962: "These new poems of mine have one thing in common. They were all written at about four in the morning—that still blue, almost eternal hour before the baby's cry, before the glassy music of the milkman, settling his bottles." The *Winter Trees* poems are particularly full of Plath's pain, as they allude to the circumstances of how her marriage failed. This event, according to Ellen Rosenberg in the *Concise Dictionary of American Literary Biography*, left Plath "bitter and devastated." "Although her health was poor, her responsibilities for the children demanding, and her emotional state depressed," Rosenberg later wrote, "[Plath] continued to write and to struggle for a stable and meaningful life. Yet she seemed unable to throw off the effects of the past months." Too depressed to continue living, Plath turned on the gas in her kitchen and asphyxiated herself on February 11, 1963.

Plath's tragic death led to an increased focus on the work she left behind. Several volumes of poetry were published after her death, and her *Collected Poems* won the Pulitzer Prize in 1982. Also among her posthumous works were two works for children; both were written in 1959, shortly before her first child was born. *The Bed Book*, published in 1976, is a clever verse telling of all sorts of unusual beds, from a "Bird-Watching Bed" to a "Tank Bed." Martha Davis Beck noted in *Hungry Mind Review* that Plath wrote for her audience "with great wit and lightness of spirit." Praising the "bouncy" verse, Michele Landsberg noted in *Entertainment Weekly* that from a poet of Plath's reputation "we expect and get some wonderful flights of invention," including an elephant bed, a pocket-sized bed, and an underwater bed. "Plath's poem is inventive and reads aloud like a dream," *Booklist* reviewer Betsy Hearne stated, while *Horn Book* contributor Anita Silvey concluded that *The Bed Book* is "one of the few good bedtime books to be published in recent years."

Another cheerful tale is related in *The It-Doesn't-Matter Suit*, published in 1996. Max Nix wants to own his own suit, one appropriate for doing everything from fishing to playing. When a brand-new "woolly whiskery brand-new mustard-yellow suit" mysteriously arrives at his house, his father and six older brothers wear the garment before Max finally gets his wish. The book "is a neat, discrete, sunny snippet," Nicci Gerrard wrote in the *Observer Review* (London), calling the overall effect "sweet." A *Publishers Weekly* critic, while finding the story one of "bland hopefulness," added that Plath "offers some clever phrases" in telling Max's story. A *Books* reviewer found the work "a delight to read," and Gerrard believed that the story helped undermine the image of Plath as "a tragic ghost who haunts our culture." While "her death engulfs her death-seduced art," the critic concluded, "small pieces of happiness like this little book remind us of her life."

■ Works Cited

Abel, Betty, "The Troubled Life and Verse of Sylvia Plath," *Contemporary Review,* March, 1988, pp. 166-67.

Alvarez, A. "Sylvia Plath," *TriQuarterly,* fall, 1966, p. 66.

Annas, Pamela J., *A Disturbance in Mirrors: The Poetry of Sylvia Plath,* Greenwood Press, 1988, pp. 158-61.

Beck, Martha Davis, review of *The Bed Book, Hungry Mind Review,* Summer, 1993, p. C18.

Bloom, Harold, editor, *Sylvia Plath: Modern Critical Edition,* Chelsea House, 1989, pp. 80-81.

Gerrard, Nicci, "The Primose Plath," *Observer Review,* February 18, 1996, p. 15.

Hearne, Betsy, review of *The Bed Book, Booklist,* September 1, 1976, pp. 41-42.

Review of *The It-Doesn't-Matter Suit, Books,* February-March, 1996, p. 27.

Review of *The It-Doesn't-Matter Suit, Publishers Weekly,* May 20, 1996, p. 258.

Kendall, Elaine, "The Foiled Biography of a Fallen Poet," *Los Angeles Times Book Review,* January 31, 1988, p. 12.

Landsberg, Michele, review of *The Bed Book, Entertainment Weekly,* February 23, 1990, p. 86.

Maloff, Saul, "Waiting for the Voice to Crack," *New Republic*, May 8, 1971, pp. 33-35.

Moss, Howard, "Dying: An Introduction," *New Yorker*, July 10, 1971, p. 75.

Oates, Joyce Carol, "The Death Throes of Romanticism: The Poems of Sylvia Plath," *Southern Review*, Volume 9, 1973, p. 509.

Orr, Peter, editor, *The Poet Speaks: Interviews with Contemporary Poets*, Routledge & Kegan Paul, 1966.

Ostriker, Alicia, "'Fact' as Style: The Americanization of Sylvia," *Language and Style*, winter, 1968, p. 202.

Perloff, Marjorie G., "'A Ritual for Being Born Twice': Sylvia Plath's *The Bell Jar*," *Contemporary Literature*, autumn, 1972, p. 512.

Plath, Sylvia, *The Bell Jar*, Harper, 1971.

Pratt, Linda Ray, "The Spirit of Blackness is In Us," *Prairie Schooner*, spring, 1973, pp. 87-90.

Rosenberg, Ellen, "Sylvia Plath," *Concise Dictionary of American Literary Biography: 1941-1968*, Gale, 1987, pp. 408-21.

Silvey, Anita, review of *The Bed Book*, *Horn Book*, October, 1976, p. 493.

West, Paul, "Fido Littlesoul, the Bowel's Familiar," *Book World*, January 9, 1972, p. 8.

■ For More Information See

BOOKS

Aird, Eileen, *Sylvia Plath: Her Life and Work*, Oliver & Boyd, 1973.

Alexander, Paul, editor, *Ariel Ascending: Writings about Sylvia Plath*, Harper, 1985.

Alexander, Paul, *Rough Magic: A Biography of Sylvia Plath*, Viking, 1991.

Barnard, Caroline King, *Sylvia Plath*, Twayne, 1978.

Broe, Mary Lynn, *Protean Poetic: The Poetry of Sylvia Plath*, University of Missouri Press, 1980.

Bundtzen, Lynda K., *Plath's Incarnations: Woman and the Creative Process*, University of Michigan Press, 1983.

Butscher, Edward, *Sylvia Plath: Method and Madness*, Seabury Press, 1976.

Hardwick, Elizabeth, *Seduction and Betrayal: Women and Literature*, Random House, 1974, pp. 120-21.

Holbrook, David, *Sylvia Plath: Poetry and Existence*, Athlone, 1976.

Kroll, Judith, *Chapters in a Mythology: The Poetry of Sylvia Plath*, Harper, 1976.

Lane, Gary, *Sylvia Plath: New Views on the Poetry*, Johns Hopkins University Press, 1979.

Melander, Ingrid, *The Poetry of Sylvia Plath: A Study of Themes*, Almqvist & Wiksell, 1972.

Newman, Charles, editor, *The Art of Sylvia Plath: A Symposium*, Indiana University Press, 1970.

Poetry Criticism, Volume 1, Gale, 1990.

Steiner, Nancy Hunter, *A Closer Look at Ariel: A Memory of Sylvia Plath*, Harper's Magazine Press, 1973.

Stevenson, Anne, *Bitter Fame: A Life of Sylvia Plath*, Houghton, 1989.

Uroff, Margaret D., *Sylvia Plath and Ted Hughes*, University of Illinois Press, 1979.

Wagner, Linda, editor, *Critical Essays on Sylvia Plath*, G.K. Hall, 1984.

PERIODICALS

American Spectator, January, 1992.

Atlantic Monthly, May, 1982, pp. 104-105.

Bulletin of the Center for Children's Books, February, 1997, p. 96.

Commentary, April, 1974, pp. 47-52.

Encounter, August, 1979, p. 42.

Harper's, January, 1972, pp. 89-91.

Nation, January 16, 1982, pp. 52-53; March 23, 1992, p. 385.

People, December 4, 1989, p. 99.*

* * *

PRESNALL, Judith (Ann) Janda 1943-

■ Personal

Born April 2, 1943, in Milwaukee, WI; daughter of Edward G. (a metal-casting pattern maker) and Tess (a homemaker, seamstress, and retail salesperson) Janda; married Lance O. Presnall (an engineer), January 21, 1967; children: Kaye Lynn, Kory Lee. *Education:* University of Wisconsin, Whitewater, B.A., 1967. Attended the University of California, Los Angeles. *Religion:* Roman Catholic. *Hobbies and other interests:* Reading, golfing, traveling, watching suspense movies, "caring for all of God's creatures."

■ Addresses

Home and office—6311 Crebs Ave., Reseda, CA 91335. *Electronic mail*—jjpresnall@aol.com.

■ Career

Writer. Kelly Services, Milwaukee, WI, secretary, 1963-66; John Marshall Jr. Sr. High School, Milwaukee, WI, business teacher, 1967-69; Pierce Community College, Woodland Hills, CA, typing teacher, 1982-86; Merit College, Van Nuys, CA, typing teacher, 1984-1988. Volunteer in newborn nursery at Tarzana Hospital, Tarzana, CA, 1995—. *Member:* Society of Children's Book Writers and Illustrators, Southern California Council on Literature for Children and Young People, California Writers Club (vice-president, 1994-96), Alpha Gamma Delta.

■ Awards, Honors

First place award, Southern California Society of Children's Book Writers and Illustrators, 1992, for *Queen Liliuokalani;* first place award, Ventura/Santa Barbara Society of Children's Book Writers and Illustrators, 1994, for *Failure Is Impossible: Susan B. Anthony;* Outstanding Science Book for Children, National Science Teachers Association/Children's Book Council, 1994, for *Animals That Glow;* Jack London Award,

JUDITH JANDA PRESNALL

California Writers Club, 1997, for meritorious service; first place award, Southern California Society of Children's Book Writers and Illustrators, 1997, for *The Giant Panda*.

■ Writings

Animals That Glow, Franklin Watts, 1993.
Animal Skeletons, illustrated by Kristin Kest, Franklin Watts, 1995.
Rachel Carson ("The Importance Of" series), Lucent, 1995.
Artificial Organs ("Overview" series), Lucent, 1996.
Circuses: Under the Big Top, Franklin Watts, 1996.
The Giant Panda ("Endangered Animals and Habitats" series) Lucent, 1998.

Contributor of articles to *Kite Tales* newsletter, *Bear Essential News for Kids* newspaper, and *My Friend* magazine; author of unpublished manuscripts, *Queen Liliuokalani* and *Failure Is Impossible: Susan B. Anthony.*

■ Sidelights

Judith Janda Presnall told *SATA:* "I have always loved the smell of books and spending hours in a cozy library. As a child, I rode my bike to the library which was about a mile away. During the 1950s you could only whisper in libraries, so they were quiet places, unlike today's large bustling, computerized rooms . . . .

"In 1985, while I was teaching at a court reporting college, I yearned to add a different dimension in my

life, so I took a general writing class at a local community college. The instructor gave us an assignment each week, and I found that most of my writing was geared for children. At first, I wrote all fiction stories, mostly picture books and stories for magazines. Being unsuccessful in selling my 'talking-animal' stories, my critique group suggested that I try writing nonfiction. In 1987, I entered and won my first contest. Writing nonfiction requires much library research, so I am back to the comfortable surroundings of my childhood . . . . "

Presnall's love for children and animals sparked her interest in writing children's books with animal and nature topics. One such book is *Animals That Glow,* published in 1993. Presnall's first book informs young children about the variety of bioluminescent animals, including fireflies, millipedes, squid, and fish. The author explains why these animals produce light, whether it's for survival purposes or for attracting prey. Presnall also addresses how bioluminescent animals are beneficial in detecting some human diseases and contamination in water. *School Library Journal* contributor Cynthia M. Sturgis praises the book for being "an informative and well-organized source for reports." Addressing the diagrams and useful captions in *Animals That Glow,* Carolyn Phelan of *Booklist* adds that the "book offers an accessible introduction to an intriguing subject."

"Besides obtaining information from books and periodicals," Presnall continued, "I gather information through on-location visits and personal interviews. This gives

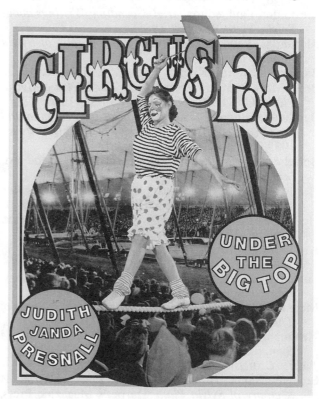

Presnall explores the excitement of a circus performer's life under the big top.

my books the authenticity that readers deserve. Writing nonfiction is exciting and an on-going learning experience. I try to give readers the sense of being 'on the scene' when they read my books...."

Presnall traveled to the eastern United States to do research for her second book, *Rachel Carson,* published in 1995. Rachel Carson is included in Lucent's "The Importance Of" series because of her crusade to bring public awareness to the dangers of chemicals. Presnall visited Carson's childhood home, her alma mater, John Hopkins University, and spoke with several of her co-workers. According to *School Library Journal* contributor Sandra L. Doggett, *Rachel Carson* is "well-researched" and "easy to read." A reviewer for *Appraisal: Science Books for Young People* contends that "the book could be a particularly good choice for students who like both science and writing."

"For *Artificial Organs,* I had the privilege of meeting Dr. Willem J. Kolff in his Salt Lake City laboratory," Presnall relayed to *SATA.* Dr. Kolff was the inventor of the first artificial kidney used on humans. While in Utah, I also met doctors who are performing scientific studies and constructing the artificial eye, heart, and arm...."

"When I was writing *Circuses: Under the Big Top,* I attended all types of events. I saw small one-ring tented circuses, huge three-ring arena-types, and the kind of circus that features contemporary high-tech theatrics and daring human acrobatics. I enjoyed interviewing some of the circus stars...." Presnall's *Circuses: Under the Big Top,* published in 1996, traces the history of circuses as far back as ancient civilization. Part of the research involved speaking to long-time circus performer Gunther Gebel-Williams and being treated to an evening "animal walk." According to *School Library*

Journal contributor George Gleason, *Circuses* is "colorful and informative," and can be enjoyed as "pleasure reading."

"I work every day to expand my writing career," Presnall explained. "When I write, I compose in longhand in a large spiral notebook. Next, I input the information into the computer. This becomes my first rough draft. It is rewritten many times before it gets to an editor's desk...."

"My advice to aspiring writers is to persist. It took me four years and 250 rejections before I sold anything! But when I visit schools and talk to children about my books and the writing process, it was well worth the effort. I have a special feeling of satisfaction to see my books in schools and libraries and to hear a child's excitement about a book that I have authored."

■ **Works Cited**

Doggett, Sandra L., review of *Rachel Carson, School Library Journal,* January, 1995, p. 142.

Gleason, George, review of *Circuses: Under the Big Top, School Library Journal,* March, 1997, p. 195.

Phelan, Carolyn, review of *Animals That Glow, Booklist,* May 15, 1993, p. 1690.

Review of *Rachel Carson, Appraisal: Science Books for Young People,* autumn, 1995, pp. 78-79.

Sturgis, Cynthia M., review of *Animals That Glow, School Library Journal,* June, 1993, p. 122.

■ **For More Information See**

PERIODICALS

Appraisal: Science Books for Young People, fall, 1993, p. 56.

Booklist, January 15, 1995, p. 939.

S

SAN SOUCI, Daniel

■ Personal

Married; wife's name Loretta; children: Yvette, Justin, Noel.

■ Addresses

Home—Oakland, CA.

■ Career

Children's book illustrator and author.

■ Awards, Honors

New York Times Best Illustrated Book, 1978, for *The Legend of Scarface: A Blackfoot Indian Tale;* Western Writers Award, 1985, for *Trapped in the Sliprock Canyon* by Gloria Skurzynski; Gold Medallion, 1986, for *Potter, Come Fly to the First of the Earth* by Walter Wangerin; Aesop Accolade List, American Folklore Society, 1995, for *The Gifts of Wali Dad: A Tale of India and Pakistan.*

■ Writings

SELF-ILLUSTRATED

North Country Night, Doubleday, 1990.
Country Road, Doubleday, 1993.

ILLUSTRATOR; WRITTEN BY ROBERT D. SAN SOUCI

The Legend of Scarface: A Blackfeet Indian Tale, Doubleday, 1978.
Son of Sedna, Doubleday, 1981.
The Brave Little Tailor, Doubleday, 1982.
The Legend of Sleepy Hollow (retelling), Doubleday, 1986.
Robert D. San Souci's The Six Swans, Simon and Schuster, 1988.
The Christmas Ark, Doubleday, 1991.
Feathertop: Based on a Tale by Nathaniel Hawthorne, Doubleday, 1992.

Sootface: An Ojibwa Cinderella Story, Delacorte, 1994.
Young Merlin, Dell, 1996.

ILLUSTRATOR

Phyllis Root, *Hidden Places,* Raintree, 1983.
White Deer of Autumn, *Ceremony—in the Circle of Life,* Raintree, 1983.
Gloria Skurzynski, *Trapped in the Sliprock Canyon,* Lothrop, 1984.
Morell Gipson, reteller, *Rip Van Winkle,* Doubleday, 1984.
The Bedtime Book, J. Messner, 1985.
Walter Wangerin, *Potter, Come Fly to the First of the Earth,* Chariot Books, 1985, reprinted as *Potter,* Augsburg Fortress, 1994.
Freya Littledale, adaptor, *The Little Mermaid,* Scholastic, 1986.
The Mother Goose Book, Little Simon, 1986.
Lilian Moore, reteller, *The Ugly Duckling,* Scholastic, 1987.
Diane Arico, compiler and editor, *A Season of Joy: Favorite Stories and Poems for Christmas,* Doubleday, 1987.
Josepha Sherman, *Vassilisa the Wise: A Tale of Medieval Russia,* Harcourt Brace, 1988.
Diane Arico, compiler and editor, *Easter Treasures: Favorite Stories and Poems for the Season,* Doubleday, 1989.
Margaret Hodges, reteller, *The Golden Deer,* Charles Scribner's Sons, 1992.
Josephine Haskell, *A Possible Tree,* Macmillan, 1993.
William O. Douglas, *Muir of the Mountains,* Sierra Club Books for Children, 1994.
Aaron Shepard, reteller, *The Gifts of Wali Dad: A Tale of India and Pakistan,* Atheneum, 1995.
David F. Birchman, *Jigsaw Jackson,* Lothrop, Lee & Shepard, 1996.
Jonathan London, *Red Wolf Country,* Dutton, 1996.
Barbara Mitchell, *Waterman's Child,* Lothrop, Lee & Shepard, 1996.

Daniel San Souci's illustrations for his brother Robert's retelling of a Native American Cinderella tale reflect his comprehensive research into mid-eighteenth-century Ojibwa village life. (From *Sootface*, written by Robert D. San Souci.)

■ Sidelights

Daniel San Souci is a highly regarded children's book illustrator who has occasionally written books as well. *Country Road,* one of his few self-illustrated picture books, tells a quiet, contemplative story about a boy's walk through the country with his father. The accompanying illustrations "are lavish double-page spreads done in realistic watercolors that highlight the animals" the two encounter on their walk, remarked Valerie Lennox in *School Library Journal.* "There's not much story," admitted Hazel Rochman in *Booklist,* but the critic added that this may well be San Souci's message to the young reader—to pay attention to the natural world, here present in the artist's detailed paintings. San Souci has also illustrated several picture books for works written by his brother, Robert D. San Souci, among them *Feathertop,* an adaptation of a tale by Nathaniel Hawthorne, *Sootface,* a rendering of an Ojibwa folktale, and *The Christmas Ark,* an original story about a Christmas celebration held at sea during the California gold rush.

In *Feathertop,* Mother Rigby, the town witch, turns her scarecrow into a handsome young man and sends him off to court the judge's daughter as a trick. But the scarecrow and the girl fall in love and the girl convinces Mother Rigby to make the transformation permanent. A *Publishers Weekly* contributor noted that the author takes constructive liberties with the original tale, and the illustrations "effectively capture the garb and architectural details of mid-eighteenth-century New England." The pictures add "brilliant colors and lively action" to the "smoothly flowing oral quality" of the text, according to Shirley Wilton in *School Library Journal.* In the San Souci brothers' *Sootface,* they present a new telling of an Ojibwa version of the Cinderella story in which the kindness and good-heartedness of Sootface win for her the love of a great invisible warrior. As with *Feathertop,* reviewers of *Sootface* found this a successful picture book. Vanessa Elder, writing in *School Library Journal,* appreciated the book's "lively" text and "full-page watercolors [that] dramatically convey the natural woodland setting" as well as the personalities of individual characters. *Booklist* contributor Carolyn Phelan observed that although this tale has been adapted many times before, this version is nonetheless "a satisfying picture book for reading aloud or alone" that could contribute to classroom projects on Native American folklore.

In this lighthearted picture book, a farmer goes on the road to exhibit his jigsaw-solving prowess, then finds that fame and fortune can't eliminate his homesickness. (From *Jigsaw Jackson,* written by David F. Birchman and illustrated by Daniel San Souci.)

Daniel San Souci has also illustrated books for a number of other children's authors. One such work is *Vassilisa the Wise,* a folktale set in medieval Russia, adapted by Josepha Sherman. In the story a beautiful and clever woman tricks the evil Prince Vladimir into releasing her husband from prison. In *Publishers Weekly,* a reviewer remarked on the book's "stately watercolors, rich in costume and architectural detail." Mary M. Burns, a contributor to *Horn Book,* likewise stated that San Souci's illustrations are "elegant and dynamic, large and authoritative, and reflect the drama and the setting." San Souci's watercolor illustrations for Josephine Haskell Aldridge's story *A Possible Tree* were also praised by reviewers. The book presents a number of animals who have been driven away from a farm as pests. Each in turn is drawn to a particular fir tree where they all nest peacefully together throughout the winter. This is "a small story made large by well-written prose and exquisite art," remarked Jane Marino in *School Library Journal.*

The Gifts of Wali Dad, an Indian and Pakistani folktale retold by Aaron Shepard, tells the story of a man whose natural frugality results in his accumulation of some wealth, with which he buys a gold bracelet that he sends to the most noble lady that can be found. She sends a gift back in return, which Wali Dad sends off to the noblest man. This exchange leads to the eventual marriage of the two gift recipients and Wali Dad's happy return to his simple life as a grass-cutter. "The illustrations convey an atmosphere of radiating generosity," remarked Mary Harris Veeder approvingly in her *Booklist* review. "Full of interesting details, the pictures support and enlarge upon the text," asserted Marilyn Taniguchi in *School Library Journal.* Another highly successful joint effort was *Red Wolf Country,* written by Jonathan London. The story relates the experiences of two wolves searching for shelter and then giving birth to a litter of cubs. "Breathtaking paintings and a dramatic text make this wildlife adventure a real stand-out," enthused Joy Fleishhacker in *School Library Journal.* A *Publishers Weekly* contributor found that the illustrator's "elegant" pictures combined with the text produce "perhaps the most compatible collaboration yet in London's series of wildlife tales."

San Souci also contributed the illustrations to David F. Birchman's *Jigsaw Jackson,* a lighthearted picture book about a farmer who goes on the road to exhibit his jigsaw-solving prowess one winter. The man finds fame and fortune, but eventually misses his animals and returns home. "Birchman relates the story with gusto, its gleeful excesses mirrored in San Souci's merry watercolors," remarked a reviewer for *Publishers Weekly*. Likewise, Christina Linz, a contributor to *School Library Journal*, commented on the author's "hilarious scenarios," adding that "there's just enough fantasy blended with realism to create some pretty hysterical pictures."

San Souci is an effective and admired illustrator whose watercolor paintings are often described as handsome creations that augment the stories they illustrate. Frequently praised for his realistic yet expressive depiction of the natural world, particularly in such works as his own *Country Road*, and in brother Robert San Souci's *Sootface*, the artist has also garnered positive critical attention for his comical rendering of characters in Robert San Souci's *Feathertop* and Aaron Shepard's *The Gifts of Wali Dad*, and for his atmospheric decorative details in such works as Josepha Sherman's *Vassilisa the Wise*.

■ Works Cited

Burns, Mary M., review of *Vassilisa the Wise, Horn Book,* July, 1988, p. 507.

Elder, Vanessa, review of *Sootface, School Library Journal,* November, 1994, p. 101.

Review of *Feathertop, Publishers Weekly,* November 2, 1992, pp. 70-71.

Fleishhacker, Joy, review of *Red Wolf Country, School Library Journal,* March, 1996, p. 178.

Review of *Jigsaw Jackson, Publishers Weekly,* April 15, 1996, p. 68.

Lennox, Valerie, review of *Country Road, School Library Journal,* March, 1994, p. 208.

Linz, Christina, review of *Jigsaw Jackson, School Library Journal,* July 1996, p. 56.

Marino, Jane, review of *A Possible Tree, School Library Journal,* October, 1993, p. 41.

Phelan, Carolyn, review of *Sootface, Booklist,* October 15, 1994, p. 433.

Review of *Red Wolf Country, Publishers Weekly,* January 1, 1996, p. 70.

Rochman, Hazel, review of *Country Road, Booklist,* October 1, 1993, p. 354.

Rochman, Hazel, review of *Red Wolf Country, Booklist,* January 1, 1996, p. 84.

Taniguchi, Marilyn, review of *The Gifts of Wali Dad, School Library Journal,* August, 1995, p. 138.

Review of *Vassilisa the Wise, Publishers Weekly,* May 13, 1988, p. 374.

Veeder, Mary Harris, review of *The Gifts of Wali Dad, Booklist,* May 1, 1995, p. 1578.

Wilton, Shirley, review of *Feathertop, School Library Journal,* December, 1992, p. 90.

■ For More Information See

PERIODICALS

Booklist, October 1, 1993, p. 352.

Publishers Weekly, September 20, 1993, p. 40.*

SAUNDERS, Susan 1945-
(Sara Hughes)

■ Personal

Born April 14, 1945, in San Antonio, TX; daughter of George S. (a rancher) and Brooksie (Hughes) Saunders; married John J. Cirigliano, September 7, 1969 (divorced, 1976). *Education:* Barnard College, B.A., 1966. *Hobbies and other interests:* Gardening, animals.

■ Addresses

Home—P.O. Box 736, Westhampton, NY 11977. *Agent*—Amy Berkower, Writer's House, Inc., 21 West 26th St., New York, NY 10010.

■ Career

John Wiley, New York City, copyeditor, 1966-67; CBS/Columbia House, New York City, 1967-70, began as proofreader and assistant to production manager, became copyeditor, then staff writer; Greystone Press, New York City, copyeditor, 1970-72; *Lighting Design and Application* (trade magazine), New York City, associate editor, 1972-76; Visual Information Systems (radio and video production company), New York City, editor, 1976-77; Random House, New York City, editor, 1977-80; freelance writer, scriptwriter, editor, copy editor, proofreader, and researcher, 1980—. Professional ceramicist. *Member:* Authors Guild.

■ Awards, Honors

Notable Children's Trade Book in the Field of Social Studies, National Council for the Social Studies/Children's Book Council, 1982, for *Fish Fry.*

■ Writings

Wales' Tale, illustrated by Marilyn Hirsh, Viking, 1980.

A Sniff in Time, illustrated by Michael Mariano, Atheneum, 1982.

Fish Fry, illustrated by S. D. Schindler, Viking, 1982.

Rat's Picnic, illustrated by Robert Byrd, Dutton, 1984.

Dorothy and the Magic Belt, illustrated by David Rose, Random House, 1985.

The Get Along Gang and the Treasure Map, illustrated by Carol Hudson, Scholastic, 1985.

Dolly Parton: Country Goin' to Town (nonfiction), Viking, 1985.

Mystery Cat, Bantam, 1986.

Sir Silver Swine and the Missing Rain, Scholastic, Inc., 1986.

The Daring Rescue of Marlon the Swimming Pig, illustrated by Gail Owens, Random House, 1986.

Mystery Cat and the Chocolate Trap, Bantam, 1986.

The Right House for Rabbit, Western Publishing, 1986.

Mr. Nighttime and the Dream Machine, Scholastic, 1986.

The Golden Goose, illustrated by Isadore Seltzer, Scholastic, 1987.

Margaret Mead: The World Was Her Family (nonfiction), Viking, 1987.

(Adaptor) Johanna Spyri, *Heidi*, Troll Associates, 1988.

The Mystery of the Hard Luck Rodeo, Random House, 1989.

Tent Show, illustrated by Diane Allison, Dutton, 1990.

Jackrabbit and the Prairie Fire: The Story of a Black-Tailed Jackrabbit, Soundprints, 1991.

Seasons of a Red Fox, Soundprints, 1991.

Tyrone Goes to School, illustrated by Steve Bjoerkman, Dutton, 1992.

"CHOOSE YOUR OWN ADVENTURE" SERIES; PUBLISHED BY BANTAM

The Green Slime, 1982.

The Creature from Miller's Pond, 1983.

The Tower of London, 1984.

Runaway Spaceship, 1985.

Ice Cave, 1985.

Attack of the Monster Plants, 1986.

The Miss Liberty Caper, 1986.

Blizzard at Black Swan Inn, 1986.

The Haunted Halloween Party, 1986.

Light on Burro Mountain, 1986.

You Are Invisible, 1989.

"MORGAN SWIFT" SERIES; UNDER NAME SARA HUGHES; PUBLISHED BY RANDOM HOUSE

Morgan Swift and the Treasure of Crocodile Key, 1985.

Morgan Swift and the Kidnapped Goddess, 1985.

Morgan Swift and the Lake of Diamonds, 1986.

"BAD NEWS BUNNY" SERIES; ILLUSTRATED BY LARRY ROSS; PUBLISHED BY SIMON & SCHUSTER

Third-Prize Surprise, 1987.

Back to Nature, 1987.

Stop the Presses!, 1987.

"SLEEPOVER FRIENDS" SERIES; PUBLISHED BY SCHOLASTIC

Patti's Luck, 1987.

Starring Stephanie, 1987.

Kate's Surprise, 1987.

Patti's New Look, 1988.

Kate's Camp-out, 1988.

Lauren's Big Mix-up, 1988.

Stephanie Strikes Back, 1988.

Lauren's Treasure, 1988.

Patti's Last Sleepover?, 1988.

Stephanie's Family Secret, 1989.

Stephanie's Big Story, 1989.

Patti's Secret Wish, 1989.

Patti, 1989.

Stephanie, 1989.

Patti Gets Even, 1989.

Lauren's Sleepover Exchange, 1989.

Kate's Crush, 1989.

A Book of U.S. Presidents, 1989.

Lauren Takes Charge, 1989.

Kate's Sleepover Disaster, 1989.

Lauren I, 1990.

Starstruck Stephanie, 1990.

Trouble with Patti, 1990.

Lauren's New Friend, 1990.

Stephanie and the Wedding, 1990.

The New Kate, 1990.

Kate's Surprise Visitor, 1990.

Lauren's New Address, 1990.

Kate the Boss, 1990.

Lauren's Afterschool Job, 1990.

A Valentine for Patti, 1991.

Lauren's Double Disaster, 1991.

The New Stephanie, 1991.

"FIFTH GRADE S.T.A.R.S." SERIES; PUBLISHED BY KNOPF

Twin Trouble, 1989.

Rent-a-Star, 1989.

"PONY CAMP" SERIES; PUBLISHED BY HARPERCOLLINS

Pam's Trail, 1994.

Maxine's Blue Ribbon, 1994.

"DOUBLE R DETECTIVES" SERIES; PUBLISHED BY HARPERCOLLINS

The UFO Mystery, 1995.

Double R Detectives No. 3, 1997.

Double R Detectives No. 4, 1997.

"BLACK CAT CLUB" SERIES; PUBLISHED BY HARPERCOLLINS

The Ghost Who Ate Chocolate, illustrated by Jane Manning, 1996.

The Haunted Skateboard, illustrated by Manning, 1996.

Curse of the Cat Mummy, 1997.

The Ghost of Spirit Lake, 1997.

The Revenge of the Pirate Ghost, 1997.

The Phantom Pen-Pal, 1997.

■ Adaptations

The Daring Rescue of Marlon the Missing Pig was adapted for videocassette recording, 1990.

■ Sidelights

Texas-born writer Susan Saunders has branded her many books for preteen readers with her love of animals, her sense of humor, and her sensitivity to the interests of young people. "I was an only child for a long time and books were my favorite entertainment, especially fairy tales from other lands, preferably with wizards, elves, dark forests, and rushing rivers," Saunders once told *Something about the Author* (*SATA*). "South Texas is semi-arid, so forests and rivers were as wonderful to me as elves." Despite the lack of dense vegetation in rural Texas, Saunders never lacked for animal companions. "Animals were and are an important part of my life," she explained. "I grew up with horses, lots of dogs, tame deer, tame—more or less—jackrabbits, and once an armadillo who really didn't work out as a pet." Animals figure prominently in both Saunders' nonfiction works, such as 1991's *Seasons of a Red Fox*, picture books like *Wales' Tale* and *The Daring Rescue of Marlon the Swimming Pig*, and numerous installments in her series of novels for preteen readers, particularly the "Pony Camp" series inaugurated in 1994.

Wales' Tale, Saunders' first children's book, was published in 1980. In the story, a young girl on her way to the local market to sell vegetables encounters a talking donkey who requests her help in ending the spell that changed him from his original form of a handsome prince. After trying several conjurers, including a neighborhood fortune-teller, the girl and donkey meet up with a love-potion-maker who concocts a special potion that transforms the donkey Wales into ... a handsome Airedale hound! The girl is relieved: "She wasn't sure she was ready for a handsome prince in her life," writes Saunders, tongue in cheek. "But a dog named Wales was a different matter."

Magic also finds its way into Saunders' picture book *A Sniff in Time.* Bored by his uneventful life as a farmer, James longs for a way to leave his landlocked home. He is visited by a wizard who tells the farmer that he will eventually live on a boat; he also offers James the power to see into the future if he will but give him a bowl of hot soup. With only turnips to give his aged guest, James is granted an abridged wish—the power to smell into the future. His new gift proves difficult to harness—he smells fire where there is not one, and rain during a drought—but at last he becomes adept enough at foretelling the future that he earns a reward from the king—a boat, which James puts on a trailer and rolls to his farm, finally content with his lot. "A very good tale for the telling," Helen Gregory commented in her review for *School Library Journal.*

Animal characters figure prominently in Saunders' *The Daring Rescue of Marlon the Swimming Pig,* as a three-hundred-pound pig goes on the lam after he discovers that he is scheduled for a visit to the livestock auction. "Briskly paced action throughout this chapter book will delight young readers," according to *Booklist* contributor Philip Wilson. In *Tyrone Goes to School,* its time for obedience training for tail-wagging Tyrone, who gets straight A's in doggy school but promptly forgets his lessons once he is out the door. Fortunately, Tyrone's young owner, the equally distractable Robert, understands the problem—a short attention span—and a helpful teacher directs both puppy and master into a schedule that allows them to settle in to their studies. While noting that the story is "a little unlikely," a *Kirkus Reviews* commentator praised *Tyrone Goes to School* as "briskly told and mildly funny," and Stephanie Zvirin deemed it a "sprightly, easy-to-read tale" in her *Booklist* review.

Saunders has created several animal characters around which she has written a sequence of entertaining stories for young readers. The Bad News Bunny is featured in books such as *Third-Prize Surprise* and *Back to Nature.* Mystery Cat, known by his friends simply as "M. C.", is introduced to readers in Saunders' 1986 story *Mystery Cat,* where the adventurous feline tempts trouble by having a daytime home with Kelly Ann McCoy and chowing down in the evening in Hilary Barnett's family

Four nine-year-olds form the Black Cat ghost-hunting club in Susan Saunders' comic tale *The Ghost Who Ate Chocolate,* illustrated by Jane Manning.

kitchen. Finally the two girls, who each thought themselves the sole owner of M. C., meet each other and become friends, agreeing to share M. C. between them. Their friendship quickly changes into a partnership after M. C. discovers a stash of counterfeit money and the girls' amateur sleuthing gets them into serious trouble. More adventures follow in the sequel, *Mystery Cat and the Chocolate Trap,* as friends Kelly Ann and Hilary attempt to discover why M. C. and his new-found friend, a pure-bred Himalayan, come home smelling like chocolate.

Among Saunders' most popular books for young readers has been her *Tent Show,* which profiles the life of nine-year-old Ellie. Ellie is disappointed after her older sister drops out of college to get married, giving up opportunities for education and a career. When she vents her feelings about her sister's choices to an elderly actress named Sara during the wedding reception, the woman tells Ellie about her own childhood, and helps the young girl to accept the fact that she cannot change or judge others' choices, but must concentrate her energies on making decisions regarding her own life. Praising the book's short chapters as a help to more reluctant readers, *School Library Journal* contributor Nancy P.

Reeder added that the elderly actress, Sara, "is particularly well developed . . . and it will be easy for readers to see the child in the adult." And in *Booklist*, Kay Weisman called *Tent Show* "a bright and funny story with memorable characters." In addition to this popular work, Saunders has written several multi-volume series for middle-graders, including "Fifth Grade S.T.A.R.S.," "Sleepover Friends," and her "Black Cat Club" books, which *School Library Journal* contributor Christina Dorr praised as "sure to satisfy early chapter-book readers."

Saunders has always loved children's books. She once explained to *SATA*, "There is a magic to them, especially picture books, that I think doesn't exist anywhere else in literature." Of her writing style, Saunders admitted: "I write in spurts: I can have an idea for a long time, but will only commit it to paper when it's almost all written in my head, or when the suspense is killing me."

■ Works Cited

Dorr, Christina, review of *The Ghost Who Ate Chocolate, School Library Journal*, November, 1996, p. 92.

Gregory, Helen, review of *A Sniff in Time, School Library Journal*, August, 1982, p. 105.

Reeder, Nancy P., review of *Tent Show, School Library Journal*, October, 1990, pp. 118-19.

Saunders, Susan, *Wales' Tale*, Viking, 1980.

Review of *Tyrone Goes to School, Kirkus Reviews*, December 1, 1992, p. 1508.

Weisman, Kay, review of *Tent Show, Booklist*, September 15, 1990, pp. 163-64.

Wilson, Philip, review of *The Daring Rescue of Marlon the Swimming Pig, Booklist*, October 15, 1987, p. 400.

Zvirin, Stephanie, review of *Tyrone Goes to School, Booklist*, March 1, 1993, p. 1240.

■ For More Information See

PERIODICALS

Bulletin of the Center for Children's Books, April, 1987, p. 156.

Kirkus Reviews, May 1, 1980, p. 578; April 15, 1982, p. 487; February 1, 1986, p. 213; May 1, 1987, p. 725; December 15, 1987, p. 1736; December 1, 1992, p. 1508.

Publishers Weekly, June 27, 1986, p. 91; December 11, 1987, p. 63.

School Library Journal, October, 1980, p. 139; September, 1986, p. 139; March, 1987, p. 165; February, 1990, pp. 92-93; April, 1993, p. 102.*

*   *   *

SAVAGEAU, Cheryl 1950-

■ Personal

Born in 1950.

■ Addresses

Agent—c/o Alicejamesbooks, 33 Richdale Ave., Cambridge, MA 02140.

■ Career

Writer.

■ Writings

Home Country (poetry), Alicejamesbooks (Cambridge, MA), 1992.

Dirt Road Home (poetry), Curbstone Press (Willimantic, CT), 1995.

Muskrat Will Be Swimming (picture book), illustrated by Robert Hynes, Northland (Flagstaff, AZ), 1996.

■ Sidelights

Cheryl Savageau's poetry is rooted in the author's Native American and French-Canadian ancestry. Savageau has garnered praise for her lyrical examinations of family relationships, poverty, and issues of gender and identity, as well as for her simple use of language and her restraint in addressing emotionally charged subjects. Savageau's debut collection of verse, *Home Country*, is divided into two sections; the first, "The Dirt Road Home," presents a view of a family primarily from a child's perspective, while the second half of the book, "The Water Flowing through Me," focuses on nature from an adult perspective. In a critique for the *Boston Review*, Sam Cornish commented: "Savageau is able to create a softness that makes the most realistic social statements seem slick and workmanlike, but the sense of detail is so acute that the reader is grateful that the material is presented this way." *Choice* contributor R. Whitman asserted: "In an era when ethnic poetry, especially by poets of mixed heritage, is fashionable, it is refreshing to find a book that is modest and honest." Whitman particularly noted Savageau's poems centering on nature, and observed that pieces such as "Beaver Woman" and "Summer Solstice" "show an increasing poetic mastery." Cornish, while praising the nature poems in "The Water Flowing through Me," remarked on the author's evocative choice of details and simplicity of language in poems from "The Dirt Road Home" section, including "The Sound of My Mother Singing" and "Hanging Clothes in the Sun." Cornish concluded: "Savageau's poems of home are insightful portraits of a real working family living out troubled lives in a racially and economically troubled society."

Savageau has also written a book for children, *Muskrat Will Be Swimming*. The story features a young Native American girl who is saddened when her classmates make fun of her and other children who live by the lake. After her grandfather tells her a folktale that reminds her of her Seneca heritage, however, she remembers how much she values her home and her special place in her community. *School Library Journal* contributor Lisa S. Murphy called *Muskrat Will Be Swimming* an "exquisite, multifaceted tribute to the power of story," and concluded that it is "a unique book with an important message."

■ Works Cited

Cornish, Sam, review of *Home Country, Boston Review,* September-October, 1992, pp. 37-38.
Murphy, Lisa S., review of *Muskrat Will Be Swimming, School Library Journal,* August, 1996, pp. 128-29.
Whitman, R., review of *Home Country, Choice,* January, 1993, pp. 796-97.

■ For More Information See

BOOKS

Contemporary Literary Criticism: Yearbook 1992, Volume 76, Gale, 1993.

PERIODICALS

American Book Review, October, 1993, p. 13.
Booklist, June 1, 1996, p. 1736.*

*　　*　　*

SCHUMAKER, Ward 1943-

■ Personal

Born February 17, 1943, in Omaha, NE; son of Lester M. (a civil engineer) and Viola (a visiting nurse; maiden name, Anderson) Schumaker; married Deborah Johnson, 1969 (divorced, 1984); children: Matthew T. *Education:* University of Nebraska at Omaha, M.F.A., 1966. *Politics:* Democrat. *Religion:* Christian.

■ Addresses

Office—466 Green St., San Francisco, CA 94133-4067. *Electronic mail*—warddraw@best.com.

■ Career

Illustrator. Worked for various magazines, including *Macworld, Boston Globe, Parents,* and *Parenting. Member:* American Institute of Graphic Artists.

■ Writings

SELF-ILLUSTRATED

All My Best Friends Are Animals Address Book, Chronicle Books, 1991.
Dance!, Harcourt Brace, 1996.
Sing a Song of Circus, Harcourt Brace, 1997.

ILLUSTRATOR

Cole Porter, *Wake Up and Dream. Let's Do It, Let's Fall in Love,* Chronicle Books, 1993.
Janet Hazen, *Mustard: Making Your Own Gourmet Mustards,* Chronicle Books, 1993.
Vivian Sathre, *Mouse Chase,* Harcourt Brace, 1995.
David Meltzer, editor, *Reading Jazz,* Mercury House, 1997.

WARD SCHUMAKER

■ Sidelights

Ward Schumaker told *SATA:* "With my son grown up and living far away, I think that by working on children's books, I fill in some of the missing joys I felt in raising him. Matthew and I read together every night while he was growing up—clear up to the age of eleven!

"I also work on children's books to fulfill a decision made when I was about seven. My mother took me to hear an author/illustrator speak about his new children's book; and, as I sat there fidgeting, it dawned on me that all this man had to do all day was write and draw pictures ... and I thought that was wonderful. Today, all I really have to do each day is draw (and sometimes write) and, while it may not always be as wonderful as I'd imagined, it's pretty great!"

Some of Schumaker's more recent self-illustrated books are *Sing a Song of Circus,* and *Dance!,* published in 1995 and 1996, respectively. Schumaker's creative words and ink drawings provide humorous tales for pre-school and early elementary school children. Both books combine quick wit with expressive illustrations that "demonstrate motion" said *Booklist* contributor Ilene Cooper reviewing *Dance!. Sing a Song of Circus* emits the same kind of "energy" asserted a reviewer for *Publishers Weekly.* The contributor also added that aside from the text, "it's clearly the visual dazzle that counts here."

Vivian Sathre's *Mouse Chase* is another well-received book credited for Schumaker's illustrations. The book depicts a cat pursuing a mouse who eventually uses its creativity to escape. The tempo of the story is upbeat and the text is fun for children to follow. Christine A. Moesch of *School Library Journal* added that Schumaker's illustrations are "simple, yet full of motion." Describing the illustrations as "aesthetically pleasing," *Booklist* reviewer Ilene Cooper applauded the "smart use of language and imagery" in the book.

■ Works Cited

Cooper, Ilene, review of *Mouse Chase, Booklist,* January 15, 1996, p. 849.

Cooper, Ilene, review of *Dance!, Booklist,* March 1, 1996, p. 1189.

Moesch, Christine A., review of *Mouse Chase, School Library Journal,* April, 1996, p. 117.

Review of *Sing a Song of Circus, Publishers Weekly,* March 31, 1997, pp. 73-4.

■ For More Information See

PERIODICALS

Kirkus Reviews, February 15, 1996, p. 300.
Publishers Weekly, January 29, 1996, p. 100.
School Library Journal, May, 1996, p. 98.

* * *

SHEMIE, Bonnie (Jean Brenner) 1949-

■ Personal

Born May 10, 1949, in Cleveland, OH; daughter of William (an engineer) and Louise (a nurse; maiden name, Lundgren) Brenner; married Milo Shemie (an engineer), 1974; children: Khuther William, Benjamin David, Daniel Naim. *Education:* Allegheny College, B.A., 1971. *Religion:* Jewish. *Hobbies and other interests:* Skiing, hiking, canoeing.

■ Addresses

Home—4474 De Maisonneuve W., Montreal, Quebec, H32 1L7, Canada. *Agent*—Tundra Books, 481 University Ave., Suite 802, Toronto, Ontario, M5G 2E9, Canada.

■ Career

Author and illustrator. Worked for various advertising agencies in Montreal, Quebec, in graphic design and illustration, 1973-76; freelance illustrator, 1976-85. Presenter at elementary schools, public libraries, Reading Association, and library and school conferences. *Exhibitions:* Shemie's works have appeared in a number of group and solo shows since 1975.

■ Awards, Honors

Choice Book citation, Canadian Children's Book Centre, and Prix d'Excellence de l'Association des Consommateurs de Quebec (for the French edition), both 1991, for *Houses of Bark: Tipi, Wigwam and Longhouse: Native Dwellings, Woodland Indians;* Choice Book cita-

BONNIE SHEMIE

tion, Canadian Children's Book Centre, 1991, for *Houses of Snow, Skin and Bones: Native Dwellings, the Far North;* Canadian Materials Notable Book citation, Canadian Library Association, 1992, for *Houses of Hide and Earth: Native Dwellings, Plains Indians;* Our Choice citation, Canadian Children's Book Centre, 1993, for *Houses of Wood: Native Dwellings, the Northwest Coast.*

■ Writings

SELF-ILLUSTRATED; PUBLISHED BY TUNDRA BOOKS

Houses of Snow, Skin and Bones: Native Dwellings, the Far North, 1989.

Houses of Bark: Tipi, Wigwam, and Longhouse: Native Dwellings, Woodland Indians, 1990.

Houses of Hide and Earth: Native Dwellings, Plains Indians, 1991.

Houses of Wood: Native Dwellings, the Northwest Coast, 1992.

Mounds of Earth and Shell: The Southeast, 1993.

Houses of Adobe: The Southwest, 1995.

Houses of China, 1996.

■ Work in Progress

A series of books about lost cities.

■ Sidelights

Bonnie Shemie is the author and illustrator of a series of books for elementary-age children on the dwellings of Native Americans. The series began with *Houses of Snow, Skin and Bones: Native Dwellings, the Far North,* a detailed look at the various types of homes built by the Inuit tribes of Alaska. In text that alternates between simple descriptions aimed at younger readers and more complex discussions intended for older children, the author places the building of homes in the context of the culture as a whole. "Shemie looks at these dwellings with admiration," noted Denise Wilms of *Booklist.* In a statement that would be echoed by reviewers of later volumes in the series, Noel McDermott in *Canadian Children's Literature* proclaimed the work "a well-written and beautifully illustrated book, in which carefully researched information is presented, clearly and accurately and without any tendency to eulogize or romanticize."

Houses of Bark: Tipi, Wigwam and Longhouse: Native Dwellings, Woodland Indians was received by commentators with similar enthusiasm. *Booklist* contributor Carolyn Phelan noted that "the softly textured artwork" creates "an appealing vision of tribal life in eastern North America." "Information given in the text is very well explained, with a deceptively simple conciseness," remarked a critic for *Junior Bookshelf* in a review of the first three books in the series. *Houses of Wood: Native Dwellings, the Northwest Coast,* the fourth book in the series, describes the dwellings built by the Indian groups who lived from northern California through British Columbia and into southern Alaska, where the region's massive trees were the most sensible resource for building materials. "Like its predecessors, *Houses of Wood* focuses on the homes while giving detailed information on other facets of the particular people's

way of life," observed Patricia Fry in *Canadian Materials.* Although Annette Goldsmith, a reviewer for *Quill & Quire,* complained about the lack of table of contents and index to help guide readers through the information in the book, she also concluded: "The subject and length are sufficiently limited, however, and the book so interesting, that this should not deter readers."

In *Mounds of Earth and Shell: The Southeast,* Shemie turned from Native homes to explore the mysterious mounds that probably served as burial sites and ceremonial and sacred places in the southeastern United States, where a few of these mounds still remain. Shemie's illustrations demonstrate what the mounds looked like during the time they were in use and offer diagrams of several mounds showing the location of artifacts found in modern times. Like the other works in this series, *Mounds of Earth and Shell* features both "clear, involving text and strong, colourful illustrations," according to *Quill & Quire* contributor Fred Boer. The book provides one of the few sources of information on the subject for children, noted Carolyn Phelan in her *Booklist* appraisal, calling *Mounds of Earth and Shell* an "attractive book."

Shemie's books for children on the architecture of Native Americans are equally admired for the author's clear presentation of useful information and the warmth and attractiveness of her precise drawings and color illustrations. "Shemie is that rare combination of writer/artist who is equally dedicated to intensive research and to art," remarked critic Patricia Fry in *Canadian Materials.* Works such as *Houses of Snow, Skin and Bones* and *Houses of Bark* have captured attention for the way in which the author integrates information about the construction of such dwellings with details about the lives of the people who built and lived in these homes. Shemie "places house-building within its cultur-

Shemie has created a series of books about Native peoples and their various types of dwellings, such as the mounds built since the earliest civilizations of North America. (From *Mounds of Earth and Shell,* written and illustrated by Shemie.)

al context," Goldsmith stated. In addition, critics have noted that the author's dual text, with simple explanations on pages with color illustrations alternating with more complex narratives on pages with line drawings, makes the books in this series useful and attractive to a broad range of students looking for information on the history of Native American dwellings.

Shemie told *SATA:* "I was very fortunate. My work was noticed at a local exhibition by the editor and owner of Tundra Books, May Cutler. She coached and cajoled me into writing as well as illustrating my books. I work at home in the basement, in the winter surrounded by heaters and bicycles, where it is quiet and I can concentrate.

"My advice to young author/illustrators: there are many wonderful topics yet to be explored. Extraordinary things are produced by ordinary people like you and me."

■ Works Cited

Boer, Fred, review of *Mounds of Earth and Shell: The Southeast, Quill & Quire,* October, 1993, p. 43.

Fry, Patricia, review of *Houses of Bark: Tipi, Wigwam, and Longhouse: Native Dwellings, Woodland Indians, Canadian Materials,* January, 1991, p. 24.

Fry, Patricia, review of *Houses of Wood: Native Dwellings, the Northwest Coast, Canadian Materials,* March, 1993, p. 57.

Goldsmith, Annette, review of *Houses of Wood: Native Dwellings, the Northwest Coast, Quill & Quire,* October, 1992, pp. 36, 38.

Review of *Houses of Snow, Skin and Bones: Native Dwellings, the Far North; Houses of Adobe: The Southwest; Houses of Bark: Tipi, Wigwam, and Longhouse: Native Dwellings, Woodland Indians, Junior Bookshelf,* June, 1996, pp. 113-14.

McDermott, Noel, review of *Houses of Snow, Skin and Bones: Native Dwellings, the Far North, Canadian Children's Literature,* No. 63, 1991, pp. 78-79.

Phelan, Carolyn, review of *Houses of Bark: Tipi, Wigwam, and Longhouse: Native Dwellings, Woodland Indians, Booklist,* January 15, 1991, p. 1058.

Phelan, Carolyn, review of *Mounds of Earth and Shell: The Southeast, Booklist,* January 1, 1994, pp. 825-26.

Wilms, Denise, review of *Houses of Snow, Skin and Bones: Native Dwellings, the Far North, Booklist,* December 15, 1989, pp. 835-36.

■ For More Information See

PERIODICALS

Bulletin of the Center for Children's Books, December, 1989, p. 96.

Junior Bookshelf, June, 1994, pp. 102-03.

School Library Journal, February, 1997, p. 125.

SHIRLEY, Gayle C(orbett) 1955-

■ Personal

Born February 2, 1955, in Ithaca, NY; daughter of Marshall (a geologist) and Jean (an office manager; maiden name, Parmenter) Corbett; married Stephen D. Shirley (a journalist), June 24, 1978; children: Colin, Jesse. *Education:* University of Montana, B.A. (with high honors), 1978. *Hobbies and other interests:* Quilting, reading, movies, walking.

■ Addresses

Home and office—Great Falls, MT. *Electronic mail*—shirleyfour @ mcn.net.

■ Career

Missoulian, Missoula, MT, reporter and editor, 1977-80; *Independent Record,* Helena, MT, reporter and editor, 1980-82; *Pinnacle* (senior citizen magazine), Helena, founder, 1982, publisher, 1982-84; Falcon Press Publishing, Helena, editor, 1984-91; freelance writer, Great Falls, MT, 1991—. Great Falls Public Library, member of board of trustees, 1995-97. *Member:* Society of Children's Book Writers and Illustrators, Falls Quilt Guild.

■ Writings

M Is for Montana, illustrated by Constance R. Bergum, ABC Press (Helena, MT), 1988.

C Is for Colorado, illustrated by Bergum, ABC Press, 1989.

A Is for Animals, illustrated by Bergum, Falcon Press (Helena), 1991.

Four-Legged Legends of Montana, illustrated by John Potter, Falcon Press, 1993.

Montana's Wildlife: A Children's Field Guide to the State's Most Remarkable Animals, illustrated by Sandy Allnock, Falcon Press, 1993.

(With Debbie Tewell) *Where Dinosaurs Still Rule: A Guide to Dinosaur Areas of the West,* illustrated by David Mooney, Falcon Press, 1993.

Four-Legged Legends of Colorado, illustrated by Potter, Falcon Press, 1994.

Four-Legged Legends of Oregon, illustrated by Potter, Falcon Press, 1995.

More Than Petticoats: Remarkable Montana Women, Falcon Press, 1995.

Charlie's Trail: The Life and Art of C. M. Russell, Falcon Press, 1996.

Contributor to magazines, including *Boy's Life, Falcon,* and *Big Sky Journal.*

■ Work in Progress

A book on remarkable women in Oregon history, completion expected in 1998; research on western history.

SHORTT, Tim(othy Donald) 1961-

■ Personal

Born December 11, 1961, in Sarnia, Ontario, Canada; son of Donald Lachlan (a petrochemical worker) and Patricia Ann (a bookkeeper; maiden name, Taylor) Shortt. *Education:* University of Windsor, B.A., 1983. *Hobbies and other interests:* Genealogical research, reading, doodling, "hanging around the library."

■ Addresses

Home—733 Talfourd St., Sarnia, Ontario, Canada N7T 1S1.

■ Career

Illustrator and writer. Plastiglide Ltd., Toronto, Ontario, quality control inspector, 1986; Sentinel Investment, Toronto, messenger, 1987; Creative Education of Canada, Sarnia, Ontario, shipper.

■ Writings

The Babe Ruth Ballet School, self-illustrated, Firefly Books (Willowdale, Ontario), 1996.

■ Work in Progress

"Awaiting inspiration on a couple of franchise characters that can support a series of books."

■ Sidelights

Tim Shortt told *SATA:* "I am a doodler. Throughout high school I sat at the back of the class, doodling all manner of goofy faces in the margins and on the covers of all my notebooks. It's a practice I continue today, so the bulk of my artistic activity is devoted to covering any nearby scraps of paper with overlapping faces and figures and ideas and sketches. My illustration pursuit, and by extension my writing, has grown out of this doodling compulsion.

"For many years I have wished to create a children's book. I can't think of another medium that offers an illustrator such a prominent role, and that allows the illustrator the freedom to invent his own individual world. I hoped a children's book was the project that would promote me from dreamy, unfocused doodler to proud, professional illustrator. I knew I would need to write this book. Although I was a novice and untutored writer, I was the only writer one-hundred-percent-compatible with my approach to illustration.

"A few years ago, I saw a series of picture book illustrations by Edward Sorel, an illustrator I have long admired. I have never seen the actual book, but a caption beside the illustrations summarized the story. It was about a little girl in the 1920s or 1930s taking a transatlantic voyage. I remember the pictures were reminiscent of old movies. Before then, I had thought of

TIM SHORTT

children's books as either suburban sandbox dramas or Neverneverland escapades. The setting of the Sorel book seemed comparatively fresh and rich.

"I began to consider books set in a similar time period, using real, historic people. I was interested, not in the great men of history, but rather in the sort of figures that fascinated me as a child, the sideshow performers of history. This is how Babe Ruth became a character in my picture book.

"Setting a book in real history provides me with a foundation for my fiction. For example, I could never have invented names as colorful as the names of the real baseball players I used in *The Babe Ruth Ballet School.* I like to see how far I can bend the historical reality, to find the point where fiction and history balance each other.

"There is a long tradition of books, stories, and movies about baseball. The most appealing aspect for me was baseball's infinite tolerance of eccentricity in the stories about it. Think of the otherworldly presences in *Angels in the Outfield* or *Field of Dreams.* I have read many other less prominent works that combine nostalgic fondness for baseball with fantastic story elements.

"I am trying to make fun books. I shy away from any serious educational intent, for fear of creating the fictional equivalent of a lecture on table manners for proper boys and girls. If I am lucky, my characters and settings will be strong enough that I'll find some substance by accident. *The Babe Ruth Ballet School* is a story about a determined nine-year-old girl. It's not about the real Babe Ruth. I've used him for his mythical stature, for his name recognition, and for his reputation as a fun-loving, big goof of a guy.

"When I began to seriously develop my book, I visited my local library to study the work of other authors and illustrators. I brought home an armload of Chris Van Allsburg's books. I saw then how strong a picture book can be.... I'm convinced that the best picture books find a way to appeal to both adults and children, so that the sharing and reading of books is encouraged. And while I'll admit achieving this delicate balance proves an elusive goal, easily overshot, it's the one I continue aiming to hit."

■ For More Information See

PERIODICALS

Quill & Quire, November, 1996.
School Library Journal, January, 1997.

* * *

SILVERMAN, Robin L(andew) 1954-

■ Personal

Born April 27, 1954, in Newark, NJ; daughter of Melvin (a dentist) and Marion Z. (a teacher) Landew; married Stephen M. Silverman (a retailer), August 18, 1974; children: Amanda Gail, Erica Leigh. *Education:* University of Pennsylvania, B.A., 1975.

■ Addresses

Office—P.O. Box 13135, Grand Forks, ND 58208-3135.
Electronic Mail—silverma @ aero.und.edu.

■ Career

Freelance writer, 1975—. Silverman's, Inc., Grand Forks, ND, marketing director, 1978—. Public speaker; Y Family Center, president, 1987-88. *Member:* Society of Children's Book Writers and Illustrators.

■ Writings

A Bosnian Family, Lerner Publications (Minneapolis, MN), 1996.

Contributor of more than eight-hundred articles and columns to magazines and newspapers.

■ Work in Progress

Unexpected Love, The Ten Gifts.

■ Sidelights

Robin L. Silverman told *SATA:* "I believe there is astonishing good inside every person on this planet. I've been looking for—and finding—it for almost twenty years. All of my books and articles, speeches, and

ROBIN L. SILVERMAN

workshops attest to the miracles that naturally occur when we stop hiding our inner light from ourselves or the world around us.

"Whenever I work, I try to remember that I am not working for myself, but for others. I keep a picture in my heart of the men, women, or children who might be reading what I write. I know they are doing so in the hope of recognizing themselves in my stories."

* * *

SIM, Dorrith M. 1931-

■ Personal

Born in 1931, in Kassel, Germany; daughter of Hans and Trude (Lindenfeld) Oppenheim; married Andrew Sim (a solicitor), December 27, 1952 (died April 18, 1992); children: Rosalind Jackson, Elizabeth Macaskill, Susan Hodgins, Ruth Bingham, David. *Hobbies and other interests:* Yoga, driving, walking, swimming, cycling, writing crosswords puzzles, working with ex-refugees, grandchildren, giving talks.

■ Addresses

Home—5 The Crescent, Prestwick, Ayrshire KA9 1AP, Scotland. *Agent*—Marlyne Malin, 5/33 Ferncroft Ave., London NW3 7PG, England.

■ Career

Freelance writer. Also worked as a secretary. *Member:* Ayr Writers' Club (founder member), Trefoil Guild (ex-Girl Guides, Brownies, etc.), Reunion of Kindertransport, Scottish Annual Reunion of Kinder, OIR (Opportunities in Retirement).

■ Writings

In My Pocket, illustrated by Gerald Fitzgerald, Harcourt (San Diego, CA), 1997.

Author of scripts for schools programs and of short stories for radio, British Broadcasting Corp. Work represented in anthologies, including *I Came Alone,* edited by Bertha Leverton and Schmuel Lowensohn, Book Guild. Contributor of articles and children's stories to magazines. Newsletter editor, Scottish Annual Reunion of Kinder.

■ Work in Progress

Continuing research on her own background, school script.

■ Sidelights

Dorrith M. Sim told *SATA:* "As a founder member of the Ayr Writers' Club, I took part in a 'memories night,' where I won first prize for the story of how I, a seven-and-a-half-year-old Jewish child, found sanctuary in Scotland through a Kindertransport out of Germany. That story, along with many of the other *kinders,* then

DORRITH M. SIM

appeared in a book called *I Came Alone.* Subsequently a Scottish 'easy reading for children' project initiated by the Scottish Association of Writers spurred me toward a manuscript titled *I Had a Handkerchief in My Pocket,* the only English sentence I could say on arrival in Britain. An author friend, Alison Prince, read it and recommended it to her agent, who found a publisher. Now, much shortened and wonderfully highlighted by Gerald Fitzgerald, my book is, for me at least, a dream come true, not only in memory of my late husband, but also as a legacy to my whole family, including eight grandchildren."

■ For More Information See

PERIODICALS

Booklist, April 15, 1997, p. 1430.
Bulletin of the Center for Children's Books, June, 1997, p. 374.
Kirkus Reviews, April 15, 1997, p. 650.
Publishers Weekly, March 17, 1997, p. 82.

*   *   *

SMITH, Patricia Clark 1943-

■ Personal

Born February 14, 1943, in Holyoke, MA; daughter of James Joseph (a project engineer) and Rita Mary (a homemaker; maiden name, Dunn) Clark; married Warren S. Smith, August 25, 1964 (divorced, 1976); married John F. Crawford (a college professor and publisher), November 26, 1988; children: (first marriage) Joshua Briggs, Caleb Michael. *Education:* Smith College, B.A., 1964; Yale University, M.A., 1965, Ph.D., 1970. *Politics:* "Leftist; registered Green Party." *Religion:* Roman Catholic.

■ Addresses

Home—2309 Headingly N.W., Albuquerque, NM 87107. *Office*—Department of English, University of New Mexico, Albuquerque, NM 87131.

■ Career

Smith College, Northampton, MA, lecturer in English, 1968-69; Luther College, Decorah, IA, assistant professor of English, 1969-71; University of New Mexico, Albuquerque, assistant professor, 1971-82, associate professor, 1982-96, professor of English, 1996—. *Member:* Phi Beta Kappa.

■ Writings

Talking to the Land (poems), Blue Moon (Tucson, AZ), 1979.
Changing Your Story (poems), West End (Albuquerque, NM), 1990.
(Editor with Paul Davis, Gary Harrison, David Johnson, and husband John F. Crawford) *Western*

PATRICIA CLARK SMITH

Literature in a World Context (anthology), two volumes, St. Martin's, 1995.

(With Paula Gunn Allen) *As Long as the Rivers Flow: The Stories of Nine Native Americans,* Scholastic, 1996.

Contributor of articles and interviews to such publications as *Working Class Women in the Academy: Laborers in the Knowledge Factory, To Speak or Be Silent: The Paradox of Disobedience in the Lives of Women, This Is About Vision: Interviews with Southwestern Writers,* and *Western Women: Their Land, Their Lives.* Has also contributed short stories to *New American Review* and *Tierra: Contemporary Short Fiction of New Mexico* and reviews to *American Indian Quarterly, The Sacred Hoop, Rio Grande Writers' Newsletter,* and *Western American Literature.*

■ Work in Progress

The Road to White Tail, a young adult novel set on the Mescalero Apache reservation in 1915. Also *On the Trail of Elder Brother: Glous'gap Stories of the Micmac,* traditional stories retold with coauthor, Micmac storyteller, Michael RunningWolf.

■ Sidelights

Patricia Clark Smith told *SATA:* "I was born on Valentine's Day, 1943, in Holyoke, Massachusetts. My family on both sides is French-Canadian, Irish, and Micmac Indian. I'm a mixed-blood person, and the more diverse [that] places are (like New Mexico), the more I feel at home there.

"When I was growing up in Massachusetts and Maine, my family told me stories, taught me the names of the birds and plants that grew around our house, and talked to me about what was happening in the world. They read to me all the time, and I became a hungry reader of everything from *Little Women* to horror comics. I made my first book when I was seven, writing the story, drawing the pictures, and sewing the pages together.

"In 1964 I graduated from Smith College in Northampton, Massachusetts, where my maternal grandmother had worked as a maid. I was the first person in my family to go to college, and often it was scary because I knew so many people were counting on me to do well. I wanted to be a writer and English professor, so I went on to Yale University, where I specialized in American literature.

"In 1971 I was hired by the University of New Mexico. I was soon asked to teach some of my classes on-site at different places on the Navajo Reservation. A lot of wonderful books by American Indian novelists and poets were being published, and I began to teach those books and publish articles about them. There was no such thing as Native American studies when I was in school, but now it is a respected field. My Native American literature classes are crowded every semester.

"Some of my Native American students, like Paula Gunn Allen, have gone on to become well-known writers. Paula and I have worked on scholarly articles together before, but *As Long as the Rivers Flow* is the first young people's book for both of us. *Scholastic* asked Paula to do the book, and she invited me to join her. We loved telling those stories! It was very important, we thought, to make readers aware of the range of Native American achievement. Some of the people we wrote about in the book are barely known, even though they were very important. Weetamoo, the Pocasset woman sachem and warrior, is a good example. She avoided war when she could, but when it became plain to her in the 1670s that the English colonists were making native ways of life impossible, she fought bravely beside Metacom (or King Philip, as the English called him) and gave the colonists a run for their money. She's my personal heroine.

"When I am not teaching or writing, I love to hang out with our seven cats, to tend my little outdoor fish pond, to cook, and to garden. My husband and I enjoy driving around the southwest and seeking different historical sights that aren't in the guidebooks, like the site of the ranch of John Chisum, the cattle rancher who knew Billy the Kid.

"Michael RunningWolf, a Micmac storyteller, and I have just finished coauthoring a collection of traditional Micmac stories about Glous'gap, the great hero of our people.

"My next book is set on the Mescalero Apache Reservation in southern New Mexico in 1915. In it, my young heroine learns about native plant medicine from her grandmother. This means doing a lot of the kind of research I love best, and right now my desk is piled high with books of Apache history and ethnology and books about native plants and their medicinal uses. A perfect day for me means being able to put aside my teaching and administrative work and settle in with the books and the word processor."

■ For More Information See

PERIODICALS

Booklist, December 1, 1996, p. 645.
Library Journal, December 1, 1979, p. 2575.

*　*　*

SORENSON, Margo 1946-
(Marcie Kremer)

■ Personal

Born in Washington, DC; married James Sorenson (an investment manager), February 17, 1967; children: Jane, Jill. *Education:* University of California, Los Angeles, B.A., 1967. *Religion:* Lutheran. *Hobbies and other interests:* Golf, skiing, reading, travel.

■ Addresses

Home and office—7133 Shannon Dr., Edina, MN 55439-2630. *Electronic mail*—MSorenso @ aol.com.

■ Career

Teacher in California and Hawaii, 1967-85; writer, Edina, MN. Johns Hopkins University, fellow, 1988—. A Better Chance (ABC) Foundation, volunteer tutor. *Member:* Society of Children's Book Writers and Illustrators, Junior League of Minneapolis.

■ Awards, Honors

Excellence in Teaching Award, Center for Academically Talented Youth, Johns Hopkins University, 1988, 1994; California Educator of the Year Award, Milken Family Foundation and California State Department of Education, 1991; Global Teaching Award, Xerox Corp., Allstate, Anheuser-Busch Co., and Immaculate Heart College's Center for International and Multicultural Studies, 1992. Quick Pick List for Reluctant Young Adult Readers Nomination, Young Adult Services Library Association, American Library Association, 1997, for *Don't Bug Me.*

■ Writings

(Under pseudonym Marcie Kremer) *Aloha, Love* (young adult romance novel), Bantam, 1995.
Danger Canyon, Perfection Learning Corp. (Logan, IA), 1996.
The Hidden Dagger, Perfection Learning Corp., 1996.
Soccer Blaster, Perfection Learning Corp., 1996.

MARGO SORENSON

Kimo and the Secret Waves, Perfection Learning Corp., 1996.
Nothing Is for Free, Perfection Learning Corp., 1996.
The Gotcha Plot, Perfection Learning Corp., 1996.
Firewatch, Perfection Learning Corp., 1996.
Time Trap, Perfection Learning Corp., 1996.
Who Stole the Bases?, Perfection Learning Corp., 1996.
Don't Bug Me, Perfection Learning Corp., 1996.
Tsunami!, Perfection Learning Corp., 1997.
Hurricane, Perfection Learning Corp., 1997.
Fight in the Fields: The Story of Cesar Chavez, Perfection Learning Corp., 1998.
Leap into the Unknown: The Story of Albert Einstein, Perfection Learning Corp., 1998.
Danger Marches to the Palace: The Story of Queen Lili'uokalani, Perfection Learning Corp., 1998.
Death of Lies: The Story of Socrates, Perfection Learning Corp., 1998.
Shatter with Words: The Story of Langston Hughes, Perfection Learning Corp., 1998.

■ Sidelights

Margo Sorenson told *SATA:* "Most kids today would rather turn on the television or a video game than read a book. The competition for readers is tough, and I try to keep that in mind when I write. For my ideas, I draw on my experiences from teaching middle school for many years, from volunteer-tutoring inner-city kids, from raising my own family, and from author visits in schools. I hope in this way I can 'hook' kids into reading by packing in lots of action that will keep them turning the pages and, even more important, by tapping into feelings and emotions they really know about."

* * *

SPELMAN, Cornelia 1946-

■ Personal

Born September 14, 1946, in Kansas City, MO; daughter of Norman L. and Elizabeth (Schneider) Spelman; married Reginald Gibbons (a poet, novelist, and professor of English); children: Samuel Spelman Chaltain, Kate Elizabeth Chaltain. *Education:* Attended University of Cincinnati, 1964-66; Emerson College, B.S., 1968; Loyola University of Chicago, M.S.W., 1987. *Hobbies and other interests:* Genealogical research, shopping for family heirlooms at secondhand stores.

■ Addresses

Home—Evanston, IL. *Office*—c/o Albert Whitman and Co., 6340 Oakton St., Morton Grove, IL 60053-2723.

■ Career

Clinical social worker at a women's health center, 1987—; therapist for individuals, families, and children. Presents parenting workshops. *Member:* National Association of Social Workers (Illinois chapter).

■ Awards, Honors

Illinois Arts Council Award, 1990, for creative nonfiction.

■ Writings

After Charlotte's Mom Died, illustrated by Judith Friedman, Albert Whitman (Morton Grove, IL), 1996.
Your Body Belongs to You, illustrated by Teri Weidner, Albert Whitman, 1997.
Always My Mommy, Always My Daddy, Albert Whitman, in press.

Author of "Talking about Child Sexual Abuse," a pamphlet for National Committee for the Prevention of Child Abuse, 1985.

■ Work in Progress

A memoir of the author's family, spanning three generations; several children's books.

■ Sidelights

Cornelia Spelman told *SATA:* "I have always loved to read, and that led inevitably to a desire to write. My happiest memories of childhood are of curling up in a big wing chair in front of the fireplace with an apple and a book—or, better yet, a stack of books. Both of my

CORNELIA SPELMAN

parents were great readers, and I'm grateful to them for promoting in me that love of books. I love the presence of books, feel most at home and happy in a room full of them, and I love libraries. When my husband and I travel, we always want to go to the local library, and we'll judge a town by its library almost before any other attribute.

"I was the youngest of five children, so I listened and watched other people a lot. It made me curious about why people behave as they do. One of the ways I satisfied that curiosity was to return to school in mid-life and study human behavior, and learn to help others by becoming a therapist. I especially like to work with young children. They are beautiful in their approach to life, and touching when they are in pain. I wrote *After Charlotte's Mom Died* because I have seen how often children are not helped with their pain. It's not hard to help them, and yet it often does not happen, probably because people don't know how, or because they are in so much pain themselves. Yet help goes so very far with children; it can make the difference for a lifetime.

"I'm working now on a long nonfiction project, which is about the stories in three generations of my own family and the profound effect that even a long-ago event in a family continues to have among its members. The sudden death of my grandfather Sam when my mother was seven affected her so deeply that it affected me, too, and resulted in my first book. I wanted finally to help that little girl who was so sad, so long ago. Every family is a kind of hidden treasure—and tomb—and the family member who becomes a writer is its archaeologist. I wish to uncover the evidence of those previous lives and to understand them. I also hold precious those objects which have survived and been passed down—my mother's diary, my grandfather Sam's worn wallet with his name on it, the cut-glass dresser dish from my great-grandmother. Then I can pass it all on, with new understanding, to my own children, and they to theirs."

■ For More Information See

PERIODICALS

Booklist, April 15, 1996, p. 1447.
School Library Journal, August, 1996, p. 130.

*   *   *

STACEY, Cherylyn 1945-

■ Personal

Born August 2, 1945, in Edmonton, Alberta; daughter of George Theodore (a refinery process operator) and Jean Angela (Puchniak) Smith; married Allen Hugh Stacey, September, 1974 (marriage dissolved, October, 1983); children: Cinnamon Rebecca and Shea Tara. *Education:* University of Alberta, B.A. (Honors in English), 1967, M.A., 1968, diploma in education, 1971. *Hobbies and other interests:* Hiking, cross-county skiing, snorkeling, traveling.

■ Addresses

Home—11611 111 Ave., Edmonton, Alberta, T5G 0E2, Canada. *Office*—Box 4400 Stn. South, Edmonton, Alberta, T6E 4T5, Canada.

■ Career

Researcher and writer on children's literature for the Edmonton Catholic Schools, 1984-95; reviewer of screenplays for various producers of film and television, 1990—. Teaching experience includes University of Alberta, Canada, 1968-70; Red Deer College, Red Deer, Alberta, Canada, 1971-72; and junior and senior high school in Dawson Creek, British Columbia, Canada, 1982. "Baby snuggling" volunteer at the University Hospital in the 1980s, and volunteer for Habitat for Humanity in the 1990s. *Member:* Writer's Guild of Alberta, Writer's Union of Canada, Canadian Society of Children's Authors, Illustrators, and Performers (CAN-SCAIP), Young Alberta Book Society, Television Film Institute.

■ Awards, Honors

Our Choice Award, Canadian Children's Book Centre, shortlist, Writer's Guild and Library Association awards, "Best of the Best" selection, Edmonton Public

Schools, 1991, all for *I'll Tell You Tuesday If I Last That Long.*

■ Writings

I'll Tell You Tuesday If I Last That Long, Tree Frog, 1989.
How Do You Spell Abducted?, Red Deer College, 1996.
Gone to Maui, Roussan, 1996.

Also author of *Sex, Lies and Southern Comfort,* a comedy produced at the 1997 One Act Festival; "Sunny Side Up," a series of columns for *Stony Plain Reporter* appearing in 1975.

■ Work in Progress

Tip of the Halo and *Beyond Spite,* two connected police procedurals centered on a Royal Canadian Mounted Police protagonist. Research into a hidden valley mentioned in a very old book.

■ Sidelights

Cherylyn Stacey told *SATA:* "I write only about things that really matter to me, things I'm trying to understand and deal with myself—like fear, becoming your own person, being 'discounted,' and—in my screenplays—issues of control. I'm always surprised when an adult

CHERYLYN STACEY

considers something I've written to be controversial; young people cluster around at readings to ask how I knew exactly what it was like for them. How can I be grappling realistically with their issues and be (as one Toronto journalist says) writing rubbish and hate literature?

"Out of all this comes my one piece of advice to aspiring writers: [Don't] worry about having everyone like what you write. For one thing, it's impossible. For another, it hardly makes sense to say anything if you're not about to tell the truth."

Stacey's novels feature young people facing difficult situations, often arising from the break-up of their parents' marriage. In *I'll Tell You Tuesday If I Last That Long*, Vicky Delorian is feeling neglected when her divorced parents begin dating other people. When her mother decides to remarry, Vicky moves in with her father during the honeymoon. "The story is narrated by Vicky and is told well," Dorothy Dodge stated in *Canadian Materials*, continuing: "Teenagers will definitely relate to the difficulties encountered with Mom." Lesley Beckett, a contributor to *Quill & Quire*, also maintained that many adolescent readers will sympathize with Vicky's situation. "Stacey is a writer with a desire to speak to teens of today's society," Beckett asserted, adding: "Look for her name in the future."

The future brought *How Do You Spell Abducted?*, a novel in which a divorced father kidnaps his three children during his two weeks of summer custody, bringing them from Canada into the United States with false custody papers. Stacey's portrayal of the father, which Alison Sutherland described in *Books in Canada* as "the wickedly accurate depiction of an irresponsible, immature man, who reacts to his own inadequacies with vindictive and, in a minor way, aggressive behaviour," engendered some controversy among Canadian reviewers. However, "if the portrait had been less plausible," Sutherland remarked, "it could have been dismissed without comment." Other reviewers also commented favorably on the realism of Stacey's story; Charlyn Lyons, reviewing *How Do You Spell Abducted?* for *School Library Journal*, found Stacey's scenario "all too representative of the times."

■ Works Cited

Beckett, Lesley, review of *I'll Tell You Tuesday If I Last That Long, Quill & Quire*, December, 1989, p. 23.
Dodge, Dorothy, review of *I'll Tell You Tuesday If I Last That Long, Canadian Materials*, May, 1990, p. 131.
Lyons, Charlyn, review of *How Do You Spell Abducted?, School Library Journal*, December, 1996, p. 124.
Sutherland, Alison, review of *How Do You Spell Abducted?, Books in Canada*, October, 1996.

■ For More Information See

PERIODICALS

Quill & Quire, September, 1996, p. 75.*

STRETE, Craig Kee 1950-

■ Personal

Born 1950, in Fort Wayne, IN; married Irmgard Van Dam (a translator), 1984. *Education:* Wright State University, B.A., 1974; University of California, Irvine, M.F.A., 1978.

■ Addresses

Home—Hollywood, CA. *Agent*—Virginia Kidd Literary Agency, 538 East Hartford St., Milford, PA 18337; Marilyn Marlow, Executive V.P., Curtis Brown Ltd., Ten Astor Pl., New York, NY 10003.

■ Career

Fiction writer and playwright. Screenwriter under various pseudonyms; foreign rights and international acquisitions editor, de Knipscheer, 1980—; *East West Players Newsletter*, managing editor, 1984-85.

■ Awards, Honors

Dutch Children's Book award nomination, 1980, for *Grootvaders Reisdoel;* first place award, Dramatist Guild/CBS New Plays Programs, 1984, for *Paint Your Face on a Drowning in the River.*

■ Writings

FOR CHILDREN

The Bleeding Man and Other Science Fiction Stories, introduction by Virginia Hamilton, Greenwillow, 1977.
Paint Your Face on a Drowning in the River (novel; also see below), Greenwillow, 1978.
Uncle Coyote and the Buffalo Pizza, In de Knipscheer (Holland), 1978.
When Grandfather Journeys into Winter, illustrated by Hal Frenk, Greenwillow, 1979.
Grootvaders Reisdoel, In de Knipscheer, 1980.
Met de Pijn die het Liefheeft en Haat, In de Knipscheer, 1983.
Big Thunder Magic, illustrated by Craig Brown, Greenwillow, 1990.
The World in Grandfather's Hands, Houghton, 1995.
(With Michelle Netten Chacon) *How the Indians Bought the Farm,* illustrated by Francisco X. Mora, Greenwillow, 1996.
They Thought They Saw Him, illustrated by Jose Aruego and Ariane Dewey, Greenwillow, 1996.
Little Coyote Runs Away, illustrated by Harvey Stevenson, Putnam, 1997.
Lost Boy and the Monster, Putnam, 1997.

FOR ADULTS

If All Else Fails, We Can Whip the Horse's Eye and Make Him Cry and Sleep (short stories), In de Knipscheer, 1976, Doubleday, 1980.
In Geronimo's Coffin, In de Knipscheer, 1978.
Spiegel Je Gezicht, In de Knipscheer, 1979.

(With Jim Morrison) *Dark Journey* (poetry), In de Knipscheer, 1979.

Two Spies in the House of Love (novel), In de Knipscheer, 1981.

Dreams that Burn in the Night (short stories), Doubleday, 1982.

Burn Down the Night (novel), Warner Books, 1982.

To Make Death Love Us, Doubleday, 1985.

Death in the Spirit House (novel), Doubleday, 1986.

Death Chants (short stories), Doubleday, 1986.

PLAYS

Paint Your Face on a Drowning in the River, produced in Los Angeles, 1984.

A Sunday Visit with Great Grandfather, produced by American Indian Community House, 1984.

The Arrow that Kills with Love, produced by American Indian Community House, 1984.

Author of plays *Dark Walkers, Love Affair, Knowing Who's Dead, In the Belly of the Death Mother,* and *Horse of a Different Technicolor.*

OTHER

Author of over twenty-five screenplays under various pseudonyms. Also author of the radio plays *Saturday Night at the White Woman Watching Hole* and *The Bleeding Man* for ZBS Productions and NPR Radio.

■ Sidelights

In addition to numerous screenplays, television scripts, stage plays, and the novels and short stories he has penned for adult readers and science fiction fans during his long writing career, Craig Kee Strete has authored several works for young readers that focus on Native American culture and concerns. In novels such as *When Grandfather Journeys into Winter* and the picture books *Big Thunder Magic* and *How the Indians Bought the Farm,* Strete illustrates the displacement felt by contemporary Native American young people who, by embracing the "white man's" lifestyle, witness the dismay and frustration of their older relatives at the gradual loss of the "old ways" of living, and also grapple with living between two cultures.

When Grandfather Journeys into Winter focuses on a small child named Little Thunder and his close relationship with his grandfather, Tayhua, a man who scorns the ways of the white man but grudgingly agrees that his grandson must be educated in white schools. Tayhua puts value in traditional objects rather than the trappings of white man's society, and when rich rancher Wilson Tanner offers a five hundred dollar reward to the man or woman able to ride a wild horse that has come into his possession, the old Native American bargains for the horse rather than the money as a reward. While Tayhua is able to break and ride the beautiful animal, he also suffers injuries that hasten his death, his journey into winter. As Little Thunder tearfully sits by his grandfather's bedside, the old man attempts to show the boy the value of his ancient culture. Strete's "easy prose, well modulated from

Craig Kee Strete and Michelle Netten Chacon

HOW THE INDIANS BOUGHT THE FARM

Pictures by Francisco X. Mora

Through this humorous trickster tale in which an Indian couple outwits a government agent who tries to take their farm away, Craig Kee Strete portrays the injustices of relocation policies enacted against Native Americans.

humor to suspense to grief, is a gift to intermediate readers," according to Gale Eaton in a review in *School Library Journal.*

A nineteen-year-old Native American man named Tall Horse is the protagonist in Strete's 1978 novel, *Paint Your Face on a Drowning in the River,* which the author would later adapt as a stage play. Unhappy with his life on the reservation, Tall Horse prepares to leave his family for white society. Emotional goodbyes that highlight the feelings of cultural loss of many Native Americans echo in the young man's goodbye to his brother Leon, a Vietnam vet who lost an arm in the war, as well as to Tall Horse's drunken grandfather and quarrelsome grandmother. Such scenes were called "high in tension and charged with interacting emotion" by a contributor to *Kirkus Reviews* due to Strete's ability to contrast the "old ways" of Native American speech with more modern communication between family members. And in 1995's *The World in Grandfather's Hands,* eleven-year-old Jimmy Whitefeather and his widowed mother also leave their Native American neighborhood, but this time unwillingly, moving to a rundown section of the city to be with Jimmy's aged grandfather. The family also relocates to the city, as Jimmy comes to realize, as a way to honor his late father's wish that his son be educated in the white man's ways, to better enable the boy to "defend us against all the lies and treacheries and untruths," according to his mother. Angry at both the burden placed on him by his father's death and the move to a grimy neighborhood, Jimmy becomes sullen, but Grandfather Whitefeather's dreams and positive view of life gradually makes the young man understand that change is a part of life. As a critic in *Kirkus Reviews* noted, "the sense of lives out of place and feelings of disconnectedness are soberingly authentic." And in her review of *The World in Grandfather's Hands* in *School Library Journal*, Jacqueline Elsner praised Strete's "deft characterization" and wrote: "Powerfully spare prose shapes this subtle, quiet, and paradoxically angry book."

In addition to novels for young adult readers, Strete has authored several picture books with Native American themes. In *Big Thunder Magic*, Nanabee the sheep strays from his home on the reservation, becomes lost, and finds himself under lock and key at a nearby zoo, requiring the ghost Thunderspirit to use the magic he stores in a sack to free his friend. The politics enacted against Native Americans by the United States government with regards to Indian relocation policies is the subject of the humorous trickster tale *How the Indians Bought the Farm*, as an Indian couple is offered a small home on a barren piece of land, but only if they can acquire sheep, pigs, or chickens to raise. The clever couple, who, as the relocation program officials know, have no money to purchase such domesticated animals, collect a moose, beaver, and a bear, which they disguise to fool the government bureaucrats, who come bearing stacks of paperwork. Young readers "will get the sense of the Indians' displacement and their respect for the wild creatures they do not own," according to *Booklist* contributor Hazel Rochman. And in *They Thought They Saw Him*, a picture book graced with colorful cartoon-like paintings by the popular illustrator duo of Jose Aruego and Ariane Dewey, a wily chameleon teaches the ways of survival in an "appealing introduction ... for budding ecologists and reptile fans," according to Ellen Mandel in her review for *Booklist*.

■ Works Cited

Eaton, Gale, review of *When Grandfather Journeys into Winter, School Library Journal*, April, 1979, p. 64.

Elsner, Jacqueline, review of *The World in Grandfather's Hands, School Library Journal*, September, 1995, p. 204.

Mandel, Ellen, review of *They Thought They Saw Him, Booklist*, April 15, 1996, p. 1447.

Review of *Paint Your Face on a Drowning in the River, Kirkus Reviews*, October 1, 1978, pp. 1075-76.

Rochman, Hazel, review of *How the Indians Bought the Farm, Booklist*, May 15, 1996, p. 1594.

Strete, Craig Kee, *The World in Grandfather's Hands*, Houghton, 1995.

Review of *The World in Grandfather's Hands, Kirkus Reviews*, June 15, 1995, p. 864.

■ For More Information See

BOOKS

Watson, Noelle, and Paul E. Schellinger, editors, *Twentieth-Century Science-Fiction Writers*, 3rd edition, St. James Press, 1991.

PERIODICALS

Booklist, September 15, 1990, p. 173.
Bulletin of the Center for Children's Books, July, 1979, p. 202; October, 1995, p. 71.
Horn Book, July-August, 1996, p. 458.
Kirkus Reviews, March 1, 1988, p. 332; April 15, 1996, p. 608.
Publishers Weekly, March 11, 1988, p. 90.
School Library Journal, October, 1978, p. 160; January, 1991, p. 82.
Voice of Youth Advocates, December, 1982, p. 40; December, 1988, pp. 242-43.

*   *   *

STROUD, Bettye 1939-

■ Personal

Born July 17, 1939, in Athens, GA; daughter of Robert Lee (an Amtrak worker) and Luna Veal Moore; married Howard B. Stroud (an associate school superintendent), December, 1989. *Education:* Fort Valley State University, B.S., 1960; University of Georgia, M.Ed., 1972, Ed.S. (library media), 1974. *Hobbies and other interests:* Travel, photography.

■ Addresses

Home and office—243 Deerhill Dr., Bogart, GA 30622. *Agent*—Jennie Dunham, Russell and Volkening, 50 West 29 St., New York, NY 10001.

■ Career

Writer. Winder Middle Grade Schools, Winder, GA, media specialist, 1960-72; Barnett Shoals School, Athens, GA, media specialist, 1972-92. Georgia Student Media Festivals, judge; Georgia Children's Book Awards, member of selection committee, 1985; Georgia Department of Education, member of instructional television panel, 1985; Georgia Library Association, member of committee for standards, 1986; Georgia Library Media Association, state president elect, 1989. Also member of Georgia Teacher Education Council, 1981-86, and President's White House Conference on Libraries, 1985. *Member:* International Reading Association, Travel Writers International Network, National Education Association, Society of Children's Book Writers and Illustrators (contact person and workshop presenter), Cassell Network of Writers, the Four at Five Writers, Georgia Association of Educators, Library Board of Athens-Clarke county, Delta Kappa Gamma.

BETTYE STROUD

■ Awards, Honors

Sandhills Writers Workshop, 1994, for *Keep Running, Lizzie*. Grants from the Southeastern Advocates of Literature for Children, 1984, and the Georgia Council for the Arts, 1995.

■ Writings

Down Home at Miss Dessa's, illustrated by Felicia Marshall, Lee and Low, 1996.
Dance Y'All, illustrated by Cornelius Van Wright and Ying-Hwa Hu, Marshall Cavendish, in press.

Contributor of articles and book reviews to *Country America, Multicultural Review, Athens Magazine, Georgia Journal,* and *The Multicultural Resource Guide.* Author of unpublished manuscript *Keep Running, Lizzie.*

■ Work in Progress

A collection of retold African American folktales; three picture books.

■ Sidelights

Bettye Stroud told *SATA:* "My writing landscape is the South, quite often the South of the past. My milieu is a mix of generations, chock full of grandparents, aunts, uncles, and extended families.

"After my mother died, I grew up with a great-aunt and uncle, but also had a father and his new family in another state. I spent a lot of time on trains, in the midst of the two families. It all made for a wonderful childhood!

"No wonder my stories are intergenerational. No wonder they swing between truck farms in the South and locomotives headed North. I hope they serve as evidence of the joy brought into the lives of young and old alike when generations come together to love, to share and to protect.

"But, present-day subjects find their way into my writing, too. More than thirty people died in my state in 1994 during the fury wrought by Tropical Storm Andrew. It was a setting I had to utilize, a subject I had to write about.

"Hopefully, in my writing, children meet the demons they have faced in their own lives and find they can be banished. They get to know protagonists who come up against obstacles and problems and somehow find solutions.

"I want children to understand all is never lost. Fears can be conquered; lost friendships can be replaced by new ones and broken hearts can be mended in time. There's always tomorrow. There's always hope.

"Like any good writer, I want the echoes of my stories to reverberate through the reader's head long after the book is closed and the reader has gone on to something else."

■ For More Information See

PERIODICALS

Booklist, December 15, 1996, p. 734.
Kirkus Reviews, September 1, 1996, p. 1329.
Publishers Weekly, September 16, 1996, p. 83.

T

TAYLOR, Cheryl Munro 1957-

■ Personal

Born August 24, 1957, in Detroit, MI; daughter of Ken Taylor (an illustrator); married Alan Brooks (a writer and computer consultant), 1986; children: Lachlan Sage. *Education:* Attended Parsons School of Design and Canberra School of Art; Rhode Island School of Design, B.F.A.

■ Addresses

Home—360 Central Park W., No. 3-B, New York, NY 10025. *Electronic mail*—chips @ panix.com.

■ Career

Art Dimensions, Detroit, MI, graphic designer, 1984; Make Tracks! (catalog for birdwatchers), Detroit, co-owner, 1984-88; Chips and Ink, Ltd. (consulting and graphic design company), New York City, co-owner, 1993—. *Member:* Audubon Society.

■ Illustrator

Linda Milstein, *Coconut Mon,* Morrow, 1995.
Gerald Hausman, *Duppy Talk: West Indian Tales of Mystery and Magic,* Simon & Schuster, 1995.
Laurie Myers, *Guinea Pigs Don't Talk,* Clarion Books, 1995.
Patricia Hubbell and Bethany Roberts, *Camel Caravan,* Morrow, 1996.
Lee Bennett Hopkins, compiler, *Song and Dance: Poems,* Simon & Schuster, 1997.
Mary Elizabeth Hanson, *Snug,* Simon & Schuster, 1998.

■ Sidelights

Cheryl Munro Taylor told *SATA:* "I'm always ready to throw on a backpack and pack off to the Catskills or China, the Himalayas or the Rockies, New South Wales or New Delhi. I don't go anywhere without the local bird guide book! In my illustrations, I only hope that my love of travel and my love of nature shine through."

■ For More Information See

PERIODICALS

Booklist, April 15, 1996, p. 1446.
Publishers Weekly, May 1, 1995, p. 57.
School Library Journal, October, 1994, p. 126; July, 1995, p. 67.

* * *

THORNTON, Yvonne S(hirley) 1947-

■ Personal

Born November 21, 1947, in New York, NY; daughter of Donald E. (a laborer) and Itasker F. (Edmonds) Thornton; married Shearwood J. McClelland (an orthopedic surgeon), June 8, 1974; children: Shearwood III, Kimberly Itaska. *Education:* Monmouth College, B.S., 1969; Columbia University, M.D., 1973, M.P.H., 1996. *Politics:* Democrat. *Religion:* Baptist. *Hobbies and other interests:* Competitive ballroom dancing, tennis, needlepoint, saxophonist, vocalist.

■ Addresses

Home—Teaneck, NJ. *Office*—100 Madison Ave., Morristown, NJ 07962. *Agent*—The Richard Parks Agency, 138 East 16th St., New York, NY 10003. *Electronic mail*—yst1@columbia.edu (Internet).

■ Career

Roosevelt Hospital, New York City, resident in obstetrics and gynecology, 1973-77; Columbia-Presbyterian Medical Center, New York City, fellow in maternal-fetal medicine, 1977-79; Uniformed Services University of Health Sciences, Bethesda, MD, assistant professor of obstetrics and gynecology, 1979-82; Cornell University Medical College, New York City, assistant professor,

YVONNE S. THORNTON

1982-89, associate professor of obstetrics and gynecology, 1989-92, assistant attending, 1982-89; New York Lying-in Hospital, New York City, assistant attending, 1982-89, associate attending of obstetrics and gynecology, 1989-92; New York Hospital-Cornell Medical Center, director of clinical services department of obstetrics and gynecology, 1982-88, director of chorionic villus sampling program, 1984-92; Rockefeller University Hospital, New York City, visiting associate physician, 1986—; Columbia University College of Physicians and Surgeons, New York City, associate clinical professor, 1995—. Director of perinatal diagnostic testing center at Morristown Memorial Hospital, 1992—; saxophonist in Thornton Sisters ensemble, 1955-76. *Military service:* U.S. Navy, medical corps, 1979-82, became Lieutenant Commander. *Member:* American Board of Obstetrics and Gynecology (diplomate), National Board of Medical Examiners, American College of Obstetricians and Gynecologists (fellow), American College of Surgeons, American Medical Association, American Society of Human Genetics, Association of Women Surgeons, Society of Perinatal Obstetricians, American Federation of Musicians, New York Academy of Medicine.

■ Awards, Honors

Daniel Webster Oratorical Competition (Washington, DC), first place, 1996; Best Audiobooks of 1996 citation, *Publishers Weekly,* for audiotape of *The Ditchdigger's Daughters;* Best Books for Young Adults citation, American Library Association, 1996, for *The Ditchdigger's Daughters.*

■ Writings

(With Jo Coudert) *The Ditchdigger's Daughters: A Black Family's Astonishing Success Story* (autobiography), Birch Lane Press, 1995.

(Editor) *Primary Care for the Obstetrician and Gynecologist,* Igaku-Shoin Medical Publishers, 1996.
Woman to Woman: Everything You Wanted to Know about Women's Health, Plume/Dutton, 1997.

■ Adaptations

The Ditchdigger's Daughters was adapted as a book on tape.

■ Sidelights

Yvonne S. Thornton, an accomplished physician, is the author of *The Ditchdigger's Daughters: A Black Family's Astonishing Success Story,* which she wrote with author Jo Coudert. Born before the climactic events of the Civil Rights movement, Thornton and her four sisters were raised by a hard-working, ditch-digging father and a house-cleaning mother, whose college education was cut short by a lack of money. Both of Thornton's parents were determined that their own daughters would be educated and successful in life, despite the odds stacked against them because they were poor, black, and female. The personification of tough love, Thornton's father instilled in his daughters the belief that through hard work and study, they could achieve anything they dreamed of; but without discipline and an education, Donald Thornton warned his girls, they would live a hard life of physical labor and little respect.

In her book, Thornton recalls how her father would drive home his point: once, when one of her sisters brought home a "C" on a test, her parents showed little reaction. Early the next morning, however, her parents woke the girl and ordered her to scrub the kitchen floor, to show her what she would be doing for the rest of her life if she did not study harder. Thornton's father also continually reminded them of the importance of being smart; society would not accept their dark skin, he told them, but if they were smart, they would gain respect and honor. "The most valuable lesson he taught us," Thornton told *Detroit Free Press* writer Cassandra Spratling, "was that the only person who can stop you from reaching your goal is you. You set a goal, you aim your sights on that goal and that's it . . . . Whatever you do, you keep going till you reach your goal."

The Ditchdigger's Daughters is Thornton's account of how she and her sisters reached their goals and fulfilled their father's dreams for their success. Each is a professional: Yvonne and one of her sisters are medical doctors, while one is an oral surgeon, another is a lawyer, and the oldest sister is a court stenographer. They financed their educations by performing as the Thornton Sisters, a musical group, with Yvonne on saxophone. Popular on college campuses, the band also garnered spots on *Ted Mack's Amateur Hour* and *Amateur Night at the Apollo Theater.*

Reviewers have warmly received *The Ditchdigger's Daughters* as an inspiring story of the power of a family's love, with most observing that the Thornton family's accomplishments are tremendous for people of

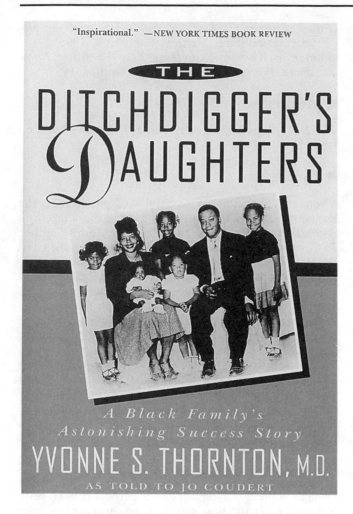

"Inspirational." —NEW YORK TIMES BOOK REVIEW

THE DITCHDIGGER'S DAUGHTERS

A Black Family's Astonishing Success Story

YVONNE S. THORNTON, M.D.

AS TOLD TO JO COUDERT

Obstetrician-gynecologist Thornton relates the story of her upbringing, during which her father inspired his six daughters to excel despite the obstacles that stood in their way.

any color or social standing. *Wall Street Journal* contributor Joseph Perkins, for example, maintained Thornton's story "shows that a family that stays together, that holds fast to traditional values, can make a quantum leap up the social mobility scale in a single generation. This holds true no matter how poor a family may start out and no matter what the family's racial heritage." Reviewer Marilyn Sanders Mobley, writing in the *Washington Post*, also appreciated the values presented in *The Ditchdigger's Daughters*. "At a moment in this nation's history when experts are lamenting the demise of the family and the loss of so-called family values," Mobley declared, "this book not only tells the story of a black family's success but also serves as a corrective to those who have underestimated the strength of the values that have historically enabled black families to survive and even thrive.... While the story of each daughter's life path is interesting, Yvonne's personal dream to become an obstetrician-gynecologist is remarkable."

■ **Works Cited**

Mobley, Marilyn Sanders, review of *The Ditchdigger's Daughters, Washington Post,* May 11, 1995, p. D2.

Perkins, Joseph, review of *The Ditchdigger's Daughters, Wall Street Journal,* September 6, 1995, p. A16.

Spratling, Cassandra, interview article in *Detroit Free Press,* April 12, 1995, pp. E1, E3.

■ **For More Information See**

PERIODICALS

Booklist, May, 1995.
New York Daily News, April 16, 1995.
New York Times Book Review, October 1, 1995, p. 29.
Philadelphia Inquirer, June 18, 1995.
Plain Dealer (Cleveland), May 14, 1995.
Publishers Weekly, April 17, 1995, p. 47.
USA Today, May 18, 1995.*

*   *   *

TREMBATH, Don 1963-

■ **Personal**

Born May 22, 1963, in Winnipeg, Manitoba, Canada; married; wife's name, Lisa (a social worker), August 25, 1984; children: Riley, Walker. *Education:* University of Alberta, B.A., 1988.

■ **Addresses**

Home—10011-104 St., Morinville, Alberta, Canada.

■ **Career**

Writer. Prospects Literacy Association, Edmonton, Alberta, Canada, special projects coordinator, 1988—. Worked variously as a tutor and writing instructor.

■ **Writings**

The Tuesday Cafe, Orca (Custer, WA), 1996.
A Fly Named Alfred, Orca, 1997.
Black Socks and Watches, Orca, 1998.

Author of bi-weekly column, "To Be a Dad," *The Edmonton Journal,* 1993-96.

■ **Work in Progress**

Sunny Taylor, a young adult novel.

■ **Sidelights**

Published in 1996, Canadian author Don Trembath's first novel *The Tuesday Cafe* is about a fifteen-year-old boy who seems to be the ideal child, until he commits an act of rebellion. Harper Winslow shocks his upper-middle-class community by setting a trash can on fire and ending up in juvenile court. After Harper is sentenced to writing an essay for arson charges, his mother signs him up for a writing workshop not realizing the class is for students with learning disabilities. It is there, however, that Harper finally encounters peers with whom he is comfortable and to whom he can

DON TREMBATH

relate. *Kliatt* contributor Jacqueline C. Rose commented that Trembath possesses a "fresh, humorous writing style" and applauded "the depth of his characters." Gerry Larson noted in *School Library Journal* that

Trembath's style, ending, and inspirational message "combine to create an appealing package." Janet McNaughton of *Quill and Quire* added that the new author is a "welcome" talent who has the ability to "create a character who tells us more about himself than he realizes."

Don Trembath told *SATA:* "I started writing stories when I was about ten or eleven. I would leave them on the dining room table and my mom and dad and all my brothers would pick them up and read them. Then they would tell me what they thought and ask if I was doing anymore. That kind of support and encouragement is crucial to a writer. I believe it went a long way in convincing me that writing would be a career path worth pursuing, that writing was something I was actually pretty good at. I think all young people should have the opportunity and encouragement to write."

■ Works Cited

Larson, Gerry, review of *The Tuesday Cafe, School Library Journal,* September, 1996, pp. 228-30.

McNaughton, Janet, review of *The Tuesday Cafe, Quill and Quire,* May, 1996, pp. 33-34.

Rose, Jacqueline C., review of *The Tuesday Cafe, Kliatt,* November, 1996, p. 11.

■ For More Information See

PERIODICALS

Voice of Youth Advocates, October, 1997, p. 248.

V–W

VIVAS, Julie 1947-

■ Personal

Born in 1947, in Adelaide, Australia. *Education:* Studied interior design and film animation at the National Art School, Australia.

■ Career

Illustrator. Worked at a veterinary clinic, then in film animation; artist; has exhibited drawings in Australia.

■ Awards, Honors

Picture Book of the Year, Children's Book Council of Australia, 1982, for *The Tram to Bondi Beach* (with Libby Hathorn), and 1989, for *The Very Best of Friends* (with Margaret Wild); Children's Book Council commendation, and New South Wales State Literary award, both 1984, International Board on Books for Young People citation for illustration, 1986, and KOALA award, 1987, all for *Possum Magic;* Boston Globe Picture Book honor, 1988, for *The Nativity;* Dromkeen Award, 1992.

■ Illustrator

Libby Hathorn, *The Tram to Bondi Beach,* Methuen, 1981, Kane/Miller, 1989.

Mem Fox, *Possum Magic,* Omnibus (Australia), 1983, Abington, 1987.

Mem Fox, *Wilfrid Gordon McDonald Partridge,* Kane/Miller, 1985.

Richard Tulloch, *Stories from Our House,* Cambridge University Press, 1987.

The Nativity (with text from the King James version of the Bible), Harcourt, 1988.

Richard Tulloch, *Stories from Our Street,* Cambridge University Press, 1989.

Sue Williams, *I Went Walking,* Omnibus (Australia), 1989, Harcourt, 1990.

Margaret Wild, *The Very Best of Friends,* Harcourt, 1990.

JULIE VIVAS

Margaret Wild, *Let the Celebrations Begin!,* Orchard Books, 1991.

Virginia Woolf, *Nurse Lugton's Curtain,* Harcourt, 1991.

Margaret Wild, *Our Granny,* Ticknor & Fields, 1994.

Ana Zamorano, *Let's Eat,* Scholastic, Inc., 1997.

Several books illustrated by Vivas have been translated into Spanish.

■ Sidelights

Australian illustrator Julie Vivas's unique watercolor works, with their rounded contours, soft edges, and fluid lines, have made her one of her country's most popular illustrators. Her gentle illustrations have graced the works of numerous authors, and have earned her awards from such prestigious organizations as the Australian Children's Book Council and the International Board on Books for Young People, as well as the praise of readers and critics alike, both in her native country and elsewhere.

A student in interior design and film animation, Vivas spent several years mixing colors and inking in and coloring artwork for an Australian animation studio before leaving in 1968 to spend four years in Spain, observing from city streetcorners and drawing the people who passed her going about their business. Returning to Australia in 1972, she exhibited the drawings she had done in Spain; it was at this point that Vivas was approached by children's book writer Libby Hathorn and asked if she would be interested in becoming an illustrator. Vivas was enthusiastic about the opportunity and readily accepted.

Taking place in the 1930s, Hathorn's *The Tram to Bondi Beach* is the story of nine-year-old Kieran, a novice newspaper carrier with dreams of working on the commuter streetcar that clatters through his city's streets each morning. The book was Vivas's first illustration project, and it took her over a year and a half of working and reworking her nostalgic, warm-toned, watercolor renderings before she felt they were ready for publication. All that hard work paid off for the young illustrator: *The Tram to Bondi Beach* was highly commended for the Australian Children's Book Council's Picture Book of the Year. Praising the work, a *Publish-*

ers Weekly reviewer noted that Vivas's "characters seem to defy the space constraints of a square page: they reach out to readers, or squabble and taunt one another, filling up backgrounds with activities and inviting a closer look."

Possum Magic, Vivas's second illustration project for young people, was particularly challenging. The story, by Mem Fox, focuses on a possum named Hush and her search through the Australian bush and beyond to discover a way to undo the mixed-up magic of befuddled old Grandma Poss that has made Hush invisible. "Rendering an invisible character and working with this broken outline was difficult," the artist explained in *Children's Book Illustration and Design.* "It was also difficult showing expressions of sadness or happiness on their faces and through their body language." To impart a feeling of airiness and lightness to her invisible protagonist, Vivas used watercolor. *Possum Magic* has, since its 1983 publication, become an Australian classic: "Fox and Vivas's Grandma Poss, with rainbow-colored slippers, round glasses and star-speckled apron, stands out as one of the most truly inspired characters ever to cross the continents," according to a *Publishers Weekly* reviewer.

The Nativity, one of Vivas's favorite illustration projects, combines her art with text from the Authorized King James Version of the Bible. Rendered in warm, earth-toned pastel and watercolor, Mary and Joseph are simple country people who are depicted going about their daily lives before visited by a somewhat scruffy Angel Gabriel—wearing unlaced workboots—and his message that Mary will bear a child. The irreverent, homey, and often humorous treatment given the Nativity story by Vivas caused one *School Library Journal* critic to remark: "Bound to provoke controversy over what is appropriate treatment of the Nativity, this book

Our granny does special exercises

to make her bottom smaller.

In this picture book illustrated by Vivas, Margaret Wild helps children appreciate the unique personalities of grandmothers. (From *Our Granny.*)

nonetheless has much to commend it." Ann A. Flowers agreed in *Horn Book,* commenting that "even though these peasant faces and bodies are far from traditionally beautiful, they cast a new and very human perspective on a beloved story and express warmth, humor, and joy."

The Very Best of Friends was the first of several fruitful collaborations between Vivas and author Margaret Wild. Published in Australia in 1989, the book depicts an elderly farm wife coming to terms with the death of her husband by focusing on gaining the trust and affection of her late husband's cat, William. Praising Vivas's illustrations as the perfect companion to Wild's moving text, a *Publishers Weekly* reviewer maintained that "her ragtag characters and soft watercolors capture the essence of an affectionate marriage ... and the pathos of death." Interestingly, the pair's next collaboration, *Let the Celebrations Begin!,* found itself the focus of some controversy over its relatively gentle depiction of one of the most horrific periods of modern history. Set in Germany's Bergen-Belsen concentration camp during World War II, Wild's story revolves around the female camp inmates' efforts to lift the spirits of the few children who had survived capture by designing toys in preparation for a celebration on the day of their liberation by Allied troops. Calling the book "a work of love" on the part of both author and illustrator, *School Library Journal* contributor Susan Scheps noted of Vivas's illustrations: "Against stark white backgrounds [she] has painted the small group of raggedly clothed, stubble-haired, thin-legged women and children; all of their faces radiate hope.... These are the survivors, and their story must be told."

Vivas's and Wild's third collaboration, a celebration of human diversity entitled *Our Granny,* met with consistent critical praise upon its publication in 1994. Told from a child's perspective, the text cataloguing the many sizes, shapes, and habits of grandmothers is full of humor, with Vivas's illustrations rising to the occasion. "A variety of women—black, white, hip, punk, and traditional—are depicted with warmth and humor, yet all have a lumpy, rounded, saggy-baggy appearance," noted Karen James, describing Vivas's characteristic style in a *School Library Journal* review. "The pictures both extend the words and focus them," added Hazel Rochman, reviewing *Our Granny* for *Booklist,* "full of surprise and warmth and laughter. This is what family values is all about."

Other books that have been enhanced by Vivas's artwork include Mem Fox's *Wilfred Gordon McDonald Partridge* and Virginia Woolf's *Nurse Lugton's Curtain.* The repetitive rhymes of 1990's *I Went Walking,* a picture book written by Australian author Sue Williams, are coupled with Vivas's imaginative animal illustrations to make a guessing game about farmyard residents for very young children. "Vivas has great comic flair," noted *Horn Book* reviewer Margaret A. Bush, "and her eloquent use of understatement produces a rich interpretation of the short, spare story line."

■ Works Cited

Bush, Margaret A., review of *I Went Walking, Horn Book,* November-December, 1990, p. 735.

Flowers, Ann A., review of *The Nativity, Horn Book,* November-December, 1988, p. 766.

James, Karen, review of *Our Granny, School Library Journal,* April, 1994, pp. 114-15.

Review of *The Nativity, School Library Journal,* October, 1988, p. 36.

Review of *Possum Magic, Publishers Weekly,* June 26, 1987, p. 71.

Rochman, Hazel, review of *Our Granny, Booklist,* January 15, 1994, p. 925.

Scheps, Susan, review of *Let the Celebrations Begin!, School Library Journal,* July, 1991, p. 75.

Review of *The Tram to Bondi Beach, Publishers Weekly,* February 10, 1989, p. 70.

Review of *The Very Best of Friends, Publishers Weekly,* March 16, 1990, p. 69.

Vivas, Julie, in *Children's Book Illustration and Design,* Library of Applied Design, 1992.

■ For More Information See

BOOKS

Children's Books and Their Creators, edited by Anita Silvey, Houghton, 1995.

PERIODICALS

Horn Book, January-February, 1988, pp. 52-53; July-August, 1989, p. 474; May-June, 1990, p. 331; May-June, 1994, pp. 322-23.

People, November 28, 1994.

Publishers Weekly, July 29, 1988, p. 232; August 31, 1990, p. 63; July 25, 1991, p. 52.

School Library Journal, July, 1989, p. 66; June, 1990, p. 106; October, 1990, p. 104; February, 1996, p. 130.

*   *   *

WHITCHER, Susan (Godsil) 1952-

■ Personal

Born January 29, 1952, in Tokyo, Japan; daughter of Augustus R. (a management consultant) and Anne (an artist; maiden name, Cleveland) White; married John Lee Whitcher (an engineer), 1980; children: Ursula Anne, Susannah Mattson. *Education:* Portland State University, B.A., 1974; attended University College (London), 1974-75; Warburg Institute (London), M.Phil, 1977; conducted Ph.D. studies at Johns Hopkins University. *Politics:* Liberal. *Religion:* "Nonaligned."

■ Addresses

Home and office—4260 Reed St., West Linn, OR 97068. *Agent*—Emilie Jacobson, Curtis Brown, Ltd.

SUSAN WHITCHER

■ Career

Writer. Whitcher told *SATA:* "I don't think I've ever had a job that could be dignified by the term 'career.' For two or three years I taught Renaissance intellectual history/literature at Johns Hopkins, but only as a graduate student teaching assistant. Other work experience includes: teaching night school, selling tourist trinkets in London, running a small English-language school in Sicily for one year, 'exotic' dancing in nightclubs, manning a domestic violence hotline, and freelance garden design." *Member:* Society of Children's Book Writers and Illustrators.

■ Writings

Moonfall (picture book), illustrated by Barbara Lehman, Farrar, Straus & Giroux, 1993.
Real Mummies Don't Bleed: Friendly Tales for October Nights (short stories), Farrar, Straus & Giroux, 1993.
Something for Everyone (picture book), illustrated by Barbara Lehman, Farrar, Straus & Giroux, 1995.
Enchanter's Glass (novel), Harcourt Brace, 1995.
The Key to the Cupboard (picture book), illustrated by Andrew Glass, Farrar, Straus & Giroux, 1997.

■ Work in Progress

Two novels, *Stealing* and *The Fool Reversed.*

■ Sidelights

Susan Whitcher writes books for young people in which fantastical elements are employed in a straightforward, almost deadpan, manner that is often found enchanting. In her first effort, *Moonfall,* a girl is certain that the moon is falling from the sky, despite her parents' reassuring explanations. Two weeks after the moon has disappeared from the sky, however, Sylvie's suspicions are borne out when she finds it in her neighbor's garden and "goes about saving the moon in a sensible, magical fashion," according to Janice Del Negro in a *Booklist* review. Critics singled out Whitcher's poetic text for special praise; although the author refuses to define the moon's qualities consistently, "children will not be stalled by the dreamlike vagaries of this debut author's text," averred a *Publishers Weekly* commentator. Indeed, Whitcher's "whimsical fantasy," when combined with Barbara Lehman's effective illustrations, yields a book that is "destined to become a read-aloud favorite in many a household," Susan Scheps predicted in *School Library Journal.*

For her next book, Whitcher again paired magical elements with deliberately ordinary language in a collection of stories for young readers called *Real Mummies Don't Bleed: Friendly Tales for October Nights.* Each story is set during the time of Halloween and features contemporary American children encountering humorous and/or frightening elements from the supernatural world. A critic for *Kirkus Reviews* commended the "original sense of the bizarre" displayed by the author in these "five fresh, witty tales."

In *Something for Everyone,* Whitcher paired up with illustrator Lehman for a second picture book, this time to tell the story of great-aunt Elsie Applebaum, who abruptly decides to retire, leaving behind a motley collection of memorabilia for her unpleasant relatives to sort through. Only Elsie's young friend, Tilda, knows what to do with the odd assortment of objects and promptly fashions them into a magic traveling machine and flies off to join Elsie. "Whitcher has poetic sensibility ... that she never overuses," noted a *Kirkus Reviews* critic. *School Library Journal* contributor Barbara Kiefer commented favorably on the way Lehman's humorous illustrations augment the author's text, making this "an agreeable book that children should find entertaining."

Whitcher is also the author of a novel for young people entitled *Enchanter's Glass,* in which an unpopular and unhappy girl finds a piece of glass that alters her perspective and leads her into a world of fantastic adventures. "Whitcher has a gift for characterization and the deft turn of phrase," maintained a *Fantasy & Science Fiction* contributor, who added: "*Enchanter's Glass* is a delight from start to finish; lyrical, with a touch of *Alice in Wonderland* absurdity and a compassionate heart."

Explaining how she began her career as a writer, Whitcher told *SATA:* "As a child, I yearned for magical

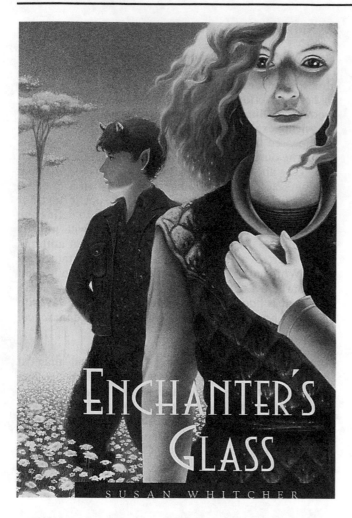

In this tale of alternate reality, Phoebe views the world differently when she looks through a chunk of magical glass and discovers that the new vision seems more believable than the old. (Cover illustration by Victor Lee.)

adventures. Later, I thought time travel might be good enough, especially if as a side effect it could make me slimmer and not need glasses. When I grew up I got contact lenses and studied history.

"I'm not saying I missed out altogether on adventures. I met a man with a huge mustache and a greasy black motorcycle. Together we traveled around Europe. We had children. I looked forward to a cutthroat university career.

"At university, I asked the school's health services to refer me to a counselor for depression. One day the counselor chided me for indulging in what she called 'magical thinking.' *Magical* thinking. I carried the phrase home with me like a gift.

"That's when I began to write stories. Halfway through writing *Enchanter's Glass* I suddenly realized why magical adventures don't just happen: not because they don't exist, but because you have to make them."

■ Works Cited

Del Negro, Janice, review of *Moonfall, Booklist,* July, 1993, p. 1978.

Review of *Enchanter's Glass, Fantasy & Science Fiction,* June, 1997, pp. 26-28.

Kiefer, Barbara, review of *Something for Everyone, School Library Journal,* November, 1995, pp. 84-85.

Review of *Moonfall, Publishers Weekly,* June 14, 1993, p. 69.

Review of *Real Mummies Don't Bleed: Friendly Stories for October Nights, Kirkus Reviews,* August 15, 1993, p. 1082.

Scheps, Susan, review of *Moonfall, School Library Journal,* October, 1993, p. 114.

Review of *Something for Everyone, Kirkus Reviews,* October 1, 1995, p. 1438.

*   *   *

WORMELL, Mary 1959-

■ Personal

Born May 3, 1959, in Glenfield, Leicestershire, England; daughter of John and Teresa Wormell; children: Lucy. *Hobbies and other interests:* Horse riding.

■ Addresses

Home—Hartwoodmyres Farm, Ettrick Valley, Selkirk, Scotland TD7 5HA.

■ Career

Writer and illustrator.

■ Writings

SELF-ILLUSTRATED

Hilda Hen's Search, Harcourt Brace, 1994.
Hilda Hen's Happy Birthday, Harcourt Brace, 1995.
Hilda Hen's Scary Night, Harcourt Brace, 1996.

ILLUSTRATOR

Dick King-Smith, *The Spotty Pig,* Farrar, Straus & Giroux, 1997.

■ Sidelights

Mary Wormell's picture books, featuring humorous tales of Hilda Hen accompanied by watercolor-washed linocut illustrations, have earned praise from book reviewers. Wormell once commented: "Hilda is a real hen. I started making prints of her which then grew into stories. She is still pecking around the farmyard." In *Hilda Hen's Search,* Hilda is looking for a good place to lay her eggs since the hen house is full, but no place she tries is quite right until she finds a child's empty dollhouse. Lynn Cockett noted in *School Library Journal* that the book's winning combination of a simple story and bold and humorous illustrations "make this book especially effective for preschool story programs."

Similarly, a *Publishers Weekly* commentator highlighted the "comforting solidity" of Wormell's illustrations, calling *Hilda Hen's Search* "a splendid debut" for the first-time author-illustrator.

The following year, Hilda Hen reappeared in *Hilda Hen's Happy Birthday,* in which the bird cheerfully travels around the farmyard, thinking that everything she meets is a birthday present for her and gratefully partaking of it, to the chagrin of everyone she meets. Children will especially enjoy "Hilda's satisfaction as she blithely leaves her trail of destruction," wrote a *Publishers Weekly* reviewer. And, as others had observed about the first Hilda Hen book, the illustrations for *Hilda Hen's Happy Birthday* "add their own humor to this gentle story," remarked Hanna B. Zieger in *Horn Book.*

"Fans of Hilda Hen will rejoice in her third adventure," predicted April Judge in a *Booklist* review of *Hilda Hen's Scary Night.* In this story, Hilda wakes from a long nap to find that night has fallen in the barnyard. She decides to brave the terrors of the dark in order to return to the hen house and encounters a snake, a monster, and a lake along the way. Dual illustrations reveal these obstacles to be a garden hose, a rocking horse, and a wading pool, noted a reviewer for *Junior Bookshelf,* who added, "the illustrations help tell the story, and the point does not have to be laboured." The next day, Hilda proudly recounts her adventures to her friends in the hen house and wonders where the monsters of the night before have gone to in the daylight. Though Gale W. Sherman in *School Library Journal* felt that Wormell's ending lacked some of the magic of the preceding pages, children who are afraid "to venture out when the sun goes down will be sympathetic" with Hilda Hen's fears, she concluded.

Wormell is also the illustrator for Dick King-Smith's picture book *The Spotty Pig,* in which young Peter the Pig, dismayed by his spots, tries a number of remedies to rid himself of them until the day he meets and falls in love with Penny, another spotty pig. Wormell's characteristic linocut illustrations are in evidence here, featuring bold outlines and happy colors, noted a reviewer for *Publishers Weekly,* calling the pictures "as cheerful as a box of new crayons, and just the thing to pair with King-Smith's droll text."

■ Works Cited

Cockett, Lynn, review of *Hilda Hen's Search, School Library Journal,* November, 1994, p. 93.

Review of *Hilda Hen's Happy Birthday, Publishers Weekly,* February 6, 1995, p. 84.

Review of *Hilda Hen's Scary Night, Junior Bookshelf,* August, 1996, p. 145.

Review of *Hilda Hen's Search, Publishers Weekly,* October 31, 1994, p. 60.

Judge, April, review of *Hilda Hen's Scary Night, Booklist,* September 15, 1996, p. 252.

Sherman, Gale W., review of *Hilda Hen's Scary Night, School Library Journal,* October, 1996, p. 110.

Review of *The Spotty Pig, Publishers Weekly,* March 10, 1997, p. 65.

Zieger, Hanna B., review of *Hilda Hen's Happy Birthday, Horn Book,* May, 1995, p. 331.

■ For More Information See

PERIODICALS

Kirkus Reviews, October 15, 1994, p. 1418.*

*   *   *

WYNNE-JONES, Tim(othy) 1948-

■ Personal

Born August 12, 1948, in Bromborough, Cheshire, England; son of Sydney Thomas (an engineer) and Sheila Beryl (a homemaker; maiden name, Hodgson) Wynne-Jones; married Amanda West Lewis (a writer, calligrapher, and teacher), September, 1980; children: Alexander, Magdalene, Lewis. *Education:* University of Waterloo, B.F.A., 1974; York University, M.F.A., 1979.

■ Addresses

Home and office—Rural Route No. 4, Perth, Ontario K7H 3C6, Canada.

■ Career

Writer. PMA Books, Toronto, Ontario, designer, 1974-76; University of Waterloo, Waterloo, Ontario, instruc-

TIM WYNNE-JONES

tor in visual arts, 1976-78; Solomon & Wynne-Jones, Toronto, graphic designer, 1976-79; York University, Downsview, Ontario, instructor in visual arts, 1978-80. *Member:* International PEN, Writers Union of Canada, Association of Canadian Television and Radio Artists, Society of Composers, Authors, and Music Publishers of Canada.

■ Awards, Honors

Seal First Novel Award, Bantam/Seal Books, 1980, for *Odd's End;* I.O.D.E. Award and Amelia Frances Howard-Gibbon award, both 1983, and Ruth Schwartz Children's Award, 1984, all for *Zoom at Sea;* ACTRA Award, best radio drama, 1987, for *St. Anthony's Man;* Governor-General's Award for Children's Literature, 1993, Canadian Library Association Children's Book of the Year award, 1993, and *Boston Globe-Horn Book* Award for Fiction, 1995, all for *Some of the Kinder Planets;* Notable Books for Children citation, American Library Association, and Mister Christie Award shortlist, 1994, both for *The Book of Changes;* Governor-General's Award for Children's Literature, 1995, Young Adult Book of the Year, Canadian Library Association, Mister Christie Award shortlist, and Books for the Teen Age citation, New York Public Library, 1997, all for *The Maestro;* Vicky Metcalf Award, Canadian Authors Association, 1997, for body of work.

■ Writings

FOR CHILDREN

Madeline and Ermadello, illustrated by Lindsey Hallam, Before We Are Six (Hawkesville, Ontario), 1977.

Zoom at Sea, illustrated by Ken Nutt, Douglas & McIntyre, 1983, illustrated by Eric Beddows, HarperCollins, 1993.

Zoom Away, illustrated by Ken Nutt, Douglas & McIntyre, 1985, illustrated by Eric Beddows, HarperCollins, 1993.

I'll Make You Small, illustrated by Maryann Kovalski, Douglas & McIntyre, 1986.

Mischief City (verse), illustrated by Victor Gad, Groundwood, 1986.

Architect of the Moon, illustrated by Ian Wallace, Groundwood, 1988, published as *Builder of the Moon,* McElderry, 1988.

The Hour of the Frog, illustrated by Catharine O'Neill, Groundwood, 1989, Little Brown, 1989.

Mouse in the Manger, illustrated by Elaine Blier, Viking, 1993.

The Last Piece of Sky, illustrated by Marie-Louise Gay, Groundwood, 1993.

Zoom Upstream, illustrated by Eric Beddows, Groundwood, 1993, HarperCollins, 1994.

Some of the Kinder Planets (short stories), Groundwood, 1993, Orchard, 1995.

(With Amanda Lewis) *Rosie Backstage,* illustrated by Bill Slavin, Kids Can Press, 1994.

The Book of Changes (short stories), Groundwood, 1994, Orchard, 1995.

The Maestro (young adult novel), Groundwood, 1995, Orchard, 1996.

(Reteller) *The Hunchback of Notre Dame,* illustrated by Bill Slavin, Key Porter Books (Toronto), 1996, Orchard, 1997.

(Reteller) Bram Stoker, *Dracula,* illustrated by Laszlo Gal, Key Porter Books, 1997.

Also author of a children's opera titled *A Midwinter Night's Dream* and a musical version of *Mischief City.* Author of regular column of children's book reviews for the Toronto *Globe and Mail,* 1985-88.

NOVELS; FOR ADULTS

Odd's End, McClelland & Stewart (Toronto), 1980, Little, Brown, 1980.

The Knot, McClelland & Stewart, 1982.

Fastyngange, Lester & Orpen Dennys, 1988, published as *Voices,* Hodder & Stoughton, 1990.

RADIO PLAYS; BROADCAST BY CANADIAN BROADCASTING CORPORATION

The Thinking Room, 1981.

The Road Ends at the Sea, 1982.

The Strange Odyssey of Lennis Freed, 1983.

The Testing of Stanley Teagarden, 1985.

The Enormous Radio (from the story by John Cheever), 1986.

St. Anthony's Man (from his own story), 1987.

Mr. Gendelman Crashes a Party, 1987.

Dust Is the Only Secret, 1988.

We Now Return You to Your Regularly Scheduled Universe, 1992.

■ Sidelights

Tim Wynne-Jones is a British-born Canadian writer whose works range from award-winning adult and young-adult fiction to such popular children's picture books as the "Zoom" series of tales about an adventurous cat. One of Canada's most popular authors among pre-schoolers and primary graders, Wynne-Jones is recognized as the creator of works that capture the mystery, fantasy, and wonder of childhood while addressing such realistic concerns as the conquering of personal fears and the relationship of children with their parents. He is known and appreciated for his rich language, zany plots, and a sophistication of theme that does not proclaim itself didactically, but that "reverberates beneath the simple surface of image and dialogue," as Gwyneth Evans noted in *Twentieth-Century Children's Writers.* A scriptwriter and composer, Wynne-Jones is also known for his work as lyricist for the television program *Fraggle Rock.*

The son of an engineer, Wynne-Jones was born in Cheshire, England, in 1948, but grew up in Ottawa, Canada. Attending the University of Waterloo, he began to study children's literature as part of a research project. A group of sociology students secured a grant to study racism and sexism in books for young readers, and Wynne-Jones, studying visual arts at the time, was included in the grant proposal as someone on the creative side of things. In an interview with Dave Jenkinson in *Emergency Librarian,* Wynne-Jones ex-

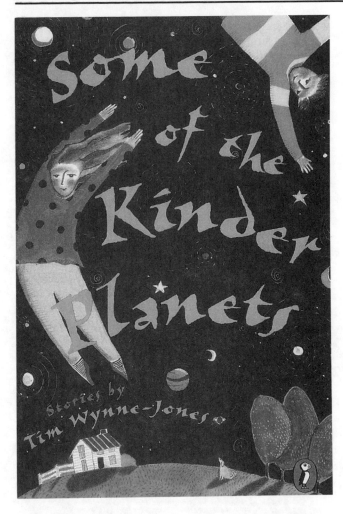

The nine stories in Wynne-Jones's collection feature young protagonists with unique personalities and interests.

plained that having examined a plethora of children's books and finding fault with many of them, "the group decided that, because they knew what was wrong with children's books, they could then write good ones. It was a great lesson in how you do *not* write a children's book." While the publishing venture created by the grant was short-lived, it did produce Wynne-Jones's first creative effort, *Madeline and Ermadello,* a "quietly charming story about a young girl's fantasies," according to Linda Smith in *In Review: Canadian Books for Children.* Ermadello is Madeline's friend, the third in a trio that includes her carpenter father, Ernie, and her next door neighbor, Barnell. But Ermadello is special: he is imaginary, and Madeline can make him be anything she wants him to be. The quiet climax to this picture book comes when Madeline introduces Ermadello to her real-life friends at a tea party. A *Children's Book News* reviewer concluded that this "is a charming story of friendship that younger readers are certain to enjoy."

Wynne-Jones's first book highlighted the elements of fantasy and wonder common to the author's subsequent efforts for children. It was several years, however, before Wynne-Jones published a second picture book. During this time he worked as a designer at a publishing

company, as a visual arts instructor at Waterloo University and York University, and as a graphic designer in his own company. He earned an M.F.A. in visual arts and was married. He also wrote and published his first adult novel, a psychological thriller, *Odd's End,* which won him Canada's prestigious Seal First Novel Award and a cash prize of $50,000. Understandably, Wynne-Jones stuck with adult fiction for his next title, *The Knot,* but he returned to children's books in 1983.

"I didn't start writing children's books because I had children," Wynne-Jones told Jenkinson in his *Emergency Librarian* interview. "I'd always had ideas for children's stories." Although a visual artist himself, Wynne-Jones does not illustrate his own books. Rather, he visualizes stories with the illustrations of other artists he respects. One such case was Ken Nutt (Eric Beddows), an acquaintance of his whose artwork Wynne-Jones wanted to see in book form. The direct inspiration for his first successful children's book was the family cat, Montezuma, or Zuma for short. Writing early one morning, Wynne-Jones observed the cat sitting on the kitchen counter batting at water from a dripping faucet. The idea for an adventure-loving and water-loving cat came to the author quickly. "The story, *Zoom at Sea,* was written in 20 minutes," Wynne-Jones told Jenkinson. "I don't quite know how those things happen." In the story, Zoom the cat goes to the home of the mysterious Maria, who helps him realize a lifelong dream of going to sea. Maria coaxes the cat as the foam gathers around him, "Go on. It's all yours." Linda Granfield, writing in *Quill and Quire,* noted that these words are "an irresistible, exciting invitation to the cat and the reader alike." Granfield added that the book was a "perfect balance of text and illustration" and served as a reminder to children and adults alike to "live our dreams."

Wynne-Jones initially had no intention of creating a sequel to this first popular "Zoom" title. However, a letter from his mother-in-law suggested further possibilities for Maria's magical powers, and *Zoom Away* was launched. In this story, a trip upstairs to Maria's attic becomes the magical metaphor for a trip to the North Pole. Zoom goes in search of the nautical tomcat, Uncle Roy, who set sail for the North Pole and has not been heard from since. Again, Nutt employed simple black and white illustrations to "complement ... perfectly" Wynne-Jones's text, according to Bernie Goedhart in *Quill and Quire.* Goedhart concluded that the two "seem destined to carve themselves a permanent niche in the world of Canadian picture-books." Though some reviewers, including Jon C. Stott in *Canadian Literature,* felt that the simple text lacked "depth," others found deeper resonances. Sarah Ellis, writing in *Horn Book,* commented that "*Zoom Away* is one of those rare picture books that combines absolute simplicity with mythic resonance.... The story is bigger than its plot." Drawing comparisons to such elemental Canadian myths as the search for the Northwest Passage and the romance involved in such adventure, Ellis concluded that the "satisfaction we feel at the book's safe ending goes beyond the satisfaction of putting a tired child to bed." Reviewing both "Zoom" books in *Canadian Children's Literature*, Ulrike Walker reminded the reader of Wynne-Jones's theory of thresholds, developmental steps that everyone must take or risk to reach maturity, and placed the books in the context of mythic test or quest tales. "The Zoom books," Walker noted, "are composed of wonderful, multi-layered mixtures of images and text that masterfully combine a comforting sense of security with an equally compelling evocation of less innocent sensual gratification." The critic concluded: "These remarkable works ... bear eloquent witness to the complex levels of realization which all of us must undergo before we reach that stage we label 'adult.'"

If Zoom travelled to the Arctic via Maria's attic, the next obvious question—and one posed by a student to Wynne-Jones—was what would a trip to the basement hold in store for Zoom? The answer came in a third "Zoom" book, *Zoom Upstream*, "a book of reunion and probably a book about death, but I don't think any child will read that into it," Wynne-Jones explained to Jenkinson in *Emergency Librarian*. Set in ancient, cat-revering Egypt, *Zoom Upstream* has Zoom following a mysterious trail through a bookshelf to Egypt where he joins Maria in a further search for Uncle Roy. It is Maria who shows Zoom five silver buttons from a sailor's coat, the clues that ultimately lead the two to Uncle Roy and safety. The book's ending is, as noted by Janet McNaughton in *Quill and Quire*, "more like a beginning," with the trio sailing away in search of the source of the Nile. "A very special book," concluded McNaughton.

With *I'll Make You Small*, Wynne-Jones moved away from the voyaging world of cats to the more prosaic but no less dangerous world of the neighborhood. Young Roland's next door neighbor is crotchety old Mr. Swanskin, who threatens to make Roland small if he catches him trespassing on his property. But when Swanskin is not seen for several days, Roland is sent by his mother to investigate, only to find the eccentric old man repairing toys he broke during his own childhood. The gift of a pie saves Roland from Swanskin's threats, and he learns the man's secret—of how he was made to feel small as child. "A child who likes scary stories, but is too young for Poe or Hitchcock, should enjoy this book," commented Bernie Goedhart in *Quill and Quire*. Appearing the same year as *I'll Make You Small* was Wynne-Jones's *Mischief City*, twenty-five poems that humorously explore subjects from a young child's frustration with adults to sibling rivalry. Joan McGrath, reviewing the book in *Quill and Quire*, felt that it was, with the illustrations of Victor Gad, "big, bold, and bright."

Another popular picture book from Wynne-Jones, and one that *Five Owls* contributor Anne Lundin compared to Sendak's *Where the Wild Things Are*, is *Architect of the Moon* (published in the United States as *Builder of the Moon*). Young David Finebloom receives an urgent message one night via a moonbeam and flies away, building blocks in hand, to repair the moon. Lundin

went on in her review to note that "Wynne-Jones's text is spare, simple, poetic," while Catherine Osborne, writing in *Books for Young People*, commented that Wynne-Jones and illustrator Ian Wallace "make a strong contending team in the moon-book category." Walker, writing in *Canadian Children's Literature*, remarked that *Architect of the Moon* "is a subtle work" and one that "does not enclose but encourages the child to take a decisive step toward change." Also writing in *Canadian Children's Literature*, Michael Steig noted that *Architect of the Moon* is a true "visual text," in which pictures and text are finely integrated and one that "achieves a highly gratifying level of literary and artistic complexity and interest."

Wynne-Jones has written several other picture books for young readers, including *The Hour of the Frog, Mouse in a Manger*, and *The Last Piece of Sky*, all of them well received, but the "Zoom" books remain his most popular achievement in that genre. He has also written juvenile and young adult fiction, including two short story collections and a young adult novel. The award-winning *Some of the Kinder Planets* consists of nine stories which tell of children making encounters with other worlds, both metaphorically and realistically.

Burl Crow finds his desolate life changed by the passionate and eccentric maestro, Nathaniel Orlando Gow. (Cover illustration by Ludmilla Temertey.)

Deborah Stevenson commented in *Bulletin of the Center for Children's Books* that the writing "is thoughtful, inventive, and often humorous," while a *Publishers Weekly* reviewer noted that "ordinary moments take on a fresh veneer in this finely tuned short-story collection." More short stories are offered up in *The Book of Changes*, a "fine collection" according to a *Kirkus Reviews* critic and "a delight" in the estimation of Annette Goldsmith, writing in *Quill and Quire*. Goldsmith added that Wynne-Jones attempted to "conjure up a sense of wonder" in these stories and that the "wonderful moments in this book ... will stay with readers." Writing in *Horn Book*, Nancy Vasilakis concluded that "Wynne-Jones tells his readers in these perceptive short stories that we all have the power to create the music of our own lives."

With *The Maestro*, Wynne-Jones again broke new ground for himself. The story of fourteen-year-old Burl and his struggle for survival, *The Maestro* was Wynne-Jones's first young adult novel. Fleeing his brutal father, Burl seeks shelter in a remote cabin by a Canadian lake. The cabin is inhabited by Nathaniel Gow, a musical genius and himself in flight from the mechanized world. Gow, patterned after the real-life Canadian musician Glen Gould, takes Burl in for a time. He also allows Burl to stay at his cabin when he returns to Toronto, and when Burl learns of Gow's subsequent death, he tries to claim the cabin for his, then goes on a mission to save Gow's final composition, confronting his father along the way. Roderick McGillis, writing in *Canadian Children's Literature*, noted that the book is "redolently Canadian," but that it also offers much more. "Its prose is dense and its themes move into challenging areas for young readers," McGillis remarked. Stevenson concluded in a *Bulletin of the Center for Children's Books* review that "Wynne-Jones has displayed a knack for the unusual made credible in his short story collections" and that it was "nice to see that skill expanded into a well-crafted and accessible novel." Writing in *Quill and Quire*, Maureen Garvie commented that *The Maestro* is "tightly and dramatically scripted" and that this first young adult novel is a "peach."

Wynne-Jones has proved himself a versatile and perceptive writer on many levels. Whether writing children's picture books, young adult titles, or adult fiction and plays, his message of the power of fantasy and fiction comes through loud and clear. As he once commented, "I like to tell stories—to entertain and instruct—about ordinary people in extraordinary circumstances or extraordinary people in very ordinary circumstances." Regarding his efforts for children, Wynne-Jones commented: "I write for children out of the child I was and am. I cannot write for an audience—where children's books are concerned, I am the Selfish Giant, shooing my audience away in order to reclaim the garden for myself!"

■ Works Cited

Review of *The Book of Changes, Kirkus Reviews,* July 15, 1995, p. 1032.

Ellis, Sarah, review of *Zoom Away, Horn Book,* May-June, 1987, pp. 378-81.

Evans, Gwyneth, "Tim Wynne-Jones," *Twentieth-Century Children's Writers,* 4th edition, edited by Laura Standley Berger, St. James Press, 1995, pp. 1049-51.

Garvie, Maureen, review of *The Maestro, Quill and Quire,* December, 1995, pp. 36-37.

Goedhart, Bernie, review of *Zoom Away, Quill and Quire,* August, 1985, p. 38.

Goedhart, Bernie, review of *I'll Make You Small, Quill and Quire,* October, 1986, p. 16.

Goldsmith, Annette, review of *The Book of Changes, Quill and Quire,* October, 1994, p. 38.

Granfield, Linda, review of *Zoom at Sea, Quill and Quire,* March, 1984, p. 72.

Jenkinson, Dave, "Tim Wynne-Jones," *Emergency Librarian,* January-February, 1988, pp. 56-62.

Lundin, Anne, review of *Builder of the Moon, Five Owls,* May-June, 1989, p.72.

Review of *Madeline and Ermadello, Children's Book News,* June, 1979, p. 2.

McGillis, Roderick, review of *The Maestro, Canadian Children's Literature,* Number 81, 1996, pp. 58-59.

McGrath, Joan, "Poems for Kids Conjure up a Cock-eyed World," *Quill and Quire,* December, 1986, p. 15.

McNaughton, Janet, review of *Zoom Upstream, Quill and Quire,* November, 1992, p. 33.

Osborne, Catherine, review of *Architect of the Moon, Books for Young Readers,* October, 1988, p. 10.

Smith, Linda, review of *Madeline and Ermadello, In Review: Canadian Books for Children,* Winter, 1978, p. 70.

Review of *Some of the Kinder Planets, Publishers Weekly,* May 1, 1995, p. 59.

Steig, Michael, "The Importance of the Visual Text in *Architect of the Moon:* Mothers, Teapots, et al.," *Canadian Children's Literature,* Number 70, 1993, pp. 22-33.

Stevenson, Deborah, review of *Some of the Kinder Planets, Bulletin of the Center for Children's Books,* May, 1995, p. 328.

Stevenson, Deborah, review of *The Maestro, Bulletin of the Center for Children's Books,* October, 1996, p. 81.

Stott, Jon C., review of *Zoom Away, Canadian Literature,* Spring, 1987, p. 160.

Vasilakis, Nancy, review of *The Book of Changes, Horn Book,* February, 1996, pp. 76-77.

Walker, Ulrike, "A Matter of Thresholds," *Canadian Children's Literature,* Number 60, 1990, pp. 108-16.

Wynne-Jones, Tim, *Zoom at Sea,* HarperCollins, 1993.

■ For More Information See

BOOKS

Children's Literature Review, Volume 21, Gale, 1990, pp. 226-31.

PERIODICALS

Booklist, April 15, 1993, p. 1524; January 1, 1994; June 1, 1994, p. 1846; March 1, 1995, p. 1241; October 1, 1995; December 15, 1996, p. 724.

Canadian Materials, January, 1994, p. 4.

Horn Book, May, 1990, p. 332; January, 1995, p. 99; May, 1995, p. 334.

Publishers Weekly, April 12, 1993, p. 61; October 30, 1995, p. 62; October 14, 1996, p. 84.

Quill and Quire, December, 1989, p. 22; October, 1993, p. 38; November, 1993, p. 38.

Reading Time, August, 1997, p. 35.

School Library Journal, August, 1990, p. 136; February, 1994, p. 92; August, 1994, p. 148; April, 1995, p. 138; October, 1995, p. 141.

—*Sketch by J. Sydney Jones*

Y

PAUL YEE

YEE, Paul (R.) 1956-

■ Personal

Born October 1, 1956, in Spalding, Saskatchewan, Canada; son of Gordon and Gim May (Wong) Yee. *Education:* University of British Columbia, B.A., 1978, M.A. 1983. *Hobbies and other interests:* Cycling and swimming.

■ Addresses

Home—922 Carlaw Avenue, Toronto, Ontario, Canada M4K 3L3.

■ Career

Writer. City of Vancouver Archives, Vancouver, British Columbia, Assistant City Archivist, 1980-1988; Archives of Ontario, Toronto, Ontario, Portfolio Manager, 1988-91; Ontario Ministry of Citizenship, policy analyst, 1991-97. Teacher in British Columbia schools, and at Simon Fraser University, University of Victoria, University of British Columbia, Vancouver Museum, and Chinese Community Library Services Society of Vancouver. *Exhibitions: Saltwater City* exhibition, Chinese Cultural Centre (CCC), Vancouver Centennial, 1986.

■ Awards, Honors

Honorable Mention, Canada Council Literature Prizes, 1986, for *The Curses of Third Uncle;* Vancouver Book Prize, 1989, for *Saltwater City;* British Columbia Book Prize for Children's Literature, National I.O.D.E. Book Award, and Parents' Choice Honor, all 1990, all for *Tales from Gold Mountain;* Ruth Schwartz Award, Canadian Booksellers Association, 1992, for *Roses Sing on New Snow;* Governor-General's Award, Canada Council, 1996, for *Ghost Train.*

■ Writings

Teach Me to Fly, Skyfighter! (stories), illustrations by Sky Lee, Lorimer (Toronto), 1983.
The Curses of Third Uncle (novel), Lorimer, 1986.
Saltwater City: An Illustrated History of the Chinese in Vancouver, Douglas & McIntyre (Vancouver), 1988, University of Washington, 1989.
Tales from Gold Mountain: Stories of the Chinese in the New World, illustrations by Simon Ng, Groundwood Books (Toronto), 1989, Macmillan, 1990.

Roses Sing on New Snow: A Delicious Tale, illustrations by Harvey Chan, Macmillan, 1992.

Breakaway (novel), Groundwood, 1994.

Moonlight's Luck, illustrations by Terry Yee, Macmillan, 1995.

Ghost Train, illustrations by Harvey Chan, Groundwood, 1996.

Struggle and Hope: The Story of Chinese Canadians, Umbrella Press (Toronto), 1996.

■ Sidelights

Born in Spalding, Saskatchewan, in 1956, Paul Yee is a Chinese-Canadian of the third generation. He grew up in the Chinatown area of Vancouver. On the dust jacket of his book, *Saltwater City,* he says he had a "typical Chinese-Canadian childhood, caught between two worlds, and yearning to move away from the neighborhood."

He received a Master of Arts degree in history from the University of British Columbia in 1983 after completing his undergraduate work there as well. Although Yee has taught informally at several institutions in British Columbia, the focus of his career has been on his work as an archivist and policy analyst. He said in an interview for *Junior DISCovering Authors* (JrDA) that "I really don't view myself as a teacher, even though I do classroom visits." An archivist takes care of historical documents that are usually stored in special areas of libraries and cultural or state institutions. These documents or papers are important for historians and other writers to research past events. A policy analyst researches and analyzes options for government decision-making.

In 1988, Yee moved to Toronto, where he became Multicultural Coordinator for the Archives of Ontario. He had been previously employed as an archivist by Vancouver City. In his interview, Yee was asked how, as an archivist, he became a writer of children's literature. "It was a fluke," he replied. "Back in 1983, I was involved in doing work for Chinatown, such as organizing festivals, exhibits, and educational programs. Even though I had written some short stories, I had not done anything in children's literature. A Canadian publishing company, Lorimer, knowing about my work in the Chinese community, asked me to write a children's book that would employ my knowledge of Chinese-Canadian life as a background. *Teach Me to Fly, Skyfighter!* was my first children's book that came out of the request by the publishing company." With his series of four related stories about children living in the immigrant neighborhoods of Vancouver, Yee "has succeeded in portraying the personalities, interests, and dreams of four 11-year-old friends whose voices ring true throughout," according to Frieda Wishinsky in *Quill & Quire.*

Yee very much enjoyed writing his first children's book. "It dovetailed with the work I was doing in building awareness of Chinese-Canadian history and community. I saw my target audience as Canadian children of

After her father's death, Choon-yi tries unsuccessfully to make a living as an artist until a ghostly presence takes her on a remarkable train trip. (From *Ghost Train,* written by Yee and illustrated by Harvey Chan.)

Chinese ancestry who needed to know more about themselves and their heritage," he said in his interview. Three years later, Lorimer worked with Yee on another book. In 1986, he won honorable mention for his second children's novel, *The Curses of Third Uncle,* from the Canada Council Literature Prizes.

The Curses of Third Uncle is a historical novel that deals with the period of the early twentieth century in which Sun Yat-Sen's revolutionary movement fought against the Chinese Empire. Dr. Sun Yat-Sen, called the "Father of Modern China," had led nine uprisings against the Empire by the time he visited Vancouver in 1910 and 1911, Yee recounts in *Saltwater City.* In *The Curses of Third Uncle,* fourteen-year-old Lillian, living in Vancouver's Chinatown, misses her father, who often travels back to China and throughout the British Columbia frontier—presumably to take care of his clothing business. He is actually a secret agent for Dr. Sun's revolutionary movement.

At one point in his travels, Lillian's father fails to return. His absence is economically hard on the family, but Lillian will not believe that her father has deserted them. Her third uncle, however, threatens to send Lillian's family back to China. In her attempts to locate her father by travelling through British Columbia, Lillian discovers that he has been betrayed by his brother, who has been paid to turn him over to his enemies. Comparing the book in the *Emergency Librarian* to historical epics such as *Shogun* or *Roots,* Christine Dewar states that Yee "has produced a story that is exciting but contrived, with an attractive and reasonably motivated heroine." *Quill & Quire* writer Annette Goldsmith similarly comments that *The Curses of Third Uncle* is "an exciting, fast-pace, well-written tale," and praises Yee for his use of legendary Chinese female warriors to reinforce Lillian's story.

Yee's next book, *Saltwater City,* was published in 1988. This book grew out of Yee's work from 1985 to 1986 as chair of the Saltwater City Exhibition Committee of the Chinese Cultural Centre. In the preface to the book, Yee writes: "The book pays tribute to those who went through the hard times, to those who swallowed their pride, to those who were powerless and humiliated, but who still carried on. They all had faith that things would be better for future generations. They have been proven correct."

Saltwater City is a history of Vancouver's Chinatown that covers a long period of time, from its beginnings in 1858 to the present. It has more than 200 photographs, many documents, deals with a large number of political, economic, and social issues, and profiles the lives of many people. Yee remarked in his interview that there were no special problems in assembling all this material: "I had done a lot of research from the Saltwater City Exhibition Committee and then there was all my previous work with Chinatown. I had worked with many people, and they were happy to tell me their stories and show me their photograph albums. Had I been an outsider, it would have been much more difficult."

Yee pointed out that "while *Saltwater City* is not a children's book, it is an extremely accessible book. It can serve as a child's book not in the sense that it is read from cover to cover, but rather as a reference book the child can open at any page and study a photograph or read a profile or sidebar." He also added that *Saltwater City* "is very much localized to the Vancouver scene. It is therefore most important to the Chinese in the Vancouver area and to the grandchildren of the people who appear throughout the book," although he noted that "it would be possible to compare some of the history to Chinese experiences in cities of the United States."

Other than commemorating the Saltwater City Exhibition, Yee said in his interview, the book serves another purpose: "The key thing in the Vancouver Chinese community is that a tremendous change is occurring. Since 1967, the arrival of many new Chinese from Hong Kong and other Asian immigrants has overwhelmed the older, established community. I felt it was necessary to recognize the earlier chapters of our history before the new waves of immigrations changed everything. I did

chapters on the newer immigrants, and their stories are different from the problems encountered earlier."

Although Yee started his career as a historian, compiling information such as that in *Saltwater City,* he had no particular difficulty in making the switch to fiction. Nevertheless, he remarked, he found that writing fiction was much more "arduous because instead of merely reporting what has happened in non-fiction, fiction requires the creation of a story" that will be believable and enjoyable. "The difference between nonfiction and fiction is the difference between reliable reporting and imaginative creating," he concluded.

Yee also said that his knowledge of folk literature comes partly from his childhood reading of western fairy tales. From those stories he remembered things such as actions happening in groups of three, a principle he makes use of in some of his stories. Other than similar memories, Yee has not relied on the formal study of children's writing to develop his own fiction.

Yee used his familiarity with traditional stories to write *Tales from Gold Mountain,* which was published in 1989. This collection of short stories has won Yee high praise from the critics. Lee Galda and Susan Cox, writing in *Reading Teacher,* believe the book "gives voice to the previously unheard generations of Chinese immigrants whose labor supported the settlement of the west coast of Canada and the United States." The book includes stories about the conflict between the manager of a fish cannery and his greedy boss; a young man who arranges the burial of Chinese railroad workers when he meets his father's ghost; a young woman's gift of ginger root to save her fiance's life; a wealthy merchant who exchanges his twin daughters for sons; and clashes between old traditions and new influences.

Betsy Hearne of the *Bulletin of the Center for Children's Books* notes that "Yee never indulges in stylistic pretensions," yet is able to dramatically blend realism and legend. She explains that Yee moves between lighter tales of love and wit to conflicts between the present and past. The result is that the stories "carry mythical overtones that lend the characters unforgettable dimension—humans achieving supernatural power in defying their fate of physical and cultural oppression." In the afterword, Yee says that he hopes to "carve a place in the North American imagination for the many generations of Chinese who have settled here as Canadians and Americans, and help them stake their claim to be known as pioneers, too."

Yee remarked in his interview that most of *Tales from Gold Mountain* was original material, with only "about five to ten percent of the tales [coming] from the stories I heard when I was growing up." He explained: "The rest comes from my imagination. It's really hard to slice up a book to say which is history and which is imagination. The Chinese stories operate within the particular context of new world history. It's not just a blend of the new with the old but the creation of a new world mythology. Every group that comes to North

America leaves an imprint of itself that can be shaped into fiction."

Denise Wilms, writing in *Booklist,* believes that Yee's stories "strikingly reflect traditional Chinese beliefs and customs in new world circumstances," and compares it to Laurence Yep's *Rainbow People. School Library Journal* contributor Margaret A. Chang also compares *Tales* to *Rainbow People* and adds that Yee's stories "will further expand and enhance understanding of the Chinese immigrant experience." The book is "told in richly evocative language," according to a *Horn Book* reviewer, and "the stories skillfully blend the hardships and dangers of frontier life in a new country with the ancient attitudes and traditions brought over from China." The critic concludes that the images of *Tales from the Gold Mountain* "will stay with the reader for a long time."

The heroine of *Roses Sing on New Snow,* Maylin, echoes the idea of the difference between the Old World and the New World when she explains to the governor of South China, who is visiting her father's restaurant in Chinatown to learn the secrets of her delicious recipes, that "this is a dish of the New World.... You cannot re-create it in the Old." In this story, the attempt to push Maylin aside so that her father and two brothers can take credit for the excellent cooking that comes from their restaurant, fails when Maylin has to be called to show the governor how the cooking is done. Yee concludes, "From that day on Maylin was renowned in Chinatown as a great cook and a wise person." In *The Bulletin of the Center for Children's Books,* Betsy Hearne notes that "vivid art and clean writing are graced by a neatly feminist ending."

Asked by *JrDA* if he felt there may have been a suggestion of a feminist twist in *Roses Sing on New Snow,* Yee replied, "Insofar as the novel shows Maylin asserting herself, I would say yes." He explained: "Children need to see representations of reality in their literature. Chinese immigration to North America has had the unique feature of being predominately male since at first the men were coming by themselves to America. That's a fact about our history. Some of the early communities were almost all male." By portraying positive female characters such as Maylin and Lillian of *Curses of Third Uncle,* Yee counters the male-dominated history with fictional female role models.

As a historian and observer of Chinese and other immigrant communities in Canada, Yee has noted significant changes in Canadian attitudes and practices toward its racial minority communities. "The change has been for the better in many ways. There are new state initiatives to improve race relations, and even the private sector is learning about managing diversity and employment equity. I am optimistic about the future." In his writing, he concluded, he strives to articulate this philosophy: "From the past, for the future."

■ Works Cited

Chang, Margaret A., review of *Tales from Gold Mountain, School Library Journal,* May, 1990, p. 121.

Dewar, Christine, review of *The Curses of Third Uncle, Emergency Librarian,* May, 1987, p. 51.

Galda, Lee and Susan Cox, review of *Tales from Gold Mountain, Reading Teacher,* April, 1991, p. 585.

Goldsmith, Annette, "Illuminating Adventures with Young People from Long Ago," *Quill & Quire,* December, 1986, p. 14.

Hearne, Betsy, review of *Tales from the Gold Mountain, Bulletin of the Center for Children's Books,* January, 1990, p. 178.

Hearne, Betsy, review of *Roses Sing on New Snow: A Delicious Tale, Bulletin of the Center for Children's Books,* July, 1992, p. 307.

Review of *Tales from the Gold Mountain, Horn Book,* July, 1990, pp. 459-460.

Wilms, Denise, review of *Tales from the Gold Mountain, Booklist,* March 15, 1990, p. 1464.

Wishinsky, Frieda, review of *Teach Me to Fly, Skyfighter!, Quill & Quire,* October, 1983, p. 16.

Yee, Paul, *Saltwater City: An Illustrated History of the Chinese in Vancouver,* Douglas & McIntyre (Vancouver), 1988, University of Washington, 1989.

Yee, Paul, *Tales from Gold Mountain: Stories of the Chinese in the New World,* Groundwood Books (Toronto), 1989, Macmillan, 1990.

Yee, Paul, telephone interview with Jordan Richman for *Junior DISCovering Authors,* August 11, 1993.

■ For More Information See

BOOKS

Seventh Book of Junior Authors and Illustrators, Wilson, 1996, pp. 352-54.

*   *   *

YODER, Dorothy Meenen 1921-
(Dot Yoder)

■ Personal

Born May 22, 1921, in Philadelphia, PA; daughter of Richard and Hilda (James) Meenen; married Daniel Miller Yoder (deceased); children: Tad Richard, Jonathan Daniel. *Education:* Attended Philadelphia Museum School of Art (now Philadelphia College of Art). *Religion:* Episcopal. *Hobbies and other interests:* "Grandparenting," choir, fire company auxiliary.

■ Addresses

Home—1103 Forest Lane, Glen Mills, PA 19342.

■ Career

Philadelphia Museum School of Art (now Philadelphia College of Art), Philadelphia, PA, teacher of nature drawing, 1944-53; Agnes Irwin School, Rosemont, PA, art teacher, 1968-82. Volunteer, Old Forge School; Girl Scout leader. Member of Christ Church, Media, PA.

■ Illustrator

UNDER NAME DOT YODER

Wags and Spunky, Family Press, 1982.

Nan Holcomb, *Andy Finds a Turtle,* Jason & Nordic, 1987.

Ralph W. Miller, Jr., *Soupy, the Featherless Duck,* KNA Press, 1989.

Nan Holcomb, *Patrick and Emma Lou,* Jason & Nordic, 1989.

Nan Holcomb, *A Smile from Andy,* Jason & Nordic, 1989.

Nan Holcomb, *Sarah's Surprise,* Jason & Nordic, 1990.

Nan Holcomb, *Andy Opens Wide,* Jason & Nordic, 1990.

Nan Holcomb, *Fair and Square,* Jason & Nordic, 1992.

Candri Hodges, *When I Grow Up,* Jason & Nordic, 1995.

Kate Chamberlin, *The Night Search,* Jason & Nordic, 1997.

■ Sidelights

Dorothy Meenen Yoder told *SATA:* "I have always been interested in both natural sciences and drawing, starting with Sunday afternoon walks with my father in the local woods, through camping experiences as a Girl Scout, to teaching nature drawing at the Philadelphia Zoo, while working at the Philadelphia College of Art. I have also enjoyed working with children as a teacher, camp counselor, Girl Scout troop leader and, of course, mother and grandmother."

*   *   *

YODER, Dot
See YODER, Dorothy Meenen